TORRES STRAIT

C.York

PAPUA
NEW
GUINEA

SOLOMON
ISLANDS

A SEA

ssel Is

GULF
OF
CARPENTARIA

CORAL SEA

SOUTH PACIFIC OCEAN

Groote Eylandt

CAPE

Wenlock R

C.Melville

Osprey Reef

Vanderlin I

YORK

PENINSULA

Willis Group

Mornington I

Mitchell R

Staaten R

Cairns

Herald Cays

Lihou Reefs

Nicholson R

Gilbert R

Bartle Frere
1622

Norman R

Hitchinbrook I

Marion Reef

ITORY

Gregory R

Leichhardt R

Flinders R

Burdekin R

SELWYN RANGE

L Dalrymple

CLARKE RA

Georgina R

QUEENSLAND

Mt Dalrymple
1259

Broad
Sound

Swain
Reefs

Saumarez Reef

Diamantina R

Thomson R

Barcoo R

DIVIDING

Capricorn Group

SON DESERT

Curtis I

Bunker Group

Tropic of Capricorn

Warburton R

CHANNEL COUNTRY

Consuelo Peak
1174

Dawson R

RANGE

Hervey
Bay

Sandy C

North

Cooper C

GREY RA

Bulloo R

Fraser I

STRZELECKI
TRACK
L Eyre South

BARRIER RANGE

Warrego R

Paroo R

DARLING DOWNS

Nth Stradbroke I

TRALIA

L Torrens

L Frome

Darling R

Barwon R

Gwydir R

PILLIGA
SCRUB

BRISBANE

Sth Stradbroke I

St Mary Peak
1180

MACQUARIE
MARSHES

Namoi R

Round Mtn
1583

C Byron

LER RA

FLINDERS RANGES

Bogan R

NEW SOUTH WALES

GREAT

DIVIDING RANGE

Lord Howe I

RE PEN

Spencer Gulf

YORKE PEN

MOUNT LOFTY RAS

Lachlan R

Port Stephens

SYDNEY

ADELAIDE

Murrumbidgee R

Port Hacking

Victor Harbor

SUNSET
COUNTRY

Murray R

RIVERINA

CANBERRA

Jervis Bay

oo I

L Alexandrina

ACT

VICTORIA

Mt Bogong
1986

Mt Kosciusko
2228

SOUTH PACIFIC OCEAN

THE GRAMPIANS

L Eildon

Green C

Port Fairy

OTWAY RA

MELBOURNE

Mallacoota
Inlet

C Otway

Wilsons Promontory

TASMAN SEA

King I

BASS STRAIT

FURNEAUX
GROUP

Flinders I

Cape Barren I

Mt Ossa
1617

TASMANIA

L Pedder

Maria I

HOBART

South Bruny I

GREAT

BARRIER

REEF

The author, **Graham Pizzey**, is highly regarded among professional and amateur ornithologists for his first *Field Guide to the Birds of Australia* and well known for other books and newpaper columns on Australian wildlife. A Member of the Order of Australia and former Honorary Associate in Ornithology at the Museum of Victoria, he has been a Council member of the Australian Conservation Foundation and the Royal Australasian Ornithologists Union and a recipient of the Australian Natural History Medallion.

The illustrator, **Frank Knight**, a member of the Society of Animal Art (New York), was with the Commonwealth Scientific and Industrial Research Organisation, mostly as illustrator, for thirty years. He has illustrated many scientific and natural history texts and books for children. In 1980 he was given a CSIRO Overseas Study Award to meet wildlife artists in Britain and USA and Canada. His work has been exhibited in group shows in the USA and Canada, plus several solo exhibitions in Australia.

The Graham Pizzey & Frank Knight
FIELD to GUIDE
the
BIRDS of AUSTRALIA

By Graham Pizzey
Illustrated by Frank Knight

Angus&Robertson
An imprint of HarperCollins*Publishers*

*This book is dedicated with respect and affection to
Rolf Baldwin and John Ponder, schoolmasters, who
first taught me to appreciate birds, and words.*

Angus&Robertson

An imprint of HarperCollins*Publishers*, Australia

First published in Australia in 1997
by HarperCollins*Publishers* Pty Limited
ACN 009 913 517
A member of the HarperCollins*Publishers* (Australia) Pty Limited Group

Text copyright © Graham Pizzey 1997
Colour plates and line drawings copyright © Frank Knight 1997

HarperCollins*Publishers*
25 Ryde Road, Pymble, Sydney NSW 2073, Australia
31 View Road, Glenfield, Auckland 10, New Zealand
77–85 Fulham Palace Road, London W6 8JB, United Kingdom
Hazelton Lanes, 55 Avenue Road, Suite 2900, Toronto, Ontario M5R 3L2
and 1995 Markham Road, Scarborough, Ontario M1B 5M8, Canada
10 East 53rd Street, New York, NY 10032, USA

National Library of Australia Cataloguing-in-Publication data:

Pizzey, Graham, 1930-.
　　The field guide to the birds of Australia.

　　Bibliography.
　　Includes index.
　　ISBN 0 207 18013 X.

　　1. Birds - Australia - Identification. I. Knight, Frank,
　　1941-. II. Title.
598.2994

Endpaper maps copyright © Commonwealth of Australia, AUSLIG,
Australia's national mapping agency. All rights reserved.
Indexes by Keyword Editorial.

Berkeley 8/10. Printed on Matt Art 105 gsm.
Printed in Hong Kong
9 8 7 6 5 4 3 2 1
99 98 97

FOREWORD

Graham Pizzey is a very good naturalist. He has an appreciation of all the ingredients of Australian flora and fauna and of their relationships with soil, climate and other elements. Birds provide an excellent indication of the state of our environment; Graham loves and has made a special study of them. In the past 40 years, I have been with him in the bush on many occasions in many parts of Australia and I know no-one who surpasses his expertise in the field. The great majority of birds in this guide he has seen and described himself, and his interpretation of their calls was an initiative he undertook early in his career.

All of us who are interested in birds need to use binoculars, but Graham refined this use by describing what he was looking at directly to a tape recorder he was carrying at the same time. Hence the immediacy of his descriptions. He is well known as a first-class photographer but he is also a competent sketcher of a bird's appearance — a talent he himself hardly acknowledges.

Graham's first book was *A Time to Look* in 1958, and I think it still gives a wonderful feeling for wildlife, including many fascinating black and white photographs. Since then there have been other books and many articles in newspapers and journals, including the Melbourne *Herald* and *The Age*, as a result of which he has a large number of appreciative admirers.

His *Field Guide to the Birds of Australia*, published in 1980, contained the best field descriptions to that time. However, this new book is more comprehensive and is easier to use. The standard of the illustrations by Frank Knight is very high and shows the same attention to detail as the text.

Graham's wife, Sue, has been a constant companion and support, and he would be the first to agree that without Sue he could not have achieved the great recognition that he has.

It is only in the past 30 to 40 years that many Australians have come to appreciate our wonderful range of flora and fauna and, in particular, their ability to understand and to learn more about birds. In this Graham has played an outstanding role. We wish him well, and long may he continue.

DR NORMAN WETTENHALL

ACKNOWLEDGEMENTS

Many people have given generous assistance in the compilation of this Guide. In particular I wish to mention Dr Norman Wettenhall. Richard Weatherly has readily shared his considerable ornithological knowledge. Murray Gunn has been a fund of sound comment. He read the entire text and compiled the gazetteer of over 900 place names. Margaret Barnard stepped into the breach many times, usually at short notice, to help out with the typing of the manuscript. I owe a continuing debt of gratitude to Stephen Marchant, whose erudite, disciplined editorial eye gave the original version of this book its stamp.

Among private individuals who gave generous financial support over the three years spent researching and writing this Guide: I wish to thank Dr Norman Wettenhall, Dr T. K. Durbridge, Professor Tom Harris, Dr Hewlett Lee (of Palo Alto, California), Hugh Mellor (UK) and Diana and Brian Snape.

The Green Mountains Natural History Association and the O'Reilly family of O'Reilly's Rainforest Guesthouse, Lamington National Park, via Canungra, Queensland, gave me generous support: many of the original observations in this book were made there. In the same sense I wish to thank Alan and Sue Robertson, of Gipsy Point Lodge, Genoa, eastern Victoria.

Among friends, correspondents and field companions to whom I am indebted, I would especially mention: Don Arnold; Mike Carter; Professor T. C. Chambers; Graeme Chapman; Chris Dahlberg; Stewart Fairbairn; Dr Stephen Garnett; Tommy Garnett; Dr David Hollands; Professor Allen Keast; Leo Joseph; Ellen McCulloch; Allan McEvey; Mimi Murphy; Lloyd Nielsen; Joan Paton, AM; Dr Douglas Robinson; Len Robinson; Dr Richard Schodde; Ken Simpson and Peter Slater; David Stewart; Glen Threlfo; Professor J. Warren and that arboreal Queensland naturalist, John Young.

I would like to acknowledge the quite remarkable sustained effort my colleague Frank Knight has made in painting his superb plates. To produce some 2638 individual bird figures and several hundred lively vignettes over a four-year period was a labour of Herculean dimension, and I salute him for it.

I wish to thank the team at HarperCollins for their care and cheerful cooperation during a long gestation, particularly, Graeme Jones, Alison Moss and Anne Reilly.

Above all, as I wrote in the first version of this Guide in 1980, I owe my greatest debt to my wife, Sue. It seems we have worked together on field guides and writings about wildlife all our married life. Mentor, librarian, computer operator, typist of endless drafts and superlative retriever of references, she has also cheerfully put up with its author withal. This book is at least hers as much as it is mine. As those who know her will readily understand, I owe her more than I can easily express.

GRAHAM PIZZEY

I would particularly like to thank people whose help was beyond what one might reasonably expect.

I must thank my colleague, Graham Pizzey, the leading writer on Australian birds, for the opportunity to work with him.

I would also like to thank members of staff at HarperCollins, especially Wendeley Harvey, Alison Pressley, Sarah Shrubb, Beverley Barnes and Anne Reilly.

The Australian National Wildlife Collection provided most of the preserved specimens, without which a serious reference book like this could not have been produced. It has been a source for a number of the most important illustrated natural history books published in Australia in recent years. Dick Schodde and John Wombey not only handed out specimens but made sure they were typical representations.

Barbara Staples, the head librarian at the Division of Wildlife and Ecology, CSIRO, was similarly and typically helpful.

Peter Shaughnessy selected me for a job that enabled me to roundtrip to the Antarctic in 1989. While on the voyage, Peter Fullagar explained how you tell prions apart and Colin Miskelly prepared hand-written illustrated notes on birds I might see on the way back. John van den Hoff spent half his first day at Davis — my only one ashore — showing me an Adelie penguin colony.

The Division of Wildlife and Ecology felt like home for most of the thirty years I spent there. Amongst the many staff members I recollect as friends I must especially thank two: Tim Ealey took me on as a technician when my only qualification was having grown up in the scrub. Harry Frith took me on a few years later as divisional illustrator, also largely in the hope that I'd learn on the job. It couldn't happen now, and even then they stuck their necks out.

FRANK KNIGHT

CONTENTS

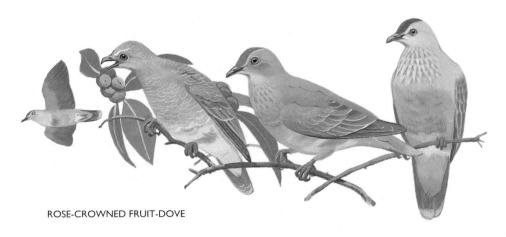

ROSE-CROWNED FRUIT-DOVE

HOW TO QUICKLY FIND YOUR BIRD

INTRODUCTION

In this guide, the text, illustrations and map relating to each of the 778 species included are arranged together to enable quick identification in the field. If you think you know, even roughly, which family your bird belongs to, try to locate it from the list opposite. The groupings and their corresponding page numbers are designed to simplify your search. Most follow the current checklist order (Christidis & Boles, *The Taxonomy and Species of Birds of Australia and its Territories*, 1994), see pp. 518–547 for a brief thumbnail sketch of every Australian bird family, a background reference to the field guide itself.

Each species entry provides essential details on field marks, habits, voice and behaviour, as well as comparisons with similar species, allowing you to cross-reference to birds that are visually similar. Information is given regarding the range and status of each bird, supported by a gazetteer of more than 900 place names (including rivers and major geographic features). A corresponding map of Australia, with longitude and latitude grid, appears in the inside back cover of the book; a detailed map of main Australian towns, mountain ranges, rivers, coastal and offshore features is found in the inside front cover.

All the information contained in this book has been organised to make it straightforward and easy to use. In order to get the most from it, and to fully appreciate the pleasure of birdwatching, do spend a little time reading the following pages of this introduction.

Colours and field markings

Colours and markings in birds' plumage are not haphazard. They have essential, practical functions. Their purpose, apart from concealment (or advertisement), is to make every species of bird recognisable to all others. They also indicate the wearer's sex, age and breeding readiness, a matter of vital importance to potential mates and rivals. Further, they can act as traffic signals: in flight, flashing white wingbars or white rumps help fast-flying flocks of petrels, swifts, waders and waterfowl to keep visual contact and avoid collisions. When flashed conspicuously, the coloured tail-panels of black cockatoos signal alarm, or sexual excitement, often with appropriate calls.

A reassuring thing to remember is that few birds share exactly the same markings. There is usually some subtle difference in these field marks to set each and every species apart. Keen-eyed humans, whose colour vision is comparable to that of birds, can readily tap into this system that the birds themselves have evolved. This book seeks to help you develop that skill.

Every species of bird, depending on its age, sex and state of moult, has consistently recognisable body-parts and plumage-structures, modelled here by a female Blue-winged Kookaburra.

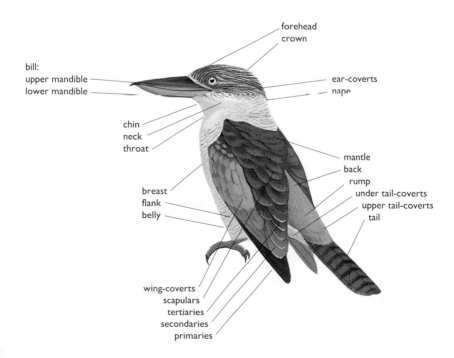

forehead
crown

bill:
upper mandible
lower mandible

ear-coverts
nape

chin
neck
throat

mantle
back
rump
under tail-coverts
upper tail-coverts
tail

breast
flank
belly

wing-coverts
scapulars
tertiaries
secondaries
primaries

Field marks

In the illustrations below, a diversity of birds model the markings they utilise in everyday life. The use of a few technical names to describe these features is unavoidable, e.g. 'wing-coverts', 'primaries', 'secondaries' or 'under tail-coverts'. Most such terms are self-explanatory.

As well as the 'working parts' of birds, there are the tracts or tufts of contrastingly coloured plumage (or bare skin) that increase the range of available field marks. For example: the area between the base of the upper part of the bill and the eye is known as the 'lores'. This marking often stands out: possession of white lores helps separate the male Grey Shrike-thrush from the female. Conversely, the same marking helps distinguish some female fairy-wrens. Other common markings are the crescent-like feather-margins or 'scallops' of Bassian Thrushes; the yellow/white eyebrows of pardalotes; the black masks of some honeyeaters; the chestnut shoulder-patches of some male fairy-wrens; and the white wingbars, pale rumps, dark central rump/tail areas of many waders; and the spread 'fingered' primaries and underwing markings which help distinguish birds of prey. The illustrations below provide a sampler of these.

You will find that these markings occur consistently within groups of related birds — more systematically than it may at first seem. In the text, the outstanding field marks of every species are emphasised by italicising the descriptive words.

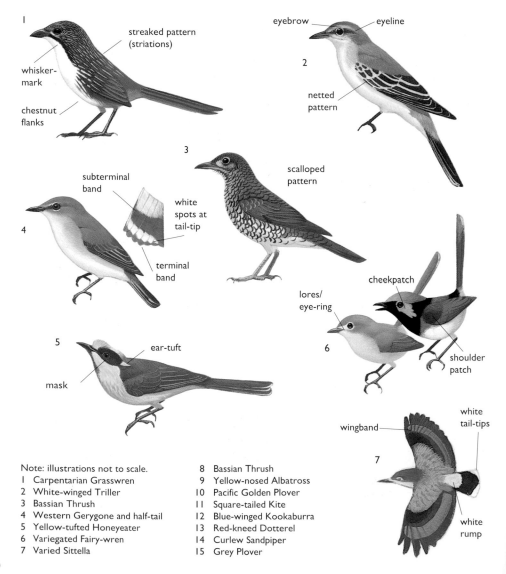

Note: illustrations not to scale.
1 Carpentarian Grasswren
2 White-winged Triller
3 Bassian Thrush
4 Western Gerygone and half-tail
5 Yellow-tufted Honeyeater
6 Variegated Fairy-wren
7 Varied Sittella
8 Bassian Thrush
9 Yellow-nosed Albatross
10 Pacific Golden Plover
11 Square-tailed Kite
12 Blue-winged Kookaburra
13 Red-kneed Dotterel
14 Curlew Sandpiper
15 Grey Plover

Recognising birds by habits and behaviour

Shape, colour and field marks are not the only means of recognising birds. Habits and behaviour can be as useful as, say, a red cap or yellow breast, in identification.

The large impressive Powerful Owl (see p. 12) of southeastern Australia often sleeps by day on large, open limbs under the leaf-canopy, clutching the half-eaten carcass of a possum. Alerted but not startled, it will follow your movements with wide-open, piercing yellow eyes.

In contrast, a Tawny Frogmouth (see p. 12) surprised by day will close its yellow eyes to slits, imperceptibly raise its feather-tufted bill skywards and slim its plumage until it looks like a dead branch with a jagged end. Only our frogmouths adopt such a pose. With other characteristics (see p. 309), it immediately identifies them.

On well-vegetated rivers and wetlands in the tropics, Comb-crested Jacanas ('Lotusbirds', see p. 14) walk on floating vegetation, spreading their weight on enormously long toes. Only jacanas (there are eight world species) have such enormous feet. Crakes and smaller rails also walk on floating vegetation, but they are generally much smaller, with smaller feet, and are more secretive and retiring.

On the bare margins of inland wetlands, companies of dark, red-legged 'waterhens' with upright square, black tails run at high speed or fly with fast, shallow wingbeats. They are Black-tailed Native-hens (see p. 15). The flightless but equally fleet-footed Tasmanian Native-hen is their only close relative. Both are unmistakable from their habit of high-speed sprinting, coupled with plumage-colours. (*Cont'd next page.*)

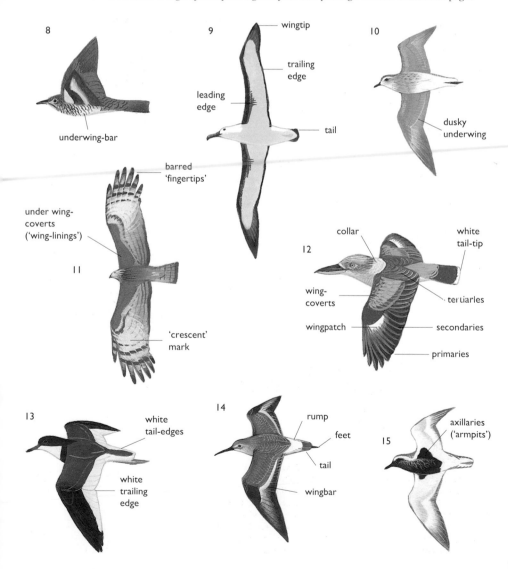

11

POWERFUL OWL

On saline lakes and commercial saltfields across southern Australia, large packs of immaculate, black-and-white waders, some with chestnut breastbands, wade and swim like long-legged gulls, feeding on brine shrimps. Their massed numbers, feeding habits and habitat help identify them as Banded Stilts, see p. 16. (But also see Black-winged Stilt and Red-necked Avocet, p. 200.)

In thundery summer weather in eastern Australia, open companies of fast-flying shapes circle high or race low over forest canopy, paddocks and roads in long, raking dives, on swept, almost blade-like wings. These are migratory White-throated Needletails from north Asia, among the earth's largest and fastest swifts. Gentler-flying Fork-tailed Swifts, also from Asia, are commoner across inland and western Australia. Both are bigger and more dashing than swallows and martins, whose flight is gentle and slipping in comparison. In contrast, the smaller swiftlets, mostly of tropical Queensland have a clipped, irregular, fluttering flight-pattern, reminiscent of small bats.

There are many such behavioural clues: several Australian robins sit upright and lower and flick their wings (and tails). Yellow Robins like to perch on vertical trunks. On the ground, Richard's Pipits gently teeter their tails up and down; Common Sandpipers do the same with greater exaggeration. Treecreepers climb trees from the base up; sittellas mostly work downwards. Gerygones (and weebills) hover outside

TAWNY FROGMOUTH

the foliage; woodswallows wag their tails, often perch in tight rows, and in some conditions, cluster like bees on tree-trunks. In territorial display, many honeyeaters fly steeply skywards singing, before dropping. Some doves fly clattering up before circling down on spread wings/tail. Our two large gulls, Pacific and Kelp, rise vertically in the wind to drop shelled molluscs onto sand or rocks, presumably to smash the shell to get at the flesh inside.

Waders probably baffle more birders than any other group. Our comparatively few resident species, such as the Red-kneed and Black-fronted Dotterels, present few problems, except in immature plumage.

But our large contingent of international migrant waders, mostly from Arctic Asia, can be extremely confusing. The group of Sanderlings on p. 17 illustrates why. First their shape and size is confusingly similar to that of other small waders. Second, when in Australia they mostly wear nondescript, nonbreeding plumage. Third, there are often immatures among them, which look substantially (or subtly) 'different'. Fourth, particularly on arrival in spring or departure in autumn, some will be in full breeding plumage, or in patchy moult, wholly different from birds in other plumages.

There is no easy solution to the problem of identifying waders, but the process of getting to know them can be highly pleasurable. It consists of equipping yourself with the best binoculars you can afford (and spotterscope and tripod if possible), locating the nearest good wader habitat, and spending as many hours as possible thoroughly familiarising yourself with the commoner species, perhaps using a bird hide at a high-tide roost. Once you have their 'jizz' firmly in mind you will find it easier to progressively add strangers. Much the same process of familiarity works with all other groups of birds. But with waders particularly, you will need regular top-ups to keep you up to scratch, as I well know.

Go quietly

To improve your chances of seeing new birds, go quietly: wear comfortable, soft, non-rustling, blending clothing — it doesn't need to be dreary. Move and speak quietly; don't chatter or fidget. Don't whisper! To a bird, sibilant sounds are more disturbing than normal speech. Learn to stand perfectly still and quiet for three (or even five) minutes at a time. In your excitement to share the sight of a bird, *don't point*. Get your binoculars onto it smoothly and quietly. Then alert your companions in a normal voice.

Binoculars

Binoculars for birding should be either one of the two standard centre focusing kinds, and be in the range of 8x30 to 10x50. The first figure refers to the magnifying power, the second to the diameter of the front lens in millimetres. Anything much less than 8x30 lacks the necessary magnifying power; anything over 10x50 (unless mounted on a tripod) is too heavy to carry all day and too hard to hold still.

A simple drill for accurate finding and focusing

Prop up the front page of a newspaper somewhere outside and stand back 10 metres. Look at the paper through your binoculars.

1. Close your right eye and focus by rotating the central or forward focusing wheel until the image of the bold type is sharp in your left eye.

2. Open both eyes, let them adjust, then look at the paper again through the binoculars.

3. Now close your left eye, and focus by rotating the right-hand eyepiece (or the rear central focusing wheel) until the bold type is sharp in you right eye.

4. Now open both eyes and look at the paper through the binoculars. You may have to make minor adjustments to the focusing systems to get a satisfactory degree of sharpness in both eyes.

5. Note the number-setting on the right eyepiece (or rear central focusing wheel), record it and use it.

6. Once through this drill, you need use only the central (or forward) focus-wheel for both eyes.

If the image of the print is double, or even slightly overlapping, or if it takes some optical effort to bring the images together, get your binoculars checked by a reputable repairer. They may have had a bump and be out of alignment — a common problem. If, on the other hand, the problem persists, have your eyes checked, buy new binoculars, or both. It is impossible to birdwatch enjoyably or effectively if you have blurry binoculars.

Finding the bird

There is a simple technique for quickly bringing binoculars to bear on a bird. Set up your newspaper again, this time about 20 metres away. With binoculars ready, look at the paper through naked eyes. Lock you eyes onto it, then smoothly lift the binoculars into your line of vision.* A magnified image of the print should leap into view, ready for sharp-focusing.

Give yourself some time to practise this movement on any distant object. You will soon perfect the ability to accurately locate the bird you wish to see, even one that's flying.

Unless in open, distant situations, do not search for birds with your binoculars. Binoculars have a visual coverage of only a few degrees; your eyes cover nearly 180 degrees. It makes far better sense to use your eyes to do the searching, *then* raise the binoculars.

Spotterscopes

Spotting scopes have at last appeared widely on the Australian scene. Mine is an outstanding, small, inexpensive, rubber-armoured Nikon Spotterscope with a fixed 20x eyepiece. Many birders, especially wader-watchers, prefer larger scopes with 15–60x zoom eyepieces.

A great many of these spotterscopes are excellent, but remember that only by using a solid (preferably tubular) tripod and a sturdy tripod-head, can one get a sufficiently steady, sharp image. If there happens to be a heat-haze, added focal power is of little use.

Bird voices

Many experienced birdwatchers learn more from their ears in two minutes than from half an hour of watching. Given the comprehensive range of bird-tapes now available, from such suppliers as the Bird Observers Club of Australia and the Royal Australasian Ornithologists Union (see p. 557), you can recognise the calls of birds of any part of the continent.

COMB-CRESTED JACANA

* Some spectacle wearers become skilled at pushing their glasses up out of the way as they raise their binoculars, but in general spectacles are a bother. If you need to wear them for normal outdoor activity — and many do — consider buying binoculars with special eyepieces: your binocular supplier should be able to advise.

BLACK-TAILED NATIVE-HEN

Listen repeatedly to these tapes, or to bird-calls in the field. If you wish to be serious about it, perhaps record, in words, in a notebook or on tape, what you *think* you heard, no matter how ridiculous the description may sound. With practice you will refine the description to a memorable version. When you hear that sound again, it will be with the warm feeling of familiarity, wherever you travel.

Tapes

Many people use tapes to lure birds, but the practice seems somewhat unsporting. From the bird's point of view, it often amounts to a rudely confident intruder broadcasting brash challenges from the very heart of the sacred breeding territory, with consequent trauma.

My friend Graeme Chapman, one of our finest bird photographers and recordists, has developed an excellent technique for reducing such trauma. With his tape recorder, he carries a small box speaker at the end of 15 metres of flex. When he wishes to attract a bird, he places the speaker in a prominent spot, rolls out the flex and sits quietly in semi-concealment.

He then starts softly playing calls of the desired species — preferably contact-notes or female calls, rather than the confident, aggressive calls of territorial males. This technique usually brings the desired bird seeking the stranger inside the odd black box, often calling vigorously in response. I have seen the technique work beautifully even on the Rufous Scrub-bird, one of our very shyest.

Be systematic

Confronted by a new bird, get your binoculars onto it (see 'Binoculars', p. 13). Systematically take in its size, shape and any outstanding features, from bill to tail-tip.

1. Note particularly its bill-size, shape and colour. Often the main tool of trade, the bill can tell you much about what kind of bird it is; so can legs and feet.
2. Check colour and markings of face, head, throat, breast, and under tail-coverts, upperparts, rump and wings. Does your bird have a white eyebrow, eye-ring, wingbars or a breastband?
3. Is its tail short, long, square, rounded, pointed or fish-shaped? Does the bird wag it gracefully sideways, quiver or teeter it quickly up and down, slowly raise and lower it, or switch it about like a fan?
4. Does your bird perch upright, crouch along the branch or cling sideways to a trunk?
5. In flight, does it undulate, fly straight and level with regular wingbeats, or is its flight broken by glides?
6. Does it hover motionless, or soar in high circles? (If so, check under-wing pattern.)
7. Does it fly with wings drooped, flat or markedly upswept?
8. Does it have tapering, pointed wings or a broad, paddle-shaped wing with distinct 'fingertips'?
9. Do its wings make a whistling sound in flight, a quick 'flop flop' sound or rustle like heavy silk?
10. If it is a waterbird, does it skitter across the surface, leap cleanly into flight, or dive?

Make notes

Record on the spot what you have seen, in a notebook or on tape. The discipline will sharpen your observing ability, defeat the tyranny of faulty memory, and become a priceless personal reference. If you can, make a rough sketch.

Bird migration

Perhaps because most of Australia lacks really harsh winters and has few land barriers, but does have irregular rainfall and periodic drought, bird migration here differs somewhat from that in Eurasia and North America. Australia certainly has traditional, regular, long distance migrants, but many Australian species make shorter summer/winter circuits, and there is much irregular nomadism.

Let's take the regulars first. Every summer, Australia enjoys the presence of a diverse company of some 80 petrels, jaegers, gulls, terns, snipe, sandpipers, waterfowl, plovers and others that breed mostly in Arctic Asia, Alaska and the North Pacific and spend their nonbreeding months here. Annually they include an estimated two million shorebirds. Some of these travellers, such as the tiny, sparrow-sized Red-necked Stint — fly some 12 000 kilometres each year from Arctic Russia to southeastern Australia and Tasmania, *and return*. In their lifetimes of up to 20 years, these birds may cover a distance that is equivalent to a return journey to the moon.

Conversely, during our winter, waters of the southern Australian continental shelf in particular host about 50 species of penguins, albatrosses, petrels, shearwaters, prions, storm-petrels and skuas that breed in summer in the sub-Antarctic and Antarctic and come here to escape the Antarctic winter. At Port Fairy on the Southern Ocean, an hour's drive south of my home, almost in one sweep of the binoculars I have watched Black-browed Albatrosses from the sub-Antarctic and wintering Common Greenshanks from Arctic Siberia, drawing the poles together.

There are also several categories of local migrant. Most breed in southern Australia (and/or Tasmania) in spring and summer, and 'winter' further north, either in inland or tropical north Australia, or in Papua New Guinea and Indonesia. A few breed only in northern Australia, and 'winter' as above. Some 25 seabirds (including the famed Short-tailed Shearwater or Bass Strait Muttonbird) breed mostly on islands around our coasts, dispersing into nearby ocean waters or undertaking a long migration during the southern winter to the northern or central Pacific, or the northern Indian Ocean.

A number of unrelated species breed in the high forests of the Great Dividing Range from western Victoria to northeast Queensland and move to lower altitudes in autumn-winter. They often make a noticeable winter presence in sub-inland or coastal towns and on farms. They include: Yellow-tailed Black and Gang-gang Cockatoos; Australian King Parrots, Crimson Rosellas; Noisy Pittas; Lewin's Honeyeaters; Flame, Scarlet and Rose Robins; Golden Whistlers; Grey Fantails; Pied Currawongs, Torresian Crows; Regent and Satin Bowerbirds and Bassian Thrushes.

Finally there is a comprehensive mixed company of quail, waterfowl, herons, kites, harriers, hawks, crakes and rails, button-quail, parrots, cuckoos, owls, a kingfisher, pardalotes, honeyeaters, chats, trillers, woodswallows and grassfinches, which breed and live in inland Australia and are highly subject to the vagaries of rainfall.

BANDED STILT

SANDERLINGS

During dry years, some of these may not breed at all, many die, and the rest must find refuge areas in order to survive. Conversely, in years of good rainfall, the resulting boom in seeds, nectar, insects and prey species of birds, mammals, reptiles and amphibians enables some species to increase their numbers several times over. A few, including Black-tailed Native-hens, Crimson Chats and White-browed Woodswallows may then 'irrupt' in large numbers, arriving and often breeding in districts where previously scarce or unknown.

Inevitably, when dry seasons return, many of these opportunists die or disperse coastwards; numbers fall, and it takes them another good run of seasons to recover.

Since the waves caused by these processes are constantly rippling through the populations of these inland-breeding species, it is difficult to precisely describe their status, beyond saying that they are nomads, influenced by irregular rainfall. That comment appears frequently in the Range and Status sections of the species entries.

In trying to understand our birds, it is instructive to keep the dominant influence of irregular rainfall in mind. For almost all our birds are, to greater or lesser degree, bound to the bumpy wheel of rainfall. It helps to make Australian birds what they are.

Distribution and maps

The most authoritative publications currently available on the distribution of Australian birds are the *Handbook of Australian, New Zealand and Antarctic Birds* (OUP and RAOU 1990–) and the *Atlas of Australian Birds* (MUP 1984).

This guide, like others, draws heavily on 'Hanzab' and Atlas data, as is frequently acknowledged in the text. I have also drawn heavily on distribution data published regularly in State and Territory bird journals. These sources are acknowledged on pp. 553–566. I have been provided with data by colleagues, and have my own data from field trips to many parts of the continent. The maps in each species entry have been compiled from these sources.

In each Range and Status section, I have given an indication of approximate limits of distribution by citing place names, and by indicating the kind of annual routine that a species follows. I believe this presents a truer picture than maps alone. Correlates of latitude and longitude (in degrees) of places named in this section can be found in the gazetteer on pp. 558–566. The map on the rear inside cover is gridded in 5° squares for approximate location of those towns, rivers, mountain ranges, and so on. In many cases, the locality, river, mountain range, cape or island, will be found on the more detailed map on the front inside cover.

In many Range and Status entries, indication of commonness or rareness is given. These judgements are arbitrary and subjective, but I hope in general give a true sketch of each species' general status. In the case of vulnerable, rare, threatened or endangered species, I have followed the determinations of *Threatened and Extinct Birds of Australia*, edited by Stephen Garnett, published jointly by the RAOU and the Australian National Parks and Wildlife Service (RAOU Report 82; second edition, April 1993).

EMU *Dromaius novaehollandiae* 1.5–2 m. Female slightly larger.

Aust. largest native bird: plumage loose, each feather divided, *pale grey–brown to almost black; bare skin of head and neck whitish to blue*, darkest in female in breeding condition; eye yellow, grey–brown or reddish; legs dark grey. Birds of se. race *novaehollandiae* have collar of pale, creamy feathers when breeding. Races in w. Aust. darker; in n., paler. **Juvenile:** to 2–3 months, greyish to buff with spotted crown, bold black or brown body stripes. **Immature:** head and neck feathered blackish; body plumage darker and patterned; matures at 18–24 months. Pairs to loose feeding companies of dozens; hundreds where food plentiful. Shy but curious; runs with bouncy flounces, up to 50 km/h in short bursts; swims well. **Similar species:** Ostrich. **Voice:** male: deep growling grunts; female: sequences of up to 10–12, single or double, loud thudding drummings; young: whistling peeps. **Habitat:** plains, scrublands, open woodlands, coastal heaths, alpine pastures, semi-deserts, margins of lakes; pastoral and cereal-growing areas. **Breeds:** April–Oct. **Eggs:** 5–11; large, dark green, granulated; laid on scanty collection of leaves, grass, bark or sticks. Male alone broods, escorts family around a large home range for up to eighteen months. **Range and Status:** Aust. mainland, now mostly absent from closely settled parts. Common in pastoral and cropping regions; State forests, National Parks. Migratory in s. WA, with coastwards movement in spring, after breeding. Tas. population, as well as King I. Emu, *D. ater*, and Kangaroo I. Emu, *D. baudinianus*, became extinct in 19th century as result of European settlement.

SOUTHERN CASSOWARY *Casuarius casuarius* 1.5–1.8 m. Female larger.

Second largest native bird: *black and shaggy, with a horn-covered, bony helmet about 17 cm high; bare skin of head pale blue; neck darker blue and purple with crimson wattles.* **Female:** wattles and skin of neck brighter. **Juvenile:** striped. **Immature:** brown then black; without helmet at first; wattle pinkish or yellowish. Singles, pairs, family parties: shy; usually seen or heard at edge of rainforest or in clearings, especially dawn and dusk. Can be aggressive if provoked. Follows tracks to fruiting trees; swims well. **Voice:** deep, thunderous booming; guttural coughing; young said to emit shrill whistles. **Habitat:** dense rainforest, especially near streams, edges and clearings. **Breeds:** June–Nov. **Nest:** collection of leaves added to rainforest litter, often at base of tree or in grass at edge of forest. **Eggs:** 3–5; very large, pale green, granulated. Male incubates and accompanies young *c.* 9 months. **Range and Status:** coastal ne. Q, from Pascoe R. s. to near Townsville. Common where habitat remains undisturbed; generally uncommon. Sedentary. Also PNG to e. Indonesia.

OSTRICH *Struthio camelus* 1.75–2.75 m. Male larger.

Largest living bird, introduced from Africa. **Male:** *black with 'wings' and tail of prominent white 'ostrich plumes'.* **Female:** *pale brown; wings dirty white.* **Juvenile:** fawn, head and neck striped black. **Immature:** grey–brown, mottled. Size, bare pink–grey head and neck and *huge ballet-dancer's thighs* render it unmistakable. Mostly in family parties: wary, runs with rudimentary wings held out, at speeds to 55 km/h. **Similar species:** Emu: smaller; neck darker, more feathered; lacks bare pink thighs. **Voice:** displaying male: hollow booming, like lion's roar. **Habitat:** pastoral lands, open mulga, saltbush, bluebush; grassed sandplains and dunes. **Breeding:** 3 (or more) females lay 20 (or more) eggs in hollow in sand. Both sexes brood. **Eggs:** very large, creamish, nearly round. **Range and Status:** introduced from S. Africa from 1869 to parts of Vic., NSW, and Younghusband Pen. (SA); also near Port Augusta, L. Alexandrina and Mundoo I. near mouth of Murray R. Most subsequently declined. Recent revival of ostrich farming has seen more birds imported, probably to every State. Two races in Africa: *camelus*, from w. and s. Sahara to Sudan; *australis* from S. Africa. Ostriches in Aust. may include both races, and/or hybrids (Marchant & Higgins, 1990).

EMU

imm.

SOUTHERN
CASSOWARY

imm.

OSTRICH

♀

♂

19

ORANGE-FOOTED SCRUBFOWL *Megapodius reinwardt* 40–50 cm

Other name: Junglefowl (erroneous).

Dark, small-headed fowl *with a short crest and powerful orange legs and feet*. Pairs, parties: active, noisy at dawn, dusk and at night. Disturbed, runs quickly, or flaps up heavily to a low branch, sits motionless with outstretched neck. **Similar species:** Brush-turkey has *bare red head and neck*; vertically fanned black tail. **Voice:** raucous loud double crow; cluckings, like protesting domestic fowl. **Habitat:** mostly lowland rainforests, beach and vine scrubs; mangroves. **Breeds:** July–March, nest-mound may be worked all year and may be used by more than one pair: large mound of earth and vegetation, or of beach sand, to 12 m in diameter and 3 m high, usually smaller. **Eggs:** 6–12; cream–white to pale pink, stained pale brown or red–brown. Laid annually by each female, singly, in deep excavations in mound; at times in decaying leaves in fissures in sun-heated rocks, or in sand. **Range and Status:** coastal n. Aust. and islands; from nw. Kimberley (WA), where patchy, to e. Arnhem Land and Groote Eylandt (NT); in Q, from Mitchell R., w. C. York Pen. and islands in Torres Strait, s. on e. coast to near Byfield; highland records Atherton Tableland. Common; sedentary. Also from Nicobar Is. (Indian Ocean) to Philippines, Indonesia, PNG, New Heb.

MALLEEFOWL *Leipoa ocellata* 55–61 cm

Other names: Lowan; Malleehen.

Large, quiet-moving fowl with greyish head/neck; *black mark down foreneck*; upperparts *barred grey, black, white, buff and pale chestnut*. Singles, pairs; mostly in scrub but also nearby grain-stubbles. Wary; 'freezes', moves quietly away, or bursts up over trees with heavy flapping. Dust-bathes, basks; rests in shade, roosts low in trees. **Voice:** male: deep, two-note bellows or booms; loud clucks. Female: high-pitched crow; soft crooning, low grunts. **Habitat:** mallee, acacia, paperbark, she oak, and other scrubs; eucalypt woodland; coastal heaths; mostly on sandy or gravel soils. **Nest:** mound, 2–5 m in diameter, up to 1.5 m high; in autumn, male fills crater with dry leaves, twigs, bark. Wet by winter rains, then covered with sand. As vegetation rots, internal temperature rises. Male works mound daily until it stabilises (*c.* 33°C). From *c.* Sept. to April, female lays 5–33 eggs, singly, at intervals of 2–14+ days, in hole excavated in mound by male, refilled by him. **Eggs:** pale pink, deepening to pale brown. Chicks hatch at 7+ weeks, dig unaided to surface; can fly and fend for themselves unaided within several hours. **Range and Status:** patchily from Pilliga scrub (NSW) sw. through mallee areas of s. NSW, nw. Vic. and Little Desert, to Murray mallee of SA, s. to Coorong; Yorke and Eyre Pens. and w. SA.; in WA, from sw. Nullarbor–Albany n. to w. coast from *c.* Moore R. to Shark Bay. Recently extinct in NT and n. SA. Sedentary. Vulnerable.

AUSTRALIAN BRUSH-TURKEY *Alectura lathami* 60–70 cm

Other name: Scrub Turkey.

Large black fowl with prominent tail flattened sideways. *Bare red head/neck with bright yellow wattle*, prominent in breeding male. (Race *purpureicollis*: bluish white wattle.) **Immature:** duller, more feathered head/neck. Singles, pairs, parties: wary; runs into undergrowth; flies heavily up into trees, with flapping leaps. Roosts high during heat of day and at night; descends with heavy flappings, grunts. **Similar species:** Orange-footed Scrubfowl: dark-feathered head/crest; orange legs. **Voice:** deep, nasal 'kyok!'; loud clucks, deep grunts. **Habitat:** tropical, temperate rainforests, scrubs; sub-inland brigalow in Q. **Breeds:** May–Nov. **Nest:** mounds average *c.* 4 m across by 1–2 m high; of leaves, etc. mixed with earth. Male regulates temperature at about 35°C. **Eggs:** white, fragile; average number in mound 12–16; laid singly, at intervals of days. One female may lay 20+ eggs per season; some in more than one mound. Incubation period *c.* 7 weeks. Young dig unaided to surface; fend for themselves. **Range and Status:** coastal e. Aust. and islands; from C. York patchily s. to Illawarra region (NSW); inland to *c.* Charters Towers-Blackall-Augathella (Q); in NSW Pilliga scrub, Boggabri. Introduced Dunk I. (Q), Kangaroo I. (SA). Race *purpureicollis* n. C. York Pen. (Q). Sedentary; common, patchy.

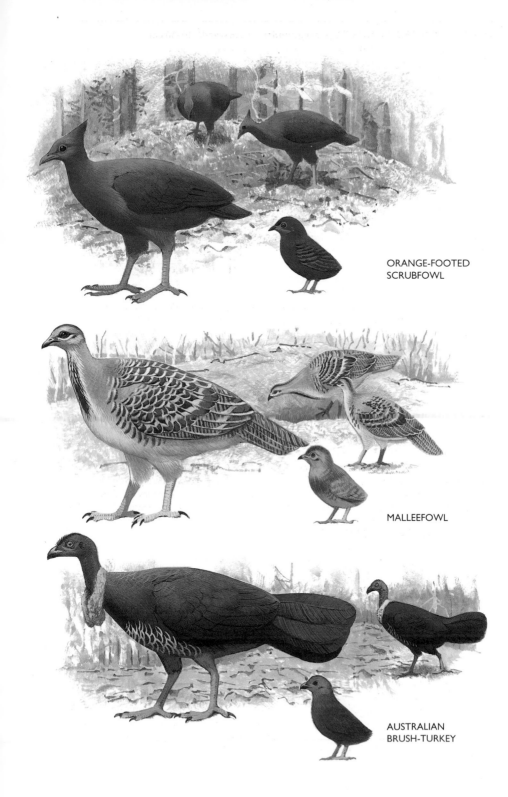

ORANGE-FOOTED
SCRUBFOWL

MALLEEFOWL

AUSTRALIAN
BRUSH-TURKEY

STUBBLE QUAIL *Coturnix pectoralis* 16–20 cm. Female larger.

Widespread quail with *long whitish eyebrows, daggerlike cream streaks on shoulders, back and breast.* **Male:** *rich buff face and throat, with black border and centre of breast.* **Female:** *face and throat fawn–white without black patch.* **Immature:** like dull adults. Singles, pairs, companies: mostly first noticed by call; flushes unexpectedly with explosive whirr; flies low, fast, far; curving slightly, skids tail-first into cover. Often active at dusk on road edges in croplands; runs in spurts. **Similar species:** Brown Quail: *uniformly darker* without strong eyebrow; *fine pattern of V-bars below;* quick chatter when flushed. Little Button-quail: smaller, rounder-winged, with heavier bill; pinkish cinnamon; belly white; chatters when flushed. **Voice:** brisk, clear 'pippy-wheat', or 'two-tweep', repeated 10–12 times/minute over 15+ minutes; others respond. **Habitat:** cereal crops and stubbles; lucerne; overgrown pastures and grasslands with thistles; saltbush, bluebush, spinifex; weedy margins of wetlands, irrigation channels, roadsides. **Breeds:** Aug.–April; dependent on rainfall. **Nest:** in scrape, with grass, etc. **Eggs:** 5–11; roundish; dirty yellow to buff or pale brown, finely smudged dark olive to red–brown. **Range and Status:** e. and se. Q (absent C. York Pen.); NSW, Vic., se. SA, w. to w. Eyre Pen.; s. WA, coastally n. to Shark Bay; rare Tas. In good conditions, moves far inland; casual Pilbara; Kimberley (WA), Top End (NT) and w. Q in good seasons. Nomadic; irruptive, part-migratory.

BROWN QUAIL *Coturnix ypsilophora* 16–22 cm

Other names: Silver, Swamp or Tasmanian Quail.

Largest native quail: face plain, *with dark 'ear-spot'; upperparts with fine silvery streaks; underparts have overall pattern of fine, dark V-bars.* Eye red on mainland, yellow in Tas., where birds are larger (race *ypsilophora*). Males grey, grey–buff to red–buff; females mostly buff–brown, heavily mottled black above. Singles, pairs, coveys of 7–8 (100+ reported in Bass Strait islands): active dawn and dusk; often on dirt roads, rank grassland. Moves fast in spurts and bounds; flushed birds explode in different directions with heavy whirr and quick flutey chatter. Flight fast, low and strong, with glides; dives headfirst into cover. **Similar species:** Stubble Quail: bolder pale streaks; *lacks barred underparts.* King Quail, female: tiny; face and throat buff; black streak under eye; flanks with sparser black crescents; flutters up more steeply. **Voice:** loud, frequent, rising, whistled crow: 'tu-weeeee', 'too-wayee' or 'bee-queek, bee-queek'; mostly morning and evening. **Habitat:** rank grasses near wetlands; drains, green pastures, clover, lucerne; rice and other stubbles; swampy coastal heaths; bracken, swordgrass, *Melaleuca* and *Banksia* thickets, tall tropical grasslands, spinifex savannah. **Breeds:** Aug.–May, timing depending on season. **Nest:** hollow, lined with stems, leaves, etc. **Eggs:** 7–11; roundish; dull blue–white to yellow–white, freckled olive, light brown. **Range and Status:** patchy but widespread in n., e., se. and sw. Aust., from Kimberley (WA) to Eyre Pen. (SA) and Tas.; also parts coastal sw. WA. Extends well inland after good rains, and may breed. Also PNG (where possibly also migratory from Aust.); e. Indonesia. Introduced NZ.

KING QUAIL *Coturnix chinensis* 12–15 cm. Male larger.

Tiny quail. **Male:** unmistakable; see plate. **Female:** darker above than most Brown Quail: *narrow dark crown with cream central streak leaves a large plain buff area on face; curving black line back from bill under eye; throat whitish buff,* distinct from patterned underparts; *fine black crescents on flanks.* **Immature:** like female; heavily spotted below. Pairs, small coveys: shy, elusive in dense habitat. Runs; flies feebly, rising steeply to a few metres, drops again, with upright body-axis; slight whirr. Looks dark on wing; lacks dash of other quail, but does make longer, direct flights, with glides. **Similar species:** Little Button-quail: pinkish cinnamon above, whiter below; bill heavier. Red-backed Button-quail: larger, paler on wing, with yellow–buff, black-spotted 'shoulders'; feeble flight similar. See Stubble and Brown Quail. **Voice:** penetrating, descending elfin crow; day or night. **Habitat:** swampy heaths, dense grasslands; growth on edges of wetlands; weedy pastures and remnants; lucerne crops, tall tropical grasslands; dry sedge-plains, rice stubbles. **Breeds:** Sept.–March in s.; almost any month in n. **Nest:** hooded scrape under tussock; lined with grass, stems, etc. **Eggs:** 4–9; very small, pale brown, olive–yellow or pale green, finely peppered red to black–brown. **Range and Status:** n., e. and se. Aust., and islands, from Kimberley (WA) to sw. Vic. Patchy and irregular; some well inland. Sedentary; dispersive. Also India, China, se. Asia to Indonesia, PNG.

STUBBLE QUAIL

♂

♀

BROWN QUAIL

race *ypsilophora*

♀

♂

KING QUAIL

♂

♀

RED JUNGLEFOWL *Gallus gallus* 40–70 cm

Domestic Fowls released on Gt Barrier Reef islands and elsewhere in 19th century reverted to type of original ancestor, the Red Junglefowl. See plate. **Voice:** high-pitched, bantam-like crow; cacklings. **Habitat:** rainforest, thick scrub and woodland. **Nest:** 'Usually on ground among fallen tree trunks, or up in cavity in the base of a large *Pisonia*' (G. Beruldsen). **Eggs:** 10–13; white. **Range and Status:** natural range: s. and se. Asia, Philippines, Indonesia. Domestic strains worldwide. Feral birds resembling ancestral type survive on Heron I., Capricorn Group (Q). Also Norfolk I. and Cocos–Keeling Is. (n. Indian Ocean).

CALIFORNIA QUAIL *Callipepla californica* 24–27 cm

Male: large, handsome quail, *with a nodding black head-plume; white forehead and eyebrow; large black throat-patch with white border.* Upper breast blue–grey; flanks grey, streaked white; underparts *whitish, cream and chestnut in centre with strong scaly pattern.* **Female:** duller, browner; no black-and-white facial pattern; shorter crest. Pairs, coveys, winter flocks of dozens: shy; runs with nodding topknot; flight explosive. **Voice:** in breeding season, a wild, 'qua-quergo', lost and plaintive; liquid 'dup dup'; soft grunts, cackles, staccato whistles. **Habitat:** rank grassland in scrubs, stunted woodlands; dense tea-tree thickets. **Breeds:** spring–early summer. **Nest:** scrape lined with grass. **Eggs:** 10–16; buff with dark spots. **Range and Status:** w. N. America; introduced to parts NSW, Vic., Tas., from 1863; also to NZ, where now widespread. In Aust., most introductions failed, but remains fairly common King I., Bass Strait. Reported near Newcastle (NSW), 1981 (Blakers et al, 1984). Also Norfolk I. Sedentary.

COMMON PHEASANT *Phasianus colchichus* 53–90 cm, incl. tail. Male larger.

Other names: Chinese, Ring-necked or Mongolian Pheasant.
Male: *head glossy dark green with 'horns', scarlet wattle and, in some, white neck-ring;* body-plumage of rich, burnished chestnut reds; wings rounded; tail long and pointed, crossed with fine black bars. **Female:** *pale brown and rich buff with dark brown and black mottlings and feather-centres; flight and tail-feathers barred paler;* no wattle or 'horns'; tail shorter. **Immature:** like dull female. Singles to small flocks, parties. Wary, runs; rockets vertically over trees with noisy flapping. **Similar species:** Pheasant Coucal. **Voice:** male: strident crow, 'korrk-kok!'; harsh note when flushed. **Habitat:** scrubby eucalypt forest and woodlands, coastal scrubs, paperbark thickets, heaths, rank grasslands, pastures, orchards, crops. **Breeds:** spring–early summer. **Nest:** scrape, lined with grass, etc., under grass, bracken, ferns. **Eggs:** 7–15; creamy olive–brown. **Range and Status:** from Caspian Sea, parts of Iran and Turkey, e. to China, Mongolia, Korea. Introduced (from England) to many locations in Aust.; few were successful. Feral populations survive on Rottnest I. (WA); King I., Bass Strait and possibly Tas. Sedentary.

WILD TURKEY *Meleagris gallopavo* 90 cm–1.25 m. Male larger.

Unmistakable, with bare pinkish grey head and expandable reddish neck wattle. Dark, with bronze, green and chestnut gloss, black barrings; primaries barred black and white; tail large, drooped, barred rufous and black. Males have larger red wattles, darker plumage and breast-tuft or 'beard' (lacking in most females). Parties; 1 male and 4–5 females; females with chicks, or groups of males. Forages on ground; when approached, runs or flies strongly. Roosts in trees. Males display with enlarged wattles, drooped wings, fanned tail. **Voice:** male: loud gobbling; contact call: sharp 'keow, keow'; yelps, croaks, trills. **Habitat:** edges of coastal scrublands, woodlands; grasslands; tree-lined windbreaks. **Breeds:** mostly spring–summer. **Nest:** a scrape, under cover of shrub, lined with grass, leaves. **Eggs:** 8–15; cream, spotted red–brown and lilac, covered when female leaves nest. **Range and Status:** e. N. America, s. to Mexico. Domesticated, widely distributed since 16th century. Introduced Aust. in 19th century. Small, semi-feral populations persist on Flinders, King Is. (Tas.). Sedentary.

INDIAN PEAFOWL *Pavo cristatus.* Male: 2–2.3 m, incl. 'train'; female *c.* 1 m.

Other names: Common Peafowl; Peacock; Peahen.
Male: unmistakable: *brilliant blue head and body;* 'train' consists of *abnormally long upper tail-coverts: glossy dark blue–green with many golden blue 'eyes';* raised fan-like and concave in display, supported by the short rufous tail-feathers. **Female:** ('peahen') grey–brown above; whitish below, patterned on breast; lacks 'train'. Singles, pairs, parties: feeds on ground; flies heavily aloft to roost; noisy. There is a non-albino white form. **Voice:** loud, discordant, descending wail or crow, sounding like 'help!'. **Habitat:** coastal scrubs, private and public gardens, sanctuaries, homesteads. **Nest:** scrape, usually under cover. **Eggs:** 3–5; brownish buff. **Range and Status:** India and Sri Lanka; long-domesticated, introduced many parts of the world, incl. Aust., Tas., King and Flinders Is. (Tas.), Kangaroo I. (SA), Rottnest I. (WA). Isolated semi-feral populations, usually near habitation, se. Q; s. Riverina (NSW).

RED JUNGLEFOWL

♀

♂

CALIFORNIA QUAIL
(scale enlarged x 2.5)

♀

♂

COMMON PHEASANT

♂

♀

WILD TURKEY

♂

♀

INDIAN PEAFOWL

♂

♀

WANDERING WHISTLING-DUCK *Dendrocygna arcuata* 55–61 cm

Other name: Diving Whistling-Duck.

Posture lower than Plumed Whistling-Duck, swimming and standing. *Black crown and nape contrast with plain yellow–buff face and neck: shoulders chestnut*; short cream flank-plumes. **Immature:** duller; centre of abdomen paler. Flocks of dozens to thousands; camps on margins of swamps and rivers; *feeds in water, dabbling, upending; companies move ahead, diving repeatedly*, to depth of 3 m. Flies in whistling mobs, looks dark and richly coloured: *chestnut shoulders and underparts, blackish underwing: note trailing black legs.* **Similar species:** Plumed Whistling-Duck: taller, paler, with pink bill and legs; brown underwing; white belly. **Habitat:** well-vegetated lagoons and swamps, flooded grasslands, pools in floodplains, river margins, well-vegetated large dams; occasionally tidal areas. **Breeds:** Jan.–May. **Nest:** scrape in ground, lined with grass; in grassland, under bush, vegetation by swamp or some distance away. **Eggs:** 6–8; cream, smooth. **Range and Status:** tropical and subtropical n. Aust.: from *c.* Fitzroy R. (WA), to se. Q; casual; NSW, Vic., sw. WA. Part-migratory. Also Philippines, Indonesia, PNG and Pacific Is.

PLUMED WHISTLING-DUCK *Dendrocygna eytoni* 41–62 cm

Elegant, erect pale brown duck *with patchy pink bill, long pink legs and upswept cream flank-plumes; sides of chest reddish, finely barred darker.* **Immature:** paler, duller. Parties to dense flocks form regular daytime camps, flying out at dusk to feed on green grasses and seeds, returning at dawn. Wingbeats slow, with characteristic wing-whistle; silhouette humped, legs trailing. *Note brown underwing, pale underparts, trailing pink legs.* In wet season (n. Aust.) and winter/spring in se. Aust., pairs disperse to feed in shallow wetlands: they dabble and upend but seldom dive; *swim with head high, flank-plumes upswept.* **Similar species:** Wandering Whistling-Duck. **Voice:** spirited whizzing whistles, lively twitterings. **Habitat:** margins of waterholes; farm dams, well-vegetated wetlands, floodplains, mangrove creeks, estuarine pools, sewage farms, grasslands, grain-stubbles, pastures, irrigated lands, ricefields. **Breeds:** Aug.–Oct., se. Aust.; Jan.–March, n. Aust. **Nest:** scrape, scantily lined with grass, plant-stems; in grass or scrub; near or far from water. **Eggs:** 10–12; white, smooth, pointed. **Range and Status:** n. and e. Aust.: extending into s. NSW and Vic.; casual far inland; sw. Vic., ne. and se. SA. Seasonally migratory or dispersive. Vagrant PNG and NZ.

SPOTTED WHISTLING-DUCK *Dendrocygna guttata* 43 cm. Not illustrated.

Dark brown above; buff–brown on face, throat and breast. *Flanks dark brown, boldly spotted white.* Bill dull red, spotted darker; legs/feet dull red–brown; posture hunched. Small to large flocks; dabbles and grazes, mostly at night. **Voice:** wheezy, nasal *zzeow.* **Habitat:** lowland marshes, mangroves (Beehler et al, 1986). **Range and Status:** Philippines, e. Indonesia, PNG, Bismarck Arch. From March–April 1995, small numbers of this widespread PNG duck were seen at the Weipa Sewerage Farm (ne. Q). On 25 December 1995, 39 birds were counted. These were the first Aust. records of this species.

AUSTRALIAN WOOD DUCK *Chenonetta jubata* 44–50 cm; span to 80 cm

Other name: Maned Duck or Goose.

Handsome, *brown-necked pale grey duck with two black stripes along back.* **Male:** *small black 'mane'.* **Female:** paler brown head with two pale stripes separated by eye. Walks easily: *short bill and longish neck and legs give it the look of a small, fine goose.* Camps by day on bare banks of dams; perches on dead logs, branches. Dabbles in shallows, often upending; feeds in grasslands, irrigated crops. Flocks fly in random order: note black belly and tail, *grey, dark-tipped wings with conspicuous white trailing panel.* Flight easy and swift as birds weave through woodland. **Voice:** female: loud, long-drawn, rising, nasal 'gnow?'; male: shorter, higher. Staccato chattering from flocks at rest or feeding. **Habitat:** grasslands, pastures, open woodlands, farm dams, lakes, wetlands, flooded pastures, coastal inlets, bays, sewage ponds, crops, ricefields, town parks. **Breeds:** Sept.–Nov. in s. Aust.; after rain elsewhere. **Nest:** of down; in hollow, over, or far from, water. **Eggs:** 9–11; cream–white. **Range and Status:** Aust. and Tas.: widespread. Has benefited greatly from farming and creation of dams. Sedentary, dispersive. Vagrant NZ.

WANDERING
WHISTLING-DUCK

PLUMED
WHISTLING-DUCK

AUSTRALIAN
WOOD DUCK

FRECKLED DUCK *Stictonetta naevosa* 48–59 cm

Other name: Monkey Duck.

At distance on water, *looks dark and broad-hulled; head blackish, large and peaked at rear; bill grey, markedly scooped.* **Male, breeding:** *bright wax-red base to bill.* Plumage *blackish brown, finely freckled pale buff to whitish; underparts paler.* **Female:** *paler; finely freckled; bill grey.* **Immature:** lighter brown, freckled buff. Parties to cohesive flocks of hundreds on open water. Where undisturbed, camps ashore, sits on stumps, fence-posts in water; feeds by filtering, upending, wading. Looks dark in flight, *with a distinctive coppery sheen; paler below, with pale wing-linings,* less gleaming white than Black Duck's: silhouette more humped, neck depressed; head larger, neck shorter, wings sharper and smaller. **Similar species:** Blue-billed Duck, female: bill blunter; head rounder. **Voice:** soft, flute-like pipe, 'whee-yu', like Black Swan. Male: short raucous roar, 'between a sniff and a snort'; female: loud discordant quack. **Habitat:** large, well-vegetated swamps; in dry periods moves to open lakes. **Breeds:** Sept.–Dec., or after suitable rainfall. **Nest:** well-constructed bowl; of stems and sticks; in lignum clump, overhanging tea-tree branch or flood-debris, or old nest of Coot. **Eggs:** 5–14; creamy, glossy, oval. Shooters' name Monkey Duck derives from habit of climbing through lignum to reach nest. **Range and Status:** breeds mostly in irregularly flooded lignum swamps in w. NSW; far sw. Q; ne. SA; also sw. WA. Disperses into coastal se. and s. Aust., nw. WA, Top End (NT) and n. Q as summer winter visitor. Rare, irruptive, nomadic.

BLUE-BILLED DUCK *Oxyura australis* 37–44 cm; span *c.* 60 cm

Male, breeding: *small rich-chestnut duck with black head, dark eye and scooped, bright pale blue bill.* Tail black, of many pointed feathers carried on surface, *or raised, fanlike.* **Female:** blackish brown, very finely barred buffish; whiter below. *Note the scooped dark grey–green bill, pale throat and slight pale line across face below eye.* **Immature:** duller, paler. Male eclipse (mostly March–July) like dark, plain female; bill patchy grey–green. Solitary, or in winter companies far from shore. Swims low, with silhouette of largish head, scooped bill, sloping stern; tail flatly submerged; dives smoothly and often. Flight rapid, direct, tail-heavy, wingbeat quick and shallow. Dives rather flies when alarmed. **Similar species:** Musk Duck, female: larger; bill more bluntly triangular; head more shaggy. See Hardhead. **Voice:** male in display: rapid, low, drumming note; female: weak quack. **Habitat:** well-vegetated freshwater swamps; large dams, lakes; in winter, more open waters. **Breeds:** Sept.–March. **Nest:** shallow cup with little down lining, often with canopy in cumbungi, pencil-rush, lignum, tea-tree over water; on ground on island; old nest of other waterfowl. **Eggs:** 5–8; light green, rough; in nest, dirtier green. **Range and Status:** se. and sw. Aust., especially Murray–Darling Basin; uncommon Tas.; casual inland and n. Aust. Mostly sedentary; young birds dispersive.

MUSK DUCK *Biziura lobata* 47–72 cm. Male larger.

Other names: Diver; Steamer.

A very strange duck. **Male:** large, low, broad and dark, with *leathery flap under bluntly triangular dark grey bill, stiff tail of 28 feathers.* **Female:** lacks bill-flap. **Immature:** at first like female. Solitary to large, open, autumn–winter companies. Swims low, *like cormorant or even platypus.* Submerges smoothly, bringing yabbies, crabs to surface. *Dozes on surface with tail spread, fanlike.* Male in display fans tail forward over back, expands under tail-coverts like powderpuff; bill raised, bill-flap expanded, rotates slowly in water, throwing foot-splashes with a loud 'k-plonk', *simultaneously uttering a grunt and a shrill, far-carrying whistle.* Female: soft grunts. Seldom on wing, but in strong breezes flies heavily. **Similar species:** Blue-billed Duck, eclipse male and female: smaller, bill scooped. **Habitat:** well-vegetated swamps; wetlands, both brackish and fresh; lakes, reservoirs, shallow bays, inlets; occasionally at sea. **Breeds:** mostly Aug.–Nov. **Nest:** rough cup of plant stems, lined with down; in cumbungi, rushes, grass on island, under low tea-tree, with canopy of surrounding growth; hole in tree at water level. **Eggs:** 1–3(4); green–white, limy; stained brown. **Range and Status:** s. Aust., from s. Q to Tas. and Bass Strait; e. and ne. SA; coastal s. WA n. to Shark Bay. Sedentary; dispersive when young, and in drought.

♂ breeding

FRECKLED DUCK

♀

BLUE-BILLED DUCK

♀

♂

♂ eclipse

Hardhead
(for comparison)

MUSK DUCK

♂

♀

♂

MUTE SWAN *Cygnus olor* 1.3–1.6 m; span 2.4 m. Male larger.
Other name: White Swan.
A very large, *wholly white swan; wings often raised in heraldic manner; bill orange with black base and knob*; in male, knob becomes larger in spring; legs and feet dark grey. **Immature:** brownish grey with knobless grey–pink bill. Flight strong, with *singing of wings*. **Voice:** hisses; rarely-heard trumpet. **Habitat:** ornamental lakes, rivers; possibly sheltered sea-coasts as in Europe. **Breeds:** Aug.–Nov. **Nest:** large heap of vegetation; on islands or among vegetation in shallows. **Eggs:** 3–7 or more; green–white, larger than Black Swan's. **Range and Status:** introduced from Europe to parts of se. and sw. Aust. and Tas.; most failed. Small breeding colonies on Northam Weir on Avon R. at Northam (WA) and reportedly at L. Leake (Tas.). Sedentary. Also introduced, and established, NZ.

BLACK SWAN *Cygnus atratus* 1–1.4 m; span 1.6–2 m. Male larger.

World's only mostly black swan; *white flight-feathers conspicuous in flight*, often visible at rest. **Male:** bill and neck longer and straighter. **Immature:** dull grey–brown with pale edges to feathers; flight-feathers dingy white, tipped black. Singles to companies of thousands. Becomes flightless during post-breeding moult, when many thousands gather on secure waters: e.g. L. George (NSW), Moulting Lagoon (Tas.) and Coorong (SA). Travelling birds frequently heard overhead at night. **Voice:** musical bugle with a break, uttered on water or in flight; softer crooning notes. **Habitat:** large open waters, fresh, brackish and salt; flooded pastures, green crops, tidal mudflats. Prefers larger permanent swamps and lakes with emergent and subaquatic vegetation; ornamental town lakes; sheltered estuaries and bays; occasionally open sea. **Breeds:** April–Oct. in s.; March–May in ne. Q; but any month after suitable rains. **Nest:** large heap; of reeds, grasses, aquatic plants, 1–1.5 m in diameter; in shallow water, on islands; occasionally in colonies. **Eggs:** 4–6 or more; greenish white. **Range and Status:** widespread and common in s. and e. Aust., Tas. and s. WA. Apparently extending breeding range into inland and Top End (NT); but still casual C. York Pen. and Gulf coast (Q), Arnhem Land and w. deserts (NT and WA). Sedentary; nomadic and dispersive. Introduced NZ and elsewhere; vagrant PNG.

CAPE BARREN GOOSE *Cereopsis novaehollandiae* 75–90 cm

Large pale ash-grey goose *with a square black tail, over which grey wing-feathers droop in short 'bustle'*. Note short black bill, *nearly covered by greenish yellow cere; white crown* and strong dusky-red legs; feet black. **Immature:** paler. Breeding pairs (on islands), family groups to summer–autumn flocks of 100+. Grazes open areas, incl. cultivated pastures and slopes of islands among rocks and tussocks; *white crown visible when head lowered*. Wary; flight powerful, in lines or random mobs, often with a harsh clamour: *wingbeats shallow; note pale patch toward dark wingtips*, black tail and under tail-coverts. Swims seldom but strongly, stern uptilted. **Voice:** both sexes utter pig-like grunts and honks. Male: loud harsh 'ark, ark-ark, ark-ark'. Imm.: reedy whistles. **Habitat:** offshore islands; improved pastures with clovers; salty ground with native succulents; camps on margins of dams; fresh or brackish swamps and lakes. **Breeds:** June–Sept. **Nest:** shallow cup; of grass, twigs, lined with down; on ground beside bush, tussock or rock. **Eggs:** 3–5; dull white. **Range and Status:** breeds from Furneaux Group and other islands, Bass Strait (Tas.), to Sir Joseph Banks Group, Neptune I., other islands in SA; Recherche Arch. and islands w. to near Albany (WA). Disperses in spring–summer to cultivated pastures on larger islands and nearby mainland areas in n. Tas.; s. and sw. Vic.; se. SA; and Eyre Pen., and near Esperance (WA); casual s. NSW. Locally migratory and dispersive. Introduced Kangaroo I. (SA), ACT and elsewhere, incl. NZ.

MUTE SWAN

imm.

BLACK SWAN

imm.

imm.

CAPE BARREN GOOSE

MAGPIE GOOSE *Anseranas semipalmata* 75–90 cm; span 1.2–1.8 m. Male larger.

Other name: Pied Goose.

Long orange–yellow legs; narrow bill, reddish facial skin and knobbed head distinguish this lanky, black-and-white, goose-like bird. **Immature**: smuttier; crown rounded, without knob. Parties to huge flocks: digs around swamp-margins; wades, swims with stern uptilted, upends; perches in heads of swamp–woodland trees. When approached, raises thickets of black necks and a fluty clamour. Flight laboured, on broad wings with *pronounced black fingertips*: note white underparts and underwings, *large black tail*; glides with lowered legs when alighting. **Similar species:** in flight, Black Swan: white wingtips; Straw-necked Ibis: white tail. **Voice:** falsetto honking, louder and higher-pitched in male. Young birds: sibilant whistles. **Habitat:** large seasonal wetlands and well-vegetated dams with rushes and sedges; wet grasslands, floodplains. **Breeds:** Jan.–April, n. Aust.; July–Nov., se. Aust. (Marchant & Higgins, 1990). **Nest:** a deep cup; on mound of floating or trampled-down vegetation; in colony in swamp. **Eggs:** 1–16, average about 8; oval, cream–white or off-white; often stained. **Range and Status:** formerly widespread in large numbers in se. Aust., coastal e. and ne. Aust. Now extends coastally (up to 300 km inland) from near Broome (WA) to about Brisbane (Q). Casual s. NSW, Vic., SA, WA; extending s. in se. Q and ne. NSW; rare, irregular Tas. Reintroduced parts Vic., where occasional reports of hundreds. Mostly sedentary; dispersive in dry season, extent of movement depending on water conditions. Also Torres Strait and s. PNG.

RADJAH SHELDUCK *Tadorna radjah* 48–60 cm; span 90 cm–1 m

Other names: Burdekin Duck; White-headed Shelduck.

Conspicuous *white duck with pale, flesh-coloured bill, pink legs, dark chestnut upperparts and breastband,* narrower in female; white plumage sometimes rust-stained. **Immature:** duller; flecked grey and brown. Pairs, parties, dry-season flocks: often perches in paperbarks over water; rests conspicuously on sandbars, mudflats. Feeds ashore or on margins of wetlands; pairs or parties dabble in shallows, frequently upending; busy, active, quarrelsome; part-nocturnal. In flight, *from below, white wings look dipped in ink; note breastband and dark tail.* Often flies through swamp woodland below canopy. **Voice:** male: hoarse whistles. Female: harsh rattling, usually in flight. **Habitat:** in wet season, most shallow waters: fresh, salt and brackish swamps, mangrove-lined coastal creeks, shallow river-margins. In dry season, concentrates on larger permanent lagoons, paperbark swamps, man-made wetlands, mangroves, tidal mudflats, estuaries. **Breeds:** Feb.–July or later, depending on wet season. **Nest:** in tree hollow usually in or near water. **Eggs:** 6–12; cream, smooth. **Range and Status:** coastal tropical n. Aust., from e. Kimberley (WA) to *c.* Rockhampton (Q), with possible break on Gulf coast (NT–Q); occasionally casual s. WA, s. SA, n. Vic., NSW, s. Q. (Range formerly extended into ne. NSW.) Sedentary; locally dispersive in dry season. Also Torres Strait islands, PNG, e. Indonesia.

AUSTRALIAN SHELDUCK *Tadorna tadornoides* 55–74 cm; span 1 m–1.3 m

Other names: Chestnut-breasted Shelduck; Mountain Duck.

Conspicuous, large, mostly black-plumaged duck with bold white, chestnut markings, large shot — green 'mirror' on wing. **Male:** white neck-ring; rich buff breast; in eclipse plumage, breast biscuit-coloured. **Female:** smaller; *breast rich chestnut; white eye-ring and white round base of bill.* **Immature:** duller, paler; head speckled white. Pairs, family parties to large flocks in which pairs persist. Grazes on short green grass; dabbles or upends in shallows; flocks loaf by day on large waters. Flight strong; *in Vs or wavering lines;* note *white panel on leading edge and white, black-tipped underwing.* After breeding, some migrate long distances to particular large waters, e.g. L. George (NSW) and Coorong (SA), to moult flight and tail-feathers, becoming temporarily flightless. **Voice:** male: deep zizzing grunts. Female: higher-pitched 'ong gank, ong gank' or strident 'ow ow ow ow'. **Habitat:** large shallow waters: fresh, brackish, saline and tidal; farmlands, pastures, stubble fields, young crops, irrigation areas, open woodlands; occasionally at sea. **Breeds:** June–Nov. **Nest:** down lining in tree hollow; on ground under vegetation; rabbit burrow, hole in cliff, shallow cave; often far from water. **Eggs:** 8–14; oval, cream, lustrous. Flightless downy young may gather in large 'crèches'. **Range and Status:** Aust. and Tas.: sparse in inland and n.; stronghold is w. Vic. and sw. WA; uncommon n. Aust. Sedentary; dispersive; locally migratory. Self-introduced NZ.

MAGPIE GOOSE

juv.

♂

♀

juv.

RADJAH SHELDUCK

♂

♀

♂

AUSTRALIAN SHELDUCK

♀

33

COTTON PYGMY-GOOSE *Nettapus coromandelianus* 34–38 cm; span *c.* 60 cm

Other name: White Pygmy-Goose.
Male: tiny, white, toylike: *note short black bill and black breastband; crown/upperparts glossy blackish green*. **Female:** duller; *dark eyeline separated from crown by conspicuous white eyebrow;* neck shaded grey; dark zone around upper breast. **Immature:** like female; browner. Pairs, parties among water-lilies; rests on logs in water; perches on trees. Flies low; male: flashing *white patch near wingtip. Female: thin white bar on trailing edge.* **Similar species:** see Green Pygmy-Goose, female. Radjah Shelduck: larger; bill and legs whitish pink. **Voice:** male, in flight: staccato coo; female: soft quack. **Habitat:** deeper freshwater swamps, lagoons, dams, with water-lilies and other semi-emergent waterplants. **Breeds:** Nov.–April. **Nest:** high, in hollow tree near water. **Eggs:** 8–15; oval, pearly-white. **Range and Status**: coastal e. Q, from Princess Charlotte Bay (e. C. York Pen.) to *c.* Brisbane. Irregular ne. NSW (where once resident); casual n. and e. Vic. Sedentary; locally dispersive in dry season. Also s. and se. Asia, Philippines, Indonesia, PNG.

GREEN PYGMY-GOOSE *Nettapus pulchellus* 34–38 cm; span to 60 cm

Male: short, pink-tipped bill; blackish cap; conspicuous white cheeks; glossy dark green neck/upperparts; *underparts seem grey–white; white feathers finely barred dark green.* **Female and immature:** duller; faint white eyebrow; cheeks, neck/underparts grey–white. **Male, nonbreeding:** cheeks smutty, not white. Pairs, small flocks on permanent wetlands among water lilies, lotus, other vegetation. Seldom ashore; rests on logs, branches. In flight, note *flickering white wedge on rear edge of dark wing near body;* dark head and neck. **Similar species:** see Cotton Pygmy-Goose. **Voice:** shrill 'pee-whit' uttered in flight; also descending 'pee-yew'; high-pitched 'whit!' and high-pitched musical trill. **Habitat:** tropical lagoons, lakes, dams with water-lilies, and other semi-emergent waterplants. In wet season, shallower swamps of spike-rush, wild rice. **Breeds:** Dec.–March. **Nest:** usually in tree hollow in or near water, up to 10 m high. **Eggs:** 8–12; white or creamy white, lustrous. **Range and Status:** coastal n. Aust., from Victoria R. (NT) to about Fraser I. (Q). Sedentary or seasonally dispersive, with local dry season congregations on permanent waters. Also Torres Strait islands, s. PNG; some e. Indonesian islands.

NORTHERN PINTAIL *Anas acuta* 50–66 cm, incl. tail; span 80–95 cm. Male larger.

Male, breeding: *elegant, long-necked slender duck* with grey–brown head, black nape, *white neck and chest*; pale grey flanks with long black and white scapulars; white flank-crescent, black under tail-coverts and *long, slender, pointed black tail with two long streamers.* **Female:** plain, pale brown head and neck; plumage scalloped buff and dark brown; tail shorter than male, brown, pointed. Flight swift: wingbeats rapid; male: brown head; white underbody and pointed tail; white trailing edge to dark green speculum. Female: browner; white belly; upper and underwings grey with white trailing edge. **Voice:** mostly silent; breeding male: short 'kree'. **Range and Status:** breeds n. Eurasia and N. America, migrating to Africa, s. and se. Asia; vagrant n. Borneo and Java; PNG and Pacific islands. Vagrant Aust.: adult male, Chandala Swamp Nature Res., 50 km ne. Perth (WA) July 1986 (Agar *et al*, 1988).

HARDHEAD *Aythya australis* 45–60 cm; span to 70 cm

Other name: White-eyed Duck.
Compact, rich-mahogany diving duck *with largish, high-crowned head.* **Male:** *eye white; bill blackish, tip crossed by blue–white band; 'stern' white.* **Female:** paler brown; *eye dark; bill blue–grey;* throat whitish. **Immature:** like female. Singles, pairs, to rafts of thousands: feeds on surface, in shallows, and in deeper water. Dives smoothly, submerges 20–30 seconds, emerges swimming rapidly; body slopes rearwards. Flight swift, with shallow flickering of slender, rear-set wings: note *flashing translucent white trailing edge to wing, white underwings and belly.* **Similar species:** see Blue-billed Duck. **Voice:** male: soft wheezy whistle; female: harsh rattle. **Habitat:** deep, permanent wetlands; large open waters; brackish coastal swamps; farm dams, ornamental lakes, sewage ponds. **Breeds:** Aug.–Dec. (se. Aust.). **Nest:** neat, well-woven cup of stems, with canopy; in reeds, cumbungi, lignum, waterside bush, stump, bole of swamp tree. **Eggs:** 9–12; creamy white. **Range and Status:** Aust. and Tas. in suitable habitat. Breeds in mainland e., se. and sw. Aust., dispersing to n. Aust., Tas. and far inland, except w. deserts, after good rains. Irregular to Indonesia, PNG, Pacific Is. and NZ. Dispersive and irruptive.

COTTON PYGMY-GOOSE

♀

♂

GREEN PYGMY-GOOSE

♀

♂

NORTHERN PINTAIL

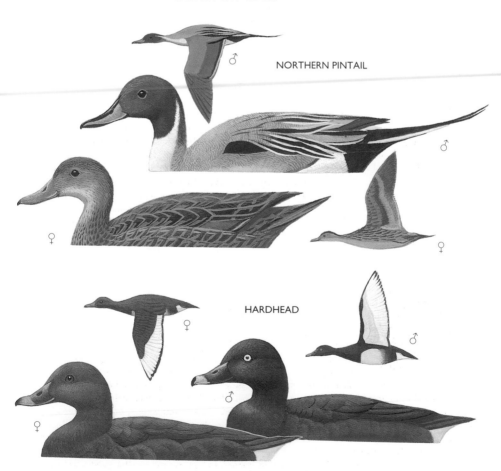

♂

♂

♀

♀

HARDHEAD

♀

♂

♂

♀

MALLARD *Anas platyrhynchos* 50–70 cm; span 85 cm–1 m

'Typical duck' of popular illustrations, member of a closely-related world group of dabbling ducks; ancestor of many barnyard breeds. **Male:** *bill yellow; head green with white neck-ring; breast purplish; wings pale grey; speculum ('wing-mirror') blue, edged black-and-white; tail white with upcurled black central feathers;* legs orange. **Female:** bill and feet dull orange; plumage paler brown, streaked and mottled darker; crown dark; *faint light eyebrow;* speculum as in male; *tail plain, whitish.* Male eclipse resembles dark female. In flight, *white underwing and whitish tail; white edges to blue speculum.*
Hybrids with native Pacific Black Duck (also a mallard) resemble latter with yellow to orange feet and Mallard speculum, or Mallard's patchy green head and curled duck-tail; females resemble female Mallard with Black Duck's facial markings. **Voice:** like Black Duck; male: quiet 'yeeb' or low 'kwck'; female: boisterous 'quack, quack-quack'. **Habitat:** deep fresh waters, rivers, ornamental lakes, ponds, farm dams. **Breeds:** Sept.–Oct. **Nest:** of grass, reeds, lined with down; usually near water, under vegetation; on ground, tree-hollow. **Eggs:** 8–15; creamy, greenish or blue–white. **Range and Status:** Eurasia, n. Africa, N. America. Introduced from England in 1860s: widespread se. Aust. and Tas. Introduced NZ, where widespread; banded NZ mallards have reached Aust.

PACIFIC BLACK DUCK *Anas superciliosa* 48–60 cm; span 80–94 cm

Other names: Brown, Grey or Wild Duck.
Familiar Aust. 'wild duck': tame in public gardens; wild and wary elsewhere. Plumage dark wood-brown with pale feather-margins: speculum dark green to purple, edged black. *Head pattern unmistakable: crown blackish; face and throat whitish to rich yellow–buff, with bold black stripe through eye, another from chin.* Pairs to flocks: dabbles, upends in shallows; forages among wetland vegetation, ashore, in wet pastures; grain stubbles. Perches on logs, dead trees over water. Flight strong with characteristic wing-whistle; *gleaming white underwing* contrasts with dark plumage. **Similar species:** Mallard, female; Grey Teal and female Chestnut Teal. **Voice:** male: quick 'raab raabraab'; when flushed, hoarse whispered 'fraank fraank'; loud 'peep' when courting. Female: hearty descending 'quark quark quark!' or quick persistent quacks. **Habitat:** any suitable water: roadside and backyard ponds, swimming pools, farm dams to tidal mudflats; prefers large permanent waters with plentiful vegetation; public gardens. **Breeds:** June–Dec., in s. **Nest:** often in stump or tree hollow, when of down only; also part-formed nests on ground, in grass, swamp-vegetation; old nest of corvid, etc. **Eggs:** 6–11; white or greenish cream. **Range and Status:** Aust. and Tas. Sedentary and nomadic. Tends to move n. in winter, s. in summer. Some exchange to and from NZ. Also Indonesia to PNG, Micronesia, Polynesia, NZ and sub-Antarctic islands.

GARGANEY *Anas querquedula* 38–41 cm

About the size and agility of Grey Teal, but distinctly marked; head somewhat shoveler-like. **Male:** head rich brown with long *curving white eyebrow; upperparts dark, with blue–grey shoulders and long, drooping black and white scapulars;* dark blue–green speculum margined white; dark-scalloped rufous-brown breast. Eclipse male like female; retains blue–grey shoulders. **Female:** strongly mottled dark brown with pale feather-margins; shoulders blue–grey, *almost pure white below; dark line from bill through eye* divides subtle whitish facial stripes. In flight, male: dark head and breast; white patch on belly; blue–grey shoulders edged white. In flight, female: head and breast sharply cut off from white patch on belly; wing like male. **Voice:** male: mechanical rattling. Female: soft quacks (overseas data). **Habitat:** well-vegetated freshwater wetlands; sewage ponds. **Range and Status:** breeds from Britain to e. Siberia. Migrates s. to Africa and through se. Asia to Indonesia and PNG. Widespread records from NT, Q, NSW, Vic. and WA suggest it may be uncommon but regular summer visitor (Oct.–March) to tropical n. Aust.; vagrant elsewhere.

♀

♂

MALLARD

♂

♀

PACIFIC BLACK DUCK

HYBRID MALLARD/BLACK DUCK

GARGANEY

♀

♂

AUSTRALASIAN SHOVELER *Anas rhynchotis* 46–53 cm; span 70–83 cm

Other names: Australian, Blue-winged or Southern Shoveler.

Look for a swimming duck with a low silhouette and *massive, dark bill*, its slope rakishly repeated by neck, wingtips and tail. **Male, breeding:** grey–blue head marked by *vertical white crescent; eye yellow; shoulder blue–grey; sides chestnut, with white flank-mark; feet orange*. **Female:** sombre brown, finely mottled darker; *pale eye-ring*; wing as male; feet yellow–brown. Male eclipse: like female; feet orange. **Immature:** like pale female. Pairs, parties, flocks with other waterfowl, often well out from shore. Flight swift, swept wings set well back; note *massive spoon-tipped bill, white underwings, blue–grey shoulders, males' conspicuous orange feet*. Courting males fly quickly up from water with audible leathery wingbeats, quickly drop back. **Similar species:** Pink-eared Duck. **Voice:** male: hoarse, repeated 'took-it'; female: quick husky quacks; when flying, a soft chatter. **Habitat:** larger waters; fresh and saline lakes, well-vegetated freshwater wetlands; coastal inlets, sewage ponds, floodwaters. **Breeds:** Aug.–Nov.; other months after rain. **Nest:** of grasses, lined with down; on ground in grass or other herbage, usually near water; occasionally in hollow stump in water. **Eggs:** 8–11; creamy or greenish white. **Range and Status:** e. Aust., mostly e. of line from Townsville (Q) to Eyre Pen. (SA); also Tas. and sw. WA. Most breed in Riverina (NSW); Vic; Tas., se. SA and s. WA. Dispersive and nomadic according to water conditions. Casual inland and n. Aust. Also NZ.

NORTHERN SHOVELER *Anas clypeata* 46–55 cm

Widespread in n. hemisphere; migrates during northern winter to Africa, Borneo, Philippines. Like Australasian Shoveler, but male has *white breast and sides of back*. Female and male in eclipse similar to Australasian in equivalent plumages, but paler, with whitish outer tail-feathers. **Range and Status:** Recent Aust. records mostly of single males, with Australasian Shovelers: NSW, Vic., SA, s. WA; vagrant NZ.

PINK-EARED DUCK *Malacorhynchus membranaceus* 38–45 cm; span 58–72 cm

Other names: Wigeon; Zebra Duck.

Poorly named small duck with *huge, square-tipped grey bill and strongly brown-barred flanks*. Pale brown with darker upperparts, *white forehead and face with clown-like dark brown patch over eye*; pink 'ear-spot' almost invisible; note white flank-mark, pale ochre 'stern'. In flight, note high-held head, huge down-held bill; flying away, note *pale trailing edge of wings; white rump and tail-tip form white double crescent*. Small to very large flocks in which pairs persist. Swims steadily ahead with bill submerged; dabbles in shallows. Feeds in rotating, locked pairs, head to tail, filtering disturbed organisms; rotating companies often spread far across surface of larger wetlands. Perches on branches, logs; associates with other ducks. **Similar species:** Australasian Shoveler. **Voice:** musical chirrup in flight and on water; also a sharp, high-pitched 'ee-jik!'. **Habitat:** shallow, temporary waters; inland lignum swamps; flooded claypans; large, bare lakes; well-vegetated freshwater wetlands; sewage ponds, commercial saltfields; coastal mangroves and saline coastal wetlands during dry periods inland. **Breeds:** any month, in suitable water conditions. **Nest:** mound of down in which eggs are buried; in hollow tree or branch, stump, log, fence-post; old nest of Eurasian Coot or other waterbird; usually over water. **Eggs:** 5–8; smooth, pointed; white or creamy. **Range and Status:** Aust.; mostly inland; rare vagrant Tas. Highly nomadic and dispersive, movements and breeding much influenced by rainfall.

♂

♂ eclipse

AUSTRALASIAN SHOVELER

♀

juv.

♂

♀

NORTHERN SHOVELER

PINK-EARED DUCK

GREY TEAL *Anas gracilis* 40–46 cm; span 60–67 cm

Most widespread Aust. waterfowl: small, mottled grey–brown; easily confused with female Chestnut Teal except for *distinctly whitish throat and area round base of bill*. In flight, note narrow white wedge on upperwing, edged by dark green speculum; underwing grey–brown, with narrow white wedge up 'armpit'. (Plumage of head, neck and underparts occasionally stained rusty from iron compounds in stagnant water: do not then confuse with male Chestnut Teal, which usually has a blackish or dark green head, and white flank-mark.) Pairs, small parties, flocks of thousands in which pairs persist. In se. Aust., flocks often include Chestnut Teal. Dabbles, upends; perches on dead timber over water. **Similar species:** Chestnut Teal, Pacific Black Duck. **Voice:** male: high-pitched, clear 'peep!' or grunt–whistle 'gdeeoo'; female: wild laughing chuckle, often at night, and raucous 'quark, quark, quark'. **Habitat:** almost any water, from coastal inlets, tidal mudflats and mangroves to isolated tanks in mallee scrub or semi-desert; newly flooded depressions, claypans and billabongs, retreating to permanent coastal wetlands in drought. **Breeds:** mostly July–Dec., in s. Aust.; any month when water conditions are suitable. **Nest:** of down, mostly in tree hollows. **Eggs:** 6–9; cream. **Range and Status:** Aust. and Tas.; strongholds are inland e. and se. Aust. and coastal and sub-inland WA. Widespread dispersal in inland and n. Aust. after good rainfall. Also Indonesia, PNG, New Cal., Lord Howe I., Macquarie I. Self-introduced NZ.

Note: Grey Teal occasionally crossbreed in the wild with Pacific Black Duck and Chestnut Teal. Hybrid progeny with the former are mid-sized between the two species, with larger, blue–grey bills than Grey Teal. They have a suggestion of Black Duck's facial marking, with indistinct pale eyebrow above a long, narrow, dark eyemark, as illustrated. Plumage is paler, more mottled than Black Duck. Hybrids with Chestnut Teal are likely to be difficult to separate with certainty in the field.

CHESTNUT TEAL *Anas castanea* 40–48 cm

Male: elegant small duck *with bottle-green head, rich chestnut body, white flank-mark, black stern*. In poor light, can look *blackish*. Male, eclipse (Feb.–April, after breeding): like dark female; head finely mottled black. **Female and immature:** like Grey Teal, but *crown darker, face and throat richer buff*, more heavily speckled; body and wings mottled darker. In flight, *narrow white wing-bar and dark green speculum above; narrow white wedge on 'armpit'*. Pairs, parties or flocks: habits like Grey Teal but prefers saline habitats. **Similar species:** Australasian Shoveler, male: huge bill, pale crescent on blue–green face; white underwing. **Voice:** male: high-pitched 'peep!' or grunt–whistle 'gdeeoo', like male Grey Teal. Female: wild laughing chuckle. **Habitat:** coastal swamps: fresh, brackish and saline; saltmarshes, tidal mudflats, estuaries; inlets, islands; freshwater wetlands, montane lakes. **Breeds:** July–Dec., other months after rain. **Nest:** lined with down; in tree hollow; grass, rushes, rock crevice; readily uses nest-boxes. **Eggs:** 7–10; lustrous, cream. **Range and Status:** se. Aust., from Rockhampton (Q) to Eyre Pen. (SA); also sw. WA; commonest duck in Bass Strait and Tas. Adults make local seasonal movements; young birds disperse far: casual Pilbara (WA), inland Aust.; Top End (NT), C. York and Townsville Common (Q), Lord Howe I. and PNG.

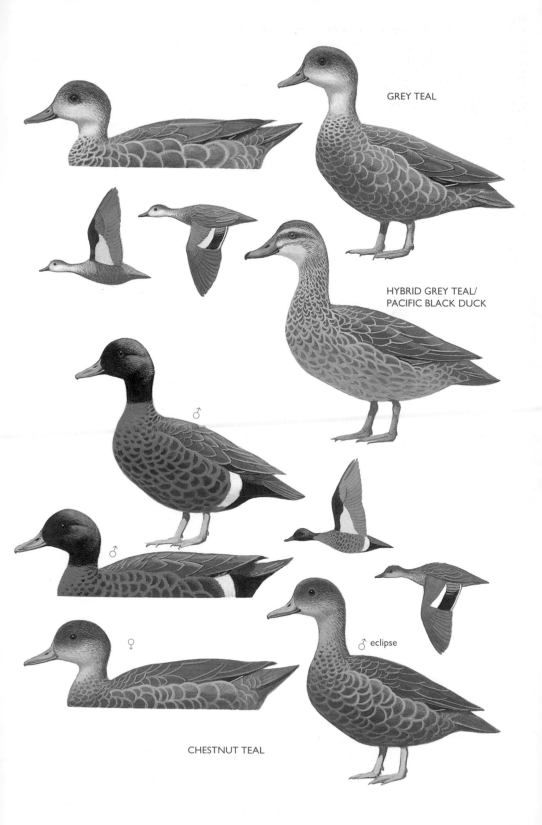

GREY TEAL

HYBRID GREY TEAL/
PACIFIC BLACK DUCK

♂

♂

♀

♂ eclipse

CHESTNUT TEAL

41

GREAT CRESTED GREBE *Podiceps cristatus* 48–61 cm

Largest grebe. *Fine sharp bill and slender, silvery white neck in all plumages.* **Breeding plumage:** *chestnut and black neck-frill; white face; pointed black 'crests'.* In autumn–winter, frill and 'crests' reduced. **Juvenile:** striped black and white head and neck. **Immature:** grey above, white face and slender neck without frill or crests. Pairs; autumn–winter companies on larger lakes, sheltered bays. Swims strongly, diving often; swift underwater. Flight low; *neck low-hung; rapidly beating shallow-flickering wings show much white.* In mating display sexes face up, shake heads, dive. **Voice:** guttural 'kar-arr', shrill 'er-wick'; trumpeting, moaning, whirring noises. **Habitat:** lakes, larger lagoons and swamps, reservoirs, floodwaters, bays, inlets. **Breeds:** Aug.–Feb. in large, well-vegetated wetlands. **Nest:** mass of waterplants and mud, anchored or resting on submerged stump on bank, or on island. Sometimes loosely colonial. **Eggs:** 3–5; glossy, green–white, limy and stained. **Range and Status:** Aust. and Tas.: irregular through inland; rare tropical n. Aust. Also Eurasia, Africa (but not Indonesia, Borneo, PNG). Sedentary, nomadic.

HOARY-HEADED GREBE *Poliocephalus poliocephalus* 29–30 cm

Breeding plumage: distinctive, with brushed-back grey 'hair', *streaked black;* eye silver; *square black 'chin'; conspicuous cream to buffish white foreneck and breast; narrow black streak down nape; greyish flanks.* Winter adult: much plainer; bill cream–grey; *brown crown cut off by whitish cheeks below eye; retains cream–white breast, diagnostic narrow black nape-streak;* flanks greyish white. **Juvenile:** striped. **Immature:** like winter adult. More gregarious than Australasian Grebe, *and more often on brackish or salt water;* in dry seasons and winter, loose flocks of hundreds on larger waters. Disturbed, may skitter and fly, rather than dive. **Similar species:** Australasian Grebe. **Voice:** usually silent; rolling guttural sounds, or soft churring. **Habitat:** brackish and salt swamps; open, bare lakes, reservoirs; larger wetlands generally; floodwaters; sheltered coastal bays and inlets, especially in winter; less likely than Australasian Grebe on small farm dams. **Breeds:** Aug.–Jan. **Nest:** smaller than Australasian Grebe; often on bottom or underwater support; frequently in loose colony, or with Whiskered Terns. **Eggs:** 2–4; greenish, oval, limy; stained brown. **Range and Status:** Aust. and Tas.; locally abundant. Scarce in n. Aust. and far inland. Nomadic; dispersive.

AUSTRALASIAN GREBE *Tachybaptus novaehollandiae* 23–26 cm

Other name: Little Grebe.

Breeding plumage: *head/neck black with chestnut stripe; oval yellow facial mark; eye yellow;* flanks pale chestnut. Winter adult: duller. **Juvenile:** striped. **Immature and first winter:** grey–brown above, border between brown crown and whitish cheeks *passes through eye.* Lacks dark nape-stripe; breast less creamy white; *flanks warmer rufous than Hoary-headed Grebe.* Territorial pairs, family parties, small autumn–winter companies. Dives often; feeds on surface and in shallows. Startled, dives rather than flies. Nestlings ride under parents' wings, even when they dive. **Similar species:** Hoary-headed Grebe. **Voice:** clear, far-carrying chitter; alarm-call, sharp 'tik!'. **Habitat:** still, shallow fresh waters generally; farm dams; freshwater wetlands with plentiful waterplants; sewage ponds; in autumn–winter in s. Aust., with Hoary-headeds on larger open waters; occasionally on sheltered bays. **Breeds:** Aug.–Dec. **Nest:** damp, floating, anchored mound of green waterplants. **Eggs:** 4–6; bluish white, limy, soon stained brown. **Range and Status:** Aust. and Tas.: widespread, common e. and sw. Aust.; irregular inland; uncommon, common tropical n. Aust. and Tas. Sedentary, nomadic; possible n. movement in winter from s. Aust. Also Indonesia, PNG, New Heb., New Cal.; related forms in NZ, Eurasia. Recently colonised NZ.

GREAT CRESTED GREBE

breeding

imm.

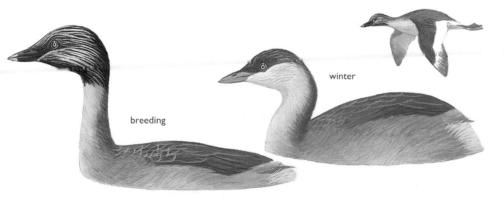

breeding

winter

HOARY-HEADED GREBE

AUSTRALASIAN GREBE

breeding

winter

MAGELLANIC PENGUIN *Spheniscus magellanicus* 71 cm

Distinctive penguin with stubby black bill and bare pink skin around eye. Black face and throat bordered by broad white band starting on forehead, encircling face and throat and ending in white front collar. *Two more black frontal bands form bold pattern on white chest.* Sexes similar; immature has grey cheeks; broad, smudgy breastbands. **Range and Status:** breeds Falkland Is. and s. S. America (s. Chile and Patagonia), wintering to s. Brazil and n. Chile; vagrant s. and e. to S. Orkneys. Once vagrant NZ (March 1972) and s. Vic. (March 1976).

KING PENGUIN *Aptenodytes patagonicus* 85–95 cm

Second largest penguin: head glossy black; upperparts silver–grey; breast white. *Note the long straight black bill with orange–rose fillet at base of lower mandible and large enclosed rich orange–yellow 'comma' on side of nape.* **Immature:** shorter black bill streaked cyclamen pink at base of lower mandible; crown tipped grey; enclosed nape-patch cream. On land looks stout and upright, bill raised aloofly; swims powerfully, 'porpoising' on surface. **Similar species:** Emperor Penguin: much larger (c. 1.0–1.3 m); bill comparatively smaller; smaller pink fillet on bill; neck marking yellower and whiter, not enclosed. Not yet recorded in Aust. waters. **Range and Status:** breeds mostly sub-Antarctic islands between 46°S and 55°S in far S. Atlantic and Indian Oceans: Macquarie and Heard Is. are nearest. Vagrant Tas., Vic., WA.

GENTOO PENGUIN *Pygoscelis papua* 70–75 cm

Medium–large penguin: head and throat slaty black; *white band from eye to eye over crown*, scattered white spots nearby; in moult, whole head may be whitish. *Bill yellow to orange, ridge black; feet yellow or orange.* **Immature:** less white on head, bill paler yellow, shorter. **Range and Status:** breeds Antarctic continent and many sub-Antarctic islands, incl. Macquarie I. Vagrant Tas.

CHINSTRAP PENGUIN *Pygoscelis antarctica* 70–76 cm

Unmistakable: white face crossed by thin black band, from behind eye across throat, *forming conspicuous angled 'chinstrap'*. Bill black; feet flesh-coloured to orange–yellow. **Immature:** smaller, face and throat greyer. **Range and Status:** breeds Antarctic Pen. and s. sub-Antarctic islands mostly in s. Atlantic, also Heard I. Disperses in winter mainly around S. America and in S. Atlantic. Vagrant Macquarie I., Tas., Vic.; mostly summer.

ADELIE PENGUIN *Pygoscelis adeliae* 70 cm

Sturdy penguin of much character: bill short, robust, brick-red, tipped black; head and throat black; no crest but *rear of crown 'peaked'; conspicuous white eye-ring*; feet flesh-pink. **Immature:** throat white; eye-ring grey. **Range and Status:** breeds around coasts of Antarctica and islands. Ranges n. to S. Georgia, Heard and Macquarie Is. Vagrant Tas., NZ, Macquarie I.

MAGELLANIC PENGUIN

KING PENGUIN

GENTOO PENGUIN

imm.

CHINSTRAP PENGUIN

imm.

ADELIE PENGUIN

imm.

LITTLE PENGUIN *Eudyptula minor* 40–45 cm. Male slightly larger.

Other names: Fairy or Little Blue Penguin.
Smallest penguin: black to blue–grey above, white below. Bill black; feet flesh-white to pinkish, soles black. **Immature:** upperparts bluer. Adults approaching moult (after breeding) become fatter, dull black above, with rusty traces. Slimmer after moulting, upperparts paler and bluer; underparts silvery *white*. Singles or parties at sea; often only head and short tail visible: 'flies' underwater, does not 'porpoise'. Concentrates shoals of small fish by circling, then charges, snapping and swallowing underwater. Comes and goes from breeding colonies in darkness. **Similar species:** Rockhopper, imm. **Voice:** at sea, an oft-heard sharp, puppy-like yap; ashore, in mating greeting or threat-display, ass-like braying, deep growls, mews. **Habitat:** oceans, bays; around jetties, piers. Roosts through year in old burrows and other nest-sites. **Breeds:** Aug.–Feb. (Vic.); April–Dec. (WA); in single pairs to large colonies mostly on islands. **Nest:** sparse, of sticks, grass, seaweed, thistle-stems; in short burrow in sand; also under vegetation, in rock cavities, under sheds, houses, boats. **Eggs:** 2; white, stained dirty greenish or brownish. **Range and Status:** only resident Aust. penguin: breeds from Carnac I. (s. WA) e. through SA and Vic. to Tas. and n. to S. Solitary I. (NSW). Dispersive when young and in winter. Most abundant Bass Strait, Tas. Best-known colony is at Summerlands Beach, Phillip I. (Vic.). Also NZ region.

ROCKHOPPER PENGUIN *Eudyptes chrysocome* 45–61 cm. Male larger.

Smallest crested penguin. Crest unmistakable: slender black feathers on crown lengthen from centre, edged by lemon-yellow plumes starting back from bill as a slim eyebrow and projecting back in *long thin strands; when dry, some wide and erect, others bend sharply and droop wispily; slicked down when wet.* Bill robust, dull orange to red–brown with flesh-pink membrane around base; eye reddish; feet pink or whitish above, black below. **Female:** bill less robust, no fleshy membrane. **Immature:** short feathers on crown, lacks yellow plumes or has them as thin pale yellow stripe only above eye; throat dirty white; bill dull brown. Singles, or small parties, off s. coast. **Similar species:** Fiordland; Erect-crested Penguins. For comparison with imm. Rockhopper, see Little Penguin. **Range and Status:** breeds in colonies on many sub-Antarctic islands, incl. Amsterdam, Macquarie I. and NZ sub-Antarctic islands. Regular winter visitor s. WA coast, Esperance to Perth; moderately common winter visitor to SA, Tas., Vic. Race most recorded is *mosleyi*, which breeds on sub-Antarctic islands in S. Atlantic.

FIORDLAND PENGUIN *Eudyptes pachyrhynchus* 55 cm

Like Rockhopper but bill heavier, no fleshy membrane around base. Crest broader than Rockhopper's, less wispy and without long black crown-feathers; begins as broad yellow eyebrow at base of bill, extends back and tends to droop down side of neck. *Diagnostic white streaks on dull black cheeks are caused by feathers parting to reveal whitish bases.* Bill and eye red–brown; feet like Rockhopper. **Immature:** bill dark grey–brown; crest very short; throat whitish; distinguished from imm. Rockhopper by white streaks on cheeks. **Range and Status:** breeds w. coasts South I., NZ: Stewart, Codfish, Solander and other NZ islands. Uncommon but possibly regular winter–spring visitor to offshore se. Aust., mostly imms. Records: Tas., Vic., NSW, SA, s. WA.

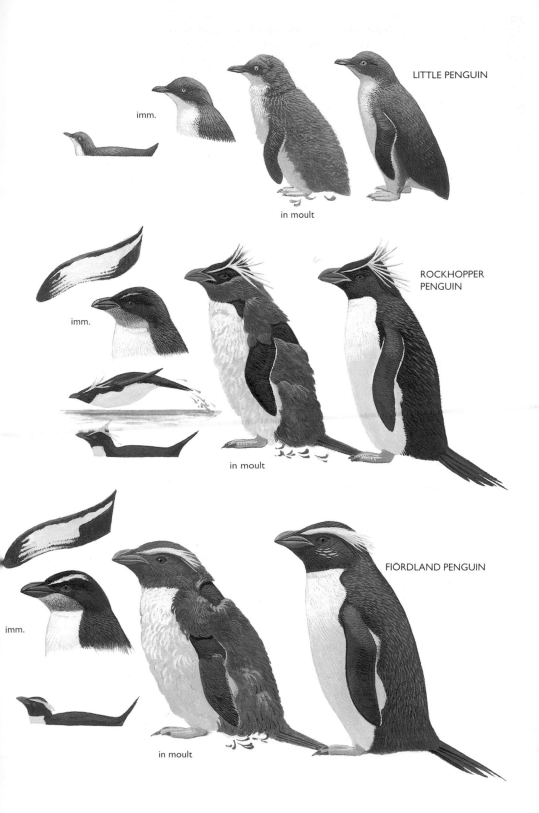

LITTLE PENGUIN

imm.

in moult

ROCKHOPPER
PENGUIN

imm.

in moult

FIORDLAND PENGUIN

imm.

in moult

47

ERECT-CRESTED PENGUIN *Eudyptes sclateri* 67 cm

Distinctive golden crest *starts above gape, widens and sweeps up to rear of crown in brush-like effect, especially when dry.* Bill red–brown, with *prominent band of white or pale pink skin along edge of lower mandible.* Eye red–brown; feet pale flesh, soles black. **Immature:** throat whitish; crest whiter and much smaller. **Similar species:** Rockhopper. **Range and Status:** breeds in NZ sub-Antarctic region on Antipodes, Campbell, Bounty Is.; disperses to NZ and Chatham I.; regular visitor Macquarie I. Vagrant Vic., s. WA.

SNARES PENGUIN *Eudyptes robustus* 50–60 cm

Similar to Fiordland Penguin; bill more robust, with membrane of pink–white skin around base. Cheeks glossy black. **Range and Status:** breeds on Snares I., NZ region, ranges n. to NZ, with stragglers w. to Macquarie I. Rare vagrant to se. Tas., se. SA.

MACARONI PENGUIN *Eudyptes chrysolophus* 70 cm

Other name: Royal Penguin.

One of the world's most abundant birds: estimated at 20+ million (Marchant & Higgins, 1990). *Bill long, massive, flesh-pink to red–brown, edged with deep pink skin at gape;* adjacent feathers sometimes tipped yellow; *face and throat white, grey or black.** Crest: *loose golden and orange plumes up to 7.5 cm long join in patch across forehead, extend back along sides of crown and untidily over eyes.* Eye red; feet as Rockhopper. **Immature:** bill smaller, dull red–brown; face and throat smutty; crest little-developed. **Similar species:** Rockhopper, imm.: smaller, bill black with pale tip; crest narrower, neater. **Range and Status:** white-faced form breeds principally Macquarie I. (Sept.–Jan.), where population may exceed 2 million. Black-cheeked forms breed in Antarctica and many sub-Antarctic islands (nearest is Heard I.). Uncommon visitor, mostly Tas., also SA and Vic.: mostly summer–autumn; moulting. Also NZ.

* White-faced birds breeding on Macquarie I. have in recent past been described as 'Royal Penguins', while mostly dark-faced forms breeding widely elsewhere in Antarctica were called 'Macaroni Penguins'. But because some of each form occur where they should not, and because no other consistent differences are evident between the two, they have provisionally been recombined (Christidis & Boles, 1994) under this species.

ERECT-CRESTED PENGUIN

imm.

SNARES PENGUIN

imm.

MACARONI PENGUIN

imm.

'ROYAL PENGUIN'

imm.

SOUTHERN GIANT-PETREL *Macronectes giganteus* 80 cm–1 m; span 1.8–2.1 m

Other names: Giant Fulmar; Nelly; Stinker.
Largest petrel: like a small ungainly brown albatross with a *massive, greenish-tipped, straw-coloured bill, surmounted by a large single nostril-tube.* Mature adult, seldom seen in Aust.: grey–brown, with head, neck and breast faded to dirty mottled whitish; eye pale grey. Note pale leading edge of underwing near body: in most Northern Giant Petrels, this area is dark brown, but becomes paler in older individuals. **Immature:** common visitor: *uniform sheer blackish brown; eye dark brown; bill more conspicuous in contrast.* A white morph (10% of total population) has sparse black spots, unlike any other seabird; rare locally. Solitary, but numbers gather where food is present, e.g. some sewage outfalls: disputes with albatrosses; occasionally ashore at stranded seals, whales. In light winds, flight inelegant, *with heavy flapping and wheeling on stiff, narrow wings; looks rather hump-backed; legs extend to tip of wedge-shaped tail.* In high winds, 'weaves' on fixed wings. Follows ships, approaches fishing boats for scraps. **Similar species:** Northern Giant-Petrel: bill horn-coloured, tipped reddish; adult has dark cap over pale face. Sooty Albatrosses. Wandering Albatross, imm.: white underwing. **Range and Status:** breeds in colonies on coasts of Antarctica and circumpolar sub-Antarctic islands between *c.* 50–60°S, incl. Macquarie I. Disperses widely over s. oceans in circumpolar pattern. Imms and sub-adults common winter–spring migrants to Aust. coasts n. to beyond Tropic, in n. WA and ne. Q; vagrant PNG. Most common May–Nov., Fremantle (WA) to Sydney (NSW). Young birds range further n. than adults, and further n. than Northern Giant-Petrel.

NORTHERN GIANT-PETREL *Macronectes halli* 80–95 cm; span 1.5–2.1 m

Other name: Hall's (Giant) Petrel.
Like Southern Giant-Petrel but adult has a subtle head pattern and bill *tipped reddish pink or orange;* eye pale grey. *Dark crown over whitish face and throat gives it a somewhat capped appearance; slight dark mask through eye.* Hybrids between Southern and Northern Giant-Petrels share features of both: at S. Georgia these have wholly pale bills, lacking either green or red tips (Marchant & Higgins, 1990). **Immature:** *uniform sooty brown; eye dark brown;* next to indistinguishable from imm. Southern, but older imms have the slightly capped look of adults; bills tipped pink or orange. Flight and behaviour like Southern Giant-Petrel; in most, *leading edge of underwing near body is dark, not pale as in adult Southern.* **Range and Status:** breeds sub-Antarctic islands, incl. Chatham, Antipodes, Campbell, Auckland and Macquarie Is., NZ region; also Stewart I. Wide circumpolar range generally n. of Antarctic convergence; downwind dispersal probably less extensive than Southern Giant-Petrel. Immature birds and some adults common May–Oct. in offshore and inshore waters from *c.* Fremantle (WA) to *c.* Sydney (NSW).

SOUTHERN GIANT-PETREL

adult

imm.

white morph

imm.

adult

white morph

imm.

adult

imm.

adult

NORTHERN GIANT-PETREL

CAPE PETREL *Daption capense* 35–40 cm; span 80–90 cm

Other name: Cape Pigeon.

Sturdy and unmistakable: bill black and short; throat and mantle black; *back, wings and rump strongly chequered black and white*; tail white with broad black terminal band. With wear, black plumage becomes brownish. Flight fast, low, direct, with quick beats of stiff wings. Noisy and quarrelsome: dives readily, in flight and from surface; floats high when swimming and feeding. Follows ships; in some localities regularly gathers near shore to feed on offal at sewage outfalls, fishing operations, but usually well offshore in Aust. **Similar species:** Antarctic Petrel: brown replaces black; pattern simpler, whiter, without chequering. **Range and Status:** breeds widely on coasts of Antarctica and many Antarctic and sub-Antarctic islands, incl. NZ region (small, dark race *australe*). Circumpolar dispersal through s. oceans to beyond Tropic of Capricorn; vagrant n. hemisphere. Regular, fairly common winter and spring (April–Nov.) migrant mostly to offshore waters of s. Aust. n. to *c*. Carnarvon (WA) and se. Q. Many beachwashed after storms: occurrence often patchy.

ANTARCTIC PETREL *Thalassoica antarctica* 40–45 cm; span *c*.1 m

Distinctive: ashy chocolate-brown above, breast and underparts white. Wings ashy brown with *broad white 'shoulder' and wingbar at rest*. In flight, this *forms a conspicuous pattern of broad brown leading edge and narrow brown trailing edge to an otherwise white wing*. Tail white with brown tips. Small to large flocks; flies fairly high with quick, shallow wingbeats and flat-winged glides. Reported to hover before plunging; feeds near, and rests on, icefloes. **Similar species:** Cape Petrel: blacker, boldly mottled white. **Range and Status:** breeds Antarctica and adjacent islands; disperses n. in winter in sub-Antarctic to about 45°S. Rare winter–spring vagrant to s. Aust. seas; recent records s. Tas., Vic.

SOUTHERN FULMAR *Fulmarus glacialoides* 45–50 cm; span 1.1–1.2 m

Other names: Antarctic or Silver–grey Fulmar or Petrel.

Graceful, thick-set grey-and-white petrel; *bill pale flesh or yellowish, nostril and tip blackish*; wings, back and tail pearl-grey; primaries blackish grey near tips, with white inner webs, providing a *marked contrast on upperwings in flight*; underwings white; feet brown or grey with flesh-pink webs. Southern close relative of well-known Northern Fulmar, *F. glacialis*, flies with *quick, shallow beats of stiff wings, and wheeling glides*; feeds in sometimes large companies at sea and at edge of pack-ice; gathers around fishing and whaling vessels, follows ships. In Aust. waters, concentrates in particular areas over continental shelf and offshore. **Similar species:** White-headed Petrel: dark bill; dark pattern on upperwing. **Range and Status:** breeds widely on coasts of Antarctica and islands mainly s. of Antarctic convergence; has wide circumpolar migratory dispersal n. to about 30°S. Uncommon, irregular visitor mostly June–Jan. to offshore waters of s. Aust., n. to se. Q and Jurien Bay (WA). At times 'wrecked' in large numbers during spring gales.

SNOW PETREL *Pagodroma nivea* 30–40 cm; span *c*. 85 cm

Pure white petrel with short black bill; black eyes, legs and feet; wings slender; tail square to slightly wedge-shaped. Flight somewhat like a gadfly-petrel but more fluttering, less impetuous and towering; searches randomly, with shallow wingbeats and occasional glides. Hovers to snap plankton at edge of pack-ice; rests on icebergs and icefloes. Beware of confusion with albino and/or leucistic plumages in other petrels. **Similar species:** White Tern. **Range and Status:** breeds Antarctica and southerly sub-Antarctic islands, mostly Oct.–April. Circumpolar distribution to limit of pack-ice. Rare vagrant to temperate seas. Two possible Aust. sight records: Newland Head (SA), 15 Sept. 1974, and Rosebud (Vic.), 6 Oct. 1974. Vagrant.

CAPE PETREL

ANTARCTIC
PETREL

SOUTHERN FULMAR

SNOW PETREL

53

GREAT-WINGED PETREL *Pterodroma macroptera* 38–43 cm; span *c.* 1 m

Other name: Grey-faced Petrel.

Large, short-necked, long-winged, dark brown petrel with *faint pale patch around the short, deep black bill.* **Immature:** paler, more extensive grey face and throat; similar to adult of NZ race *gouldi* 'Grey-faced Petrel'. This race has *more distinct paler patch extending over forehead, cheeks and throat.* Often solitary; ignores ships, but companies gather around fishing trawlers. Flies spectacularly with high-towering arcs, sweeping descents, 'like oversized swift': *'wrists' carried well forwards, slender wingtips angled back; tail a short, pointed wedge;* underwing brownish; feet black. Noisy around breeding islands; aerial chases day or night. At Aust. colonies breeding adults are present most of the year; active and noisy Feb.–Aug. **Similar species:** Providence Petrel: greyer, with shadowy mark across upperwings; on underwing, white patch on base of primaries, adjacent smaller white crescent. Kermadec Petrel, dark morph: more compact; white shafts and bases of primaries form prominent wingpatch visible above and below; feet pink. Kerguelen Petrel: smaller, greyer, with paler inner leading edge, dark wing-linings and contrasting silvery sheen to underside of primaries. Shearwaters have longer, more slender bills; heads/necks protrude further. **Breeds:** May–Nov. in Aust. (WA). **Nest:** she oak needles, grass, etc.; in burrow *c.* 1 m long or under rock, creeper, tree-roots or scrub. **Egg:** 1; white, smooth, without gloss. **Range and Status:** breeds sub-Antarctic islands in S. Atlantic, s. Indian Oceans; nominate race breeds from Recherche Arch. to Eclipse I. in s. WA. Race *gouldi* breeds islands off North I. (NZ); regular in Tasman Sea and offshore waters of se. Aust., where abundant in spring–summer–autumn (Marchant & Higgins, 1990). The species as a whole is common in offshore waters of s. Aust. from *c.* Geraldton (WA) to se. Q. Mostly nominate race in WA and SA, where uncommon; both races Vic., Tas., to se. Q.

KERGUELEN PETREL *Lugensa brevirostris* 33–36 cm; span *c.* 80 cm

Short black bill, abrupt forehead, large head, tapering body and wings and uniform greyish colouring make confusion unlikely. In flight, note silvery flash from underside of flight feathers, and tapering, pointed tail. Solitary; feeds mostly at night. By day, soars and floats high; flight somewhat swift-like: weaving, with very fast, raking glides on slightly downheld wings, with bursts of energetic wingbeats. **Similar species:** Great-winged Petrel: larger, browner; face usually greyer. **Range and Status:** breeds few sub-Antarctic islands in S. Atlantic and s. Indian Oceans; large circumpolar dispersal from Antarctic pack-ice to about 30°S. Mainly winter (June–Sept.) visitor to offshore waters of s. Aust. from about Fremantle (WA) to Tas. and e. Vic., with numbers beachwashed. Rare on e. coast, with beachwashed and sight-records from s. coast NSW to se. Q (Fraser I.); mostly late winter–spring. Migratory, dispersive.

PROVIDENCE PETREL *Pterodroma solandri* 40 cm; span *c.* 1 m

Other names: Bill Hill Muttonbird; Brown-headed Petrel.

Robust, greyish petrel with browner head, wings and tail; subtly scalloped white on face and forehead; underwing dark grey; *base of primaries and under wing-coverts white, forming large and small whitish crescents, split by a brown loop.* Flight often slow and easy, but in high winds displays typical gadfly weaving and arcs. **Similar species:** Great-winged Petrel: underwing wholly dark. Kermadec Petrel, dark morph: face and head pale; prominent white shafts to primaries. Herald Petrel: all morphs have complex underwing pattern from white bases of primaries and secondaries and their coverts. **Range and Status:** breeds Lord Howe I. (May–Nov.). Formerly bred Norfolk I., where exterminated in 1790s by European settlement; in 1985 discovered breeding on nearby Philip I. (Marchant & Higgins, 1990). Annual winter–spring migration to N. Pacific, e. to California, apparently by nonbreeding and immature birds. During same period, (breeding birds?) occur in offshore waters of e. Aust., over continental shelf, from se. Tas. and e. Vic. to Fraser I. (Q). Regular offshore from s. coast NSW to se. Q , April–Oct. Migratory and dispersive.

GREAT-
WINGED
PETREL

nominate
race

race
gouldi

KERGUELEN PETREL

PROVIDENCE PETREL

55

KERMADEC PETREL *Pterodroma neglecta* 38 cm; span *c*. 90 cm

Shorter, with squarer tail than other gadfly-petrels. Flight leisurely with deep wingbeats followed by long, unhurried glides, banking in broad arcs (Harrison, 1983). Bill short, black; feet whitish flesh to bluish, tips of webs black; eye blackish. A species of several colour-morphs, which may interbreed. Dark morph: largely brown. Intermediate morph: body whitish, mottled darker about face. Pale morph: largely white head and body; *brown tail*. All have wings brown above, with prominent white shafts to primaries; grey–brown underwing with pale leading edge near body and a *broad white patch (toward blackish wingtip)* formed by conspicuous white bases to primaries and primary coverts, *crossed by a brown loop*. **Similar species:** Herald, White-headed and Providence Petrels. **Range and Status:** breeds across S. Pacific from Lord Howe (Ball's Pyramid) and Norfolk Is. to Juan Fernandez I. (se. Pacific Ocean). Disperses throughout warmer Pacific waters. Rare visitor summer–autumn–winter to coastal e. Aust. from se. Q to about Jervis Bay (NSW). Vagrant.

WHITE-HEADED PETREL *Pterodroma lessonii* 40–46 cm; span *c*. 1 m

Robust, long-winged, white-bodied petrel with *sturdy black bill and black eye-patch. At rest and in flight, note contrasting dark grey wings.* Pearl-grey wash on crown deepens to mid-grey on back; wings with a broken M band above; *rump and tail pearl-grey to whitish*; underwing grey; legs and feet flesh-white. Solitary or in small groups: patrols low with shallow, stiff-winged beats interspersed with glides. In high winds flight is fast and wheeling in great sweeps, with stiff pointed dark wings bowed; ignores ships; feeds much at night. **Similar species:** Soft-plumaged Petrel, pale morph: smaller; grey head joins breastband in hooded look; upperparts and upper surface of tail darker grey; underwing shows pale leading edge near body, dark grey under wing-coverts, pale bases of flight-feathers. Kermadec Petrel, pale morph: smaller; upperparts and tail brown; bases and shafts of primaries form white patch in flight. Grey Petrel: larger; bill longer, yellowish; head and upperparts more uniformly grey. **Range and Status:** breeds Crozets and Kergulen Is. (s. Indian Ocean); Auckland, Antipodes and Macquarie Is. (NZ region). Wide circumpolar dispersal n. to *c*. 30°S. Uncommon winter visitor (mostly May–Sept.) to offshore waters of s. Aust., n. to *c*. NW Cape (WA) and se. Q. But a few present most months; beachwashed, or far at sea over continental shelf. Migratory and dispersive.

KERMADEC
PETREL

white-
headed
morph

pale
morph

intermediate
morph

dark
morph

WHITE-HEADED
PETREL

57

SOFT-PLUMAGED PETREL *Pterodroma mollis* 33–36 cm; span *c*. 90 cm

Combination of *dark grey underwing band and grey breast band across white underparts* is diagnostic. Forehead whitish, mottled darker, and with *broad, blackish eye-mark*; back dark blue–grey; wings similar, with dark brownish slate M band; tail grey. (Rare wholly grey form breeds Marion I. (S. Atlantic); not recorded Aust.) Bill black; legs flesh-pink; webs tipped black. Common, flies fast in small parties near surface. Usually ignores ships. **Range and Status:** breeds sub-Antarctic islands in S. Atlantic and s. Indian Oceans, sub-tropical islands in N. Atlantic, Antipodes I. and in NZ region and possibly Macquarie I. Wide migratory dispersal in S. Atlantic and s. Indian Oceans between *c*. 30 and 50°S. Common winter visitor to Aust. seas, from s. WA n. to *c*. NW Cape (where most common), around s. coasts and Tas.; scarce n. to *c*. Q (Maryborough). Beachwashed records all states; increasing number of offshore sight-records on s. coasts, most months. Winter–spring gales produce many beachwashed birds.

HERALD PETREL *Pterodroma arminjoniana* 37 cm; span *c*. 95 cm

Other name: Trinidade Island Petrel.

Pale morph mostly seen in Aust.: *head ashy brown, darker before and behind eye, sides of forehead and throat white.* Upperparts dark grey–brown with shadowy dark M band across wings. White below, smudged grey across chest in indistinct band. *Dark grey underwing has white leading edge near body and thin median white stripe broadening into white patch at base of primaries, forming diagnostic dark M band on underwing.* Bill black, deep, narrow, with strongly hooked nail at tip; feet pale flesh with outer half of webs and toes black. Dark morph has wholly grey–brown head and body, with suggestion of paler underwing markings; legs, feet black. Intermediate forms between the two. Solitary or small parties: flies somewhat like a tropical shearwater, close to surface, with leisurely wingbeats and glides. At breeding islands, performs a high speed courtship flight, with dives and loops. **Range and Status:** breeds on islands across *c*. Pacific near Tropic, e. from Chesterfield Reefs, Raine I. and possibly other islands in Coral Sea to Easter I.; also islands in Indian Ocean (incl. N. Keeling I.) and S. Atlantic. Disperses through equatorial and N. Pacific. Vagrant e. Aust.: beachwashed or offshore sight-records from se. Q to se. NSW, mostly summer–autumn.

TAHITI PETREL *Pseudobulweria rostrata* 39 cm; span *c*. 95 cm

Distinctive, stocky, tropical gadfly-petrel with robust black bill; *head, upperparts and upper breast glossy dark brown, forming a hood sharply cut off from white breast, underparts and central under tail-coverts.* In flight, wings slightly bent; underwing in good view shows blackish brown wing-linings cut off sharply by whitish or silvery under wing-coverts, *which form a pale, curved, shallow bar along centre of wing*; underside of flight feathers dark with silvery gloss. Legs and feet pink and black. Singles or open companies with other species. Flight relaxed, close to surface; banking glides interspersed with deep, easy wingbeats; seldom above horizon. **Similar species:** Herald Petrel: all morphs have whitish patch at base of primaries and pale underwing bar; white-bellied morphs have pale area round bill and throat. Kermadec Petrel: pale (white-bellied) morphs have pale heads; all show large whitish patch near tip of underwing and white primary shafts on upperwing. Soft-plumaged Petrel: pale (white-bellied) morph has white around bill and throat. **Range and Status:** breeds New Cal., Society and Marquesas Is.; wide pelagic dispersal across Pacific from Japanese waters to sw. N. America. Offshore summer–autumn sight-records from outer Gt Barrier Reef (Q) to Sydney (NSW); beachwashed se. Q and ne. NSW. Offshore reports from nw. WA and NT. Regular visitor. Uncommon.

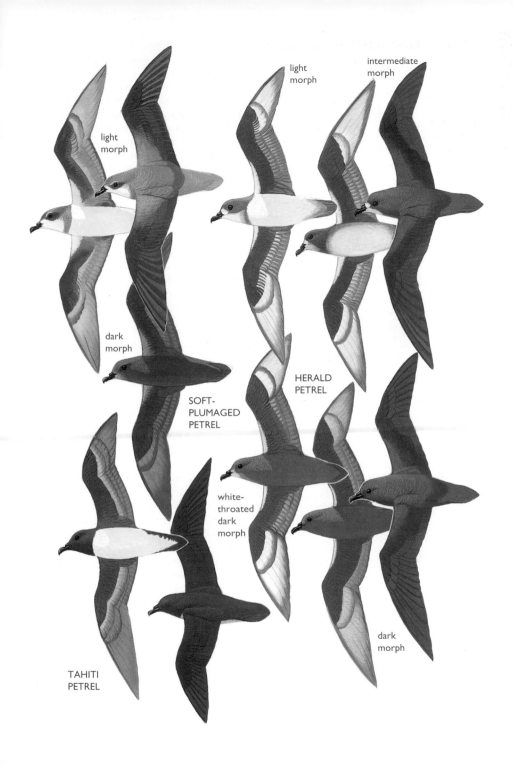

light
morph

intermediate
morph

light
morph

dark
morph

HERALD
PETREL

SOFT-
PLUMAGED
PETREL

white-
throated
dark
morph

dark
morph

TAHITI
PETREL

MOTTLED PETREL *Pterodroma inexpectata* 35 cm; span *c.* 85 cm

Other names: Rainbird; Scaled Petrel.

Medium-sized, fairly thickset gadfly-petrel with long, narrow wings. Grey above, with frosty 'scaling'; crown and eyepatch darker; scalloped white area over bill joins white throat; blackish shoulders expand in flight into prominent shallow M band across slender grey upperwings. From below, made unmistakable by white throat, grey–brown breast, *large grey patch on belly*, heavy angled black bar across white underwing, extending outward along leading edge. Bill black, short and hooked; feet flesh pink, ends of webs black. Singles, small parties; rarely flocks: usually far from land. Flight fast, towering, impetuous, bounding, with quick, shallow wingbeats and long, fast arcs. **Range and Status:** breeds s. NZ coastal islands and Snares I. Migrates in winter to far N. Pacific. Disperses s. during summer to Antarctic zone of pack-ice. Rare vagrant se. Aust. (mostly Sept.–April), offshore sight-records or beachwashed, from se. SA round Tas. to ne. NSW.

BLACK-WINGED PETREL *Pterodroma nigripennis* 28–30 cm; span *c.* 67 cm

Forehead and underparts *white; dark mark below eye; blue–grey of crown, nape and back extends as collar on foreneck.* In flight, a broad, blackish brown M band angles across grey wings and rump; repeated by V-shaped black tip to tail. *Underwing pure white, with heavy black margins and wingtip*: thick black margin on leading edge swings inwards as an *angled black bar across innerwing.* Bill black, short; legs and feet flesh-pink (sometimes bluish) with tips black. Singles to loose flocks, with other petrels, shearwaters; sometimes follows ships. Flight over breeding colony 'fast swooping, and erratic, often wheeling in steep arcs and inclined loops ... with frequent rolls from side to side. Rapid, fairly deep wingbeats are followed by banking and gliding, with wingtips swept back at the "wrists".' (Klapste, 1981) Reported to frequently alight on ships in mid-ocean (Falla et al, 1979). **Similar species:** Cook's Petrel: paler, with greyer head, smaller eyemark; white underwing with finer black margins and crossbar. Gould's Petrel: large angular black cap but *no collar*; underwing has *finer* black margins and bar. **Breeds:** Oct.–April. **Egg:** 1; white; in burrow *c.* 1 m long; in colony on island, among shrubs or trees. **Range and Status:** breeds Lord Howe and Norfolk Is. (recent); possibly colonising islands on e. coast, e.g. Capricorn Group (Q); Muttonbird I. (NSW). Also breeds NZ region and New Cal. Present Tasman Sea in spring–summer: beachwashed and offshore sight-records from Capricorn Group (Q) to e. Vic. Casual Tas. and w. Vic. Dec.–April. In May–Sept. migrates to nc. Pacific, from Japan to Hawaii, and coastal c. America (Marchant & Higgins, 1990).

COOK'S PETREL *Pterodroma cookii* 25–30 cm; span *c.* 65 cm

Small, pale gadfly-petrel with *unusually long, slender black bill.* Forehead white, *extending as slight eyebrow above darkish eyemark below and behind eye. Crown and upperparts uniformly pale to mid-grey* (darker when worn), with frosty look from light scalloping. Grey upper wing and back crossed by a rounded, blackish brown M band, narrowest across rump. Tail grey, *finely edged white*, central feathers tipped blackish brown. Underparts and underwing white, with fine black margins and tips, heavier margin on leading edge angles across innerwing toward body in tapering black curve. Legs and feet bluish with yellow webs, black tips. **Immature:** grey feathers of upperparts have more distinct pale fringes. Flight languid and rolling (in light airs) to fast and erratic with steep banks, alternately showing white underparts and upperwing pattern (Tuck, 1980), or fluttering with bounding, swooping arcs. Feeds with shearwaters, storm-petrels; does not flock or follow ships. **Similar species:** Black-winged Petrel. **Range and Status:** Oct.–April on Little and Great Barrier Is. and Codfish I. (NZ region); disperses into Pacific to w. coasts of Baja California, Peru and Chile. Rare spring–summer visitor (Oct.–Feb.) to offshore e. Aust. Beachwashed or offshore sight-records from se. Q to c. NSW. Vagrant.

MOTTLED
PETREL

BLACK-WINGED
PETREL

COOK'S
PETREL

61

WHITE-NECKED PETREL *Pterodroma cervicalis* 39–43 cm; span *c*. 1 m

Slender grey, black and white gadfly-petrel: face and body white *with black cap to below eyes, separated from grey back by broad diagnostic white collar.* Back and upperwings grey with subtle pale scaled pattern and crossed by bold M band joining dark primaries and forming dark, pointed loop over rump; tail grey to blackish; pale outer edge when spread. Underparts white with small greyish rear half-collar *behind broad white rear collar*; underwing white with narrow black margins; slightly heavier margin on leading edge angles inwards across white innerwing toward body in tapering black bar. Legs and feet flesh-pink, toes black. Singles to parties: flight leisurely, strong and wheeling, arcing high above horizon in high winds; wrists well forward, wingtips slightly below level of wing; large tail prominent. **Similar species:** smaller gadfly-petrels have dark crowns and napes; more impetuous flight. Cook's has grey crown/nape. Buller's Shearwater ditto, lacks angled black line on underwing. **Range and Status:** breeds Oct.–June, only Macaulay I. in Kermadec group: migrates across N. Pacific and into Tasman Sea. Beachwashed; offshore and pelagic sight-records Lord Howe I. and in e. Aust. from s. NSW to se. Q, mostly Aug.–Feb. Autumn records after cyclones.

GOULD'S PETREL *Pterodroma leucoptera* 30 cm; span *c*. 70 cm

Contrastingly marked small, slight petrel: in flight note *sooty black crown extending in angled patch onto white foreneck; dark M band across dark blue–grey upperwings and rump, above a paler band formed by wing-coverts;* tail-tip black. Underwing white, with narrow black edges, *broader on leading edge and angled inwards in tapering bar across innerwing.* Singles or small flocks: flies with quick wingbeats and glides, banks; weaves in higher winds. **Similar species:** Black-winged and Cook's Petrels. **Breeds:** Oct.–May. Nests on ground in rocks, crevices, under fallen palm fronds, between buttress roots. **Egg:** 1; chalk-white. **Range and Status:** nominate race (*c*. 500 pairs) breeds Aug.–May only on Cabbage Tree I. off Port Stephens (NSW), apparently dispersing through offshore waters of se. Aust. Beachwashed specimens and offshore sight-records of singles and small flocks from se. Q to Vic., Tas., and SA, and far s. of sw. WA, mostly Nov.–April. In nonbreeding season (June–Sept.) birds leave Cabbage Tree I. and probably disperse to feeding locations in n. Tasman Sea and adjacent Pacific (Marchant & Higgins, 1990). Other races breed New Cal. (*caledonica*); New Heb. (*brevipes*), Fiji Is., and possibly elsewhere, dispersing across Pacific to w. coast S. America. Race *caledonica* is a scarce vagrant to se. Aust.

BLUE PETREL *Halobaena caerulea* 26–32 cm; span *c*. 65 cm

The only small petrel with square white tail-tip: resembles a dark-headed, long-winged prion: blue–grey above, white below; white forehead and throat contrast with blackish crown extending below eye, down nape and forming a large dark patch on side of neck, *separated from earmark by white notch.* Conspicuous dark M band (broken at rump) crosses pale blue–grey upperwings; scapulars and secondaries finely tipped white. *Underwings wholly white, without black margins.* Tail blue–grey with narrow subterminal *dark band and conspicuous square white tip.* Legs and feet blue with pink webs. **Immature:** browner, forehead greyer. In open flocks, or with other petrels, prions; follows ships. Flight buoyant, gentle, hugs contours of waves with long running glides on bowed wings; in high winds, weaves, banks, rises over horizon in high arcs, white underparts alternating with blue upperparts. **Similar species:** Gould's Petrel: larger, unbroken patch on head; distinctive underwing pattern; no white tail-tip. Prions: head-markings differ; bill grey; crown grey: eyebrow white over dark eyemark; dark tail-tip either narrow or broad. **Range and Status:** breeds (Sept.–March) on sub-Antarctic islands: Marion, the Crozets, Kerguelen, Macquarie; islands off S. America; S. Georgia. Some colonies very large. Huge circumpolar dispersal s. to Antarctic pack-ice, n. to *c*. 30°S. Regular winter visitor to offshore waters of s. Aust. mostly July–Oct.; records n. to *c*. Fremantle (WA) and Sydney (NSW); vagrant Fraser I. (Q). Commonly beachwashed after storms.

WHITE-
NECKED
PETREL

GOULD'S
PETREL

BLUE PETREL

ANTARCTIC PRION *Pachyptila desolata* 25–30 cm; span *c.* 64 cm

Other name: Dove Prion.
Like Broad-billed Prion but bill *does not display combs when closed; has straight sides.* **Range and Status:** breeds Antarctica and sub-Antarctic islands, incl. Auckland and Macquarie Is. Ranges n. to 35°S, occasionally across equator. One of the most abundant sub-Antarctic seabirds. Common winter–spring visitor (May–Oct.) to offshore waters of s. Aust. from s. WA to Tas. and to se. Q: many beachwashed. Vagrant s. Gt Barrier Reef.

SALVIN'S PRION *Pachyptila salvini* 25–30 cm; span *c.* 58 cm

Other name: Medium-billed Prion.
Smaller than Broad-billed. Bill-comb visible, giving snarling look. Sides of bill less prominently bowed than Broad-billed, more so than Antarctic. **Range and Status:** breeds Prince Edward, Marion, Crozets, Amsterdam, St Paul Is. (s. Indian Ocean). Disperses eastward through sub-Antarctic; common winter/spring visitor to offshore s. Aust., from s. WA to Tas., Vic. and s. NSW; many beachwashed June–Oct. Less common se. Q.

FULMAR PRION *Pachyptila crassirostris* 28 cm; span *c.* 60 cm

Very like Fairy Prion: more sturdily built, usually paler. Bill deeper, more swollen; lower mandible more robust; nail larger and more curved; space between nail and nostril tubes *less* than in Fairy. **Range and Status:** breeds sub-Antarctic islands (NZ region); Heard I (s. Indian Ocean). Beachwashed nw. Tas., Sept. 1996. Unconfirmed records Vic., s. NSW. Vagrant.

SLENDER-BILLED PRION *Pachyptila belcheri* 25–26 cm; span 56 cm

Grey crown, slightly darker than blue–grey upperparts; broad white eyebrow emphasised by broad, dark grey line through eye, curving down neck. In flight, *white sides to head and only faint M band on wing;* narrow, dark tail-tip. Bill slender, combs not exposed; sides straight when viewed from above. **Range and Status:** breeds Crozets and Kerguelen Is. (s. Indian Ocean); Falkland Is. (S. Atlantic) and islands off s. S. America. Possibly Macquarie I. Ranges n. in winter to *c.* 30°S. Uncommon winter/spring visitor from s. WA to Tas., NSW to se. Q. Commonest on sw. and s. coasts; some beachwashed.

BROAD-BILLED PRION *Pachyptila vittata* 28–32 cm; span *c.* 60 cm

Largest prion, *with grotesquely broad, frogmouth-like, blue–grey to blackish bill; 'comb' visible when closed, giving snarling look;* sides bow strongly outwards. At rest, note blackish 'shoulder' and conspicuous blackish M band; *tail bluntly wedge-shaped, with medium–broad blackish tip and edges.* **Similar species:** Fairy Prion: bill finer; head paler; dark tail-tip broader. **Range and Status:** breeds Aug.–Feb. on NZ coastal islands; Chatham and Snares Is.; also Gough I. and Tristan da Cunha in S. Atlantic. Rare, mostly winter visitor (June–Sept.) sw. WA to Tas., s. NSW; vagrant se. Q.

FAIRY PRION *Pachyptila turtur* 23–28 cm; span *c.* 56 cm

Smallest prion: bill narrow and short with strong hook narrowly separated from nasal tubes. Plumage differs from all except Fulmar Prion: *less dark shading on crown, less distinct dark eyemark and wide, blackish tail-tip, up to half length of tail.* Bounces over surface picking up plankton; tilts, flits from wave to wave; 'hydroplanes' with wings spread, head underwater; swims underwater with half-closed wings, bobs up to swallow food on surface. In strong winds, *open flocks weave at high speed on fixed wings, blue and white surfaces alternating.* **Breeds:** Sept.–March, mostly in island colonies. **Nest:** small chamber, sometimes lined with plant material; in slender burrow 60+ cm long; under vegetation or in rock crevice. **Egg:** 1; matt white. **Range and Status:** breeds coastal NZ and many islands; also s. Indian and S. Atlantic Oceans. Breeds islands round Tas., (also on North Head); in Bass Strait, off Wilsons Prom., w. to Lady Julia Percy I. and Lawrence Rocks (w. Vic.). Common offshore se. Aust. w. to Eyre Pen. (SA) and n. to c. Q, where less common; rarest in s. WA. Present through Bass Strait and Tas. most months, with a winter peak. Gales drive many ashore.

ANTARCTIC
PRION

SALVIN'S
PRION

FULMAR
PRION

BROAD-
BILLED
PRION

BROAD-
BILLED
PRION

SLENDER-BILLED PRION

FAIRY
PRION

BLACK PETREL *Procellaria parkinsoni* 46 cm; span *c.* 1 m

Gracefully proportioned, deep-bodied *sooty black petrel; bill seems piebald from a distance*: horn-coloured with greenish yellow tinge, black along ridge of upper mandible, along cutting edge, and on tip; legs and feet black. In flight, black toes protrude just beyond tip of short, wedge-shaped tail. Seldom follows ships but gathers at fishing boats. **Similar species:** Westland Black, White-chinned and Great-winged Petrels; Flesh-footed Shearwater. **Range and Status:** breeds (mostly Nov.–May) on Great and Little Barrier Is. (NZ); formerly in mountainous parts of NZ mainland. Migrates into e. tropical Pacific, March–Nov. Summer visitor to offshore waters of se. Aust.; rare but possibly regular. Recent sight-records from Sydney to e. Vic., Nov.–April.

WESTLAND PETREL *Procellaria westlandica* 50–55 cm; span *c.* 1.4 m

Nearly identical to Black Petrel, but larger, longer-billed, broader-winged, more heavily 'bull-necked'. Mostly solitary except near breeding colony. Flight rather heavy in light winds with low coursing over surface, interspersed with languid wingbeats. In higher winds, 'weaves' on flexed wings. *Bill whitish to yellowish horn with dark ridge and cutting edge, dark 'nail'*; legs and feet black. **Similar species:** White-chinned Petrel: birds lacking white chin easily confused. Note *deeper bill with pale, not black, tip.* Flesh-footed Shearwater: bill, head and neck more slender and shapely; *base of bill and feet pink.* **Range and Status:** breeds in winter (April–Nov.) in mountains near Barrytown on w. coast, South I. (NZ). Disperses e. into Pacific. Rare visitor to offshore waters of se. Aust.: beachwashed and pelagic sight-records from se. Q to e. Vic. and Tas., mostly winter. Vagrant s. Vic., se. SA.

WHITE-CHINNED PETREL *Procellaria aequinoctialis* 55 cm; span *c.* 1.4 m

Large, blackish brown petrel *with robust pale bill and irregular (in some, wholly absent) white patch on chin*; underwing brown. Bill longish, rather deep; whitish, bluish, yellowish or greenish horn, incl. the strongly hooked tip; with dark nostril and blackish ridge; feet black. One of the commonest petrels of southern oceans: flight languid on broad wings, near surface; aggressive, dives well, follows ships. (A rarer race, *conspicillatus*, 'Spectacled Petrel', has band of white over crown and broad white whisker-mark; chin white. No Aust. records.) **Similar species:** Black and Westland Petrels have black-tipped bills but are not easily distinguished from a wholly dark White-chinned. See also Great-winged Petrel, Flesh-footed Shearwater. Giant Petrels are much larger, with longer, heavier, less piebald bills. **Range and Status:** breeds (Nov.–May) on sub-Antarctic islands in NZ region and in s. Indian and S. Atlantic Oceans. Common on s. and se. shipping routes in winter. Huge circumpolar dispersal s. to Antarctic pack-ice and n. to 40–30°S. Beachwashed and offshore sight-records from se.Q–ne. NSW to Perth (WA). Most records from offshore e. Vic., mostly May–July; se. Tas., March–April.

BLACK
PETREL

WESTLAND
PETREL

WHITE-CHINNED PETREL

GREY PETREL *Procellaria cinerea* 45–51 cm; span 1.2 m

Robust, slender-winged, shearwater-like petrel: ashy grey above, washed brownish; darker on head, wings and tail. *Colour of crown shades into whitish grey-washed underparts below eye-level; underwing grey; flight feathers blackish with silvery sheen below; under tail-coverts grey*, contrasting with white underparts; tail blackish. Bill grey–green or greenish yellow with black nostril and ridge; feet flesh-coloured or bluish brown, webs yellow, tipped black. Flies high, wheeling and albatross-like, on stiff, slender wings; feet protrude a little, *giving slightly forked-tail look*. Dives often, from height; 'flies' underwater with half-open wings; emerging, 'shakes itself like a dog'. Follows ships at a distance; attracted to fishing boats by offal. **Similar species:** White-headed Petrel: shorter black bill; whiter head with black eyemark; white tail. **Range and Status:** breeds Sept.–March on many sub-Antarctic islands, incl. Campbell and Antipodes Is. (NZ region). Formerly bred Macquarie I., but exterminated, probably by feral cats. Circumpolar dispersal from Antarctic to offshore waters of southern continents n. to (or beyond) 30°S. Rare visitor offshore waters from s. WA, se. SA, w. Vic., and Tas., most months. Vagrant n. NSW.

BULLER'S SHEARWATER *Puffinus bulleri* 40–46 cm; span *c.* 1 m

Other names: Grey-backed or New Zealand Shearwater.
Large, long-billed, long-necked, wedge-tailed shearwater with blackish brown crown, ash-grey upperparts and *contrasting blackish broad M band across wings, dark wingtips and large, dark wedge-shaped tail. Note ashy white leading edge of upperwing near body, and similar crescent across upper wing-coverts; pale rump.* Underparts and underwing white, with grey–brown sides of neck. Bill dull slate-blue; legs and feet fleshy-white, tipped black. Singles or open companies: flight drifting, leisurely, somewhat albatross-like; wings slightly bowed, 'wrists' carried well forward. **Similar species:** Wedge-tailed Shearwater, pale (white-breasted) morph: upperparts more uniform grey–brown, with faint M band. **Range and Status:** breeds Sept.–May only Poor Knight Is. off North I. (NZ) in large numbers. In nonbreeding season migrates to N. Pacific, returning down w. coast of N. and S. America and c. Pacific. Regular, scarce late spring–summer visitor offshore se. Aust.; beachwashed and sight-records from e. Tas. to se. Q, mostly Oct.–March. Reported ashore in burrows, Montague and Cabbage Tree Is. (NSW).

STREAKED SHEARWATER *Calonectris leucomelas* 48 cm; span *c.* 1.2 m

Very large shearwater with a large, pale grey, dark-tipped bill. *Combination of brownish, obscurely-streaked crown and hindneck, and white forehead and face, give it a helmeted look.* Upperparts brown; flight feathers dark brown; obscure dark M band across upperwings and rump; tail large and wedge-shaped; dark brown under whitish upper tail-coverts; underwing white with broad black trailing edge and large dark tip. Singles or scores (mostly off n. Aust.); may form 'rafts'. Associates with Wedge-tailed, Flesh-footed Shearwaters, gannets, terns, mostly well offshore. Takes flight on approach of boat, keeps wary distance. Flight leisurely, wingbeats deep, purposeful, almost laboured, with brief glides on down-arched wings. In high winds wings flexed more from 'wrist'; birds arc high and weave in more typical shearwater-manner (Carter, 1983). **Similar species:** see Buller's Shearwater, White-necked Petrel, Wedge-tailed Shearwater, pale morph. **Range and Status:** breeds March–July on islands off Korea and Japan, migrating to waters off Malaysia, Sri Lanka, and PNG. In Aust., abundant off n. coasts, Nov.–May. Now apparently regular summer visitor to w. and e. coasts s. to *c.* Geraldton and Albrohos region (WA); and on e. coast s. to *c.* Wollongong (NSW), mostly Jan.–March. Less common further s.: specimen and sight-record s. of Gabo I. in e. Bass Strait; beachwashed Airey's Inlet (Vic.).

GREY PETREL

BULLER'S
SHEARWATER

STREAKED
SHEARWATER

69

BULWER'S PETREL *Bulweria bulwerii* 26–28 cm; span *c.* 70 cm

Distinctive small, sooty brown, shearwater-like petrel with *short bill, head and neck, long, slender body and long wedge-shaped tail, usually carried in a blunt point.* Flies with 'wrists' well forward, like Wedge-tailed Shearwater, which it resembles, though much smaller: *conspicuous pale fawn patch on dorsal surface of wing.* Flight gentle and erratic, low to sea, with frequent changes in direction, at times with bat-like zig-zagging (Marchant & Higgins, 1990), or of several beats interspersed with glides on slightly bowed wings. **Similar species:** Wedge-tailed Shearwater. Matsudaira's Storm-Petrel: white shafts to primaries form small white patch on leading edge of upperwing. **Range and Status:** breeds in N. and c. Pacific, from China and Japan e. to Hawaii and Marquesas, and in ne. Atlantic Ocean. Migrates to tropical seas in Sept.–April, incl. n. Indian Ocean. Sight-records in Aust. waters include birds between nw. WA and Christmas I. in Indian Ocean; off outer Gt Barrier Reef e. of Cardwell (Q), Nov. 1985; off Cape Nelson (Vic.), Sept. 1986. Vagrant.

WEDGE-TAILED SHEARWATER *Puffinus pacificus* 38–46 cm; span *c.* 1 m

Common 'muttonbird' of our warmer coastal waters: responsible for crooning, wailing sounds often heard at night on Gt Barrier Reef islands. Distinguished by *buoyant gentle flight on broad wings, close to water, 'wrists' well forward; longish wedge-shaped tail looks pointed in flight and protrudes beyond wingtips at rest.* Bill dark grey (a few are pale horn-coloured, with dark tip); *feet flesh-coloured,* not extending beyond tail-tip in flight. Note that some birds from region of Shark Bay (WA), se. Q and elsewhere are *white-breasted, with greyer brown upperparts and a faint dark M band across upperwings; underwings white, mottled darker on leading edge near body;* flight-feathers dark. **Similar species:** Flesh-footed Shearwater: bigger, with squarer tail; bill pinkish with dark tip; wings straighter. Sooty and Short-tailed Shearwaters: smaller; wings more slender; tail short; legs black; flight more impetuous. For pale morph, see Buller's Shearwater. **Breeds:** Oct.–May in crowded colonies. **Nest:** sparse, of grass, feathers; in long 1–2 m burrow in sand under roots, crevice under rock, creepers, bushes or in palm logs. **Egg:** 1; large, white. **Range and Status:** in WA, breeds from Carnac and Rottnest Is., n. to Montebello Group and Forestier I.; common. In e. Aust. from Montague I. (NSW) to Raine I. (Q); Lord Howe, Norfolk Is. and in Coral Sea. Common from s. of Sydney to C. York, Gt Barrier Reef (Q), and Coral Sea. Rare across n. Aust.; vagrant s. Aust. Also NZ, Pacific and Indian Oceans. Part migratory; mostly *absent* from se. Q–NSW June–Aug.

BULWER'S
PETREL

pale
morph

dark
morph

WEDGE-TAILED
SHEARWATER

SOOTY SHEARWATER *Puffinus griseus* 46–54 cm; span *c.* 1 m

Other name: New Zealand Muttonbird.

Looks bigger, slimmer than Short-tailed, *with longer bill (longer than 4 cm); flight seemingly slower;* whitish underwing stripe noticeable in good light. But take care: some lack this, while some Short-taileds have reflective pale underwings. Unlike Short-tailed, it moults in summer; thus in s. Aust. in summer, check any dark shearwaters with gaps in flight feathers. Flight direct on stiff, straight wings, with slower wingbeats than Short-tailed, and long, slicing glides. In high winds, weaves in arcs, wings more flexed.

Similar species: Flesh-footed Shearwater: pale bill with dark tip; feet pink; underwing blackish brown. White-chinned Petrel: piebald bill; blackish brown underwing. **Breeds:** Sept.–April. **Nest:** of grass, etc.; in burrow 1–3 m long; usually beneath tussocks. In Aust., typically on high land. **Egg:** 1; large, white. **Range and Status:** predominantly a NZ species, breeding on many NZ islands, and Macquarie I.; also off Chile and far s. S. America. In se. Aust., some breed from Montague I. to Broughton I. (NSW); also Courts, Tasman and Breaksea Is. (Tas.). Present off e. NSW and Tas., mostly Oct.–Feb.; uncommon autumn–winter, Vic.; mostly Oct.–Feb, SA; June–Oct. s. coast WA. Winter migration to N. and e. Pacific; circumpolar dispersal in sub-Antarctic and Atlantic. Vagrant British Isles.

SHORT-TAILED SHEARWATER *Puffinus tenuirostris* 40–43 cm; span 90 cm

Other names: Slender-billed Shearwater; Bass Strait or Tasmanian Muttonbird.

Dark smoky brown, with paler throat and silky gloss on underwings. Some have whitish underwing (but see Sooty Shearwater). Bill slender, shorter than Sooty (shorter than 3.5 cm); tail short, rounded; in flight, black toes extend just past tail-tip. Some flocks immense, passing offshore in undulating streams; become churning masses on sea when feeding; rest on surface in dark rafts. In light winds, birds search randomly with easy beats and glide on stiff, straight wings; in high winds, flight is fast and weaving on fixed wings, with bursts of wingbeats. **Similar species:** Sooty, Wedge-tailed and Flesh-footed Shearwaters. **Breeds:** Oct.–April. **Nest:** sparse, of grass, leaves, etc.; in burrow 0.5–2 m long, usually under tussocks; typically in island colony. **Egg:** 1; large, white, laid between 19 Nov. and 1 Dec.; incubation 52–55 days; chick remains in nest *c.* 94 days. Returning birds circle en masse and drop to burrows after dark, depart before dawn. **Range and Status:** breeds in several tens of millions on islands from Recherche Arch. (WA) e. through SA and Vic., Tas. and through Bass Strait, n. to Broughton I. (NSW). Migrates May–Aug. to N. Pacific, via n. of NZ and Japan, returning via w. coast N. America, arriving home last week in Sept. Common to very abundant in summer off e. Aust., from n. NSW, s. round Tas. and w. to s. WA, n. to *c.* Busselton. Less common n. NSW and e. Q, though conspicuous offshore as southbound passage migrant, Aug.–Nov.

FLESH-FOOTED SHEARWATER *Puffinus carneipes* 40–46 cm; span *c.* 1.3 m

Other name: Lord Howe Island Muttonbird.

Large-headed, robust, graceful, blackish brown shearwater. *Bill large, pale flesh or whitish green, tipped blackish; legs and feet pale pink* (do not extend beyond tail). Underwing brown; tail short, squarish or fan-shaped. Flight languid, with easy, shallow wingbeats and glides near surface; note pale bases to primaries on underwing. Singles, open companies or rafts: dives from surface, swims underwater; attends fishing boats. **Similar species:** Wedge-tailed Shearwater: *dark* bill; flesh-coloured feet; wings broad, 'wrists' carried well forward; *tail longer, pointed.* Sooty and Short-tailed Shearwaters: faster; bills and legs black; underwings paler. Great-winged Petrel: short; dark bill; grey face; dark feet. White-chinned Petrel, dark form: pale bill; feet dark. Black Petrel: more thick-set, with piebald black and yellow horn bill; feet black; toes protrude. **Breeds:** Oct.–May. **Nest:** scraps of vegetation in burrow *c.* 1–2 m long. **Egg:** 1; large white. **Range and Status:** breeds on Lord Howe I. and in s. WA in Recherche Arch. and islands w. to C. Hamelin. Common Nov.–April from *c.* Bunbury (WA) to coastal SA; autumn–spring migrant on w. coast n. to *c.* Carnarvon (WA). In e. Aust. common n. NSW to se. Q in summer; in Q, offshore autumn–spring passage migrant. Rare Vic., Bass Strait and Tas. Pacific birds migrate to n. and ne. Pacific; WA birds probably to n. Indian Ocean. Also breeds NZ and S. Atlantic.

SOOTY
SHEARWATER

SHORT-
TAILED
SHEARWATER

FLESH-FOOTED
SHEARWATER

MANX SHEARWATER *Puffinus puffinus* 30–38 cm; span *c*. 80 cm

Other name: Common Shearwater (North Atlantic).

Medium-sized white-breasted shearwater with longish bill: plumage black (brownish black, when worn) above, contrasting sharply with white underparts, boundary lying *just below eye; foreneck white with a neat white 'notch' extending onto black hindneck behind blackish ear-coverts*; sides of upperbreast smudged brown. Bill noticeably long, slender and hooked at tip; grey at base with darker tip; feet pinkish-flesh. Closely related to Fluttering Shearwater but larger, bill bigger; flight more characteristic of larger shearwaters: stiff-winged gliding broken by few rapid shallow wingbeats. **Range and Status:** breeds ne. Atlantic, Mediterranean and ne. Pacific. Migrates to coasts of Brazil, Argentina; w. and S. Africa. One Aust. specimen: a bird banded on Skokholm, Wales, Sept. 1960 recovered dead Venus Bay (SA), Nov. 1961. Possible sight-records: offshore e. Vic., Dec. 1976 and off Sydney (NSW), Oct. 1984. Two beachwashed NZ, June 1972 and Jan. 1985.

FLUTTERING SHEARWATER *Puffinus gavia* 33–37 cm; span *c*. 76 cm

Much the commonest small white-breasted shearwater in se. Aust. waters: *blackish brown above, fading to pale brownish or rusty in worn summer plumage; underparts and underwing white, but leading edge near body and axillaries (armpit) smudged brownish*. Bill slender; smudgy border of dark crown passes below eye, extends onto side of neck as partial collar. Legs and feet blackish with pale flesh or whitish inner surface. Especially in winter, often seen from shore in se. Aust. in large flocks, flying near surface: rapid fluttering wingbeats broken by quick glides; overall impression is of most weight forward of wings, less behind; feet protrude slightly. In strong winds, 'weaves' in stiff-winged shearwater manner. Spends much time on water, in rafts; dives, swimming underwater with half-closed wings. **Similar species:** Hutton's, Manx and Little Shearwater. **Range and Status:** breeds Aug.–Dec. on many NZ offshore islands: migrates to coastal waters (occasionally bays and harbours) of se. Aust. from se. Q to Eyre Pen. (SA). Commonest April–Sept., but some all months. Casual s. WA.

HUTTON'S SHEARWATER *Puffinus huttoni* 36–38 cm; span *c*. 78 cm

Very like the Fluttering Shearwater; slightly larger, with darker blackish brown upperparts smudging onto sides of neck in *more distinct partial collar*. In flight, *head and collar appear dark; leading edge of white underwing greyish brown, expanding over axillaries (armpits) on underwing near body; remainder of white on underwing variably washed greyish*. Odd birds mix with Fluttering Shearwaters, or form large flocks, travelling in open formations, or coursing in wide circles; diving from low flight, swimming underwater to feed. On wing, flight-action and shape like Fluttering Shearwater, with long head/body and shorter rear end. **Range and Status:** breeds Sept.–April in South I. (NZ). Adults sedentary; young birds migrate to Aust. and extend to nw. WA and Torres Strait; may spend first 2 years in Aust. waters. Present offshore se. Aust. all months; in WA ranges n. to *c*. Dampier mostly April–Dec.; rare visitor se. Q. (Dec.–Aug.); winter visitor Torres Strait.

MANX
SHEARWATER

FLUTTERING
SHEARWATER

HUTTON'S
SHEARWATER

LITTLE SHEARWATER *Puffinus assimilis* 25–30 cm; span *c.* 63 cm

Smallest Aust. shearwater: flies low, fast and straight, with very rapid wingbeats and banking glides. *Smaller and finer-billed than Fluttering Shearwater; blue–black above. In Aust. races, junction between black crown and white face is above eye-level, with dark eye exposed in white face.* Underwing white with narrow black margin on trailing edge; under tail-coverts white; *legs and feet cobalt blue with pinkish webs.* Singles or (especially in sw. Aust.) flocks. Spends much time on water; dives, swims to depths of 10+ m on half-open wings. **Similar species:** Fluttering and Hutton's Shearwaters: larger; dark crown extends over eye and onto side neck; 'armpits' more or less smutty. Diving-Petrels. **Breeds:** June–Nov. **Nest:** in burrow or under rocks. **Egg:** 1; large, white. **Range and Status:** in Aust., race *tunnei* breeds in WA, on islands from Recherche Arch. to Abrolhos group. Race *assimilis* around Lord Howe and Norfolk Is. Other races breed in NZ, coastal and sub-Antarctic islands, Kermadecs, s. Indian and S. Atlantic Oceans. Moderately common offshore waters of s. WA; uncommon to rare spring–summer, coastal waters of SA, Vic., Tas., NSW and se. Q. Sedentary.

AUDUBON'S SHEARWATER *Puffinus lherminieri* 27–33 cm; span *c.* 70 cm

Like Little Shearwater, but browner and larger; closer to Fluttering in size and *in black of crown covering the eyes. Has unique combination of black under tail-coverts and undertail, with flesh-coloured feet.* Flight reported to be smoother and more gliding and casual than Little, and with fewer wingbeats. Underwing white like Little, *but with long dark tip and heavier black borders.* **Range and Status:** breeds on islands in tropical Atlantic, w. Indian and Pacific Oceans, from near Japan through many island groups in c. Pacific. Nearest to e. Aust. are New Heb. and Fiji Group (Harrison, 1983). One sight-record off c. coast NSW, Feb. 1987; other possible sight-records. Vagrant.

COMMON DIVING-PETREL *Pelecanoides urinatrix* 20–25 cm; span *c.* 40 cm

Tubby little blackish petrel with short, stout bill, short tail and dusky white underparts and underwings. Singles or small flocks: *bursts quail-like out of sea ahead of boat, flies low on whirring short wings before plunging back into sea and 'flying' underwater, using wings as flippers.* On surface swims low, like miniature penguin. Comes and goes from breeding islands in darkness. Many are beachwashed: in hand note two elongated nostril-holes, separated by a ridge (septum): a small crossbar on that ridge is *at rear end* of nasal opening; in South Georgian Diving-Petrel, crossbar is at *centre* of nasal opening. **Breeds:** July–Dec. in Aust. **Nest:** in burrow *c.* 0.5 m long in soil or rock crevice; in loose colony on oceanic island. **Egg:** 1; dull white. **Range and Status:** in Aust., breeds from Seal Island Group and nearby islands off Wilsons Prom., w. to Lady Julia Percy I. and Lawrence Rocks (Vic.); also Tas.: where islands s. to Maatsuyker I. are its Aust. breeding stronghold. Disperses into onshore and offshore waters w. to Spencer Gulf (SA); regular in bays and shelf waters of Vic., Tas., and NSW n. to c. Port Stephens; casual se. Q. Race *exsul*, 'Kerguelen Diving-Petrel', vagrant s. WA. Also breeds in s. Indian, S. Atlantic Oceans and many islands in NZ region, incl. Macquarie I. Sedentary and dispersive.

SOUTH GEORGIAN DIVING-PETREL *Pelecanoides georgicus* 18–21 cm; span *c.* 32 cm

Similar to Common Diving-Petrel but slightly smaller; indistinguishable at sea. Has variable whitish blotches on head/neck; narrow white tips to scapulars form indistinct line across base of upperwing in flight; white, rather than grey, inner edges of primaries; faint white tips to secondaries in fresh plumage. For differences in hand, see Common Diving-Petrel. Breeds Codfish I. and Auckland Is. (NZ region); and sub-Antarctic islands in s. Indian, S. Atlantic Oceans. Some colonies in Crozets group number millions (Marchant & Higgins, 1990). One Aust. record: Bellambi Beach (NSW), Dec. 1958; possible s. NSW sight-records. Vagrant.

LITTLE SHEARWATER

AUDUBON'S
SHEARWATER

COMMON
DIVING-PETREL

SOUTH GEORGIAN
DIVING-PETREL

WANDERING ALBATROSS *Diomedea exulans* 1.1–1.35 m; span 2.5–3.5 m

Longest-winged ocean bird, somewhat hump-backed in flight: adult always has *white (or pale) back, white dorsal surface of wings near body, and white underwings*. Except in fully mature old males, white tail usually has black edges; pink toes protrude in flight. From afar, resembles a flying white cross. Seen close, note large, shapely pale-flesh bill, and very fine grey barring on white plumage of head/body. **Female:** smaller, slightly duller; crown usually smutty; greyer fine barring and/or pink wash on neck and breast. **Juvenile:** very different — *uniform dark brown with contrasting clown-like white face and white underwings* (see Amsterdam Albatross, below). Becomes whiter in untidy, mottled annual stages; dorsal surface of wing becomes patchy black-and-white *from body out along centre of wing*, often with a large white inboard patch on upperwing. Mature (9–11+ years) males are *white with black flight-feathers*. Singles, or loose groups disputing floating food with other albatrosses and/or Giant-Petrels. On water, looks very large and white. *In flight, sheer size, enormously long wings, languid wingbeats and effortless sailing distinguish it from all but Royal and Shy Albatrosses*. **Similar species:** Royal Albatross easily confused — see entry. All smaller albatrosses have dark backs. Sooty Albatrosses and Giant-Petrels lack imm. Wanderer's clear-cut, clown-like white face and white underwing. **Range and Status:** several distinctive races breed on sub-Antarctic islands mostly in s. Indian Ocean and NZ region, nearest being Macquarie I. Regular visitor to coastal and shelf waters n. to Fremantle (WA) and Whitsunday Group (Q); common in s. Records every month, mostly June–Nov. Usual race in Aust. is *exulans*.

Note: Breeding population on Amsterdam I. in s. Indian Ocean, formerly regarded as a race of Wandering Albatross, is now tentatively treated as a separate species, Amsterdam Albatross (*D. amsterdamensis*). It differs from Wandering in *not acquiring* white adult plumage, but remaining coloured like a juv. Wandering. The bill is also distinctive: pale pink like Wandering, but with *brownish green tips and conspicuous dark brown cutting edge* (Marchant & Higgins, 1990). Adults of some other breeding populations, e.g. on Antipodes and Campbell Is., s. of NZ, are claimed also to retain dark plumage, and may be mistaken for juvs. Birds from these populations may occur in sw. and s. Aust. waters.

imm.

imm.

old adult

imm.

WANDERING
ALBATROSS

ROYAL ALBATROSS *Diomedea epomophora* 1–1.2 m; span 3–3.5 m

At all ages like *adult* Wandering Albatross, with no separate immature plumage. Head and body pure white, usually *without* smutty marks or fine grey barring. Nominate race *has white back and mostly black upperwings at first, with white starting to spread outwards from body along leading edge of wing.* In contrast, Wandering becomes whiter along *centre of wing*, with a large chequered white patch forming on innerwing. Old adult nominate Royals are white, with mostly black flight-feathers; white tail. **Female:** smaller and duller. **Immature:** black tips to white tail; note *contrast of white back and mostly black wings.* Smaller race *sanfordi: upper surface of wings almost wholly black, clear-cut from edge of white back*; tail white or with few black flecks. Juvenile: like juv. of nominate race. In both races and all ages, underwing like Wandering, except that in nominate race, leading edge of under wingtip is white. The following features are useful at close range: *on bill, note the black cutting edge to upper mandible; swollen, forward-directed nostril tubes, and black eyelids.* **Range and Status:** nominate race: 'Southern Royal Albatross' breeds Campbell I. and in the Auckland Is. (NZ region). Race *sanfordi* 'Northern Royal Albatross', breeds Otago Pen. (NZ), and Chatham Is. Wide, possibly circumpolar distribution when not breeding, especially to continental waters of s. S. America in winter; ranges n. to *c.* 35°S. In *offshore waters* of s. Aust., nominate race moderately common all months, mostly se. NSW, Tas., Vic. In se. SA, mostly May–Sept.; race *sanfordi* predominant. Casual s. WA and n. NSW.

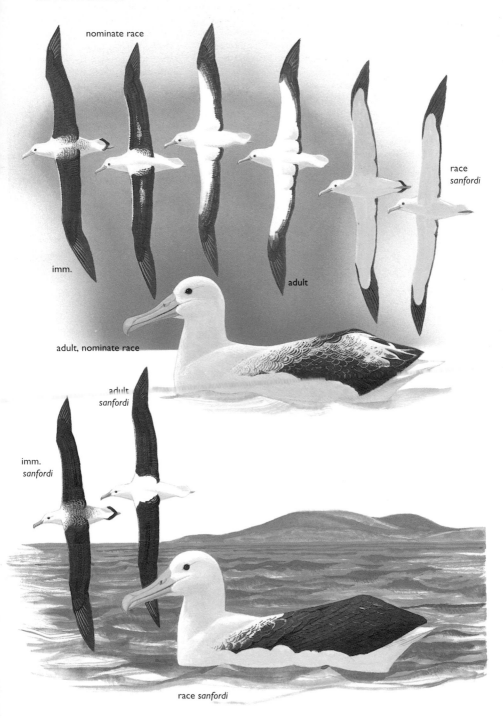

nominate race

race
sanfordi

imm.

adult

adult, nominate race

adult
sanfordi

imm.
sanfordi

race *sanfordi*

BLACK-BROWED ALBATROSS *Diomedea melanophris* 84–94 cm; span 2.1–2.5 m

Other name: Mollymawk.

Compact mollymawk, *with darkest underwing of all*. Wings, back and tail slaty black; *underwing has broad black margins, into which white central streak merges in squarish blocks; bill yellow, tipped pink; small black brow over dark eye gives it a 'sharp' look*. NZ breeding race *impavida* has honey-coloured eye: heavier black brow gives it a 'scowling' look; *impavida* also has broader black leading edge to underwing. **Immature:** bill blackish; crown and nape suffused grey; *smudgy collar around foreneck; underwing nearly black*. **Subadult:** bill yellowish with dark tip; develops narrow white streak up underwing. Follows ships, attends fishing-boats. Flight tighter and more controlled, less casual, than larger albatrosses. **Similar species:** Shy Albatross. Grey-headed Albatross, imm.: differs from imm. Black-browed: grey head and neck cut off cleanly from white breast; underwing more white. **Range and Status:** most abundant albatross; circumpolar breeding on many sub-Antarctic islands, incl. Macquarie and Heard Is. Ranges n. to coasts of all southern continents (vagrant n. hemisphere). Regular winter–spring migrant n. to *c.* Geraldton (WA) and to Tropic in Q. Commonest May–Oct. Race *impavida* breeds Campbell I. (NZ region); visits offshore se. Aust. in winter.

YELLOW-NOSED ALBATROSS *Diomedea chlororhynchos* 71–82 cm; span 1.8–2 m

Other name: Mollymawk.

Smallest mollymawk; *long, slender, glossy black bill has bright yellow line along upper ridge to orange tip*. Head and neck slender, usually white (race *bassi*); cheeks and nape washed pearl-grey; black eyemark larger (race *chlororhynchos*). Wings blackish brown above; back greyish brown; *underwing white, with narrow, even, clean-cut black margins, slightly wider on leading than trailing edge*. **Immature:** *bill wholly black*; in sub-adult, bill-ridge yellow, tip black. **Similar species:** Buller's Albatross: prominent broad gold stripes on top *and bottom* of bill; head/neck greyer, contrasting with white crown; somewhat broader black leading edge on underwing. Black-browed Albatross, imm.: separated from imm. Yellow-nosed by smutty collar around foreneck, much darker underwing. Gregarious, feeds with its own species and other albatross. Flight swift, wheeling and manoeuvrable. **Range and Status:** breeds more northerly sub-Antarctic islands; regular migrant May–Oct. to s. Aust. waters n. to NW Cape (WA) and to near Tropic in Q. Commonest WA, where flocks of adults occur; uncommon Gt Aust. Bight, common near St Vincent Gulf (SA); rare Bass Strait, common e. coast. The race usually seen in Aust. is *bassi*.

*Note: seafarers long used the name 'Mollymawk' to distinguish the smaller black-and-white albatrosses from the large, stately Wandering and Royal Albatrosses. 'Mollymawk' is still useful as a group name and is so used by some birders.

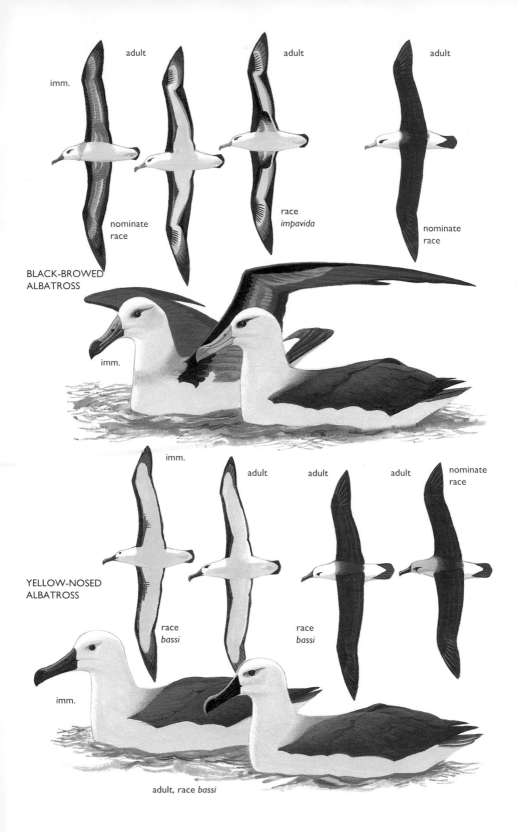

adult

imm.

adult

adult

adult

nominate
race

race
impavida

nominate
race

**BLACK-BROWED
ALBATROSS**

imm.

imm.

adult

adult

adult

nominate
race

**YELLOW-NOSED
ALBATROSS**

race
bassi

race
bassi

imm.

adult, race *bassi*

SHY ALBATROSS *Diomedea cauta* 90–100 cm; span 2.1–2.6 m

Other name: White-capped Albatross; Mollymawk.

Largest mollymawk: back and wings grey–black. Flies in the casual, hump-backed, lanky, droop-winged manner of Wandering, and has a similar *mostly white underwing with narrow black margins; all races have a distinct black 'thumb print' next to body under leading edge of underwing.* When close, note thin black eyebrow and delicate grey wash over face; *white crown and nape give it a capped look.* Bill: pale greyish straw, with yellowish tip; bill of imm.: lead-grey, tipped darker; darker grey wash on cheeks and on sides of neck, in partial collar. Race *salvini*, 'Grey-backed Shy Albatross': bill olive–grey, *with prominent ivory-horn stripe along top of bill to tip*; lower half of bill *has distinct blackish spot near tip*, and ivory-horn stripe along underside. Grey–brown wash on cheeks and sides of neck; back paler grey than upper surface of wings; underwing shows broader black wingtips. Race *eremita*, 'Chatham I. Shy Albatross': smaller; bright yellow bill *has distinct black spot near tip of lower mandible*; sooty grey wash on crown, cheeks and neck; wings and back darker. Nominate race occurs as singles and open companies: follows ships at distance, approaches fishing boats for scraps. Circles feeding dolphins, watching for floating, headless carcasses of discarded cuttlefish. **Similar species:** Wandering and Black-browed Albatrosses. **Breeds:** Sept.–April. **Nest:** very large cup of earth and droppings, vegetation and bones; in colony on island. **Egg:** 1; very large, white-flecked, red–brown at large end. **Range and Status:** the only albatross with Aust. breeding stations: nominate race breeds Albatross Rock, Bass Strait; the Mewstone and Pedra Branca, s. Tas. and Auckland I. (NZ region). Dispersal mostly local but crosses S. Pacific to w. coast S. America and s. Indian Ocean to S. African waters. Vagrant through tropics to Red Sea and N. American Pacific Coast. Common all months (but mostly winter) on coasts of Vic., Tas., s. NSW and SA; uncommon in se. Q and WA n. to Carnarvon; casual ne. Q. Race *salvini* breeds Snares and Bounty Is. (NZ region) and Crozet Is. in s. Indian Ocean; disperses to w. coast S. America and s. Indian Ocean; rare S. Atlantic. Sight-records from NSW to s. WA but some may be of imms. of nominate race. Race *eremita* breeds Chatham I.; dispersing into S. Pacific; rare vagrant se. Aust.; s. Tas.

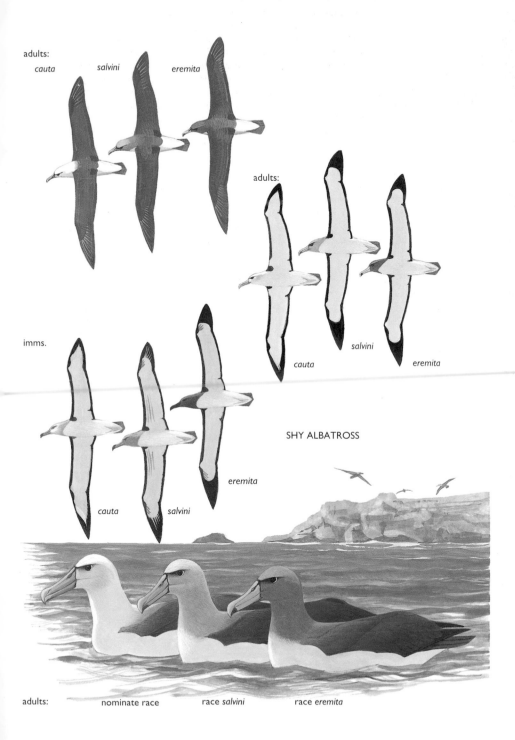

adults:

cauta *salvini* *eremita*

adults:

cauta *salvini* *eremita*

imms.

cauta *salvini* *eremita*

SHY ALBATROSS

adults: nominate race race *salvini* race *eremita*

BULLER'S ALBATROSS *Diomedea bulleri* 76–81 cm; span 2–2.13 m

Other name: Mollymawk.

Like a lightly built Grey-headed Albatross with *paler grey head and more distinct dark area in front of eyes; forehead and crown white, giving it a more distinctly capped appearance. Bill distinctive: long, slender and blackish, with broad yellow ridge and underside*, widening at base of upper mandible. Upperparts paler than Grey-headed; *underwing has greater central area of white*; pattern somewhat like Yellow-nosed — wide black margin on leading edge, much narrower on trailing edge. **Immature:** bill dark horn, with blackish tip, then like dull adult; neck and back brownish grey with smutty collar around foreneck, darker than crown. Distinguished from imms of Grey-headed and Black-browed by underwing pattern. **Range and Status:** nominate race *bulleri* breeds only on Solander and Snares Is.; race *platei* breeds only on Chatham and Three Kings Is. (all in NZ region). Ranges e. to coasts of Chile and Peru and n. to offshore waters of se. Aust. Regular, uncommon autumn–winter migrant to offshore waters from e. Tas. and e. Bass Strait n. to *c.* Coffs Harbour (NSW); casual s. Vic. and se. SA.

GREY-HEADED ALBATROSS *Diomedea chrysostoma* 70–85 cm; span 2.1–2.4 m

Other name: Mollymawk.

Darkish blue–grey head and neck cut off from white breast; black bill tipped pink, with narrow golden stripe along top and bottom. Some have nearly white heads, confusable with similar-sized sub-adult Black-browed; *underwing somewhat like Black-browed, but more sharply outlined; black on leading edge wider than on trailing edge.* **Immature:** browner; bill looks all-black; ridge and stripe along bottom become yellow, tip remains black; head and neck lead-grey, indistinctly cut off from white breast; *white of underwing heavily clouded dark grey at first.* **Similar species:** Buller's: more slender; has broader more conspicuous bill stripes; whiter forehead; whiter underwing. Black-browed Albatross, imm. **Range and Status:** breeds many sub-Antarctic islands, incl. Macquarie and Campbell Is. (NZ region). Southerly, circumpolar distribution; uncommon winter–spring migrant to offshore and inshore waters of s. Aust. n. to se. Q and s. WA, mostly May–Nov. Most regular in small numbers to se. SA, Vic., Tas., se. NSW; some beachwashed.

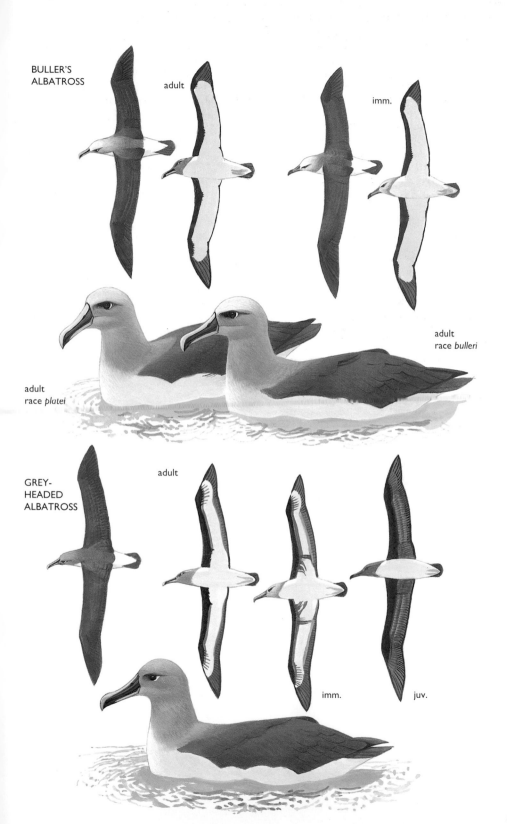

BULLER'S
ALBATROSS

adult

imm.

adult
race *bulleri*

adult
race *platei*

GREY-
HEADED
ALBATROSS

adult

imm.

juv.

SOOTY ALBATROSS *Phoebetria fusca* 84–89 cm; span *c.* 2 m

Sooty brown albatross with very slender wings and pointed, wedge-shaped tail. Bill slender and straight; black with a *pale-yellow to orange stripe on lower mandible*; head slightly darker than body; partial fine white ring around eye. Shafts of primaries and central tail-feathers white. Adults in worn plumage have nape, back and sides of neck paler, some nearly whitish, inviting confusion with Light-mantled. **Immature:** lacks white shafts and has *conspicuous buff–brown nape*; less pronounced bill-stripe is yellow, grey, bluish or violet. Follows ships on southern sea-routes, may fly among or alight on, rigging. **Similar species:** Wandering Albatross imm. Giant-petrels: pale heavy bills; bodies bulkier, hump-backed without Sooty's elegant taper. **Range and Status:** breeds sub-Antarctic islands in S. Atlantic and s. Indian Oceans, dispersing between 55°S and 30°S, with eastward extension to Aust. offshore waters. Rare but probably regular, mostly autumn–winter, migrant n. to se. Q and NSW, Tas., Vic. and SA; often on southern shipping routes.

LIGHT-MANTLED SOOTY ALBATROSS *Phoebetria palpebrata* 78–90 cm; span 1.8–2.3 m

Like Sooty Albatross *but back and underparts pearly grey in 'Siamese-cat' contrast to dark, smoky brown head, wings and tail*; (thicker) eye-ring and white shafts like Sooty. Bill shorter, heavier than Sooty, with blue or violet stripe. **Immature:** like adult but pale areas in plumage whitish, not buff; primaries lack white shafts; stripe in bill brown to blue, eye-ring duller. Some of the few sight-records on Aust. sea-routes probably refer to imm. Sooties. In flight has an evident two-tone appearance, and a noticeably shorter bill than Sooty, with blue bill-stripe. But positive field-identification chancy because of overlap of shadings of both adults and imms. **Range and Status:** breeds circumpolar sub-Antarctic islands, incl. Auckland, Campbell, Antipodes and Macquarie Is. (NZ region). Ranges s. to Antarctic pack-ice and n. to *c.* 35°S. Rare, mostly winter–spring, visitor offshore: beachwashed and sight-records SA, Tas., Vic., NSW, s. Q. Vagrant.

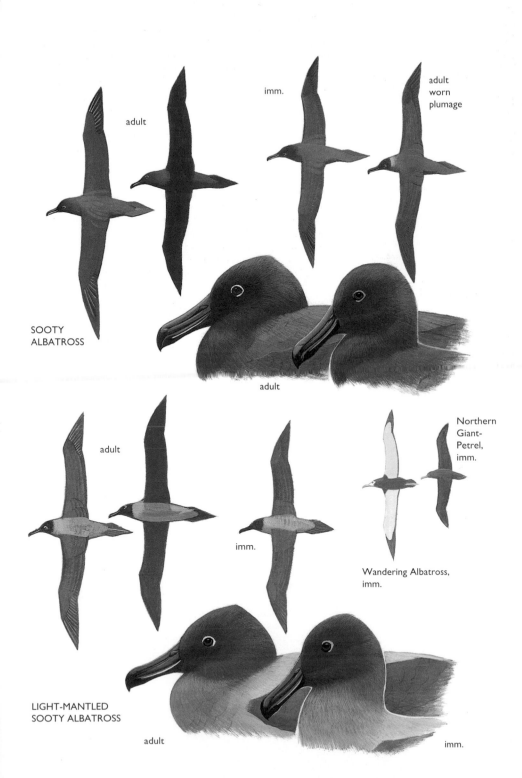

adult

imm.

adult
worn
plumage

adult

SOOTY
ALBATROSS

adult

adult

Northern
Giant-
Petrel,
imm.

imm.

Wandering Albatross,
imm.

LIGHT-MANTLED
SOOTY ALBATROSS

adult

imm.

WHITE-BELLIED STORM-PETREL (DARK MORPH) *Fregetta grallaria* 18–22 cm; span 46–48 cm

Wholly sooty black *except for white mottling on centre of belly and under tail-coverts*; under wing-coverts slightly paler. Intermediate morphs show continuous variation between dark and light morphs (Marchant & Higgins, 1990). Differs from Wilson's Storm-Petrel in *absence* of conspicuous white rump; is larger, heavier, with broader wings, shorter legs. Differs from Matsudaira's Storm-Petrel in *absence* of white mark on forewing, and in having a square, rather than forked tail. Flight erratic and bouncing. **Range and Status:** breeds on islets around Lord Howe I., where the only known polymorphic breeding population exists, a significant percentage being dark morph birds. (For further distribution data, see pale morph entry, next page.)

WILSON'S STORM-PETREL *Oceanites oceanicus* 15–19 cm; span 38–42 cm

Sooty brown, *with white upper tail-coverts* forming a broad V shape, and overflowing onto flanks; short rounded wings and tail black; grey wing-coverts form *pale loop across dorsal surface of innerwing in flight*; underwings brown; tail black, *squarish when open*, often carried 'dished'. Bill black, slender and short, with inconspicuous nostril-tube; legs and feet black with bright yellow webs, tipped black. Sustained flight strong, swallow-like and direct, well above waves, feet protruding slightly beyond tail. When feeding, pats surface; dances, wings raised, head down, or drags feet in water as sea-anchors when gliding into wind on raised wings. Rarely alights, but then swims buoyantly, high in water. **Range and Status:** one of earth's most widespread, abundant birds. Breeds Nov.–May in Antarctica and many sub-Antarctic islands. Migrates n. April–June to 'winter' in tropics and n. hemisphere; extends over all oceans. Appears on n. passage over shelf waters of Tas., se. and sw. Aust. in late autumn; common in winter offshore n. Aust. from ne. Q to the Kimberley (WA); returns s. Sept.–Nov. Vagrant Port Phillip (Vic.) after storms, Nov. 1994. Migratory.

LEACH'S STORM-PETREL *Oceanodroma leucorhoa* 19–25 cm; span 45–48 cm

Resembles Wilson's Storm-Petrel, but paler, slimmer, *tail longer and more forked*. White 'saddle' on *upper tail-coverts is smaller*, and divided by indistinct greyish line or indented by blackish upper tail-coverts. Little white shows on edge of under tail-coverts. Wings longer than Wilson's, with slight pale brown bar across upper wing-coverts. Flight erratic, bounding and butterfly-like on narrow, sharply angled wings; feet do not extend beyond tail-tip. Some lack white rump, but can be separated from Matsudaira's Storm-Petrel by *absence* of white mark on forewing. **Range and Status:** breeds Greenland, Atlantic and Pacific coasts of N. America, Alaska, n. Asia, Japan. Migrates into tropical waters. Few Aust. records: w. Vic., June 1965; Swan R. (WA), April 1978. Sight-record, Fremantle, May 1979; beachwashed Bremer Bay (WA), July 1984. Vagrant.

MATSUDAIRA'S STORM-PETREL *Oceanodroma matsudairae* 23–26 cm; span 56 cm

Large, dark brown, fork-tailed northern storm-petrel with buffish angled bar across dorsal surface of innerwing, *but no white in plumage except on shafts of primaries which, in flight, form a small white patch on the leading edge of outer-wing*. Wings slender and angled, flight strong but slow with glides, less erratic than smaller species. When feeding, carries wings in shallow V and dips to surface (Harrison, 1983). **Range and Status:** breeds Volcano and Bonin Is. (Pacific Ocean, s. of Japan). Migrates s. in June–Dec., passing through Indonesian Arch. to n. Indian Ocean. Specimens and sight-records from Indian Ocean waters off nw. Aust.: Seringapatam Reef; wsw. of Ashmore Reef and over continental shelf, Lacepede Is., near Montebello I. and off Dampier (WA); mostly July–Oct. Rare but perhaps regular winter–spring offshore visitor. Migratory.

dark
morph

WHITE-BELLIED
STORM-PETREL

WILSON'S
STORM-PETREL

LEACH'S
STORM-PETREL

MATSUDAIRA'S STORM-PETREL

WHITE-FACED STORM-PETREL *Pelagodroma marina* 18–21 cm; span 38–43 cm

The only storm-petrel with white forehead, face and underparts; broad dark mark through eye. Bill slender, with prominent nostril-tube; legs long and black; feet with yellow or buff webs. Singles or open flocks: in flight, *black flight feathers and square dark tail contrast with grey shoulders and back*; underwing white. Feeding into wind, trails long legs in water; flutters, dips, picks food from surface. Also feeds while swimming or rests in flocks on calm water, floating high, wingtips up-slanted. Direct flight swift, wheeling, *feet protrude a little*. Seldom seen near land by day. **Similar species:** pattern and colour very like a prion; take care. **Breeds:** Oct.–Feb. **Nest:** scanty lining of grass in very slim burrow like rat-hole, *c.* 1 m long; usually in colony. **Egg:** 1; white, finely flecked red–brown. **Range and Status:** breeds late spring and summer on many coastal islands in s. Aust. from Abrolhos group (WA) at least to Broughton I. (NSW); Bass Strait and Tas. islands; also Kermadecs; NZ and NZ sub-Antarctic islands; N. and S. Atlantic. Part of Aust. population winters n. Indian Ocean and Arabian Sea; some e. coast birds range into Pacific. Present offshore s. Aust. in summer; apparently absent in winter. Migratory.

GREY-BACKED STORM-PETREL *Garrodia nereis* 16.5–19 cm; span 39 cm

Very small, greyish storm-petrel with head to upper breast sooty grey–brown, sharply cut off by white underparts; underwing white, with broad black leading edge. *Back, dorsal surface of innerwings and rump ashy grey, feathers slightly margined white, giving scaled or frosted look. Tail grey, square, with broad blackish terminal band.* Bill small, with inconspicuous nostril-tubes. Sustained flight fast and direct, with rapid, bat-like fluttering low over waves (Marchant and Higgins, 1990). When feeding, flight buoyant, with rapid erratic darting and hovering. **Similar species:** White-faced Storm-petrel: white forehead, face and throat; dark eyemark. **Range and Status:** breeds islands in NZ region; also Macquarie, Kerguelen and islands in s. Indian Ocean and S. Atlantic. NZ population visits offshore waters of se. Aust., in all months, but mostly winter. Records from Eyre Pen. (SA), w. and e. Vic., Tas., and c. coast NSW. Flocks of hundreds reported beyond continental shelf.

WHITE-BELLIED STORM-PETREL (PALE MORPH) *Fregetta grallaria* 18–22 cm; span *c.* 47 cm

Sooty black above and on throat, mantle paler; *rump white, joining sharply cut-off white underparts. Underwings white, margined dark brown; tail black, square.* Intermediate morphs intergrade continuously from dark to pale morph, but usually have some white on centre of belly. Small and compact; nostril-tube conspicuous; flight erratic; *feet do not extend beyond tail-tip in flight.* **Range and Status:** breeds Lord Howe I. (see previous page) and Kermadec Is. (NZ), and islands in Pacific and S. Atlantic Oceans; disperses n. into tropics. Birds breeding around Lord Howe I. are pale, intermediate and dark morphs in the proportion of 1:4:5 (Marchant and Higgins, 1990). This is the only known polymorphic breeding population. Known breeding populations elsewhere are of pale morphs only. Birds from Lord Howe I. and Kermadecs may disperse into Coral, Tasman Seas and e. into Pacific. A few winter–spring sight-records claimed for shelf waters of s. Q and se. coast NSW, mostly April–Sept. Vagrant.

BLACK-BELLIED STORM-PETREL *Fregetta tropica* 19–22 cm; span 46 cm

Like White-bellied Storm-Petrel: differs in *irregular band of dark brown down centre of white abdomen*, difficult to see in flight. Unlike White-bellied, feet extend beyond tail-tip in flight. **Range and Status:** breeds Nov.–April on circumpolar sub-Antarctic islands, incl. NZ region, ranging n. to about 30°S in winter. Migrates into S. Atlantic, s. Indian and S. Pacific Oceans, to beyond equator in n. Indian Ocean. In s. and e. Aust. mostly a passage migrant, well offshore. In Vic., Tas. and SA, mostly late spring–summer visitor (Oct.–Feb.). Mostly winter–spring visitor to coastal waters of s. to ne. NSW, se. Q and far offshore waters of Gt Barrier Reef and Coral Sea. Vagrant s. WA (April). Migratory.

WHITE-
FACED
STORM-
PETREL

GREY-
BACKED
STORM-
PETREL

WHITE-
BELLIED
STORM-
PETREL

White-bellied,
intermediate
morph

BLACK-BELLIED
STORM-PETREL

White-bellied,
pale morph

RED-TAILED TROPICBIRD *Phaethon rubricauda* 86 cm, incl. tail 40 cm; span *c*. 1 m

Other name: Red-tailed Bosunbird.

Largest tropicbird: silky white, some with a pink flush; robust bill red, orange or, rarely, yellow; tail mostly white; two elongated, stiff, ribbon-like central tail-plumes, *bright red*. Difficult to see afar, their 'absence' gives a *stubby silhouette*. Black feet are used as rudders in flight. **Immature:** black bill; black-mottled upperparts; no red tail-plume. Mostly solitary at sea; usually far offshore; flies high, fluttering wingbeats broken by glides. High-dives like a gannet, submerging completely. Over breeding grounds, birds hover in group-displays, tails depressed, feet extended. **Similar species:** White-tailed Tropicbird: smaller; bill yellow–orange; bolder black wing bars; *tail white*. Imm. White-tailed smaller than imm. Red-tailed, with yellow tones in dark bill; more black on outer primaries. **Voice:** mostly silent at sea; guttural cackles, croaks, in aerial display with mate near nest-site. **Habitat:** tropical seas, islands and coasts; seldom near land except at nesting sites. **Breeds:** most months in tropics; Oct.–June near C. Naturaliste, sw. WA (Marchant and Higgins, 1990). **Nest:** a scrape; in shaded cavity in cliff or under bush on shore. **Egg:** 1; stone-coloured, heavily spotted red–brown. **Range and Status:** in e. Aust., breeds Raine I. (Coral Sea); Herald Cays and Coringa Islets, Gt Barrier Reef; Lord Howe and Norfolk Is. and widely through Pacific Ocean; also Cocos Keeling Is., Christmas I. and Ashmore Reefs (Indian Ocean). In s. WA, small colony persists Sugarloaf Rock, near C. Naturaliste; nesting attempted on mainland WA beaches. Possible recent breeding Neptune Is. (SA). Probably regular summer visitor to offshore waters n. of Wollongong (NSW) and C. Naturaliste (WA); casual summer–autumn, sometimes well inland, in s. NSW, Vic., Tas., SA, mostly after tropical storms, cyclones. Dispersive. Vagrant NZ.

WHITE-TAILED TROPICBIRD *Phaethon lepturus* 63–82 cm, incl. tail 40 cm; span 90–95 cm

Other names: Golden or White-tailed Bosunbird.

Smaller than Red-tailed Tropicbird: typical form is silky white, *usually with yellow bill and longer, flexible white tail-streamers, with longer black comma-shaped eyebrow, and much more black on wings* (parts of scapulars, secondaries and outer primaries). Note that Christmas I. (Indian Ocean) population includes a golden morph, commonly known as 'Golden Bosunbird': bill orange–pink or yellow; golden or apricot wash to plumage, incl. underwings. **Immature:** (typical form) smaller, more finely mottled and barred black above than Red-tailed; larger black patch on outer primaries; at first lacks streamers; bill dull yellow with dark tip. Flight strong, direct, with rapid wingbeats, seldom glides. Hovers over fish before plunging, gannet-like. Floats high, tail raised; follows ships. **Similar species:** Red-tailed Tropicbird; bigger; bill and tail-streamers red; less black on upperwings. **Voice:** rattling calls in flight; harsh screams at nest. **Range and Status:** off nw. WA, nearest breeding stations are Ashmore Reefs; Cocos–Keeling I. and Christmas I. Ne. of Aust., nearest breeding stations are Fiji–New Cal., Tuamotu Is. and Walpole I. Regular offshore nw. Aust. s. to *c*. Dampier. In e. Aust., uncommon offshore from Torres Strait s. to Ballina, (Q); ne. NSW, mostly Jan.–April, following tropical cyclones; casual s. to Bateman's Bay (some well inland); s. Vic. and s. WA, NZ. Dispersive. Also breeds elsewhere in tropical Indian Ocean, c. and w. Pacific Ocean, Atlantic Ocean, and Caribbean.

RED-TAILED TROPICBIRD

imm.

Caspian Tern
(for comparison,
not to scale)

imm.

WHITE-TAILED
TROPICBIRD

golden morph

CAPE GANNET *Morus capensis* 90 cm; span 1.8 m

Nearly identical to Australasian Gannet, *except for a fine black streak down centre of throat and foreneck; most have all-black tails*. Breeds on islands off S. Africa, ranging n. in winter. In Aust., vagrant C. Leeuwin (WA), Oct. 1986 and Wedge Light platform, lower Port Phillip Bay (Vic.) from Jan. 1986 on, interbreeding with local birds. Also reported Lawrence Rocks off Portland (Vic.). Vagrant.

AUSTRALASIAN GANNET *Morus serrator* 91 cm; span 1.7–2 m

Other names: Australian Gannet; Diver.

Spectacular high-diving white seabird of s. Aust. coasts. Note its *racy tapering outline, buff-washed head and black flight-feathers; only central tail-feathers black*. Fishing gannets fly on narrow, pointed, crank-shaped wings 15–50 m above sea, bills downpointed: sighting prey, they plunge spectacularly. Companies wheel over shoaling fish, plunging in salvos. Travelling gannets fly in lines, with alternating easy wingbeats and glides, and slice along the face of combers, gaining 'lift'. They rest on calm water in white rafts and on platforms of pile lights or high steep slopes of islands; otherwise seldom ashore. **Immature:** very different — grey–brown with *plentiful 'salt-and-pepper' white spots; head and body become patchy white and brown*. Adult plumage assumed over two years, first with *less* yellow on head; at one stage with mottled blackish brown wings, back and tail; whitish head/body. The *pattern* then is albatross-like, but the whole 'jizz' is 'gannet'. **Similar species:** Cape Gannet: nearly identical; black streak down throat; tail more black. Red-footed Booby, white morph: lacks deep yellow–buff head; tail white; feet red. Masked Booby: white head; black face and tail. **Breeds:** July–Feb. **Nest:** pedestal of compacted earth, guano, seaweed. **Egg:** 1; blue–white, limy; becoming stained brown with incubation. **Range and Status:** coastal waters of s. Aust. and NZ. In Aust. breeds Pedra Branca, Eddystone Rock (s. Tas.); Black Pyramid and Cat I. (Bass Strait); also Lawrence Rocks, on navigation platforms in lower Port Phillip Bay (Vic.); attempts to form mainland breeding colony, Portland Bay (Vic.). Widespread on s. coasts during summer, n. in winter to *c.* NW Cape (WA) and Mackay (Q). Local population far outnumbered by migrant adults and imms from NZ. Sedentary, migratory and dispersive, some are present at colonies all year.

CAPE GANNET

adult

imm

juv.

adult

adult

imm

juv.

adult

juv.

imm.

AUSTRALASIAN
GANNET

adult

ABBOT'S BOOBY *Papasula abbotti* *c.* 80 cm

Off-white plumage, black panda-like eyepatch, black wings, flank mark and tail and black outer ends of blue webbed feet make it unlikely to be confused with any other species. **Male:** bill pale grey, tipped black. **Female:** bill pink, tipped black. **Immature:** like male; bluer around eye. In flight, underwings nearly all-white, save for black margin at tips; tail black above and below. Outline racy, wings long and narrow, but blunt-ended; tail fairly short. Flies easily, with glides and occasional wingbeats; takes flying fish and squid. Ashore perches (and nests) high in leafy rainforest trees. **Breeds:** April–Dec. or longer. **Nest:** substantial shallow cup of sticks, in leafy tree, high in rainforest. **Egg:** 1; chalk-white. **Range and Status:** breeds Christmas I. (n. Indian Ocean) and perhaps elsewhere in region, apparently dispersing into nearby seas, n. to waters off Java. World population estimated *c.* of 2000–3000 only. May extend to Aust. seas. Rare and threatened.

MASKED BOOBY *Sula dactylatra* 74–86 cm; span 1.7 m

Robust white booby *with dark brown flight-feathers and tail; facial skin and base of bill blue–black,* rest of bill bright yellow in male, dull green–yellow in female; eye yellow (dark in Lord Howe and Norfolk I. birds); feet blue–grey or blue–green. **Juvenile:** ashy brown above and on neck, *upperparts crossed by mottled white bars;* wing-linings and underparts white, merging into brown breast. Bill dull brown, blue–black at base and on facial skin; eye, legs and feet dark. Usually well offshore; often solitary: flies high and dives strongly.
Similar species: juvs of other boobies show less contrast of dark head with white underparts; have less scaly pattern above. Juv. Brown Booby has grey bill; pale eye. Australasian Gannet; Red-footed Booby, white morph. **Breeds:** most months. **Nest:** scrape in sand, occasionally with pebbles or grass-roots. **Eggs:** 2(3); limy, blue–white. Usually only one nestling raised. **Range and Status:** breeds Bedout and Adele Is. (WA); Pandora Cay and Raine I. (ne. Q); Swain and Wreck Reefs (ce. Q); also many stations in sw. Coral Sea; Norfolk and Lord Howe Is. Disperses s. to Dampier Arch. (WA) and *c.* Brisbane (Q); casual NSW and SA. Fairly common in oceanic waters of main range, usually well offshore; uncommon coastally. Also tropical Pacific, Indian and Atlantic Oceans.

ABBOTT'S BOOBY

♂

♀

Abbott's
Booby

Masked
Booby

Australasian
Gannet
(adult)

juv

adult

Masked
Booby
(adult)

♀

MASKED
BOOBY

♂

juv.

RED-FOOTED BOOBY *Sula sula* 66–80 cm; span *c.* 1.4 m

Smallest booby, with light and dark colour-morphs and intermediates; *adult always has bluish bill, lolly-pink at base, and bluer skin around eye; feet flesh-pink to cherry-red; tail white in adults of all Aust. forms.* In flight looks slender with longish white tail. **Light morph:** white with *distinctive black patch on outer underwing;* black flight-feathers (birds in Coral Sea colonies have black primaries and white secondaries); some have a golden wash on head/body. **Intermediate morph:** head and body dull white to light buff; back and wings chocolate-brown or grey; tail white. **Dark morph:** head and body ashy-grey or ash-brown; wings and back grey; tail whitish. **Immatures, all morphs:** *wholly mottled brown;* bill black, often tinted dull blue; legs and feet dark grey, becoming red; tail grey–brown. Differs from most other boobies by nesting and roosting in trees, seldom on ground; perches in ship's rigging. In flight, 'wrists' carried well forward, giving leading edge of inner wings a scooped look. Flies fast: dives from heights of 7–8 m, pursues flying fish on wing; may forage at sea at night. **Similar species:** Brown Booby, imm.: paler underwing and abdomen; tail brown. Both Masked Booby and Australasian Gannet *lack white morph's black underwing-mark, red feet, wholly white tail.* **Breeds:** any month. **Nest:** bulky, rather untidy platform of sticks, grass; in low bush or tree, occasionally on ground. **Egg:** 1; chalky, green–white. **Range and Status:** in Aust. region, breeds Raine I. (n. Q), cays in sw. Coral Sea and on Gt Barrier Reef s. to Capricorn Group; also Ashmore Reefs, Christmas I. (n. Indian Ocean). Straggler to coastal waters of Q–ne. NSW, s. to c. Ballina, especially after cyclones. Casual coastal NT. Local; uncommon; dispersive. Also tropical Indian, Pacific and Atlantic Oceans.

BROWN BOOBY *Sula leucogaster* 65–76 cm; span 1.4 m

Small dark brown booby with *sharply cut-off white belly and underwings.* **Male:** bill creamy grey with blue base and facial skin. **Female:** yellow bill and facial skin; blue spot before eye. Legs and feet of both sexes green–yellow. **Immature:** same pattern but less contrast; bill and facial skin dark blue–horn; legs and feet yellowish. Singles or in small flocks: flies close to waves with casual wingbeats and glides; often dives from low levels, takes fish from waves in flight. Roosts on coral cays, buoys, beacons, trees, ships' rigging. In s. Q and n. NSW, look for it with flocks of gannets. **Similar species:** Australasian Gannet, imm.: larger, more patchy. Masked Booby, imm.: barred above; less clear-cut contrast below; lower neck white; bolder brown bar on white underwing. Red-footed Booby, imm.: more uniformly dark; feet dark grey, becoming red. **Breeds:** all year, with autumn and spring peaks. **Nest:** scrape in sand or low collection of sponges, seaweeds; on edges of cliffs and in small clearings on islands, on ground. **Eggs:** 2, rarely 3; chalky, green–white. **Range and Status:** common: in nw. WA, breeds from Ashmore Reef (n. Indian Ocean) s. to Bedout I.; in Q, from Raine I., off ne. C. York Pen., to Bunker Group, s. Gt Barrier Reef. Common offshore s. to Moreton Bay (Q) and Dampier Arch. (WA); uncommon on NSW coast; casual Vic. Dispersive. Also widespread tropical Pacific, Indian and Atlantic Oceans.

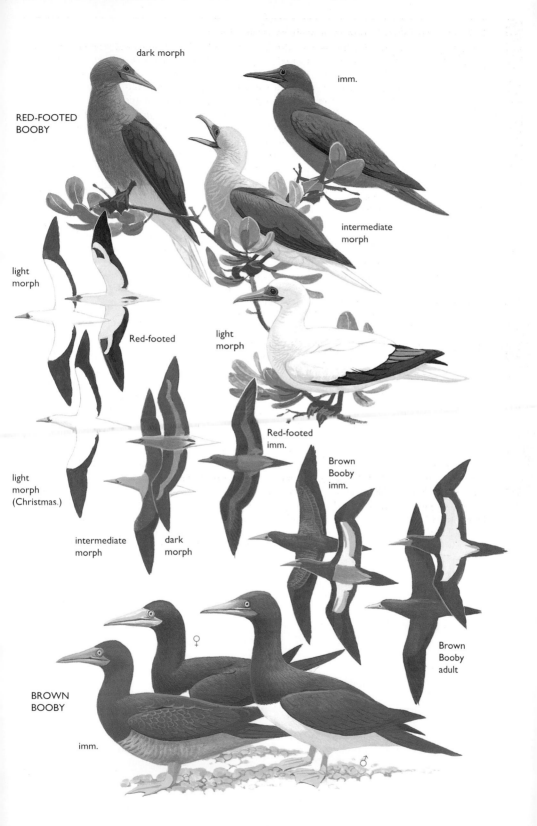

RED-FOOTED
BOOBY

dark morph

imm.

intermediate
morph

light
morph

Red-footed

light
morph

light
morph
(Christmas.)

intermediate
morph

dark
morph

Red-footed
imm.

Brown
Booby
imm.

Brown
Booby
adult

BROWN
BOOBY

♀

imm.

♂

DARTER *Anhinga melanogaster* 86–94 cm; span 1.2 m

Other name: Snake-bird.

Differs from cormorants in *stiletto-bill, snake-like kinked neck, pointed patterns in dark plumage and larger black tail.* **Male:** *black,* with white neck-streak. In breeding plumage, chestnut neck markings richer; long pointed plumes on upper wing-coverts and scapulars. **Female:** *head and neck pale grey with white streak; foreneck and breast cream–white.* **Immature:** like pale female; neck greyish. Young males develop black neck, with contrasting whitish belly. Singles or pairs; open companies: dries wings on dead branches, logs, navigation piles. On approach, snake-like neck writhes about. Flight distinctive — *wingbeats rapid, shallow, every few strokes broken by glides;* often soars high on slender black wings, square black tail *fanned.* **Similar species:** Great Cormorant: hooked bill heavier; throat-pouch yellow; back and wings coppery brown with dark feather-margins; deeper, steadier wingbeats. **Voice:** brassy clanging; alarm-note: mechanical clicking. **Habitat:** larger shallow waters, fresh and salt: rivers, lakes, swamps, lagoons, reservoirs, tidal inlets, estuaries; seldom open sea. **Breeds:** spring–summer, but any month. **Nest:** bulky platform of sticks; in dead or live tree over water, usually in small colony. **Eggs:** 4–5 (6); green–white, chalky. **Range and Status:** mainland Aust., patchy according to habitat and rainfall; sparse in w. and s. inland. Moves coastward in winter in n. Aust., summer in s. Aust. Vagrant Tas. and NZ. Also Africa, s. Asia to PNG.

GREAT CORMORANT *Phalacrocorax carbo* 72–92 cm; span 1.3–1.5 m

Other names: Black or Big Black Cormorant; Black Shag.

Largest cormorant, with slender, dark horn, hooked bill; *ochre–yellow throat-pouch and facial skin.* **Breeding plumage:** glossy black, with fine white streaks on neck, *white chin and flank-mark;* wing-feathers coppery brown, patterned by dark margins. **Nonbreeding:** duller, without white markings. **Immature:** dull brown, with dull yellow throat pouch; foreneck and breast dirty white. Singles to large flocks: wary; dries wings on trees over water, piers, sandspits, buoys; roosts in public gardens with lakes. Fishes in clear water, submerging smoothly from surface. Flight strong and direct, in lines or Vs, with measured wingbeats; glides in unison. **Similar species:** Pied Cormorant, imm.: paler below; bill paler; yellowish mark in front of eye. Little Black Cormorant: bill black and slim; facial skin black; wingbeats quicker. **Voice:** querulous rising croaking, and rapidly repeated guttural coughing. **Habitat:** large waters: coasts, bays, estuaries; rivers and lakes, reservoirs; farm dams, irrigation impoundments, spillways and regulators. **Breeds:** most months. **Nest:** bulky platform of sticks, weed; usually in treetop colony over water, with other cormorants, herons or spoonbills; occasionally on ground or cliff. **Eggs:** 3–4; greenish white, chalky. **Range and Status:** Aust. and Tas., widespread; irregular through w. inland; rare n. Aust. Sedentary and nomadic. Also Indonesia, PNG, NZ. Cosmopolitan.

LITTLE BLACK CORMORANT *Phalacrocorax sulcirostris* 58–64 cm; span *c.* 1 m

Other name: Little Black Shag.

Small, slim, wholly black cormorant with dark grey slender bill and dark facial skin. Breeding plumage more bronzed, head and neck sparsely flecked white, but no solid white in plumage. Forms flocks, especially autumn–winter. Active when feeding; locates fish from the air, wheeling and settling progressively, driving together, diving in rising frenzy, leapfrogging those in front. Dries wings in companies, typically on fallen trees over water, sandspits. *In flight, wingbeats quicker than Great Cormorant;* moves in fast-flying undulating strings or Vs. **Similar species:** Great Cormorant: horn-coloured bill; ochre–yellow throat pouch. Glossy Ibis: flying flocks can be confused, but note drooping necks, legs. **Voice:** usually silent, away from nest. **Habitat:** coastal waters, bays, inlets, mangroves, rivers, swamps, lakes, reservoirs. **Breeds:** spring–summer, s. Aust.; summer–autumn, n. Aust., but any month when conditions suitable. **Nest:** rough platform of sticks, leaves, bark, waterplants; in colony, some large, in trees over water, with other cormorants, herons, spoonbills. **Eggs:** 4; greenish white, chalky. **Range and Status:** Aust. and Tas.: mostly coastal but through inland when water conditions suitable. Common; sedentary and nomadic. Also Borneo, Indonesia, PNG, New Cal., NZ.

DARTER

♀

♂

imm.

♂

♀

adult
breeding

GREAT
CORMORANT

adult
breeding

imm.

LITTLE BLACK
CORMORANT

BLACK-FACED CORMORANT *Phalacrocorax fuscescens* 60–70 cm; span *c.* 1 m

Other names: Black-faced Shag; White-breasted Cormorant.

White-breasted sea-cormorant with black flank-mark: *black of crown reaches green eye; bill dark grey; throat-pouch and facial skin black.* **Breeding plumage:** hind neck finely streaked white. **Immature:** browner; face buff; foreneck smutty. Singles to occasional large companies on offshore rocky islands, buoys, isolated jetties, breakwaters. On wing, has *pot-bellied look, small head carried level with body;* flight straight and swift with rapid shallow wingbeats, close to water. **Similar species:** Pied Cormorant, imm.: bill paler than imm. Black-faced; facial skin yellowish; white plumage smutty. Little Pied Cormorant, imm.: much smaller; stubby bill yellow on sides. **Voice:** mostly silent away from nest. **Habitat:** coastal waters: islands, larger bays, deep inlets; ashore mostly on isolated rock-stacks, remote rocky headlands; *seldom on beaches.* **Breeds:** Sept.–Feb. **Nest:** scanty to substantial, of dry seaweed, driftwood, grass, pigface; in colony on rock shelf or rock-face of island or stack. Largest colonies in SA. **Eggs:** 2; pale green, chalky. **Range and Status:** coasts of s. Aust. from far e. Vic. to *c.* C. Leeuwin (WA). Common Bass Strait, coasts of Tas., and Vic., w. from Wilsons Prom. through SA, where abundant in Gulfs. Possible break in Gt Aust. Bight. Resident Recherche Arch., and coastally w. from Israelite Bay to Hopetoun (WA). Casual Green Cape and Montague I. (NSW). Sedentary.

PIED CORMORANT *Phalacrocorax varius* 66–80 cm; span *c.* 1.5 m

Other name: Yellow-faced Cormorant.

Largest white-breasted cormorant: *bill long, slender, horn-coloured.* **Breeding plumage:** *facial skin orange–yellow between eye and bill, reddish on chin; eye-ring blue; white facial plumage extends to just above eye.* Looks whiter than Little Pied, with slab-sided white neck; bold black flank-mark when perched. **Immature:** smutty brown of upperparts extends onto white face and neck, often with patchy band across upper breast; bill dark horn; yellow patch between eye and bill. Singles, small parties, companies of thousands on w. coast. Wary, roosts on piles, dead trees over water, lonely sandspits, mangroves. Flight strong, direct, in V-skeins in company; wingbeats slower than Little Pied. **Similar species:** Black-faced Cormorant: black bill and facial skin. Little Pied: much smaller; bill stubbier, yellower on sides; long white eyebrow; no adult flank-mark. Distinguish Little Pied Cormorant, imm., from Pied imm. by size, and stubbier, part-yellow bill; smutty black plumage of crown covers eye. **Voice:** at breeding colony; guttural cacklings, croakings and screams. **Habitat:** coastal waters with sloping shorelines: estuaries, bays, tidal inlets; large inland lakes and rivers, irrigation ponds, coastal mangroves and offshore islands SA and WA; often far inland in n. and e. Aust. **Breeds:** all seasons. **Nest:** flat bulky mass of seaweed, sticks; in colonies on ground on islands, mangroves, trees over water; on beacons. **Eggs:** 2–5; dirty green–white. **Range and Status:** Aust. mainland, casual King I. (Tas.). Abundant coastal WA and SA e. of Bight; moderately common Vic., NSW and Q on coastal lakes, estuaries and Murray–Darling basin. Sedentary and nomadic. Also NZ.

LITTLE PIED CORMORANT *Phalacrocorax melanoleucos* 58–64 cm; span 84–92 cm

Smallest Aust. cormorant: *bill stubby, yellow-sided; white eyebrow extends back from bill over eye to side of face; adult lacks black flank-mark.* **Breeding plumage:** *head-plumes fuller, black crown-feathers often raised in low, spiky crest.* **Immature:** bill grey–brown, yellowish on sides; plumage dull black and white, smutty black extends from crown to below eye, and onto neck; looks slimmer-headed than adult; *has a black flank-mark.* Singles to companies: roosts and nests communally; usually fishes alone. Flies randomly in companies: white underparts often stained rusty from impurities in water. **Similar species:** Pied Cormorant: larger, paler bill; yellow and red facial skin; black flanks. **Voice:** querulous cooing, seldom heard away from roosts or colonies. **Habitat:** coasts, islands, inlets, estuaries; inland waters of all kinds; rivers, floodwaters, house dams, roadside ditches. **Breeds:** almost any month, mostly spring–summer in se. and sw. Aust. **Nest:** small shallow structure of sticks (and green eucalypt leaves); alone or in colonies of few to thousands; in trees, bushes, from 1 m above water; occasionally on ground or ledges on islands. **Eggs:** 2–5; chalky, blue–white. **Range and Status:** Aust. and Tas. in suitable habitat; casual Lord Howe I. Sedentary and nomadic. Also Malaysia, Indonesia to PNG, Solomons, New Cal.; NZ and some sub-Antarctic islands. The Aust. race is *melanoleucos.*

BLACK-FACED
CORMORANT

imm.

PIED
CORMORANT

imm.

LITTLE PIED
CORMORANT

imm.

CHRISTMAS FRIGATEBIRD *Fregata andrewsi* 94–97 cm; span 2–2.3 m

Other name: Christmas Island Frigatebird.
Male: like Great Frigatebird with inflatable scarlet throat-sac. But *lower abdomen white, in shield-shaped patch which does not extend to underwings.* **Female:** like female Great Frigatebird, but white on breast *forms partial rear collar and extends to lower belly, and in 'spurs' onto black underwing near body.* **Immature:** difficult to distinguish from other imm. frigatebirds; young male has white belly and black-and-white 'scaled' breast (Harrison, 1983). **Habitat:** tropical seas, oceanic islands, coasts. **Range and Status:** breeds April–June, Christmas I. (Indian Ocean). Ranges through tropical Indian Ocean to coasts of India; se. Asia to Java, Sumatra, Borneo, Philippines. Sight-records, Darwin, Jan. 1974. Vagrant.

GREAT FRIGATEBIRD *Fregata minor** 86 cm–1 m; span 2–2.3 m. Female larger.

Other names: Man-o'-war Bird or Hawk.
Male: *wholly glossy black,* with small, collapsed scarlet throat-sac inflatable into huge scarlet balloon in display; brownish upper wing-coverts. Bill grey; eye-ring black; feet dull pink. **Female:** bill dull pink; eye-ring red (*blue* in Herald Cays, ne. Q (F.T.H. Smith)). *Throat greyish; breast white; abdomen black;* underwing wholly black. **Immature:** not safely identified from other imm. frigatebirds: blackish brown above with pale brown wing-coverts; head and breast variably rusty or whitish; underwings black. Behaves like other frigatebirds but roosts in bushes and trees, seldom on ground. **Similar species:** Lesser Frigatebird; Christmas Frigatebird. **Habitat:** tropical and subtropical seas, coastlines and islands. **Breeds:** differing seasons according to location. **Nest:** platform of sticks in top of shrub or tree. **Egg:** 1; white, large, smooth and glossy. **Range and Status:** breeds islands in Coral Sea, incl. outer Gt Barrier Reef. Largest local breeding stations are Christmas and Cocos–Keeling Is. in Indian Ocean. Scarce coastal n. Aust.; regular on islands of Gt Barrier Reef and offshore s. to Fraser I. (Q); casual coastal se. Q and ne. NSW, mostly after cyclones. Seasonally dispersive. Straggler to c. coastal NSW, Vic., s. WA. Also tropical Pacific, Indian and Atlantic Oceans.
*When described in 1789, named Lesser Pelican, *Pelecanus minor*. Under rules governing scientific names, the specific name *minor* must stand, though a smaller frigatebird, Lesser, was later described.

LESSER FRIGATEBIRD *Fregata ariel* 70–82 cm; span 1.8–1.9 m. Female larger.

Other name: Man-o'-war Bird.
Male: overall glossy black with inflatable scarlet throat-sac like Great Frigate bird; brownish bar across upperwing-coverts; underparts *black, with distinctive white 'spurs'.* Bill grey; eye-ring black; feet blackish or reddish brown. **Female:** bill greyish or flesh-coloured; eye-ring red; feet red or pinkish. Upper breast and part rear collar white, extending in white 'spurs' on underwing; *black throat forms prominent wedge on white breast.* **Immature:** head and neck deep-ginger; breast blackish; abdomen whitish, *extending a little onto wings.* **Similar species:** Great Frigatebird: male wholly black; female has grey throat merging into white breast. **Habitat:** tropical and subtropical seas, coasts and islands. **Breeds:** any month, depending on location. **Nest:** small, flat; of sticks, grass; in trees, shrubs or on ground. **Egg:** 1; white, chalky. **Range and Status:** breeds islands and cays off tropical n. Aust., from Capricorn Group (Q) n. to Quoin I. and Raine I. (Coral Sea); Manowar I. in Gulf of Carpentaria, to Bedout I. (WA) and coastally s. to NW Cape; also Ashmore Reefs and Cocos–Keeling I. (Indian Ocean). Seasonally dispersive. Regular summer–autumn visitor coastal w. Aust., s. to se. Q; irregular after tropical cyclones s. to c. NSW coast (*c.* 83 seen, Ballina, NSW, April 1989); casual s. to Merimbula (NSW); Vic. Also breeds islands in Coral Sea, Christmas I., and other islands in c. Pacific, n. Indian Ocean and S. Atlantic.

CHRISTMAS FRIGATEBIRD

juv.

juv.

♀

♂

juv.

♂

GREAT FRIGATEBIRD

♀

juv.

♀

♂

juv.

♂

imm.

♀

imm.

♂

♂

LESSER FRIGATEBIRD

GREAT-BILLED HERON* *Ardea sumatrana* 1–1.2 m

Huge dark grey to bronze–brown heron with heavy dark brown bill, yellowish below, at base: eye and facial skin yellow; throat whitish; legs grey. **Breeding:** facial skin grey; silvery plumes on foreneck, crest and back. **Immature:** browner; feathers edged rufous; no crest. Shy and solitary: feeds along quiet, usually remote, tidal, mangrove-lined waterways and mudbanks, margins of large rivers; faithful to certain confined locations. Flight heavy: note dark wings, folded neck and long, trailing legs. **Similar species:** young Black-necked Stork has even more massive *black bill; flies with neck extended.* **Voice:** deep, prolonged, resonant, guttural roar, 'like an angry bull' or thunder; often at night. Alarm call: harsh croaks. **Habitat:** mangrove-overhung creeks and rivers, tidal mudflats, tree-surrounded swamps; ascends larger rivers (e.g. Katherine Gorge, NT). **Breeds:** in solitary pairs, any month; principally spring, autumn. **Nest:** massive, untidy, flattish structure on low mangrove fork; occasionally to *c.* 12 m above ground in riverside tree; within foliage canopy; constructs several nests in territory. **Eggs:** 2; dull blue–green. **Range and Status:** coastal n. Aust.: from *c.* Derby (WA) to McArthur R. on Gulf (NT), and from Gregory R. and C. York Pen. s. to *c.* Rockhampton (Q); formerly bred Fraser I.; vagrant s. to Yamba (NSW). Sparse; sedentary. Also se. Asia to PNG.
* See pp. 110–111 for other herons.

BLACK-NECKED STORK *Ephippiorhynchus asiaticus* c. 1.4 m; span c. 2 m

Other name: Jabiru.
Striking tall black-and-white bird with *massive, slightly upturned, glossy black bill, glossy green–black head and neck and lanky red legs.* Eye: male black, female yellow. **Immature:** browner; bill dull grey. Singles, pairs, family parties: strides through water sweeping or probing with part-open bill; runs after fish with wings raised. Flies straight with slow wingbeats; soars high, looking skeletal: note extended dark head and neck, black panel on long, translucent, white wings, extended long red legs. **Similar species:** Great-billed Heron, imm.: smaller, with shorter, sharper bill; more uniformly bronze–brown; flies with neck folded. **Voice:** dull booms; sharp bill-claps. **Habitat:** coastal wetlands, mangroves, tidal mudflats, floodplains, open woodlands, irrigated lands, bore-drains, sub-artesian pools, farm dams, sewage ponds. **Breeds:** Oct.–May. **Nest:** large flat pile of sticks, grass, rushes, high and exposed in tall live or dead tree. **Eggs:** 2–4; whitish. **Range and Status:** coastal and subcoastal n. Aust., from Port Hedland (WA) to c. coast NSW; sparse s. of Q border; has bred s. to Shoalhaven R. Vagrant Vic. and inland. Mostly sedentary. Also India, se. Asia, Indonesia, PNG.

AUSTRALIAN PELICAN *Pelecanus conspicillatus* 1.5–1.9 m; span 2.4–2.6 m

Huge black-and-white bird with *very large bill and pink bill-pouch*, red in mating displays. **Female:** smaller. **Immature:** black parts browner. Singles to flocks: swimming groups encircle fish, plunging heads in unison; single birds swim stealthily up to fish with head low, neck folded. On wing, looks like rotund flying-boat, head drawn back, bill resting on breast; note *white panel on black upperwing, white V on rump.* Flies in lines or Vs, with intervals of wingbeats and glides; flocks slow-wheel to great heights on flat, slender wings; skims over calm water in long, sailing glides. Perches on piles, logs, dead trees, light-stanchions; tame where fed. **Voice:** gruff croaks. **Habitat:** large shallow waters: fresh, brackish and saline, coastal and inland; occasionally open sea; also islands, mudflats, sandspits. **Breeds:** almost any month, mostly Aug.–Nov. in s. Aust. **Nest:** a scrape, progressively lined with sticks, grass, seaweed; in small to very large isolated colonies, usually on bare islands, coastal or inland; occasionally in vegetation over water. **Eggs:** 2–3; chalky, dull white. **Range and Status:** Aust. and Tas.: common in suitable habitat; inland movements influenced by rainfall. Dispersive; highly nomadic. Also New Heb., Solomon Is., PNG, Indonesia; vagrant NZ.

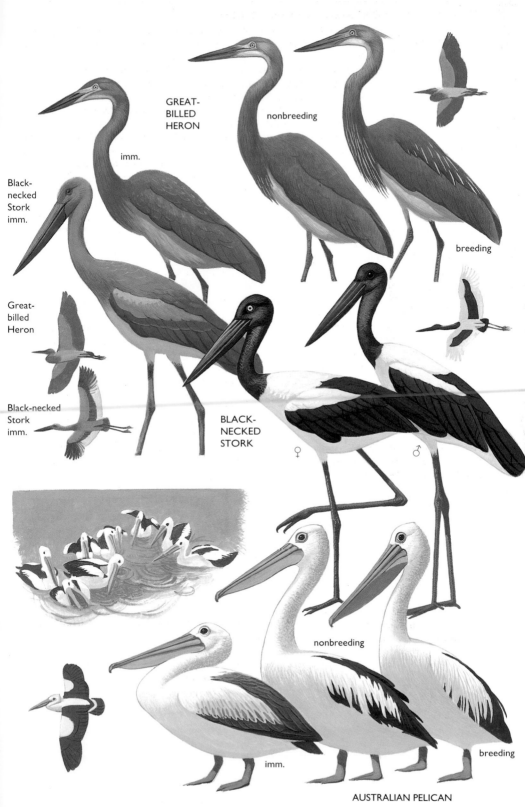

GREAT-
BILLED
HERON

nonbreeding

imm.

Black-
necked
Stork
imm.

breeding

Great-
billed
Heron

Black-necked
Stork
imm.

BLACK-
NECKED
STORK

♀   ♂

nonbreeding

breeding

imm.

AUSTRALIAN PELICAN

WHITE-NECKED HERON *Ardea pacifica* 76 cm–1.06 m; span to 1.6 m

Large heron with long *white head/neck contrasting with slate-black wings/body; plum-coloured breeding-plumes on back/breast. Bill and legs black; double line of black spots down foreneck;* streaked black below. **Immature:** head/neck buffy white, more spotted on foreneck; lacks plumes. Singles, loose companies to hundreds, in shallow fresh water and grasslands. Flight stately, slow-beating; neck folded; looks big, dark, long-winged in air; easily identified by *two prominent white patches ('landing lights') on leading edge of each wing.* **Similar species:** White-faced Heron; Pied Heron, imm. **Voice:** guttural croak. **Habitat:** shallow fresh waters: claypans, flooded pastures, farm dams, roadside puddles; occasionally home fish-ponds; rarely tidal areas. **Breeds:** mostly Sept.–Dec. in s. Aust.; any month after good rain. **Nest:** rough, shallow structure of sticks; in living tree, e.g. river red gum, 3–18 m over water. Singles or small colonies; often with cormorants, spoonbills. **Eggs:** 3–4; blue–green. **Range and Status:** mainland Aust., irregular Tas.; regular winter–spring movements in many regions; vagrant PNG, NZ.
Note: Grey Heron, *Ardea cinerea*, of Eurasia and Africa, is widespread in Indonesia, with unconfirmed Aust. records. Look for a *tall (90 cm) yellow-billed grey heron with white head, bold black 'eyebrows' that extend back in long black head-plumes; black shoulders; pale grey breast with pointed plumes, strong black streaks down centre of foreneck. Flight stately with neck folded: note pale underparts and contrasting black belly; long yellowish grey legs.*

WHITE-FACED HERON *Egretta novaehollandiae* 66–70 cm; span 1.06 m

Other name: 'Blue Crane' (erroneous).
Familiar small, pale grey heron *with white face and yellow legs.* **Immature:** paler grey; *only throat white.* Flight stately, sometimes with neck briefly extended: note *two-tone contrast of pale grey body and darker flight feathers.* Singles to autumn companies: wades in shallow water, on roadsides, farm dams, etc. Perches on fence-posts, trees, telephone poles, house roofs. **Similar species:** White-necked Heron; Eastern Reef Egret (dark morph). **Voice:** gobbling, gravelly croaking. **Habitat:** shallow wetlands: fresh, brackish or salt; farm dams, pastures, grasslands, crops, shores, saltmarsh, tidal mudflats, boat-harbours, beaches, golfcourses, orchards, garden fishponds. **Breeds:** Sept.–Nov. in se. and sw. Aust. **Nest:** untidy, shallow; of sticks in leafy branch 5–12 m high; sometimes far from water. **Eggs:** 3–5; pale blue. **Range and Status:** Aust. and Tas.: mostly winter visitor to Top End (NT), C. York Pen.–Torres Strait. Dispersive or part-migratory. Also Indonesia, PNG, Pacific, sub-Antarctic islands. Vagrant Macquarie I. Also NZ.

PIED HERON *Ardea picata* 43–50 cm

Other names: Pied Egret.
Elegant, *small, yellow-billed, yellow-legged, dark slate-grey heron with contrasting white throat and neck; crested dark cap pulled well down over eyes.* **Immature:** *lacks crest; head/neck white,* often smutty; body and wings red–brown to dark blue–grey. Singles to flocks, some large; imms may outnumber adults: dashes after prey, stands motionless or stabs while hovering. Flocks fly in bunches, with quick wingbeats, necks folded; dash about in air. **Similar species:** White-necked Heron. **Voice:** loud 'awk', usually in flight. **Habitat:** margins of, and floating vegetation on, wetlands, lakes, freshwater lagoons; ricefields, tidal rivers, mudflats, mangroves, sewage ponds, stockyards, garbage tips, freshly burned ground. **Breeds:** Feb.–May. **Nest:** small, shallow platform of sticks; to 5 m high, in live tree over water; in colony, small to large, with other herons, egrets, cormorants. **Eggs:** 3–4; deep blue–green. **Range and Status:** coastal/subcoastal n. Aust., from c. Wyndham (WA) (casual s. to Broome); to c. St. Lawrence (Q). Wide winter movement to n. coasts may extend in migration to Indonesia. Winter visitor Torres Strait. Casual inland NT, SA and Murray Valley (NSW). Dispersive; part-migratory. Also PNG to Borneo.

EASTERN REEF EGRET (DARK MORPH)* *Egretta sacra* 60–70 cm; span 90 cm–1 m

Uniform dark grey, with small, white streak on throat. Bill grey–horn; legs grey, washed yellow. **Immature:** browner grey. **Breeding plumage:** longer grey plumes on nape (forming small crest), back and breast. See Eastern Reef Egret, white morph, for other details (pp. 112–113). **Similar species:** White-faced Heron, imm.: more extensive white throat; clearer yellow legs; more distinctly pale grey with blackish flight-feathers. See also Striated Heron, pp. 118–119.
*For white morph, see p. 112–113.

breeding

WHITE-NECKED
HERON

imm.

nonbreeding

adult

WHITE-FACED
HERON

imm.

PIED HERON

imm.

EASTERN
REEF EGRET
dark morph

imm.

CATTLE EGRET *Ardea ibis* 48–53 cm; span *c.* 90 cm

Sociable small egret: habitually feeds around cattle, horses, etc., snapping up insects, frogs, etc. they disturb. Head large, 'jowls' deep; leggy and quick; walks with back-and-forward head-movement, but at rest can look hunched and chunky. **Nonbreeding:** white, some with *buff wash*; bill and eye yellow; legs greyish yellow or black. **Breeding plumage:** *spiky orange–buff plumes on head, breast and back; bill orange–yellow; in display at nest, bill and facial skin flush red; eyes/legs red.* Some singles, but mostly parties to loose flocks: flies in bunches, wingbeats quick, legs protrude length of tarsus; associates with other egrets.

Similar species: Intermediate Egret, nonbreeding: taller, with longer legs; often in deep pastures, or swamp-vegetation, but seldom so intimately with large mammals; wingbeats slower; legs protrude further. Little Egret. **Voice:** querulous croaks. **Habitat:** stock paddocks, pastures, croplands, garbage tips, wetlands, tidal mudflats, drains. **Breeds:** Nov.–Jan. in s. Aust.; March–May in n. Aust. **Nest:** small, untidy platform of sticks in foliage in swamp-woodland; usually in company with others, sometimes thousands. **Eggs:** 3–6; white, tinged blue. **Range and Status:** colonised NT (probably from Indonesia) in 1940s as part of worldwide expansion. Now widespread from Kimberley (WA) to coastal se. Aust. Breeds in summer in warmer parts of range; mostly winter–spring migrant to Vic., Tas., SA, s. WA. Also PNG and NZ. Cosmopolitan.

LITTLE EGRET *Egretta garzetta* 56–65 cm; span *c.* 90 cm

Fine small egret, about size of White-faced Heron: the slender bill is always *black, with part-yellow base to lower mandible and bright yellow facial skin.* Legs and feet dark grey, with *yellow soles in Aust. race: a difficult field mark.* **Nonbreeding:** filmy plumes reduced, or absent, *but some retain head-'ribbons'.* **Breeding plumage:** facial skin briefly pink or red in courtship; *note twin ribbon-like head-plumes, and abundant, erectile, filmy plumes on back and breast.* **Immature:** lacks plumes and ribbons; yellow–green facial skin, grey–green legs. Solitary, or loose companies: often feeds near other egrets, spoonbills or ibises, pursuing prey disturbed by them. Feeds actively, stirs with feet; possibly using flash of yellow on soles to disturb prey; *dashes after small fish in shallow water with raised wings.* **Similar species:** Cattle and Intermediate Egrets; Eastern Reef Egret, white morph: bills seldom black. (See Great Egret, breeding, p. 114.) **Voice:** a croaking 'kark'. **Habitat:** tidal mudflats, saltmarshes, mangroves, freshwater wetlands, sewage ponds. **Breeds:** Oct.–Feb. (se. Aust.); March–April (n. Aust.). **Nest:** scanty, of sticks; in colony often with other waterbirds, over water; occasionally far from water, in introduced cypress. **Eggs:** 3–5; pale blue–green. **Range and Status:** coastal n., e. and se. Aust.; inland and to s. WA when conditions suitable. Common in n., uncommon in s.; winter visitor Tas. Nomadic or migratory. Also Africa and s. Eurasia to PNG. Vagrant NZ.

EASTERN REEF EGRET (WHITE MORPH) *Egretta sacra* 60–70 cm; *c.* 95 cm

Other name: Eastern Reef Heron.

Workman-like beach and reef-dwelling heron, *with long bill (for a heron) and fairly short legs.* Two colour-morphs (for dark morph, see pp. 110 and 111). White morph: bill yellowish, with grey or horn-coloured upper mandible; *legs dull yellow–grey.* Immature similar. White morph predominates in tropics, but in NSW, SA and s. WA, birds are mostly grey. **Breeding plumage:** (both morphs): longer plumes on nape (forming small crest), back and breast. Singles, family groups, small colonies: stoops, crouches, wings part-spread in canopy over water; stirs with foot; chases prey or jabs at it while flying. Flight direct and low, wingbeats rather rapid; *feet protrude just beyond tail-tip.* **Similar species:** (white morph); all egrets are more slender, with finer bills and longer legs; generally more gracefully proportioned. Away from nest-colonies, most have either yellow or black bills, or black-tipped, yellow bills. **Voice:** hoarse croaks. **Habitat (both morphs):** islands, rocky shores, exposed coral reefs, beaches, tidal rivers, inlets, mangroves. **Breeds:** mostly Sept.–Feb. **Nest:** untidy structure of sticks; in trees in island woodlands; on ground under scrub, or among rocks, caves, ledges; in single pairs to small colonies. **Eggs:** 2–3; pale green to blue–white. **Range and Status:** coasts and islands of Aust., now *absent or rare* from coasts of Vic. and Tas. *except* far e. Vic. (Mallacoota); uncommon SA (Parker et al, 1979). Common on Q coast and Gt Barrier Reef. Sedentary; dispersive. Also se. Asia to PNG, w. Pacific islands and NZ.

CATTLE EGRET

'breeding flush' colouring

nonbreeding

breeding plumage

breeding plumage

LITTLE EGRET

nonbreeding

breeding plumage

imm.

EASTERN REEF EGRET
white morph

GREAT EGRET *Ardea alba* 76 cm–1 m; span *c.* 1.5 m

Other names: Large or White Egret; White Crane.

Tallest egret, with a gaunt, lanky, leaning-forward look. *When stretched out, head and neck nearly one and a half times as long as body.* For most of year, bill pale to rich yellow, sometimes with dark tip. Note flat crown, *yellow facial skin and gape pointing back under eye*; blackish legs. **Breeding plumage:** *bill black; facial skin pea-green; erectile 'aigrette' plumes cascade down over back to beyond tail-tip, but none on breast.* Some develop plumes and breed while retaining yellow bill; some black-billed birds without plumes are seen.

Solitary, small parties; in parts, e.g. floodplains of n. Aust., very large companies in wet season. Usually forages in water, moving with cautious deliberation; freezes motionless for long intervals before making lightning thrust. Occasionally seizes fish from surface in hovering flight. *Sustained flight steady with stately wingbeats, neck usually folded; trailing legs extend far beyond tail.* **Similar species:** Intermediate Egret: head and neck about equal length of body; wingbeats quicker. **Voice:** deep guttural rattling croaks. **Habitat:** shallows of rivers, estuaries; tidal mudflats, freshwater wetlands; sewage ponds, irrigation areas, larger dams, etc. **Breeds:** Nov.–Feb. in s. and e.; March–May in n. Aust. **Nest:** scanty platform of sticks; in treetop colony over water in swamp-woodland, mangroves. **Eggs:** 3–5; blue–green. **Range and Status:** Aust. and Tas. in suitable habitat; casual Lord Howe I., Macquarie (and other) sub-Antarctic islands. Dispersive. Cosmopolitan.

INTERMEDIATE EGRET *Ardea intermedia* 56–70 cm

Other name: Plumed Egret.

Smaller, daintier, more graceful than Great Egret: *extended head and neck about equal to body-length.* Head rounder, bill shorter and deeper: line of gape extends to just below eye, not past it. **Nonbreeding:** bill yellow, occasionally reddish; legs black below 'knee'; yellow, grey or reddish above. Unlike Great Egret, *may have a wisp of fine plumes on breast.* **Breeding plumage:** splendid and unmistakable; a veil of long, filmy, erectile plumes on back and breast; bill and legs temporarily flush deep rose-red; facial skin pea-green. Often

solitary in s., but in e. and n. Aust. forms open companies to hundreds. Forages in taller vegetation than other egrets. Hunts quietly; peers with neck extended, stirs with foot. Flies with quicker wingbeats than Great Egret, legs protrude less far: flies in random bunches. **Similar species:** Cattle Egret, nonbreeding: smaller, more chunky and 'jowly'; wingbeats quicker. Great and Little Egrets. **Voice:** rattling croak. **Habitat:** freshwater wetlands, pastures and croplands, tidal mudflats, floodplains. **Breeds:** Nov.–Jan. in se. Aust., March–May in n. **Nest:** small, untidy, flattish cup of sticks: 3–10 m high in fork; usually with other egrets in riverine forest, swamp-woodland; mangroves. **Eggs:** 3–5; pale green. **Range and Status:** common, widespread breeding species in better-watered parts of coastal n. Aust., from Kimberley (WA) to *c.* Brisbane (Q), ne. and central coast NSW. Generally uncommon in se. Aust., but breeds Macquarie Marshes and Murray Valley (NSW–Vic.) and irregularly at Bool Lagoon (se. SA). Scarce visitor s. Vic.–s. SA; scarce and irregular in WA s. of Kimberley; casual Tas., Norfolk I.; vagrant NZ. Winter visitor to PNG from Aust. Dispersive; part migratory. Also Africa to se. Asia, PNG and Solomons.

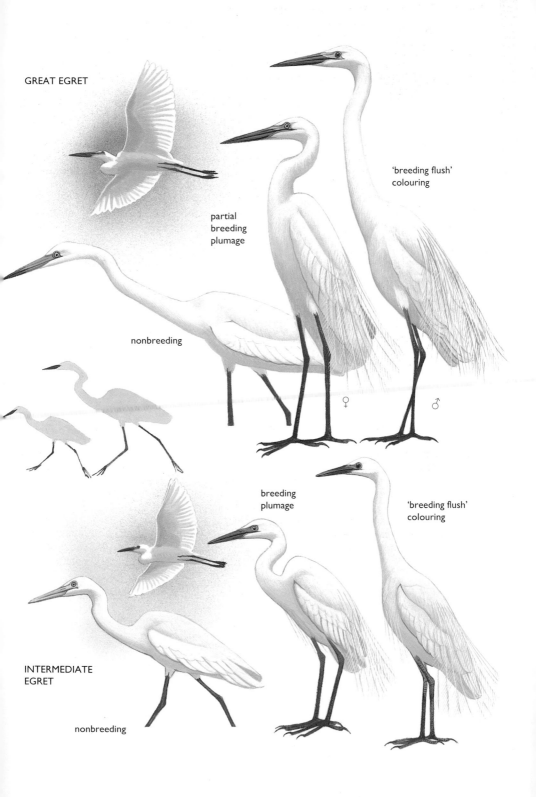

GREAT EGRET

'breeding flush' colouring

partial breeding plumage

nonbreeding

breeding plumage

'breeding flush' colouring

♀   ♂

INTERMEDIATE EGRET

nonbreeding

NANKEEN NIGHT HERON *Nycticorax caledonicus* 56–64 cm; span to 1.1 m

Other name: Rufous Night Heron.

Stocky, stooped heron, with large head, *short neck and short yellow legs; crown black; upperparts rich cinnamon; underparts whitish, washed buff.* **Breeding plumage:** two or three slender white head-plumes. **Juvenile:** heavily streaked pale brown and buff–white, with *rows of large, white and buff spots on wings*; often mistaken for a bittern. **Immature:** gains adult plumage by stages: crown black; plumage washed cinnamon with pale spots above, streaks below. Companies roost in leafy trees, on rivers, lakes, city parks and gardens, even leafless exotic poplars and willows, usually near water. At dusk, moves out in slow-flapping, loose flocks, like flying-foxes. May forage by day, seizing prey while wading or occasionally while hovering. **Similar species:** Australasian Bittern: bigger, browner, with dark neck-streak; fine black patterns on wings *without white spots*; rarely in trees. Striated Heron: smaller; reddish morphs are deeper grey–buff below, *with dark spots and white streaks down centre of breast.* **Voice:** loud, peevish 'kyok!', often at night. **Habitat:** shallow margins of rivers, wetlands, mangrove-lined estuaries, offshore islands, floodwaters, garden trees. **Breeds:** Sept.–Feb. in s.; March–April in n. **Nest:** loose structure of sticks; in colony over water, in mangroves, swamp-woodlands, river red gum forests; often with egrets, cormorants. **Eggs:** 2–5; light blue–green. **Range and Status:** mainland Aust. in suitable habitat; nomadic in response to rainfall. Regular, huge breeding colonies in Murray Valley (NSW–Vic.), coastal NT; smaller numbers elsewhere. Uncommon Tas. Also Indonesia to PNG, Solomons, New Cal., sw. Pacific. Vagrant NZ.

LITTLE BITTERN *Ixobrychus minutus* 25–35 cm; span to 50 cm

Tiny, handsome bittern. **Male:** black crown, back and tail, *set off by pale chestnut neck and large buff shoulder-patch.* **Female:** duller; crown and back rich brown; paler below, streaked brown. **Immature:** browner, more streaked. Singles, pairs: secretive; partly nocturnal; crouches with humpty-dumpty look; climbs in reeds and cumbungi. Forages among dense low swamp-vegetation and on floating waterplants. When disturbed, raises bill skywards and freezes. Flushes awkwardly with legs trailing, flashing conspicuous shoulder-patch: settles into typical neck-folded heron-flight. **Similar species:** Striated Heron: larger; no shoulder-patch; habits and habitat differ. Yellow Bittern. **Voice:** male in spring reported to utter a monotonously repeated 'hoch'; when flushed, a deep 'koh!'. **Habitat:** reed and cumbungi-choked sections of freshwater swamps, lakes, rivers; tussocks in wetland areas; well-vegetated lakes in city parks. **Breeds:** Oct.–Jan. **Nest:** small, shallow, loosely constructed platform in rushes or cumbungi, over water; sometimes in loose colony. **Eggs:** 5; large, white, glossy. **Range and Status:** breeds in spring–summer in inland se. Aust. — Macquarie Marshes and Riverina (NSW); Bool Lagoon (SA); coastal nw. WA (Kununurra) and sw. WA. Patchy and apparently very uncommon; irrupts coastwards in drought, e.g. Sydney (NSW) region in summer 1994–95; possibly winter migrant to PNG. Migratory or dispersive. Also Afro–Asia to PNG and NZ.

YELLOW BITTERN *Ixobrychus sinensis* 30–37 cm; span *c.* 50–60 cm

Other name: Chinese Little Bittern.

Very small yellow–brown bittern: *bill longer and more slender than Little Bittern.* **Male:** buff–brown, not blackish, *contrasting less with the yellow–buff shoulders.* Note black crown, black marks at bend of wing; *black primaries and tail, separated by grey rump*; underparts streaked pale sandy. **Female:** duller; breast whitish, broadly streaked brown. **Immature:** like female, with heavier streaks below. *In flight, black crown, fawnish wings with black primaries, buff back and black tail give piebald look.* In field, female and imm. probably indistinguishable from ditto Little. Said to be solitary in habits (Japan); in Borneo, climbs in riverside bamboos; flicks tail sideways and downwards; raises crown feathers (Smythies, 1968). **Voice:** reported to utter soft, staccato 'kakak kakak' in flight (MacKinnon & Phillipps, 1993). **Range and Status:** one Aust. specimen Kalgoorlie (WA), 1967, after tropical cyclone; other unconfirmed records. Potential summer visitor from Indonesia and/or PNG, as a summer migrant from Asia. Vagrant.

NANKEEN NIGHT HERON

breeding

imm.

juv.

adult

♂

♀

imm.

LITTLE BITTERN

♂

♂

♀

♂

imm.

♀

♀

YELLOW BITTERN

STRIATED HERON *Butorides striatus* 43–51 cm; span *c.* 70 cm

Other name: Mangrove Heron.

Dumpy little heron with large head and bill, black cap extends down nape in drooped crest: note *black and white marks down centre of foreneck.* Bill grey, yellowish below; *short legs and feet dull yellow, orange when breeding. Plumage variable: dark grey above, paler or buffish below, to red–brown above and pink–brown or buff below* (mostly Pilbara–Onslow region (WA), but varying with colour of local soil). **Immature:** upperparts dark grey–brown; *wing-feathers with buffish white flecks;* underparts streaked. Hunts furtively on exposed mud; stalks fish or crabs in stealthy crouch; *may deliberately drop leaf, fruit, etc. as bait;* plunges from perches. Disturbed in trees, freezes bittern-like, bill skywards. Tame around boat areas. *Flies low, with quick beats of rounded wings, neck folded; yellow feet protrude from stubby tail.* **Similar species:** Nankeen Night Heron; Little Bittern. **Voice:** sneeze-like 'kew!', 'tch-aah', startled, scratchy 'kew, kew, chit, chit, kew', like Swamphen; explosive 'hoo!'. **Habitat:** mangroves, tidal waterways, mudflats near same; exposed reefs, jetties, piles, anchored boats, sea-walls. In n. Aust., floodplain wetlands, swamp-woodlands; freshwater lakes. **Breeds:** Sept.–March. **Nest:** flimsy platform of sticks in horizontal fork, usually of mangrove; 3–9 m high. **Eggs:** 2–4; blue, green chalky or mud-stained. **Range and Status:** suitable habitat in coastal n. and e. Aust., from Shark Bay (WA), casual s. to far e. Vic; occasionally well inland. Sedentary. Also widespread Americas, Afro–Asia, PNG, Polynesia.

BLACK BITTERN *Ixobrychus flavicollis* 54–66 cm

Sooty black bittern with *slender head, neck and stiletto-like dark bill*, yellowish below; eye usually yellow; legs dark. **Male:** *bold white then golden-yellow patch from throat down sides of neck; black and white streaks down centre of foreneck and breast.* **Female:** browner, less brightly marked. **Immature:** duller, browner; rufous feathers of upperparts finely edged buff. Singles or pairs: secretive; keeps to leafy cover and shade near water by day. Disturbed, runs or creeps along branches; may point bill skyward and freeze. When startled into flight looks black and chunky; neck folded, tail short; wingbeats fairly quick. **Similar species:** Striated Heron. **Voice:** loud, pronounced 'w-h-o-o-o-o', repeated. **Habitat:** shadowy, leafy waterside trees: callistemons, casuarinas, paperbarks, eucalypts, mangroves, willows; tidal creeks, sheltered mudflats, oyster-slats. **Breeds:** Sept.–April. **Nest:** untidy platform of sticks on sheltered horizontal branch over water. **Eggs:** 3 (5); whitish or pale blue–green; rounded. **Range and Status:** coastal n., e. and sw. Aust., Torres Strait and Christmas I. (n. Indian Ocean). From Pilbara (WA) to far e. Vic., where a few pairs breed (e.g. near Gipsy Point); rare s. of Sydney (NSW) and far sw. WA. Casual to Wingan Inlet (Vic.) and inland rivers in NSW. Sedentary. Also India, se. Asia to PNG, Bismarck Arch.

AUSTRALASIAN BITTERN *Botaurus poiciloptilus* 66–76 cm; span 1–1.2 m

Other name: Australian or Brown Bittern.

Secretive, heavy-set heron-like bird: *upperparts patterned dark brown, buff and black like old leaves;* underparts streaked brown and buff; legs green, rather short. *Note paler eyebrow and throat and broad, dark brown mark down side of neck.* **Immature:** paler. Part-nocturnal: usually solitary, but loose companies in suitable habitat. Forages over water in dense cover, sometimes from platforms in wetland vegetation; wades stealthily with neck extended. Disturbed, vanishes slowly into cover, or slims plumage, points bill skywards and 'freezes', streaked underparts matching dead reeds. Occasionally flies over swamps by day on broad, slow-beating wings: neck folded, tail short, green legs just protruding. **Similar species:** imm. Nankeen Night Heron is often mistaken for 'a bittern'; note *pattern of pale spots on wings.* **Voice:** like distant foghorn — deep, double 'woomph!', often at night; when put to flight a hoarse 'cra-ak!'. **Habitat:** in, or over, water in tall reedbeds, sedges, rushes, cumbungi, lignum; also ricefields; drains in tussocky paddocks; occasionally saltmarsh, brackish wetlands. Seldom in trees. **Breeds:** Sept.–Dec. **Nest:** shallow saucer in platform of trampled waterplants over water in reeds, etc.; sometimes several pairs in proximity. **Eggs:** 4–6; green–brown. **Range and Status:** coastal and subcoastal se. Aust., especially Murray–Murrumbidgee region; se. SA; Tas., far s. WA; casual Kimberley (WA). Sedentary; occasionally irruptive following heavy rains and floods, or drought elsewhere. Uncommon. Also NZ, New Cal., etc.

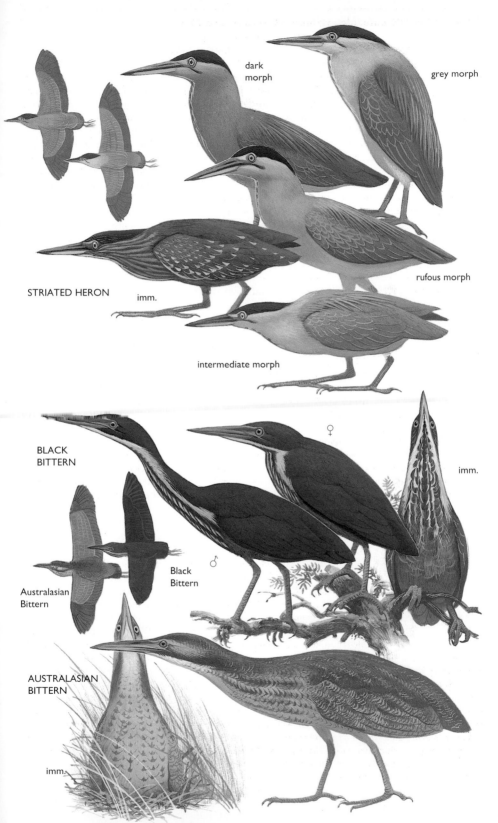

dark
morph

grey morph

rufous morph

STRIATED HERON

imm.

intermediate morph

BLACK
BITTERN

♀

imm.

Australasian
Bittern

Black
Bittern

♂

AUSTRALASIAN
BITTERN

imm.

119

GLOSSY IBIS *Plegadis falcinellus* 48–61 cm; span *c.* 90 cm

Small dark ibis: at a distance looks like a black curlew. **Breeding:** rich purplish brown, glossed bronze or green; distinctive white line borders facial skin. **Nonbreeding:** browner and duller; facial border less bold; head and neck streaked white. **Immature:** bill shorter, straighter; white mark on crown; plumage browner; pale mottlings on head and neck. Flocks of dozens to hundreds: feeds in shallow wetlands. Flies in long, swift, undulating lines, Vs, or bunches; often dashes about erratically, with sudden glides. Flocks can resemble Little Black Cormorants, but note *drooping bills, necks and legs.*
Voice: long, harsh, crow-like croak; grunts. **Habitat:** well-vegetated wetlands, wet pastures, ricefields, floodwaters, floodplains; brackish or occasionally saline wetlands, mangroves; mudflats; occasionally dry grasslands. **Breeds:** Oct.–Dec. in s. Aust.; Feb.–April in n. **Nest:** shallow platform of leafy sticks; in colony (some very large) over water in trees (incl. mangroves), shrubs, cumbungi, lignum or reeds, trampled into platforms. Often with other waterbirds. **Eggs:** 3–6; dull, deep green–blue. **Range and Status:** n. and e. Aust., most numerous in n.; movements often erratic but fairly regular spring–summer breeding migrant to s. Murray–Darling region (NSW, Vic.) and adjacent se. SA. Most breeding occurs in this region, Macquarie Marshes (NSW) and in s. Q. Many apparently move n. in autumn, and range far inland after good rains. Nonbreeding visitor to sw. WA and Tas. Migratory, nomadic and irruptive. Cosmopolitan; NZ.

STRAW-NECKED IBIS *Threskiornis spinicollis* 58–76 cm; span 1–1.2 m

Iridescent black upperparts and sides of breast contrast with white 'collar', underparts and tail. Note strawlike tuft of breast-plumes. **Female:** *bill shorter;* black breastband. **Immature:** bill shorter and straighter; head closely feathered black; neck feathered white. Loose flocks walk in 'fronts' across grasslands or feed in shallow wetlands. Flocks wheel high, mostly black wings contrasting with *snow-white wing-linings, underparts and tail.* Flies in Vs or long, undulating lines. Settles in dead trees by day; roosts in heads of leafy trees in woodlands and forests. **Voice:** hoarse coughs, grunts. **Habitat:** grasslands, sometimes far from water; freshwater wetlands, flooded areas, irrigated pastures, crops, playing fields, airfields, sewage ponds, croplands; tidal mudflats or saltmarsh (seldom). **Breeds:** Sept.–Nov. in se. Aust. **Nest:** shallow cup of sticks, reeds, over water in colony in trampled cumbungi, lignum, rushes, reeds, paperbarks; on ground on islands; some colonies of many 1000s. **Eggs:** 4–5; white, dirty. **Range and Status:** e., n. Aust. and WA; breeds widely, but largest numbers in Murrumbidgee–Murray Valley region (NSW), s. Vic. and se. SA; nonbreeding visitor Tas. Widespread movement to n. Aust. in winter; uncommon to absent in arid regions. Part-migratory; dispersive; nomadic; movements influenced by rainfall. Vagrant Lord Howe and Norfolk Is. Winter migrant to Indonesia and PNG.

AUSTRALIAN WHITE IBIS *Threskiornis molucca* 65–76 cm; span to 1.25 m

Other name: Sacred Ibis.
White with bare black head and ibis-bill; black tips to flight-feathers. **Breeding:** pink marks on black neck, yellowish breast-plumes, bare scarlet skin on underwing; *lacelike wing-plumes over yellowish white tail.* Female smaller; bill shorter. **Immature:** bill shorter, straighter; feathered black on head and neck; no wing-plumes. Singles to large flocks: feeds in pastures, freshwater wetlands, tidal areas; *plumage often soiled.* Flies in undulating lines or Vs with quick wingbeats and glides, often with Straw-neckeds; flocks wheel high.
Voice: harsh barks, shouts. **Habitat:** freshwater wetlands, irrigated areas; margins of dams, floodplains, brackish and saline wetlands, tidal mudflats; pastures, lawns, orchards, garbage tips, public gardens. **Breeds:** June–Dec., s. Aust.; Sept.–April n. NSW–s. Q. **Nest:** compact shallow cup of sticks, reeds, etc.; in colonies, some large, over water in dense trees; on island; in trampled reeds, cumbungi, lignum, mangroves; artificial structures in town environs. **Eggs:** 2–4; white, dirty. **Range and Status:** e., se. and n. Aust.; recent expansion to Tas. and sw. WA. Most breed in Murrumbidgee–Murray Valley (NSW), Vic. and se. SA. Some colonies to 10 000+: smaller in n. Aust. Has benefited from establishment of pastures, farm dams. Sedentary; dispersive. Vagrant NZ.

GLOSSY IBIS

imm.

STRAW-NECKED
IBIS

imm.

AUSTRALIAN
WHITE IBIS

imm.

ROYAL SPOONBILL *Platalea regia* 74–80 cm

Usually spotless white bird with distinctive *black, spoon-bill and black legs*. **Breeding plumage:** small red mark along black forehead; rich yellow mark above each eye *and conspicuous flowing white head-plumes;* breast lightly washed buff. **Nonbreeding:** lacks coloured markings and head-plumes; retains black bill and legs. **Immature:** bill shorter; tips of flight feathers black. Singles; small to occasional large flocks in suitable habitat. Flies with steady wingbeats; silhouette rather flat, with extended neck inclined upward, legs extended. Flocks fly in echelons, occasionally soar high. **Similar species:** Yellow-billed Spoonbill: always has whitish bill, greyer legs. **Voice:** usually silent; near nest, soft purring grunts. **Habitat:** larger shallow waters, inland and coastal: well-vegetated shallow freshwater wetlands; floodplains, billabongs, sewage ponds, irrigation storages, tidal mudflats, estuaries, saltmarshes, saltfields, mangroves, islands. Visits farm dams less frequently than Yellow-billed. **Breeds:** Sept.–Nov. in s.; Feb.–April in n. **Nest:** shallow platform of sticks; in small, loose colony, often with other waterbirds, usually over water in heads of trees such as paperbarks, mangroves; also in lignum, cumbungi. **Eggs:** 3 (4); dull white, spotted yellow–brown or red–brown. **Range and Status:** e. and n. Aust., except waterless, treeless and densely vegetated regions; scarce in s. WA; rare nomadic visitor, Tas.; vagrant Lord Howe and Norfolk Is. Sedentary; dispersive. Vagrant Indonesia, PNG; self-introduced NZ.

YELLOW-BILLED SPOONBILL *Platalea flavipes* 76–92 cm; span *c.* 1.3 m

Unlike Royal, white plumage often soiled; flattened *spoon-bill dull yellow to flesh-white; legs similar* (but often muddy). **Breeding plumage:** fine black line edges the pale grey facial skin; breast-plumes longer; sparse dark lacelike plumes from inner wings. **Nonbreeding:** lacks plumes. Mostly solitary: unlike Royal, seeks out small, isolated fresh waters. Forages in muddy water, scything submerged bill-tips from side to side more slowly than Royal; rests on banks of dams or in dead trees; occasionally forages in dry grassland. Flies steadily or with alternate shallow wingbeats and glides; silhouette rather flat, neck inclined upwards, legs extended; occasionally soars high. **Voice:** a feeble reedy grunt. **Habitat:** small fresh waters: farm dams, roadside pools, inland claypans and tanks; irrigated areas: channels, regulators, ricefields. Seldom on tidal areas but occasionally saline wetlands. **Breeds:** Sept.–Jan. in s.; March–May in n. **Nest:** platform of sticks in live or dead tree over water, often in river red gum; cumbungi, lignum. Sometimes in colony, but often solitary. **Eggs:** 2–3; dull white. **Range and Status:** widespread coastal n., e., se. and sw. Aust., extending far inland after good rains. Most breed spring–summer in Murrumbidgee–Murray Valley region of NSW, Vic. and se. SA, dispersing to inland and n. Aust. and Tas. Vagrant Lord Howe and Norfolk Is., NZ.

adult

ROYAL SPOONBILL

nonbreeding

breeding

imm.

imm.

nonbreeding

breeding

imm.

YELLOW-BILLED SPOONBILL

BLACK-SHOULDERED KITE *Elanus axillaris* 33–38 cm; span to 90 cm

Beautiful pale grey hawk with *pure white head, body and tail, black shoulders and red eyes. Cere and legs yellow. A black 'comma' mark in front of eye extends over and to rear of eye.* **Immature:** deep-buff head and upper breast; back and wings mottled buff or brown, *with prominent white tips;* eye brown; progressively whiter, with buff zone around breast. Singles, pairs, family parties: perches conspicuously on dead and living trees, fence-posts; hovers near roadsides. Flight direct, with quick, shallow wingbeats broken by sailing glides on upswept 'gull' wings; underwing white except for bold black mark near 'wrist', and blackish wingtip. Hovers frequently, often with feet dangling: parachutes onto prey, wings held up in a deep V. **Similar species:** Letter-winged Kite. **Voice:** clear 'chee', with a sob, uttered repeatedly; in aggression, a harsh 'skairr!'; around nest, 'kik kik kik', etc. **Habitat:** grasslands with trees; farms, cereal-stubbles, market gardens, roadsides, sewage farms, overgrown vacant land, suburban paddocks, coastal wastes. **Breeds:** mostly spring, but any time when food abundant, with 2–4 successive broods. **Nest:** smallish, compact, deep cup of sticks; usually 7–12 m up in eucalypt or exotic pine. **Eggs:** 3–4; oval, cream–white, heavily blotched chocolate-brown. **Range and Status:** mainland Aust.; vagrant Tas. Nomadic and irruptive in response to local abundance of introduced house mouse. Closely related forms in PNG and other continents.

LETTER-WINGED KITE *Elanus scriptus* 30–38 cm; span 90 cm

Superficially like Black-shouldered Kite but note *conspicuous black bar forming a shallow W across whiter, partly translucent underwing.* Flight more tern-like, with deeper, looser wingbeats. *Crown greyer than Black-shouldered, eyes larger and deeper red; black 'comma' mark does not extend in point past eye; legs and feet whitish.* **Immature:** crown and upperparts grey–brown; sides of head, upperparts and upper breast washed buff, upperparts *without* white tips as in imm. Black-shouldered; eye brown. Pairs, loose flocks: roosts by day in leafy trees, *normally hunts mostly at night.* **Voice:** harsh, rasping 'karrr'; alarm-call: high, clear whistle. **Habitat:** grasslands, with trees; tree-lined watercourses. **Breeds:** typically in loose colony; often in coolibahs on inland watercourses; mostly spring, but whenever food abundant. **Nest:** May refurbish nest of another raptor, or crow, lining it with food-pellets, wool, over dead gum leaves. **Eggs:** 2–5; white to buff, spotted, smeared red or brown, mostly at large end. **Range and Status:** s. Barkly Tableland (NT); Georgina R.–Diamantina R. drainage of far w. Q to L. Eyre Basin of ne. SA. When populations of long-haired rat, *R. villosissimus*, increase, kites breed repeatedly. When rats decline, kites disperse. May then occur almost anywhere except driest deserts, hunting house mice, etc., and may breed, but probably few survive. Irruptive, nomadic; generally rare.

PACIFIC BAZA *Aviceda subcristata* 36–45 cm; span 80 cm

Other name: Crested Hawk.
Note the slim black crest on plain grey head; yellow eyes. Breast white with bold dark-brown bars; tail with dark bars. In flight, undersides of *long, paddle-shaped wings show white, conspicuously barred flight-feathers, black trailing edge, orange–buff wing-linings and under tail-coverts; undertail pale grey with broad black terminal band.* **Immature:** browner above, with rusty feather margins; upper breast buff, bars on breast thinner; undertail strongly barred. Pairs, family parties: often tame and approachable around camp-grounds, suburbs; soars over territory in shallow circles on *flat wings,* performs spectacular tumbling displays, calling plaintively. Hunts around leafy trees, plunging into foliage after prey. **Voice:** weak piping; in flight, mellow double whistle, 'ee-choo, ee-choo', descending (Hollands, 1984). **Habitat:** leafy trees on rainforest fringes; open forest and woodland; timbered watercourses; well-treed suburbs. **Breeds:** Oct.–Dec. **Nest:** flimsy, on horizontal, often leafy branch up to 30 m high. **Eggs:** 2–5; shaped like a top; blue–white or green–white, smeared, blotched, spotted light brown. **Range and Status:** coastal n. and e. Aust., from w. Kimberley (WA) to Top End (NT), and from C. York (Q) s. to c. Newcastle and Sydney (NSW); rare s. of Grafton. Sedentary; locally dispersive. Generally uncommon. Also e. Indonesia, PNG, Solomons.

BLACK-SHOULDERED KITE

juv.

Black-
shouldered

LETTER-WINGED KITE

juv.

Letter-
winged

imm.

imm.

PACIFIC BAZA

BLACK KITE *Milvus migrans* 48–55 cm; span to 1.2 m

Other names: Fork-tailed Kite; Kite-Hawk; Pariah Kite (India).

Floats overhead on long, drooped wings with prominent spread 'fingertips'; twists, tilts its long, forked tail. Plumage mud-brown; *slight pale patch at base of primaries; undersides of wings and tail faintly barred paler brown. Beware:* when soaring high, the spread, triangular tail suggests a 'square-tailed' kite. At rest, note *dark mark around eye, pale forehead and throat, fawn band across 'shoulder', very short legs.* **Immature:** *streaked and spotted* fawn. Scavenges around towns, stockyards, garbage-tips, slaughter-houses; climbs sky in huge, wheeling companies. Irruptive in response to locust or mouse plagues; attracted to bushfires; swoops low into smoke to seize prey. **Similar species:** Square-tailed Kite. Whistling Kite: paler fawn, with contrasting black flight-feathers; rounded tail; different wing-pattern and call. **Voice:** stuttering trills and whinnies. **Habitat:** grasslands, gibber-deserts, sandhills, timbered watercourses, beaches, tidal flats, airfields, homestead environs. **Breeds:** July–Dec., s. Aust.; almost any month in n. Aust. **Nest:** usually in tree on watercourse; singly, or in loose colony; flattish, untidy, of sticks, may be lined with wool, dung; often refurbishes old nest of other raptor or crow. **Eggs:** 2–3; spotted, blotched red–brown. **Range and Status:** n. and especially e. inland Aust., s. to *c.* Murray R.; casual to coastal se. and sw. Aust. Vagrant Tas. Sedentary; dispersive; irruptive. Widespread and familiar Africa, Eurasia, PNG.

BRAHMINY KITE *Haliastur indus* 43–51 cm; span 1.2 m. Female larger.

Other name: Red-backed Kite.

Adult unmistakable: *deep chestnut with whitish head, neck and breast.* Flight slow and soaring on rounded wings with *black tips and rounded, pale-tipped tail.* **Juvenile:** brown; head and breast streaked; upperparts scalloped buff: in flight, *pale patch at base of dark flight-feathers* extends along centre of underwing, separating brown wing-linings from blackish trailing edge; whitish tip to tail. **Immature:** like browner patchy adult: overhead, belly and under tail-coverts chestnut. Singles, pairs, loose companies: scavenges along beaches; seizes fish or offal from surface, reptiles or insects from ground or foliage. **Similar species:** compared with imm. Brahminy, imm. Whistling Kite is rangier and its paler plumage contrasts more with black flight-feathers; different underwing pattern and call. Black Kite; Little Eagle. **Voice:** stuttered 'peeah-h-h'; peevish trills, mews and squeals. **Habitat:** beaches, tidal sandflats and mudflats, estuaries, coastal forests, mangroves, islands, large rivers, harbours, environs of coastal towns. **Breeds:** April–June, n. Aust.; Sept.–Nov., s. Aust. **Nest:** bulky, of sticks, seaweed, grass, etc.; in top of tree, often mangrove. **Eggs:** 1–2; dull bluish white, with hairlike blackish lines, rusty spots. **Range and Status:** coastal n. Aust. and islands, from *c.* Carnarvon (WA) to Myall Lakes (NSW). Uncommon s. of C. Byron (NSW). Sedentary. Also s. Asia to PNG, Solomon Is.

WHISTLING KITE *Haliastur sphenurus* 50–60 cm; span 1.2 m. Female larger.

Other name: Whistling Eagle (erroneous).

Small-headed, sandy-fawn large hawk *with browner wings, contrasting black flight feathers, and long, plain, pale, rounded tail.* Underwing pattern distinctive: broad, pale brown leading edge turns at right angles near end of wing and crosses to trailing edge, separating black outer primaries from black secondaries. Pale streaks on head and body; traces of large pale spots on wings; legs/feet bone-coloured, unfeathered. **Immature:** more heavily streaked; wings with large pale spots. Singles, pairs, small travelling companies: soars buoyantly in small circles on drooped wings with prominently spread black 'fingertips', 'wrists' well forward; *tail long and rounded,* fanned when soaring. Body rises and falls with wingbeats, but effortlessly glides, circles and floats. Takes live prey, e.g. young rabbits; swoops to pick fish or carrion from water; pirates food from ibises, herons. **Similar species:** Black and Brahminy Kites. Little Eagle: larger-headed, thicker-set, with feathered legs, triangular underwing pattern (see plate); soars on flatter wings, head/neck extend further; tail squarer. Brahminy Kite, imm. **Voice:** distinctive shrill whistling call: first note leisurely, descending, followed by *staccato upward burst;* peevish mews. **Habitat:** open forests and foothills, usually near water; timbered watercourses; lakes, swamps, tidal inlets, estuaries, mudflats. **Breeds:** June–Oct., s. Aust.; Feb.–May, n. Aust.; any time after rain. **Nest:** bulky, of sticks; high in eucalypt or exotic pine; re-used year after year until large. **Eggs:** 2–3; blue–white, blotched red–brown. **Range and Status:** Aust. and coastal islands; casual Tas. Common. Sedentary; migratory or nomadic to coastal n. Aust. in dry season; s. in autumn in s. Aust. Also PNG, New Cal.

imm.

BLACK KITE

imm.

BRAHMINY KITE

imm.

juv.

imm.

WHISTLING KITE

SQUARE-TAILED KITE *Lophoictinia isura* 50–56 cm; span to 1.3 m

Often solitary, but in pairs when nesting. Usually seen *sailing, harrier-like, over woodland and forest canopy in search of bird nestlings*, its main food. Note whitish, streaked, downpointed head, reddish brown wing-linings and underparts; *very long, upswept paddle-shaped wings, with large cream crescent at base of long, broadly barred 'fingertips'. Tail long and square, dark grey above, with sparse bars and broad dark tip;* when worn, can look forked. Perched, note *blackish brown upperparts, pale band across wing,* shadowy, barred wingtips *extending well beyond tail-tip;* underparts rufous, heavily streaked black; small, short, legs and feet flesh–white. **Immature:** head rounder; *head and body rich orange–brown; eye brown;* upperparts mottled black; flight pattern like adult. **Similar species:** Black Kite, imm. Black-breasted Buzzard and Red Goshawk. **Voice:** 'a thin, high, single-noted whistle' (Olsen et al, 1993); 'hoarse contralto yelp' near nest (Hollands, 1984). **Habitat:** heathlands, woodlands, forests; tropical and subtropical rainforest; timbered watercourses; hills and gorges. **Breeds:** July–Nov. **Nest:** large, loose; of sticks; 15–25 m up in leafy tree. **Eggs:** 2–3; dull white, blotched lavender and red–brown. **Range and Status:** uncommon to rare and sparse (perhaps least rare in s. WA in summer). In coastal and sub-coastal se. Aust. (incl. Murray R. region in SA) and sw. WA, it is a rare but regular breeding migrant, arriving *c.* Sept., departing by *c.* April, apparently to n. Aust. Mostly a nonbreeding winter visitor to coastal and sub-coastal n. Aust., but in e. Q, widely scattered breeding occurs (earlier than in s.). Sedentary; part-migratory. Rare.

BLACK-BREASTED BUZZARD *Hamirostra melanosternon* 51–61 cm, span *c.* 1.5 m. Female larger.

Other name: Black-breasted Kite.

Impressive large raptor: sails effortlessly, rocking in wind, on long upswept (and often backswept) wings. Note *black breast, chestnut underparts, large white 'window' at base of spread black primaries, short, plain buff–grey tail.;* little obvious barring on wings or tail. Pairs perch conspicuously in dead trees, long wings extending well beyond tail. **Immature:** head and body sandy buff, finely streaked with black; wing-linings ditto; broad, pale line along centre of wing contrasts with plain, pale grey underside of secondaries, white 'bull's-eye' and unbarred black primaries; tail plain buff–grey. **Similar species:** imm. Spotted Harrier, Red Goshawk and Square-tailed Kite can all be confused with imm. Buzzard, but all have barred flight-feathers and/or tail-feathers. Little Eagle, imm.: different underwing pattern; legs feathered; tail larger, more barred; glides on flat wings. **Voice:** 'a repeated harsh, scraping sound'; also 'repeated loud, hoarse yelp' (Hollands, 1984). **Habitat:** grasslands, sandhills, gibber deserts; timbered watercourses and waterholes; tropical woodlands; sparsely vegetated offshore islands, coasts. **Breeds:** Aug.–Nov. **Nest:** very large, shallow; of sticks; in tall tree, often dead, near water. **Eggs:** 2–3; whitish, blotched mauve and dark brown. **Range and Status:** e. inland Aust., coastal n. and w. Aust.: sparse but locally common; summer visitor to s. inland; se. Q, s. NSW, s. WA. Sedentary; dispersive.

RED GOSHAWK *Erythrotriorchis radiatus* 50–61 cm; span to 1.35 m. Female much larger.

Large rich reddish 'goshawk'; size of Little Eagle, *with whitish, dark-streaked head, richly black-mottled upperparts, prominent rusty red 'trousers', powerful yellow legs and feet, barred grey tail.* Sits upright, wings nearly reaching tail-tip. Flies with quick, strong beats and glides: slightly bowed wings longer, more pointed than Brown Goshawk; tail shorter, squarer when closed, rounded when soaring; note contrast of *rusty wing-linings with whitish, black-barred undersurface of flight-feathers and tail.* **Immature:** head red–brown like body; *in flight, reveals unbarred white base of plain black primaries* (underside of secondaries and tail lightly barred); legs and feet flesh white. **Similar species:** Black-breasted Buzzard, imm.: underparts sandier; longer wings more upswept, with bolder, unbarred white 'bull's-eye' and black wingtips; *mostly plain grey secondaries; tail shorter, plain grey.* Square-tailed Kite, adult and imm.: pale undersides of flight-feathers have fewer, bolder bars; grey undertail is scarcely barred, but has *dark terminal band.* Little Eagle, imm.: dark facial pattern and short rear crest; underwing pattern bolder; wings blunter, flatter; legs feathered. **Voice:** female: harsh crowing, like Noisy Friarbird. Male: higher-pitched yelp. Staccato, high-pitched alarm-call, like Masked Lapwing (Hollands, 1984). **Habitat:** open forests, woodlands, especially near rivers, wetlands; rainforest fringes. **Breeds:** April–Sept. **Nest:** of sticks; in a heavy fork of live *Eucalypt* or *Melaleuca*, 10–20 m+; or old nest of crow or magpie. **Eggs:** 1–2; blue–white, smeared grey, brown or lavender. **Range and Status:** coastal and subcoastal n. and ne. Aust., from Kimberley (WA), formerly s. to Sydney but now rarely seen s. of Q–NSW border. Rare, declining.

SQUARE-TAILED
KITE

imm.

imm.

BLACK-BREASTED
BUZZARD

imm.

RED
GOSHAWK

♂

imm.

♀

129

COLLARED SPARROWHAWK *Accipiter cirrhocephalus* 30–40 cm; span to 76 cm. Female larger.

Colours and markings of adult and immature are similar to same stages of Brown Goshawk. Best identified by size, shape and style of flight. Much smaller and finer than goshawk, except in n. Aust., where males of small goshawk race *didimus* are overlapped by female sparrowhawks. Head of sparrowhawk smaller; expression wide-eyed, without goshawk's beetle-brow; *tail is shorter, squarer, slightly forked when folded; legs/feet more slender, with very long middle toe.* Some males tiny, seemingly thrush-sized. Singles, pairs: differs from goshawk in faster, flicking, *more flexible flight on more shapely wings, with longer, backswept primaries.* In direct, travelling flight, often undulates like a cuckoo-shrike. Courting, dashes about sky in loops, dives and twists. Relentless in tail-chases, preys on birds up to the size of rosellas, bronzewing. **Similar species:** Australian Hobby: darker, with more slender, pointed, rakish wings. Note: Nankeen Kestrel is erroneously called a 'sparrowhawk'. **Voice:** shrill, rapid 'kikikikiki', like alarm-call of White-plumed Honeyeater; near nest, thin squeals, mews. **Habitat:** forests, woodlands, river margins, inland scrubs, timbered gorges, farmlands, shelterbelts, leafy suburban gardens. **Breeds:** Aug.–Dec. **Nest:** shallow platform of small sticks, lined with eucalypt leaves; 10–30 m up in living tree; or in old nest of crow. **Eggs:** 2–4; white or green–white; faintly blotched brown and buff. **Range and Status:** Aust. and Tas: widespread; uncommon or seldom recognised. Also PNG, Aru I. (Indonesia).

BROWN GOSHAWK *Accipiter fasciatus* 40–50 cm; span 70 cm to *c.* 1 m. Female larger.

Other name: Australian Goshawk.

Powerful *yellow-eyed hawk with heavy beetle-brow; long, yellowish legs, powerful feet and talons.* **Adult**: *powdery grey–brown above with rufous rear-collar; underparts finely barred rufous and white.* **Juvenile:** *dark brown above,* off-white below with *heavy brown splashes on upper breast; dark brown V-bars on flanks become bold rufous bars in imm. (second year) plumage.* Bars become narrower and paler and extend to upperbreast in adult. Singles, pairs: flies heavily with quick wingbeats and glides on broad, slightly arched wings; *note longish rounded tail.* Slips through trees, along hedges, to surprise prey; ambushes from cover. Aggressive when nesting. In sunny weather, *soars high on slightly upswept wings with straight trailing edge, tail fanned.* N. Aust. race *didimus* smaller, paler. **Similar species:** Collared Sparrowhawk. Brown Falcon. **Voice:** male: rapid 'kikikiki!'; female: deeper; mellow 'yuik-yuik-yuik'. **Habitat:** open forests, woodlands, scrublands and margins; farmlands, golf-courses, sewage farms, parks, gardens. **Breeds:** Sept.–Dec. **Nest:** flattish; of sticks, lined with green leaves; 6–20 m up in living tree; mistletoe-clump, or old nest of other raptor. **Eggs:** 2–4; plain blue–white, faintly blotched red–brown. **Range and Status:** Aust. and Tas: common, widespread. Sedentary and part-migratory; suspected winter movement to n. Aust., overlapping range of sedentary tropical race *didimus*. Also Christmas I. (n. Indian Ocean), PNG, New Cal.

GREY GOSHAWK *Accipiter novaehollandiae* 40–54 cm; span to 1.1 m. Female larger.

Other name: Variable or White Goshawk.

Powerful hawk of two colour-morphs: (1) *pure white; eyes bright yellow or dark red;* (2) *grey above, whitish below, finely barred grey; eyes dark red.* Both morphs have bright yellow cere and legs. Immatures like adults, but grey morphs browner above, somewhat more heavily barred on breast, flight feathers and tail. Singles, pairs: watches from live, or emergent dead, trees; flies with quick, shallow wingbeats and glides on slightly depressed wings. Soars with wings slightly upswept; silhouette distinctive: wings broad and blunt, trailing edge notably convex in centre; tail shorter than Brown Goshawk. **Similar species:** Grey Falcon, Black-shouldered Kite. **Voice:** Female: deep mellow 'yewik, yewik, yewik, yewik', slower than Brown Goshawk. Male: higher-pitched, staccato, slower than Brown. **Habitat:** rainforests, forests; forest gullies and valleys; taller woodlands, timber on watercourses; open country in autumn dispersal. **Breeds:** Sept.–Dec. **Nest:** large, shallow, of sticks; high in live tree. **Eggs:** 2–3; blue–white. Morphs may interbreed; has interbred with Brown Goshawk. **Range and Status:** Aust. and Tas.; patchy in coastal n. Aust., from Kimberley (WA) to C. York Pen. (Q); more regular in rainforests of e. Aust. to e. and sw. Vic., and w. Tas.; casual Adelaide, Kangaroo I. (SA). Grey morph predominates on e. coast; white morph across n. Aust. and in Tas., w. Vic. Sedentary; seasonally dispersive. Uncommon to rare. Also e. Indonesia, PNG, Solomon Is., etc.

imm.

imm. ♀

COLLARED
SPARROWHAWK

adult ♀

BROWN
GOSHAWK

♀ race
didimus

imm.

imm.

♀

GREY GOSHAWK

♂ grey morph

♀ white
morph

OSPREY *Pandion haliaetus* 50–65 cm; span to 1.7 m. Female larger.

Other name: Fish Hawk.

Graceful large fishing hawk with *white head/body, brown wings*: note *bold dark brown mark through eye, down neck; female has brown-streaked 'necklace'.* **Immature:** heavier streaked buff breastband; upperparts mottled buff. Singles, pairs, family parties: perches on dead trees, piles, masts. Patrols over water on long, arched wings; hovers, plunges spectacularly from 10–50 m, entering feet-first. Taking flight, shakes water from plumage, carries fish torpedo-like: note *white underwing, with black mark at 'wrist'.* **Similar species:** White-bellied Sea-Eagle imm.: more patchily marked; lacks Osprey's heavy, dark eyemark; wings broad and upswept, with cream crescent at base of primaries; short buff tail with (or without) broad brown subterminal band. **Voice:** plaintive, 'pee-ee'; squeals. **Habitat:** coasts, estuaries, bays, inlets; islands and surrounding waters; coral atolls, reefs, lagoons, rock cliffs, stacks. Ascends larger rivers (e.g. Murray R., SA); ventures far inland (Finke R., NT). **Breeds:** April–July, n. Aust.; July–Sept., s. Aust. **Nest:** large, of sticks, seaweed, rope, etc.; high in tree (live or dead) or on pylon; on islands, on ground; added to for many seasons, becomes tall. **Eggs:** 2–3; dull white, capped with reddish blotches. **Range and Status:** coasts and islands of Aust.: now rare or absent far s. NSW, Vic., Tas., Bass Strait and far se. SA, though breeds Yorke and Eyre Pens and Kangaroo I. (SA). Breeds n. from c. Newcastle–L. Macquarie (NSW); all coastal Q; Gt Barrier Reef; n. Aust., and WA, possibly *except* Eighty Mile Beach, extends e. to Kangaroo I. (SA). Sedentary; dispersive. Cosmopolitan.

WHITE-BELLIED SEA-EAGLE *Haliaeetus leucogaster* 70–90 cm; span c. 2 m. Female larger.

Other name: White-breasted Sea-Eagle.

Very large white and grey eagle with unfeathered cream legs and feet. Soars in majestic circles: *broad, upswept wings and short white tail, dark at base, give it the look of a huge butterfly; underwings divide into white and blackish triangles.* **Juvenile:** (first year) head buffish and 'spiky', contrasting with patchy cream and dark brown body and wings; underwing pattern also patchy, but note large *cream half-moon at base of primaries; grey–white tail with broad dark brown subterminal band and pale tips.* **Immature:** (second and third years) patchy buff–white head and body and grey–brown wings; tail plain buff–grey; later like adult. Singles, territorial pairs, family parties: watches from large trees over coasts, rivers, lake-shores. Hovers low over prey, or makes sloping power-dive from a height (or high perch) to seize fish, waterbird or offal from surface; unlike Osprey, seldom enters water. **Similar species:** Osprey: bold dark eyemark; slimmer, arched wings with black 'wrist'-mark. Wedge-tailed Eagle: blacker; larger, diamond-shaped black tail. **Voice:** far-carrying metallic clanking; mated pairs duet. **Habitat:** coasts, islands, estuaries, inlets, large rivers, inland lakes, reservoirs. **Breeds:** May–Aug., n. Aust.; June–Dec., s. Aust. **Nest:** huge, of sticks; in tall live tree near water; on ground on island, remote coastal cliff. **Eggs:** 2; white, some smeared yellowish. **Range and Status:** coastal Aust. and Tas.; larger rivers, lakes and storages, some far inland. Sedentary; dispersive. Also India, se. Asia to PNG, Solomon Is.

OSPREY

imm.

sub-
juv. adult

imm.

juv.

WHITE-BELLIED
SEA-EAGLE

133

LITTLE EAGLE *Hieraaetus morphnoides* 45–55 cm; span to 1.30 m. Female larger.

Sturdy small eagle with broad head and subtle facial pattern: *blackish crown, eyebrow and cheeks and short black crest on nape*; long, closely feathered legs and square-cut tail; pale band across upperwing when perched and in flight. **Pale morph:** in flight, *broad, pale diagonal bar across underwing* separates rufous wing-linings from dark, triangular secondaries and joins white patch inside dark wingtip; square-cut tail finely barred darker. **Dark morph:** *dark sandy brown or reddish brown wing-linings leave a dark, barred triangle on trailing edge*, cut off by pale, barred bases to primaries. **Immature:** brighter buff (pale morph) or brighter rufous (dark morph) than respective adults. Singles, pairs: flies steadily, with easy, slow wingbeats, or quick beats and level glides. *Soars in tight circles on flat wings, 'fingertips' upturned, tail fanned and square-cut; head and neck extend well forward of wing;* often glances up over shoulder. Territorial males perform high, linked, 'fish-hooks' display on closed wings, with quick upshoots, uttering quick, disyllabic whistle (see Voice). More than most raptors, attracts mobbing magpies, woodswallows, etc. **Similar species:** Whistling Kite: flight more floating on drooped wings, 'wrists' well forward with prominent spread 'fingertips'; longer, rounder pale tail; wing-pattern differs. Brahminy Kite, juv. Red Goshawk: much finer barred pattern on underside of flight-feathers; yellow unfeathered legs with rich rusty 'trousers'. **Voice:** quick disyllabic or trisyllabic 'pip-it, pip-it', or 'pip-it-it'; piping notes 'kleep kleep kleep'; complaining chitter when mobbed. **Habitat:** plains, foothills, open forests, woodlands and scrublands; river red gums on watercourses and lakes. **Breeds:** July–Oct., s. Aust.; April–July, n. Aust. **Nest:** of sticks; compact; high in leafy tree; may use old nest of other raptor or corvid. **Eggs:** 1–2 (3); white or bluish-white, blotched and smeared red–brown. **Range and Status:** mainland Aust.; vagrant Tas. Uncommon. Adults sedentary or part-migratory in autumn–winter; young dispersive. Also PNG.

WEDGE-TAILED EAGLE *Aquila audax* 90 cm–1.1 m; span to 2.8 m. Female larger.

Other name: Eaglehawk.
Huge, dark eagle with long, closely feathered legs and long, diamond-shaped tail; male blacker than female. *Old adults are mostly black, with varying degrees of chestnut nape; tawny band across wing.* Immatures and sub-adults to c. 5 years browner, patchy; hind-neck and wing-coverts pale golden brown to straw-coloured. Singles, pairs, family parties: companies at dead kangaroos, etc. Perches conspicuously on live or dead trees, telephone poles, or ground. Flies with easy, powerful wingbeats and glides on upswept wings; soars high in majestic circles, large tail prominent; wings noticeably upswept, *underwing showing a line of white down centre of wing* at junction of feather-tracts, and whitish bases of primaries. Parties soar and skirmish in wind over steep hills, gorges, peaks. Conspicuous territorial display of linked, U-shaped dives on half-closed wings, toppling forward into another dive at apex of each vertical recovery. **Similar species:** Black-breasted Buzzard: white 'window' in wing; short grey tail; legs not closely feathered. Juv. White-bellied Sea-Eagle: underwing patchy brown and cream–buff; cream half-moon at base of primaries; short, pale tail with or without dark, subterminal band. **Voice:** feeble, high-pitched 'pseet-you, pseet-you'; screams in aggressive encounters. **Habitat:** mountain forests to nearly treeless plains; occasionally over lakes, beaches, cities. **Breeds:** June–Oct. **Nest:** huge; of sticks, lined with fresh eucalypt leaves; in fork or limb, often high, but in inland and on islands, in bush or on ground. Territorial pairs may build several nests over time, using some as feeding platforms. **Eggs:** 1–3 (4); whitish, blotched buffish, spotted or streaked red–brown and lavender. Many nests produce only one fledgling as stronger young frequently kill smaller siblings. **Range and Status:** Aust. and Tas. Sedentary, dispersive. Also s. PNG.

GURNEY'S EAGLE *Aquila gurneyi* 73–90 cm; span to 1.9 m. Female larger. Not illustrated.

Blackish brown eagle with a dark, rounded tail. Legs feathered 'dark buffy greyish' to toes (Rand & Gilliard, 1967). Bill slate-grey with black tip; eye dark yellow; feet dull yellow. **Immature:** head brown, tipped buff; eye brown; upperparts grey and brown; underparts buff, washed reddish brown and dark brown; legs feathered white. Gliding and soaring, the long, rounded wings are held nearly flat; the large, rounded tail, is 'faintly marked below with broad paler bands' (Beehler et al, 1986). **Voice:** 'medium, high-pitched, slightly nasal piping' (Beehler et al, 1986). **Habitat:** lowland forests, coastal floodplains, forested offshore islands, mangroves. **Range and Status:** coastal PNG and islands. Sight-record Feb. 1987, Boigu I. (Torres Strait) (Garnett, 1987).

dark
morph

pale
morph

imm.

LITTLE EAGLE

imm.

pale morph

dark morph

WEDGE-TAILED EAGLE

imm.

135

SPOTTED HARRIER *Circus assimilis* 50–61 cm; span to 1.2 m

Other name: Smoke Hawk.

Smoke-grey above; facial disc chestnut, outlined in grey; underparts chestnut, plentifully spotted white; long, grey tail, with four or five bold black bands and broad black tip; legs long, yellow. **Juvenile:** *very different — reddish buff; facial disc outlined with blackish streaks; buff mark on nape; upperparts mottled and barred black; cluster of buff crescents on 'shoulder' becomes a pale upperwing-band in flight.* Flight feathers black; *rump mottled paler; tail banded dark grey;* underparts paler buff, finely streaked blackish on breast, with broader red–brown streaks below. N.B. juvs moulting into imm. plumage briefly have whitish buff body, with head and neck heavily streaked dark brown, giving a hooded appearance (Marchant & Higgins, 1993). **Immature:** *grey upperparts with buff feather-margins; underparts chestnut, streaked paler; tail dark grey, barred darker.* Singles or pairs: *flies, glides slowly and low over grassland and crops, on broad, upswept wings, head downpointed;* note *long, boldly barred, trough-shaped tail, bluntly wedge-shaped at tip.* Hovers low with wings slowly beating, tail fanned, long legs trailing. Soars high, often lowers legs; overhead, note contrast of black, unbarred spread 'fingertips' and white undersides of flight feathers, regularly barred black. Unlike other harriers, perches and nests in trees. **Similar species:** Swamp Harrier: old, pale males (some with grey hoods) confusable, *but rump always white;* most have unbarred grey tails (but *barred* wingtips). **Voice:** at nest 'a sharp, high-pitched "wik wik wik"' (Hollands, 1984). **Habitat:** grassy plains, crops and stubblefields; bluebush, saltbush, spinifex associations; scrublands, mallee, heathlands; open, grassy woodlands. **Breeds:** Aug.–Dec. or Feb.–April. **Nest:** usually in live tree. **Eggs:** 3–4; white or blue–white, smeared, blotched rusty. **Range and Status:** mostly inland and sub-inland e. and se. Aust. and coastal WA. Dry season visitor to coastal n. Aust.; summer–autumn (and irregular winter) visitor to coastal s. Aust. Vagrant Tas. Nomadic; irruptive in response to local abundance of rodents, quail, etc. Sedentary; dispersive; irruptive; part-migratory.

SWAMP HARRIER *Circus approximans* 50–61 cm; span to 1.45 m. Female larger.

Other names: Marsh Harrier; Swamp Hawk.

Large, small-headed, long-legged brown hawk with a distinct facial disc, buff-streaked breast and white rump. Sits tall and slim on fence-posts, ground, swamp vegetation. *Sails low over crops, etc., on upswept long wings, head downpointed, rocking a little; white rump readily visible.* Both sexes become greyer with age; old males have ash-grey inner primaries and *unbarred* ash-grey tail; breast buff to whitish with buff streaks; underwing whitish; wingtips grey, *barred black.* Some pale males have slate-grey hood. **Female:** browner; underparts more rufous; wings broader, curved trailing edge has broader black margin (Marchant & Higgins, 1993); shadowy bars on grey wingtips and tail. **Immature:** *chocolate-brown with rufous tones; cream streaks on nape sometimes form a large, pale mark; small, pale rufous rump; underwing blackish with rufous tones; large whitish patch at base of primaries; tail has shadowy bars.* Singles, pairs, family parties: over territory in spring, males soar high, calling and cutting spectacular loops and circles with wings in a stiff V. **Similar species:** Spotted Harrier; Papuan Harrier, female and imm. **Voice:** short, high 'kyeow!'; thin repetitive calls. **Habitat:** swamps and wetlands, tall grasslands, grain-crops, coasts, islands, heathlands, saltmarsh, bracken, bore-drains. **Breeds:** Sept.–Feb. **Nest:** low heap of grasses, sticks, rushes; in tall grass, grain-crop; cumbungi, other dense, low vegetation on ground or over water. **Eggs:** 3–5; blue–white, rounded. **Range and Status:** breeds mostly Tas., Vic., s. SA and far s. WA. Migrates n. from Tas. and s. coastal districts in autumn, or makes local winter movements. Winter visitor to inland and coastal n. Aust., possibly to PNG, e. Indonesia. Also Norfolk, Lord Howe Is.; NZ and sub-Antarctic islands; Macquarie I.; Cocos–Keeling Is. (Indian Ocean); Pacific islands.

PAPUAN HARRIER *Circus spilonotus* 48–53 cm. Female larger.

Other names: Eastern Marsh Harrier; Pied Harrier; Spotted Marsh Harrier.
Male: striking pale grey harrier *with black hood, back, shoulders and throat, with black streaking onto white upperbreast and hind-neck; wings silver–grey, barred black with black wingtips; tail plain silver–grey.* **Female:** like small female Swamp Harrier; *tail more heavily barred.* **Immature:** like imm. Swamp Harrier, but *with larger white patch on nape.* Female and imm. probably not safely separated from Swamp Harrier. **Similar species:** some male Swamp Harriers have grey hoods; also remember 'hooded' stage imm. Spotted Harrier. **Range and Status:** the Papuan race, *spilothorax,* of the widespread Eastern Marsh Harrier, of s. Siberia, n. Mongolia, ne. China, Manchuria. Unconfirmed but probable Aust. sight-records: Top End (NT); C. York Pen., Atherton Tableland and Daintree R. (Q); Torres Strait; Lord Howe I.

adult

sub-
adult

juv.

SPOTTED
HARRIER

adult

juv.

SWAMP
HARRIER

♂

♀

juv.

♂

♀

juv.

PAPUAN
HARRIER

♂

♀

juv.

♂

♀

juv.

BLACK FALCON *Falco subniger* 45–55 cm; span to 1.2 m. Female larger.

Big, sooty brown falcon, with *broad, pointed wings and long rounded tail*; strong whitish legs/feet part-hidden by long, blackish 'trousers'. Old birds acquire whitish forehead and throat, fine whitish barring on base of primaries and under tail-coverts. **Immature:** paler feather-margins. Singles, pairs, family parties: usually seen in open country; perches on fence-posts, dead trees; looks small-headed, broad-shouldered, rather crouched. Flies with easy, shallow beats of *sharply pointed, casually drooped broad wings that are widest at 'wrists'; trailing edge straight.* Black wing-linings show little contrast with underside of flight and tail-feathers. *Tail usually held narrowly folded in flight; but when fanned, looks large and ample; note diagnostic small notch at each corner.* Circles over driven sheep, quail-shooters, harvesting machines, waiting for quail, pipits to flush; tail-chases or 'stoops' at astonishing speed. Often pirates prey from other raptors. **Similar species:** Brown Falcon, dark morph; Black Kite. **Voice:** mostly silent: thin, cackling screams near nest, with crowing character of Brown Falcon (Hollands, 1984). **Habitat:** plains, grasslands, foothills, timbered watercourses, wetland environs; crops; occasionally over towns and cities. **Breeds:** June–Dec., in old (or usurped) nest of other raptor or corvid. **Eggs:** 3–4 (5); reddish white, freckled, spotted, blotched red–brown. **Range and Status:** e. inland Aust.; migrates to coastal se. Aust. (and sparsely into s. WA) in late summer–autumn; coastal n. and ne. Aust. in winter. Uncommon. Nomadic; dispersive. Vagrant NZ.

BROWN FALCON *Falco berigora* 40–50 cm; span to 1.2 m. Female larger.

Sits upright on dead trees, fence-posts, telephone poles or wires on long, skinny, greyish legs. Plumage ranges from dark, nearly uniform sooty brown to light red–brown above, whitish below. *Note four constant features:* (1) *double 'teardrop', enclosing pale cheekpatch;* (2) copious red–buff barring and scattered buff spots on flight and tail-feathers; (3) somewhat glossy undersides of flight feathers look *markedly paler* than wing-linings; (4) in all plumages, always has red–brown to dark brown 'trousers', *even when these are isolated from otherwise whitish breast and underparts.* Cere, eye-ring and legs usually greyish, but some grey-crowned, pale morph birds have bright yellow cere, orbit and legs. **Immature:** yellow–brown wash on forehead, throat, rear part-collar and breast; irregular brown blotches below; upperparts with buff nape-streaks; buff tips to flight feathers. Singles, pairs, companies: perches upright, big-headed, narrow-shouldered on dead trees, posts, phone wires. Hovers clumsily: makes sloping glides to seize prey on ground; hunts on foot. *Usually flies slowly, with deep, 'rowing' beats of broad, bluntly tapered gull-wings; soars on strongly upswept wings, tail fanned.* Can fly fast on backswept wings, but lacks shallow flicker of typical falcon. *Display noisy: dives spectacularly, dashes, cackling, about sky; wings in stiff V, body swinging.* **Similar species:** Black Falcon; Peregrine, imm.; Brown Goshawk. **Voice:** noisy: screeches, hoarse chuckles, rattles and high-pitched cacklings, like laying hen. **Habitat:** open woodlands, plains, gibber deserts, alpine meadows, forest clearings, farmlands, croplands, roadsides, coastal dunes. **Breeds:** April–Oct., n. Aust.; Aug.–Nov., s. Aust. **Nest:** may renovate nest of other raptor, or corvid; tree-hollow. **Eggs:** 2–3; buff–white, heavily mottled red–brown. **Range and Status:** Aust., Tas. and offshore islands. Common. Sedentary; nomadic; irruptive. Also PNG.

NANKEEN KESTREL *Falco cenchroides* 30–35 cm; span to 80 cm. Female larger.

Other names: 'Sparrowhawk'; Windhover.

Hovers *with tail fanned, black tail-band visible from below;* hangs motionless in stiff breezes with slender wings crooked back, tail closed and raised. *Pale rufous ('nankeen') above, with black flight-feathers; whitish below, with black 'teardrop' down through eye.* **Male:** crown and tail pale grey. **Female:** crown and tail as upperparts; tail finely barred black. **Immature:** like mottled female. Singles, pairs, family parties, open companies: perches on dead trees, fence and telephone posts. Hovers over grasslands; soars in air-currents around city buildings, spires. **Similar species:** Black-shouldered Kite; Brown Falcon, pale morph with yellow cere, legs. **Voice:** shrill, rapid 'keekeekeekeekee'; wavering 'keer, keer, keer'. **Habitat:** grasslands, plains, gibber deserts, foothills, high plains, beach-wastes, dunes, cliffs, farmlands, ploughed land, crops, roadsides, grain silos, railyards, buildings. **Breeds:** Aug.–Dec. **Nest:** in tree hollow; ledge or cavity in cliff or building; old nest of other raptor, corvid, babbler or chough. **Eggs:** 3–4 (5); pale buff, closely mottled red–brown. **Range and Status:** widespread mainland Aust.; in Tas., uncommon, nonbreeding visitor. Sedentary, part-migratory, nomadic: with movement to n. Aust. in winter, s. Aust. in summer; down from high country in autumn. Irruptive in response to local abundance of house mice, grasshoppers. Also Lord Howe I., PNG, Indonesia, where possibly winter migrant.

old adult

♀

BLACK
FALCON

♂

imm.

BROWN
FALCON

dark
morph

light
morph

juv.

♂

♀

NANKEEN KESTREL

PEREGRINE FALCON *Falco peregrinus* 36–47 cm; span to 95 cm. Female larger.

Other names: Black-cheeked Falcon; Duck Hawk.
Famous falcon: crown and cheeks black; upperparts slate–blue; underparts white or buff; breast and underwings *finely barred black, leaving prominent white or buff 'bib'*. Cere, eye-ring and legs yellow. **Immature:** browner; feather-margins buff; buff below, *streaked blackish brown*; cere, eye-ring and legs bluish. Singles, pairs, family parties: perches high, on dead limbs, cliffs, broadcasting pylons. Soars high, wings flat and elliptically tapered; tail fanned; 'bib' prominent; *looks wide-hipped, tail broad and ample*. Wingbeats quick and shallow, broken by glides; 'stoops' spectacularly on birds such as pigeons, galahs, or teal, streaking across sky on nearly closed wings. Chases with hard, lashing strokes of backswept wings. **Similar species:** Australian Hobby; Brown Falcon; Grey Falcon. **Voice:** hoarse, staccato, complaining 'chak-chak-chak-chak', male's noticeably higher-pitched; near nest, high, thin 'keer-keer-keer'. **Habitat:** cliffs, gorges, timbered watercourses, environs of rivers, wetlands, plains, open woodlands, pylons, spires, buildings. **Breeds:** Aug.–Nov. **Nest:** on cliff ledge or crevice; large tree-hollow or nest of other raptor or corvid; ledge of city building. **Eggs:** 2–3; pale buff, finely marked reddish chestnut. **Range and Status:** Aust. and Tas.: uncommon. Sedentary; dispersive when young. Cosmopolitan, *except* NZ.

AUSTRALIAN HOBBY *Falco longipennis* 30–35 cm; span to 90 cm. Female larger.

Other name: Little Falcon.
Small, swift, dark falcon: wings and square-cut tail proportionally longer and narrower than Peregrine, with sharper bend on trailing edge. Forehead, throat and peaked half-collar whitish or buff, tinged rufous; upperparts dark slate–blue; *underparts orange–buff, with rufous streaks, blue–grey V-bars on flanks. Unlike adult Peregrine, has blue cere and eye-ring.* **Immature:** more rufous forehead, collar and breast; upperparts browner, with rufous feather-margins and tail-barrings. Race *murchisonianus*, of inland, n. and w. Aust.: pale blue–grey above with whiter half-collar and larger white 'bib'; sandier underparts. Flies down birds like starlings, swallows, pipits, with lashing wingbeats; soars at dusk for flying insects. **Similar species:** Peregrine: larger, with broader wings, hips and tail; flies higher, soars more; has larger white or pale buff 'bib'. Imm.: browner, buffish feather margins, streaked brown below; *lacks* peaked half-collar. **Voice:** shriller, higher-pitched 'kek kek kek kek' than Peregrine, accelerating into a rapid-fire 'kee-kee-kee-kee-kee'. Male higher-pitched than female. **Habitat:** open woodlands, grasslands with trees; environs of wetlands, lakes, rivers, timbered watercourses; foothills, city parks, well-treed suburbs. **Breeds:** Aug.–Nov. **Nest:** in usurped nest of other raptor or corvid, usually in tall living tree. **Eggs:** 2–4; heavily marbled red–brown. **Range and Status:** mainland Aust. and Tas.; uncommon; some migrate in autumn–winter to n. Aust., New Britain, s. PNG, e. Indonesia. Sedentary; seasonally dispersive; part-migratory.

GREY FALCON *Falco hypoleucos* 30–44 cm; span to 90 cm. Female larger.

Pale grey inland falcon with rich yellow cere, eye-ring, legs and feet. **Immature:** mottled darker above, bolder streaks on whitish breast; cere and eye-ring bluish; legs and feet yellow. Singles, pairs, family parties: male slender and dashing; the larger female can look bomb-like and heavy-shouldered; *wings broad, tapering, with slight banana-like upsweep when soaring. Underwings whitish with dark tips*; tail proportionally larger than Peregrine's. Flight leisurely, with casual 'over-arm' wingbeats, or fast and questing. 'Stoops' from high on birds like crested pigeons, pursues them at treetop level, or hunts from perches. **Similar species:** Grey Goshawk. **Voice:** mostly quiet; but hoarse, 'chak-chak-chak-chak', not unlike Brown Falcon. **Habitat:** lightly treed inland plains; gibber deserts, sandridges, pastoral lands, timbered watercourses; seldom in driest deserts. **Breeds:** June–Nov. in refurbished nest of another raptor or corvid, usually high in leafy eucalypt on watercourse or waterhole. **Eggs:** 2–3; pink–buff, heavily marbled red–brown. **Range and Status:** resident or nomadic visitor to inland parts of all mainland States, especially in Simpson Desert–Strzelecki Track region of NT, SA, w. Q and far w. NSW; nw. coast of WA from *c*. Shark Bay to e. Kimberley; ne. coast near Townsville (Q). Rare to very rare: sedentary, dispersive or part-migratory, with apparent movement to n. Aust. in autumn–winter, towards coast or better-watered habitats in drought. Vagrant s. PNG.

PEREGRINE FALCON

adult

imm.

imm.

♂

♀

AUSTRALIAN HOBBY

adult

imm.

♂

♀

imm.

race
murchisonianus

GREY FALCON

♀

♂

imm.

Eagles, large Kites and Harriers, overhead

1. OSPREY: mostly white below with long brown eyemark and black 'wrist-mark' on underwing; females and young birds have brownish necklace. Wings long, slightly crank-shaped; hovers, plunges.

2. WHITE-BELLIED SEA-EAGLE: broad, upswept wings divide into dark grey and white triangles; note small half-white tail. Resembles huge grey-and-white butterfly.

2a. WHITE-BELLIED SEA-EAGLE, IMM.: variably dark brown, buff and white: cream 'half-moons' at base of primaries; buff–white tail with or without broad V-shaped subterminal band.

3. WEDGE-TAILED EAGLE: very large, dark, with pale line along underwing at bases of flight-feathers; large, diamond-shaped tail; majestic soaring flight on upswept wings.

4. BLACK-BREASTED BUZZARD: broad upswept wings with white 'bulls-eyes' contrast with black, *unbarred, wingtips; black breast and short, plain buff–grey tail.*

4a. BLACK-BREASTED BUZZARD, IMM.: sandy buff head/body and wing-linings; pale line along centre of wing, grey secondaries. White 'bulls-eye', *unbarred black primaries; unmarked buff–grey tail.*

5. SQUARE-TAILED KITE: head whitish; underparts/wing-linings red–brown; long, almost 'paddle-shaped' wings have *cream crescent at base of primaries;* flight feathers boldly barred; long, square, grey tail has dark subterminal band.

5a. SQUARE-TAILED KITE, IMM.: head/body rich orange–brown. Confusable with imm. Black-breasted Buzzard, but note kite's *barred flight feathers and tail.*

6. LITTLE EAGLE, PALE MORPH: broad, pale diagonal bar across underwing separates sandy wing-linings from dark, triangular secondaries, and joins a pale patch inside dark wingtip.

6a. LITTLE EAGLE, DARK MORPH: dark, red–brown wing-linings leave blackish barred triangle on trailing edge, cut off by pale, barred bases to primaries; undertail barred.

7. WHISTLING KITE: 'fingertips' spread; 'wrists' carried well forward. On underwing, pale brown leading edge joins pale inner primaries at right angles, separating black wingtips from black secondaries.

8. BLACK KITE: floats on long, drooped wings with spread 'fingertips', twisting and tilting its large, forked tail. Pale base of primaries; undersides of wings/tail faintly barred.

9. BRAHMINY KITE: unmistakable, with whitish head, neck and breast, chestnut body and undersurfaces, rounded black wingtips, pale tips to tail.

9a. BRAHMINY KITE, IMM.: large pale area along midwing, joining pale base of unbarred black primaries. Some have chestnut belly and under tail-coverts.

10. SWAMP HARRIER, FEMALE: underparts rufous–brown, streaked darker; bowed trailing edge of underwing has black margin. Underside of flight feathers and tail grey with shadowy bars.

10a. SWAMP HARRIER, MALE: paler than female; breast and wing-linings whitish, streaked buff–brown; underwing whitish, underside of wingtips ash-grey, obscurely barred darker; tail ash-grey, *unbarred.*

10b. SWAMP HARRIER, IMM.: dark rufous to chocolate brown below, with blackish flight feathers; large whitish base to primaries; tail with shadowy dark bars.

11. PAPUAN HARRIER, MALE: small, silver–grey and white harrier with black hood and wingtips. But take care: see 'hooded' stage of imm. Spotted Harrier; ditto old male Swamp Harrier.

11a. PAPUAN HARRIER, IMM.: similar to imm. Swamp Harrier: identification doubtful without experience.

12. SPOTTED HARRIER: underparts and wing-linings chestnut with plentiful white spots; spread wingtips jet black, *unbarred;* underside of wings white, with regular fine black barrings. Tail pale grey *with bold black bars, broad black pointed tip.*

12a. SPOTTED HARRIER, IMM.: body and wing-linings reddish buff, streaked darker. Underwing and tail shaped and patterned like adult. (Placed near Black-breasted Buzzard/Square-tailed Kite, for comparison.)

Hovering Kites; Falcons; Goshawks, etc., overhead

1. LETTER-WINGED KITE: *thick black bar along underwing* forms a shallow W; primaries grey, secondaries translucent. Flight looser, more tern-like, than Black-shouldered.

2. BLACK-SHOULDERED KITE: note bold black mark near 'wrist' and broad blackish tip to underwing. Flight direct, with quick, shallow wingbeats broken by sailing glides on upswept 'gull' wings.

3. NANKEEN KESTREL: underparts whitish, with fine dark shaft-streaks; under wingtips darker. Hovers frequently with tail fanned, subterminal black tail-band and finer barrings visible from below.

4. AUSTRALIAN HOBBY, MALE: wings and square-cut tail proportionately longer, narrower than Peregrine's, with sharper bend on trailing edge; underparts orange–buff, with *rufous streaks*.

4a. AUSTRALIAN HOBBY, IMM. FEMALE: larger than male, underparts darker rufous than adult's.

5. PEREGRINE FALCON: broad wings taper; underparts white or buff; breast and underwings appear greyish from very fine black barring, leaving gleaming white or buff 'bib'. Looks wide-hipped, tail broad.

5a. PEREGRINE FALCON, IMM.: browner than adult; underparts fawn to buff, plentifully *streaked* blackish brown.

6. GREY FALCON: underparts greyish white, with darker wingtips; flight feathers and tail indistinctly barred. Soars with wings slightly upswept. Direct flight effortless, with quick, shallow wingbeats.

6a. GREY FALCON, IMM.: mottled darker above, whiter below, with fine, darker streaks; undersides of wings/tail more noticeably barred.

7. BLACK FALCON: Flies with easy, shallow wingbeats and glides on casually drooped, broad, pointed wings and long, narrow tail 'notched' at corners. Dark wing-linings show less contrast with underside of flight feathers than dark morph Brown Falcon. (Head *smaller* than shown here.)

8. BROWN FALCON: sooty brown, patchy brown, reddish or whitish below, but always with brown or red–brown thighs ('trousers'). *Note contrast between dark wing-linings and pale, barred, slightly glossy undersides of flight-feathers and tail.* Flight often sluggish, with steady 'rowing' wingbeats.

9. GREY GOSHAWK: pure white or grey, latter finely barred. Flies on flat, blunt, broad wings, *convex on centre of trailing edge*; tail shorter than Brown Goshawk.

10. BROWN GOSHAWK, ADULT MALE: quick, shallow beats and glides on broad, slightly arched wings; longish, blunt tail. Soars on slightly upswept wings with straight trailing edge, tail fanned.

10a. BROWN GOSHAWK, IMM. FEMALE: larger than male; plumage browner and darker; bolder brown splashes on breast, heavier brown V-bars on flanks.

11. COLLARED SPARROWHAWK, ADULT MALE: smaller, finer than Brown Goshawk, with slightly longer, hooked-back outer primaries; tail shorter, squarer at tip. Flight faster, more flexible and flicking.

12. RED GOSHAWK: flies strongly below woodland canopy; *red–brown underparts and wing-linings contrast strongly with barred whitish undersides of flight and tail feathers.* Soars on slightly upswept wings.

13. PACIFIC BAZA: soars on flat, paddle-shaped wings: orange–buff wing-linings and undertail-coverts contrast with whitish underwing and conspicuously barred wingtips. Breast barred.

13a. PACIFIC BAZA, IMM.: browner and buffer; tail barred, with more shadowy terminal band.

SARUS CRANE *Grus antigone* 1.2–1.5 m; span to *c.* 2.5 m

Like a large Brolga, but with *deep scarlet skin from base of bill and sides of head down upperneck; crown bare and grey; no black dewlap; eye deep red; legs dull pink or red, occasionally grey.* Plumage of upperneck may be paler and there are some white feathers in 'bustle'. In flight, primaries are darker than rest of wing, forming a square, blackish, broad wingtip. (Most Brolgas have darker trailing edge.) **Immature:** light rufous wash over head and upperneck; legs grey–pink. In foraging, flocking, displays and other behaviour, as well as habitat, resembles Brolga. **Voice:** like Brolga, but higher-pitched. **Breeds:** Dec.–July. **Nest:** mass of reed, rush stems, grass straw, on ground in shallow wetland, or on mound; or platform of vegetation. **Eggs:** usually 2; glossy pale bluish white. **Range and Status:** Asian species, first (surprisingly) recorded in Aust. near Normanton (Q) in Oct. 1966. Has since expanded rapidly. Now extends from se. Gulf coast n. to near C. York; e. from *c.* Burketown to Atherton Tableland, s. to Townsville–Ayr and inland to *c.* Julia Ck. Smaller numbers on w. Gulf lowlands, Top End (NT) and Kimberley (WA); possibly extending s. into the Pilbara (Karratha). Locally common on Atherton Tableland in ne. Q, where it forms roosts of many hundreds (e.g. Bromfields Swamp, near Malanda). Mostly sparse elsewhere. Part migratory; dispersive. Also India to se. Asia and Philippines.

BROLGA *Grus rubicundus* 70 cm–1.3 m; span 1.7–2.4 m

Other names: Australian Crane; Native Companion. Note that White-faced Heron is incorrectly called a 'blue crane'.

Tall, silver–grey native crane with 'bustle' of feathers over rump; bill straight, horn-coloured; *eye yellow;* bare head pale grey on forehead and crown, *pale red round rear of head, with distinctive blackish 'haired' dewlap under chin* (larger in male); *legs dark grey.* **Juvenile:** bill brownish; head *lightly feathered* buff–grey. **Immature:** skin of rear of crown flesh-pink, later becoming pale orange; no dewlap. Pairs, parties to companies of many hundreds; in n. Aust, occasionally thousands. Wades in shallow, vegetated wetlands, plunges head underwater to dig for roots, corms; also in grasslands, claypans, crops, grain-stubbles. Famed for 'dancing' displays. Flight distinctive: neck and legs extended, wingbeats slow, majestic, often with upward flick; *all flight-feathers dark.* Post-breeding companies of hundreds, consisting of families and unmated birds, congregate annually in flocking areas, often remote from nest-sites. **Similar species:** Sarus Crane: larger; no dewlap; deeper scarlet extends down neck; legs pink; in flight, only primaries darker than rest of wing. **Voice:** far-carrying whooping trumpet, uttered in flight or when standing; mated pairs point bills skyward in antiphonal duets, ending in staccato cacophony; male lifts wings in 'tent' while calling; also yelps, hoarse staccato croaks. Calls at distance confusable with Channel-billed Cuckoo. **Habitat:** well-vegetated shallow freshwater wetlands; small, isolated swamps in eucalypt forests; floodplains, grasslands; paddocks, ploughed fields, irrigated pastures, stubbles, crops; desert claypans; bore drains; environs of towns in n. and inland Aust.; sometimes tidal areas, mangroves, beach-wastes. Roosts at night in shallow, bare swamps, fresh or saline. **Breeds:** July–March, s. Aust.; Sept.–June, n. Aust. **Nest:** usually of grasses, plant-stems, sticks; on small island in wetland or standing in shallow water; eggs occasionally laid on bare ground. **Eggs:** usually 2; white, often spotted and blotched brown and lavender. **Range and Status:** n. and e. Aust.; vagrant NZ. Now sparse, uncommon or rare, except in n. Aust., where still abundant. Locally, seasonally migratory; dispersive. Also s. PNG.

SARUS CRANE

juv.

juv.

♀

♂

BROLGA

RED-NECKED CRAKE *Rallina tricolor* 23–29 cm

Unmistakable, with *green bill, bright chestnut neck and dark olive–brown back, wings and underparts*, latter with obscure pale bars; in flight *underwings strongly barred black and white*. Singles, pairs, groups: shy; active at dawn, dusk, and at night; forages in forest litter and in shallow rainforest streams and pools. Swims, dives; runs, head-down, rather than flies. Noisy, especially at night and in overcast weather: maintains permanent territories. **Similar species:** Red-legged Crake: underparts and under tail-coverts strongly barred black and white; red legs. Bush Hen, imm.: bill stouter; throat whiter; under tail-coverts buff. **Voice:** described by C. B. Frith as 'a very loud series of sharp "keck" notes which diminish in power and clarity'. Neighbouring birds respond. Also incessant 'clock, clock, clock', by pairs at night; pig-like grunts. **Habitat:** rainforests, especially with dense understorey of ferns, vines, etc.; mostly near watercourses; also vine-thickets, drier monsoon forests, lantana, dense gardens. **Breeds:** Nov.–March. **Nest:** collection of leaves on ground or between buttress-roots; or a cup of twigs, vine tendrils, broad leaves; on stump, in fern, among vine tangle, or in fork, up to 2 m high. **Eggs:** 3–5 (6); smooth, dull white. **Range and Status:** ne. Q, from C. York s. to about Paluma; inland to Atherton Tableland. Possible break in range n. of Cooktown. Casual s. to Eungella NP, inland of Mackay (Q). Sedentary in southern part of range; some migrate through Torres Strait to PNG in winter, where also widespread resident in lowlands and foothills (Beehler et al, 1986). Also e. Indonesia; Bismarck Arch.

RED-LEGGED CRAKE *Rallina fasciata* 19–25 cm

Other name: Malay Banded Crake.

Distinctive: head, neck and breast soft chestnut-brown; wings dark red–brown with black and white barring on wing-coverts, secondaries and primaries; underparts and under tail-coverts *boldly barred black and white*. Bill greenish yellow, red at base; eye red; *legs bright red*. **Female:** duller, bars on underparts narrower. **Immature:** head and neck brownish; barrings less distinct. Elusive crake of dense waterside habitats, perhaps most likely to be discovered by call. **Similar species:** Red-necked Crake. **Voice:** 'a loud series of *pek* calls, given at intervals of (roughly) half seconds, usually at dawn and dusk' (Lekagul & Round, 1991). **Habitat:** environs of streams in tropical forests and secondary growth; vegetation in nearby swamps and watercourses; paddyfields. **Range and Status:** from Assam to parts of se. Asia and Taiwan; Borneo, Philippines, to e. Indonesia. Vagrant Aust.: only record to date was of an emaciated live male found on board a pearling lugger at Broome, 16 July, 1958, following strong north-east winds and heavy seas (Serventy, 1958). Occurrence of this (and other) small Asian crakes in nw. Aust. is likely, especially in summer.

BUSH-HEN *Amaurornis olivaceus* 24–28 cm

Secretive small gallinule: plain olive–brown above, greyish below, with *rufous–buff under tail-coverts*. Bill olive–yellow with grey frontal shield; when breeding, *bill pea-green, shield orange*; legs dull yellow. Female duller. **Immature:** duller. Singles, pairs, family parties: part-nocturnal, keeps to dense cover, emerges on overcast mornings, evenings. Wades in shallows; swims; walks hunched or stands tall, flicking tail. Runs when disturbed but when migrating may fly distances at night. **Voice:** noisiest when breeding: 'Eight to ten loud harsh, shrieking (and crowing) notes each of one second duration, followed by five or six muted notes'; often uttered in response to some loud noise. Also a 'wailing, cat-like duet'; low, piping and clicking notes (Clarke, 1975) Also a mellow, rapid, high-pitched 'pleak-pleak-pleak-pleak' repeated *c.* 12 to 20 times, with liquid chorus. **Habitat:** rainforest fringes, swamp-forests; low scrub in flooded areas; roadside vegetation, tall grass, lantana thickets, canefields, gardens. **Breeds:** Oct.–April. **Nest:** platform or cup of grasses in tall grass, rank growth, with canopy. **Eggs:** 4–7; dull white, pinkish cinnamon, freckled chestnut, grey or brown, mostly at large end; underlying shadowy lilac, chestnut. **Range and Status:** coastal n. Aust. and islands, from Kimberley (WA) to Top End (NT): C. York Pen. (Q); coastal e. Aust. to s. of Ballina (NSW); casual inland and Torres Strait islands. Sedentary, part-migratory; nomadic: movements influenced by rainfall. Also Philippines, e. Indonesia, PNG, Solomons.

RED-NECKED
CRAKE

imm.

tail of
adult

RED-LEGGED
CRAKE

imm.

tail of
adult

BUSH-HEN

imm.

tail of
adult

BUFF-BANDED RAIL *Gallirallus philippensis* 28–33 cm

Other names: Banded Landrail or Rail.

Elegant rail *with red–brown bill, white eyebrow and rich chestnut stripe from bill through eye to nape; grey breast crossed by buff band; underparts and undertail finely banded black and buff–white.* **Immature:** duller; lacks chestnut nape and breastband. Singles, pairs, families: shy, mostly keeps to cover. Walks hunched or elegantly tall; tail flicked when nervous. Ventures from low, dense vegetation to forage on edge of water, bare wettish ground or saltmarsh. Runs fast: in flight, note extended neck, rounded wings, trailing legs. Active, flies at night: arrives unexpectedly in homestead gardens; tennis-courts, cattle-yards. **Similar species:** Lewin's Rail: longer pink bill; no white eyebrow or breastband; wings barred. **Voice:** high-pitched double cheeps, like House Sparrow, or Galah; territorial call 'coo-aw-ooo-aw-ooo-aw' like braying donkey; repetitive sharp clicks; coos; thudding grunts; 'crek's, squeaks and rattles. **Habitat:** fringes of rainforest; rank vegetation in swamps, marshes, creeks; wet paddocks, scrubby woodlands, heathland, crops, rank pastures; samphire in brackish swamps, saltmarsh; environs of tourist resorts; garbage-tips, lawns, well-vegetated gardens. On islands, mangroves; drier, more open habitats. **Breeds:** Aug.–March; any month after rains. **Nest:** cup of grass and leaves in tussock or sedge. **Eggs:** 5–8+; off-white to buff, spotted and blotched red–brown, heavily at large end; underlying lilac–grey blotches. **Range and Status:** e., se. and coastal n. Aust.; Kimberley and coastal WA and many islands; vagrant Tas. Erratic inland and drier coastal areas in good seasons. Sedentary; dispersive. Also Lord Howe, Norfolk Is.; PNG to Philippines; Cocos–Keeling Is. (Indian Ocean); many Pacific islands; NZ.

LEWIN'S RAIL *Rallus pectoralis* 21–27 cm

Other name: Lewin Water Rail.

Tubby, dark rail with a *longish pink, dark-tipped bill and fiery chestnut nape and shoulders; breast plain olive–grey; part of wing, underparts and undertail black, finely barred whitish.* **Female:** duller, crown more streaked. **Immature:** duller; bill blackish; upperparts more heavily streaked black, with little if any chestnut on nape; more spotted below. Singles, pairs, family parties: secretive, uses runs in dense cover, usually near water. Potters on ooze near cover, probing, seldom flicks tail. Wades, swims, dashes to cover; flies feebly with legs trailing, *showing fiery nape and barred dark flanks,* but apparently travels far at night. **Similar species:** Banded Rail: shorter red–brown bill; white eyebrow; buff breastband; undertail more boldly barred black and white. **Voice:** loud, sustained chorus of 'pluke pluke pluke' or 'crek crek crek'; answered by others, accelerating and becoming louder, declining; ringing, anvil-like 'jik-jik-jik', almost a song; also rapid thudding grunts, like galloping horse; sharp alarm-note. **Habitat:** swamp woodlands; rushes, reeds, rank grass in swamps, creeks, paddocks; wet heaths, treeferns; samphire in saltmarshes. **Breeds:** Aug.–Jan. **Nest:** compact cup of fine grass and rushes, some with trampled ramp or canopy of interlaced stems, near or over water; in tussock, sedge or rush-clump. **Eggs:** 4–6; stone-coloured, spotted pinkish brown and lavender–grey. **Range and Status:** patchy in suitable habitat in coastal e. Aust., from c. Port Douglas (Q) to se. SA, Mt Lofty Ras. and Kangaroo I. (SA); casual, s. Eyre Pen.; inland to w. slopes of Divide: mostly in se. Aust. and Tas. Vagrant Top End (NT). Presumed extinct in s. WA. Uncommon, seasonally dispersive or nomadic. Also Philippines, PNG; NZ sub-Antarctic islands.

CORNCRAKE *Crex crex* 25–27 cm

Other name: Landrail.

Sturdy buff–yellow rail with grey behind eye, on throat and on breast; shoulders bright chestnut, flanks barred buff and chestnut; undertail plain grey–buff. Bill short, pink–horn; legs and feet pinkish. In flight, chestnut shoulders and underwing; legs dangle at first. **Immature:** more buffish. Solitary; skulking; runs swiftly; sneaks fast through undergrowth; active morning·and evening. **Voice:** male: persistent, rasping 'rerrp, rerrp', usually at night: 'like passing thumbnail along teeth of comb'. **Habitat:** hayfields, crops, water-meadows. **Range and Status:** Europe to w. Siberia, migrating to Africa and sw. Asia. Vagrant Aust.: Randwick (NSW), June 1893, and on ship off Jurien Bay (WA), Dec. 1944. Vagrant NZ.

BUFF-BANDED
RAIL

imm.

tail of
adult

LEWIN'S RAIL

imm.

tail of
adult

CORNCRAKE

imm.

tail of
adult

SPOTLESS CRAKE *Porzana tabuensis* 17–21 cm

Compact blackish crake with black bill, red eye, plain olive–brown wings/back; finely barred under tail-coverts; legs dull red. **Immature:** throat dull white; eye brown; legs grey. Singles, pairs, companies: forages in cover on swamp-margins; flicks tail, *swims, dives.* Startled, dashes through cover or flies with legs trailing. **Voice:** single, sharp 'kek!'; shrill machinegun chitter; loud, explosive purring, like motor-cycle, or air bubbling from submerged bottle. **Habitat:** well-vegetated freshwater wetlands with rushes, reeds, cumbungi; salt-swamps, saltmarsh; mangroves. On islands, drier, scrubs, beaches. **Breeds:** Aug.–Dec. **Nest:** shallow cup of grass, plants, often with flimsy canopy; on ground under vegetation, in rush or tussock in water. **Eggs:** 3–5; light cream to pale brown or grey, mottled chestnut, lavender–grey. **Range and Status:** mostly coastal se. Aust., coastal WA, Tas and many islands. Winter visitor to coastal NT, ne. Q; irregular inland in good seasons. Uncommon; nomadic, migratory. Also se. Asia, Philippines to PNG, Oceania; NZ, sub-Antarctic islands.

AUSTRALIAN SPOTTED CRAKE *Porzana fluminea* 19–23 cm

Dark crake *with fine white streaks on olive–brown upperparts; white under tail-coverts. Bill olive green with red base;* eye red; face blackish; *throat/breast dark grey;* flanks barred black/white; legs green. **Juvenile:** duller; upperparts spotted white; underparts greyish. Singles, pairs, open companies: ventures from tussocks, reeds on shallow margins of rivers, wetlands, saltmarshes. Wades, swims, walks on floating plants. **Similar species:** Baillon's Crake. **Voice:** staccato, high-pitched double notes, descending; wheezing; whirring chatterings. **Habitat:** drying fresh, brackish or salt swamps with cover of water ribbons; sedges, bullrushes, clumps of rush or tussocks; 'samphire' around saltmarshes, saltfields, salt lakes, inland and coastal. **Breeds:** Aug.–Jan.; autumn where conditions favourable. **Nest:** shallow cup, with ramp of trampled material and canopy of grass, rush-stems, etc.; in rushes, water-ribbons; over water. **Eggs:** 4–5 (6); olive–brown, spotted red–brown and black. **Range and Status:** mostly se. Aust. and coastal WA; uncommon Tas. Fairly common in se. Aust., especially Murray–Murrumbidgee region; extends far inland when conditions suitable, e.g. Alice Springs. Sparse WA; irruptive n. to Kimberley; scarce coastal n. Q. Dispersive; irruptive; influenced by rainfall.

BAILLON'S CRAKE *Porzana pusilla* 15–16 cm

Tiny crake with *streaked, tawny yellow upperparts, pale grey face/breast. Flanks, under tail-coverts barred black/white.* Bill and legs green; eye red. **Immature:** duller. Walks over floating vegetation; flicks angled short tail, *showing barred black and white under tail-coverts.* Swims; flies with rapid wingbeats, legs dangling. **Similar species:** Australian Spotted Crake. **Voice:** harsh 'krek-krek'; high-speed, repetitive clicks with whirring 'chirr'; soft, whining notes. **Habitat:** vegetated freshwater wetlands; waterside trees and shrubs. **Breeds:** Aug.–Feb. **Nest:** shallow cup of rushes, water-plants, grass, leaves, with part-canopy, trampled approach-ramp: in tussock, water-ribbons, bush, over or beside water. **Eggs:** 4–8; oval, brown–olive, mottled darker. **Range and Status:** breeds mostly s. of Brisbane (Q) and e. of Eyre Pen. (SA), incl. Murray–Murrumbidgee region; also coastal WA; rare Tas. Possible winter migration from s. to coastal n. Aust. may extend to PNG and beyond. Also NZ; vagrant Macquarie I; Eurasia, Africa e. to Japan, s. to Philippines.

WHITE-BROWED CRAKE *Porzana cinerea* 17–18 cm

Tropical crake *with black cap and two white lines on blackish face; under tail-coverts plain warm buff.* **Immature:** browner, with faint cap; buffer on neck. Singles, pairs: forages in shallows, walks on floating vegetation, climbs in branches, flicks tail; associates with other rails. **Voice:** nasal grunts, squeaks; soft 'churr'; chattering 'cutchee cutchee', in chorus. **Habitat:** reeds, rank grass, water-lilies, floating vegetation in swamps; mangroves, woodland edges near or over water; sewage ponds. **Breeds:** most months. **Nest:** shallow cup of rushes; on platform with canopy of stems; among swamp vegetation; tussock in water, low branches. **Eggs:** 4–5 (6); oval, green–white to yellow–brown, with fleecy dots, spots, blotches of yellow–brown to dull chestnut. **Range and Status:** coastal n. Aust. and islands from e. Kimberley (WA) to *c.* Townsville (Q). Probable winter migrant to PNG. Also Malaysia to New Cal. Fiji, Samoa.

SPOTLESS CRAKE

imm.

tail of adult

AUSTRALIAN SPOTTED CRAKE

imm.

tail of adult

BAILLON'S CRAKE

imm.

tail of adult

WHITE-BROWED CRAKE

imm.

tail of adult

DUSKY MOORHEN *Gallinula tenebrosa* 35–40 cm

Other name: Waterhen.

Common waterhen of town lakes and well-vegetated wetlands: *yellow-tipped scarlet bill and bill-shield; dark eye; legs red above 'knee', red or greenish below with long, slender toes; white under-edges of tail.* Some have white streaks on flanks. **Nonbreeding:** bill-shield duller, legs greener below 'knee'. **Immature:** browner, with blackish green to dull orange bill and legs; white tail-edges. Pairs, loose colonies: forages ashore and on surface; flicks tail, swims with head jerking; skitters. Flies apparently feebly; legs trailing. Noisy, aggressive, with frequent fights and chases. **Similar species:** Eurasian Coot: bill and 'shield' white; plumage all-grey. Purple Swamphen: blue, with massive all-red bill, all-white 'stern'. Black-tailed Native-hen: green–orange bill; yellow eye; erect, wholly black tail; all-red legs. **Voice:** rapidly repeated, resonant, 'kok's; strident 'kerk!'; repeated shrieks, taken up by other birds. **Habitat:** well-vegetated wetlands; town lakes, parks, farm dams, irrigation storages, bore drains; rivers with sloping, grassy margins; trees or scrub on banks; introduced willows; brackish wetlands; mangroves in dry periods. **Breeds:** Aug.–March. **Nest:** bulky saucer of sticks, stems, bark, grass; in rushes, reeds; in or near water in vegetation, or on stump, tree bole, roots; or low branches of waterside tree. Builds resting platforms. **Eggs:** 7–10; buff or sandy, blotched, spotted purplish brown. **Range and Status:** e., se. and sw. Aust.; spreading in Tas.; uncommon coastal nw. and n. Q; vagrant NT. Common; sedentary, dispersive; vagrant NZ. Also Borneo, Indonesia, PNG. Probably conspecific with Eurasian race *chloropsis*, which has white streaks on flanks.

PURPLE SWAMPHEN *Porphyrio porphyrio* 44–48 cm

Other names: Bald Coot; Eastern or Western Swamphen; Pukeko.

Large, conspicuous waterhen with *robust scarlet bill and forehead-shield, deep-blue head and breast; flicks tail, exposing snow-white under tail-coverts; long reddish legs.* Race *bellus* (s. WA), neck/breast paler blue. **Immature:** duller; bill blackish red. Territorial groups to open companies on margins of wetlands, nearby paddocks; climbs, roosts in vegetation over water; constructs feeding platforms. Aggressive between groups: takes eggs/young, scavenges dead birds, fish. **Similar species:** Dusky Moorhen: black with yellow-tipped scarlet bill and 'shield'. **Voice:** high-pitched rasping screeches; nasal 'nerk's; cooings, unusual liquid thuds. **Habitat:** margins of swamps, lakes; shallow rivers with dense rushes, reeds, cumbungi; familiar on town lakes; lawns, golf-courses, sewage ponds, bore drains, airports. **Breeds:** July–Dec., s. Aust; after rain, n. Aust. **Nest:** bowl-shaped, in shallow platform of rushes and grass; often with open canopy of stems; on trampled-down reeds, water-ribbons, cumbungi. **Eggs:** 3–5; sandy buff, blotched, spotted chestnut with underlying spots of grey. Groups nest cooperatively. **Range and Status:** race *melanotus*: widespread in e. and coastal ne. Aust., from *c*. Cooktown (Q), s. to Eyre Pen. (SA); also Tas. and coastal islands; less common across coastal n. Aust. Extends far inland when conditions suitable; vagrant PNG. Race *bellus*: sw. WA. Sedentary; dispersive. Also Lord Howe and Norfolk Is.; NZ region; Melanesia, New Cal.; w. Polynesia; Indonesia, Eurasia, Africa.

EURASIAN COOT *Fulica atra* 35–38 cm

Unmistakable plain slate-grey waterhen, darker on head, *with pure white bill and bill-shield; legs silver–grey, toes with flattened lobes* to assist swimming, diving. **Immature:** grey–brown, whitish below; bill greyish. Pairs, family parties, flocks: feeds ashore, in shallows, or far out on large waters in 'rafts'. *Dives for plant food;* skitters when taking off: *sustained flight swift, with rapid, shallow wingbeats;* travels mostly at night. Aggressive. **Similar species:** Dusky Moorhen, Purple Swamphen: reddish bills; white under tail; neither habitually dives when foraging. **Voice:** noisy; harsh notes, a sharp 'kyik!' or 'kyok!'; repeated raucous screeches, 'tok's, etc. **Habitat:** large, fresh, brackish, occasionally saline waters, with underwater vegetation; permanent wetlands, town lakes, reservoirs, sewage ponds, brackish coastal swamps; occasionally on sheltered coastal inlets or sheltered waters around offshore islands. **Breeds:** Aug.–Feb. in s. Aust., but any time when conditions suitable. **Nest:** of sticks, swamp-vegetation, grass, lignum; on bottom in shallow water or on low island, stump or log; singly or in companies. **Eggs:** 6–7; stone-coloured, finely and evenly dotted black. **Range and Status:** Aust. and Tas. except driest deserts, but principally e. and se. Aust., coastal and subcoastal WA. Common; often very abundant. Nomadic; dispersive. Casual Norfolk, Lord Howe and Macquarie Is. Also NZ, PNG, Eurasia, n. Africa.

DUSKY MOORHEN

imm.

PURPLE SWAMPHEN

imm.

EURASIAN COOT

imm.

155

BLACK-TAILED NATIVE-HEN *Gallinula ventralis* 30–36 cm

Other name: Barcoo Bantam.

Dark, fleet-footed native hen with an erect, black, square 'bantam's tail'; green–red bill; white streaks on flanks; red legs. Singles, parties to companies of thousands: runs swiftly across paddocks and margins of swamps, claypans; 'camps' under nearby trees, lignum, etc.; tame around homesteads. Swims readily; *flies strongly with rapid shallow wingbeats, legs trailing.* **Similar species:** Dusky Moorhen: yellow-tipped scarlet bill and shield; tail has white edges. Tasmanian Native-hen. **Voice:** usually silent, but utters single, very high-pitched note, like striking silvery anvil, at *c.* 2 second intervals. Also a rapid, harsh, scratchy, metallic chorus of 'yapyapyapyap'. **Habitat:** open margins of wetlands, lakes, rivers; wet claypans, *especially in lignum*; open woodland; pastures, crops, gardens. **Breeds:** June–Dec., but any month after flooding rains. **Nest:** flattish structure of grass; on ground among bushes or lignum; often near others. **Eggs:** 5–7; pale green, with brown dots and bold blotches of chestnut-brown; underlying spots of lavender–grey. **Range and Status:** s. and inland e. Aust.; mostly inland of Divide and s. of Tropic; well-established from Murray–Darling region and L. Eyre basin to se. SA; coastal and sub-coastal WA. After flood rains, occurs almost anywhere: small to large numbers arrive sometimes overnight, breed and quickly depart. Scarce, mostly summer, visitor Kimberley (WA), Top End (NT); n. Q. (but not C. York Pen.). Casual coastal e. Aust. Vagrant Tas., NZ. Dispersive; irruptive, opportunistic in response to rainfall.

TASMANIAN NATIVE-HEN *Gallinula mortierii* 43–50 cm

Other name: Narkie.

Large flightless native hen confined to Tas.: *upperparts olive–brown;* erect tail black; underparts grey; belly and under tail-coverts black; *whitish patch on flank. Bill heavy, yellow–green; legs grey.* **Immature:** bill grey; upperparts browner; underparts spotted white. Singles, pairs, parties: active, noisy, demonstrative and aggressive; jerks tail up and down. When disturbed runs swiftly across roads, paddocks; swims and dives readily to escape. **Similar species:** Black-tailed Native-hen; casual Tas.; darker, with red legs. **Voice:** rasping, hacksaw-like cacophony, often from many birds, day and night; also deep, bubbling grunts. **Habitat:** farmland with short grass, tussocks; edges of wetlands, streams, lakes; margins of woodlands; roadsides. May become a pest in nearby crops. **Breeds:** July–Jan. **Nest:** platform of tussocks pulled up by the roots and trampled down, or shallow saucer of grass, roots, leaves and twigs; in undergrowth, long grass or tussocks; occasionally floating and anchored in reeds. **Eggs:** 6–9; stone-coloured, blotched and finely spotted chestnut, with paler underlying markings. **Range and Status:** endemic to Tas., mostly n. and e.; mostly absent from w. and sw.; introduced Maria I. Common; sedentary.

CHESTNUT RAIL *Eulabeornis castaneoventris* 44–52 cm. Male larger.

A particularly large, unusual rail with a long, *yellowish bill, grey head, chestnut body, longish pointed tail and longish pale yellow legs.* The Q–NT population has *chestnut upperparts, wings and tail;* in nw. WA (Derby to Cambridge Gulf), *uniform olive–grey to olive upperparts, wings and tail* (Marchant & Higgins, 1993). Singles, pairs, family parties: wary; forages slowly over exposed mud and mangrove roots at low tide. Runs dodging to cover when disturbed, seldom flies. **Voice:** a loud, raucous 'whack, whacka, wak-wak' repeated steadily. (Ragless, 1977); also emu-like drumming notes and loud, sustained squealing. **Habitat:** coastal mangroves; tidal creeks and exposed mud. **Breeds:** Sept.–Dec. **Nest:** cup of sticks or grass, leaves, etc.; *c.* 20 cm across, in a heap or platform of dry sticks in crotch of mangrove, *c.* 2 m from mud. **Eggs:** 4; long, oval; pink–white, dotted reddish-chestnut and purple; some darker markings as though beneath surface. **Range and Status:** coastal n. Aust. and islands, from *c.* Derby (WA) to Top End (NT), to se. Gulf of Carpentaria. Reported Weipa (Q), June 1996 (Stewart & Nielsen, 1996). Sedentary. Also Aru I.

BLACK-TAILED NATIVE-HEN

TASMANIAN NATIVE-HEN

CHESTNUT RAIL

AUSTRALIAN BUSTARD *Ardeotis australis* 76 cm–1.5 m; span 1.6–2.1 m. Male larger.

Other names: Plains or Wild Turkey.

Lordly, upstanding large bird of open country. **Male:** crown black; *neck and breast grey–white, with bold black breastband; bend of wing patterned black and white.* **Female:** smaller; narrow, browner crown; neck/breast greyer, no breastband. Singles, pairs, groups: in n. Aust., companies of dozens (occasionally hundreds) where grasshoppers, crickets, house mice abundant. *Moves in stately walk, with bill aloofly raised.* 'Taxies' into wind; flight powerful, large body sags, slow-beating broad wings and trailing legs distinctive. Rests unseen in tall grass or scrub in heat of day; moves out to feed at evening. Male display: conspicuous; extends expanded, white-plumaged breast-sac to ground, fans tail forward over back; 'marks time' so that pendulous breast-sac swings and twists conspicuously. Points bill skywards, balloons throat, roars like a distant lion. **Voice:** croaks while feeding; hoarse bark in alarm. **Habitat:** grasslands, spinifex, open scrublands, grassy woodlands, sandhills, pastoral lands, burned ground; occasionally crops, airfields. **Breeds:** Aug.–Nov., s. Aust.; all months, n. Aust. **Eggs:** 1–3; buff to green–buff; on open bare ground; by bush, stones, tussock. **Range and Status:** mainland Aust.; once widespread: still common away from settlement in parts of e. inland, inland, n. Aust. and WA. Now mostly extinct in settled districts of s., se. Aust. and sw. WA but casual wanderers still occur. Nomadic, dispersive, in response to rainfall; regular movement s. in summer; to n. coastal Aust. in winter. Also s. PNG.

BUSH STONE-CURLEW *Burhinus grallarius* 55–59 cm; span 80 cm–1.05 m

Other names: Bush Thick-knee; Southern Stone-curlew; Weeloo; Willaroo.

Unusual, bush-dwelling wader, more often heard than seen. Grey–brown above (washed pale rufous in n. Aust.), buff–white below, *strongly streaked darker; dark mark along wing over a broader pale zone.* Bill blackish, forehead whitish; *broad white eyebrow over thick black line from below eye down neck; eye large, yellow.* Pairs, groups to loose flocks. Shy, watchful: moves weirdly, slowly, often with head lowered. 'Freezes' stick-like, lies flat with neck extended, walks deliberately away or runs furtively. Flies with *quick, stiff beats of long, bowed wings, revealing prominent white patch across black primaries.* Active at night, often on country roads; wing-patches luminous in headlights. Tame near habitation: golf-courses, resort islands. **Similar species:** Beach Stone-curlew. **Voice:** usually at night: a far-carrying, eerie whistling call (or chorus) that starts low and quietly — a drawn-out 'wee–eeer', repeated up to 5 times; rises, becomes a high-pitched, drawn-out 'keeleeoo', quickens, breaks, descends, often ends in a chorus of 'wee-wiff; wee-wiff; wee-wiff', by several birds. Other groups respond. Screeches in flight. **Habitat:** open woodland, dry watercourses with fallen branches, leaf-litter, sparse grass; sandplains with spinifex and mallee; coastal scrub, mangrove fringes, golf-courses, rail-reserves; timber remnants on roadsides; orchards, plantations; suburbs, towns, cities in Q; resort islands. **Breeds:** Aug.–Jan.; earlier in n. Aust. **Eggs:** 2; on bare ground; stone-coloured, blotched dark brown, grey. **Range and Status:** e., se., n., coastal WA, many coastal islands; vagrant Tas. Absent from s. inland and Nullarbor region. Rare to wholly extinct in settled parts of coastal se. Aust. More abundant in subtropics (incl. Brisbane suburbs) and across n. Aust. Sedentary, locally dispersive; vulnerable in s. Aust. Also s. PNG.

BEACH STONE-CURLEW *Esacus neglectus* 56 cm

Other name: Beach Thick-knee.

Large wader with stately, bustard-like carriage and heavy, black-tipped yellow bill; *prominent black-and-white pattern on head, bar on shoulder*, heavy yellow–green legs; eye large, yellow. Singles, pairs or parties: active dusk, dawn and at night; feeds deliberately, with short runs. Keeps ahead of observer or flies some distance along beach on *surprisingly white, downcurved wings with broad black wingbar and black rear edge*; wingbeats slow, rather stiff; toes trail beyond tail. **Similar species:** Bush Stone-curlew. **Voice:** like Bush Stone-curlew but higher pitched, harsher. Alarm-call: sharp but feeble 'klee' or 'klee-klink'. **Habitat:** open undisturbed beaches; exposed reefs, tidal mudflats and sandflats; coastal lagoons, mangroves; occasionally canefields near tidal areas. **Breeds:** Sept.–Nov. e. Aust.; July–Oct., n. Aust. **Egg:** 1; laid on sand, usually just above high-tide mark, and vulnerable. Creamy white, streaked and blotched olive–brown. **Range and Status:** coastal n. and e. Aust. and coastal islands: from *c.* Shark Bay (WA) to Nambucca Heads (NSW); casual s. to Norah Head, s. coast and far e. Vic. Nowhere common, rare s. of Cairns, but seemingly extending range s. in NSW. Sedentary. Also Malaysia, Philippines to PNG, New Cal.

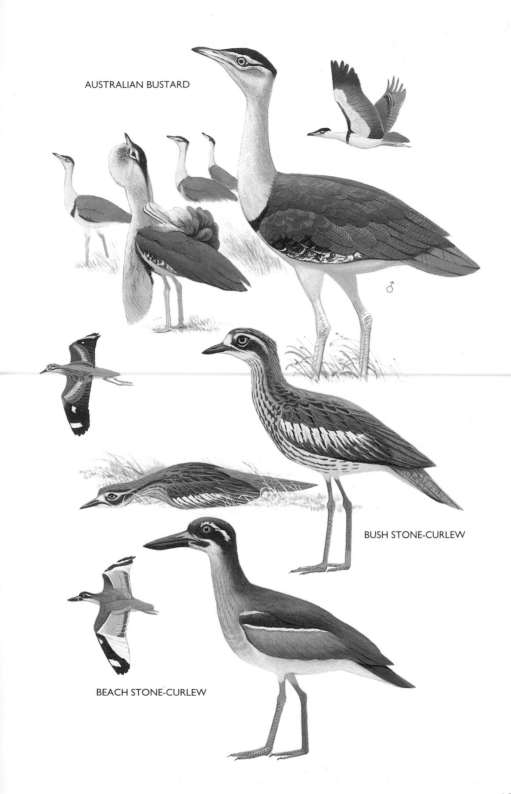

AUSTRALIAN BUSTARD

♂

BUSH STONE-CURLEW

BEACH STONE-CURLEW

PAINTED BUTTON-QUAIL *Turnix varia* 17–19 cm. Female larger.

Female: *note red eye; bright chestnut shoulder-patch; fine white eyebrow, white spots on face/neck; large cream–white spots on creamy grey breast;* legs deep yellow. **Male:** duller, less chestnut. Singles, pairs, coveys: feeding birds rotate while scratching in leaf-debris, forming 'soup-plate' depressions. Runs quickly, head high; flushes with a whirr, flies fast, *weaving through trees on longish, pointed wings, showing grey–brown rump and tail.* **Similar species:** Red-backed, Black-breasted, Buff-breasted Button-quail. **Voice:** female: deep swelling 'oom', starting at *c.* 1 second intervals, accelerating/rising through sequence of 10–30 calls; contact call: rapid soft drumming. **Habitat:** scrublands, open woodlands with branch, leaf debris; tussocks, stones; heathlands, farm regrowth, mallee. **Breeds:** spring/autumn. **Nest:** depression lined with grass, leaves, with part-canopy; by tussock, log, base of tree or rock. **Eggs:** 4; whitish, freckled blue/brown; sparser red–brown spots. **Range and Status:** e. and se. Aust., Tas. and s. WA: from Atherton Tableland (ne. Q) to Tas., w. to Eyre Pen. and Kangaroo I., n. to s. Flinders Ras. (SA). In sw. WA, n. to Shark Bay, incl. coastal islands. Sedentary; nomadic.

BLACK-BREASTED BUTTON-QUAIL *Turnix melanogaster* 16.5–19 cm. Female larger.

Female: *head and breast black, with massed white half-moons on upperbreast.* Upperparts marbled chestnut, with black ladders, white streaks. Bill grey, longish, stout; eye cream–white; legs/feet yellowish. **Male:** *whitish face/neck finely dotted black; plentiful white half-moons over mottled black and chestnut upperbreast.* Pairs, coveys: makes 'soup-plate' depressions. Approached, freezes, walks quietly, runs or bursts up, glides, runs. **Similar species:** Painted Button-Quail. **Voice:** male: soft clucks. Female: deep, low 'oo-oom oo-oom oo-oom'; low, tremulous drumming; deep 'chucks'. **Habitat:** leaf-litter in drier rainforests, vine thickets; scrubby woodlands of eucalypts, she oaks, bottle-trees, brush box, brigalow and other *Acacias*; thickets of lantana on rainforest fringes, hoop pine plantations; grain stubbles. **Range and Status:** Patchy in suitable habitat in se. Q–ne. NSW, on or e. of Divide: from Fraser I. and Nanango-Bunya Mts region (Q) s. to Legume, Nightcap Ra. NP/Rocky Ck Dam, n. of Lismore (NSW). Formerly widespread. Sedentary, rare and local; dispersive.

CHESTNUT-BACKED BUTTON-QUAIL *Turnix castanota* 15–19 cm. Female larger.

Large button-quail with big, bone-coloured bill; yellow eye/legs. **Female:** *upperparts cinnamon–rufous,* with *sparse* black, chestnut and white ladders; wings mottled black and white; *rump plain cinnamon–grey; breast olive–grey, spotted cream;* underparts whitish. **Male:** plainer cinnamon–rufous *back, rump and tail.* Singles, pairs, coveys of 6–20: nocturnal and crepuscular (Marchant & Higgins, 1993). Runs with neck extended, head raised; in flight, *note dark leading edge to wing, plain cinnamon–rufous to grey back, rump and tail.* **Voice:** low 'ooms'. **Habitat:** tropical woodlands with sparse grass; slopes, hills, escarpments, ridges; taller grasses, spinifex, vine-thickets. **Breeds:** Nov.–June (Olsen et al, 1993). **Nest:** open or partly domed; of grasses/leaves; in depression among grass, or tussock. **Eggs:** 4; glossy green–white, freckled light brown, dark brown, blue–grey and black, mostly at large end. **Range and Status:** coastal nw. Aust., from Kimberley (WA) through Top End and Melville I. (NT). Sedentary.

BUFF-BREASTED BUTTON-QUAIL *Turnix olivii* 18–22 cm. Female larger.

Large button-quail with big greyish bill; yellow eyes/legs/feet. **Female:** *upperparts, rump, tail sandy cinnamon;* back/wings darker, with black and chestnut laddering; *underparts plain olive–buff.* **Male:** neck freckled black and white; wings mottled white. Pairs, coveys flush from underfoot, scatter before dropping. In flight, *sandy cinnamon rump/tail.* **Voice:** booming '. . . ooom, ooom, ooom', starting low, rising and accelerating lasting *c.* 30 secs. Also 'a rapid deep humming "gug-gug-gug", and (male) deep, rapid whistling, "chu-chu-chu"' (White, 1922). **Habitat:** drier ridges/slopes in eucalypt woodland; stony ground with sparse grasses, small shrubs. **Breeds:** Dec.–May. **Nest:** oval, with side entrance, of grasses. **Eggs:** 3–4: glossy white, minutely spotted, blotched black, red–brown, blue–grey. **Range and Status:** ne. Q, from *c.* Pascoe R. s. to Atherton Tableland. Rare; seasonally nomadic.

PAINTED BUTTON-QUAIL

♀

♂

BLACK-BREASTED BUTTON-QUAIL

♀

♂

CHESTNUT-BACKED
BUTTON-QUAIL

♀

BUFF-BREASTED BUTTON-QUAIL

♀

LITTLE BUTTON-QUAIL *Turnix velox* 12–14 cm. Female larger.

Very small *with heavy blue–grey bill, pale cream eye.* **Female:** *pinkish cinnamon above* with whitish streaks; *whitish fawn below,* washed buff across breast; *flanks, belly white*; legs pinkish. **Male:** pale brown, *with darker pattern on crown/upperparts,* dark scallops on sides of neck/breast. **Immature:** breast more scalloped. Singles, loose flocks: runs like mouse, squats; flies low, fast: note pale central area in darkish wings (Marchant & Higgins, 1993), *cinnamon rump, white flanks and underparts.* **Similar species:** King Quail, female; Red-backed, Red-chested Button-quail. **Voice:** high-pitched 'oom, oom', day/night. When flushed, quick 'chek chek'. **Habitat:** grassy plains, creekflats, woodlands; burned areas; saltbush, spinifex; mulga, mallee; margins of wetlands; crops, pastures, stubble. **Breeds:** any month. **Nest:** scanty; of grass, some hooded; in hollow by tuft, shrub. **Eggs:** 3–4; rounded, buff–white, spotted, blotched purple–brown, slate–grey, chestnut. **Range and Status:** mainland Aust. *except* coastal far n. Aust.; sparse se. of Divide. Summer migrant to subcoastal s. Aust. Nomadic; irruptive; abundant inland in good years.

RED-CHESTED BUTTON-QUAIL *Turnix pyrrhothorax* 12–16 cm. Female larger.

Small with *stout silver–grey bill, cream–white eye.* **Female:** *underparts rich orange–buff*; crown, face, upperparts grey–brown, finely patterned black, rufous, with cream streaks. **Male:** whiter throat/belly; *fine black crescents on sides of breast/flanks.* Singles, pairs, coveys: flushes with chatter; note *chunky silhouette, orange–buff underparts/flanks; paler inner wingpatch, dark flight-feathers* (Marchant & Higgins, 1993). **Similar species:** Little, Red-backed Button-quails. **Voice:** sharp 'chek chek' when flushed; repeated 'ooms' increasing in speed. **Habitat:** grasslands, open woodlands: native pine; mulga; spinifex between mallee ridges; lucerne; cereal stubbles with weeds, thistles. **Breeds:** Sept.–Feb. in se. Aust.; Feb.–July in n. **Nest:** of grass, sparsely domed by tussock; in lucerne, grain-stubble. **Eggs:** 4; buff–white, freckled slate grey, chestnut; blotched brown. **Range and Status:** nw., n., e. and se. Aust., far inland in good seasons; spring–summer visitor s. NSW, Vic., se. SA. Nomadic; irruptive. Uncommon.

RED-BACKED BUTTON-QUAIL *Turnix maculosa* 12–15 cm. Female larger.

Note slim, pointed yellowish (or grey) bill, white eye. **Female:** *face, neck, shoulder-patch, rear collar rich rusty; wing-coverts/flanks rusty to yellow–buff, with large black spots.* **Male:** *face/neck pale yellow–buff*; rear collar less rusty; *wing-coverts, flanks yellow–buff with prominent black spots, crescents.* **Immature:** *black-mottled breast, flanks, wing-coverts*; bill blackish; eye brown. Singles, pairs, coveys: flutters to cover or flies fast on angled wings, *buff wing-panels contrast with dark flight-feathers.* **Similar species:** Red-chested Button-quail. **Voice:** female: high-pitched, cooing, 'oom', each note upslurred; starts at one per second, accelerates, rises through *c.* 20–25. **Habitat:** grasses, sedges near water; grassy woodlands, rainforest edges; black soil plains; spinifex; cereal crops, lucerne, gardens. **Breeds:** spring to early winter. **Nest:** scantily lined hollow under tussock, shrub. **Eggs:** 2–4; glossy, pale slate-grey, spotted brown, blotched dark grey. **Range and Status:** coastal n. and e. Aust. (and many islands) from w. Kimberley (WA) to Top End (NT); C. York Pen. (Q) and Torres Strait Is., s. on e. coast to Manning R. (NSW); casual s. NSW, Vic. Sedentary; dispersive. Also Solomon Is., s. PNG, Indonesia, Philippines.

PLAINS-WANDERER *Pedionomus torquatus* 15–19 cm. Female larger.

Lankier than a button-quail, with slimmer yellow bill, pale eye, angular head, slender neck. *Legs yellow, longish, with hind-toe.* **Female**: *white-spotted black collar above rufous breastband.* **Male**: plainer; light brown above, patterned with brown rosettes; fawn–white below with *blackish crescents.* Singles, pairs, family parties: 'freezes', cranes tiptoe, or runs crouching through grass. Flushes reluctantly, showing *pale, angled wing-coverts, white wingbar across dark flight-feathers*; alights waveringly with trailing legs. **Voice:** low, resonant 'moo' or 'oo'; soft clucks. **Habitat:** sparse, treeless, lightly grazed native grasslands/herbfields with bare ground; old cereal crops; short lucerne; sparse saltbush, low shrubland (Baker-Gabb, 1993). **Breeds:** early spring, late summer, in s.; autumn–early winter (Q). (Marchant & Higgins, 1993). **Nest:** scanty, of dry grass in scrape, some with woven canopy. **Eggs:** 4; pointed, stone-coloured, freckled, blotched, smudged brown, slate-grey. Male incubates; broods young. **Range and Status:** stronghold is s. NSW Riverina: patchy, inland NSW/Q; s. NT; n., se. SA, n. Vic. Rare; vulnerable.

LITTLE BUTTON-QUAIL

RED-CHESTED BUTTON-QUAIL

RED-BACKED BUTTON-QUAIL

PLAINS-WANDERER

LATHAM'S SNIPE *Gallinago hardwickii* 28–31 cm

Other names: Australian or Japanese Snipe.

The only true snipe known to regularly visit se. Aust.: note the long (7.5 cm), straight bill and large dark eye, set high in head. Plumage intricately marked rufous, black and buff, with bold brown stripes and cream streaks; *flanks barred; belly and underparts whitish*. Small parties, occasional large companies. Shy: forages on marshy ground, ramming bill vertically into mud with rapid sewing-machine action. Disturbed, freezes, or bursts up in fast, zigzagging flight, alarm-call flushing others; may dash wildly into sky, or quickly drop to cover. Note *the long bill, conspicuous white belly*. **Similar species**: safely identified from Swinhoe's and Pin-tailed Snipe only in hand: has 18 or fewer tail-feathers; Swinhoe's has 20+; Pin-tailed 24–28. Narrow outer 'pin' feathers on sides of tail (specialised sound-producing feathers erected in diving display flights over breeding territories) are most distinctly barred. Length of extended wing: Latham's: 15.2 cm and over; Swinhoe's under 15 cm; Pin-tailed *c*.13.2 cm. See also Painted Snipe. Note that godwits and other long-billed sandpipers are incorrectly called 'snipe'. **Voice:** when flushed: quick, explosive 'chak!' or 'zhak!', like sudden tearing of sandpaper. **Habitat:** soft wet ground or shallow water with tussocks and other green or dead growth; wet parts of paddocks; seepage below dams; irrigated areas; scrub or open woodland from sea-level to alpine bogs over 2000 m; 'samphire' on saltmarshes; mangrove fringes. **Range and Status:** breeds Japan (Hokkaido and Honshu); Kurile Is., and Sakhalin I. Regular summer migrant to Aust. arriving in ne. Q July–Aug. Stronghold is from se. Q, through NSW, Vic., Tas. and s. SA, Kangaroo I., w. casually to Eyre Pen. and Ooldea; numbers peak in this region Dec.–Jan. Mostly coastal and subcoastal, but substantial inland movement through Murray–Darling region. Some overwinter. Uncommon: locally common. Small numbers to Darwin (NT) and coastal WA, s. to s. WA. Generally uncommon; migratory. Also PNG, Lord Howe I., NZ. Vagrant Macquarie I.

PIN-TAILED SNIPE *Gallinago stenura* 25–27 cm

Other name: Pintail Snipe.

Smallest true snipe known to regularly visit Australia. Bill shorter, more slender than Latham's and Swinhoe's, without bulbous tip. Upperparts duller, browner, more uniform; 'dark, richly patterned', with narrower, fainter white lines on back. Neck and breast yellow–brown with fine dark speckling. Mostly solitary: reported to pick, rather than probe when feeding, and to often rise silently when flushed, *flying heavily and slowly, with feet trailing beyond tip of short tail*. Rarely zigzags or flies high: *pale feathers on upper wing-coverts form a pale patch, contrasting with the brown flight-feathers; underwing dark with broad brown and narrow white bars*. In hand, note 24–28 tail-feathers, incl. 6–9 pairs of pin-like outer tail-feathers less than 2 mm wide, like 'a row of tiny paintbrushes'. **Voice:** said to be less explosive than other snipe; variously described as 'scaap'; 'squik'; 'squok'; or a nasal 'pench'. **Habitat:** boggy edges of vegetated wetlands; sewage and other ponds; stubbles, grasslands with shrubs, pastures. **Range and Status:** breeds from ne. Russia across n. Siberia: winters India, Burma, se. Asia to Borneo, Sumatra, Java. Probably regular, uncommon summer migrant (Aug.–March) to coastal nw. and w. Aust. from Darwin (NT) to Kimberley (WA); casual s. to about Perth.

SWINHOE'S SNIPE *Gallinago megala* 26–29 cm

Other names: Chinese or Marsh Snipe.

Slightly smaller than Latham's Snipe, *with broad white tips to tail-feathers*. In hand has 20+ tail-feathers, incl. four pairs of 'pin' feathers, 2–4 mm wide. Note limited Aust. range. **Voice:** reported to have a sharp, rasping alarm-note. **Habitat:** wet grassy ground; edges of reedy swamps. **Range and Status:** breeds c. Siberia and Mongolia: winters widely from s. Asia to PNG, mostly e. of the wintering range of Pin-tailed Snipe. Probably regular summer migrant to tropical n. Aust.; records from Wyndham and L. Argyle region (WA) to Top End (NT), s. to c. Newcastle Waters, L. Woods and Brunette Ck; in Q, s. to Camooweal, e. to Iron Ra., e. C. York Pen.

LATHAM'S
SNIPE

PIN-TAILED
SNIPE

SWINHOE'S
SNIPE

BAR-TAILED GODWIT *Limosa lapponica* 38–46 cm. Female larger.

Large, pale, brown-streaked wader with a long, tapering, slightly upturned bill, pink at base with blackish tip; dark grey legs. **Female:** bill longer. **Breeding plumage:** male: *head/body chestnut or brick-red; upperparts richly patterned black and buff.* Female: *head/body deep buff.* **Nonbreeding (both sexes):** *fawn rear eyebrow; upperparts pale grey–brown, subtly streaked and mottled; paler below, finely streaked.* Singles, parties, flocks, spread out widely over mudflats when feeding. Rams bill to hilt in soft ground; wades deep. Sometimes roosts in mangroves. Flight swift, often in staggered lines or chevrons low to water. Race *baueri*, the usual form in e. Aust., has no pale wingbar, but *whitish rump and whitish, finely-barred tail, and finely dark-barred underwing* which looks greyish in flight. **Similar species:** Asian Dowitcher: straight untapering black bill; larger white eyebrow; heavier markings above. Black-tailed and Hudsonian Godwits. **Voice:** scratchy 'ketta-ket'; soft 'kit-kit-kit'. **Habitat:** tidal mudflats, estuaries, sewage ponds, shallow river margins, brackish or saline inland lakes, flooded pastures, airfields. **Range and Status:** the race *baueri* of this widespread wader, breeding in ne. Siberia and nw. Alaska, is thought to migrate mostly to Indonesia, PNG, e. Aust.; NZ and islands. Widespread summer migrant to e. Aust. and Tas. (Sept.–April): mostly on coasts, but regular inland passage; often overwinters. The race *menzbieri*, breeding in c. Siberia, occurs in WA.

BLACK-TAILED GODWIT *Limosa limosa* 36–43 cm

Slightly smaller than Bar-tailed but *legs longer; bill longer and straighter, pink with black tip.* **Nonbreeding:** *more evenly grey and buffish; less streaked.* **Breeding plumage:** male: *head, neck and breast buffish to rusty; eyebrow cream; upperparts richly patterned black and rusty; flanks barred black and white.* Female: *head/neck buffish.* **Immature:** richer buffish neck and breast; buff edges to dark feathers of upperparts. Small parties to companies of hundreds; often with Bar-tails: *compare bills and look for Black-tail's white underwing when stretching.* Feeding movements unhurried; probes mud deeply. Flight swift, often low over water, occasionally erratic: note *bold white wingbar across black flight-feathers; white underwing, white rump and black tail; legs extend further beyond tail than Bar-tailed.* **Similar species:** Hudsonian Godwit: shaped more like a Bar-tailed Godwit, incl. slightly upturned bill; note black 'armpits' (axillaries) and dusky underwings; white wingbar much less conspicuous. **Voice:** staccato, slightly harsh 'witta-wit' or 'reeta reeta reeta'; when feeding, single 'kuk'. **Habitat:** tidal mudflats, estuaries, sandspits, shallow river margins, sewage ponds; inland on large shallow fresh or brackish waters. **Range and Status:** the race *melanuroides* of this widespread wader breeds from Mongolia to ne. Siberia, migrating to s. and se. Asia, Indonesian region; occasional PNG and NZ. Regular summer migrant to Aust. (Sept.–May); common from nw. WA to Gt Barrier Reef (Q) and c. NSW coast; widespread but scarce in s. Aust.; vagrant Tas. Records from s. NT, w. Q, w. NSW and nw. Vic. indicate regular inland passage. Some overwinter.

HUDSONIAN GODWIT *Limosa haemastica* 37–42 cm

Shaded like a darkish Black-tailed Godwit, but neck and legs shorter, bill more like Bar-tailed Godwit, usually slightly upturned. In all plumages, five features help identify it: (1) *distinctly pale face and eyebrow;* (2) in flight, or when stretching, *dusky black 'armpits' and under wing-coverts;* (3) *short white wingbar, visible above and below;* (4) *narrow white band across rump;* (5) *narrow whitish tips to black tail.* **Nonbreeding:** neck streaked grey and blackish brown; upperparts grey–brown; paler below; remnant coarse dark bars on wings and flanks. **Breeding plumage:** male: *feathers of upperparts have bold buff–white notches and flecks; breast and underparts oxblood red with heavy dark bars on flanks; under tail-coverts barred black and white.* Female: *much paler red below, with white blotching.* **Immature:** as nonbreeding; buff edges to feathers above. In Aust., has been met singly, with other godwits. **Voice:** flight-calls: a low, double 'ta-it' or sharp but not far-carrying 'kit-keet' (Falla et al, 1979). **Habitat:** tidal mudflats and estuaries; waterways in mangroves; saltmarsh, freshwater wetlands. **Range and Status:** breeds Alaska to Hudson Bay, Canada: winters far s. S. America; some reach NZ almost annually. In Aust., summer vagrant Hunter R. (NSW) (from Dec. 1982) and near Adelaide (SA) (from Sept. 1986).

imm.

BAR-TAILED GODWIT

♂ breeding

♀
non-
breeding

♀ breeding

imm.

♂
non-
breeding

BLACK-TAILED GODWIT

♀ breeding

imm.

♂ nonbreeding

HUDSONIAN GODWIT

EASTERN CURLEW *Numenius madagascariensis* 60–65 cm

Other names: Australian, Far Eastern or Sea Curlew.
Largest migrant wader, *distinguished by very long (18 cm), pink-based, downcurved bill, nearly half length of body; brown rump and tail.* **Female:** bill longer (up to 20 cm). In flight, bill very prominent; note finely dark-barred *brown rump and tail. Underwing pale brown, closely barred darker.* Solitary to large, dispersed companies: aloof and wary. Flocks fly in drawn-out lines or Vs, calling hauntingly. Active at night, especially at low tide. **Similar species:** Eurasian Curlew: bill shorter; rump and underwing white. Whimbrel. **Voice:** haunting, sometimes grating 'curlee, curlee' or 'crooee, crooe', mostly in flight; also a musical, bubbling running trill, rising then falling. **Habitat:** estuaries, tidal mudflats, sandspits, saltmarshes, mangroves; occasionally fresh or brackish lakes; bare grasslands near water. **Range and Status:** breeds ne. Asia: common summer migrant (Aug.–May) to coasts of n., e., and se. Aust. and Tas.; less common SA and s. WA; seldom inland. Many overwinter. Also NZ. Declining.

EURASIAN CURLEW *Numenius arquata* 50–60 cm

Other names: Common or European Curlew.
Slightly smaller than Eastern Curlew, with shorter bill (c. 14 cm); note *white, dark-barred tail and white rump extending up back in wedge conspicuous in flight.* Siberian race *orientalis* has *mostly unbarred whitish wing-linings and underparts.* Habits, voice, habitat: generally as Eastern Curlew, with which it may associate. **Similar species:** Whimbrel: smaller; bill less curved; crown divided by pale streak; underwings closely barred darker. Calls differ. **Range and Status:** breeds from w. Europe to sw. Siberia, winters s. Europe, Africa; occasional e. to Malaysia, Borneo. In Aust., sight-records Darwin (NT) and s. WA. Vagrant.

WHIMBREL *Numenius phaeopus* 38–43 cm

Bill shorter and less curved than curlews; dark brown crown split by buff–grey central stripe, bordered by whitish eyebrows. In flight, *white rump extends in wedge up lower back, underwing brownish, chequered darker; wingbeats quicker.* Call distinct: a shrill, rapid, tittering 'ti-ti-ti-ti-ti-ti'. Occasionally grating 'croo-ee' like Eastern Curlew. Solitary, or small flocks, often with other waders. Difficult to approach without putting to noisy flight (but tame on Gt Barrier Reef islands). Roosts in trees and mangroves. Birds differ in size — beware of seeing 'Little Curlews' on size alone. **Similar species:** Eurasian Curlew (race *orientalis*); American Whimbrel; Little Curlew. **Habitat:** estuaries, mangroves, tidal flats, coral cays, exposed reefs, flooded paddocks, sewage ponds, bare grasslands, sportsgrounds, lawns. **Range and Status:** widespread Eurasian wader; race *variegatus* breeds ne. Siberia, wintering from se. Asia to PNG, Aust. and NZ. Regular summer migrant (Aug.–April) to coastal Aust.; common in n. and e.; uncommon and local in se. and sw.; casual Bass Strait and Tas. Many overwinter, especially in n. Aust. Note: American Whimbrel, *N. hudsonicus*, regular summer visitor to NZ, probably rare vagrant to coastal e. Aust.

LITTLE CURLEW *Numenius minutus* 30–36 cm

Other name: Little Whimbrel.
Tiny curlew: *bill shortish, slightly downcurved, tip dark grey, base pink. Crown peaked at rear; dark brown, divided by fawn central stripe. Broad buffish eyebrow widens behind eye. Subtle dark eyeline runs back from bill, dividing buffish eyebrow from similarly coloured cheek.* Diamond-shaped brown centres to feathers with pale edges on back and wings; underparts fawn, lightly streaked brownish on foreneck and sides of breast; fawn–white flanks have sparse, shadowy barrings; underparts unmarked. At rest, wingtips equal tail-length. Small to huge flocks in grasslands of n. Aust., its world winter stronghold: wary, walks rapidly; squats, freezes or flushes with quick calls. Flight easy, buoyant: note *brown rump and longish, brown tail; whitish shafts on notably blackish outer primaries; holds wings up on landing.* Tame near settlement. **Similar species:** Eskimo Curlew *N. borealis.* (Not recorded in Aust.) **Voice:** rapid, hoarse 'tit-tit-tit-tit', less shrill than Whimbrel; 'tchew-tchew-tchew', harsher, lower pitched than Common Greenshank. **Habitat:** dry grasslands, floodplains, margins of drying swamps; tidal mudflats, airfields, playing fields, crops, commercial saltfields, sewage ponds. **Range and Status:** breeds Arctic Siberia: migrates from s. China to s. PNG and n. Aust. in Sept., returning by April. Very large numbers disperse over grasslands of n. WA, NT and nw. Q in wet season; singles or small parties casual to c., e. and se. Aust. in summer; vagrant Tas.

EASTERN CURLEW

EURASIAN CURLEW
(race *orientalis*)

N. American race
hudsonicus

WHIMBREL

imm.

LITTLE CURLEW

imm.

LESSER YELLOWLEGS *Tringa flavipes* 23–26 cm

Slim, elegant, yellow (or orange) legged wader, between Wood Sandpiper and Common Redshank in size. *Buff-spotted dark grey above, white below washed and finely streaked brownish on neck and breast. Bill slim, straight; roughly equals length of leg above knee.* Long-legged, high-stepping and graceful: digs and probes in shallows; walks, runs. Flight easy, wingbeats slow and elastic, but may zigzag and tumble. Note *unspotted trailing edge of wing; square white rump; tail whitish, barred brown.* **Similar species:** Wood Sandpiper: smaller, browner with longer white eyebrow; bill, neck and legs shorter. Stilt Sandpiper and Wilson's Phalarope: similar flight pattern but upperparts paler, plainer grey; tails unbarred. **Voice:** quiet 'tew' or 'tew tew', louder in alarm; like Common Greenshank but flatter, less penetrating. **Habitat:** shallow margins of muddy wetlands; marshy areas in paddocks or crops; ricefields, sewage ponds, saltmarshes, tidal mudflats. **Range and Status:** well-known N. American wader. Breeds e. Alaska to e. Canada: winters s. to Chile and Argentina (Aug.–May). Vagrant Japan, NZ, Aust. Sight-records of single birds from inland and coastal se. SA; s. Vic.; e. NSW and se. Q, Aug.–April.

COMMON REDSHANK *Tringa totanus* 27–29 cm

Like a small, brown-and-white Common Greenshank: *bill finer and straighter, orange–red at base, tip black; legs orange–red.* **Breeding plumage:** head and neck heavily streaked black, with *short whitish eyeline and eye-ring;* upperparts dark grey–brown; underparts white, heavily streaked and barred darker. **Nonbreeding:** eyeline plainer; upperparts grey–brown, mottled darker; underparts paler, more lightly streaked. **Immature:** feathers of upperparts notched buff; base of bill and legs more orange–yellow. Singles with other waders, or in small flocks in n. Aust. Perches on low objects; nervous — stretches neck, bobs head; noisy. Flight fast and direct, with clipped wingbeats, showing *contrasting pattern of blackish upperparts and pointed white rump, flanked by a broad white arc on the trailing edge of each wing.* Tail finely barred black and white; red feet extend beyond tail-tip. On alighting, holds wings briefly above back. **Similar species:** Spotted Redshank: bill finer, *slightly turned down at tip, red on lower base only;* in flight, no white arcs on wings; secondaries spotted white; legs longer. See Ruff. **Voice:** musical, down-slurred 'tleu-hu-hu'; alarm call a volley of strident, high-pitched repeated yelping 'teuk' or 'chip' notes. **Habitat:** tidal sandbars and mudflats; mangroves; freshwater swamps and lagoons; saltfields. **Range and Status:** breeds from British Isles to e. Asia: migrates to Africa, s. and se. Asia, Indonesian region. Uncommon but perhaps regular, mostly summer migrant to coastal n. Aust.; records Broome (WA), Darwin (NT), Cairns (Q); casual s. Aust. (se. SA; Boort, Vic.). Some overwinter.

SPOTTED REDSHANK *Tringa erythropus* 29–32 cm

Graceful, *very finely built,* long-legged wader. **Breeding plumage:** unique: sooty black with fine white margins and toothings to wing-feathers; white wedge up back; underwings white; tail barred white. Note the slender bill, *slightly drooped at tip and scarlet at lower base; legs dark red.* **Nonbreeding:** slender black bill, orange–red at lower base; orange–red legs; short white eyebrow over strong black mark from bill to eye; upperparts uniform grey with darker flight-feathers toothed white; underparts whitish grey. **Immature:** like nonbreeding; base of bill and legs paler orange–red; upperparts washed browner; face and underparts finely barred grey and white. Seen singly in Australia; in Eurasia often in dense packs, swimming and upending like Avocets. Shy: swims readily; feeds actively by picking, probing or sweeping bill from side to side. Flight fast, direct; *wingtips blackish, inner trailing edge spotted white; conspicuous white wedge extends high up back, dark-barred white rump and tail; orange–red legs extend far beyond tail-tip.* **Similar species:** Common Redshank: bill straight, not drooped; in flight, white arcs on each trailing edge. **Voice:** on being flushed, a loud 'chit, chit, chew-it, chew-it, chew-it, chew-it, chew-it'; also 'chew-it' and 'chit' calls uttered separately (Carter & Sudbury, 1993). **Habitat:** muddy margins of lakes, reservoirs; sewage ponds; shallow ephemeral freshwater swamps. **Range and Status:** breeds Arctic Eurasia: migrates to c. Africa, Persian Gulf, India, se. Asia, Borneo. Aust. sight-records: (mostly Oct.–April) Top End (NT); Port Hedland, and Eighty Mile Beach (WA); Hunter R. (NSW) and Seaford (Vic.). Vagrant.

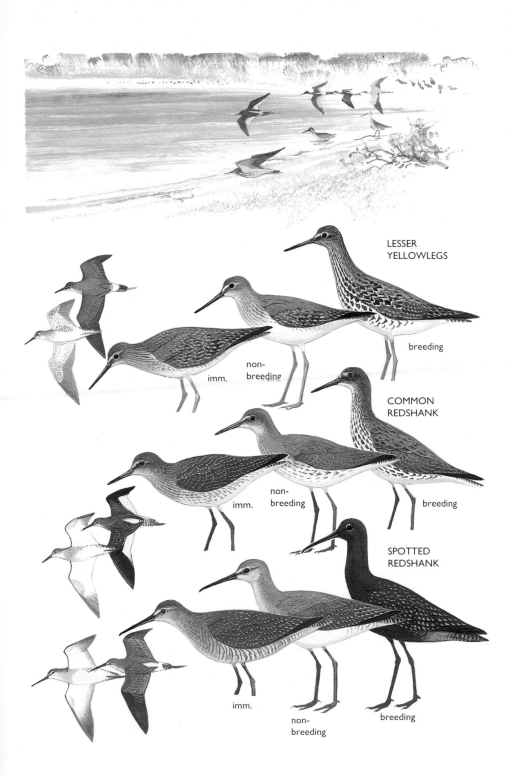

LESSER
YELLOWLEGS

breeding

non-
breeding

imm.

COMMON
REDSHANK

non-
breeding

imm.

breeding

SPOTTED
REDSHANK

imm.

non-
breeding

breeding

COMMON GREENSHANK *Tringa nebularia* 30–34 cm

Large, pale, nervous wader with *medium-long, slightly upturned bill, lead-grey at base, with black tip; grey–green legs*. **Nonbreeding:** very pale, with slight dark mark below and behind eye; wings and back pale grey–brown with fine white feather-margins and 'toothings'; *grey extends to sides of upperbreast*; lower breast and underparts white. **Breeding plumage:** head, neck and breast more heavily streaked grey–brown; upperparts with scattered, white-notched black feathers. **Immature:** like breeding, with buffish edges to feathers of upperparts. Singles, small parties, occasional flocks. Nervous: dashes about while feeding; bobs head, flushes with ringing alarm calls alerting other waders. Flight fast with clipped wingbeats: *white wedge up back, and white rump, contrast with dark wings, no wingbar; tail white, barred grey–brown; underwing wholly white*; toes protrude beyond tail. **Similar species:** Marsh Sandpiper: smaller; bill *straight, black, needle-like*; whiter on face, head and neck; slender yellow–green or grey–green legs protrude further in flight. See also Nordmann's Greenshank, Lesser Yellowlegs. **Voice:** strident, ringing 'tew-tew', or 'tew-tew-tew' with sobbing intonation, instantly alerting other waders; often at night. **Habitat:** mudflats, estuaries, saltmarshes, margins of lakes; wetlands, claypans, fresh and saline; commercial saltfields, sewage ponds. **Range and Status**: breeds from Scotland to s. and ne. Siberia: winters s. Europe, Africa, s. and se. Asia to PNG, Aust. and NZ. Regular, widespread summer migrant to Aust. and Tas. (Sept.–April). Mostly coastal, but inland in suitable habitat. Some overwinter.

NORDMANN'S GREENSHANK *Tringa guttifer* 29–33 cm

Other name: Spotted Greenshank.

Like Common Greenshank with *heavier bill, thicker at base; yellowish green on basal half, blackish towards tip; legs clear yellow to greenish or brownish yellow; noticeably shorter than Common Greenshank's*, partially webbed between toes. **Nonbreeding:** paler above than Common Greenshank; head and neck finely streaked grey; upperparts grey–brown with fine white feather-margins, contrasting with browner scapular area of wing. **Breeding plumage:** head and neck heavily streaked blackish brown with dark eyeline and partial white eyebrow before eye; upperparts brownish black with white edges and toothings to feathers; *sides of throat, breast and belly finely, then more heavily, spotted and scalloped blackish brown*. **Immature:** washed brownish, feathers of back spotted and fringed pale buff; sides of breast washed buffish. Stance horizontal; runs after prey with head lowered, bill level, like Terek Sandpiper; wades deep. Wary; flies strongly: *whitish rump extends up back in pointed wedge; white tail finely barred darker; white underwings contrast more with dark upperparts; feet barely extend beyond tail-tip*. **Similar species:** Common Greenshank. Great Knot (breeding) has rich chestnut markings on upperparts; heavier black markings on breast; bill slightly downcurved. **Voice:** a hoarse, piercing 'keyew', sometimes repeated. **Habitat:** tidal mudflats, sandspits, sewage ponds. **Range and Status**: breeds: Sakhalin I. and possibly e. Siberia: migrates to coasts from Assam and Bangladesh, Thailand, Hong Kong, China, Japan, Borneo, Philippines. Sight records: Top End (NT). Vagrant.

MARSH SANDPIPER *Tringa stagnatilis* 22–25 cm

Other name: Little Greenshank.

Like a small, finely built Common Greenshank with *straight needle-like black bill, and proportionately longer and more stilt-like yellow–green, grey–green or yellow legs*. **Breeding plumage:** feathers of upperparts have dark brown centres and buff–grey edges, notches and bars; flanks with fine dark V-bars. **Nonbreeding:** face and foreneck *whiter than Common Greenshank, with no dark eyeline*; feathers of upperparts finely margined paler; *black shoulders and flight-feathers contrast more with grey of wings than Common Greenshank*. Singles, parties, occasional flocks: active, wades deep; swims, head high, busily picking food off surface. Flight fast, *wingbeats clipped; note dark shoulder and wingtips; white rump extends up back in long wedge; white tail lightly barred; legs protrude further than Common Greenshank*. **Similar species:** Wilson's Phalarope, nonbreeding: grey 'phalarope-mark'; shorter yellow legs; in flight, white rump forms saddle between grey back and greyish tail. Wood Sandpiper: browner, with white eyebrow, white-spotted upperparts, yellow legs. **Voice:** sharp 'yip-chik'; musical 'chiff, chiff'; twittering trills; a soft 'teeoo'. **Habitat:** salt, brackish or freshwater wetlands; sewage ponds, commercial saltfields, bore-drains, mangroves, tidal mudflats, estuaries. **Range and Status**: breeds Austria to n. Mongolia: migrates to Africa, India, se. Asia, Indonesia; vagrant NZ. Regular summer migrant (Aug.–May), mostly to coastal Aust.; widespread but very scattered throughout inland. Fairly common in n.; mostly rather uncommon in s. and Tas.

non-
breeding

breeding

imm.

COMMON
GREENSHANK

imm.

breeding

NORDMANN'S
GREENSHANK

non-
breeding

imm.

breeding

MARSH
SANDPIPER

non-
breeding

WOOD SANDPIPER *Tringa glareola* 20–23 cm

Nervous, dainty wader found mostly in shallow fresh waters, often among dead timber. Note *longish straight black bill, dark line from bill to eye under long white eyebrow and whitish eye-ring; longish yellow–green legs.* **Nonbreeding:** grey–brown above with plentiful white spots and 'notching' on wing-feathers; whitish below, washed grey across breast. **Breeding plumage:** crown and upperparts rich grey–brown, heavily spotted white; throat white; foreneck and breast streaked grey–brown. **Immature:** upperparts warmer brown, spotted buff. Singles, pairs or parties, occasional flocks: bobs head, flicks tail; flushes with clear calls, flight fast and twisting with clipped wingbeats; typically zigzags high into sky: note *light grey underwing, white rump, barred at sides and across dark surface of tail; yellow feet extend beyond tail.* **Similar species:** Marsh Sandpiper: whiter, with longer legs and needle-like bill; lacks distinct eyebrow. Common Sandpiper: lacks white spots above; has white 'hook' around bend of wing. **Voice:** shrill, excited 'chiff-chiff-chiff', less strident than Common Greenshank; liquid 'tlui'. **Habitat:** muddy margins of wetlands; tidal mangroves; margins of tidal mudflats; saltmarshes, sewage ponds. **Range and Status**: breeds n. Eurasia to ne. Siberia: regular summer migrant to Aust. (Sept.–April). Moderately common n. Aust., uncommon regular migrant to s. Aust.; sparse through inland in suitable habitat. Vagrant Tas.

GREEN SANDPIPER *Tringa ochropus* 21–24 cm

Like a bulkier, more contrastingly marked Wood Sandpiper, *with longer dark bill, shorter white eyebrow and comparatively shorter, greenish legs.* **Breeding plumage:** *upperparts dark olive–brown to blackish green with sparse white spots; rump and tail pure white, end of tail with 3 or 4 dark brown bars.* Upperbreast and flanks heavily streaked dark brown, cut off sharply by white underparts. **Nonbreeding:** similar, upperbreast paler. **Immature:** spotted deep-buff above. Forages quietly in small freshwater wetlands and ditches; teeters, stance 'hunched, horizontal'; disturbs easily, zigzags skywards in snipe-like escape flight with 'jerky deep wingbeats' (Hayman et al, 1986). Note *broad, blackish brown wings above and below, contrasting with square-cut white rump and broadly barred end of tail.* Unlike Wood Sandpiper feet barely protrude beyond tail-tip in flight. **Voice:** a high-pitched, ringing 'tlueet, weet-weet'. **Range and Status:** breeds Scandinavia to e. Siberia: migrates to c. Africa, India, se. Asia, Borneo, Philippines, occasionally PNG. Vagrant, (unconfirmed) NT.

COMMON SANDPIPER *Actitis hypoleucos* 19–22 cm

Dainty sandpiper of *horizontal stance and constant nervous teetering.* Bill fine, brown with buff base; *eyebrow and eye-ring whitish, with slight dark eyeline;* legs grey–green tinged yellow. Bronze–brown to grey–brown above, very finely barred darker; white below *with distinct white 'hook' around bend of closed wing;* sides of upperbreast washed brown. **Immature:** finely barred buff and black above. Solitary birds to occasional small parties: feeds in ooze and margins of shallow water; perches rocks, branches, boats, jetties, piles. Flight distinctive: quick and fluttering, with clipped, shallow wingbeats, broken by glides on downcurved wings; note *broad white wingbar and white sides of brown rump and tail.* **Similar species**: Wood Sandpiper: greyer, spotted white above; white rump; no white 'hook'; no wingbar. **Voice:** plaintive, piping 'twee-wee-wee', like Varied Sittella or Welcome Swallow; a single, rising 'weeep'. **Habitat:** shallow, pebbly, muddy or sandy edges of rivers and streams, coastal to far inland; dams, lakes, sewage ponds; margins of tidal rivers; waterways in mangroves or saltmarsh; mudflats; rocky or sandy beaches; causeways, riverside lawns, drains, street gutters. **Range and Status**: breeds from British Isles to e. Siberia and n. Japan: winters s. Europe, Africa, India, s. and se. Asia to Indonesia, PNG; vagrant NZ. Regular, widespread but mostly uncommon summer migrant to Aust. (Aug.–May), more common in n. and e. Aust. and on w. coast than in se. and Tas. Some overwinter.

imm.

breeding

WOOD SANDPIPER

non-breeding

non-breeding

imm.

GREEN
SANDPIPER

imm.

non-breeding

breeding

COMMON SANDPIPER

GREY-TAILED TATTLER *Heteroscelus brevipes* 24–27 cm

Nonbreeding: elegant, evenly grey-shaded wader, mid-grey above, whitish below; *washed grey across breast.* Bill straight, grey, yellowish at base, with a short nasal groove; dark line extends from bill through eye under longish white eyebrows that nearly meet across pale forehead; shortish legs dull grey–yellow or orange–yellow. **Breeding plumage:** underparts white; *breast and flanks finely barred dark grey; belly and central under tail-coverts remain unbarred.* **Immature:** feathers of upperparts finely notched white. Singles, or with other waders; small to occasionally large companies at roosts. Nervous: bobs head, wags rear of body up and down. Note that wingtips just equal length of tail-tip (Bunkport, 1995). Perches snags, rocks, oyster-frames; flies, calling, low across water with clipped wingbeats; alighting, raises wings, showing *grey underwings.* **Similar species:** see Wandering Tattler. Wood Sandpiper: freckled white above; white rump and finely barred white tail; whitish underwing. **Voice:** drawn-out, liquid 'tlooeep' or 'weet-eet', more scratchy 'peet, peeppeeppeep' or strident 'klee klee, klee klee, tooee, tooee'. **Habitat:** estuaries, tidal mudflats, mangroves; wave-washed rocks and reefs; shallow river-margins, coastal or inland. **Range and Status:** breeds c. and e. Siberia; regular summer migrant (Sept.–April) to coastal n. Aust. from about Shark Bay (WA) to about Sydney (NSW); less common on s. coasts, but regular Corner Inlet and Westernport (Vic.). Casual inland, e.g. Finke R. (NT); uncommon Tas. Some overwinter, mostly in n. Also Solomons to Fiji; NZ.

WANDERING TATTLER *Heteroscelus incanus* 26–29 cm

Uncommon summer migrant to Aust.: usually solitary, or with Grey-tailed Tattlers. Wary and alert: in nonbreeding plumage, can (with care) be distinguished from Grey-tailed Tattler by: (1) *darker grey upperparts*; (2) *heavier bill*, with longer nasal groove than Grey-tailed; (3) *shorter white eyebrows that do not meet on forehead and rarely extend beyond eye*; (4) at rest and when feeding, *wingtips usually extend beyond tail-tip* (Bunkport, 1995); (5) differing call. Tends to fly with clipped beats of down-arched wings. **Breeding plumage:** darker above than Grey-Tailed Tattler; *underparts, incl. flanks and under tail-coverts, more heavily barred dark grey* (except centre of belly); traces of barring may persist in nonbreeding plumage. **Voice:** rippling, whimbrel-like trill of 6–10 accelerating, descending notes of decreasing volume; usually uttered in flight. **Habitat:** quite specific: prefers coral islands and cays of Gt Barrier Reef; rocky reefs, islands and wave-washed rocks and rock-platforms; occasionally to other tidal areas. **Range and Status:** breeds ne. Siberia, Alaska and n. Canada: migrates to e. Asia, C. and S. America and widely to islands in c. and sw. Pacific, s. to NZ. Uncommon but probably regular summer migrant (Sept.–March) to region of Gt Barrier Reef, Lord Howe I. and Norfolk I. and coasts of n. and e. Aust. from about Darwin (NT) to n. NSW; casual s. to Moruya district (s. NSW).

TEREK SANDPIPER *Xenus cinereus* 21–25 cm

Distinctive wader with *longish, slightly upcurved black bill*, dull orange–yellow at base, and *short orange–yellow legs.* **Breeding plumage:** grey–brown above; *shoulder darker, with two black lines along back*; grey–brown on sides of breast; underparts white. **Nonbreeding:** plainer pale-grey above, shoulder darker; white bar often visible on secondaries; white below, faintly streaked on breast. Singles, small parties, with other waders or in high-tide roosts of hundreds, sometimes in mangroves. Can look squat and hunched, but when alert stands upright, revealing longish neck. *Active: jerks tail, bobs head, dashes about after small crabs, etc. in crouched posture, bill lowered, tail raised*; probes rapidly with bill. Flight strong and direct: note *grey rump and tail, broad white trailing edge of wings near body contrasting with dark wingtips.* **Voice:** pleasant musical trill, 'teerrr-da-weet, teerrr-da-weet-a-weet'; rapid high-pitched 'tee-tee-tee'; fluty 'du-du-du-du-du!' **Habitat:** tidal mudflats, estuaries; shores and reefs of islands; coastal swamps, commercial saltfields. **Range and Status:** breeds from Finland to ne. Siberia: migrates to Africa, India, se. Asia, Borneo to PNG, Aust. and NZ. Regular summer migrant to coastal Aust. (Aug.–April); fairly common from n. WA to Hunter R. (NSW); mostly scarce and/or local elsewhere; vagrant Tas. Some overwinter.

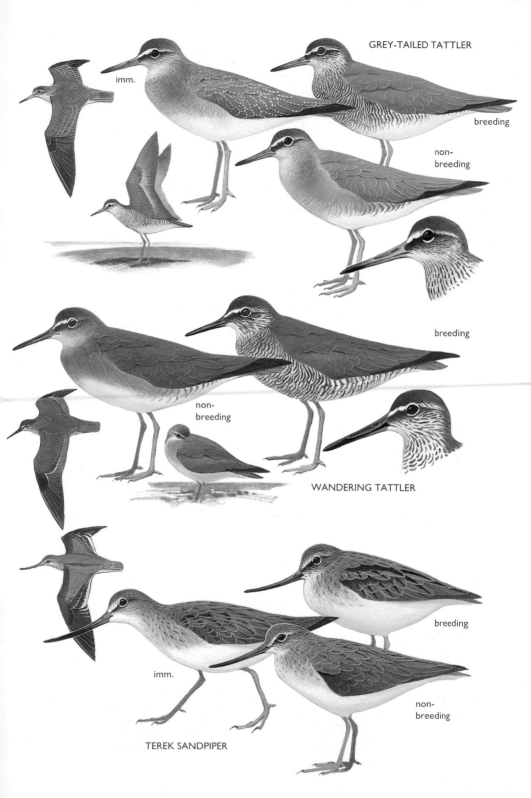

GREY-TAILED TATTLER

imm.

breeding

non-
breeding

WANDERING TATTLER

non-
breeding

breeding

TEREK SANDPIPER

imm.

breeding

non-
breeding

ASIAN DOWITCHER *Limnodromus semipalmatus* 33–36 cm. Female larger, bill longer.

Other name: Asiatic Dowitcher.
Like small Bar-tailed Godwit, with *long, straight, black bill, brown at base, blunt and swollen at tip*; shorter black legs. **Nonbreeding:** *grey above, feathers of back and wings heavily marked black, with pale margins*; white below, flanks *lightly barred black*. In flight, look for a *pale grey wedge up back, and a broad pale grey panel along inner hindwing. Rump and tail white, barred blackish, heaviest on tail. In contrast to other dowitchers the underwing is mostly white*, and feet protrude beyond tail in flight. **Breeding plumage:** *head/body reddish chestnut; upperparts black, chestnut and buff; flanks barred black; belly and under tail-coverts white.* **Immature:** like nonbreeding, but warmer toned, with buff margins to feathers of upperparts; buff wash on neck and breast. Singles, with godwits, or open flocks. Actions stiffer than godwit: carries bill sloping downwards; ramming it to the hilt in mud, with rapid action; neck rigid, whole body tilting (King et al, 1980). **Similar species:** Bar-tailed Godwit; Long-billed Dowitcher. **Voice:** quiet: a plaintive, yelping 'yow'. **Habitat:** tidal mudflats, beaches, commercial saltfields, sewage ponds. **Range and Status:** breeds c. and e. Siberia, Mongolia, ne. China: winters from Persian Gulf to coastal mudflats of Indonesia. Scarce but regular summer migrant to coastal n. Aust. (Sept.–April); most abundant from Top End (NT) to Port Hedland (WA). Casual elsewhere: Cairns (ne. Q), Moreton Bay (s. Q), s. Vic.; some overwinter. Vagrant PNG.

LONG-BILLED DOWITCHER *Limnodromus scolopaceus* 26–30 cm. Female larger, bill longer.

Slightly larger than a Grey-tailed Tattler: despite name, *a smaller, shorter billed wader* than Asian Dowitcher. Bill slightly downturned at tip; dark grey, some olive–yellow at base; legs *greenish yellow*. **Nonbreeding:** cap dark grey; white eyebrow wider before eye than behind; dark eyeline; upperparts dark grey–brown, with fine pale margins to wing-feathers. *Dingy grey–brown wash across upper breast contrasts with white underparts*; sparse dark V-bars on flanks; *under tail-coverts finely barred blackish*. In flight, note *conspicuous white wedge up back; white rump and tail finely barred blackish; shortish white wingbar on innerwing, paralleled by a longer white trailing edge. Underwing white, finely barred blackish (looks grey in flight); only toes project beyond tail-tip.* **Breeding plumage:** head and *all* underparts dull rusty, *with prominent paler eyebrow*. Cap chestnut, finely streaked black; upperparts black with chestnut, buff and white fringes; black neck-streaks become fine bars on breast; coarser V-bars on flanks and under tail-coverts. **Immature:** feathers of upperparts fringed chestnut with white toothings; breast washed buff with darker streaking, sparse brown V-bars on flanks. **Similar species:** Asian Dowitcher. Short-billed Dowitcher, *L.griseus*, American species nearly identical to Long-billed, can be separated by distinctive call: a rapid, whistled 'chu chu chu', 'which may suggest the mutter of Turnstone' (Cramp, 1983). Not yet recorded in Aust. **Voice:** differs from Asian: a sharp, thin 'keek', 'keek-keek-keek' or throaty 'keekery'. **Habitat:** shallow, muddy freshwater pools, with grass or marginal vegetation (Cramp, 1983); tidal estuaries. **Range and Status:** breeds ne. Siberia, n. Alaska and nw. Canada: migrates to s. N. and C. America. Vagrant se. Asia, Indonesia, Aust. First confirmed Aust. record: a bird in nonbreeding plumage, captured Corner Inlet (Vic.) 18 June 1995 (Campbell & Minton, 1995).

RUDDY TURNSTONE *Arenaria interpres* 21–25 cm

Tubby, distinctive wader with slightly upturned, *short black bill and short orange legs*. **Breeding plumage:** *unmistakable — black, white and orange tortoise-shell pattern*; male brighter than female. **Nonbreeding:** grey–brown above, white below with *smutty black 'cloverleaf' bib on upperbreast; legs orange*; often has traces of orange in upperparts. **Immature:** like nonbreeding adult, but more dusky, with scaly pattern of pale feather-margins. Solitary, small parties or with other waders; abundant in Gt Barrier Reef (Q) and Roebuck Bay (WA), where winter flocks of 20–200+ gather. Potters slowly, or bustles, flipping shells and bulldozing heaps of seaweed with bill. Sturdy on wing, with frequent noisy aerial chases, showing *conspicuous white wing-panel, white lower back and tail crossed by two black bars*. **Voice:** guttural, rattling 'kititit'; ringing 'kee-oo'. **Habitat:** tidal reefs and pools; weed-covered rocks; pebbly, shelly and sandy shores with stranded seaweed; mudflats; occasionally inland on shallow waters, sewage ponds, commercial saltfields, open or ploughed ground. **Range and Status**: breeds high Arctic: migrates to all s. continents. Regular summer migrant (Aug.–April) to coastal Aust.; some inland. May overwinter, some in breeding plumage. Also Lord Howe, Norfolk, Christmas and other islands; NZ. Vagrant Macquarie I.

imm.

breeding

ASIAN
DOWITCHER

non-
breeding

imm.

breeding

LONG-BILLED
DOWITCHER

non-
breeding

imm.

breeding

non-
breeding

RUDDY TURNSTONE

RED KNOT *Calidris canutus* 23–26 cm

Note: bird is 'red' (chestnut) only in breeding plumage. **Nonbreeding:** *low-slung, full-bellied grey wader with straight, slightly tapering black bill roughly equal to length of head; legs short, dull green.* Note *pale area around bill and slight pale eyebrow; darkish mark back from bill through eye widens on ear-coverts; fine pale feather-edges on upperparts,* and *slight* dark streaks and bars on breast and flanks. Parties with other waders, or dense flocks; feeds steadily with rapid downthrusts, head often submerged. Massed packs perform swift aerobatics: note *thin white wingbar and finely dark-barred white rump, which* looks grey; tail grey. **Breeding plumage:** *face and body rust–red to chestnut; upperparts beautifully spangled black, buff and silver; female duller.* **Immature:** buffer than nonbreeding with *stronger scaly pattern* above. **Similar species:** see Great Knot. Sanderling: smaller, whiter with blackish shoulder; *runs more on black legs;* larger white wingbar; dark centre to white rump. **Voice:** throaty 'knut-knut'; mellow whistling 'tooit-wit'. **Habitat:** tidal mudflats, sandflats, beaches, saltmarshes, flooded pastures, ploughed lands. **Range and Status:** breeds around Arctic Circle. Birds from n.–c. and ne. Siberia and n. Alaska are regular, widespread, mostly coastal, summer migrants to Aust. and Tas. (Aug.–April). Abundant in n., fewer in s. and inland; some overwinter. Also NZ; Macquarie I.

GREAT KNOT *Calidris tenuirostris* 26–28 cm

Other names: Slender-billed or Stripe-crowned Knot.
Larger and smaller-headed than Red Knot, with longish, heavy-based, slightly decurved black bill, longer than head. **Nonbreeding:** *grey–brown above, more heavily and patchily streaked and mottled than Red Knot; white below, with scattered spots and streaks.* **Breeding plumage:** distinctive; *upperparts chestnut, buff, brown and grey; large black spots on chest* sometimes form black band. **Immature:** *upperparts dark brown with buff feather-margins; breast and flanks buffish, with dark brown spots.* Parties, compact flocks; often with other waders. Feeds slowly, deeply probing mud or sand. Flight strong and direct: note *faint white wingbar, blackish carpel area of upperwing; whitish rump with darker mottlings;* tail grey–brown. **Similar species:** Red Knot: bill shorter, more distinct dark eyeline, white eyebrow. Asian Dowitcher: much longer, heavier bill. **Voice:** usually silent, but said to utter a double whistle; other calls resemble Red Knot's. **Habitat:** tidal mudflats; sandy ocean and bay shores; estuaries; shallow saline and freshwater wetlands. **Range and Status:** breeds ne. Siberia: migrates to India, s. and se. Asia, Indonesia, PNG, and NZ (where rare). Regular summer migrant (Sept.–March) to coastal Aust. and Tas. (straggler); inland in nw. Q, nw. Vic. Common Top End (NT) to coastal nw. WA; where flocks of 20 000 gather at some high-tide roosts. Some overwinter, especially in n. Aust.

SANDERLING *Calidris alba* 19–21 cm

Nonbreeding: *whitest sandpiper: pale grey above with fine black streaks; face and underparts white. Bill and legs black (no hind-toe); shoulder-patch and primaries black.* **Breeding plumage:** *pale around base of bill; head, neck and upperbreast pale rusty buff to deep rosy chestnut, cut off sharply by white underparts;* head streaked dark brown; dark spots on breast; upperparts *with bold black feather-centres, fringed and tipped buff or white.* Moulting birds often patchy. **Immature:** more heavily marked: streaked black on crown and nape; sides of breast washed buff; upperparts *have angular black feather-centres with white, grey or buff margins.* Small to large flocks favour particular ocean beaches: plump, low-slung and active, potters round beach-debris, *chases retreating waves,* 'ploughs' or jabs bill repeatedly into sand; often with stints, Hooded Plover, etc. Flight rushing, direct: in all plumages *shows largest white wingbar of any sandpiper, contrasting with black wing-coverts and flight-feathers in flickering effect; rump white with blackish centre;* tail grey with dark, pointed central feathers. **Similar species:** Red-necked Stint: much smaller, but easily confused: in nonbreeding plumage is less contrasting grey, black and white, with finer white wingbar and less positive black shoulder. Hooded Plover, imm.; Grey Phalarope, nonbreeding. **Voice:** liquid 'twik-twik'; soft, querulous 'ket ket ket'. **Habitat:** broad ocean beaches of firm sand 'where waves ebb and flow', depositing strands and heaps of seaweed; often near river mouths; also inlets, tidal mudflats, coastal lagoons. **Range and Status:** breeds around Arctic from Spitsbergen e. to Iceland: migrates to coasts of s. continents. Regular summer migrant (Sept.–May) to coastal Aust. and Tas. Patchy, regular on certain beaches; occasional inland. Some overwinter; may assume breeding plumage.

imm.

breeding

nonbreeding

RED KNOT

imm.

breeding

nonbreeding

GREAT KNOT

nonbreeding

SANDERLING

breeding

imm.

moulting
adult

RED-NECKED STINT *Calidris ruficollis* 13–16 cm

Nonbreeding: *tiny plain grey–brown and whitish wader with black legs and straight, gently tapering black bill, slightly swollen at tip.* Shadowy dark line from bill through eye separates small white area over bill and subtle whitish eyebrow from whitish throat. Upperparts grey–brown with fine dark shaft-streaks; underparts whitish *with grey–brown zone on sides of upperbreast.* **Breeding plumage:** *face, throat, neck and upperbreast plain, unmarked salmon-pink to pinkish chestnut, leaving small pale area round base of bill.* (Moulting birds may have dark mottlings across breast.) Feathers of back and mantle *grey with black centres at first* ('pre-breeding'), *then acquire bright chestnut and white fringes; but wing-coverts and tertiaries mostly remain grey–brown.* **Immature:** like nonbreeding, but brighter, *with warm buff feather-margins, especially on mantle, upper wing-coverts and tertials.* Less richly patterned than imm. Little Stint, and without such bold white Vs on back. Parties or large, dense flocks wheel, plunge and run about, feeding with sewing machine action. In flight, *strong white wingbar diffuses on blackish primaries*, sides of rump white, rump and centre of tail black *and pointed.* **Similar species:** Little Stint; Sanderling. Western Sandpiper: bill longer, downcurved; crown, ear-coverts and edges of mantle pale chestnut. Long-toed Stint: browner, with brown breastband; legs greenish yellow. **Voice:** a weak 'chit, chit' or quick, high-pitched trill. **Habitat:** tidal mudflats, saltmarshes; sandy or shelly beaches; saline and freshwater wetlands, coastal and inland; saltfields, sewage ponds. **Range and Status:** breeds Arctic Siberia and n. Alaska: migrates to Indonesia, PNG, NZ and sub-Antarctic islands. Abundant summer migrant (Aug.–April) to coastal and inland Aust. and Tas.; most in nw. and se. Many overwinter.

LITTLE STINT *Calidris minuta* 12–14 cm

Nonbreeding: very like Red-necked Stint, but note: (1) slightly thinner and more tapering black bill; (2) black legs are often longer; (3) crown higher and rounder; (4) neck fractionally slimmer and longer; (5) upperparts browner, with more dark speckling on head and more obvious buff–grey zone on sides of upperbreast, *leaving white throat;* (6) broader dark feather-centres; *wing-feathers (incl. tertials) often retain orange–chestnut fringes;* (7) wings and tail shorter than Red-necked, held higher when standing and feeding; (8) in flight, white wingbar does not diffuse onto primaries. **Breeding plumage:** orange–chestnut wash on head, neck and across white breast; *throat white. Feathers of wings and back have bold blackish centres, edged bright chestnut, with cream V on edges of back.* **Immature:** crown rufous, with white eyebrow and snipe-like sub-streaks; black feathers of upperparts (*incl. wings*) edged bright rufous and white; white V on edges of back; pale orange wash across chest; throat and underparts white. Singles, often with Red-necked Stint: feeds mouse-like; stands tiptoe to peer; runs, probes; often wades, swims. **Voice:** repeated 'chit' or 'tit', quiet, high-pitched 'tsee-tee'. **Habitat:** tidal mudflats, saltmarshes, saltfields; muddy margins of freshwater and saline wetlands; sewage ponds. **Range and Status:** breeds Arctic Eurasia: winters Europe, s. Asia; vagrant Japan, Brunei, PNG. Summer vagrant (Sept.–March) to Aust., mostly in 'reverse' breeding plumage; records NT, SA, Vic., and NSW, coastal and inland.

nonbreeding

pre-breeding

breeding

imm.

imm.

RED-NECKED STINT

nonbreeding

imm.

imm.

LITTLE STINT

breeding

183

LONG-TOED STINT *Calidris subminuta* 13–15 cm

Like a tiny, neat, long-necked Sharp-tailed Sandpiper, *with slender, long greenish yellow (olive, or grey) legs, and long central toe.* Short, blackish bill may have *yellow, brown or greyish base.* **Nonbreeding:** long white eyebrow, *dusky mouse-brown above from crown back; blackish feather-centres margined buff–grey; white below, streaked grey–brown across upperbreast.* **Breeding plumage:** cap chestnut; *some with split white eyebrow; upperparts, incl. tertials, black with buff/chestnut/white margins;* breast creamish, sharply streaked brown to flanks; underparts whitish. **Immature:** brighter, buffer; longer white eyebrow; feathers of upperparts fringed orange–rufous; white edges to scapulars may form a distinctive V on back, like Little Stint. Mostly singles with other waders, but in WA flocks to 100+. Unobtrusive: feeds slowly, stance horizontal; creeps with 'knees' bent, or quick mouse-like runs; picks food from surface; sometimes probes. Stands tiptoe, cranes neck, freezes or hides in vegetation. Flight snipe-like, zigzagging, towering: note dark wings, thin white wingbar, *white-edged black rump; yellow toes extend beyond dark grey tail.* **Similar species:** Least Sandpiper, *C. minutilla* (not yet recorded in Aust.): more compact, wingbar stronger; legs/toes shorter; call differs: thin 'kree-eet'. Temminck's Stint: greyer, *outer tail-feathers white;* yellow legs shorter; voice differs. **Voice:** trilling 'chee', 'crreeet' or 'chrreee-chrreee'; also a chirrup, like House Sparrow. **Habitat:** tussocky, weedy margins of shallow wetlands, coastal and inland; sewage ponds, weed on tidelines, tidal mudflats. **Range and Status:** breeds Siberia to far N. Pacific: migrates to s. and se. Asia; PNG. Regular, uncommon summer migrant to inland and coastal Aust. (Aug.–April); most abundant in WA. Vagrant Tas. Some overwinter.

TEMMINCK'S STINT *Calidris temminckii* 13–15 cm

White edges to longish tail, conspicuous in flight, separate it from other stints. The only other stint with yellow (or grey–green or green) legs is Long-toed Stint. **Nonbreeding:** dark mottled grey–brown above; *throat whitish with grey–brown breastband, cut off by white underparts.* Bill slender, tapering, slightly drooped, *often yellowish, grey–green or pale brown at lower base, tipped darker;* legs yellow to grey–green or green. **Breeding plumage:** crown buff–brown, streaked darker; feathers of upperparts *with angular black centres broadly edged buff;* include scattered grey feathers. *Sides of neck and breast washed buff–brown, streaked darker.* **Immature:** like nonbreeding; upperparts have *fine buff or rusty feather-edges.* Solitary in Aust., mostly on freshwater: forages deliberately, stooped, horizontal, slender, longish; on approach crouches, or flies high, fast and twisting, with clipped wingbeats: note *distinct white wingbar and prominent white edges to rump and white outer tail-feathers,* like a small greyish Common Sandpiper. **Similar species:** Long-toed Stint: plumages brighter; white lines on back. **Voice:** a short, hard, trilled 'tirr', or longer 'trrrit'. **Habitat:** muddy, sparsely vegetated margins of mostly freshwater wetlands. **Range and Status:** breeds from n. Scotland and n. Scandinavia across Arctic Eurasia to ne. Siberia: winters e. Mediterranean, Egypt, tropical Africa, India, se. Asia to Borneo, where uncommon but regular winter visitor. Possible summer vagrant to Aust.

imm.

imm.

non-
breeding

breeding

LONG TOED STINT

imm.

imm.

breeding

non-
breeding

TEMMINCK'S STINT

185

WESTERN SANDPIPER *Calidris mauri* 14–17 cm

Nonbreeding: somewhat like a Red-necked Stint, but *bill longer than head, broad at base, finer and usually slightly drooped at tip*. This feature and its chesty shape recall a small Dunlin. Sides of face pale; dark eye accentuated by shadowy darkish area from bill around eye; legs black, longish; *feet part-webbed — an important field mark*. Upperparts clear grey, with fine dark streaks and pale feather-margins; underparts white *with breastband of fine dark streaks*. **Breeding plumage:** *distinctive pale rusty crown and ear-coverts; scapulars rich rusty, spotted black, forming V on back*. **Immature:** *very bright; sides of breast washed buff streaked darker; mantle blackish, with rusty edges; rusty inner scapulars contrast with grey outer scapulars; tertials edged rusty*. Solitary, or with other small waders (dense flocks in N. America). Tame: wades deep, immerses bill. In flight, note rusty V on back; thin white wingbar; white sides to dark rump; tail blackish. **Similar species:** Red-necked Stint, nonbreeding: bill shorter, straighter; grey wash on sides of breast. **Voice:** described as a shrill, short, penetrating 'krreep', 'cheet', or a high, raspy 'jeet'. **Habitat:** tidal mudflats, shallow wetlands. **Range and Status:** breeds ne. Siberia and Alaska: migrates to s. N. America, Gulf coasts and S. America. Vagrant Europe, Japan. Several unconfirmed se. Aust. sight-records: a wader photographed near Byron Bay (NSW) 9–10 Nov. 1995 was possibly of this species.

WHITE-RUMPED SANDPIPER *Calidris fuscicollis* 17–19 cm

The only stint-sized sandpiper with a white rump. Bill longer than Red-necked Stint; black, with yellow–brown base, fine and slightly decurved. **Nonbreeding:** longish white eyebrow; crown and upperparts uniform darkish grey–brown; chin and underparts white, *with a zone of dark streaks across chest. Standing and feeding, note the dark, pointed and very long wingtips, extending beyond tail-tip; with the short black legs, they give the bird a graceful, drawn-out, horizontal look*. Flight twisting; note *thin, short, white wingbar and narrow white band across grey–brown upper tail-coverts, contrasting with dark-centred grey–brown tail; feet barely protrude*. **Breeding plumage:** washed rufous on crown, ear-coverts and back; underparts streaked, with arrowheads on flanks. **Immature:** *brighter, white eyebrow contrasts with chestnut wash on crown, ear-coverts and back; white lines edge mantle and scapulars*. Associates with other waders, but feeds apart; wades in shallows; picks, probes; *long wingtips describe arcs as it feeds*. **Similar species:** Curlew Sandpiper: larger, bolder white wingbar, larger, higher white rump. Baird's Sandpiper: similarly long-winged, but more buffish and mottled; lacks white rump. **Voice:** mouse-like squeak, 'jeet'. **Habitat:** shallow, muddy parts of freshwater and tidal wetlands. **Range and Status:** breeds Arctic Alaska and Canada: migrates to s. S. America. Vagrant Europe and elsewhere; summer records se. and sw. Aust.; also NZ. Vagrant.

BAIRD'S SANDPIPER *Calidris bairdii* 14–17 cm

Like a *slender, long-winged, 'scaly' buff–brown, broad-chested stint with short blackish legs. Bill black, slender, slightly decurved; some are greenish yellow at base*. **Nonbreeding:** head and neck grey–buff, streaked darker; long buff–white eyebrow; throat white; *upperparts have scaly pattern of fawn or buff–grey fringes to dark-brown feathers; wingtips dark, longer than tail. Breast grey–buff, streaked darker, cut off by white underparts, with white centre*. **Breeding plumage:** *upperparts more strongly patterned by shield-shaped black feather-centres with buff and white fringes; breast buffish with blackish spots, and finely streaked brown*. **Immature:** head and breast washed buff; upperparts have finer scaly pattern of dark brown feather-centres neatly margined buff-white. Quiet and likely to be solitary, with other waders: picks, probes to depth of bill; wades; carriage horizontal; *long dark wingtips describe arcs as bird feeds*. Approached, raises head high; in flight, looks brown, spindle-shaped, with long dark wings (Curry, 1979); note *faint white wingbar, black rump with white edges; grey–brown tail*. **Similar species:** White-rumped Sandpiper: bill heavier, longer; plumage less buff; rump white. See also Sanderling. **Voice:** shrill repeated 'kreep'. **Habitat:** tidal mudflats, beaches with seaweed; edges of shallow wetlands, fresh and saline. **Range and Status:** breeds far ne. Siberia, Arctic N. America e. to Greenland; winters S. America and around Pacific; vagrant NZ. Sight-records most Aust. States, coastal and sub-inland: sw. NSW; e. Tas.; w. Vic.; se. SA; s. WA; Top End (NT).

imm.

breeding

non-
breeding

WESTERN SANDPIPER

WHITE-RUMPED SANDPIPER

imm.

non-
breeding

breeding

non-
breeding

BAIRD'S SANDPIPER

imm.

SHARP-TAILED SANDPIPER *Calidris acuminata* 17–21 cm. Males larger, some notably.

Nonbreeding: bill straight or *slightly* decurved; pale grey–brown, *seldom longer than head.* Legs dull olive–yellow, yellow or olive–grey; crown dull chestnut; dark eyeline back from bill widens and becomes browner on ear-coverts, *accentuating widening pale rear eyebrow; long feathers of upperparts have pointed dark centres, pale brown margins.* Underparts whitish buff, sparsely streaked brown. **Breeding plumage:** *long dark feathers of upperparts have rufous and buff–white edges;* neck and upperbreast *buffish, heavily streaked brown, but not cut off like Pectoral; scattered dark 'boomerangs' on lower breast and on flanks.* **Immature:** bright rufous cap isolated by large whitish rear-eyebrow; feathers of upperparts margined chestnut, buff–yellow and white; neck and breast washed orange–buff, with fine dark streaks. In flight, slight whitish wingbar; rump dark brown with white sides; tail wedge-shaped, dark brown in middle, brownish at sides; *toes protrude slightly beyond tail-tip in flight.* Small parties, flocks of hundreds with other waders. Much variation in size. **Similar species:** Pectoral Sandpiper; Ruff. **Voice:** on taking flight, a dry 'trit-trit'; musical twitter, 'trrt wheeteet'. **Habitat:** tidal mudflats, saltmarshes, mangroves; shallow fresh, brackish or saline inland wetlands; floodwaters, irrigated pastures and crops; sewage ponds, saltfields. **Range and Status:** breeds Arctic Siberia: migrates to s. and se. Asia, PNG; sw. Pacific islands, NZ and sub-Antarctic islands, incl. Macquarie I. Widespread summer migrant to coastal and inland Aust. and Tas. (Aug.–April); a few overwinter. In coastal n. Aust., mostly a passage migrant.

PECTORAL SANDPIPER *Calidris melanotos* 19–23 cm. Males larger, some notably.

Larger relative of Sharp-tail: looks 'different': plainer, browner, longer-necked, rounder-crowned. *Bill slightly longer than head,* heavier and olive–yellow at base, slightly decurved, tipped dusky; legs pale to deep yellow, usually brighter than Sharp-tail's. *Heavy brown or blackish streaking or mottling on neck and breast cut off sharply by whitish underparts.* Solitary, or with Sharp-tails and easily overlooked; occasionally in small flocks. Shy: cranes upright, or freezes flat. In flight, zigzags like snipe, uttering distinctive calls: note indistinct white wingbar, *large, oval white patches on edge of rump,* dark centre to rump and tail; *toes do not protrude beyond tail-tip in flight.* **Similar species:** Ruff, nonbreeding: taller, smaller headed, plainer-faced, with 'Oriental' look; lacks cut off zone across breast. See also Baird's Sandpiper. **Voice:** a deep, reedy, musical 'chirp' or 'chirrup', like Budgerigar; harsher and different from Sharp-tail. **Habitat:** *prefers shallow fresh waters,* often with low grass or other herbage; swamp margins, flooded pastures, sewage ponds; occasionally tidal areas, saltmarshes. **Range and Status:** breeds ne. Siberia and American Arctic: most migrate to S. America, but some to Japan, Pacific islands, PNG, NZ and Aust. Regular, uncommon summer migrant to Aust. and Tas. (Aug.–May); mostly se. Aust., Murray–Darling Basin and w. Vic.; coastal and inland.

COX'S SANDPIPER *Calidris paramelanotos* c. 19 cm

Recently described from coastal se. Aust.: a natural hybrid between Curlew Sandpiper and Pectoral Sandpiper. Resembles *a pale, short-necked Sharp-tailed Sandpiper with bill like a Curlew Sandpiper,* but straighter; some have yellowish base. Legs yellow–green, brownish green or dark olive–green. **Nonbreeding:** head and neck pale grey–brown, finely streaked darker; *pale eyebrow from bill over eye more distinct than Sharp-tail's but much less obvious than Curlew Sandpiper's; ear-coverts tinged rusty.* Feathers of upperparts grey–brown, fringed grey; underparts white, *breast streaked grey–brown (not sharply cut off as Pectoral).* When moulting into breeding plumage ('pre-breeding'), *ear-coverts and neck are washed rufous; feathers of upperparts black, fringed buff and pale chestnut, tipped grey; breast washed rufous; head, breast and flanks streaked darker; underparts white.* **Immature:** like nonbreeding, with scaly pattern from fine pale feather-margins on upperparts. In flight, smaller white wingbar than Curlew Sandpiper; *sides of rump extensively white, may converge like those of Ruff;* centre of rump and tail dark; tail grey, with pointed black central feathers; toes extend to tail-tip. Mixes with other waders: probes rapidly; seldom runs. When standing upright, neck shorter than Sharp-tailed or Pectoral, *but wingtips extend beyond tail.* **Similar species:** Sharp-tailed, Pectoral and Curlew Sandpipers. **Voice:** 'trilt', like Pectoral, but shriller (F. Smith, 1982). **Habitat:** muddy edges of wetlands, fresh, brackish and saline, coastal and inland; sewage ponds, saltfarms, tidal mudflats. **Range and Status:** breeding: no data. Summer migrant to mostly se. Aust. from unknown breeding grounds, possibly e. Siberia. Specimens from SA: sight records: Q, NSW, Vic., Tas., SA and WA.

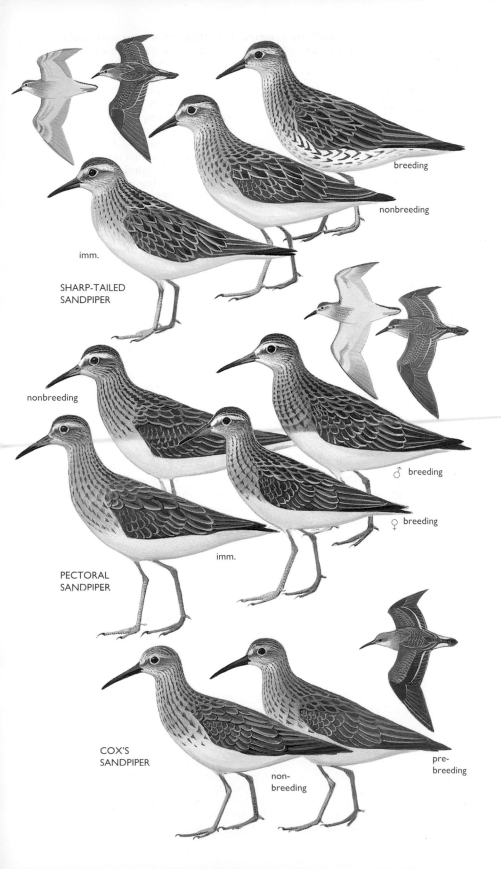

breeding

nonbreeding

imm.

SHARP-TAILED
SANDPIPER

nonbreeding

♂ breeding

♀ breeding

imm.

PECTORAL
SANDPIPER

COX'S
SANDPIPER

non-
breeding

pre-
breeding

BROAD-BILLED SANDPIPER *Limicola falcinellus* 16–18 cm

Note shapely black bill, longer than head, stout at base, broadening and turning down near tip. Legs shortish, grey, greeny brown or yellowish. **Nonbreeding:** dark eyeline in pale face; *dark centre-line on crown margined (in some) by snipe-like whitish eyebrows splitting near eye.* Upperparts grey with dark shoulders; dark feather-centres with pale fringes; underparts white, streaked darker across breast. **Breeding plumage:** *cream double streaks along crown and back;* black feathers of upperparts edged bright cinnamon and buff; breast washed buff–brown; dark arrowheads on flanks. **Immature:** feather-margins on upperparts broader pale buff; breast washed buff; flanks unstreaked. Solitary, with other waders; occasional small flocks: unobtrusive; runs, feeds deliberately with jabbing action, bill downpointed. Wades deep, at times with head under. In flight note distinctive bill, black leading edge of upperwing, white wingbar, white-edged dark rump. **Similar species:** see Curlew Sandpiper; Dunlin, nonbreeding. **Voice:** short trill 'trii-trii-trit'; also 'tzit' and 'trr'. **Habitat:** tidal mudflats, reefs, saltmarsh, freshwater wetlands, sewage ponds; favours muddy ooze. **Range and Status:** breeds Arctic Eurasia: winters Africa, India, se. Asia, Indonesia to PNG. Scarce summer migrant mostly to coastal Aust. (Sept.–April); small numbers inland. Vagrant NZ.

DUNLIN *Calidris alpina* 16–22 cm

Somewhat like a chesty, short-legged Curlew Sandpiper with heavier black bill, *decurved at tip;* less distinct pale eyebrow. **Nonbreeding:** grey–brown above streaked darker; short, indistinct pale eyebrow; breast grey, finely streaked darker, cut off fairly sharply from whitish underparts; legs short, black. **Breeding plumage:** bright chestnut above, mottled and streaked black; *face and underparts whitish with large black patch on centre of white underparts.* **Immature:** head/breast washed buff with lines of dark spots on lower breast and flanks; underparts whitish; feathers of back and scapulars black with rusty and buff margins; whitish lines at edges of mantle. In flight, all plumages: *bold white wingbar and conspicuous black centre to white rump.* Feeds actively, posture hunched. **Similar species:** Curlew Sandpiper; Broad-billed Sandpiper. **Voice:** 'treep', 'teerp', or a nasal, rasping 'cheezp'. **Habitat:** tidal mudflats, rocks, islands, saltfields, sewage ponds. **Range and Status:** breeds widely in far n. hemisphere: migrates to *s. coasts of n. hemisphere.* Unconfirmed Aust. sight-records.

CURLEW SANDPIPER *Calidris ferruginea* 20–22 cm. Female, bill longer.

Nonbreeding: elegant, medium sized, uniformly grey–brown wader with *slim, longish, evenly downcurved black bill, long white eyebrow, white rump and longish black legs.* **Breeding plumage:** *pale patch around bill; head and body deep rosy chestnut;* upperparts richly marked buff, chestnut and black; white rump sparsely barred darker. Moulting birds show patchy, scaly, chestnut pattern. **Immature:** buffer; upperparts *neatly 'scaly' from fine whitish feather-margins.* Small to large flocks, with other waders. Active: wades deep; submerges head; groups chase in flight; flocks wheel. *In flight* (all plumages): *bold white wingbar and rump.* **Similar species:** Dunlin, nonbreeding; Broad-billed Sandpiper; Stilt Sandpiper. **Voice:** liquid 'chirrup'; musical 'tirri-tirri-tirri' in aerial chases. **Habitat:** tidal mudflats, saltmarsh, saltfields; fresh, brackish or saline wetlands; sewage ponds. **Range and Status:** breeds ne. Siberia: migrates to Africa, s. and se. Asia, Indonesia, PNG, NZ. Widespread, common summer migrant to Aust. (Aug.–April); mostly coastal, but many inland. Some overwinter.

STILT SANDPIPER *Micropalama himantopus* 18–23 cm

About size of Curlew Sandpiper, with *longer, more robust, tapering black bill,* slightly drooped and swollen at tip, and *longer, spindly yellow–green legs.* **Nonbreeding:** white eyebrow above slim dark eyeline; upperparts deep grey–brown, patterned by fine, pale feather-margins (and some dark feathers); neck and underparts white, with short grey streaks throughout. **Breeding plumage:** dark, richly patterned, with *distinct rusty ear-patch;* underparts barred dark brown. **Immature:** buffer; with chestnut fringes on scapulars; underparts buff–grey to whitish, mottled darker on sides of breast; legs grey–yellow. In flight, thin white wingbar; *dark upperparts cleanly cut off from white rump (mottled in breeding plumage);* underwing white; yellow feet trail beyond tail. Forages unhurriedly; probes bill straight up and down, often submerges head; wades deep, swims. **Voice:** quiet, soft 'dew'; rattling 'kirr'. **Habitat:** wetlands, saltfields, dead snags, sewage ponds. **Range and Status:** breeds Arctic Alaska, Canada; winters s. N. America; c. S. America. Summer vagrant to Aust. Sight-records: Top End, and s. NT; s. Vic; c. NSW.

BROAD-BILLED SANDPIPER

non-
breeding

breeding

breeding

DUNLIN

imm.

nonbreeding

Dunlin

Curlew Sandpiper

CURLEW
SANDPIPER

imm.

non-
breeding

breeding

STILT SANDPIPER

breeding

breeding

imm.

nonbreeding

191

BUFF-BREASTED SANDPIPER *Tryngites subruficollis* 18–21 cm

About the size of Sharp-tailed Sandpiper but more plover-like: bill fine, black, shorter than head, which is small and round; neck longish; carriage upright, walks with head jerking. *Plumage throughout year sandy–buff from head to under tail-coverts with dark spots on breast near bend of wing. Eye large and dark in plain buff face*; pale diffuse eye-ring; *legs yellow to orange–yellow.* Crown streaked dark brown; *upperparts strongly 'scaly', with bold black feather-centres and fine grey-to-buff margins.* **Immature:** duller, more spots on neck. Usually solitary, loosely with other waders; occasional small flocks: note habitat. Flight graceful: *white underwing contrasts with buff body; note dark band on under primary-coverts;* rump brown; *short, rounded brown tail has pale tips.* On settling, wings often held aloft, displaying white underwing. **Similar species:** Ruff, nonbreeding: lankier; bill longer; dark streak through eye; less spotted on sides of breast. Sharp-tailed Sandpiper: less buff; differing head-pattern; more spots or 'boomerangs' on *flanks.* Baird's Sandpiper: smaller, horizontal, greyer; breast heavily marked; wings longer than tail; legs short, black. **Voice:** subdued, sharp 'chek-chek' or 'pik', like stones chipped together; low trilled 'pr-r-reet'. **Habitat:** short grasslands, dry ground; margins of freshwater or saline wetlands; occasionally tidal mudflats. **Range and Status:** breeds Arctic N. America and far ne. Siberia: winters S. America; vagrant Europe, Asia. Rare, mostly summer visitor to se. and s. Aust. and Tas. Vagrant.

UPLAND SANDPIPER *Bartramia longicauda* 28–32 cm

Other names: Bartram's Sandpiper; Upland Plover.

Unusual, small-headed, thin-necked, upstanding wader that looks like a sandpiper and behaves like a plover. Pale brown above, mottled darker; paler around the large dark eye and on throat and underparts. *Bill slightly downcurved, yellowish at base; legs long, dull yellow; tail longish and pointed, barred black at edges.* Flight rather stiff; *brownish wing-coverts and narrow white trailing edge contrast with black wingtips; underwing boldly barred black and white; rump and longish wedge-tail dark in centre, pale on sides; feet protrude beyond tail.* Holds wings up on alighting. Perches posts, stumps. **Similar species:** Ruff: shorter, more curved bill, yellowish only at base; plainer buff–grey head and neck; in flight shows pale wingbar and wholly white, unbarred underwing; larger white ovals on sides of rump. Feet extend beyond shorter tail. See also Sharp-tailed and Pectoral Sandpipers. **Voice:** Mellow, whistled 'kip-ip-ip-ip' and a rolling 'pulip pulip'. **Habitat:** grassy paddocks, plains. **Range and Status:** breeds N. America: migrates to S. America; vagrant Europe, Russia, Aust. (once) and NZ.

RUFF (REEVE) *Philomachus pugnax* 20–30 cm. Male much larger.

Male is called a Ruff, the smaller, duller female a Reeve. **Nonbreeding:** tall, with long neck, small head and simple head-pattern: *pale patch around elongated base of bill; fine dark horizontal streak through eye imparts a made-up, 'Oriental' look. Bill slightly longer than head, tapering to a knob, often downcurved; black, yellow–green or orange–red at base with dark tip; legs long; yellow, orange–red; green, brown or grey; feet part-webbed.* Upperparts buff–brown to grey–brown, with *scaly pattern from buff margins to dark feather-centres;* breast white to sandy, washed grey–brown or buff. **Breeding plumage:** (seldom in Aust.). Ruff: spectacular, variegated black, chestnut, grey, black or white ruffs and ear-tufts; moulting birds patchy. Reeve: rich buff–brown, patchy black above; black to chestnut bars or mottling on breast. **Immature:** buffer; golden brown above with black diamond pattern. Often with Sharp-tails and other waders: feeds deliberately and apart; round-shouldered, loop-necked and pot-bellied. Flight easy, with strong, well-spaced wingbeats and glides: *thin white wingbar and (conjoined) large white oval patch on each side of dark rump;* toes extend beyond tail-tip; underwing white. **Similar species:** Sharp-tailed and Pectoral Sandpipers: note head and breast-patterns. Buff-breasted Sandpiper: bill shorter, face plainer buff, without eyeline; sides of breast more spotted; rump and tail brown, with much narrower pale edges. **Voice:** mostly silent: a low 'tu-whit'. **Habitat:** fresh, brackish and saline wetlands; tidal mudflats, saltfields, sewage farms. **Range and Status:** breeds France to ne. Siberia: winters Europe, Africa, s. Asia and Aust. and Tas. Regular, uncommon, summer migrant (Sept.–April), mostly to coastal Aust. and Tas.; some inland.

imm.

BUFF-BREASTED
SANDPIPER

UPLAND
SANDPIPER

♂ non-
breeding

♀ breeding

RUFF

♀ imm.   ♂ imm.

RED-NECKED PHALAROPE *Phalaropus lobatus* 18–19 cm

Other name: Northern Phalarope.

Nonbreeding: dainty grey, black and white, small-headed, long-necked wader, *with black needle-like bill about same length as head.* Body 'duck-like', flat and broad. *Conspicuous black 'phalarope mark' curves through eye onto ear-coverts.* Rear of crown and hindneck sooty-grey. *Upperparts grey, with white lines along edge of mantle; feathers of wings and wing-coverts fringed paler;* underparts white. **Breeding plumage:** unmistakable — see plate (male resembles paler, faded female). **Immature:** like dark nonbreeding adult; forehead dark, connecting with 'phalarope mark'; neck and breast washed pinkish buff; feathers of upperparts fringed golden-buff. In Aust. mostly seen singly, with other waders; but flocks of dozens in nw. WA, often of one sex. Feeds while swimming, floating high and gull-like, neck slanting forwards, head nodding; actions fussy, often 'spins'. When feeding ashore, jabs mud; note horizontal carriage, short legs; toes less lobed than other phalaropes. Flight low, erratic, on fluttering, downcurved wings like Common Sandpiper: *note white wingbar on dark wings, white lines on back, prominent white edges to dark rump, dark tail.* **Similar species:** Grey Phalarope: bill thicker, often yellowish at base; more robust, with paler, plainer grey upperparts; moulting immature difficult. **Voice:** soft, repeated 'chuk', 'chek' or 'twit', in flight. **Habitat:** in Aust., shallow pools; in commercial saltfields; tidal mudflats, beaches, saltmarsh, freshwater wetlands. **Range and Status:** breeds around Arctic; winters at sea. East Siberian population migrates to Celebes Sea from s. Philippines, e. to PNG and Bismarck Arch. Irregular summer migrant to Aust. (Aug.–April), regular in nw. WA, but many sight-records in se. Aust. Odd birds overwinter, acquiring breeding plumage.

GREY PHALAROPE *Phalaropus fulicaria* 20–22 cm

Other name: Red Phalarope.

Nonbreeding: more robust than Red-necked Phalarope, with distinctly thicker black bill, often yellowish at base; legs greyish; toes lobed. Head often all-white, with patchy black 'phalarope-mark' and black patch on crown or nape; upperparts uniform blue–grey; bend of wing and flight-feathers darker, edged paler. **Breeding plumage:** unmistakable — see plate (male resembles pale female). **Immature:** like dark, nonbreeding adult, but golden-buff fringed brown feathers of upperparts can resemble Red-necked; *initially lacks 'phalarope-mark'.* Solitary in Aust. and often tame; swims buoyantly like small gull, 'spins' or 'dips' to either side when feeding; may feed along waters edge. Comes ashore to rest and preen with other waders. Flight strong and direct, body robust. *Note white wingbar, white shafts of primaries, white edges to grey rump; tail grey.* **Similar species:** Other phalaropes. At distance on water, can be mistaken for small gull. **Voice:** in flight, a low 'whit' or 'twit', singly or in series. **Habitat:** in Aust. recorded in shallow brackish, inland pondages; shallow coastal saltmarsh and flooded saline claypans. **Range and Status:** breeds Arctic Eurasia and Alaska: winters at sea off tropical and subtropical w. Africa and S. America (Chile). Vagrant over huge area, incl. India, se. Asia, Aust. and NZ. Sight records n. and s. Vic. (Feb.; July), s. SA (March and July); some acquire breeding plumage. Vagrant.

WILSON'S PHALAROPE *Steganopus tricolor* 22–24 cm

Nonbreeding: like a nonbreeding Marsh Sandpiper; black needle-like bill longer than small head, rotund body and *heavier, shorter, pale yellow legs.* Crown and nape grey; white forehead runs into white eyebrow; slight grey 'phalarope-mark' extends from below eye to nape. Wing-feathers grey with pale edges; wingtips blackish; underparts grey–white. **Breeding plumage:** unmistakable, see plate (male resembles paler, less boldly marked female). In flight (in breeding plumage), both sexes show uniformly dark upperwing, square white rump, dark tail. **Immature:** like nonbreeding but crown and upperparts dark brown, fringed buff; legs pinkish yellow. More than other phalaropes, feeds ashore or on floating weed; runs about with lurching gait, picking insects; head down, tail up. Note long, needle-like bill, small head, longish neck, broad phalarope 'hull', pot-bellied look. Swims high in water, flattens neck to stab insects; rotates. Flight swift, erratic: *pale grey upperparts and blackish outer-wings* contrast with square white rump; feet just extend beyond grey tail. **Similar species:** Red-necked Phalarope; Marsh Sandpiper. **Voice:** low nasal 'wurk' or 'chek chek chek'. **Habitat:** coastal saltfields, evaporation basins, freshwater wetlands. **Range and Status:** breeds inland N. America from sw. Canada to California: migrates to S. America. Vagrant Europe and Antarctic. Aust. sight records: s. NSW, s. Vic. Vagrant.

RED-NECKED PHALAROPE

imm.

♀ breeding

nonbreeding

GREY PHALAROPE

♀ breeding

imm.

moulting

imm.

nonbreeding

WILSON'S PHALAROPE

imm.

non-
breeding

nonbreeding

♀ breeding

COMB-CRESTED JACANA *Irediparra gallinacea* 20–26 cm. Female larger.

Other names: Lily-trotter; Lotusbird.

Walks across floating plants on *enormously long, dull green toes and claws; bill reddish, tipped black; pink-to-red comb on forehead; face and foreneck white, bordered yellow–buff; above a broad black breastband.* **Immature:** comb small and pink; crown ginger–brown; no buff on foreneck or dark breastband. Singles, pairs, open companies on waterlily leaves and other floating aquatic-vegetation: active and often excitedly noisy, with much chasing. Walks with back-and-forward head-movement: bobs head, flicks tail. Flies swiftly with quick shallow wingbeats, long legs and feet trailing. Swims; submerges to escape predators. **Voice:** thin squeaky chitter or piping, often uttered in flight. **Habitat:** floating vegetation of permanent, well-vegetated wetlands and dams; occasionally feeds along muddy wetland-margins. **Breeds:** Dec.–April in n.; Sept.–Jan. in e. Aust. **Nest:** low heap of wet, floating vegetation. **Eggs:** 4; highly polished yellow–brown or red–brown, covered with maze of black lines. Adults may carry eggs/young under wings during transfer to new site. **Range and Status:** coastal n. and e. Aust. from Kimberley (WA) to Hunter R. (NSW); well inland in parts, e.g. Mt Isa (Q); vagrant Mudgee, Sydney region and s. coast, NSW. Common n. Aust.; local and uncommon in s. Sedentary. Also se. Borneo to PNG, New Britain.

PHEASANT-TAILED JACANA *Hydrophasianus chirurgus* 31–39 cm. Not illustrated.

Nonbreeding: large lotusbird, grey–brown above with no comb or crest; foreneck, wings and underparts white; *sides of neck yellowish, with distinct black line through eye and down neck to form a black breastband; tail shorter than the long, pointed wingtips, which turn up like spurs.* Legs and feet blue–grey. **Breeding plumage:** (unlikely to be seen in Aust.) white face, neck and wings contrasting with *black and yellow nape, black underparts* and long, downcurved, black, 'pheasant' tail adding c. 18 cm to length. Gregarious in nonbreeding season: flocks of 50–100 in suitable habitat. **Habitat:** floating and/or emergent vegetation on lakes, ponds, marshes, reservoirs, ricefields. **Voice:** peculiar nasal or musical mewing. **Range and Status:** breeds India, Sri Lanka, se. Asia to Philippines, s. Borneo; 'regular but rare winter visitor' to Sumatra, Java. Two Aust. sight-records in Pilbara and Kimberley regions (WA). Vagrant.

PAINTED SNIPE *Rostratula benghalensis* 22–30 cm. Female larger.

Note longish, *slightly drooping bill, pinkish and swollen at tip; long cream or white eyepatch*; cream line along middle of crown; legs olive–grey. **Female:** *dark smoky brown neck and breast cut off by creamy white 'horse collar' extending in two cream lines along back.* Upperparts patterned bronzy grey–green; unmarked white below. **Male:** greyer, markings less contrasting, with *distinct banded pattern of cream–buff spots on wings.* **Immature:** like male; throat paler, bill shorter, greyer. Singles, pairs, occasional flocks in suitable habitat. Part-nocturnal; skulks rail-like, feeds deliberately; jerks rear of body up and down. Disturbed, 'freezes' or flies fast and low on rounded wings, feet trailing; note *black wingbar across patterned upper wing-coverts, white wingbar below.* Occasionally flies higher and faster, but lacks dash of Latham's Snipe. **Similar species:** Latham's Snipe: longer, straighter bill; bursts up with a tearing call and flies very fast, with tilting zigzags. **Voice:** when startled into flight, loud repeated 'kek!'. In display, female utters musical 'booo', like blowing over neck of a bottle. **Habitat:** well-vegetated shallows and margins of wetlands, dams, sewage ponds; wet pastures, marshy areas, irrigation systems, lignum, tea-tree scrub, open timber. **Breeds:** Aug.–Dec. in s.; May–Oct. in Q; probably any time after good rains. **Nest:** scrape or well-made saucer of twigs, reeds, grasses; on small hummock above water-level, usually in cover; may have light canopy of stems, grasses. Sometimes several nests in proximity. **Eggs:** 4; rounded, tapered, creamy buff, blotched black, brown, underlying grey. Only male incubates. **Range and Status:** mostly se. Aust., s. of Brisbane-Adelaide; scarce and erratic over much of inland., n. Q, NT and coastal WA; vagrant Tas. Rare. Dispersive or irruptive in response to rainfall; possibly part-migratory, moving n. into Q in summer (Marchant & Higgins, 1993), but recent winter sight-records from Leeton (NSW) and Mt Carbine (ne. Q). Also Africa; s. and se. Asia, Japan, Indonesia; vagrant NZ.

COMB-CRESTED JACANA

breeding

imm.

PAINTED SNIPE

♂

♀

PIED OYSTERCATCHER *Haematopus longirostris* 42–51 cm

Other names: Eugerie-bird, Redbill, Seapie, Wongbird.

Sturdy conspicuous wader; *black with sharply cut-off white belly and rump; straight scarlet bill; red legs*. In flight, note *broad, short, angled white wingbar, white rump and belly*. **Immature:** bill dusky; feathers of upperparts with brownish edges; legs paler. Singles, pairs, autumn and winter flocks: wary, usually well away from cover; indulges in noisy aerial chases. Known to fishermen on n. NSW and Q coasts from habit of opening bivalves wedged in wet sand. Lures intruders from nest with injury-feigning distraction display. Often active at night. **Voice:** brisk, ringing 'peepapeep, peepapeep' or 'kleep, kleep', usually in flight; musical tittering and piping in courtship. **Habitat:** undisturbed sandy, shellgrit or pebble beaches; sandspits and sandbars, tidal mudflats and estuaries, coastal islands. Occasionally rocky reefs, shores, rock-stacks; brackish or saline wetlands. Also grassy paddocks, golf-courses or parks near coast; probes for worms in wet short grass. **Breeds:** Aug.–Jan. **Eggs:** 2–3; stone-grey, spotted black–brown with grey underlining marks; laid in shallow scrape in sand on open beach or among low growth behind beach. **Range and Status:** suitable habitat on coasts and islands of Aust. and Tas.; more common in s. Aust. than in n. Vagrant inland, Norfolk I. and Lord Howe I. Common: sedentary and dispersive. Closely related forms from Old World to PNG and NZ.

SOOTY OYSTERCATCHER *Haematopus fuliginosus* 40–52 cm

Other names: Black Oystercatcher; Redbill; Black Redbill.

Sturdy sooty black wader with scarlet bill and dull pinkish legs. Race *ophthalmicus* of n. Aust. has larger, bare fleshy eye-ring and longer bill. **Immature:** bill and eye-ring orange–brown; wing-coverts bordered brownish; legs grey. Habits like Pied Oystercatcher but more solitary, usually singles, pairs or in small autumn and winter flocks of 20+; *favours more rocky habitats than Pied*. Occasional lone birds associate with flocks of Pieds and sometimes interbreed. **Voice:** somewhat like Pied Oystercatcher but less noisy; calls sharper. **Habitat:** intertidal rocky and coral reefs, mostly on ocean shores; breeds mostly on offshore islands; occasionally frequents sandspits and tidal mudflats, mostly when not breeding. **Breeds:** June–Jan. **Eggs:** 2–3; stone-coloured, spotted and blotched purple–brown; larger, darker than Pied Oystercatcher's; laid in depression in sand among rocks, seaweed, pigface, shells, usually on island. **Range and Status:** suitable coasts and islands of Aust. and Tas. Less common than Pied. Sedentary.

PIED
OYSTERCATCHER

imm.

imm.
nominate
race

race
fuliginosus

race
ophthalmicus

SOOTY OYSTERCATCHER

BLACK-WINGED STILT *Himantopus himantopus* 33–38 cm

Other names: Pied or White-headed Stilt.

Aust. race of a widespread cosmopolitan species: *adult's black nape and extremely long, slender pink legs are unmistakable.* **Immature:** crown/nape washed blackish grey. Pairs, small parties, open companies of hundreds: often with Red-necked Avocets, but seldom in such huge, compact flocks as Banded Stilt. Wades in shallows, occasionally swims. *In flight, wings black above and below; trailing pink legs nearly double length of body.* Noisy and demonstrative near nest; bobs head, flutters overhead with trailing legs. **Similar species:** Banded Stilt, nonbreeding and imm. **Voice:** repeated falsetto 'yap' or 'boo', mostly when nesting; imm. has thin whistle. **Habitat:** fresh and brackish swamps; shallow river or lake margins; flooded claypans; dams, sewage ponds, commercial saltfields, saltmarsh, tidal estuaries, mudflats. **Breeds:** mostly Aug.–Dec. in se. Aust., but almost any month after rain. Often in autumn-winter in tropics. **Nest:** of water-plants, weeds, often built up; in open colonies on low hummocks in water, among dead bushes, at times floating; or in depression on dry ground, with little lining. **Eggs:** 3–4; dark olive, blotched and spotted dark brown. **Range and Status:** widespread in suitable habitat across mainland Aust. *except* waterless deserts, Nullarbor Plain. Scarce Kimberley region (WA) and parts of C. York Pen.(Q). Seasonally dispersive or nomadic, according to rainfall. Moves inland in response to autumn–winter rainfall; coastward into se. and sw. Aust. after winter–spring rains; casual Tas., especially in mainland drought. Casual Lord Howe I., Norfolk I. Also PNG, NZ, Eurasia, Africa, N. America, Hawaii.

BANDED STILT *Cladorhynchus leucocephalus* 36–45 cm

Specialised, native wader with *slim, straight black bill, white head, neck and body* and (in breeding plumage), *broad dark chestnut breastband and black belly-stripe;* legs orange–pink. Nonbreeding adults and grey-legged immature birds have *wholly white breast.* Mostly in large, compact flocks, sometimes tens of thousands; also small parties or lone birds, usually with other waders, e.g. Red-necked Avocets; some reach e. coast. Flocks spread wide over shallow lakes; wading, upending like ducks or swimming like buoyant black-and-white gulls. *Flight swift, in close-packed flocks that stream, twist and dive:* note *indented white panel on trailing edge of black wing, trailing orange–pink legs.* **Similar species:** Black-winged Stilt; Red-necked Avocet. **Voice:** wheezy puppy-like bark. **Habitat:** shallow salt lakes, saltmarshes, tidal mudflats, commercial saltfields; occasionally flooded claypans, shallow freshwater lakes. **Breeds:** irregularly and intermittently, when water conditions suitable, *in huge, close-packed colonies on low islands in large inland salt lakes in s. WA and SA.* **Eggs:** 3–4; laid on scrape; white to fawn or brown; scrawled black, blotched chestnut. Downy young in thousands known to walk cross-country as lakes dry up. **Range and Status:** s. inland and coastal s. and w. Aust., n. to near Tropic in WA and s. NT. Straggler to coastal se. Q, NSW and e. Vic; vagrant Tas. Dispersive, nomadic and irruptive: movements influenced by effect of weather on water-levels, salinity and food-organisms, particularly brine-shrimps. Tends to move coastward in summer in s. WA, SA and s. and w. Vic.

RED-NECKED AVOCET *Recurvirostra novaehollandiae* 40–48 cm

Elegant native wader with unmistakable *long, upturned fine black bill, rusty head, white body and black-and-white wings.* Legs long, pale blue–grey; feet webbed. **Immature:** duller, pale around bill; brownish buff on wings. Parties, occasional large flocks: wades, swinging bill from side to side, locating shrimps, insects, fish by touch. Swims, upends like a small duck. In flight, *note flickering effect of black-tipped white wings with angled black bar on upperwing; legs trail well beyond tail. Flying away, two black bars down white back are diagnostic.* Often roosts and feeds with stilts. Demonstrative when nesting. **Voice:** musical, fluty 'toot toot'. **Habitat:** estuaries, tidal mudflats; fresh, brackish and salt swamps and lakes; claypans, commercial saltfields, sewage ponds. **Breeds:** mostly Aug.–Dec. in single pairs, loose colonies. **Nest:** scrape, with scant lining of sticks, rootlets; often near small bush or on hummock in shallow water. **Eggs:** 4; dark olive to creamy stone, blotched, spotted black, stained grey. **Range and Status:** widespread but irregular across s. Aust. from c. NSW coast (Hunter R.) to about Port Hedland (WA); many coastal habitats, e.g. w. Port Phillip Bay (Vic.) visited regularly. Breeding strongholds are s. inland NSW–n. Vic., se. SA and inland s. WA. Regular, mostly uncommon visitor to parts of coastal n. Aust., from n. WA to e. Q. Dispersive and nomadic; moves toward coast in summer (s. Aust.) and in dry season (n. Aust.). Vagrant Tas.; NZ.

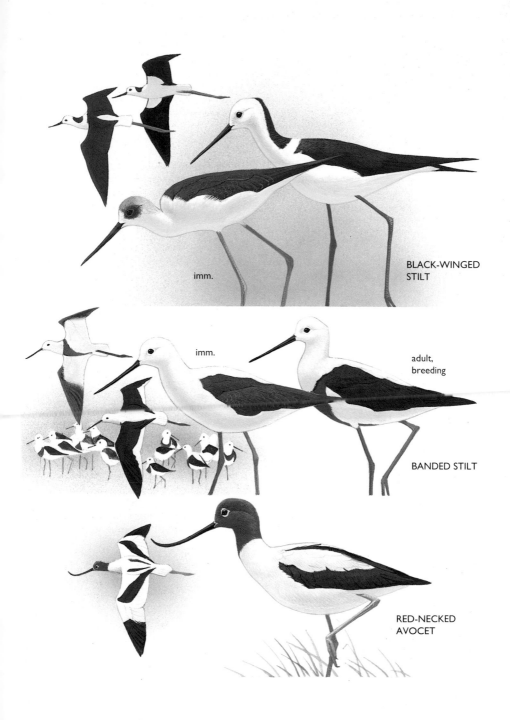

imm.

BLACK-WINGED
STILT

imm.

adult,
breeding

BANDED STILT

RED-NECKED
AVOCET

EURASIAN GOLDEN PLOVER *Pluvialis apricaria* 26–29 cm; span 67–76 cm

Largest, deepest-bodied of three world Golden Plovers; not yet admitted to full Aust. list but should be kept in mind as a possibility. Almost the size of Grey Plover; *bill and legs relatively shorter than Pacific Golden Plover*. In all plumages, differs in flight from Pacific and American Golden Plovers *in pure white underwings; on upperwings, narrow white wingbar splits into white streaks on bases of inner primaries; toes do not protrude beyond tail-tip in flight*. At rest, wingtips extend beyond tail-tip. **Nonbreeding:** *most 'golden' Golden Plover*, with indistinct pale eyebrow and dark 'ear-spot'. Gold feather-margins spangle entire upperparts and *upperbreast, cut off fairly sharply by unmarked white centre of belly and under tail-coverts.* **Immature:** like adult nonbreeding; duller, with finer spanglings; flanks and belly finely fringed black in subtle 'scaly' effect. **Breeding plumage:** face, throat, narrow centre breast and patch on belly *smutty grey to jet black, but under tail-coverts always white. Narrow white band runs across forehead, down sides of face, widening on sides of neck and flanks to white under tail-coverts*, with golden spangling and fine black barring down flanks. Some birds have whitish face and breast and only centre of belly black. **Voice:** flight-call, liquid 'too-eee' or 'tlui'. **Range and Status:** breeds from Iceland and n. British Isles to n. Scandinavia and Arctic Russia, e. to Khatonga R., s. of Tamyr Pen. (Marchant & Higgins, 1990). Migrates to n. Africa, Mediterranean region, Caspian Sea.

PACIFIC GOLDEN PLOVER *Pluvialis fulva* 23–26 cm; span 60–72 cm

Other names: Eastern or Lesser Golden Plover.

Smallest and most delicately built golden plover, but stands more upright, on *proportionately longer legs than American or Eurasian Golden Plovers*; wingtips extend just beyond tail-tip. **Nonbreeding:** *pale buff forehead and face with distinct whitish to yellow–buff eyebrow*; ear-coverts and upperparts brownish; yellow–buff spanglings on brown plumage of crown, back, wings and tail; breast buff–white with/without gold or white spangles; belly and under tail-coverts whitish. **Immature:** like nonbreeding adult; eyebrow more yellowish buff; crown and upperparts streaked and mottled brown, and plentifully spangled yellow; breast buff, mottled brown; *flanks lightly barred brownish*; underparts whitish. **Breeding plumage:** face and breast black with *narrow white border extending down flanks*; belly and under tail-coverts white, or white, blotched black. Newly-arrived and soon-to-depart birds in moult are often patchy black below. Singles, small parties, occasional large open companies. In flight (nonbreeding), *dusky grey–brown underwing; toes extend beyond tail-tip. The brown, gold-speckled upperparts show indistinct pale wingbar and white shafts on primaries.* **Similar species:** American and Eurasian Golden Plovers. Grey Plover, imm. and nonbreeding. Oriental Plover: plainer, no spangling or wingbar; eyebrow and legs longer; note habitat. **Voice:** a musical 'too-weet'; whistling 'tlooi'; rough scratchy 'kree kree kree'. **Habitat:** estuaries, mudflats, saltmarshes, mangroves; rocky reefs and stranded seaweed on ocean shores; margins of shallow open inland swamps; sewage ponds, short-grass paddocks, sports-grounds, airfields, ploughed land. **Range and Status:** breeds ne. Siberia and w. Alaska; regular common widespread summer migrant (Aug.–April) to PNG, Aust. and islands, incl. Norfolk and Lord Howe Is; also NZ. Mostly coastal, but many inland records; some overwinter coastally, especially in Q.

EURASIAN GOLDEN PLOVER

non-breeding

imm.

♂ breeding

♂ breeding

PACIFIC GOLDEN PLOVER

♂ breeding

♂ moulting

non-breeding

imm.

AMERICAN GOLDEN PLOVER *Pluvialis dominica* 24–28 cm

Larger, heavier-billed but comparatively shorter-legged than Pacific Golden Plover; approaches Grey Plover in size and appearance. When standing, exposed primaries extend further beyond tail than Pacific; tertiaries shorter, in relation to tail-tip (Alstrom & Colston, 1991). **Nonbreeding:** upperparts grey–brown; breast greyish; underparts whitish; *eyebrow white and obvious, especially behind eye; lacks yellow tones on face and breast*. Yellow spangles on upperparts *reduced or absent*. In flight, wings long; *underwings greyish, with darker grey 'armpits' (axillaries); white wingbar inconspicuous: rump does not differ from back; toes do not extend beyond tail-tip*. **Immature:** more brightly and evenly patterned than nonbreeding adult, and more yellowish on neck, breast, wings and back; more distinctly marked underparts, with some barring. Differs from imm. Pacific by much less yellow on eyebrow, neck, wings and back. **Breeding plumage:** in full breeding plumage, *male has wholly black, or white-mottled black, underparts and under tail-coverts*; white band from forehead down sides of neck and breast *widens into a prominent white patch, cut off by the black flanks*. Moulting birds are patchy black below. Habits, habitat, etc. as for Pacific Golden Plover. **Range and Status:** breeds Arctic N. America; winters in inland S. America. Unconfirmed sight-records in coastal e. Aust. incl. Cairns (Q); Byron Bay (NSW); Anna Plains (n. WA).

GREY PLOVER *Pluvialis squatarola* 28–31 cm; wingspan 71–83 cm

Other name: Black-bellied Plover.

Big plover of strong, graceful flight; at rest often has 'hunched, dejected appearance'. Carriage horizontal: note large head and large, dark eye, heavy black bill with somewhat bulbous tip. **Nonbreeding:** pale grey above, finely mottled darker, with whitish forehead and eyebrow, whitish rump, strongly barred white tail; underparts whitish grey. **Breeding plumage:** distinctive — upperparts deep grey, strongly chequered white; *face, throat and breast jet black; broad white band runs from forehead over eyes to nape, broadening into a conspicuous white patch on side of neck; under tail-coverts always snowy white*. Birds in moult look patchy; head whitish. **Immature:** more warmly coloured than adult, with fine brownish feather markings on head, neck and breast and fine yellow–buff margins to feathers of crown, mantle and wings, like American (especially) and Pacific Golden Plovers. But note *white rump and barred white tail*. In flight, all plumages, *distinctive black 'armpit' patch contrasts with mostly white underwing; strong white wingbar and black carpal patch on upperwing; white rump, barred tail*. Shy: singles or small parties, mostly aloof from other waders; usually forages far out on exposed mudflats, sandspits. In a few places, e.g. Mud I. (Vic.), se. Gulf of Carpentaria (Q) and nw. WA, in flocks of hundreds. **Similar species:** Pacific Golden Plover, nonbreeding: smaller, buffer, more upright; indistinct pale wingbar in flight; underwing grey–brown; no distinct pale rump. See also American Golden Plover. **Voice:** plaintive, drawn-out 'tlee-o-weee', usually in flight. **Habitat:** mudflats, saltmarsh; tidal reefs and estuaries; rarely inland. **Range and Status:** breeds around Arctic: migrates to s. hemisphere. Regular summer migrant (Aug.–April), mostly to traditional sites in coastal Aust. and islands. Local; not uncommon in some areas, but generally sparse. Occasional inland, apparently on passage. Some young birds overwinter. Also PNG, NZ.

♂ moulting

♂ breeding

non-
breeding

imm.

AMERICAN
GOLDEN PLOVER

♂ moulting

non-
breeding

GREY PLOVER

♂
breeding

imm.

nonbreeding

RINGED PLOVER *Charadrius hiaticula* 18–20 cm

Small Eurasian sand-plover. **Nonbreeding:** bill short, blackish; yellowish on under-base. *Cap brown; forehead and rear eyebrow white; blackish brown 'mask' is separated by complete white collar from brown upperparts; incomplete broad brown breastband widest at sides of upperbreast.* **Breeding plumage:** *bill orange–yellow with black tip; legs orange–yellow (dark when muddy). Some birds have narrow orange eye-ring. Black double forehead band extends onto ear-coverts; breastband black below white collar.* In flight, note white collar, prominent white wingbar, white edges to brown rump and tail, which has a broad black tip, edged white. Active: forages on exposed sand or mud; rarely wades. In flight, wingbeats regular and pumping. **Similar species:** Little Ringed Plover; Black-fronted Dotterel; Double-banded Plover; Red-capped Plover. **Voice:** described as a clear 'dzerwit', and a fluted 'too-ee' in flight. **Habitat:** level sandy or muddy shores. **Range and Status:** breeds from British Isles to Arctic Siberia; ne. Canada, Greenland and Iceland. Migrates to Mediterranean, Africa; Siberian race *tundrae* to China, Japan, Malaya, n. Borneo. Rare, mostly summer migrant to Aust.; records NT, Q, NSW, Vic., SA. Vagrant NZ.

LITTLE RINGED PLOVER *Charadrius dubius* 14–16 cm

Smaller and more slender than Ringed Plover; resembles a slim, longish Red-capped Plover *with a yellow eye-ring and proportionately longer yellow or pale pink legs.* **Nonbreeding:** *brown crown separated by small dark band from white forehead; blackish mask separated from brown crown by slim, white rear eyebrow. There is a slim, complete white collar and incomplete dark brown band around upperbreast, broken in middle, deepest at sides of upperbreast.* **Immature:** similar, markings less definite; buffish forehead; lacks pale eyebrow; scaly pattern from pale feather-margins. **Breeding plumage:** *flesh-coloured area at base of dark bill; white upper margin to black forehead band; pale yellow eye-ring; narrow black breastband under slim white collar.* Singles, pairs: usually on edge of water or mud; more active than Ringed Plover — runs, freezes, wades. **Voice:** clear, descending 'pee-ooo', with emphasis on first, sharp syllable. **Habitat:** open muddy or sandy shores of lakes, swamps, tidal areas; sewage ponds, farm dams. **Range and Status:** breeds across Eurasia from Spain to Japan, s. to Mediterranean, Persian Gulf, s. and se. Asia. Migrates to Africa, Malayan Pen., Philippines, Indonesia, PNG. Rare but regular summer migrant (Sept.–March) to Aust., especially Top End (NT), but casual all States, particularly WA. Most belong to the migratory n. Eurasian subspecies *curonicus*. (A non-migratory race, *dubius*, breeds from Philippines to PNG and New Ireland.)

RED-CAPPED PLOVER *Charadrius ruficapillus* 14–16 cm

Other names: Red-capped Dotterel; 'Sandlark'; 'Sandpiper'.
Male: forehead white; *crown and nape fox red; margined black, black mark from bill to eye and another on upperbreast.* **Female:** head and nape sandier, black markings less distinct. **Immature:** paler; with scaly pattern to upperparts. Singles, pairs; runs along edge of water on twinkling black legs; autumn companies with other small waders, in flocks that wheel and plunge; now brown, now white. Note pure white underparts, *thin white wingbar, tail blackish in centre, edged white.* **Similar species:** Double-banded Plover; Ringed Plovers; Red-necked Stint. **Voice:** brisk 'tik!', singly or accelerating into rapid buzz; sharp peeps. **Habitat:** broad sandy and shelly beaches; bare margins of saline wetlands and lakes, inland and coastal; saltmarsh; tidal mudflats and sandflats; adjacent dune-wilderness; occasionally shallow freshwater wetlands, inland and coastal. **Breeds:** July–Jan. s. Aust.; all months n. Aust. **Eggs:** 2–3; pale sandy to greenish stone; blotched and mottled grey, lavender, dark brown and black; laid in scrape in sand, shingle or bare ground; scantily lined with shells, stones, plants. **Range and Status:** Aust. and Tas. in suitable habitat, coastal and inland. Sedentary; nomadic. Vagrant NZ.
Note: the closely related, slightly larger Kentish Plover, *C. alexandrinus* (15–17.5 cm), breeds from n. Africa through Eurasia to the Americas (where known as Snowy Plover). Adult whiter than Red-capped, less fox-red on head/shoulders. Male breeding: bill black, *longer and heavier; legs longer and greyer. Note blackish mask above narrow white complete collar; black 'epaulette' from shoulder to sides of upperbreast.* Female: browner; mask and shoulder markings dark brown. Nonbreeding: plumage markings browner. Juvenile: like nonbreeding; feathers of upperparts scaled with dark fringes. In flight shows white rear collar. Migrates as far s. as Indonesia; vagrant Aust. Sight-record, Top End (NT), Nov. 1988 (Marchant & Higgins, 1993).

nonbreeding

RINGED PLOVER

imm.

breeding

non-
breeding

breeding

imm.

LITTLE RINGED PLOVER

non-
breeding

breeding

imm.

distraction display

RED-CAPPED PLOVER

DOUBLE-BANDED PLOVER *Charadrius bicinctus* 17.5–19 cm

The only wader to breed in NZ and winter in Aust. Mostly seen here in **nonbreeding plumage:** buffish grey–brown above, *with broad, brownish mark from bill below eye widening on ear-coverts; forehead and eyebrow whitish to yellow–buff, tending to loop downwards behind eye; yellow–buff wash on nape suggests rear collar.* Underparts whitish, *with traces of (or complete) slim brownish breastband at sides of upperbreast;* some show traces of chestnut lower breastband. Bill black; legs dull yellow–grey or grey–green. In flight note thin white wingbar, white shafts to primaries, pale sides to brownish rump and tail. **Immature:** like nonbreeding: facial area and collar more yellow–buff; upperparts with pale buff feather-margins. **Breeding plumage:** (mostly seen on arrival and before departure) male: *forehead and underparts white with black head-markings; sharp black band across lower throat and well-separated broad chestnut band across breast.* Female: *head-markings and upper breastband brown.* Mostly in open companies; on bare or sparsely grassed areas, near or far from water. **Similar species:** Lesser Sand Plover; Red-capped Plover; Ringed Plover. **Voice:** incisive, high-pitched 'pit', or 'chip chip'. **Habitat:** wide beaches, tidal mudflats, saltmarsh; wide, sparsely vegetated margins of shallow saline and freshwater wetlands; paddocks with sparse vegetation; ploughed fields, airfields. **Range and Status:** breeds NZ and islands. Part of South I. population migrates annually to mostly s. Aust. and Tas., Norfolk I. and Lord Howe I. (Feb.–Sept.). Commonest in se. Aust. and Tas., incl. inland Vic., NSW and SA; casual n. to Cairns (Q) and w. to Shark Bay (WA).

LESSER SAND PLOVER *Charadrius mongolus* 19–21 cm

Other names: Mongolian Sand Plover; Mongolian Plover or Dotterel.

Easily confused with Greater Sand Plover: see below. **Nonbreeding:** *Bill black, robust: length equals distance from bill to eye;* legs dark grey, tinged greenish; grey–brown above with white forehead; blackish mask; broad, dark grey partial breastband. (Moulting birds often show pinkish flush on breast). In flight, narrow white wingbar and edges to rump and tail; *toes barely extend beyond tail-tip.* **Immature:** browner, markings less distinct; forehead and eyebrow washed buffish; buff feather-margins on upperparts. **Breeding plumage:** male: *strong black mask extends from forehead through eye onto ear coverts; white throat; bright rusty chestnut sides of neck extend in broad chestnut zone across upperbreast.* Female: head and breast-markings duller, browner. N.B. *See Plate for racial differences.* Singles, parties, flocks of hundreds, with other waders, incl. Greater Sand Plover. Forages on mud, sand or open areas of short grass; pure flocks gather at high-tide roosts; with other waders. **Similar species:** Greater Sand Plover; Double-banded Plover. **Voice:** short 'drrit' or 'drit, drit, derreet'; a soft 'tikit'; trills. **Habitat:** tidal mudflats and sandflats; gently sloping sandy and shelly beaches; saltmarsh, estuaries, atolls, reefs, mangroves, airfields. Occasionally inland on freshwater lakes, swamps, bore-drains, etc. **Range and Status:** breeds c. and ne. Siberia; regular summer migrant (Aug.–May) to mostly coastal Aust., Tas. and NZ; scattered inland occurrences. Regular in low thousands in certain locations, e.g. se. Gulf of Carpentaria and Moreton Bay (Q).

GREATER SAND PLOVER *Charadrius leschenaultii* 20–25 cm; span 53–60 cm

Larger than, but similar to, Lesser Sand Plover. Note: (1) *proportionately larger head;* (2) *larger bill, longer than distance from bill to eye;* (3) *longer pale, greenish or yellowish grey legs;* (4) in **nonbreeding plumage**, *paler, sandier upperparts;* partial grey–brown breastband forms band on sides of upper breast; (5) in **breeding plumage**, *male: black mask encloses white forehead; paler chestnut on rear and side-neck and breast; chestnut breastband paler and narrower.* Female: *head-markings less distinct; breastband smuttier, less complete.* Solitary or with other waders, especially Lesser; larger flocks in nw. Aust. Favours open, undisturbed areas but often less nervous than other waders: on approach lowers head, slinks away or flies a short distance. Flight strong: *prominent white wingbar splits onto inner primaries; white underwing; dark rump with whitish sides; tail sandy grey–brown, darker towards end, tipped white; unlike Lesser, toes clearly extend beyond tail-tip.* **Similar species:** Oriental Plover. Double-banded Plover. **Voice:** quiet, clear, mellow 'tweep tweep'; melodious trill. **Habitat:** wide, sandy or shelly beaches; sandspits, tidal mudflats, reefs, sand-cays, mangroves, saltmarsh, dune wilderness, bare paddocks; seldom far inland. **Range and Status:** breeds (in three races) from Turkey to s. Siberia; regular summer (Aug.–May) migrant to Aust., Tas., commonest in nw. WA, where flocks of thousands occur; smaller numbers coastally in all states; some overwinter. Also PNG, NZ, oceanic islands.

non-
breeding

breeding

imm.

DOUBLE-BANDED
PLOVER

nominate
race
nonbreeding

race *atrifons*
nonbreeding

♂
nominate
race
breeding

♂ race *atrifons*
breeding

LESSER
SAND PLOVER

imm.

nonbreeding

♂ breeding

GREATER SAND
PLOVER

ORIENTAL PLOVER *Charadrius veredus* 22–25 cm; span 46–53 cm

Nonbreeding: resembles a small, slender, uniformly shaded Pacific Golden Plover with *long legs and wings:* upperparts plain sandy–olive, *with buff–white eyebrow and buffish rear-collar; whitish underparts have distinct buff–grey zone across upperbreast; at rest, wingtips extend beyond tail-tip.* Flight strong and graceful, or erratic, with swift turns; *underwing always grey–brown; upperwing has no obvious wingbar; tail dark brown, narrowly tipped white; feet extend beyond tail.* **Breeding plumage:** *eyebrow, face and throat cream or buff–white, merging into orange–buff upperbreast; this in turn merges into a black breastband cut off sharply by white underparts.* **Immature:** like nonbreeding adult, *with pale buff margins to wing-feathers.* Singles or small parties; open flocks in inland and coastal n. Aust., often with pratincoles. Wary, erect; runs, bobs head; stands on rocks, stumps. **Similar species:** Pacific Golden Plover: dark brown upperparts are spangled gold, buff, grey or white. Greater Sand Plover: more compact; bill heavier; at rest, wings just extend to tail-tip; in flight, *underwing white; toes* extend beyond tail-tip. Australian Pratincole: chestnut belly; white rump; short black tail. Oriental Pratincole: white rump; forked tail. Both pratincoles have shorter, curved bills. **Voice:** in flight, loud, deliberate 'chip-chip-chip'; melodious trills; short, piping 'klink'. **Habitat:** open plains; bare, rolling country, often far from water; ploughed land; muddy or sandy wastes near inland swamps or tidal mudflats; bare claypans; margins of coastal marshes; grassy airfields, sportsfields, lawns. **Range and Status:** breeds Mongolia and Manchuria; regular summer migrant to Aust. (Sept.–March). Records all states but most regular and abundant across coastal and n. inland.

CASPIAN PLOVER *Charadrius asiaticus* 18–20 cm; span 55–61 cm

Nonbreeding: like small, slim Oriental Plover, with two regular differences, both visible in flight: *on upperwing, pale wingbar on inner primaries; on underwing, whitish wing-linings contrast with brown undersides of flight-feathers.* **Breeding plumage:** male: *white forehead, eyebrow, face and throat with contrasting brown crown, nape and ear-coverts; clear-cut black-edged orange–buff breastband is separated from whitish underparts by heavier blackish lower band.* Female: breast paler, lacks black band. **Immature:** like nonbreeding adult; feathers of upperparts scaled with buff or rufous fringes. Habits like Oriental Plover. Legs usually *olive–grey,* but can be pinkish, yellow, or yellow–brown to slate-grey. **Voice:** soft piping 'tyk tyk tyk' and a shrill, whistling 'kwhit' or 'kuwit' (Cramp, 1983). **Habitat:** inland plains with sparse grass, especially where recently burned; wide, bare wetland margins. **Range and Status:** breeds steppes and semi-deserts of e. Caspian Region: migrates to e. and s. Africa. Vagrant Aust.: specimen, Pine Creek, Sept. 1896: unconfirmed sight-record, Darwin Sept.–Oct. 1974. Other sight-records: Finnis (NT) 5 Oct. 1994; Cleveland Bay, Townsville (Q) Oct.–Nov. 1995.

♂ breeding

nonbreeding

ORIENTAL PLOVER

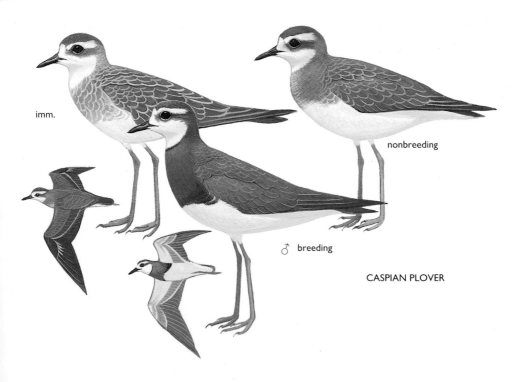

imm.

nonbreeding

♂ breeding

CASPIAN PLOVER

HOODED PLOVER *Thinornis rubricollis* 19–23 cm

Other name: Hooded Dotterel.

Tubby, small plover of ocean beaches (and inland salt lakes in s. WA). *Black hood and throat, and white rear collar* distinguish adult from all other waders. **Immature:** lacks hood; scaly, silvery grey above with white rear collar, smudgy grey 'lapels'; pinkish base to bill and eye-ring; pinkish or pale yellow legs. Pairs, family parties, larger winter flocks: potters around jetsam and edges of spent waves; turns its back on observer, squats in footprints; runs, or flies briskly out over waves to settle further along. In flight note *flashing broad white wingbar crossing black flight-feathers, white tail with black hourglass pattern*. **Similar species:** Sanderling: lacks white rear collar; bill and legs black; shoulder dark. **Voice:** short, piping 'pert peet'; a barking 'kew kew' in flight. **Habitat:** broad sandy ocean (and occasionally bay) beaches, with plentiful seaweed and jetsam; adjacent dune wilderness; weedy rock-shelves and reefs; occasionally tidal flats. In SA and WA, coastal and inland salt lakes. **Breeds:** Sept.–Jan. **Eggs:** 2–3; pale stone, blotched blackish brown, lavender; laid in scrape in sand, often near beach-debris. **Range and Status:** confined to suitable habitat from *c.* Jervis Bay (NSW), s. through Bass Strait and Tas. (a stronghold), w. to Bight coast of SA. In WA, coastally w. from Israelite Bay, n. to Jurien Bay, casual to Abrolhos and Shark Bay; inland on salt lakes to *c.* L. Barlee (WA), and in s. SA. Sedentary; locally dispersive.

RED-KNEED DOTTEREL *Erythrogonys cinctus* 17–19 cm

Black 'hangman's' hood and breastband enclose pure white throat and bib; fine white line separates wing from chestnut flank-mark. Bill dull red tipped blackish; upper leg dull red, lower dark blue–grey. **Immature:** brown above, plain white below, with white collar; later gains brownish breastband. Singles, pairs, parties, occasional widespread companies: *typically feeds in water, wading to full length of legs; swims, submerges head; bobs head, stands tall*. In flight, *note strong contrast of black plumage with white throat and wing-linings; broad white trailing edge and white-edged tail*; feet extend well beyond tail-tip. **Voice:** high-pitched 'chet chet', running to a musical trill in flight. **Habitat:** shallow freshwater wetlands; claypans, floodwaters, sewage ponds (especially those with small shrubs), tussocks, rushes, lignum. Also brackish waters, salt swamps; seldom tidal. **Breeds:** Oct.–Jan., but any month when water conditions are suitable. **Nest:** a scrape, or well constructed cup of twigs, plant-stems; in or near water, under shrub or tussock. **Eggs:** 4; stone-coloured, with dense wavy streaks and blotches of black and dark brown. **Range and Status:** throughout mainland Aust. in suitable habitat; regular in Murray–Darling basin. Visits coastal areas mostly during dry periods inland; may remain to breed. Nomadic; irruptive. Vagrant Tas. and NZ. Also s. PNG.

BLACK-FRONTED DOTTEREL *Elseyornis melanops* 16–18 cm

Other name: Black-fronted Plover.

Widespread native wader of disruptive patterns: *black forehead extends back through centre of crown and through eyes under long white eyebrow, joining bold black Y on white breast*. Upperparts brownish, *with dark chestnut 'shoulder-bar'*. Bill red to orange, tipped black; eye-ring red; legs flesh-pink to yellowish. **Immature:** lacks breastband and black forehead but has black mask under bold white eyebrow; shoulder-bar paler chestnut; more white on wings. Singles, pairs, parties: usually on gravel, sand or mud near shallow freshwater; gravel or stony roads. Stands horizontal; bobs head, tips, runs; occasionally swims. Active; vocal at night: when courting, brisk aerial chases with excited churring. Flight easy, undulating, jerky and dipping, on 'oversize wings': note *white wingbar, chestnut wingpatch and rump, black tail edged and tipped white*. **Similar species:** Red-kneed Dotterel: black hood, white bib; white trailing edge in flight. Hooded Plover: head black with white rear collar. See also Ringed and Little Ringed Plovers; Inland Dotterel. **Voice:** liquid 'dip!'; tinkling rattles and churrings, often in flight. **Habitat:** shallow bare freshwater wetlands; sandbars and margins of rivers; open ground, on pebbles, gravel, mud, branch and leaf-debris, inland claypans, receding shallow floodwaters; sewage ponds, farm dams in bush, stone and gravel roads. Less commonly on saltmarsh, brackish lakes, sandy seashores or mudflats. **Breeds:** Aug.–Feb., but almost any month when conditions suitable. **Eggs:** 2–3; yellow–white to stone colour, closely scribbled dark brown and lavender, laid in scrape in sand, shingle, bare ground among leaf-litter; gravel road. May be lined with small sticks, etc. Some away from water. **Range and Status:** Aust. and Tas: widespread in suitable habitat; absent from waterless regions. Sedentary; locally dispersive. Also NZ.

imm.

HOODED PLOVER

imm.

RED-KNEED
DOTTEREL

distraction
display

imm.

BLACK-FRONTED
DOTTEREL

213

MASKED LAPWING *Vanellus miles* 35–38 cm

Other name: Masked or Spurwinged Plover.

Well-known by appearance, aggressive habits and penetrating calls. Race *novaehollandiae* (formerly 'Spurwinged Plover'): crown and *back of neck black, extending broadly down sides of upperbreast.* Nominate race *miles* of n. Aust. (formerly 'Masked Plover') noticeably *whiter: yellow facial wattle much larger and more conspicuous; crown black, tapering on nape; neck and underparts white.* Intermediates, resulting from interbreeding of the two races (see below) have mid-sized wattles, variable amount of black on side of neck.

Pairs to large, vocal flocks in autumn. Noisy: with much interaction and upright posturing when courting. Aggressive when nesting; dives at intruders; sharp, black-tipped yellow bony spurs on 'shoulders' used against predators. Flies with quick beats: broad wings white below with black flight-feathers; *rump and tail white with broad black sub-terminal band.* **Similar species:** Banded Lapwing: bold black breastband; zigzag wing-markings. **Voice:** well-known *metallic,* grating, staccato 'kekekekekek' or single, piercing, repeated 'kek!'; often at night. In display, running, rattling trills. **Habitat:** swamp-margins, flooded ground, paddocks with dams, beaches, airfields, orchards, gardens, factory grounds, pebbled flat roofs. **Breeds:** June–Oct. in s.; Nov.–May in n. Aust. **Eggs:** 3–4; yellow–olive to dark olive, spotted, blotched, brown–black; laid in scrape or shallow cup of twigs, grasses, pebbles or dry cow-dung; on ground or small hummock in water. **Range and Status:** nominate race breeds tropical n. Aust. from *c.* Dampier (WA) to about Cairns (Q). Race *novaehollandiae:* all se. Aust., n. to about Mackay (Q), casual n. to *c.* Cairns. The two races interbreed in a broad zone across n. inland. Both casual in s. WA. Nominate race vagrant/migrant to s. PNG and islands; *novaehollandiae* has colonised NZ, Lord Howe I. Common; sedentary, nomadic or part-migratory. Also e. Indonesia; Christmas I. (Indian Ocean).

BANDED LAPWING *Vanellus tricolor* 25–28 cm

Other names: Banded or Black-breasted Plover.

Mostly seen on stony open ground and/or with short grass, or on ploughed land. Smaller than Masked Lapwing: black cap broken by bold white line through eye, curving onto nape; *black sides of neck extend in prominent black breastband,* enclosing white throat. Small parties, occasional large winter flocks: wary and usually far from cover; seldom wades. In heat of day, seeks shade of stumps, fence-posts. *Takes flight with quick, clipped wingbeats, wild cries. White bar across base of black flight-feathers gives zigzag appearance; tail white, with black subterminal band.* **Similar species:** Red-kneed and Black-fronted Dotterels. **Voice:** wild, plaintive cries, higher-pitched than Masked Lapwing; quick, metallic 'er-chill-char, er-chill-char'; strident 'kew-kew, kew-kew'; often at night. **Habitat:** bare or ploughed paddocks; new crops, plains, airfields; stony ground and other areas of very short grass; margins of dry swamps; occasionally beaches. **Breeds:** June–Oct.; other months after rain. **Eggs:** 3–4; rounded at large end, tapering: deep olive–green to stone coloured, spotted and blotched brown or blackish brown, underlying grey marks; laid in scrape, sparsely lined with grasses, rootlets, pieces of dung. **Range and Status:** Aust., mostly s. of Tropic and inland of Gt Divide; casual n. to Cairns–Mt Isa (Q), Alice Springs (NT), Ashburton R. (WA); also Tas. Patchy in suitable habitat; scarcer in n.; vagrant w. deserts in good seasons. Sedentary; dispersive or nomadic.

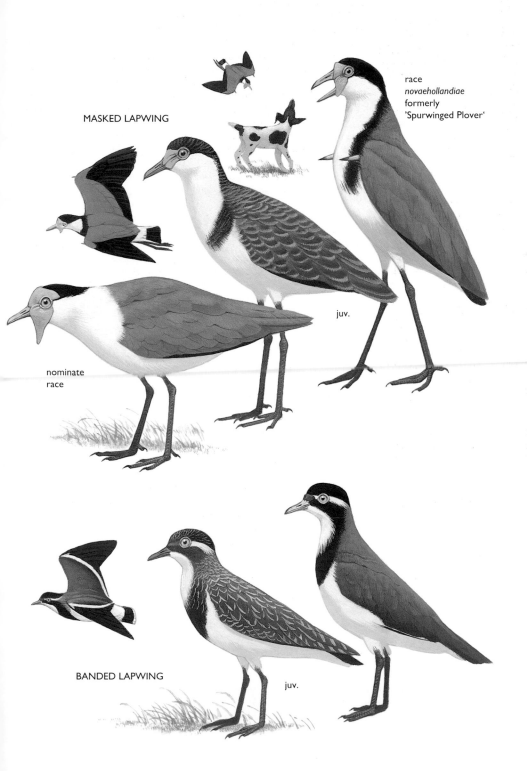

MASKED LAPWING

race
novaehollandiae
formerly
'Spurwinged Plover'

juv.

nominate
race

BANDED LAPWING

juv.

INLAND DOTTEREL *Charadrius australis* 19–20 cm; span 43–47 cm

Disruptively patterned wader of arid inland and drier coasts. Adult unmistakable — see Plate. **Immature:** *breastmarking indistinct or is plain buff–white below, running to chestnut on flanks.* Parties and small, close flocks: posture upright; runs from observer, freezes, bobs head; sometimes seen day or night on outback roads. Flies, crouches flat or runs behind plants. In hot weather seeks shade of small shrubs; feeds mostly at night. Flight low, swift; note contrast of buff underwing, *dark belly and white under tail-coverts; rump and tail brownish.* **Similar species:** Australian Pratincole; Oriental Pratincole; Buff-breasted Sandpiper. *All lack dotterel's Y-shaped breast-pattern.* **Voice:** described as a fairly sharp, pleasant 'quik', singly or oft-repeated; a somewhat guttural, trill 'kroot', or 'krrr krik, krrr krik' in flight. **Habitat:** stony, sparsely vegetated plains and uplands; gibber, stock-routes, outback roads, bare pastures, crops, golfcourses; occasionally ploughed land. Seldom near water, but drinks at claypans, stock-tanks, etc. at dusk. **Breeds:** pairs to loose colonies; almost any month depending on location and rainfall. **Eggs:** 3; variably oval, cream to buff–brown or light olive, heavily streaked and blotched dark brown, with underlying violet marks; in scrape, ringed with sandy soil, pebbles, stems, dung-pellets. On leaving nest, bird kicks this debris over eggs; young shelter in holes, burrows. **Range and Status:** in inland parts of all mainland States, mostly s. of Tropic, extending patchily to coast from se. SA to c. Exmouth Gulf, casual n. to Dampier Arch. (WA). Vagrant e. coast and Gulf coast (NT). Nomadic: movements influenced by plant-growth following rainfall.

AUSTRALIAN PRATINCOLE *Stiltia isabella* 22–24 cm; span 50–60 cm

Slim, graceful, upstanding *sandy–olive wader with extremely long, narrow, pointed black wings; deep chestnut and black patch on flanks.* **Breeding plumage:** note short, arched, red tipped black bill; legs long, grey, dull reddish or brown. **Nonbreeding:** duller, bill mostly blackish; blackish spotting on throat; smaller flank-marks. **Immature:** browner with shorter black primaries; sandy fringes to feathers of upperparts. Singles to open companies beside outback roads. Runs easily on long legs; pursues insects – leaps, swerves; on approach, bobs head, rocks rear of body up and down. Flight swift and tern-like on very slender, swept, black-tipped wings: note *black underwings, chestnut flanks, white underparts; long legs protrude noticeably beyond the short, white, black-centred tail.* **Similar species:** Oriental Pratincole: dark-rimmed cream throat-patch, *reddish tan wing-linings;* white, black-forked tail. **Habitat:** vicinity of water on inland plains to coastal floodplains; stony ground with sparse low shrubs; claypans; bare margins of swamps; stock-tanks, stockroutes, airfields. **Voice:** sweet 'weetweet' or shrill, tern-like 'quirree-peet'. **Breeds:** in loose colonies mostly Sept.–Dec., but any month after suitable rain. **Nest:** bare patch, ringed with small stones, plant-material, dung-pellets. **Eggs:** 2; pale stone to creamy white, spotted and blotched grey, brown, black. **Range and Status:** n. and inland e. Aust., from about Eighty Mile Beach (WA) to Rockhampton (Q), s. to coastal SA; casual in inland WA and Nullarbor Plain. Breeds mostly s. of Tropic, migrates n. in autumn–winter to n. Aust.; Torres Strait, PNG, Indonesia, Borneo. Vagrant NZ.

ORIENTAL PRATINCOLE *Glareola maldivarum* 23–24 cm; span *c.* 60–65 cm

Other name: Swallow Plover.
Olive–brown above, pale buff–grey to white below, with white rear end of body ending in short, black-forked white tail; legs dark grey. **Breeding plumage:** short, arched black bill, scarlet at base; yellow buff throat neatly margined with a fine black/white line. **Nonbreeding:** bill mostly black, with streaked, indistinct black border to creamish throat. **Immature:** feathers of upperparts edged buff; throat whitish; breast mottled grey. Singles to huge open companies: runs on shortish grey legs on open ground; stands on tiptoe; feeds on insects on ground and when hawking on swept, sickle wings, with easy, fluid wingbeats, swoops and twists: note *reddish-tan wing-linings, pale underparts without chestnut patches and short, black-forked, white tail.* In flight, tail can simply look pointed. **Habitat:** plains; shallow wet and dry edges of open bare wetlands; tidal mudflats, beaches. **Voice:** tern-like 'kyik'. **Range and Status:** breeds Pakistan, India, parts of se. Asia, China, Japan and Philippines: migrates to spend Nov.–Feb. or later, from coastal nw. WA to Top End (NT) and Gulf country of nw. Q; Torres Strait and PNG. Within Aust. nomadic according to rainfall, huge companies (tens of thousands) suddenly appearing over plains, then moving on. A few reach coastal s., se. and e. Aust.; vagrant NZ.

imm.

INLAND DOTTEREL

nonbreeding

breeding

AUSTRALIAN PRATINCOLE

imm.

breeding

nonbreeding

ORIENTAL PRATINCOLE

GREAT SKUA *Catharacta skua* 61–66 cm; span 1.5 m

Other name: Antarctic Skua.

Like a stout brown gull with a hooked black bill, *broad wings and large white patch at base of primaries, conspicuous in flight*. Plumage darkest after moult, patchily paler with wear: *head plain brown; nape and neck sparsely streaked buff, with pale flecks; some have pale buff or rufous streaks and fringes to feathers of breast and upperparts*. Many seen in Aust. waters in winter are in untidy stages of wing-moult. **Immature:** redder brown, mottled; smaller white wingpatch. Singles, occasional parties or flocks (mostly in s. WA): follows ships for discarded refuse; circles fishing boats; sometimes tame, mostly wary. Enters harbours in winter gales; rarely ashore. Flight powerful, hawk-like, with regular, easy wingbeats, 10–15 m above water; *tail bluntly wedge-shaped, carried slightly dished, with small notch between two slightly projecting central feathers*. Pirates food from gannets, shearwaters, even albatrosses; accelerates wingbeats, hurtles after victim and despite size follows with close twists, seizing tail or wingtip, until food disgorged. **Similar species:** South Polar Skua, dark morph: smaller; paler round base of bill; plumage blackish brown without buff body-streaks; *pale head and/or nape emphasises dark cap*. Pomarine Jaeger, dark morph, nonbreeding: less bulky; note dark cap and blunt tail-projections; wingpatch smaller. (Great Skua population of n. hemisphere, *C. skua skua*, has more distinct black cap.) **Voice:** described as 'quee-kek-kek-kek'. **Habitat:** mostly offshore waters; occasionally on beaches at dead seals, whales. **Range and Status:** southern races breed on Antarctic Peninsula; also s. S. America and on circumpolar sub-Antarctic islands n. to Macquarie I.; South Island and Stewart I., NZ. Regular winter migrant to Aust. waters n. to *c.* Shark Bay (WA) and Sandy Cape (Q), arriving April–May, most departing late June to early Aug.; some remain until Oct.–Nov. Sparse, uncommon.

SOUTH POLAR SKUA *Catharacta maccormicki* 53 cm; span 1.3 m

Smaller than Great Skua, with finer bill and smaller head, but still a powerful, bulky seabird, less streaked than Great Skua. Most are identifiable *by pale patch around base of bill, pale nape accentuating dark face/throat, or wholly pale, milk-coffee tone of head, neck and breast*. **Immature:** bill blue or blue with blackish tip; feet blue. Head grey to grey–brown, *with distinctive pale fawn to grey–buff collar*; body and wings greyer than adult (some whitish) *with light grey or buffish feather-margins. In flight, much patchy white on base of primaries and secondaries*. Harasses shearwaters, albatrosses; kills and eats small petrels and other seabirds. **Range and Status:** breeds Antarctic peninsula and adjacent islands (dark morph); further s. on Antarctic continent (pale and intermediate morphs). Some breed further s. than any other bird; vagrant S. Pole. Migrates in winter to n. Indian Ocean, n. Pacific, N. Atlantic (Harrison, 1983). Present in offshore Aust. waters in small numbers June–Nov. Observations off s. NSW suggest offshore migration (Barton, 1982).

GREAT SKUA

imm.

imm.

SOUTH POLAR SKUA

imm.

dark
morph

imm.

pale
morph

intermediate
morph

ARCTIC JAEGER *Stercorarius parasiticus* 41–46 cm, incl. tail (*c.* 10 cm or more); span *c.* 1.1–1.25 m

Smaller than Pomarine Jaeger with slimmer bill; *wings narrower than length of tail; two broad, pointed central tail-feathers may extend 10 cm+ beyond tail-tip.* N.B. *Nonbreeding adults and imms. usually lack these or have short points only.* Flight dashing, falcon-like on backswept wings; intercepts terns, gulls; follows every turn until food disgorged, often seizes it in mid-air. Plumage: has dark, light and intermediate morphs. **Breeding plumage:** *dark morph:* uniform dark brown; white patch at bases of four outer primaries; tail-plumes broad and pointed. *Pale morph:* blackish cap, cream rear collar; wings grey–brown with white flash on outer primaries; breast white with partial dark breastband; tail-plumes may be present. *Intermediate morph:* includes features of both. **Nonbreeding:** tail-points short. *Dark morph:* like Breeding but some have pale-barred tail-coverts. *Pale morph:* upperparts scalloped buff or white; tail-coverts above and below barred brown. **Immature:** usually lacks tail-points; bill pale grey, tipped black; plumage patchy — upperparts brown, obscurely barred on back and rump; underparts/underwings untidily barred brown and white. In flight, white at base of *four outer primaries.* Mostly offshore, in shipping lanes; small parties float together; stand on drifting planks, boxes. **Similar species:** see Long-tailed and Pomarine Jaegers. **Voice:** nasal, squealing 'eee-air'. **Habitat:** offshore waters; bays, harbours; follows ships; seldom ashore. **Range and Status:** breeds throughout Arctic: migrates to coasts of s. continents. Arrives s., e. and w. Aust. Oct.–Nov., departs late April. While present, is local, sedentary.

POMARINE JAEGER *Stercorarius pomarinus* 46–52 cm, incl. tail-plumes (c. 10 cm); span 1.25–1.4 m

Other name: Pomarine Skua.

Plumages like Arctic Jaeger, but *bigger, heavier, with more robust bill. Wings broader (wider than tail-length); larger white wingpatch at base of primaries.* **Breeding plumage:** *two broad, twisted, spoon-shaped central feathers extend c. 10 cm beyond tail-tip.* (Shorter (or broken) in nonbreeding plumage, *mostly lacking,* or only thick blunt points, in imms.) **Immature:** bolder barring on white rump, underwing and under tail-coverts than imm. Arctic. Solitary, occasional small flocks: disputes floating offal with larger petrels, albatrosses, usually without Arctic's spectacular aerial pursuits. Behaves like a large gull, flies steadily 10–15 m above sea with little gliding. **Similar species:** see Arctic Jaeger. Great Skua: more robust, plumage more streaked; lacks Pomarine's suggestion of dark cap and pale rear collar; tail broader, without plumes. **Voice:** disputing food, a sharp, gull-like 'which-yew, which-yew'. **Habitat:** oceans, offshore waters, entrances of harbours, bays. **Range and Status:** breeds Finland to e. Siberia; Arctic Alaska, Canada, Greenland. Migrates to oceans, offshore waters of s. continents. Arrives in Aust. offshore waters Oct.–Nov. Departs April–May. Uncommon.

LONG-TAILED JAEGER *Stercorarius longicaudis* 50–55 cm, incl. tail-plumes (15–20 cm); span *c.* 1–1.17 m

Small, slender jaeger: short grey bill tipped black; head/neck short. Wings slender (*narrower than tail-length*). Flies higher than other jaegers; ignores ships; flight airy, buoyant, dipping, like tern, small falcon or shearwater. Less piratical than Arctic, but pursues smaller gulls, terns. Swims buoyantly, wingtips, tail-tip raised. **Breeding plumage:** *blackish cap separated from grey upperparts by broad, creamish rear collar; some have partial dark breastband; tail-plumes very long (up to 20 cm) and whippy. In flight, dark trailing edge and wingtips contrast with grey upperwing; underwing grey, with white shafts to only two outer primaries.* (Rare dark brown morph similar to Arctic.) **Nonbreeding:** like dull Breeding, with *pale barring on upper tail-coverts; dark barring on throat, flanks and under tail-coverts; most retain slender, elongated central tail-plumes.* **Immature:** two-tone bill; plumage like imm. Arctic, but greyer, breast whiter with brown breastband, grey–brown barring on flanks, under tail-coverts and underwings; tail longish, slightly wedge-shaped; tail-points visible on two central feathers. **Habitat:** (on migration) oceans, offshore waters, entrances to bays, harbours. **Range and Status:** breeds Arctic: migrates to oceans, offshore waters of s. continents. Regular, scarce summer migrant (Oct.–May) mostly to offshore waters of se. Aust. and Tas. Numbers fluctuate; 'wreck' of dozens in NZ in 1983 coincided with unprecedented numbers off Sydney that year.

pale morph,
breeding

imm.

dark morph,
breeding

ARCTIC JAEGER

imm.
pale morph

non-
breeding

imm.
dark morph

dark
morph

summer

winter

pale
morph,
breeding

POMARINE JAEGER

pale
morph,
breeding

non-
breeding

dark morph,
breeding

imm.

imm.
dark
morph

imm. pale
morph

pale morph,
breeding

dark
morph,
non-
breeding

dark
morph,
breeding

LONG-TAILED JAEGER

pale morph,
breeding

adult, non-
breeding

imm.
pale
morph

imm.
dark
morph

pale morph,
breeding

PACIFIC GULL *Larus pacificus* 58–66 cm; span 1.3–1.5 m

Other name: Mollyhawk.

Note the *massive yellow bill, broadly tipped scarlet; yellow legs; upperwings and wingtips wholly black with narrow white inner trailing edge; white tail crossed by broad black subterminal band. Beware: some moulting adults in autumn have stumpy, all-white tails.* **Juvenile:** *dark brown;* bill glossy black; eye dark; legs grey–brown. **Immature:** Year 2: forehead paler brown; *pale margins to feathers form large ovals; rump paler; tail darker; bill horn-coloured with dark brown tip;* eye and legs grey–brown. Year 3: forehead whiter; *tail nearly black; rump whitish;* bill cream with dark tip; eye white; legs yellowish. Year 4: like smutty adult. Singles, pairs, occasional loose companies: flies or sails steadily, high along tidelines; rises vertically 10–15 m in wind to drop molluscs on rocks, sand; follows fishing boats. **Similar species:** Kelp Gull; Great Skua. **Voice:** shouted 'ow! ow!'; muffled 'auk, auk'; gruff chuckles; whining stutters. **Habitat:** coasts, bays, offshore islands, coastal farmland, swamps, garbage tips; some follow rivers inland. **Breeds:** Sept.–Dec., in pairs, loose colonies, on offshore islands. **Nest:** cup of sticks, stalks, grasses, in elevated position. **Eggs:** 2–3; olive–brown, blotched brown, grey. **Range and Status:** s. coastal Aust., from *c.* Sydney (NSW), Tas., w. to *c.* Port Hedland (WA); casual further n. Breeds offshore islands in s. Vic.; e. to Furneaux Group (Bass Strait); Tas., s. SA, s. WA, n. to Shark Bay (WA). Adults sedentary; young dispersive. Being displaced by Kelp Gull in se. Tas.

KELP GULL *Larus dominicanus* 55–60 cm; span 1.28–1.4 m

Other names: Dominican Gull, Southern Black-backed Gull.

Bill slimmer than Pacific, red spot on lower tip only; legs green–grey to yellowish. Wing has wider white trailing edge; single white 'window' in wingtip; white tips to primaries; tail all-white. N.B. Birds in sub-adult plumage may temporarily have clear-cut black tail-band, confusable with Pacific Gull: check other features. **Juvenile:** bill and eye black; *brown plumage streaked paler on head/neck; wing-feathers have angled pale edges, forming small diamond patterns;* in flight, wide pale trailing edge; tail brown, obscurely banded darker; broad black terminal band. **Immature:** bill pale creamy-horn, with dark tip, then yellowish; eye yellowish white; head/body brownish, then smutty white; wings brownish black *without white windows; tail all white, or dark terminal band.* Gregarious: noisy, aggressive; follows fishing boats; drops molluscs on rocks. **Similar species:** Pacific Gull. Lesser Black-backed Gull, *Larus fuscus:* vagrant? Melville Bay (NT), Oct. 1973: wings/back greyer; *outer two primaries* have white windows. **Voice:** yelping or laughing 'yo-yo-yo-yo-yo-yo-yo', heard in nearly every film with coastal/marine scenes. **Habitat:** coasts, bays, beaches, reefs, islands. **Breeds:** Sept.–Dec., in pairs, loose colonies, on islands. **Nest:** bulky cup of plant-stems, grasses, seaweed; on ground, near rock, tussock. **Eggs:** 2–3; drab grey–green, blotched, speckled dark brown, dark grey. **Range and Status:** occurs locally and patchily in coastal se. and s. Aust. and Tas.; small breeding colonies Moon I., Five Is., and Sydney–Port Kembla region (NSW); Seal Rocks (Vic.); s. WA w. to Esperance. Larger colonies (*c.* 200 pairs) on islands s. of Hobart (Tas.), where replacing Pacific Gull. Dispersive. Casual Cairns, Townsville (Q); Jurien Bay (WA). Also NZ, s. S. America, S. Africa, many sub-Antarctic islands.

BLACK-TAILED GULL *Larus crassirostris* 46–48 cm; span 1.2 m

Other name: Japanese Gull.

Medium-sized gull with *yellow bill tipped red, banded black;* legs yellow–green; back/wings *slate grey with black tips;* tail white with *broad black subterminal band.* **Nonbreeding:** head/nape greyer. **Immature:** tawny brown with pale front of head/neck; *flight feathers and tail black* with fine white tips; rump *nearly white;* underparts whitish; bill pink with black tip; legs pinkish. Sub-adult: head streaked grey, upperparts greyer; tail like adult; in flight (adults, sub-adults), *white trailing edge to inner wing.* **Similar species:** Pacific Gull, Kelp Gull. **Voice:** 'plaintive mewing' (Harrison, 1983). **Habitat:** sea coasts. **Range and Status:** breeds s. China, Taiwan, Japan. Vagrant Aust.: Darwin (NT) (April); Port Phillip Bay (Vic.) (March–Sept.). Vagrant.

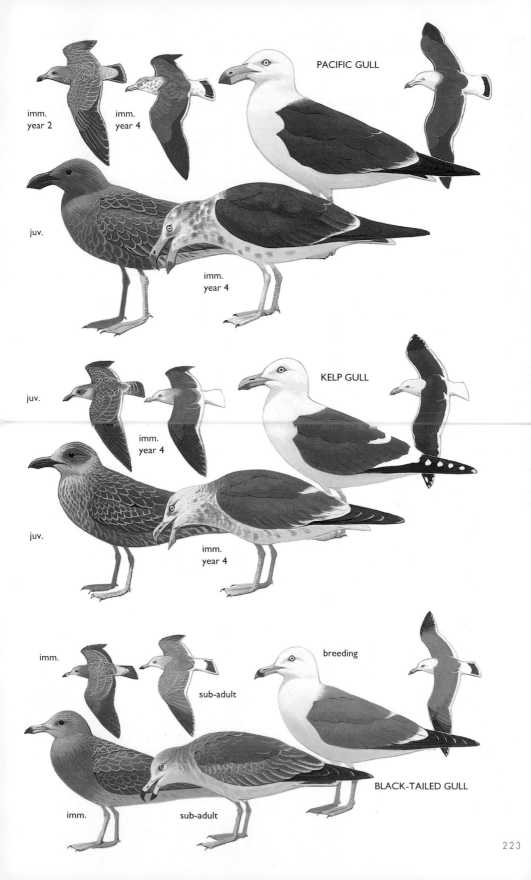

imm.
year 2

imm.
year 4

PACIFIC GULL

juv.

imm.
year 4

juv.

KELP GULL

imm.
year 4

juv.

imm.
year 4

imm.

sub-adult

breeding

BLACK-TAILED GULL

imm.

sub-adult

SILVER GULL *Larus novaehollandiae* 38–43 cm; span 94 cm

Familiar Aust. 'seagull': in s. Aust., increasingly common around settlement, from availability of food scraps and garbage. Bill and legs scarlet; eye white; upperparts pale silver-grey; *primaries white at base, then black with white tips; white 'windows' in three outer primaries; tail white.* **Juvenile:** bill, eye and legs black; wings mottled buff and brown; small brownish ear-patch; each secondary with black subterminal panel, forming broken black line along trailing edge in flight; dusky subterminal spots on tail-feathers. **Immature:** bill dull yellow–brown with dark tip; legs yellow–brown. **Sub-adult:** bill and legs dull red. Flocks, especially where food plentiful: parks, streets, fishing centres, rubbish-tips, vessels near coast. In gales, shelters on town-lakes, sportsgrounds, airfields. **Voice:** short, harsh, guttural 'korr' or 'keow'; longer, harsh, descending 'karrr-karrr-karrr'. Imms: peevish squeals, trills. **Habitat:** waters near coast; beaches, reefs, jetties and piers; town lakes, public gardens, sewage ponds; streets in towns and cities; sportsgrounds, garbage tips, to which many gulls commute long distances. **Breeds:** Aug.–Dec. **Nest:** saucer of seaweed, rootlets, plant-stems; on ground, low shrub, rocks, salt-piles, jetties, old boats, etc. **Eggs:** 1–3; pale brown or bluish to dark olive–green; blotched, spotted, striped dark brown and black. **Range and Status:** Aust., Tas: very abundant in s., less so in n.; extends far inland, some breeding. Sedentary and dispersive. Vagrant Norfolk I. Also New Cal., NZ, some sub-Antarctic islands, S. Africa.

BLACK-HEADED GULL *Larus ridibundus* 34–37 cm; span 1–1.1 m

Nonbreeding: like small Silver Gull with dark tip to scarlet bill, smutty crescent on ear-coverts *and separate smutty bands over crown and nape;* tail white; legs scarlet. Wing-pattern diagnostic: *white leading edge, fine black margin to wingtip contrasts strongly with 4–5 white outer primaries. These and grey inner primaries have partial black webs and broad black tips, forming a bold black trailing edge to wingtip. Underside of flight feathers mostly slate grey, contrasting with black-margined white outer primaries.* **Breeding plumage:** *dark eye and white rear eyelids contrast with chocolate-brown hood; nape white.* **Juvenile:** bill pink tipped black; legs pink–grey; yellow–brown bands across crown and nape; lower hind-neck, mantle and wing-coverts yellow–brown; centres of feathers on wing-coverts black, forming netted pattern. Flight-pattern as adult, except for mottled wing-coverts and dusky trailing edge to secondaries. **Immature:** whiter and greyer; bill orange, tipped black; legs orange–red; smaller marks on crown and ear-coverts; mottled wing-coverts; underwing pattern like adult except for smutty trailing edge and dark tip to tail. Gregarious and abundant in much of Europe, Eurasia. **Similar species:** Silver Gull: imm. also has dark spot on ear-coverts, but wing-pattern differs. Franklin's Gull: adult and imm. wing-pattern diagnostic. Imm. Franklin's has wholly dark grey primaries and fine white trailing edge on dark secondaries. Also see adult wing-pattern. **Voice:** high-pitched harsh screams in quick succession; variable long call described as 'kreeooo' or 'kraaahr' (Cramp, 1983). **Habitat:** coasts, sewage ponds. **Range and Status:** widespread from Iceland and British Isles, through Eurasia to Japan and Kamchatka Pen., migrating to Mediterranean, E. Africa, India and se. Asia s. to n. Borneo, Philippines. Vagrant; mostly to n. Aust. and WA.

SILVER GULL

imm.

adult

juv.

imm.

BLACK-HEADED
GULL

juv.

nonbreeding

breeding

juv.

nonbreeding

FRANKLIN'S GULL *Larus pipixcan* 32–36 cm; span 85–95 cm

Nonbreeding: like a small Silver Gull *with a dark grey rear-hood, prominent broad white rear 'eyelids', darker grey back and wings, with black primaries prominently tipped white.* In flight, wingtips black, tipped white: on both upperwing and underwing, a variable *white trailing edge curves across wingtip, separating grey wing from black outer primaries.* **Breeding plumage:** bill deep red; legs dusky red; hood brownish black, emphasising heavy white 'eyelids'. Some show pink flush on underparts. **Immature:** bill blackish red; rear white 'eyelids'; forehead white; rear crown and face blackish; wingtips unmarked blackish; *grey secondaries and inner primaries have black subterminal band and pale tips; tail has broad blackish subterminal band, except on outer tail-feathers.* Mostly singles in Aust., with other gulls; flight graceful; catches insects on wing, picks food from surface in flight; in n. America, follows plough. **Similar species:** imm. Laughing Gull: black tail-band extends across outer tail-feathers. **Voice:** shrill 'kuk-kuk-kuk'; also high, nasal 'kear, kear' (American data). **Habitat:** coasts, beaches, tidal flats, freshwater wetlands. **Range and Status:** breeds Canadian prairies and inland N. America; migrates to w. S. America. Wanders widely: sight-records of adults and imms from s. WA, SA, coastal and inland NSW, s. and ne. Q (Cairns Esplanade); mostly summer. Vagrant.

LAUGHING GULL *Larus atricilla* 36–40 cm; span 1.05 m

Nonbreeding: *seemingly longer than Silver Gull, with longer, drooping black bill (some orange-tipped); long, slender black wingtips extend beyond tail, all but outer two primaries finely tipped white; legs blackish.* Head/body white, washed greyish with *whitish eyelids and speckled, shadowy rear hood; upperparts grey–brown; rump and tail white.* **Breeding plumage:** bill dark red with black ring near orange tip; *white 'eyelids' stand out against distinctive black hood.* In flight, *all flight-feathers except two outer primaries have narrow white trailing edge; rump and tail white.* **Immature:** bill/legs black; rear of head brownish grey; forehead and throat white; breast washed grey–brown; mantle grey–brown; wing-coverts brownish, with pale feather-margins; in flight, wingtips black; rest of wing has narrow white trailing edge, with dark subterminal band on secondaries; underwing dusky; *note broad black subterminal band on white tail, extending from edge to edge.* Singles, pairs; with other gulls, waders. Scavenges along tidelines; flight powerful, wingbeats 'jerky' (Harrison, 1983). **Similar species:** Franklin's Gull. **Voice:** strident laugh, or variety of low chuckles. **Habitat:** coasts, tidal flats. **Range and Status:** breeds coastal e. N. America, and California: migrates to ne. Brazil and down Pacific coast to n. Chile. Vagrant Hawaii, Samoa, elsewhere in Oceania. Two (or more) present on Esplanade, Cairns (n. Q), at intervals of months in recent years possibly having followed ships across Pacific. Vagrant.

SABINE'S GULL *Larus sabini* 27–32 cm; span 90 cm–1 m

Small tern-like gull with slightly forked tail and *a unique upperwing pattern of black, white and grey triangles; underwing grey.* **Nonbreeding:** bill short and thin, black with yellow tip; head white with *shadowy eye-marking and partial rear hood; upperparts grey; black wingtips tipped white; body, rump and forked tail, white;* legs short, dark grey. **Breeding plumage:** *black-bordered, dark grey hood;* bill and legs as above; *eye-ring red.* **Immature:** bill black; forehead white; grey rear hood extends onto nape; upperparts, shoulders and wing-coverts grey–brown, with black bars and white tips to feathers; *tail white with black fork;* some have dusky bar on underwing; legs yellowish or pinkish grey. Singles, with other gulls, terns. Flight tern-like: picks food from surface of water or mud in flight; scavenges around boats. **Habitat:** ocean waters, coasts, bays, beaches. **Voice:** harsh, grating and tern-like 'k-year'. **Range and Status:** breeds arctic: winters oceanic regions in s. hemisphere. Siberian birds travel se. through n. and e. Pacific to Peru Current of S. America; n. American and Greenland birds through e. Atlantic to Benguela Current off Namibia, S. Africa. Many young overwinter there (Cramp, 1983). Sight-records Darwin (NT); se. SA; s. NSW; all autumn–winter. Vagrant.

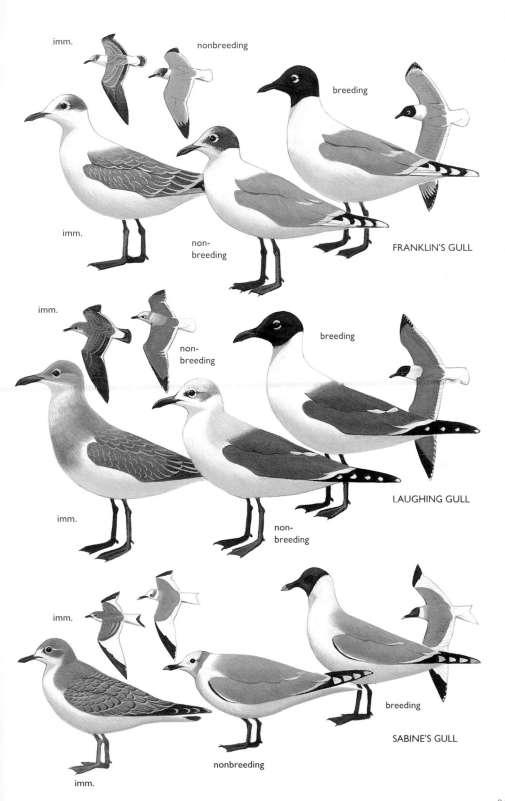

imm.

nonbreeding

breeding

imm.

non-
breeding

FRANKLIN'S GULL

imm.

non-
breeding

breeding

imm.

non-
breeding

LAUGHING GULL

imm.

breeding

nonbreeding

SABINE'S GULL

imm.

WHISKERED TERN *Chlidonias hybrida* 25–27 cm; span 70 cm

Largest marsh tern. **Breeding plumage:** *bill dark red; legs red; black cap pulled well down; cheeks white (hence 'whiskered'); upperparts pearl-grey; throat/breast silver-grey; underparts smutty black.* **Nonbreeding:** bill, legs black/dull red; plumage paler — forehead white; crown streaked black; *black line through eye widens on rear crown; ear-coverts white but no obvious pale rear collar;* underparts white. **Juvenile:** heavily mottled dark brown on mantle/shoulders. **Immature:** like nonbreeding, with darker shoulder-patch, *paler rump*. Open companies *work into wind, swooping and dipping over shallow wetlands, crops;* often fly fast cross-country, like waders. **Similar species:** White-winged Black Tern, nonbreeding. Common Tern, nonbreeding. **Voice:** grating 'kittitt' or 'ki-ik'. **Habitat:** vegetated and open wetlands; brackish, saline lakes; saltfields, irrigated lands, sewage ponds; occasionally offshore. **Nest:** small pile of floating vegetation, or on small island; in loose colony. **Eggs:** 2–3; glossy, pale stone; spotted, blotched grey, black. **Range and Status:** summer breeding migrant to s. Aust. (Sept.–March); some overwinter: migrates in autumn–winter through n. Aust. to PNG, Indonesia, possibly Philippines. Vagrant Tas; NZ. Also Eurasia, Africa, Asia.

WHITE-WINGED BLACK TERN *Chlidonias leucoptera* 22–24 cm; span 66 cm

Smaller than Whiskered: flight more fluttering, wings rounder, short tail barely forked. **Breeding plumage:** bill, legs red; head/body black; wings grey with white shoulder, black wing-linings; rump/tail white. **Nonbreeding:** bill black; legs pinkish black; *smutty black crown extends onto ear-coverts, some have dark patch only on ear-coverts; white rear collar and whitish rump contrast with grey back and tail; underwings whitish, or with patchy black under wing-coverts.* **Juvenile:** back mottled dark brown; rump grey–white; *outer primaries black; dark leading and trailing edges of wings contrast with paler grey centre of upperwing.* Parties, open flocks with other terns, especially Whiskered. **Similar species:** Whiskered Tern, Black Tern. **Voice:** buzzing 'kee-eek'; rapid 'kik-kik-kik'; sharp 'kik'. **Habitat:** large wetlands, coastal and inland; saltfields, sewage ponds, estuaries, coastal waters. **Range and Status:** breeds Eurasia: migrates to Africa, s. and se. Asia, Indonesia, PNG and NZ. Nonbreeding summer migrant to n., e. and se. Aust. (Sept.–May), at times well inland on extensive freshwater wetlands. Irruptions into sw. WA after tropical cyclones. Many acquire breeding plumage before departure; some overwinter. Casual Lord Howe I.

BLACK TERN *Chlidonias nigra* 22–24 cm; span 66 cm

Breeding plumage: bill, legs reddish; *head/body black, with grey wings, rump and tail. In flight, underwings greyish white.* **Nonbreeding:** like White-winged, but: (1) bill finer, tail longer; (2) head blacker, extending over eye and ear-coverts; (3) distinctive dark mark on side of upperbreast near wing; (4) narrow white rear collar; (5) uniformly mid-grey upperparts. In flight, note white rear collar, diagnostic dark mark on sides of upperbreast, dark leading edge to upperwing near body; wing-linings grey–white, never patchy black — although breast/flanks may be speckled black. **Juvenile:** bill yellowish at base; legs yellow–brown; back mottled brownish black; in flight, upperwing less contrasting than imm. White-winged; rump greyer. **Voice:** quiet; squeaky, 'kik', 'ki-ki-ki' or 'keek keek'. **Habitat:** coastal seas, estuaries, coastal lakes, freshwater wetlands, ricefields, rivers, lakes. **Range and Status:** breeds Europe, w. Siberia; N. America: migrates to Africa, S. America, s. and se. Asia. Rare summer–autumn straggler mostly to coastal Aust.: sight-records Cairns (ne. Q); e. NSW; s. WA and Anna Plains, nw. WA.

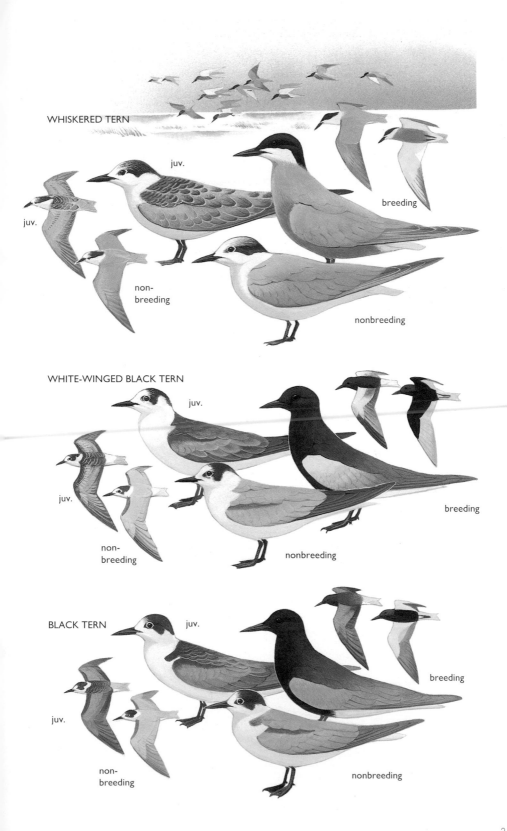

WHISKERED TERN

juv.

juv.

breeding

non-
breeding

nonbreeding

WHITE-WINGED BLACK TERN

juv.

juv.

non-
breeding

nonbreeding

breeding

BLACK TERN

juv.

juv.

non-
breeding

nonbreeding

breeding

229

CASPIAN TERN *Sterna caspia* 48–55 cm; span 1.1–1.4 m

Largest tern, with *robust scarlet bill*. **Breeding plumage:** forehead/crown black. **Nonbreeding:** forehead white; rear crown, ear-coverts streaked brownish. **Juvenile:** bill orange with blackish tip; ear-coverts/crown streaked blackish brown; upperparts mottled. In flight: *long wings darker at tip; tail short, white, slightly forked.* Patrols 10–15 m high with easy beats; swoops, hovers, plunges. Noisy, aggressive over nest. **Voice:** deep, harsh 'kraa-uh'; 'kah'. **Habitat:** coastal, offshore waters; beaches, mudflats, estuaries, larger rivers, reservoirs, lakes; *some inland.* **Breeds:** Sept.–Dec. in s.; any month in n.; pairs, colonies on sandspits, islands. **Eggs:** 1–2; creamy grey to pale brown, lightly spotted, blotched blackish, dark brown; in scrape with seaweed, grass, sticks. **Range and Status:** Aust., incl. Tas: seldom numerous; some breeding companies 200+. Nomadic, part-migratory. Cosmopolitan.

GULL-BILLED TERN *Sterna nilotica* 37–43 cm; span 1–1.2 m

Bill black, deep; at rest, wingtips extend beyond tail; legs black, long. **Breeding plumage:** black cap pulled down over eyes. **Nonbreeding:** head white, ear-coverts black. **Juvenile:** streaked darker on crown; mottled above. Singles, parties: in flight *note broad whitish wings with dark trailing edge at tip; tail short, forked.* Swoops/skims gracefully, plucks prey from surface of water, ground; seldom plunges. **Similar species:** Caspian Tern. **Voice:** throaty 'ka-huk', or 'tirruck-tirruck'. **Habitat:** fresh, brackish wetlands; beaches, mudflats, inland swamps, lakes, grasslands, crops, ploughed lands, airfields. **Breeds:** Sept.–May, small colonies on islands in inland lakes mostly in s. Aust., but large colony *c.* 800 nests reported, Barkly Tableland (NT). **Eggs:** 2–3; buff–white, grey–green; blotched purplish red, brown, lilac; in scrape, lined with twigs, feathers. **Range and Status:** cosmopolitan race *macrotarsa* mostly sparse, but present all months coastal e. Aust. s. to *c.* Hunter R. (NSW). Summer breeding visitor to se. Aust.; breeds well-inland and in w. Aust. when conditions suitable; scarce and patchy in s. WA; mostly winter visitor coastal n. Aust., PNG. Vagrant Tas., Lord Howe I., NZ. Nomadic. Race *affinis*: nonbreeding summer migrant (Sept.–April) from Asia to n. and e. coasts, s. to Hunter R. (NSW): smaller, greyer, shorter legged; usually in nonbreeding plumage.

CRESTED TERN *Sterna bergii* 44–48 cm; span 95 cm–1.05 m

Bill long, straw-yellow; legs black. **Breeding plumage:** *shaggy black cap separated from bill by white saddle*; upperparts deep silver-grey. **Nonbreeding:** duller; front of head white. **Immature:** *bill greenish straw; forehead white; cap smutty; upperparts/shoulders heavily mottled; flight-feathers, tail-tips dusky grey; in flight, pale patch on upperwing contrasts with dark leading edge and wingtips.* Singles, flocks: flies on rakish narrow wings with deep, easy beats; plunges; often offshore. Spectacular paired mating flights. **Similar species:** Lesser Crested Tern. **Voice:** rasping 'carrik' or 'kirrik'. **Habitat:** coastal, offshore waters; beaches, bays, inlets, tidal rivers, salt swamps, lakes, larger rivers. **Breeds:** Sept.–Jan. e. and s. Aust.; most months n. and w. Aust. **Eggs:** 1 (rarely 2); stone-coloured, scrawled, blotched black, red–brown, umber, shadowy grey; in scrape or on rock; in colony (some thousands) on island. **Range and Status**: coastal Aust., and Tas.; abundant in s. Aust. Sedentary; dispersive. Also Fiji–Philippines; s. and e. Asia; Red Sea–s. Africa, where known as Swift Tern.

LESSER CRESTED TERN *Sterna bengalensis* 37–42 cm; span *c.* 90 cm

Smaller, paler than Crested, with *orange bill.* **Breeding plumage:** *black cap extends nearly to base of bill*; white spots on forehead. **Nonbreeding:** bill duller; *forehead white, streaked black on crown.* **Immature:** dark shoulder-mark, mottled brownish above; outer primaries, outer tail-feathers sooty. **Voice** (and behaviour): like Crested Tern. **Habitat:** offshore waters; islands, cays, reefs, beaches. **Breeds:** Oct.–Dec.; April–May, depending on location. **Egg:** 1; light stone-coloured, blotched, spotted dark purple, underlying lavender marks; in scrape, in colony, on island. **Range and Status:** coastal n. Aust.: from Shark Bay (WA) to *c.* Brisbane (Q); breeds from Bedout and Adele Is. (WA) to Capricorn group, s. Gt Barrier Reef (Q); casual NSW, sw. WA. Also Solomons–PNG–Indonesia to Red Sea, w. Mediterranean. Sedentary.

breeding

CASPIAN TERN

juv.

juv.

GULL-BILLED TERN

breeding

breeding

juv.

nonbreeding

breeding

CRESTED TERN

breeding

nonbreeding

juv.

LESSER CRESTED TERN

breeding

breeding

breeding

nonbreeding

231

ROSEATE TERN *Sterna dougallii* 35–38 cm; span *c.* 75 cm

Breeding plumage: beautiful small tern *with long white tail-streamers. Bill long black, some with red base; longish legs red; black cap pulled down over bill, nape;* upperparts pearly grey; white underparts *suffused pink.* In flight, three black outer primaries form *narrow dark leading edge to wingtip, with white trailing edge.* **Nonbreeding:** bill black; forehead white; crown mottled, rear crown black; light grey bar on shoulder; shorter tail-streamers; legs orange–red. In flight, note grey shoulder-bar, black wedge on outer leading edge, white trailing edge to primaries. **Immature:** like nonbreeding; shoulder bar greyer; outer primaries black; legs black. Singles, small flocks with other terns; gulls, waders. Flight buoyant; *wingbeats shallower, quicker than Common/Arctic; white tail longer.* **Similar species:** White-fronted Tern: bigger, forehead whiter; black crown more domed. Common/Arctic Terns: bodies slightly larger; bills, legs, tails shorter; crowns rounder: *dark trailing edge to primaries; dark edge to outer tail-streamers.* **Voice:** rasping 'aach, aack'; soft 'chuick'. **Habitat:** offshore waters, islands, coral reefs, sand cays, beaches, tidal inlets. **Breeds:** Aug.–Dec.; April–June, depending on location. **Eggs:** 1–2 (3); stone-coloured, spotted, blotched dark brown, grey; in rock-cavity; scrape in sand; in colony. **Range and Status:** breeds islands near Fremantle, and Abrolhos Group (WA), n. into tropics; on Gt Barrier Reef (Q), s. to Bunker/Capricorn Groups. Casual s. to C. Leeuwin (WA) and Ballina (NSW). Sedentary; seasonally dispersive. Also Torres Strait, New Cal., Solomons, PNG, s. and e. Asia; Europe, n. Africa, N. America.

WHITE-FRONTED TERN *Sterna striata* 38–42 cm; span *c.* 80 cm

Breeding plumage: black cap separated from bill by *white saddle; white rear collar;* some have rosy wash over breast. At rest, *white line along upper edge of folded primaries; tail white, deeply forked; long streamers extend past wingtips.* **Nonbreeding:** *smaller, paler than Crested Tern; bill black, slender, with whitish tip; legs red–brown; head domed, forehead white, black cap extends forward through eye; primaries grey (outer primary has black outer web); greyish tail deeply forked.* **Immature:** mottled white on forehead/crown; cap smutty; *mantle, wing-coverts strongly barred black; broad black shoulder-bar; primaries/tail dark grey with black tips; in flight, pale grey secondaries form wedge between black wingtips and black shoulders; dark back contrasts with pale grey rump.* Mostly winter visitor, often with Crested Terns. Flight buoyant, wingbeats choppy; hovers, swoops to pick food from surface, rarely plunges; follows fishing boats. **Similar species:** Common/Arctic Terns, nonbreeding: bill shorter; upperparts greyer; in flight, *dark trailing edge to primaries.* Roseate Tern, nonbreeding: grey shoulder-bar; wingbeats shallower, more fluttering; note range. **Voice:** high-pitched 'siet' or 'zitt'. **Habitat:** offshore waters; bays, reefs, islands. **Breeds:** Oct.–Dec. (NZ). **Nest:** scrape in sand, shingle, depression in vegetation. **Eggs:** 2; pale stone, blotched grey below surface; bolder black splodges. **Range and Status:** breeds NZ, sub-Antarctic islands: regular migrant (March–Oct.) to offshore and coastal NSW, Vic., Tas.; casual n. to Rockhampton (Q), w. to Adelaide (SA); accidental inland. N.B. small numbers breed Nov.–Feb. on islets off s. Furneaux Group, Tas.

BLACK-NAPED TERN *Sterna sumatrana* 30–32 cm; span *c.* 60 cm

Small, *pale grey/white tern with longish fine black bill/legs; black line through eye widens onto nape; fine black edge to outer primary; tail long, white, forked.* Underparts may be washed pale pink. **Immature:** bill blackish yellow; crown streaked grey–brown; nape-mark indistinct above whitish collar; upperparts heavily marked with blackish fringes to pale grey feathers of mantle; flight-feathers, tail grey. In flight, looks very white, with fine black leading edge to wingtip; wingbeats short, choppy, with diving swoops to surface. Often with Roseate and other terns, noddies. **Similar species:** Little Tern, nonbreeding and imm.: greyer above, darker shoulder-mark and flight-feathers; wingbeats quicker. Roseate Tern, nonbreeding: larger; greyer above, with longer black nape, grey shoulder-bar; legs orange–red. **Voice:** sharp, high-pitched 'tsii-chee-chi-chip'. **Habitat:** tropical, subtropical seas: forages over lagoons, edges of reefs; coasts, mostly offshore. **Breeds:** Oct.–Dec., in colonies on islands, cays. **Eggs:** 2 (3); white; spotted, blotched purplish black, mauve–grey, blackish with underlying lavender; in rock-crevice, scrape in coral or shingle beach; under roots, vegetation. **Range and Status:** coastal n., ne. Aust., from Capricorn Group (se. Q), n. and w. to islands off Cobourg Pen. (NT) (Blakers et al, 1984). Occasional s. in winter to Bribie, Stradbroke Is. (se. Q) and w. to *c.* Darwin (NT); casual Broome (WA). Sedentary, dispersive. Also Torres Strait, tropical Indian and w. Pacific Oceans.

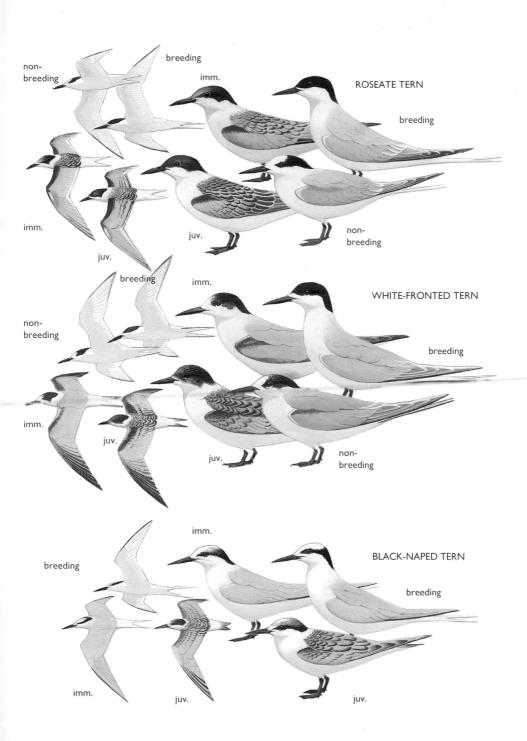

non-
breeding

breeding

imm.

ROSEATE TERN

breeding

imm.

juv.

juv.

non-
breeding

breeding

imm.

WHITE-FRONTED TERN

non-
breeding

breeding

imm.

juv.

juv.

non-
breeding

imm.

breeding

BLACK-NAPED TERN

breeding

imm.

juv.

juv.

COMMON TERN *Sterna hirundo* 32–38 cm; span 80 cm

Not widely 'common' in Aust., but locally abundant in summer. **Nonbreeding:** bill black; legs black or orange–red; forehead white, mottled dull black on crown; black cap extends forward through eye; at rest, note *blackish shoulder-bar, long, upswept blackish wingtips, equal to length of greyish forked tail, outer webs black. Flight very buoyant, body rising and sinking at each wingstroke: hovers, dips, plunges, quickly flutters up:* note dark shoulder-bar, dark trailing edge of wing near body, narrow dark wedge on leading edge of wingtips. On underwing, smudgy black tips to outer primaries *form broad dark bar along outer trailing edge,* adjacent outer *secondaries become a translucent triangle on trailing edge.* **Breeding plumage:** bill black *(red in nominate race);* legs may be reddish. Cap black; upperparts whiter; *underparts washed pearl-grey.* Rump and tail white with *fine black outer webs to long streamers.* In flight overhead, *translucent white outer secondaries contrast with broad grey trailing edge to outer primaries.* **Immature:** dark shoulder-bar; in flight, *dark tips to secondaries form grey line along upperwing; outer primaries dark grey; tail pale grey, outer edges blackish.* **Similar species:** Arctic, Roseate Terns. White-fronted Tern: larger, whiter, no black on tail; imm.: stronger patterns; mostly winter visitor. **Voice:** excitable, brisk 'kik-kik-kik-kik'; or 'keer-keer-keer-keer'; high-pitched 'keeee-yaah'. **Habitat:** offshore waters, beaches, reefs, bays, estuaries, sandflats, saltfields, sewage ponds, freshwater wetlands. **Range and Status:** breeds across n. hemisphere. Race *longipennis* of n. and e. Siberia regular summer migrant (Sept.–April) to coastal nw., n., e. and se. Aust., from Port Hedland (WA) to Adelaide (SA). Many imms overwinter. Banded adults of European nominate race recovered in s. WA, Vic.

ARCTIC TERN *Sterna paradisea* 33–38 cm; span *c.* 80 cm

Very like Common Tern: *bill shorter, deeper; forehead higher; neck shorter; legs very short.* Solitary to small flocks: on wing, looks 'neckless'; flight very light and graceful, with 'springy' wingbeats. **Nonbreeding:** bill black, sometimes red at base; forehead/crown white, with black wedge widening through eye to rear of head and nape; birds in moult have white patch in centre of black crown, look 'capped' (Carter et al, 1994). *Upperparts pale grey; shoulder-bar; deeper grey; rump/tail white; outer streamers grey with narrow black outer web.* In flight, overhead, underparts white; *flight-feathers translucent; black leading edge to outer primary and dark tips to all primaries form sharp black line on both edges of wingtip.* **Breeding plumage:** seldom seen in Aust.: bill blood-red; legs red; full black cap; upperparts whiter, primaries greyish, wings otherwise as above; breast pearly grey; *long tail-streamers have thin black outer edge; at rest, extend well beyond wingtips.* **Immature:** darker grey above than imm. Common, with fainter dark shoulder-bar; rump and tail white. Overhead, *secondaries white;* outer primaries dark grey; tail shorter, with thin grey outer web. **Similar species:** Common, Roseate, Antarctic Terns. **Voice:** rising, double-syllabled 'kee-yahr'; higher, whistled 'kee-kee'. **Habitat:** more oceanic than Common; but occurs on beaches, tidal mudflats, saltmarsh, reefs, bays, inlets; at times storm-driven inland. **Range and Status:** breeds widely across far n. hemisphere: migrates s. through Atlantic and e. Pacific to Antarctic pack ice — world's longest annual migration. Many remain several seasons in s. Singles to flocks, often mixed with other terns: recorded in s. Aust. all months, from Fremantle (WA), to s. Q, exceptionally n. to Cairns (Q). Birds banded in Russia, Scandinavia, UK have been recovered here.

ANTARCTIC TERN *Sterna vittata* 40–42 cm; span c. 80 cm

Bulkier than Common/Arctic Terns: bill longer, heavier; legs longer; wings and tail shorter; attains breeding plumage at opposite time of year (Oct.–April). Flight easy, undulating; dives vigorously, sometimes vertically. **Breeding plumage:** bill coral–red; legs orange–red; *blue–grey above and below, with white facial streak between black cap and grey underparts. Rump, under tail-coverts and deeply forked tail white.* In flight, tips of black outer primaries form black trailing edge, but outer web of tail-feathers *pale grey, not edged black.* **Nonbreeding:** large white forehead; rear crown blackish; *bill and legs dusky pink. Some birds in moult have smoke-grey breastband* (Harrison, 1983). **Immature:** like nonbreeding; bill and legs black; dark shoulder-bar, underparts whitish, lightly washed grey–brown across breast. **Voice:** shrill, high-pitched; described as 'chit-chit-churr' (Harrison, 1983). **Range and Status:** breeds Antarctic Peninsula and sub-Antarctic islands, incl. Macquarie I., and NZ region. Migrates in winter to S. America, S. Africa; rare vagrant SA, Vic.

non-breeding

breeding

imm.

COMMON TERN

breeding

nonbreeding

imm.

juv.

juv.

breeding

imm.

non-breeding

ARCTIC TERN

breeding

nonbreeding

imm.

juv.

juv.

non-breeding

breeding

imm.

ANTARCTIC TERN

breeding

imm.

juv.

nonbreeding

juv.

FAIRY TERN *Sterna nereis* 21–25 cm; span *c.* 50 cm

Very like Little Tern in habits and appearance, especially in immature plumage, when difficult to separate. *Fairy is paler and chunkier; bill deeper from top to bottom; legs shorter (at rest, 'knees' are nearly hidden in plumage); flight feathers only slightly greyer than wing.* **Breeding plumage:** large white forehead *with no white eyebrow.* Black of crown extends *bluntly (not in sharp wedge)* a short way from eye to bill; whole crown and nape black. *Bill and legs orange–yellow; upperparts whitish; all flight-feathers whitish grey.* **Nonbreeding:** *base and near-tip of bill blackish, central part dull yellow; only forehead white; crown and nape black; faint grey shoulder-mark; primaries mid-grey.* **Immature:** like nonbreeding, with white forehead and crown; bill black; legs dull orange–brown; fainter shoulder-bar. Small to large flocks (thousands in nw. WA) but now mostly in small numbers in s. and se. Aust. Flight and feeding behaviour like Little Tern. **Similar species:** other small terns are best distinguished by foraging and flight-styles: no other local *small* terns have yellow bills. **Voice:** like Little Tern: hard, loud 'tchi-wick'; excited 'kirrikiki-kirrikiki'; rapid, high-pitched 'ket-ket-ket-ket'. **Habitat:** as Little Tern. **Breeds:** Sept.–Jan., in single pairs, small to large colonies; on beaches, islands, rock platforms. **Eggs:** 1–3; paler, rounder than Little; cream–yellow, splotched umber and grey. **Range and Status:** predominantly an Aust. species: breeds from n. of Broome (Lacepede Is.) (WA) and Pilbara coast, where locally very abundant, coastally s. and e. in much smaller numbers to e. Vic. (has bred Mallacoota Inlet and se. NSW), Bass Strait islands, n. and e. Tas. Casual n. to Botany Bay (NSW) and Admiralty Gulf (WA) (Blakers et al, 1984). Breeding range is overlapped by that of Little Tern in e. Tas. and e. Vic., w. to about St Vincent Gulf (SA), with some interbreeding. Birds on Heron I. and elsewhere on Gt Barrier Reef may be migrants from New Cal.; casual ne. Q (Bowen, (Nov.)) and Cairns (July). Also breeds NZ.

LITTLE TERN *Sterna albifrons* 21–24 cm; span *c.* 50 cm

Breeding plumage: bill pale yellow, usually *with black tip; forehead white, extending back over eye in short, sharp white eyebrow; cap black, with slim black wedge from eye to bill; wings pale grey, with two or three outermost primaries black;* legs yellow. **Nonbreeding:** bill black, with some yellow at base; large white forehead goes back over eye; *blunt* black mark in front of eye as in Fairy Tern; *crown white, black band around nape;* legs dull yellow. In flight, blackish shoulder-bar forms dark inner leading edge; *black outer primaries form dark wedge on wingtip.* **Immature:** bill black; less black in front of eye; forehead and crown white, nape-band black; back and wings 'scaled'; shoulder mottled smutty black; primaries dark; legs blackish or yellowish black. Small to large flocks: *flies with very quick, deep beats of narrow, pointed wings; hovers rapidly; parachutes down on stiff, upheld wings before plunging.* In flight, short, white forked tail often forms a single spike. Note: *in summer, in nw., n. and e. Aust., migratory Asian-breeding Little Terns in nonbreeding plumage mingle with local Little Terns in breeding plumage.* **Similar species:** Fairy Tern. **Voice:** excited sharp, high-pitched 'kweek!'; urgent 'tee-eep tee-eep tee-eep'; chitterings. **Habitat:** coastal waters, bays, inlets, saline or brackish lakes, saltfields, sewage ponds near coast. **Breeds:** mostly Sept.–Jan., in se. Aust.; May–July (Gulf of Carpentaria and se. Asia); in colonies on islands, sandspits, beaches, dune-wastes. **Eggs:** 1–2 (3); stone-coloured, spotted, blotched dark brown, umber and grey; in scrape in sand or shell-debris. **Range and Status:** coastal nw., n., e. and se. Aust., from about Shark Bay (WA), to e. Tas., and w. to Yorke Pen. (SA). The race most widespread in Aust. is *sinensis*. In Aust. it breeds from near Broome (WA); on islands in Gulf of Carpentaria; in ne. Q and some Gt Barrier Reef islands, to se. Aust: in recent decades small numbers have extended breeding range to c. Vic., e. Tas. and s. SA, overlapping eastern limits of Fairy Tern, which breeds in mixed colonies with it, occasionally interbreeding. This race also breeds from PNG to s. and se. Asia. Flocks of Asian-breeding Little Terns (also mostly *sinensis*) are summer migrants (Aug.–April) to n. and e. Aust., s. to about Shark Bay (WA) and Sydney (NSW); fewer to Vic., SA. Little Terns are scarce in se. Aust. in winter, as Asian birds depart and local birds apparently migrate coastally north. Little and Fairy Terns in se. and e. Aust. have suffered serious decline caused by beachgoers, dogs, vehicles intruding on beach nest-sites. Please keep clear of any beach area where they gather. Observe warning notices.

FAIRY TERN

breeding

breeding

imm.

non-
breeding

juv.

juv.

nonbreeding

LITTLE TERN

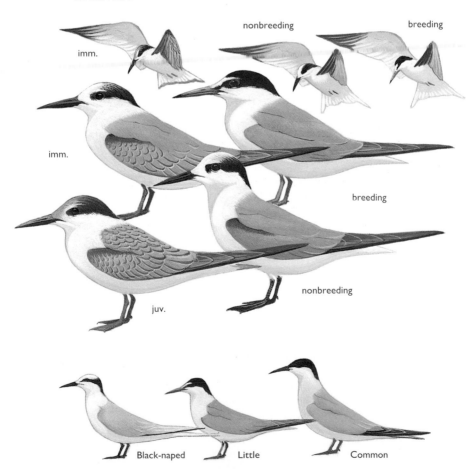

imm.

nonbreeding

breeding

imm.

breeding

juv.

nonbreeding

Black-naped   Little   Common

SOOTY TERN *Sterna fuscata* 40–46 cm; span *c.* 90 cm

Other name: Wideawake.
Black, with white forehead, underparts, tail-streamers. **Juvenile:** *sooty-grey with white scallops on upperparts; dark breast, white underparts;* tail dark, edged white, with shallow fork. Flocks skim and dip offshore, soar high; seldom plunge. **Similar species:** Bridled Tern. **Voice:** nasal 'ker-wack-wack'; endlessly at colonies. **Habitat:** tropical, subtropical seas; islands; cays. **Breeds:** spring, autumn or aseasonally. **Nest:** scrape in sand, coral debris, in colony, often immense. **Egg:** 1; white, cream, spotted, blotched dark brown, chestnut, shadowy grey. **Range and Status:** breeds n. from Abrolhos Group (WA) to n. Gt Barrier Reef, Coral Sea; Norfolk I., Lord Howe I. Has bred SA. Occurs coastally after cyclones from *c.* Townsville (Q) to s. NSW: *many are young birds;* some inland; casual Vic., SA. In WA, casual s. to C. Leeuwin. Migratory; dispersive. Also Indian, Pacific, Atlantic Oceans.

BRIDLED TERN *Sterna anaethetus* 38–42 cm; span 76 cm

Greyer than Sooty, *with white eyebrow,* partial pale collar; more white in tail. **Juvenile:** buff–white feather-margins; entire underparts pale. More solitary than Sooty: feeds offshore; dips, plunges. **Voice:** puppy-like double yap. **Habitat:** tropical, subtropical seas; offshore islands; rarely coasts. **Breeds:** autumn, winter or spring–summer; in pairs, loose colonies. **Nest:** scrape under ledge, bush; among coral blocks. **Egg:** 1; cream–white, spotted, blotched dark red–brown, indistinct blue–grey. **Range and Status:** breeds islands off w., n. and e. Aust., from C. Leeuwin (WA) to Bunker Group in s. Gt Barrier Reef (Q). (Has bred Baudin Rocks, SA.) Fairly common offshore in summer, and on Gt Barrier Reef; uncommon s. to Q–NSW border. Also PNG–se. Asia; Indian, Atlantic Oceans.

COMMON NODDY *Anous stolidus* 38–45 cm; span c. 85 cm

Largest, brownest noddy: *white cap cut off sharply by black mark between bill and eye; underwing pale with dark edges.* **Juvenile:** lacks cap; has pale mottling on wings. **Voice:** ripping 'karrk'; 'kwok, kwok'; 'eyak!'. **Habitat:** tropical, subtropical seas; cays, reefs, buoys and piles. **Breeds:** spring, autumn. **Nest:** cup of dry seaweed, grass, twigs; shells, in low shrub; scrape in coral sand. **Egg:** 1; dull white, blotched red–brown, purplish; finely spotted black. **Range and Status:** in island colonies, some huge, from Abrolhos Group (WA), n. to Timor Sea; Torres Strait, Coral Sea; s. on Gt Barrier Reef to Bunker Group; also Norfolk I., Lord Howe I. Dispersal after breeding little-known. Casual s. to Stradbroke I. (Q), coastal NSW and s. WA; vagrant, Vic. Winter visitor Top End (NT). Also tropical Pacific, Indian, Atlantic Oceans.

BLACK NODDY *Anous minutus* 33–36 cm; span c. 65 cm

Other name: White-capped Noddy.
Blackish brown with long, slender bill; white cap sharply cut off by black face between bill and eye; underwing darker; tail greyer than Common Noddy; *wingbeats quicker.* **Juvenile:** forehead white; wing-coverts tipped buff. **Voice:** nasal, rattling 'chrrr'; tern-like 'kik-kirrik'. **Habitat:** tropical, subtropical oceans; woodlands on islands; cays. **Breeds:** aseasonally, in colonies. **Nest:** mass of leaves, seaweed; guano; in leafy tree. **Egg:** 1; creamy white, spotted, blotched red–brown, purplish grey. **Range and Status:** inhabits regular island colonies (some huge) in e. Aust. on Capricorn, Bunker Groups, s. Gt Barrier Reef; Norfolk I., possibly Lord Howe I.; also Quoin I. (ne. Q) and Coral Sea. Adults sedentary; young dispersive. Casual Stradbroke I. (Q); e. NSW, Top End (NT). Also PNG, Indonesia, Philippines; tropical Pacific, Atlantic.

LESSER NODDY *Anous tenuirostris* 30–34 cm; span c. 60 cm

Small Indian Ocean noddy: *pale grey crown shades evenly between bill and eye and down neck; black area around eye does not extend to bill.* **Juvenile:** forehead pale, underparts fringed paler. **Voice:** soft rattling 'churrr's. **Habitat:** tropical, subtropical oceans; mangroves. **Breeds:** Sept.–Jan.; in island colonies, some large (*c.* 10 000). **Nest:** deep platform of seaweed, leaves, guano, on branch of mangrove; dries hard with use. **Egg:** 1; pale stone, blotched chestnut; shadowy dark brown. **Range and Status:** ■ See map for Black Noddy. Breeds Abrolhos Group (WA); Ashmore Reefs. (off nw. Aust.). Sedentary, but winter beachwashed s. to C. Naturaliste (WA). Also Madagascar, Seychelles.

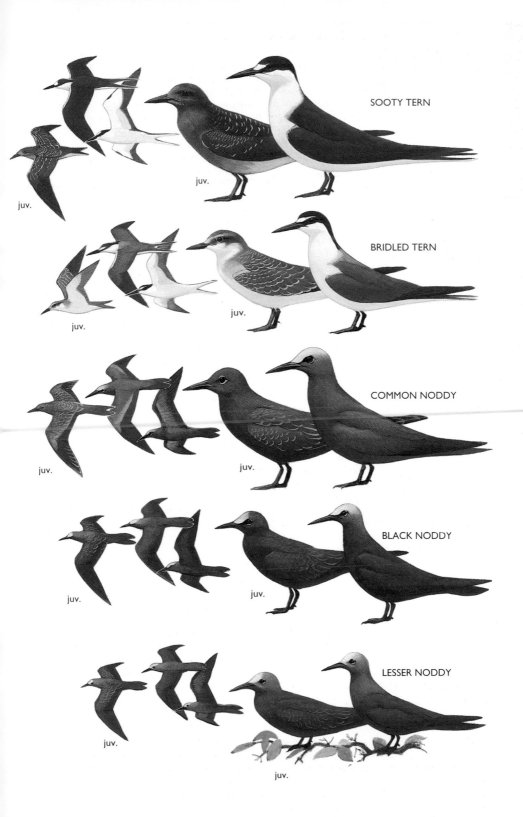

SOOTY TERN

juv.

juv.

BRIDLED TERN

juv.

juv.

COMMON NODDY

juv.

juv.

BLACK NODDY

juv.

juv.

LESSER NODDY

juv.

juv.

WHITE TERN *Gygis alba* 30–33 cm; span c. 76 cm

Other names: Love Tern, White Noddy.

Fairy-like, ethereal, *all-white tern*: overhead (against blue sky), wings and lightly forked tail part-translucent. Eye dark brown, emphasised by fine black eye-ring. Bill black, deep blue at base, seemingly uptilted; feet black with small bluish webs. **Juvenile:** black spot before and around eye; upperparts washed brown or grey; shafts of flight and tail-feathers blackish. Flight airy, or swift and darting: compact flocks hover low and dip, catching small fish as they jump. **Similar species:** Grey Ternlet. **Voice:** guttural 'heech, heech'; other notes described as rattling, wheezing, twanging. **Habitat:** oceanic islands; tropical and subtropical seas. **Breeds:** Sept.–Feb. **Egg:** 1; pale green–grey, with brown scrawls and underlying grey blotches, *laid and incubated in depression on branch of forest tree or palm frond up to 10 m above ground*. **Range and Status:** Norfolk, Lord Howe (recently) and Kermadec Is. Casual coastal e. Aust. from se. Vic. to ne. Q, summer–autumn–winter after storms, some up to 30 km inland. Also tropical, subtropical Pacific, Indian and Atlantic Oceans.

GREY TERNLET *Procelsterna cerulea* 25–30 cm; span c. 50–60 cm

Other name: Grey Noddy.

Graceful small noddy with *white head merging into pale grey neck and underparts; back and wings pale blue–grey*; flight-feathers slate-grey; *tail grey, tapered, slightly divided at tip*. Bill and eye black, with black eye-ring in front of eye, slimmer white part-ring behind. Legs long and black with yellow webs to largish, gull-like feet. Overhead, wing-linings white, margined slate-grey; tail grey. Note: uncommon dark morph birds are darker grey, with pale grey head/neck. **Juvenile:** washed brownish above and below. Compact flocks dip and flutter over surface near breeding islands. Flight graceful and fairylike; occasionally settles on water. **Similar species:** White Tern. **Voice:** rolling or purring 'cror-r-r'. **Habitat:** oceanic islands and surrounding seas. **Breeds:** Sept.–Feb. **Egg:** 1; white, laid on sheltered cliff ledge, crevice or in rock cavity. **Range and Status:** tropical and subtropical Pacific Ocean, incl. Lord Howe and Norfolk Is. Casual alive or beachwashed e. coastal Aust., usually after storms. Large flock reported from Ballina (ne. NSW), March 1995, after cyclone.

WHITE TERN

juv.

juv.

BLACK-
NAPED
TERN

dark morph

dark
morph

juv.

GREY TERNLET

SPOTTED TURTLE-DOVE *Streptopelia chinensis* 28–32 cm

Other names: Chinese, Indian Turtle-Dove; Spotted Dove.

Head *pale grey; white-spotted black patch on hind-neck; breast pinkish grey.* **Immature:** plainer; no chequered patch. Singles, pairs, companies: feeds on ground, walking sedately. Flight direct: *note blue–grey shoulders, broad white tail-tips.* Displaying males clatter up at steep angle, circle down on spread wings/tail. **Similar species:** Bar-shouldered Dove: blue–grey face/foreneck; barred copper nape; flies with head raised, showing coppery flight-feathers. Laughing Turtle-Dove (WA): reddish fawn, no rear collar; black-streaked breastband. **Voice:** mellow, rough 'coocoo, croo(oo)', or more emphatic 'coo-coo, krroo, kook!'. **Habitat:** streets, parks, gardens, railyards, wheat silos, agricultural areas, open woodlands, tropical scrubs, secondary growth, scrubby creeks. **Breeds:** mostly Sept.–Jan. in se. Aust.; autumn in n. **Nest:** scanty platform of twigs, rootlets; 1–15 m in shrub, dense tree, often exotic; ledges, level surfaces in buildings. **Eggs:** 2; white, slightly glossy. **Range and Status:** Locally common in and near settlement in coastal e., se. Aust. and Tas. (Hobart, Launceston): from Cooktown (Q) to Adelaide and Port Lincoln (SA); also sw. WA, Perth–Pemberton; Kalgoorlie; Esperance. Sedentary; expanding. Two races, *tigrina* and *chinensis*, of Burma–Malaya and s. China, were introduced from 1860s on; now much hybridised, but *tigrina* persists around Cairns (Q) (Blakers et al, 1984).

LAUGHING TURTLE-DOVE *Streptopelia senegalensis* 25–27 cm

Other name: Senegal Dove or Turtle-Dove.

Small reddish fawn dove with grey-washed head/neck and *black-speckled, deep-buff band across lower throat; shoulders and wings blue–grey.* **Immature:** duller, plainer. Singles, pairs; small flocks after breeding. Tame: walks quietly, hunched. Flight swift, level, showing prominent white tail-margins. Display-flight like Spotted Turtle-Dove. **Voice:** bubbling, laughing 'coo-oo, coocoo'. **Habitat:** urban areas, country towns, parks, gardens, railyards, roadsides, farms and farmyards, especially in WA wheatbelt. **Breeds:** Sept.–March, any month after rain. **Nest:** smaller than Spotted Turtle-Dove. **Eggs:** 2; white, ditto. **Range and Status:** Africa to India: introduced Perth (WA), from 1898; now through WA wheatbelt, e. to *c.* Southern Cross; n. to beyond Geraldton, casual Shark Bay; s. to Albany; populations Kalgoorlie, Esperance. Follows spilled grain along roads, rail routes (Blakers et al, 1984). Also Rottnest, Garden Is. Common; sedentary.

FERAL PIGEON *Columba livia* 33–36 cm

Other names: Domestic or Homing Pigeon; Rock Dove.

Typically blue–grey, with purplish/green sheen on neck; *two curved black bars (or black chequering) on wing; rump pale grey;* tail-tip dark. But endlessly variable: plain, barred or chequered red–brown to sandy; white, black or mixtures. Influence of cultivated strains shows in enlarged wattles, neck-ruffs, ballooning crops, feathered legs, fan-tails; somersaults ('tumbles') in flight. **Immature:** cere brownish; eye brown; plumage duller. Singles, pairs, flocks: feeds on ground, often around park benches; wheels high, *showing white underwings.* Males in display clap wings together, sail with wings upheld in deep V. **Voice:** deep 'coo roo coocoo'; 'rackitty-coo'; persistent 'oom's. **Habitat:** city buildings, grain installations, bridges, railyards, wharves, streets, parks, gardens, roadsides, open woodlands, paddocks, ploughed land, stubblefields, dunes, beaches, cliffs, islands, river red gums. **Breeds:** all year. **Nest:** scanty; of twigs or grass; on ledge or cavity, under eaves, roof-beams, girders, in guttering, crevice in rock, tree hollow. **Eggs:** 2; white, oval, glossy. **Range and Status:** probably introduced early in European settlement: now widespread in villages, towns, cities and homesteads inland. Wild ancestor, Rock Dove, *C. livia*, widespread Europe, n. Africa, s. and w. Asia.

SPOTTED TURTLE-DOVE

imm.

LAUGHING
TURTLE-DOVE

imm.

FERAL PIGEON

'Red Chequer'   ' Blue Chequer'   'Blue Bar'

DIAMOND DOVE *Geopelia cuneata* 19–22 cm

Tiny blue–grey dove with *red eye-ring and fine white spots on grey–browm* wings. **Female:** eye-ring smaller; markings browner; some have uneven rufous wash. **Immature:** duller, browner; with irregular open, *barred pattern of black, buff and grey–white on upperparts; some white spots on wings;* eye-ring fawn; eye brown; legs grey. Pairs, parties, winter flocks: feeds on ground in quick, toddling run; often in hot sun. Flushes with whistling 'frrr' of wings: flight undulating, fast, direct, almost like Budgerigar, *showing chestnut flight feathers; white belly, white outer tail-feathers more prominent than Peaceful Dove.* **Similar species:** Peaceful Dove: eye-ring blue–green; plumage closely scalloped black and white across breast; *wing-linings* chestnut. **Voice:** mournful, falsetto, slow, *level* four-note coo, 'oh-my-papa'; also plaintive, slow, high-pitched 'coo-cooooo'. **Habitat:** drier grassy woodlands, scrub near water, wooded watercourses. **Breeds:** any month after rain; mostly spring in s. Aust. **Nest:** fragile platform of twigs, grasses, rootlets; in low shrub or scrubby tree; stump; occasionally on ground. **Eggs:** 2; white, rounded. **Range and Status:** drier parts of all mainland states, except driest deserts; mostly absent from coastal s. Aust., s. WA (s. of Murchison R.) and Nullarbor Plain: scarce C. York Pen. (Q). But moves coastwards during dry periods inland, mostly in summer in se. Aust., winter in n. Fairly common; patchy; nomadic.

PEACEFUL DOVE *Geopelia striata* 19–21 cm

Tiny, widespread, grey–brown dove *with fine black-and-white scalloping on upperbreast.* Eye greyish white; blue–grey eye-ring connects with bill, cere. **Immature:** paler, less barred; eye grey–white with dull grey eye-ring. Pairs, parties, autumn–winter flocks: feeds on ground; tame in streets, gardens. Flushes with a 'frrr' of wings; flies in a quick, undulating, flip-flip style; note *chestnut wing-linings and dark grey undersides of flight feathers* — reverse of Diamond Dove's wing-pattern; less extensive white tips to black outer tail-feathers. **Similar species:** Diamond Dove: red eye-ring; white spots on wings. See imm. Diamond. Bar-shouldered Dove: bigger; coppery hindneck; *unbarred* grey breast. **Voice:** well-loved, falsetto, musical 'doodle-doo', also a falsetto 'co-co-coo'; emphatic 'croorrr!' in display. **Habitat:** scrublands, especially acacias; open, grassed woodlands near water; scrubby, lightly-timbered watercourses; rainforest-fringes, agricultural country, roadsides, parks, gardens, fowlyards, railyards. **Breeds:** mostly Oct.–Jan. in s. Aust.; March–June in n. **Nest:** scanty, of sticks; up to 7 m on horizontal branch or fork in leafy shrub or tree; citrus in orchard, pepper-tree near homestead. **Eggs:** 2; white, rounded. **Range and Status:** coastal e., n. and nw. Aust.: from se. SA to Kimberley and Pilbara (WA), coastally s. to *c.* Murchison R. Absent from, or sparse sw. WA and Nullarbor region; w. deserts; c. Aust.; w. SA; s.–c. Vic., where replaced by Spotted Turtle-Dove. Sedentary. Also s. PNG–Malaysia.

BAR-SHOULDERED DOVE *Geopelia humeralis* 26–30 cm

Other name: Pandanus Pigeon.
Bigger than Peaceful Dove: *unbarred blue–grey upperbreast contrasts with black-barred coppery nape;* eye-ring grey, red–brown when breeding. **Immature:** duller, washed coppery on blue–grey neck; eye-ring buff. Pairs, parties: feeds mostly on ground. Flight swift, level, direct, with loud wing-whistle. *Carries head high; note pale-copper shoulders, blue–grey fore-neck, chestnut patch on flight-feathers, cinnamon wing-lining;* white tail-edge narrower than Spotted Turtle-Dove (but display-flight similar). **Similar species:** Peaceful Dove: smaller; lacks copper nape; *has fine scallopings across breast; in flight, wing-linings chestnut, flight-feathers dark grey.* Spotted Turtle-Dove: spotted white rear-collar. **Voice:** high-pitched, melodious 'coolicoo'; emphatic 'hook, coo!, hook, coo!, hook!' **Habitat:** vegetation near water: tropical, subtropical scrubs, inland and coastal; gullies, gorges, scrubby vegetation, mangroves, by creeks, swamps; eucalypt woodlands, crops, plantations, lantana, *Pandanus* thickets, well-treed gardens. **Breeds:** mostly Sept.–Jan. in s.; Feb.–April in n. **Nest:** scanty platform of twigs, grasses; usually in shrub, low tree, mangrove or vine scrub. **Eggs:** 2; white, rounded, glossy. **Range and Status:** e. and coastal n. Aust. (and islands) from Illawarra–Blue Mts region (NSW), where increasing, to Pilbara region (WA), coastally s. to *c.* Onslow. In lowland e. Aust., inland to upper Barcoo–Warrego Rs (Q); casually s. to lower Murrumbidgee R.–Wilcannia (NSW). Vagrant nw. Vic. Also Torres Strait, s. PNG. Sedentary.

DIAMOND DOVE

imm.

♂

♀

PEACEFUL DOVE

imm.

BAR-SHOULDERED DOVE

imm.

245

BROWN CUCKOO-DOVE *Macropygia amboinensis* 38–43 cm

Other name: Brown or Pheasant Pigeon.

Graceful, long-tailed pigeon: *coppery-brown above, buffish cinnamon below with broad shadowy bars under tail*. **Male:** rose/green wash on neck. **Female:** subtle smutty pattern on neck-breast. **Immature:** buff feather-margins on upperparts; crown, underparts more chestnut, latter with faint black barrings. Birds n. of Cooktown (Q), smaller; males have greyish heads. Pairs, parties, feeding companies: not shy; often feeds in low shrubs beside roads or tracks in rainforest, secondary growth in clearings. Flight strong, graceful with easy wingbeats. Display flight like Spotted Turtle-Dove. **Voice:** mellow, high-pitched, repeated 'cuckoo-rork', rising at end ('did you walk?'), repeated frequently; rolling 'c-croor' in display. **Habitat:** highland and lowland rainforests, mostly on margins; brigalow/softwood scrubs; secondary growth; thickets of wild tobacco, inkweed, lantana. **Breeds:** mostly spring–early summer. **Nest:** scanty, of twigs laid crosswise; in understorey shrub or tree, head of *Pandanus*, palm, treefern, vine tangle; often near edge of tracks. **Egg:** 1; creamy white. **Range and Status:** coastal e. Aust. and islands: from Pascoe R. (and Weipa–Aurukun), C. York Pen., s. to near Bega (NSW); inland to Atherton Tableland–Chinchilla–Toowoomba (Q); Tenterfield–Liverpool Ra.–Budawang Ra. (NSW). Casual e. Vic. (Mallacoota Inlet, Bairnsdale). Common; seasonally, locally nomadic. Also Bismarck Arch.–PNG–Indonesia, Philippines.

TOPKNOT PIGEON *Lopholaimus antarcticus* 40–46 cm

Other name: 'Flock Pigeon'.

Big, pale grey pigeon (smaller in ne. Q) with *curious backswept 'hair-do', grey in front, ginger behind*. Flight-feathers and long tail slaty-black; *tail crossed by narrow buff–grey band*. **Immature:** plainer; bill brown; crest smaller; tail-band less definite. Parties, flocks of hundreds fly easily, strongly, over rainforests, valleys, circling effortlessly, *like big Feral Pigeons with large, banded tails*. Feeds actively on fruits in canopy, clambering, flapping, skirmishing; flocks rest in open (often dead) trees above canopy, with pattering sound of excreted seeds on foliage below. Crosses open country to isolated figs, camphor laurels. **Similar species:** White-headed Pigeon: note tail. **Voice:** seldom heard; soft, rumbling grunt; when skirmishing, short screech, like distant flying fox or pig. **Habitat:** rainforests, palms, native figs; nearby eucalypt forests, woodlands; fruiting trees in open country; orchards, e.g. cherries. **Breeds:** July–Jan. **Nest:** flat, loose, bulky, of long twigs; 3–30 m in leafy tree, usually in rainforest. **Egg:** 1; white, large, oval, slightly glossy. **Range and Status:** coastal e. Aust., from C. York to far s. coast NSW, on and e. of Divide. Fairly common from Atherton Tableland (ne. Q) to ce. NSW; scarce n. of Cooktown; casual far e. Vic. to Mallacoota region; Gippsland Lakes and Tas. unprecedented numbers (flocks to *c.* 40) in the dry summer of 1994–1995. Movements influenced by seasonal availability of rainforest fruits, or absence of same.

EMERALD DOVE *Chalcophaps indica* 23–28 cm

Other names: Emerald Pigeon, Green Dove, Green-winged Pigeon.

Small *dark pinkish brown to purplish brown pigeon with bronzed emerald-green wings; flight-feathers dark brown*; two pale grey bars cross lower back; bill and legs orange to maroon. **Male:** white shoulder-patch. **Female:** browner; grey mark on shoulder; less distinct bars on rump. **Immature:** brown, barred rufous and black on body, greenish on wings. Singles, pairs, parties: feeds unobtrusively on ground in shady cover; tame around settlement. Moves ahead of observer on forest tracks; departs with clatter; flight, low, fast; weaves through tree-trunks showing *buff underwing and chestnut patch on flight-feathers*; settles, remains motionless. **Voice:** 6 or 7 low-pitched moaning coos, starting softly, rising; also nasal 'hoo-hoo-hoon'. **Habitat:** edges/clearings in rainforest; tropical, subtropical scrubs; wet eucalypt forest; lantana, coastal heaths, scrubs, mangroves, fruiting trees, farms, gardens; drier habitats in winter. **Breeds:** spring–early summer in se. Aust.; late dry season, early wet in n. Aust. **Nest:** scanty platform of twigs in shrub, tree limb or fork; fern, vine or lantana, up to 5 m. **Eggs:** 2; creamy-white. **Range and Status:** coastal n. and e. Aust. and islands: race *longirostris* from c. Walcott Inlet, Kimberley (WA) through Top End (NT); race *chrysochlora* from C. York Pen. (Q), s. through coastal e. Aust. to *c.* Shoalhaven R. (NSW), casual s. Vic. and sw. WA; also Lord Howe and Norfolk Is. Common, dispersive, nomadic. Also New Cal., PNG to se. Asia.

BROWN
CUCKOO-DOVE

♀

♂

imm.

TOPKNOT PIGEON

imm.

EMERALD DOVE

♂

♂

imm.

♀

♀ race *longirostris*

race *chrysochlora*

COMMON BRONZEWING *Phaps chalcoptera* 32–36 cm

Pale fringes to feathers of upperparts make distinct scaly pattern; note bronzed fiery orange/green patch on wing. **Male:** forehead yellow–buff; crown purple–brown; white line curves from bill under eye; neck/breast pink–grey. **Female:** duller; forehead grey, emphasising white line on face; underparts greyer; less bronze on wing. **Immature:** duller, without bronze. Singles, pairs, open companies: feeds on ground under seeding wattles, grain-stubble at edge of scrub. Wary; departs with clatter or settles, head-bobbing, on limb. Weaves through trees at speed, with wing-whistle; *showing rich-cinnamon wing-linings.* At dawn/dusk, flies far to drink at creeks, isolated tanks, dams, etc.; comes for grain in farmyards, gardens. **Similar species:** Brush Bronzewing: smaller; uniform dark olive–brown above with rich chestnut nape; two blue–green bars cross wings; face/throat pattern differs. **Voice:** when breeding, monotonous, fugitive but carrying, swelling 'oom', repeated *at c. 3-second intervals*; lower-pitched, slower than Brush Bronzewing; much slower than Painted Button-quail. **Habitat:** forests, woodlands, mallee, native cypress scrubs, acacia thickets, coastal tea-tree, banksias and heaths; in summer, alpine woodlands to over 2000 m, coastal and inland. **Breeds:** mostly July–Jan. **Nest:** scanty platform or substantial saucer of twigs, rootlets; up to 12 m on horizontal branch, fork, mistletoe clump; near ground on stump; or on old nest of babbler, chough, magpie. **Eggs:** 2; white, oval. **Range and Status:** widespread Aust., and Tas. in suitable habitat; stronghold is se. and sw. Aust.; scarce in driest deserts, Nullarbor region (WA) and C. York Pen. (Q). Common; sedentary, locally nomadic.

BRUSH BRONZEWING *Phaps elegans* 28–31 cm

Dark olive–brown above with rich chestnut nape and shoulders; two curved bronzed blue/green bars across wing; underparts blue–grey. **Male:** forehead chestnut–buff; crown grey; *bold chestnut line back through eye joins nape, margined white below; rich chestnut throat-patch.* **Female:** duller, forehead grey; nape less chestnut; throat-patch smaller. **Immature:** greyer, duller, with fine cream fringes to wing-coverts. Singles, pairs: feeds quietly on ground at edge of scrub, roadsides; flight swift; *looks very dark; note rich chestnut shoulders, rusty flight-feathers.* **Similar species:** Common Bronzewing: larger; has distinct scaly pattern above; lacks chestnut tones and throat-patch; has *white eyeline;* larger, bronzed orange–green wingpatch. **Voice:** muffled 'whoop!', shorter, higher-pitched than Common Bronzewing; *at shorter intervals (c. 45–50 per minute);* incessantly when breeding. **Habitat:** dense scrubs, heaths, forest; woodland with scrubby understorey; mallee; alpine woodlands in summer. Drier, sparser scrubs near coast and on coastal islands. **Breeds:** Sept.–Jan. **Nest:** scanty, of twigs and rootlets; in shrub or tangle of fallen branches and leaves, near or on ground under cover. **Eggs:** 2; white. **Range and Status:** coastal se. and sw. Aust., from Fraser I. (Q) to Bass Strait islands and Tas.; Eyre Pen. and Kangaroo I. (SA), inland to w. slopes of Divide and Vic.–SA mallee. In s. WA, mostly w. and s. of Esperance–Dongara; also Recherche Arch., Abrolhos Group and other islands. Locally common; generally scarce. Sedentary.

WONGA PIGEON *Leucosarcia melanoleuca* 36–40 cm

Stately grey ground-feeding pigeon *with prominent white forehead: breast grey and white in a bold double V;* underparts white, boldly spotted black. **Immature:** duller, browner, bill blackish. Singles, pairs, parties: early and late in day feeds on forest floor or margins of cover. During day perches; calling often. Freezes, or flies with a clatter, settling on branch with back to observer. May then (or when brooding on nest) slowly raise tail, expand speckled under tail-coverts, resembling broken dead wood. Flies with tilting glides on flat wings, with quick flips. **Voice:** far-carrying, high-pitched, monotonous, whistling 'wonk', endlessly repeated in breeding season; imitated by blowing through cupped hands. **Habitat:** rainforests, wet eucalypt forests; dense timbered gullies; open, drier woodlands; brigalow, other inland acacia scrubs; roadsides; newly planted crops near cover; thistle-beds, banana plantations; quiet gardens near bush. **Breeds:** mostly Oct.–Jan.; any month when conditions suitable. **Nest:** shallow platform of sticks, twigs and stems; on horizontal fork up to 16 m. **Eggs:** 2; large, white and rounded. **Range and Status:** e. coastal Aust. and highland areas up to *c.* 1800 m, from *c.* Eungella NP, inland of Mackay (Q), to w. Gippsland (Vic.); inland to Carnarvon Gorge NP (Q), Mudgee–Tumut (NSW); Powelltown (Vic.); casual w. to Mt Macedon (Emison et al, 1987) and St Andrews. Locally common; generally uncommon. Sedentary.

imm.

♀

♂

COMMON
BRONZEWING

imm.

♀

♂

BRUSH
BRONZEWING

imm.

WONGA
PIGEON

CRESTED PIGEON *Ocyphaps lophotes* 30–34 cm

Other name: 'Topknot'.

Our only *grey pigeon with slender black crest. Wings wavily barred black; bronzed green/purple wingpatch edged white; tail longish, dark grey, tipped paler.* **Immature:** duller, no bronze on wing. Singles, pairs, open flocks; feeds quietly on ground, runs with crest erect, perches on dead trees, fences, overhead wires. Flight swift; *bursts of whistling wingbeats with flat-winged, tilting glides;* tips tail on alighting. Display-flight like Spotted Turtle-Dove. **Similar species:** Spinifex Pigeon. **Voice:** 'whoop!', repeated; singly in alarm. **Habitat:** pastoral and farming lands, watercourses, stubble-fields, croplands, weed-grown paddocks, roadsides, homestead gardens, farmyards, sportsgrounds, railyards, beaches, suburban golf-courses, urban areas. **Breeds:** mostly spring–summer, but almost any month. **Nest:** frail platform of twigs; in shrub or tree, up to 5 m. **Eggs:** 2; oval, white, glossy. **Range and Status:** originally a dweller of inland and w. Aust., has expanded coastwards with settlement: now widespread on Aust. mainland; forests of Gt Dividing Range inhibit spread into coastal far se. Aust. but becoming established in outer se. suburbs of Melbourne (Vic.). Scarce in driest deserts, n. C. York Pen. (Q), Top End (NT), Kimberley (WA). Common; sedentary.

SPINIFEX PIGEON *Geophaps plumifera* 20–24 cm

Other names: Red Spinifex or Plumed Pigeon.

Plump little rusty-buff pigeon with *tall sandy crest and wavy black barrings on wings.* **Immature:** duller, plainer. Nominate race: underparts white. Race *ferruginea*, 'Red Spinifex Pigeon': underparts *rusty-buff*. Pairs, small flocks: runs, dodges through rocks, grasses; flushes with sudden whirr or clatter; flies low, fast, with flips, glides, exposing *large copper patch on rounded wings, blackish outer tail-feathers*. Tame around habitation, camp-grounds. **Voice:** soft, high-pitched 'coo' or 'cooloo-coo'; deep guttural 'coo-r-r-r'. **Habitat:** near water in rocky, hilly country; spinifex, *Triodia*, on sandridges; acacia scrubs, grassy woodlands, creekbeds, etc. **Breeds:** spring–summer, or after rain. **Eggs:** 2; white; laid on ground in shelter of spinifex clump, low bush. **Range and Status:** n. inland Aust. Nominate race: s. C. York Pen., Gulf coast, Q–NT; inland through sw. Q–n. SA; most NT, *except* far Top End, to Kimberley (WA). Race *ferruginea*: nw. WA, from Eighty Mile Beach–Pilbara s. to *c*. Gascoyne R., inland to *c*. Meekatharra. Common; sedentary.

CHESTNUT-QUILLED ROCK-PIGEON *Petrophassa rufipennis* 28–32 cm

Plumage red–brown to dark brown, *primaries mostly pale chestnut*, forming a streak sometimes visible at rest, and noticeable *wingpatch in flight*. **Juvenile:** duller. Singles, pairs, parties that chase along ledges, preen and doze together. Feeds, drinks, at foot of escarpment: flies up to take refuge among rocks with clatter or musical loud whirr, stiff flips and tilting glides on flat wings. **Similar species:** White-quilled Rock-Pigeon. **Voice:** low coos; loud 'coo-carook'. Alarm-call: sharp, high-pitched single coo (Frith, 1982). **Habitat:** sandstone escarpments, with gullies, gorges, tumbled rocks; eucalypts, figs, other softwoods, pockets of rainforest; nearby grassy woodlands. **Breeds:** mostly dry season. **Nest:** platform of sticks on ledge or crevice in rock-face; hollowed, lined with thick pad of spinifex, leaves, stems. **Eggs:** 2; creamy white, elliptical, smooth, glossy. **Range and Status:** w. Arnhem Land (NT), from *c*. Oenpelli s. to upper Katherine R., mostly in Kakadu NP. Locally common; sedentary.

WHITE-QUILLED ROCK-PIGEON *Petrophassa albipennis* 26–29 cm

Blackish brown in Kimberley, becoming lighter, redder eastward into NT (Frith, 1982). Has less pale mottling than Chestnut-quilled: only face, throat, finely mottled white. White bases of outer primaries, barely visible at rest, become *white wingpatch in flight*. Note: small reddish race *boothi* of w. NT shows less white in wing. **Juvenile:** duller. Singles, pairs, small flocks: runs, squats motionless, merging into rocks. Behaviour, Voice, Habitat: like Chestnut-quilled. **Breeds:** probably throughout year, with peaks in wet and early dry seasons (Frith, 1982). **Nest:** of sticks, leaves, stalks of spinifex, loosely arranged; on shaded rock-ledge, horizontal crevice in cliff. **Eggs:** 2; creamy white, smooth, glossy, elliptical. **Range and Status:** Kimberley (WA), from inland of Derby s. to Argyle Downs, e. into w. NT on upper Victoria R. and Stokes Range, where race *boothi* occurs. Sedentary.

CRESTED PIGEON

imm.

SPINIFEX PIGEON

nominate
race

imm.

race *ferruginea*

CHESTNUT-QUILLED ROCK-PIGEON

WHITE-QUILLED
ROCK-PIGEON

western form

eastern form

SQUATTER PIGEON *Geophaps scripta* 26–29 cm

Dull-brown, ground-dwelling pigeon with *vertical black-and-white facial pattern; dark eye.* Pale feather-margins give wings subtly scaly pattern; *whitish sides to grey breast form distinct V.* Skin around eye orange–red in race *peninsulae* of ne. Q, blue–grey in nominate race over rest of range; feet dull blue or purplish. Immature duller. Parties, small flocks: squats, runs twisting through grass with neck craned, *crown-feathers raised in small, rough crest.* Bursts up with clatter or whirr, *showing broad dark tips of outer tail-feathers;* flies fast with quick wingbeats and tilting glides; settles on ground or horizontal branch where it squats, or stands erect, motionless. Said to be attracted to cattle camps to feed on ticks; tamer near settlement. **Similar species:** Partridge Pigeon: note range. **Voice:** low, quiet, conversational double 'coos'. **Habitat:** never far from water in grassed woodlands; foothills, watercourses, riverflats, grassy plains; environs of homesteads. **Breeds:** any month, but mostly May–June, in early dry season. **Nest:** depression in ground, lined with grass. **Eggs:** 2; creamy white, rounded. **Range and Status:** e. Q, in suitable habitat, *except* settled parts of coastal and higher-rainfall areas, far sw. and n. C. York Pen. Extends short way into n. NSW; occasional further s.; in general, rare s. of *c.* Gympie–Charleville. Locally common in n.; generally uncommon; much reduced by settlement, competition from stock, predation by foxes/cats, pot-hunting. Sedentary, part-nomadic.

PARTRIDGE PIGEON *Geophaps smithii* 25–28 cm

Squat, dull-brown pigeon with distinctive head-pattern: *heavy black bill; white eye; prominent red facial skin (yellow–ochre in Kimberley race blaauwi) outlined in white; breast pinkish brown with prominent white sides, forming large V.* **Immature:** duller, eye brown, facial skin grey. Pairs, small flocks (occasionally large): runs with feathers of crown raised in rough crest, 'freezes' or suddenly explodes with a roar, rocketting steeply up through trees or dispersing in different directions, showing broad dark tail-tips. Settles on high branch or planes fast and low on set level wings, with occasional shallow 'flip'. **Similar species:** Squatter Pigeon: note range. **Voice:** soft, rolling, double 'coo'. **Habitat:** woodlands with short grass; open rocky or sandy ground by streams, watercourses; roadsides; areas of newly-burned grass or bush; seldom far from water. **Breeds:** March–Oct., with peak in May–June (Frith, 1982). **Nest:** depression on ground; lined with grass. **Eggs:** 2; creamy white or greenish white. **Range and Status:** coastal nw. Aust.: from Kimberley (WA), s. to Cockatoo Spring; Top End (NT), s. to Mataranka–Mallapunyah; possibly into extreme nw. Q; also coastal islands, e.g. Melville I. Locally common. Sedentary.

FLOCK BRONZEWING *Phaps histrionica* 26–31 cm

Other name: Flock Pigeon.

Long-winged, sandy-coloured pigeon, usually seen in rapid flight over plains. **Male:** sandy-copper above, blue–grey below; *head black with conspicuous white forehead, ear-mark and bib.* **Female:** duller, browner; forehead dull white, smutty area on lower throat bordered by whitish bib. **Immature:** like dull female with pale feather margins, browner on breast. Flocks feed on ground far from cover, unexpectedly flush with roar. Single birds or parties traverse sky on long, lashing, backswept wings; courting males fly with quick shallow wingbeats, *glide with wings held up in stiff V.* When locally abundant, at end of day, undulating, shearwater-like flocks fly to water, settle short distance away and walk in. Thirsty latecomers may drop directly into water and drink while spreadeagled, before springing off. (May carry water to young in wet plumage.) **Habitat:** treeless grassy plains; saltbush, spinifex, open mulga, tanks, bore-drains, flooded claypans, watercourses, river pools. **Breeds:** July–Oct. **Nest:** scrape by low bush or tussock; many in proximity. **Eggs:** 2; creamy white. **Range and Status:** Barkly Tableland, e. NT, and adjacent Q, e. to *c.* Hughenden–Longreach; casual to e. coast near Townsville; w. to s. Kimberley region (WA). Casual s. to Pilbara and Shark Bay (WA); L. Eyre Basin (SA); Darling R. (NSW), occasional s. to *c.* Ivanhoe. Once in flocks of 100 000+, so numerous that eggs stained wool of resting sheep; by early 1900s feared extinct from habitat loss, foxes, feral cats, pot-hunting. Since 1950s, again in occasional flocks of thousands. Patchy; nomadic.

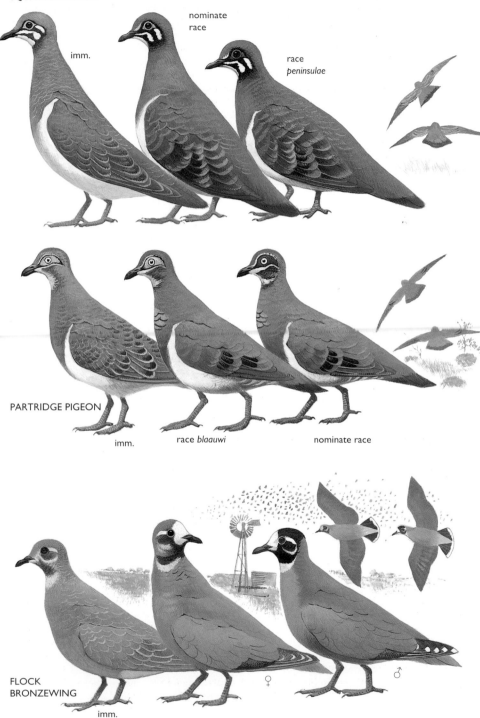

SQUATTER PIGEON

imm.

nominate
race

race
peninsulae

PARTRIDGE PIGEON

imm.

race *blaauwi*

nominate race

FLOCK
BRONZEWING

imm.

♀

♂

BANDED FRUIT-DOVE *Ptilinopus cinctus* 33 cm

Other names: Banded, Black-banded, Black-backed Fruit-Dove or Pigeon.
White-headed, black-backed, tree-dwelling pigeon *with short pale bill; black breastband; underparts blue–grey;* tail black, *broadly tipped pale grey.* **Immature:** greyer, with buffish fringes to wing-feathers. Singles, parties or small flocks: shy; when feeding in fruiting trees, e.g. native figs, may reveal itself by flapping. Flight strong, undulating. Perches on emergent limbs over woodland. **Similar species:** Pied Imperial-Pigeon. **Voice:** deep boom or hoot, lasting *c.* 1 second, repeated at intervals of 4–5 seconds (Frith, 1982). **Habitat:** rainforest pockets in sandstone escarpments; nearby eucalypt woodlands. **Nest:** flimsy, of short sticks; 2–7 m high, on horizontal fork near end of branch in leafy shrub or tree; on escarpment, in rainforest. **Egg:** 1; white, sub-elliptical, smooth, not glossy. **Range and Status:** nw. Arnhem Land (NT), from Oenpelli s. to upper S. Alligator R.; elsewhere in Top End lowlands. Sedentary; uncommon. Also Indonesia.

PIED IMPERIAL-PIGEON *Ducula bicolor* 38–44 cm

Other names: Nutmeg, Torresian Imperial or Torres Strait Pigeon.
Large tree-dwelling white pigeon with pale bill, slaty-black flight feathers and lower tail; head may be soiled brownish by fruit. Singles, parties, large flocks: conspicuous in emergent trees. In ne. Q. *in spring–summer, flocks commute daily from breeding islands to mainland rainforests to feed on fruit, returning at dusk.* Flies with continuous beats of *long, dark-tipped wings.* Displaying males fly steeply up, stall, tip forward, glide down. **Similar species:** White-headed Pigeon: black back, wings, rump and tail. Banded Fruit-Dove. **Voice:** deep 'mrrroooo!', starting with a 'cluck!'; also 'roo-ca-hoo'; low, moaning 'up-oooo'. **Habitat:** rainforests; adjacent eucalypt woodland; coastal scrubs, creeks, rivers, mangroves; vegetated cays and islands. **Breeds:** Aug.–Jan., in colony in mangroves, vines, palm fronds, mostly on well-vegetated offshore islands (some breed inland). **Nest:** substantial, of mangrove shoots, sticks; on horizontal fork 1–5 m high. **Egg:** 1; large, white. **Range and Status:** coastal n. Aust. and many islands, incl. Gt Barrier Reef, from Kimberley (WA) to near Broad Sound (Q). Kimberley population resident, non-migratory (Blakers et al, 1984). Population from Top End (NT) to e. Q migratory (Garnett, 1984), arriving from Indonesia–PNG in Aug., departing Feb.–April. Numbers once huge; slaughter at nest-colonies decimated populations in 19th century; slowly recovering with improved protection.

ELEGANT IMPERIAL-PIGEON *Ducula concinna* 43–45 cm

Other name: Blue-tailed Imperial-Pigeon.
Beautiful big tree-dwelling pigeon, a newcomer to Aust. list. Bill black; eye golden; *head, neck, entire breast soft grey–white; under tail-coverts rich chestnut; legs, feet red. Wings to tail blue–green.* In flight, *blackish underwings contrast with pale body;* wingbeats slow, deep. **Voice:** 'staccato hoarse grunt, loud upslurred growl and low-pitched upslur' (Diamond & Bishop, 1994). **Habitat:** mangroves, coastal forests, savannah woodland; also a Darwin (Nightcliff) garden. **Range and Status:** breeds on small outer islands in e. Indonesia, se. to Aru Is. group. Vagrant Darwin (NT), Sept.–Nov. 1993 and subsequently. Possibly 'caught' in flocks of Pied Imperial-Pigeons migrating from Indonesia.

WHITE-HEADED PIGEON *Columba leucomela* 38–41 cm

Other names: Baldy, Baldy Pigeon.
White head/breast contrast with glossy blackish upperparts, wings and tail. Bill red, tipped paler; eye pale orange or yellow; eye-ring, legs red. **Female:** duller, greyer. **Immature:** crown, nape, breast grey. Singles, pairs, small flocks: often seen in swift direct flight across open country or through rainforest. Feeds on fruit in canopy, low vegetation, on ground in open under trees; fallen grain in cornfields. Perches (and calls) high in rainforest. Visits bird tables. **Similar species:** Topknot and Pied Imperial-Pigeons. **Voice:** loud, gruff, explosive 'WHOO! uk, WHOO! uk, WHOO!', breath indrawn on the 'uk'; gruff, melancholy 'ooms'. **Habitat:** tropical, subtropical rainforest, scrubs; timber on watercourses; isolated trees, secondary growth, street trees. **Breeds:** mostly Oct.–Dec. **Nest:** scanty platform of twigs; usually high in canopy. **Egg:** 1; cream-white. **Range and Status:** coastal e. Aust. from Cooktown (Q) to c. Bermagui (NSW), inland to Bunya Mts NP (Q). Casual e. Vic, w. to c. Powelltown. Common; locally nomadic, increasing and expanding range, probably assisted by success of introduced camphor laurel, privet, etc.

imm.

BANDED FRUIT-DOVE

ELEGANT
IMPERIAL-
PIGEON

PIED IMPERIAL- PIGEON

WHITE-HEADED
PIGEON

♀

♂

imm.

SUPERB FRUIT-DOVE *Ptilinopus superbus* 22–24 cm

Other names: Purple-crowned Fruit-Dove or Pigeon; Superb Fruit-Pigeon. Gorgeous small foliage-dwelling pigeon. **Male:** crown rich purple; hindneck fiery orange; *blue–black breastband separates grey upperbreast from cream–white underparts. These are partly barred green at sides; green tail has grey tips.* **Female:** *green with blue–purple patch on crown; no breastband.* **Immature:** green with yellow edges to wing-coverts and *broad white broken areas below.* Singles, pairs, parties: feeds low or high in dense trees, elusive in foliage. Listen for call, falling fruit or wing-whistle in quick short flights. **Similar species:** Rose-crowned Fruit-Dove: belly apricot–yellow; tail tipped yellow. **Voice:** 5 or 6 clear, deep 'whoop's; also a low 'oom', uttered in series *but not accelerating.* **Habitat:** rainforests and fringes; scrubs, mangroves, wooded stream-margins, lantana thickets, isolated figs, pittosporums, lilly pillies, blackberries. **Breeds:** mostly Sept.–Jan. **Nest:** flimsy, of twigs; among branchlets or on fork up to *c.* 8 m. **Egg:** 1; creamy-white. **Range and Status:** coastal e. Aust. and highlands: from C. York (Q) to s. coast NSW (Moruya); casual inland to Scone–Delegate (NSW); c. and w. Vic.; n. and e. Tas. Breeds n. of Proserpine (Q) and probably further s. May migrate to PNG in winter. Many also inexplicably migrate s. through Sydney to s. coast NSW in all months, with peak in April–May, frequently hitting windows at night; many are young birds. Also Bismarck Arch., PNG, e. Indonesia.

ROSE-CROWNED FRUIT-DOVE *Ptilinopus regina* 20–25 cm

Other names: Red-crowned Fruit-Dove, Fruit-Pigeon or Pigeon. Gorgeous small foliage-dwelling pigeon with *pink or rose-red cap separated by a yellow line from grey-textured head and neck.* Often seen from below in rainforest *when apricot–yellow underparts and yellow tail-tip immediately identify it.* **Female:** duller. **Immature:** mostly green with yellow margins to wing and tail-feathers; *yellow abdomen.* Singles, pairs, parties: inconspicuous in foliage. Climbs after fruit; displays and skirmishes on exposed branches. Listen for calls, falling fruit, or quick, whistling flights. Sustained flight very swift, direct. **Similar species:** Superb Fruit-Dove: underparts patchy *white-and-green;* male has black breastband; female dark blue crown. Wompoo Fruit-Dove: purple breast cut off by yellow underparts; tail grey below, *without* yellow tip. **Voice:** surprisingly loud, explosive: begins with a slow, repeated 'hook-coo'; descends into a rapid, accelerating staccato 'coo-coo-coo-coo'. Also swelling 'OO!, uk-COO, uk-COO'. **Habitat:** rainforests, vine scrubs; adjacent eucalypt forests and woodlands; swamp woodlands, mangroves, berry or fruit-bearing trees in farms, gardens, public and private. **Breeds:** Nov.–April. **Nest:** frail platform of twigs, low in vines or other understorey vegetation; paperbark, etc., up to 8 m. **Egg:** 1; pure white, oval. **Range and Status:** coastal nw., n. and e. Aust. and coastal islands, from n. Kimberley (WA) to Arnhem Land, e. to Pellew Group (NT), and from C. York Pen. (Q) s. to *c.* Hunter R. (NSW); casual s. coast NSW, s. Vic. and Tas. Fairly common; migratory, dispersive and nomadic. Also s. PNG, s. Indonesia.

WOMPOO FRUIT-DOVE *Ptilinopus magnificus* 35–50 cm

Other names: Bubbly Jock, or Mary; Green or King Pigeon; Magnificent Fruit-Dove; Wompoo Fruit-Pigeon or Pigeon. Magnificent big pigeon, often hard to see in foliage until it moves: *head and neck grey; upperparts green, with curving yellow line across wing-coverts; breast plum–purple, cut off by rich yellow underparts; tail green above, grey below.* Singles to companies at ripening fruit: feeds high in canopy or low, often first revealed by call or falling fruit. Flight swift, direct, exposing yellow wing-linings. **Voice:** typical phrase is a deep, gruff, bubbling 'wollack-a-woo', 'bok-bok-oo', or quieter 'wompoo'. (Rudely paraphrased, 'bollocks are blue'.) Shorter sharp 'pack pack' sounds when feeding. **Habitat:** rainforests, monsoon forests; adjacent eucalypt forest; fruiting trees on scrubby creeks or in open country. **Breeds:** Oct.–Feb. **Nest:** very flimsy; usually on slim, leafy, horizontal branch, *Acacia,* or palm frond, 2–10 m high in thick scrub, often over stream. **Egg:** 1; largish, white, often visible through nest. **Range and Status:** coastal e. Aust. and forested coastal islands: from C. York (Q) to *c.* lower Hunter R. region (NSW), formerly s. to Illawarra; mostly on and e. of Divide. Races in ne. Q and PNG *smaller.* Fairly common in Q, scarcer in NSW. Sedentary, with nomadic feeding movements. Also PNG, adjacent islands; crosses Torres Strait irregularly (Garnett, 1984).

SUPERB FRUIT-DOVE

♂

imm.

♀

♂

ROSE-CROWNED FRUIT-DOVE

♂

imm.

♀

♂

WOMPOO FRUIT-DOVE

imm.

PALM COCKATOO *Probosciger aterrimus* 56–64 cm

Large, slate-black cockatoo with huge, dark grey bill and orange–pink facial skin, scarlet when excited; crest-feathers long, slender, erectile. **Female:** bill, facial patch smaller. **Juvenile:** facial patch paler; underparts, wing-linings scalloped pale yellow; bill paler. Singles, pairs, parties: perches in emergent trees, calling, displaying, sometimes upside-down, wings, crest spread. Flies with full, slow beats of broad wings, bill tucked onto breast; glides on downcurved wings. Occasionally feeds on ground. In territorial display, drums on hollow trunks with short stick held in foot, or clenched foot (Wood, 1984). **Similar species:** Red-tailed Black Cockatoo: *red or orange panels in tail*; female has yellow–orange spots and bars. **Voice:** whistling 'hweet-kweet', deep, mellow, far-carrying; harsh deep screech; also high-pitched 'surprisingly human-like . . . *howlloww*' (Frith, 1993). **Habitat:** edges of tropical lowland rainforest, eucalypt and swamp woodlands; *Pandanus*. **Breeds:** Aug.–Jan. **Nest:** layer of splintered twigs; high in hollow tree-trunk. **Egg:** 1; white. **Range and Status:** C. York Pen. (Q), s. to Archer R. on w. coast and Princess Charlotte Bay in e. Fairly common; sedentary. Also PNG, Aru Is.

GLOSSY BLACK-COCKATOO *Calyptorhynchus lathami* 46–51 cm

Other name: Casuarina Cockatoo.
Small, blackish brown cockatoo with broad, bulbous bill; low, rounded crest; blacker wings. **Male:** bill blackish; clear red panel in tail. (Some have sparse yellow feathers on head.) **Female:** *bill dark grey; irregular yellow patches on head, crest and/or neck; red tail-panel edged yellow, usually barred black.* **Immature:** tiny yellow spots on cheeks, upper, under wing-coverts; fine yellow barring on throat, abdomen, under tail-coverts (Courtney, 1986); tail like female. Pairs, family trios, small flocks: *feeds mostly in she oaks, audibly crunching seed-capsules*; flies high or through dense woodland, wingbeats quicker than Red-tailed; *tail-panels spectacular when birds turn or alight*. **Similar species:** Red-tailed Black-Cockatoo: bigger, blacker, with larger, helmet-like crest; female *spotted yellow on head/wings, barred yellow–orange on breast/ underparts*. Wingbeats slower; calls louder; note Range. **Voice:** *feeble, drawn-out, soft trumpet, like distant* Red-tailed. **Habitat:** she oaks (mostly allocasuarinas) in forests, woodlands, timbered watercourses. In ne. Vic., inland NSW and Q, in hilly, rocky ridge country. Also in eucalypts, native cypress (*Callitris*), brigalow (*Acacia*) scrub. **Breeds:** March–Aug. **Nest:** layer of woodchips in large hollow, often high. **Egg:** 1; white, oval. **Range and Status:** se. Aust.: from *c.* Eungella NP (Q) to Wingan Inlet–Snowy R. (e. Vic.); vagrant w. to Gippsland Lakes (Vic.). Ranges inland to *c.* Augathella–Tambo (Q); Cobar–Hillston– Griffith (NSW); Warby Ras.–Strathbogies (Vic.). Isolated population, Kangaroo I. (SA), occasionally vagrant to adjacent SA mainland, e.g. 20 birds, McLaren Vale, July 1995. Sedentary; declining.

RED-TAILED BLACK-COCKATOO *Calyptorhynchus banksii* 50–64 cm

The only black cockatoo in much of n. and far inland. **Male:** black, with clear *scarlet panels in tail*. Bill blackish, very robust (especially in race *macrorhynchus* of Kimberley (WA) and Top End (NT)); *crest helmet-like, erectile.* **Female and immature:** *bill whitish; yellow spots on head, neck, wings; breast-feathers barred orange–yellow; tail-panels orange–yellow, barred black.* Pairs to flocks of hundreds; sometimes thousands: feeds in foliage and on ground; in s. WA, associates with other black-cockatoos. *Flight steady, level, with majestic, deep, slow wingbeats. Conspicuous at water early, late in day.* **Similar species:** Glossy Black-Cockatoo. **Voice:** far-carrying, drawn-out trumpet: 'kreee', like rusty windmill. **Habitat:** tall open forests; woodlands (in w. Vic.–se. SA, dependent on remnant Brown Stringybark, *Eucalyptus baxteri*); grasslands, scrublands, floodplains, river margins, wetlands; river red gums on watercourses. **Breeds:** July–Oct.; March–April in s. Aust.; April–July in n. **Nest:** decayed debris in tree-hollow, usually high. **Egg:** 1, occasionally 2; white. **Range and Status:** several populations, ranging in size and bill-structure from the large, massive-billed *macrorhynchus* of tropical n. Aust. to the smaller *samueli* of inland e. Aust.: (1) tropical n. Aust., from Kimberley (WA) to most Q; casual coastal ne. NSW; regular s. to Darling R. in w. NSW; casual further s. and e. to Ivanhoe, Nyngan, Narrabri; (2) Central Ras, s. NT and nw. SA (Everard Ras.); (3) far sw. Vic. and far se. SA; (4) WA, from forests of far sw., n. through wheatbelt to Hamersley Ras.–e. Pilbara. Rare and declining in se. Aust.; common interior and w. Aust.; recovering in WA. Sedentary; seasonally nomadic, part-migratory.

PALM
COCKATOO

GLOSSY BLACK-
COCKATOO

♀

♂

juv.

race
samueli

♂

♀

race
macrorhynchus

♂

♀

RED-TAILED BLACK-COCKATOO

SHORT-BILLED BLACK-COCKATOO *Calyptorhynchus latirostris* 53–60 cm

Other name: White-tailed Black-Cockatoo.

Dull black cockatoo with pale feather margins; *white patch on ear-coverts and white panels in long tail*, often exposed in flight. **Male:** *bill black; eye-ring reddish; dull white ear-patch; less distinct feather-margins.* **Female:** *bill whitish; eye-ring grey; clear-white ear-patch; broader pale margins to breast-feathers.* Confined to WA: closely related to Yellow-tailed Black-Cockatoo of e. Aust. Differs from Long-billed Black-Cockatoo (see below) in *shorter, broader bill* adapted for cracking seed-capsules of hakeas, dryandras, banksias, grevilleas; feeds much on ground. **Habitat:** open forests, woodlands, scrublands, wheatbelt and sandplain areas; taller, denser karri, *Eucalyptus diversicolor*; exotic pine plantations in summer–autumn dispersal; gardens. **Breeds:** July–Nov. **Nest:** decayed wood-debris in large hollow in eucalypt, from near ground to over 20 m. **Eggs:** 2; oval, white; usually only one offspring survives. **Range and Status:** confined to sw. WA, from *c.* lower Murchison R. to *c.* Israelite Bay in se., inland to L. Moore–Merredin–Norseman. Breeds in n. Darling Ras. and wheatbelt, disperses coastwards in summer–autumn, returning in winter. Locally nomadic.

LONG-BILLED BLACK-COCKATOO *Calyptorhynchus baudinii* 53–60 cm

Other name: Baudin's Cockatoo.

Identical to Short-billed Black-Cockatoo, *except for its long, finely curved, narrow bill*, adapted to removing seeds from the deep seed-capsules of the marri gum, *Eucalyptus calophylla*, tearing wood to expose wood-boring 'white grubs' and removing seeds from banksia (and other) cones. Pairs, small flocks; larger flocks of hundreds or more in nonbreeding season (Jan.–June); causes damage in apple, pear and almond orchards. Flight and calls similar to Short-billed. **Similar species:** see Short-billed and Red-tailed Black-Cockatoos. **Habitat:** forests, woodlands, pine plantations, orchards. **Breeds:** July–Nov. **Nest:** on decayed debris, in hollow of isolated eucalypt, usually at some height. **Eggs:** 1–2; white, oval. **Range and Status:** heavier forested areas of sw. WA. from *c.* Gin Gin, n. of Perth, through Darling Ra. to Stirling Ra. NP, in tall karri forests and mixed jarrah/marri forests and woodlands of sw. corner. Locally, seasonally nomadic.

YELLOW-TAILED BLACK-COCKATOO *Calyptorhynchus funereus* 55–65 cm

Large black cockatoo with *pale feather-margins, and large pale yellow panels in long tail*. **Male:** *bill blackish; eye-ring reddish; dull yellow spot on ear-coverts.* **Female:** *bill whitish; eye-ring grey; bright yellow spot on ear-coverts; yellow tail-panels spotted and etched brown.* **Immature:** browner, pale feather-margins more prominent; bill pale; eye-ring grey. Pairs, family trios; autumn–winter flocks of hundreds: in coastal e. Aust. tears out sapwood of acacias, eucalypts, casuarinas, grasstrees, exposing 'white grubs'; flocks feed on ground and in foliage on seed-capsules of hakeas, banksias, exotic pines. Flight *buoyant with slow, deep wingbeats*, long tail prominent. Demonstrative on wing, wheeling, spreading, flashing yellow tail-panels, calling. **Similar species:** Red-tailed, Glossy Black-Cockatoos. **Voice:** weird, far-carrying, squealing, 'why-lar' or 'wee-lar'; much conversational chuckling and 'giggling' from flocks in flight. Harsh screeches in alarm; grinding, begging sounds from young. **Habitat:** temperate rainforests, eucalypt forests; woodlands from sea-level to above snowline; heathlands, banksia, hakea, acacia woodlands and scrubs; shelterbelts, plantations of eucalypts, exotic conifers, e.g. radiata and Aleppo pines. **Breeds:** Nov.–Feb. in s. Aust.; March–Aug. in n. NSW and Q. **Nest:** on decayed debris; in large tree-hollow, usually high. **Eggs:** 1–2; white, oval; usually only one offspring survives. **Range and Status:** se. Aust. and Tas.: from Eungella NP and (coastally) from *c.* Rockhampton (Q), to Kangaroo I. and s. Eyre Pen. (SA); inland to *c.* Blackall–Cunnamulla (Q), Walgett–Moulamein (NSW); e. and s. Vic., nw. to Little Desert NP. Moderately common; seasonally nomadic or migratory; widespread autumn–winter movements from high country to lowlands (incl. city suburbs).

LONG-BILLED
BLACK-COCKATOO

SHORT-BILLED
BLACK-COCKATOO

♀

♂

♂

YELLOW-TAILED
BLACK-COCKATOO

♀

♂

MAJOR MITCHELL'S COCKATOO *Cacatua leadbeateri* 35–40 cm

Other names: Major Mitchell, Pink Cockatoo.
Beautiful *pink-washed white cockatoo* with whitish bill; upswept whitish crest *spreads in bands of scarlet and yellow.* **Male:** eye dark brown. **Female:** eye red; crest has broader yellow band (except in WA race *mollis*, which has little or no yellow in crest). Pairs to family parties; flocks of several hundreds where food abundant. Feeds on ground, on seeds of small melons; in foliage on seeds, e.g. of acacias, saltbush, native cypress. *Wingbeats shallow, fluttering and irregular, with glides on downcurved wings; note sunset-pink underwing and undertail.* Often with Galahs, Little Corellas. **Similar species:** Sulphur-crested Cockatoo: whiter; bill black; crest yellow; underwings washed yellow. Little and Long-billed Corellas. **Voice:** distinctive stuttered, quavering, falsetto cry; in alarm, harsh screeches. **Habitat:** near water on timbered watercourses; surrounding grasslands, gibber, saltbush; mulga and other acacias; stands of native cypress, casuarinas; larger mallee eucalypts with suitable nest-hollows; mallee associated with riverine woodlands, e.g. of black box, coolibahs, river red gums. **Breeds:** Aug.–Dec. in s. Aust.; May–Aug. in Q; April–June in n. Aust. **Nest:** on decayed debris, bark-fragments, pebbles; in tree-hollow. **Eggs:** 2–4; white, oval. **Range and Status:** arid and semi-arid interior Aust., from inland Q, NSW and Vic., to w. Coast (WA) and Gt Aust. Bight. Widespread, but much less abundant than other white cockatoos. Sedentary; locally nomadic.

GANG-GANG COCKATOO *Callocephalon fimbriatum* 33–36 cm

Owl-like small dark grey cockatoo patterned by pale margins to rather square feathers; olive wash on wings. **Male:** *light red head and raffish crest.* **Female:** head/crest grey; breast-feathers fringed light red. **Immature:** like female; wings, undertail barred, marbled whitish yellow; imm. males patchy light red on head/crest. Pairs, family parties, flocks: inconspicuous in foliage, often first noticed by growls, cracking and dropping of eucalypt seed-capsules. Also eats green pods of acacias, walnuts in gardens, hawthorn seeds in hedges, 'spitfire' larvae of sawflies, leaf-gall larvae. Not shy: when flushed, swoops low, often swings steeply up into next tree. Flight loose, tilting with deep wingbeats. **Voice:** short, raven-like growls when feeding; in flight, *loud, stuttered, creaky growls, with rising inflection, like rusty hinge.* **Habitat:** wetter forests and woodlands, from sea level to over 2000 m on Divide; timbered foothills and valleys; timbered watercourses, coastal scrubs, farmlands, suburban gardens. **Breeds:** Oct.–Jan. **Nest:** decayed debris in tree-hollow in dense woodland or forest. **Eggs:** 2–3; white, rounded. **Range and Status:** se. mainland Aust., from mid n. coast, Hunter Region and c. Tablelands (NSW) s. to w. Vic.; inland to *c.* Merriwa–Bathurst–Wagga (NSW); e. and c. Vic. w. to Grampians region, stringybark forests of far sw. Vic. and adjacent se. SA. Rare visitor Tas. and some Bass Strait islands; formerly resident King I. Fairly common in suitable habitat. Sedentary; seasonally nomadic or part-migratory: in autumn–winter, wide dispersal from highlands through coastal and sub-inland woodlands, farmlands, urban areas.

GALAH *Cacatua roseicapilla* 34–38 cm

Pale grey above, with cap-like crest; pink to deep rose-red below. Male: eye dark brown; female: eye red. Nominate race *roseicapilla* has whitish crown and crest; deep red eye-ring; race *assimilis*, confined to WA, has pinker crest; pale grey eye-ring; *whiter rump and tail.* **Immature:** (both races) breast washed grey; eye-ring grey. Pairs to very large, noisy flocks: wingbeats 'change gear' after take-off; flight swift and tilting, often flies wildly, pink then grey. Feeds on ground and in low foliage of saltbush, shrubs and trees; a pest in grain, haystacks, domestic fruit or nut trees. Flocks gather at spilt grain on country roadsides, railyards, grain silos. Waters and roosts in noisy antic companies; in rain hangs upside down from wires with wings spread. **Voice:** high-pitched, splintered 'chill chill'; harsher screeches. **Habitat:** open country with suitable trees; watercourses, town parks, playing fields, beaches. **Breeds:** July–Dec. in s. Aust.; Feb.–June in n. Aust. **Nest:** in tree-hollow, living or dead; strips bark from a large area around entrance; adds green eucalypt leaves and twigs; occasionally hole in cliff. **Eggs:** 2–5; white, oval. **Range and Status:** widespread on mainland Aust. in suitable habitat; absent only from driest deserts and denser forests. Range has expanded coastwards since European settlement: self-introduced and consolidating in Tas., via King I. Common to very abundant. Sedentary, with local foraging movements; young birds dispersive, nomadic.

MAJOR
MITCHELL'S
COCKATOO

♂

♀

GANG-GANG
COCKATOO

♀

♂

GALAH

race *assimilis*

nominate race

LONG-BILLED CORELLA *Cacatua tenuirostris* 38–41 cm

Note long, curved whitish bill, red forehead and throat-bar, pink tinge in under-feathers, bare whitish skin around eye; short, cap-like crest usually folded. Singles to flocks of thousands: flight swift, pigeon-like, with quick, shallow wingbeats. Looks large-headed, slender-winged; yellow wash on underwing, undertail. Digs for roots, corms, especially of introduced onion weed, *Romulea* sp.; *head and breast often mud-stained.* Damages sprouting grain-crops, stacked hay. **Similar species:** Little Corella. Sulphur-crested Cockatoo. **Voice:** quick, quavering, falsetto 'currup!'; harsh screeches. **Habitat:** river red gums in woodlands and on watercourses; pastoral, cropping country; sprouting cereal crops, grain-stubbles, hay windrows. **Breeds:** July–Nov. **Nest:** on decayed debris; in tree hollow. **Eggs:** 2–3; dull white, oval, **Range and Status:** once widespread inland se. Aust. but declined with pastoral settlement. Heartland is Vic. western district but in recent decades has extended w. to near Mt Lofty Ras. (SA); e. through Geelong–Melbourne–Shepparton (Vic.); n. into Riverina and e. through Jerilderie–Albury (NSW). Adults sedentary; young dispersive. Feral flocks resident near Sydney, n. coast NSW, Brisbane, etc.

WESTERN CORELLA *Cacatua pastinator* c. 47 cm

Other name: Western Long-billed Corella.

Closely resembles Long-billed Corella, but note range. Parties to flocks: digs for corms, roots, especially of introduced onion weed, *Romulea* sp. **Similar species:** Little Corella: shorter bill; less red on face, none on throat. **Voice:** like Little Corella. **Habitat:** wheat; sheep farming country, with remnant native forest; woodland, scrub, sandplain heath. **Breeds:** Aug.–Oct. **Eggs:** 1–3 (4); laid on disturbed wood-mould on floor of tree-hollow. **Range and Status:** s. WA: (1) Albany–Boyup Brook region of far s. WA; (2) ne. of Perth, between Northam and Dongara; Moora and Burakin in w. and e. After breeding, flocks move locally; some to coasts near Perth, Albany, return to breeding areas by March (Smith & Moore 1992). Uncommon. Sedentary, with seasonal feeding movements.

LITTLE CORELLA *Cacatua sanguinea* 35–39 cm

Small white cockatoo with short, cap-like crest usually folded; *whitish-horn bill; blue–grey bare skin around eye; pink stain between bill and eye* (faint in nominate race of nw. WA, Top End (NT)); *underfeathers of head and throat pink.* Pairs to immense noisy flocks in trees by water and feeding on ground. Flight direct, pigeon-like, wings slender; underwings/undertail washed yellow. **Similar species:** Long-billed, Western Corellas. **Voice:** noisy, high-pitched, falsetto 'currup'; screeches. **Habitat:** rangelands, pastoral country: sandhills with spinifex; gibber, saltbush, mulga, mallee, native cypress; crops, stubble, timbered watercourses, dams, tanks, mangroves, offshore islands, cliffs, towns. **Breeds:** Aug.–Oct. in s.; May–Oct. in n. **Nest:** on decayed debris; in tree-hollow, cavity in cliff, termite-mound. **Eggs:** 3–4; white, oval. **Range and Status:** widespread inland, n. and w. Aust; s. to Geraldton–Mt Magnet (s. WA) and to c. n. Vic.–s. NSW; scarce higher rainfall areas of e. Aust. Expanding into ranges of Western and Long-billed Corellas. Common to very abundant. Local feral flocks from aviary escapes/releases near major e. coastal cities; se. Vic., Tas. Sedentary; nomadic. Also s. PNG.

SULPHUR-CRESTED COCKATOO *Cacatua galerita* 44–51 cm

Other name: White Cockatoo.

Familiar, noisy 'white cockatoo' with *blackish bill, upswept yellow crest;* faint yellow cheekmark; underwings, undertail washed yellow. Parties to flocks of hundreds: adaptable — feeds on ground in grasslands, or in rainforest trees, e.g. Hoop Pines. Flies on broad, *rounded wings with steady, or stiff, irregular wingbeats, flap-flap-glide sequences, fast swoops.* **Similar species:** Corellas, Pink Cockatoo. **Voice:** raucous, shattering screeches; sharp squawks, whistles. **Habitat:** tropical, temperate rainforests; palm forests, swamp woodlands; eucalyptus forests and woodlands; river red gums in pastoral country and on watercourses; mangroves, farmlands, crops, city parks, gardens. **Breeds:** Aug.–Jan. in s.; May–Sept. in n. **Nest:** on decayed debris in tree-hollow, usually high; hole in cliff. **Eggs:** 2–3; white, oval. **Range and Status:** coastal, subcoastal n. and e. Aust., Tas.; introduced to s. WA before 1935. (Blakers et al, 1984). Common to abundant: local flocks enhanced by aviary escapes/releases now common around cities. Sedentary. Also PNG, islands; introduced NZ.

LONG-BILLED
CORELLA

LITTLE
CORELLA

WESTERN
CORELLA

SULPHUR-CRESTED
COCKATOO

RAINBOW LORIKEET *Trichoglossus haematodus* 25–32 cm

Other names: Blue Mountain Parrot; Red-collared Lorikeet.
Familiar large lorikeet: race *moluccanus* of e. and se. Aust. has scarlet bill, *streaky blue head, yellow–green nape, blue belly, and red–orange chest and 'trousers'*. Race *rubritorquis*, 'Red-collared Lorikeet' of tropical n. and nw. Aust.: *nape orange–red, belly black*, breast orange–yellow. **Immature:** duller; bill blackish. Pairs to flocks: feeds noisily in foliage and blossoms of eucalypts, banksias, paperbarks, etc.; nectar-feeders in gardens. Raids ripe garden fruit, loquats, pears, etc. Gathers in noisy roosts. In flight looks *fast, dark and colourful with swept wings and long, pointed tail: note red wing-lining and yellow underwing-bar.* **Similar species:** no other Aust. parrot has streaked blue head and orange chest. **Voice:** rolling musical screech, deeper than Musk Lorikeet; harsher screeches; raucous chatterings. **Habitat:** rainforest, eucalypt forests, woodlands, paperbark woodlands, coastal banksia scrubs, heaths, mangroves, plantations, gardens, street trees. **Breeds:** June–Jan. in e. Aust. **Nest:** on decayed debris; in tree hollow, often high. **Eggs:** 2–3; white, oval. **Range and Status:** race *rubritorquis*, 'Red-collared Lorikeet': coastal n. Aust., from Kimberley (WA) to w. C. York Pen. (Q). Race *moluccanus*: coastal e. Aust. from C. York (Q) to Eyre Pen. (SA); vagrant Tas. Common to abundant. Established around Perth (WA) and elsewhere from releases or aviary escapes. Sedentary; nomadic. Also New Cal., New Heb., Solomons to PNG, e. Indonesia.

SCALY-BREASTED LORIKEET *Trichoglossus chlorolepidotus* 22–24 cm

Only lorikeet with *unmarked green head; neck and breast have distinctive yellow scaly pattern*; bill and eye red. **Immature:** bill *brownish*; less yellow in plumage. In flight, *note orange–red wing-linings*. Associates with other lorikeets; has same general habits. **Similar species:** in flight, Purple-crowned Lorikeet and Swift Parrot also show red wing-lining, but one is smaller, the other long and slender; calls differ. **Voice:** rolling screech, higher-pitched, thinner than Rainbow Lorikeet. **Habitat:** coastal eucalypt woodlands and forests; paperbark and banksia woodlands; flowering street trees; agricultural lands, suburban gardens. **Breeds:** May–Feb. **Nest:** on decayed debris in tree hollow. **Eggs:** 2–3; white, oval. **Range and Status:** coastal e. Aust., from C. York (Q) s. to Illawarra region (NSW); inland to c. Augathella–Charleville (Q); Warrumbungle NP–Parkes (NSW). Common to abundant. Sedentary and nomadic. N.B. Local populations, probably based on aviary escapes, established elsewhere, e.g. Melbourne's e. and se. suburbs. In these areas interbreeds with Rainbow and other lorikeets, producing variable intermediate forms.

VARIED LORIKEET *Psitteuteles versicolor* 17–20 cm

Softly but gorgeously coloured small tropical lorikeet: *pale green, with deep-scarlet cap; white 'goggles'; lime-green ear-patch and pink breast, with plentiful fine, lime-green streaks.* **Female:** duller, with olive–green crown. **Immature:** dull green; pink on forehead. Pairs, parties, small flocks: quieter than other lorikeets. Flight very swift, showing *pale green wing-linings.* Gathers in flowering eucalypts and paperbarks; *scarlet crowns prominent when hanging to feed*; ventures far over grasslands to feed on blossoms of isolated trees such as 'kapok', *Cochlospermum* sp. **Voice:** thin rolling screech, less strident than Rainbow or 'Red-collared Lorikeet'. **Habitat:** tropical eucalypt, paperbark woodlands; flowering trees on foothills and coastal plains; trees on watercourses and in grasslands. **Breeds:** April–Aug. **Nest:** on decayed debris or fragmented eucalypt leaves; in tree hollow. **Eggs:** 2–4; white, oval. **Range and Status:** tropical n. Aust., and coastal islands, from Kimberley (WA), Top End (NT), e. to n.–c. Q and w. C. York Pen.; exceptionally e. to Atherton region (ne. Q); good seasons inland cause irregular inland movements to Channel Country of sw. Q and elsewhere. Common Top End (incl. around Darwin) and Kimberley (WA); less common Q. Nomadic, irregular.

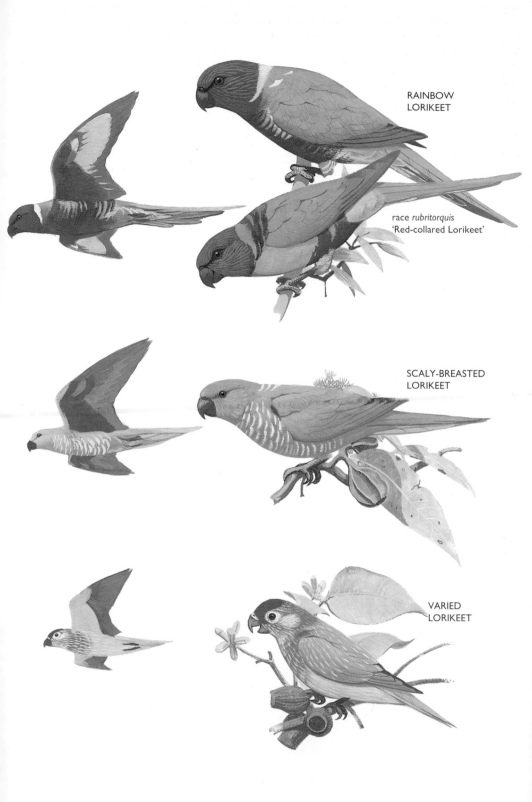

RAINBOW
LORIKEET

race *rubritorquis*
'Red-collared Lorikeet'

SCALY-BREASTED
LORIKEET

VARIED
LORIKEET

LITTLE LORIKEET *Glossopsitta pusilla* 15–16.5 cm

Tiny green lorikeet with black bill and red patch covering forehead/throat, but not *ear-coverts*; eye orange–yellow. **Immature:** duller, bill brown, less red. Pairs, flocks: a bird of treetops, hard to see as it threads mouse-like through foliage, blossoms. Flight bullet-like, showing *pale green wing-linings; yellow–orange underside of tail*. Often with other lorikeets; may raid soft fruits. **Similar species:** Musk, Purple-crowned Lorikeets; Fig-parrot. **Voice:** quick, insect-like 'zit' or 'zit zit', shorter than Purple-crowned. **Habitat:** forests, woodlands; large trees in open country; timbered watercourses, shelterbelts, street trees.

Breeds: July–Jan. **Nest:** on decayed debris; in small hole in eucalypt, often high. **Eggs:** 4–5; white, rounded. **Range and Status:** coastal e. Aust., from *c.* Cooktown (Q) to se. SA; inland to Carnarvon Ra. NP (Q), Warrumbungle NP–West Wyalong–Deniliquin (NSW); most Vic., except nw.; w. to Mt Lofty Ra.–Adelaide Plains–Yorke Pen. (SA) as uncommon, irregular visitor (more regular in far se. SA). Vagrant Tas. Nomadic.

PURPLE-CROWNED LORIKEET *Glossopsitta porphyrocephala* 15–17 cm

Tiny lorikeet with black bill and blue–purple crown: *forehead and ear-coverts apricot–yellow; breast pale blue*. **Immature:** forehead cream; ear-coverts yellow. Parties to flocks, often with Musk, Little Lorikeets: scurries mouse-like through leaves, blossoms, from treetops to near ground. Flight bullet-like: note *crimson flanks/underwings*. **Similar species:** Little Lorikeet: red patch around bill; green underwings. **Voice:** thin, 'ziit' or 'ziit-ziit'; mellower, longer, more buzzing than Little. **Habitat:** like Musk Lorikeet, but ranges widely through inland mallee when in blossom. **Breeds:** Aug.–Dec. **Nest:** on decayed debris; in small hole in eucalypt; several may nest nearby. **Eggs:** 3–4; white, rounded. **Range and Status:** e. Vic. to s. WA, coastally n. to *c.* Geraldton; inland to s. Riverina–mallee areas of sw. NSW; s. Flinders Ras. (SA); Gt Victoria Desert–Menzies–Payne's Find (WA). Casual se. NSW, w. slopes of Divide in NSW–se. Q; Shark Bay (WA). Fairly common, locally abundant. Nomadic.

MUSK LORIKEET *Glossopsitta concinna* 20–23 cm

Sturdy lorikeet with *brilliant scarlet patch from forehead extending back over ear-coverts*. Bill blackish at base, tipped red; eye orange. **Female:** duller. **Immature:** bill dark brown; cheek orange. Pairs to flocks; often with other lorikeets. Flight swift: looks bomb-shaped; note *pale green wing-linings*; may raid soft fruit, grapes, unripe corn. **Similar species:** Little Lorikeet: tiny; bill black; red patch only around bill; quick 'zit' calls. **Voice:** rolling screech, tinnier, higher-pitched than Rainbow; chatterings. **Habitat:** eucalypt woodlands, drier forests on foothills, plains, roadside timber, shelter-belts, timbered watercourses. **Breeds:** Aug.–Dec. **Nest:** on decayed debris; in tree-hole, usually high. **Eggs:** usually 2; white, rounded. **Range and Status:** coastal e. Aust., from *c.* Rockhampton (Q) to s. Eyre Pen. (SA); inland to w. slopes, plains; also e. Tas. Uncommon; locally common; nomadic. Established around Perth (WA), from aviary escapes/releases.

SWIFT PARROT *Lathamus discolor* 23–26 cm

Slender mid-green parrot related to rosellas, with nectar-eating habits of lorikeets. *Bill pale-horn; eye yellow; crown and cheeks bluish*; note red areas in plumage, and long, *spiky, dusty-red tail*. **Immature:** duller, with pale wingstripe; undertail cream–yellow. Small, tight flocks weave fast through woodlands, *calling distinctively*, or travel high, with random turns; note *red wing-linings and spiky tails*. Often with lorikeets; feeds on blossom-nectar, lerp-insects in foliage, tail often stabbing skywards; also eats soft fruits, berries; sometimes forages in grass. At times, where nectar plentiful, still gathers in hundreds, and forms noisy, crowded roosts. **Similar species:** lorikeets chunkier, with red or black bills; mostly shorter, wedged tails; calls differ. **Voice:** bursts of high-pitched, tinkling chattering; piping 'pee-pit, pee-pit, pee-pit'. **Habitat:** forests, woodlands, plantations, banksias, etc.; street trees, parks, gardens. **Breeds:** Sept.–Dec. **Nest:** in tree hollow, 6–20 m high, often several pairs nearby. **Eggs:** 3–5; white, rounded. **Range and Status:** breeds only in Tas: most migrate in March–June to se. Aust., w. to Mt Lofty Ra. (SA), n. to *c.* Bowen in coastal e. Q; inland to Griffith–Warialda (NSW), Chinchilla (Q). Nomadic on mainland. Returns Tas. Aug.–Oct.

LITTLE
LORIKEET

PURPLE-
CROWNED
LORIKEET

MUSK
LORIKEET

SWIFT
PARROT

DOUBLE-EYED FIG-PARROT *Cyclopsitta diophthalma* 13–16 cm

Smallest Aust. parrot, *with robust, pale grey, blackish-tipped bill,* yellow sides of upperbreast, blue outer primaries, a touch of red on secondaries, and very short tail; eye dark brown. The three Aust. races are geographically well-separated and can be told apart by head-markings. **Race marshalli:** 13 cm. **Male:** red forehead and red cheeks with blue lower edge. **Female:** no red on head; blue forehead; blue whisker-mark encloses creamish patch on cheek. **Race coxeni:** 16 cm. **Male:** blue on forehead nearly replaces red; red cheek-patch smaller. **Female:** no red on forehead; red cheek-patch duller. **Race macleayana:** 14 cm. **Male:** small red patch on forehead separated from red cheek by *pale blue between bill and eye;* violet–blue whisker-mark borders red cheek. **Female:** like male, but cheek not red. Pairs to small flocks; quiet, hard to locate when feeding; they creep through foliage; sometimes revealed by calls and sounds of falling pieces of fruit as they attack native figs to remove seeds; they eat other fruit, berries, fungi, lichens, insect-larvae; and bathe in wet foliage, like lorikeets. Flight swift and darting, over and through canopy; flocks reported to roost communally when not breeding. **Similar species:** Little Lorikeet: bill finer and black; *single red patch surrounds bill; no blue in plumage;* likely to be confused only with male *marshalli.* **Voice:** quick, penetrating 'ziiit ziiit', longer, more splintered than Little Lorikeet, perched and in flight; also chattering twitters. **Habitat:** rainforests; adjacent eucalypt woodlands and coastal scrubs; timber on watercourses, paperbark woodlands; occasionally visits figs, loquats and other fruit-trees in gardens and plantations. **Breeds:** Aug.–Nov. **Nest:** on debris in a hole excavated in decayed wood in the trunk or branch of a tree, at heights to *c.* 10 m, sometimes much higher. **Eggs:** 2; white, rounded, unglossy. **Range and Status:** race *marshalli:* lowland rainforest on ne. C. York Pen. (Q), in vicinity of Lockart and Claudie Rs. and probably beyond. Race *macleayana:* highland and lowland rainforests from Cooktown s. to Eungella NP, near Mackay (Q). Race *coxeni:* highland, and sparse remnant lowland, rainforests, from *c.* Maryborough (Q) to Macleay R. (NSW). Sedentary; locally nomadic. Northern races still moderately common; race *coxeni* has declined seriously from clearing of lowland rainforest; now rare and endangered.

Little Lorikeet
(for comparison)

race *marshalli*

♂

DOUBLE-EYED FIG-PARROT

♀

race *coxeni*

♂

race *macleayana*

♂

♀

ECLECTUS PARROT *Eclectus roratus* 40–43 cm

Other name: Red-sided Parrot.

Large tropical parrot with 'reversed' colouring. **Male:** *bright green with orange bill; red flanks;* flight-feathers, bend of wing blue; wing-linings scarlet; dark tail tipped yellow; eye pale yellow. **Female:** *wine-red, with blue eye-ring, shoulders; broad blue band across breast; bill black;* wing-linings blue; tail-tip orange; eye pale yellow. **Immature:** like adults, bill brownish. Pairs, small flocks: noisy; forages high in rainforest on fruits, blossoms; may circle up, screeching. Flight direct, with deliberate wingbeats, glides, wings not raised above body-level (Forshaw, 1981). Roosts in noisy companies. Overhead in poor light can look black. **Voice:** flight-call, harsh rolling screech 'kraach-krraak' or 'kar!, kar!, kar!'; wailing cry, flute-like whistle (Forshaw, 1981). **Habitat:** rainforest; nearby eucalypt woodlands. **Breeds:** Aug.–Jan. **Nest:** in tree hollow, usually high. **Eggs:** 2; white, oval. More than one pair may attend nest; one tree may house several nests. **Range and Status:** e. C. York Pen. (Q), from Pascoe R. s. to McIlwraith Ra. Locally common. Sedentary. Also Solomons, PNG, e. Indonesia.

RED-CHEEKED PARROT *Geoffroyus geoffroyi* 20–25 cm

Compact, bright green parrot. **Male:** *forehead/face bright rose-red; crown/nape violet–blue;* wing-lining sky-blue; abdomen/undertail yellow–green. Bill red above, grey below; eye yellow. **Female:** head olive–brown; bill grey; eye pale yellow. **Immature:** head green; eye brown; imm. males show traces of adult colours, incl. bill. Pairs, parties: heard more than seen in rainforest canopy; flutters, hangs to reach fruits, flowers. Perches in emergent trees, calling (Forshaw, 1981). *Flight fast, starling-like.* **Voice:** piercing metallic 'hank'; guttural chatterings; screeches like Rainbow Lorikeet. **Habitat:** rainforest, scrubs; nearby eucalypt woodlands. **Breeds:** Aug.–Dec. **Nest:** in hole excavated in rotten wood of tree or palm. **Eggs:** 2–3; white rounded. **Range and Status:** e. C. York Pen. (Q), from Pascoe R. s. to Rocky R. Locally common. Sedentary. Also PNG, e. Indonesia, PNG.

AUSTRALIAN KING-PARROT *Alisterus scapularis* 41–44 cm

Male: *brilliant scarlet head/body; dark green wings with pale green band.* Bill red above, black below; eye yellow. **Female:** *upperparts and upperbreast dark green (some have pale wing-band); lower breast scarlet;* bill red-grey; eye yellow. **Immature:** like female; eye brown; young males become patchy red. Parties, small flocks, mostly of green birds: feeds quietly in foliage on fruit, palm shoots, blossoms, mistletoes; on ground. Raids fruit in orchards; bananas, corn, sorghum, potatoes, acorns. Tame in gardens, farmyards, resorts. Flight strong, easy, erratic with deep pumping wingbeats. **Similar species:** Crimson Rosella. **Voice:** brassy 'chack! chack!'; male, drawn-out, ringing 'sweee'; alarm-screeches. **Habitat:** rainforests, palm forests, eucalypt forests, dense gullies, clearings, coastal woodlands; regrowth with berry-bearing shrubs; crops, potato-fields, orchards, parks, gardens. **Breeds:** Sept.–Jan. **Nest:** in tree hollow, with high entrance. **Eggs:** 3–5; white, rounded. **Range and Status:** coastal e. Aust., from *c.* Cooktown (Q) to Otway Ras. (Vic.), inland to *c.* Carnarvon Ra. NP (Q), Warrumbungle NP (NSW), Wodonga–Daylesford (Vic.). Common to uncommon; disperses to lowlands in autumn–winter. Sedentary; dispersive.

RED-WINGED PARROT *Aprosmictus erythropterus* 30–33 cm

Male: *bright, 'fluorescent', green with scarlet shoulder; black mantle; blue lower back,* tail green, square, tipped yellow. **Female:** pale green with *scarlet band across wing; blue rump.* Both sexes: bill scarlet or coral. **Immature:** like female but paler. Pairs, small flocks, mostly near water; feeds in foliage and blossoms; associates with rosellas, ringnecks. Wary; flies noisily to distant trees with erratic, lashing wingbeats. **Similar species:** Superb Parrot, female; King Parrot, female. **Voice:** flight-call, rapid brassy 'ching-ching' or 'ching-chink'; thin screeches. **Habitat:** grassy woodlands, rainforest fringes, mangroves, timbered watercourses, mulga, brigalow, casuarina, native-cypress scrubs, crops. **Breeds:** Aug.–Feb. in NSW; April–July in n. **Nest:** in tree-hollow, usually near water. **Eggs:** 3–6; white. **Range and Status:** e., ne. and n. Aust., from Pilbara (WA) to C. York Pen. (Q), s. nearly throughout Q, to e. inland NSW, far ne. SA. Common, nomadic, dispersive. Also s. PNG.

ECLECTUS PARROT

♀ ♂

RED-CHEEKED PARROT

imm. ♀ ♂

AUSTRALIAN
KING-PARROT

imm. ♂ ♀ ♂

RED-WINGED
PARROT

imm. ♀ ♂

SUPERB PARROT *Polytelis swainsonii* 36–42 cm

Slender, long-tailed, bright green parrot. **Male:** *forehead/throat yellow, cut off by scarlet crescent;* eye yellow. **Female:** green, *washed blue–grey on cheeks, bend of wing; undertail black/pink.* **Immature:** like female; eye brown. Pairs, family parties; flocks, some of males only. Feeds on ground in grassy woodland; stubbles, spilt grain on roadsides; on fruits, seeds; blossoms of acacias, eucalypts, mistletoes. Flight swift, with swept wings, long slim tail. **Voice:** rolling 'currack currack'. **Habitat:** river red gums, black box, yellow box, river oak, mostly near rivers; mallee, stubbles, pastures, gardens. **Breeds:** Sept.–Dec. **Nest:** hollow of river red gum, yellow box; near water. **Eggs:** 4–6; white, rounded. **Range and Status:** NSW Riverina, to far n. Vic. (principally Barmah Forest), w. to *c.* Balranald, n. to Lachlan R., e. to *c.* Cowra–Yass–Albury (NSW). Autumn–winter migration to region of Namoi R. (nc. NSW). Dispersive; part-migratory.

REGENT PARROT *Polytelis anthopeplus* 38–41 cm

Male: *note strikingly gold shoulders, black flight-feathers, soft-red band on inner wing; long black tail.* **Female and immature:** greener, less red on wing; undertail black/pink. Race *westralis,* greener, duller. Pairs; autumn/winter flocks: feeds on ground and in, blossoms of eucalypts, acacias, mistletoes, unripe grain, spilt grain on roadsides; roosts communally. Flight swift, on swept wings, long tail. **Similar species:** Superb Parrot, Yellow Rosella. **Voice:** rolling, grating 'carrak'; soft warblings. **Habitat:** in e. Aust., river red gum and black box forests; adjacent mallee–spinifex; native cypress, farmlands, weedy clearings, vineyards, crops, stubble, golf-courses. In sw. WA, wheatbelt farmlands, timbered watercourses, clearings in woodlands, forests; saltbush. **Breeds:** Aug.–Jan.; autumn. **Nest:** in hollow of large eucalypt, or stump. **Eggs:** 4–6; white, rounded. **Range and Status:** nominate race: inland se. Aust., w. to Murray Bridge–Morgan (SA), n. and e. to Pooncarie–Balranald (NSW), s. to Swan Hill–Wyperfeld NP (Vic.). Race *westralis:* sw. WA, w. and s. of Israelite Bay–Shark Bay. Seasonally nomadic: either race may move well n. and inland beyond stated limits after good rains. Sedentary; nomadic.

PRINCESS PARROT *Polytelis alexandrae* 34–46 cm. Male longer.

Other names: Alexandra's Parrot, Princess Alexandra's Parrot.
Male: soft olive–green with *pale blue crown, pink throat, lime-green shoulders, sky-blue rump and long, slim blue–green tail.* **Female and immature:** duller, tail shorter. Pairs, small flocks: feeds in foliage, blossoms, and on ground. Flight easy, wingbeats irregular, with *long streaming tail; perches along limbs.* **Voice:** long rolling call; cackling chatterings; sharp 'queet, queet'. **Habitat:** spinifex with eucalypts, acacias, desert oaks, desert poplars, hakeas, mistletoes; parakeelia, other succulents around salt lakes; often far from fresh water. **Breeds:** Sept.–Jan., or after rain. **Nest:** eucalypt hollow on watercourse; desert oak; several pairs nearby. **Eggs:** 4–6: white, glossy, rounded. **Range and Status:** w. inland Aust.: from sw. Q–s. NT, to Gt Victoria Desert (SA–WA), w. to Gibson–Gt Sandy Deserts (WA). Arrives to breed where long absent; 'disappears' again after breeding. Numbers present recent years on n. Canning Stock Route (WA) and Gt Victoria Desert (WA–SA). Rare, highly nomadic; irregular.

COCKATIEL *Nymphicus hollandicus* 30–33 cm

Other names: Cockatoo-parrot; Quarrion.
Male: *distinctive with pale yellow crest and face, orange–red earspot; otherwise grey with prominent white shoulders.* **Female:** head greyer; outer tail-feathers/underwing pale yellow, finely barred grey; flight feathers toothed white. **Immature:** like dull adults. Pairs, parties, flocks: feeds on ground; settles on dead trees, often *along* limbs. Flight easy; with swept wings, longish tail. **Voice:** rolling chirrup, hence Aboriginal 'Quarrion'; penetrating 'queel, queel'. **Habitat:** near water in open woodlands; scrublands, plains; timber on watercourses; spinifex, sorghum, sunflowers, stubbles, spilt grain on roadsides. **Breeds:** Aug.–Dec. in s. inland, autumn–winter in n. **Nest:** in tree-hollow, near water. **Eggs:** 4–7; white, rounded. **Range and Status:** mainland Aust., *except* C. York Pen. (Q), wetter coastal areas, forests, driest deserts. In spring–summer, moves from inland to breed in better-watered pastoral, cereal-growing country; visits coastal n. Aust. in dry season. Highly nomadic: movements influenced by rainfall.

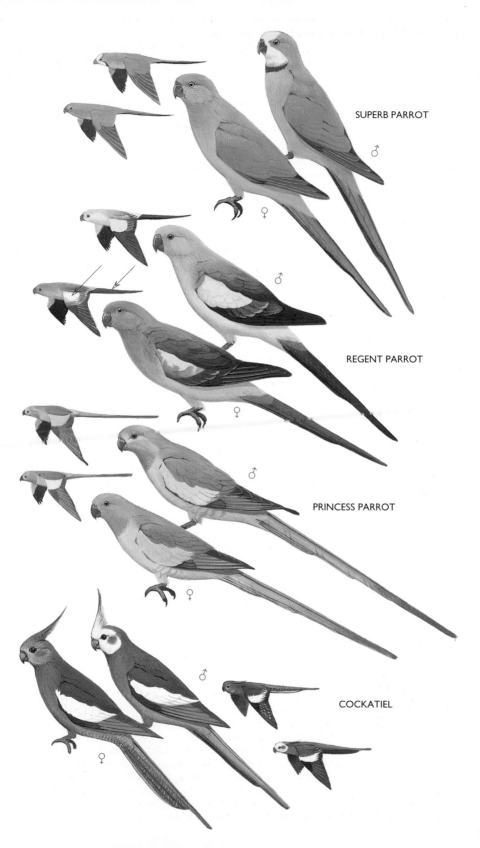

SUPERB PARROT

♂

♀

REGENT PARROT

♂

♀

PRINCESS PARROT

♂

♀

COCKATIEL

♂

♀

YELLOW ROSELLA *Platycercus elegans flaveolus* 30–34 cm

Pale yellow: forehead red; cheeks and shoulder blue; mantle mottled black; tail blue with whitish margins; some have reddish wash on breast. **Immature:** *washed olive green; pale wingstripe in flight.* Pairs, small flocks: feeds on ground; in foliage, blossoms of eucalypts, acacias; peppercorns; orchards, gardens. In flight, *yellow plumage contrasts with pale/dark blue wingpatches.* **Similar species:** Adelaide Rosella. **Voice:** ringing 'rik-rik'; bell-like 'ding-ding, didit'. **Habitat:** near water in grassy woodlands of river red gums; black, grey, yellow box; mallee, clearings, farmland, roadside timber, shelterbelts, parks, gardens. **Breeds:** Aug.–Jan. **Nest:** in tree-hollow; often over water. **Eggs:** 4–5; white, rounded. **Range and Status:** near rivers in s. NSW, n. Vic., se. SA: Murray R., Darling R.(upstream to *c.* Tilpa); Lachlan, Upper Bogan, Murrumbidgee, Edward, Wakool, Goulburn Rs., etc. Common; sedentary: interbreeds with Adelaide Rosella near Morgan–Mannum (SA). Now regarded as race *flaveolus* of Crimson Rosella.

ADELAIDE ROSELLA *Platycercus elegans adelaidae* 34–36 cm

Natural hybrid of Crimson/Yellow Rosellas: some are yellow with reddish forehead/breast; blue cheeks, shoulders and tail-edges; others washed red on mantle, merging into yellow neck and rump. Birds in s. Flinders Ras. (SA) are usually pale, others variable. **Immature:** olive–green; *forehead, throat, under tail-coverts dull red;* pale wingstripe in flight. Habits like Crimson Rosella. **Habitat:** timbered valleys; open forests, woodlands; timbered watercourses, mallee, farmlands, roadsides, parks, gardens. **Breeds:** Nov.–Feb. **Range and Status:** Fleurieu Pen., Mt Lofty Ras.–Adelaide Plains–s. Flinders Ras., e. to L. Alexandrina–Murray R. (SA). Common; sedentary. Interbreeds with Yellow Rosella near Mannum–Morgan (SA).

CRIMSON ROSELLA *Platycercus elegans* 32–37 cm

Other name: Red Lowry.

Showy common parrot: *crimson with blue cheeks, shoulders, tail; back mottled black.* **Immature:** usually outnumber adults: golden-olive with patchy crimson forehead, throat, under tail-coverts; *blue cheek-patch, shoulder, blue–white tail-edges;* in flight, pale wingbar. In n. NSW–Q, juveniles resemble adults, with greenish fringes to feathers of mantle. Race *nigrescens* in ne. Q smaller, darker. Pairs, small flocks: feeds in foliage, cracking seed-capsules: treeferns, etc., and on ground. Flight swooping, *with flashing two-toned blue wings/tail;* wingbeats often deep, exaggerated. Tame in parks, gardens, resorts. **Similar species:** King Parrot. **Voice:** ringing 'trip-klee'; slow, bell-like 'klee-kleekeee'; in flight, raucous clanging 'klee klee klee'. **Habitat:** rainforests, eucalypt forests, fern-gullies; alpine and other woodlands; farmlands, timbered watercourses, coastal scrubs, roadsides, parks, gardens. **Breeds:** Sept.–Jan. **Nest:** in tree-hollow, often high; cavity in building. **Eggs:** 5–8; white, rounded. **Range and Status:** Nominate race: mountains of ne. Q, from Atherton Tableland to Eungella NP. Nominate race: from Cooroy (Q) to sw. Vic.–Kingston (SA) (isolated race on Kangaroo I.); inland to *c.* Stanthorpe (Q); Warrumbungle NP–Narrandera (NSW); Cobram–Little Desert (Vic.). Wide autumn–winter dispersal to lowlands, incl. urban areas. Common; seasonally dispersive. Introduced Norfolk I., NZ.

GREEN ROSELLA *Platycercus caledonicus* 32–38 cm

Robust blue-cheeked rosella: confined to Tas. region where it replaces Crimson Rosella. **Male:** *rich yellow with red forehead; blue cheeks; upperparts dark green with black mottling; rump olive–yellow;* shoulder, edge of wing, tail blue. **Female:** greener, duller. **Immature:** duller olive, with pale wingstripe. Pairs; autumn–winter flocks; mixes with Eastern Rosellas. Feeds in foliage of eucalypts, treeferns, wattles; blackberries, thistles; orchard fruit, grain crops; on ground in clearings, pastures. Flight strong, sometimes high; *note rich yellow head and underparts.* **Voice:** 'kussik, kussik'; bell-like contact note; shrill alarm-calls. **Habitat:** forests, woodlands, farmland; timber along rivers; briar-scrub, hawthorn hedges, crops, orchards, gardens. **Breeds:** Nov.–Feb. **Nest:** in tree-hollow; building cavity. **Eggs:** 4–8; white, rounded. **Range and Status:** Tas.; Flinders, King, Hunter Is.; Kent Group. Common. Sedentary, with local winter movements.

YELLOW ROSELLA

imm.

ADELAIDE ROSELLA

imm.

CRIMSON ROSELLA

imm.

GREEN ROSELLA

imm.

277

NORTHERN ROSELLA *Platycercus venustus* 28–30 cm

Pale lemon rosella with black cap, blue and white cheekpatch, blue and black shoulders. Bold lemon fringes to black feathers of back; dark 'scaly' margins to yellow feathers of underparts; red under tail-coverts. **Immature:** duller; red marks on head/breast; in flight, pale wingbar. Pairs, small flocks: feeds on ground and in foliage; flight strongly undulating. **Similar species:** Hooded Parrot. **Voice:** high-pitched 'trin-see, trin-see'; chattering. **Habitat:** usually near water in grassy tropical woodlands and clearings; paperbarks, acacia scrublands, hill country, timber along watercourses, mangroves, roadsides, crops; occasionally gardens. **Breeds:** June–Sept.; any month after rain. **Nest:** in tree-hollow, usually near water. **Eggs:** 2–4; white, rounded. **Range and Status:** n. Aust.: Kimberley (WA), e. from c. Derby–Fitzroy Crossing; through Top End (NT), s. to Katherine–McArthur R., coastally, and on some islands e. to Nicholson R., far nw. Q. Sedentary; uncommon.

PALE-HEADED ROSELLA *Platycercus adscitus* 28–32 cm

Palest-headed Australian parrot. Nominate race (ne. Q): white or yellow–white with large white, and small blue, cheekpatches; mantle feathers black, edged yellow–white; lower breast blue–white; under tail-coverts red; *rump yellowish.* Race *palliceps* (s. Q–ne. NSW): *deeper yellow above; cheeks white; breast and rump pale blue–grey.* **Immature:** like dull adults; female and imm. have traces of pink. Pairs, small flocks: feeds on ground and in foliage, blossoms; crops, orchards. Flight undulating; *note rump colour:* yellowish in n. Q; blue–grey in s. Q; turquoise in ne. NSW–se. Q, from cross-breeding with Eastern Rosella. **Voice:** flight-call, hard 'crik crik'; rapid, ringing, high-pitched 'fee fee fee'. **Habitat:** open forest, woodlands, scrublands, timbered watercourses, grasslands, clearings, roadsides, farmlands, orchards, crops, lantana thickets. **Breeds:** Sept.–Jan., or after rain. **Nest:** in tree-hollow, stump, fence-post. **Eggs:** 3–5; white, rounded. **Range and Status:** ne. Aust.: from C. York Pen. (Q) w. to Gilbert R.–Longreach (Q) and exceptionally to Bourke (NSW); s. to Tweed R. (NSW), exceptionally s. to Gunnedah. Common. Sedentary.

EASTERN ROSELLA *Platycercus eximius* 29–34 cm

Other name: White-cheeked Rosella.
Trademark 'rosella': *bright scarlet head/body with white cheeks;* back yellow, mottled black; shoulders blue; underparts yellow and pale green; under tail-coverts red; *rump bright greenish yellow.* **Female:** duller, patchy green on crown/upperparts. **Immature:** more patchy green; pale wingstripe in flight. Race *cecilae* of ne. NSW: golden nape/mantle; *pale turquoise rump.* Pairs, small flocks: often on roadsides, fences; raids fruit, nuts, in orchards, gardens. When disturbed, flies noisily to trees; flight strongly undulating; *note bright rump.* **Voice:** brisk 'pink-pink'; slow, ringing 'pee-p-peeee'; soft chatterings. **Habitat:** open grassy forests, woodlands; nearby grasslands; timbered watercourses, farmlands, crops, roadsides, parks, gardens. **Breeds:** mostly Aug.–Feb. **Nest:** in tree-hollow; stump, fence-post, burrow in bank; termite-mound. **Eggs:** 4–7; white, rounded. **Range and Status:** se. Aust. and Tas.: from c. Kingaroy (se. Q) to c. Keith (se. SA); inland to Moree–Hay–Euston (NSW) and w. on Murray R. Nominate race and *cecilae* intergrade n. of Hunter R. (NSW). Introduced Adelaide–Mt Lofty Ras. (SA); NZ. Common; sedentary.

WESTERN ROSELLA *Platycercus icterotis* 25–28 cm

Smallest rosella; confined to sw. WA. **Male:** *red head/body with yellow cheekpatch;* feathers of mantle black, fringed red, grey–green. **Female:** greener, cheekpatch duller; forehead red, touches of red, green, yellow below. **Immature:** greener, no cheekpatch. Race *xanthogenys:* redder, greyer above. Pairs, parties: quiet; feeds in foliage of shrubs, trees, and on ground; flies up to nearest tree. Flight gentle with few undulations; female and imm. show pale wingbar. **Voice:** soft 'chink chink'. **Habitat:** open forest, woodland with grassy clearings; trees on watercourses; farmlands, crops, roadsides, orchards, homestead-gardens. **Breeds:** Aug.–Dec. **Nest:** in tree-hollow. **Eggs:** 3–7; white, rounded. **Range and Status:** sw. WA, s. and w. of Dongara–Israelite Bay, e. to Southern Cross–Norseman. Nominate race: better-watered coastal districts. Race *xanthogenys:* drier parts inland; some intergradation. Fairly common. Sedentary; coastward movements in summer.

PALE-HEADED ROSELLA

race *palliceps*

nominate race

NORTHERN ROSELLA

EASTERN ROSELLA

♀

♂

♂

♀

WESTERN ROSELLA

RED-CAPPED PARROT *Purpureicephalus spurius* 35–38 cm

Other name: King Parrot (WA only).
Gaudy, with distinctive long, pale bill. **Male:** *dark green above with crimson cap, lime-green cheeks and rump,* blue-purple breast, red underparts. **Female:** duller; crown/cheeks green; breast pale mauve. **Immature:** duller; traces of adult colours. Pairs, parties: forages on ground under trees and in foliage. Bill specialised to remove seeds from deep gumnuts of marri, *E. calophylla,* and seeds of other eucalypts, casuarinas, grevilleas, hakeas; pest in orchards. Flight undulating, fluttering, with *contrasting lime-green rump/dark upperparts;* female and imm. show pale wingbar. **Similar species:** Western Ringneck: dark rump. **Voice:** grating, rosella-like 'checkacheck'; harsh clanging screeches. **Habitat:** eucalypt forests, woodlands, shelterbelts, trees in farmlands; timbered watercourses, roadsides, orchards, parks, gardens. **Breeds:** Aug.–Dec. **Nest:** in eucalypt hollow, usually high. **Eggs:** 4–6; white, rounded. **Range and Status:** s. WA, s. and w. of Moore R.–L. Grace–Esperance. Common. Sedentary, with local movements.

EASTERN RINGNECK *Barnardius barnardi* 32–36 cm

Other name: Mallee Ringneck.
Brilliant blue–green head/body and 'shoulders' contrast with dark blue–grey mantle. Note red forehead, yellow rear collar, orange–yellow breast-patch. **Female:** duller; back grey–green. **Immature:** brownish above. Eastern-Western Ringneck hybrids in Flinders Ras. (SA) have brownish heads, *green* backs. Small race *macgillivrayi,* 'Cloncurry Ringneck': paler blue–green, underparts yellower; no red forehead. Pairs, family parties: feeds on ground and in foliage, on seeds, blossoms of eucalypts, acacias, mistletoes, eremophilas, grevilleas. Flight undulating, wingbeats deep, showing *flashing turquoise shoulders and rump.* **Similar species:** Western Ringneck: head blackish; upperparts dark green. **Voice:** flight-call: clanging 'kling-kling-kling' or 'put-kleep, put-kleep, put-kleep'. **Habitat:** edges, clearings, in mallee, eucalypt woodland, native cypress, mulga, bulloak scrubs; river red gums on watercourses, lakes; farmlands, stubbles, gardens. **Breeds:** Aug.–Dec. in s. Aust.; Feb.–June in n. (*macgillivrayi*). **Nest:** in eucalypt hollow. **Eggs:** 4–6; white, rounded. **Range and Status:** e. inland Aust. from c. Port Augusta (SA), n. through Flinders Ras.–L. Eyre Basin; to Windorah–Winton (Q), e. to Blackall–Goondiwindi; Moree–Dubbo–Wagga (NSW); s. to Kerang–Little Desert–Edenhope (Vic.); Naracoorte–Kingston (SA), but not Mt Lofty Ras. Race *macgillivrayi*: Cloncurry region (nw. Q), from Boulia–Kynuna n. to Gregory Downs, w. to upper Nicholson R. (NT). Common. Sedentary; locally nomadic.

WESTERN RINGNECK *Barnardius zonarius* 34–37 cm

Other names: Port Lincoln Parrot or Ringneck; Twenty-eight Parrot.
Robust, dark green parrot with blackish head and yellow rear-collar. **Nominate race:** belly *yellow.* **Immature:** head browner; imm. female: pale wingstripe in flight. **Race *semitorquatus,* 'Twenty-eight Parrot':** larger, darker; small red forehead mark; *underparts green.* **Race *occidentalis*** (not illustrated): paler; head plain grey–black; upperparts bluer; under tail-coverts yellow. In this widespread complex, most forms interbreed: expect to see birds with intermediate features. Pairs, parties: feeds on ground and in foliage, blossoms; usually near water. *Flies strongly with strident calls, head raised, with marked undulations and exaggerated deep wingstrokes.* Pest in crops, orchards, vineyards, but eats many insects, larvae. Escapes often from aviaries; feral in urban areas. **Similar species:** Eastern Ringneck. **Voice:** strident, ringing 'put-kleepit-kleepit'; rapid 'kling-kling-kling-kling', like striking silvery anvil. Alarm-note: sharp 'vatch!'. Race *semitorquatus*: distinct triple-note 'twenty-eight'. **Habitat:** forests; woodlands; river red gums on watercourses; inland mallee, mulga, desert oak, spinifex, farmlands, roadsides, homestead-gardens, orchards, parks, gardens. **Breeds:** Aug.–Dec. in s. Aust.; July–Sept. in n. Aust. **Nest:** in tree-hollow. **Eggs:** 4–7; white, rounded. **Range and Status:** w. half of continent n. and w. from Eyre Pen.–Flinders Ras. (SA). In NT, it extends n. to L. Woods, e. to NT–Q border; w. into arid se. Kimberley (WA). In WA s. of Kimberley, it extends throughout State, incl. w. deserts in good seasons. Race *occidentalis* ranges from c. Marble Bar–de Grey R. s. to Geraldton–L. Way. Race *semitorquatus* occupies sw. WA. Common. Sedentary, with seasonal and/or drought-induced movements.

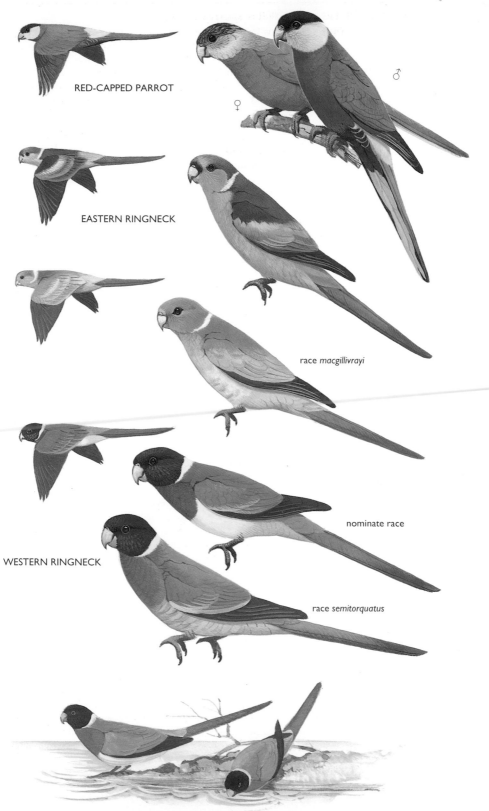

RED-CAPPED PARROT

♀ ♂

EASTERN RINGNECK

race *macgillivrayi*

nominate race

WESTERN RINGNECK

race *semitorquatus*

BLUE BONNET *Northiella haematogaster* 27–35 cm

Other names: Bulloak Parrot, Little Blue Bonnet, Naretha Parrot.
Pale grey–brown parrot *with deep blue forehead, face and bend of wing.* **Nominate race:** *shoulder blue and deep olive–yellow;* red patch on belly and thighs; *under tail-coverts pale yellow.* **Race haematorrhous:** *dark red patch on shoulder;* lower breast pale yellow; *thighs, centre of belly and under tail-coverts, dark red.* **Race narethae, 'Little Blue Bonnet':** smaller, plumage more olive–green; two-tone blue on head; shoulder red and *olive–yellow; belly and thighs pale yellow; under tail-coverts red.* Females and imms. of all races are less colourful, with pale wingstripe in flight. Pairs, parties: stance upright; feeds much on ground, flies with sharp alarm-calls. Flight undulating, erratic, with rapid, shallow wingbeats; note *blue flight-feathers, blue–white outer tail-feathers; lemon underparts with more or less red.* **Similar species:** Paradise Parrot. **Voice:** flight-call: harsh 'jak, jakajak' or 'chakchakchakchak'; piping whistles. **Habitat:** open woodlands, scrubs, often far from water: native cypress, belar, sheoak, bulloak; mulga, other acacias; sugarwood; larger, open mallee; saltbush, grasslands, timbered watercourses, farmlands, crops, roadsides, rail sidings, homesteads. Race *narethae*: belar, *Casuarina cristata*, with acacias; low eucalypts. **Breeds**: July–Dec., or after rain. **Nest:** in low hollow of acacia, casuarina, eucalypt. **Eggs:** 4–7; white, rounded. **Range and Status:** inland se. Aust.: from n. Eyre Pen. (SA) to nw. SA (Everard Ras.), e. to s. Q, from Eyre Ck, w. of Birdsville, ne. to Windorah–Blackall, e. to Roma–Condamine–Texas; in NSW, e. to Warialda–Gunnedah–Wellington–Wagga Wagga–Corowa; s. to Rochester–Dimboola (Vic.); w. to Bordertown–Yorke Pen. (SA). Race *haematorrhous* ne. part of range in n. inland NSW–s. Q, forming a large zone of intergradation with nominate race. Pale race, *pallescens* (not illustrated): L. Eyre region (SA). Race *narethae* is isolated on n.–nw. Nullarbor Plain (se. WA). Common to uncommon. Sedentary.

RED-RUMPED PARROT *Psephotus haematonotus* 25–28 cm

Other name: Grass Parrot.
Male: *head/neck brilliant emerald-green; lower back brick-red; underparts yellow.* **Female:** pale grey–green, dull white below; bend of wing blue; *rump green.* **Immature:** like dull adults; female and imm. have pale wingbar. **Race caeruleus:** male paler, bluer, whiter below; female paler. Pairs; flocks, in which pairs persist: feeds in foliage, blossoms, and on ground on grass seeds, spilt grain on roadsides; when disturbed, flies to fence-wires, trees, with pleasing calls. Flight undulating, *exposing male's red rump, yellow belly.* **Similar species:** Mulga Parrot. **Voice:** flight-call, cheery 'chee chlip, chee chlip', with slight break; pretty warbling song. **Habitat:** usually near water: farm paddocks with living and/or dead trees; grassy woodlands, pastoral country; river red gums on watercourses; mangroves, crops, stubbles, farmyards, roadsides, playing fields, suburban allotments. **Breeds:** Aug.–Jan. in s.; after rain inland. **Nest:** in tree hollow, fence-post, stump. **Eggs:** 4–6; white, rounded. **Range and Status:** race *caeruleus* farthest-inland: on timbered watercourses in Cooper Ck–Coongie Lakes region (ne. SA), e. to lower Barcoo R. (Q) (Forshaw, 1981). Main population from s. Q to e. SA; absent from forests of Divide, wetter coastal areas. With clearing of woodlands, has expanded coastwards; now resident parts of all e. mainland capitals. Common. Sedentary; dispersive.

MULGA PARROT *Psephotus varius* 25–31 cm

Other name: Many-coloured Parrot.
Male: *slender, brilliant emerald parrot with yellow on forehead and shoulder; red mark on centre of nape and rump; pale green band across lower back;* scarlet/yellow patch on belly, thighs. **Female:** dull brownish green; *red mark on nape and shoulder; green rump.* **Immature:** like dull female; in flight, female and imm. show pale wingbar. Pairs, family parties: feeds on ground near trees, and in foliage of saltbush, mulgas, eucalypts. Shy, keeps more to cover than Red-rump. Flight *audibly swift, undulating, direct;* with quick, interrupted wingbeats, distinctive calls; note male's scarlet belly. **Similar species:** Red-rumped, Swift Parrots. **Voice:** brisk, distinctive flight-call, 'swit swit'. **Habitat:** vicinity of water; in mulga, mallee, other scrubs; saltbush with belts of trees; timbered watercourses. **Breeds:** Aug.–Nov. **Nest:** in tree-hollow; near ground in low woodland, taller trees on watercourses. **Eggs:** 4–5 (7); white, rounded. **Range and Status:** suitable habitat across interior of s. Aust.: to parts of w. and s. coasts, from c. NW Cape (WA) to the lower Murray R. (SA); n. through Pilbara (WA); inland to se. Tanami Desert (NT); in Q, n. to Windorah–Tambo, e. to c. Chinchilla; in NSW, e. to Moree–Coonabarabran–Cowra–Corowa; in nw. Vic., e. to L. Boga, s. to Little Desert NP; most SA, *except* far se., Fleurieu Pen., and Mt Lofty Ras. Sedentary; locally nomadic.

BLUE BONNET

race
narethae

race *haematorrhous*

nominate race

RED-RUMPED PARROT

♂

♀

♂

♀

MULGA PARROT

♂

♂

♀

283

GOLDEN-SHOULDERED PARROT *Psephotus chrysopterygius* 25–27 cm

Other names: Ant-bed, Ant-hill Parrot.
Male: *slender, upright turquoise-blue parrot; small blackish cap is separated from bill by pale yellow forehead;* back/wings pale brown with *golden shoulder-patch; belly/under tail-coverts salmon-pink.* **Female:** pale bitter-green; bronze wash on green crown/nape; cheeks blue–grey; lower breast, flanks/rump pale blue; belly/under tail-coverts *pink.* **Immature:** like female; young males greener, with darker crowns, turquoise cheeks. Females and imms. show pale wingstripe in flight. Singles, pairs, small parties: feeds chiefly on ground, on grass-seeds; when disturbed, flies up to trees; flight swift, slightly undulating. Rests in foliage during midday heat. **Similar species:** Hooded Parrot. **Voice:** chirruping calls; soft, pleasing whistle: 'chee chee' or 'cheer-weeo'. **Habitat:** open eucalypt, paperbark woodlands; grasslands with termite-mounds. **Breeds:** March–Aug. **Nest:** cavity excavated at end of narrow tunnel in termite-mound (magnetic or conical), often on seasonally inundated ground. **Eggs:** 5–6 (4–7); white, rounded. **Range and Status:** endemic to C. York Pen. (Q), where formerly widespread. Now mostly in area of c. Pen., total population reduced to *c.* 150 pairs or *c.* 1000 birds of all ages after breeding (Garnett & Crowley, 1995). Declining from reduction in burning frequency causing encroachment by paperbark and other scrub on habitat, resulting in increased predation of breeding adults and young by birds such as Pied Butcherbirds. Sedentary.

HOODED PARROT *Psephotus dissimilis* 25–27 cm

Like Golden-shouldered Parrot, *but male has entire crown black to below eye; more golden yellow on shoulder.* **Female:** pale yellow–green; forehead/face pale blue; neck/upperbreast yellow–green; *under tail-coverts pink.* **Immature:** like female but duller; bill yellowish at first; young males have darker heads, brighter colouring. Pairs, parties, occasionally flocks: perches in trees, incongruously on telephone wires; feeds much on ground. Flight swift, undulating; dark upperparts contrast with golden shoulders, turquoise rump. **Similar species:** Golden-shouldered Parrot (note range); Northern Rosella. **Voice:** described as 'chu-weet' in flight (Forshaw, 1981). Alarm-call: sharp metallic 'chissik-chissik' or 'chillik'. **Habitat:** dry, open woodlands; paperbarks, spinifex; eucalypts in rocky, open grasslands bordering watercourses; usually with termite-mounds. **Breeds:** April–June. **Nest:** in cavity in termite-mound, reached by short tunnel. **Eggs:** 2–5; white, rounded. **Range and Status:** confined to Top End (NT), e. to w. edge of Arnhem Land escarpment (formerly e. to *c.* McArthur R.). Patchy, uncommon; now mostly reported at w. end of range, from upper S. Alligator R., w. to Pine Creek and s. to about Mataranka. Sedentary.

PARADISE PARROT *Psephotus pulcherrimus* 27–30 cm

Other names: Ant-hill or Soldier Parrot.
Exceedingly beautiful small, long-tailed parrot. **Male:** bright turquoise-green with *scarlet forehead; crown and nape blackish 'like a tight little cap'; dark brown above with scarlet shoulders;* underparts and under tail-coverts scarlet; *rump/flanks turquoise-blue;* tail bronze-green and blue above, margined white. **Female:** duller, paler; less scarlet on shoulder; *face/breast buff–yellow with brownish orange markings;* rump turquoise-blue; underparts pale blue; under tail-coverts reddish. **Immature:** like poorly coloured adults. Female and imm. show pale wingbar in flight. Pairs, family parties: reported to feed quietly on ground, flying up into nearby trees when disturbed. Posture upright when perched, hence earlier name, 'Soldier Parrot'. Flight undulating, *with contrasting dark brown upperparts and blue rump.* **Similar species:** Blue Bonnet, race *haematorrhous:* pale grey–brown, with blue 'face' and bend of wing; lower breast lemon; calls differ. **Voice:** described as short, sharp, musical whistle, uttered before taking flight; metallic 'queek', repeated; also an animated musical song. **Habitat:** grassy eucalypt woodlands; scrubby grasslands; with low, rounded termite-mounds. **Breeds:** Sept.–Dec.; March–April. **Nest:** in chamber in terrestrial termite-mound, reached by tunnel *c.* 4 cm in diameter; occasionally in creekbank, stump. **Eggs:** 3–5; white, rounded. **Range and Status:** formerly sub-coastal se. Q and ne. NSW: from *c.* Inverell (NSW) n. to *c.* Rockhampton (Q). Once fairly common; declined from habitat changes due to grazing, burning, drought, bird-trapping; introduced cat and fox. Last confirmed breeding was near Gayndah (Q) in 1922. Probably extinct.

GOLDEN-SHOULDERED
PARROT

♀

♂

♂

HOODED
PARROT

♀

♂

PARADISE PARROT

♀

♂

285

BLUE-WINGED PARROT *Neophema chrysostoma* 20–23 cm

Soft olive–green with yellowish facial mask; *blue forehead-band stops at eye; note large dark blue shoulder-patch.* Underparts pale yellow; *some have orange belly.* **Female:** duller; forehead-band smaller. **Immature:** duller; less blue; pale wingbar in flight. Pairs, parties, companies: feeds quietly on ground; flits along, settles (often on fence-wires). Darts skyward, calling. Flies high, with quick, wader-like hesitation in wingbeats; other neophemas fly similarly. **Similar species:** Elegant, Rock, Orange-bellied Parrots. **Voice:** *double,* silvery, tinkling 'brrrt brrrrt'; startled, staccato burst, 'chappy-chappy-brrt-chippy-chippy-brrt'. **Habitat:** open woodlands, coastal scrubs; dune, saltmarsh vegetation; mallee, mulga, saltbush, wetland-edges, alpine meadows, airfields, saltfields, golf-courses, paddocks, crops, orchards. **Breeds:** Oct.–Feb. **Nest:** in tree hollow or stump; several pairs nearby. **Eggs:** 4–6; white, rounded. **Range and Status:** breeds e., n. Tas.; s. Vic., n. to Grampians NP; and in se. SA. Migrates in March–April to inland NSW, sw. Q and e. SA w. to Eyre Pen.; returning Aug.–Oct. Uncommon.

ROCK PARROT *Neophema petrophila* 21–23 cm

Dullest grass-parrot. **Male:** *brownish olive, yellower below; forehead band dark blue; facial mask pale blue to behind eye; wing edged blue;* some have orange belly. **Female:** duller. **Immature:** duller, pale wingstripe in flight. Pairs to flocks of 100+: feeds on ground among low growth; flits, settles on rocks, shrubs; *posture upright;* darts skywards, fast and high. **Similar species:** Blue-winged, Orange-bellied Parrots. **Voice:** rapid 'tsit, tsit, tsit'. **Habitat:** granite, limestone islands; coastal dunes, scrubs, grasslands, swamps, wastelands, golf-courses; coastal railyards, for grain. **Breeds:** Aug.–Feb. **Nest:** *mostly on rocky offshore islands;* among rocks or under vegetation. **Eggs:** 4–5; white, rounded. **Range and Status:** coasts, islands of s. Aust., from Coorong (SA) to Shark Bay (WA); possible break on Bight coast. Common, sedentary; autumn–winter dispersal from islands to nearby coasts.

ELEGANT PARROT *Neophema elegans* 22–24 cm

Golden olive, with yellow facial mask: *forehead-band dark blue, narrowly edged pale blue, extends just past eye; narrow, dark/light blue band around bend of wing;* underparts buttercup yellow; some have orange belly. **Female:** duller; mask olive–yellow; less blue. **Immature:** no band or mask; pale wingbar. Solitary, pairs, small flocks: quiet; flight quick, with flitting wingbeats; yellower than Blue-winged, shows *golden-olive rump, yellow outer tail-feathers.* **Similar species:** Blue-winged, Orange-bellied Parrots; female Turquoise, Scarlet-chested Parrots. **Voice:** single sharp 'tsit'; feeble twitterings. **Habitat:** open forests, woodlands, scrublands; river red gums on watercourses; saltbush, mallee, mulga; clearings with rank growth; saltmarsh. **Breeds:** Aug.–Dec. **Nest:** in tree-spout. **Eggs:** 4–5; white, round. **Range and Status:** disjunct: (1) se. SA, incl. Flinders Ras. and adjacent far sw. NSW; rare in w. Vic. (e. to Ararat region); (2) sw. WA, s. and w. of c. Esperance–Merredin–Geraldton. Common to rare; part-nomadic.

ORANGE-BELLIED PARROT *Neophema chrysogaster* 20–22 cm

Male: *robust, rich green grass parrot;* orange belly-patch not always visible. Mid-blue forehead-band stops at eye; 'mask' yellow–green; bright blue around bend of wing; tail dark blue–green, outer feathers yellow. **Female:** duller, with less blue; green wash on breast; less orange on belly. **Immature:** duller; pale wingbar. Parties, small flocks: feeds on ground, perches on low shrubs; sometimes with Blue-winged Parrots. Wary; dashes skywards, calling; looks *dark, sturdy;* travels far, flies high. **Similar species:** Blue-winged, Elegant Parrots. **Voice:** soft tinklings; when flushed, distinctive buzzing, metallic, explosive 'zizizizizizizizi'. **Habitat:** in sw. Tas., button-grass; sedges on wet peat plains; breeds in eucalypt woodland on margins of coastal plains. On mainland favours small islands, peninsulas in coastal areas; with saltmarsh plants; coastal pastures, golf-courses; crops of millet and sunflowers; dunes, beaches. **Breeds:** Nov.–Dec. **Nest:** in tree-hollow. **Eggs:** 4–6; white, rounded. **Range and Status:** breeds sw. Tas.: migrates n. in March–April via King I. to coastal s. Vic.–se. SA; casual e. to Gippsland Lakes (Vic.), w. to Yorke Pen. (SA). Returns Tas. mid-Oct. Rare, local: total wild population c. 150+ birds (Garnett, 1993). Endangered.

BLUE-WINGED PARROT

♀ ♂

ROCK PARROT

♀ ♂

ELEGANT PARROT

♂ ♀

ORANGE-BELLIED PARROT

♀ ♂

BOURKE'S PARROT *Neopsephotus bourkii* 18–22 cm

Other names: Night or Sundown Parrot.
Male: *soft-brown with whitish eye-ring and pale fringes to wing-feathers; underparts washed deep pink.* Forehead band and bend of wing mid-blue; *flanks, sides of rump and under tail-coverts pale blue.* **Female:** duller; no blue on forehead, less on wing. **Immature:** like female; less pink; adult and imm. females show pale wingstripe in flight. Pairs, flocks: feeds quietly on ground and in foliage. When disturbed, freezes or darts quickly to nearby tree (often dead tree), matching colour of wood. In flight, *note pale blue underwing and flanks, white edges to tail.* At dusk, dawn, and in total darkness, flocks fly fast through scrub to water, uttering soft calls, wings whistling softly. **Similar species:** Peaceful, Diamond Doves. **Voice:** flight-call, mellow 'chu-wee'; soft chirrupy twitter; shrill metallic alarm-call. **Habitat:** mulga, other acacia scrubs; native cypress; open eucalypt woodlands. **Breeds:** Aug.–Dec. **Nest:** decayed debris in low hollow of acacia, casuarina. **Eggs:** 3–6; white, rounded. **Range and Status:** widespread across s. interior, from about Blackall–Cunnamulla (Q) and Walgett–Hillston (NSW), to w. coast WA, between *c.* Moore R. and NW Cape; n. to Devil's Marbles (NT), s. to Port Augusta–Gt Victoria Desert. Moves further s. and e. in dry periods inland. Locally abundant; patchy, irregular. Nomadic.

TURQUOISE PARROT *Neophema pulchella* 19–21 cm

Male: *grass-green with bright blue forehead and cheeks;* brilliant two-tone blue band around bend of wing contrasts *with dark brick–red shoulder-patch; underparts and tail-edges rich yellow.* **Female:** *facial mask whitish;* no *red* on wing; pale wingstripe. Old birds of either sex may have orange belly. **Immature:** like dull adults. Pairs, small flocks: feeds quietly in low grass, weeds; flits ahead of observer, flies up to nearby trees. Flight swift, direct or erratic, fluttering; shows bright green upperparts, buttercup-yellow underparts and outer tail-feathers. **Similar species:** Scarlet-chested, female: has *blue* mask. Blue-winged, female: duller olive; slight blue forehead-band; olive-yellow mask. **Voice:** weak tinkling flight-call; high-pitched 'peet' like Azure Kingfisher; musical twittering. **Habitat:** open grassy woodland, with dead trees, near permanent water and forested hills (Morris, 1980); coastal heaths; pastures with exotic grasses; weeds, roadsides, orchards. **Breeds:** Aug.–Dec. and April–May. **Nest:** in dead stump or spout of eucalypt. **Eggs:** 4–5; white, rounded. **Range and Status:** slopes, lowlands of Divide in se. Aust., from Cooloola NP and Gayndah (Q) to n. and far e. Vic.: approximate inland limits are Chinchilla (Q): Moree–Nymagee–Hillston–Deniliquin (NSW), upper Murray Valley–Warby Ras.–Bendigo (Vic.). Reaches e. coast (and Sydney outskirts) approx. from Hunter R. to s. of Nowra, patchily down s. coast to far e. Vic., w. to Snowy R. Consolidating after decades of decline; locally common; part-nomadic.

SCARLET-CHESTED PARROT *Neophema splendida* 17.5–22 cm

Male: unmistakable — *head bright deep blue; chest deep scarlet;* underparts rich yellow. **Female:** *blue face (incl. 'mask'); green upperparts contrast with yellow underparts.* **Immature:** like female but duller; young males darker on face; in flight, females show pale wingstripe. Pairs, small parties to large flocks: quiet; feeds on ground on seeds of grasses, herbs, shrubs, incl. acacias. When disturbed, flits to settle on ground or tree. Flight erratic and fluttering or swift and direct, *showing rich yellow margins of blackish outer tail-feathers.* Seldom at water: apparently gains moisture from dew or succulent plants. **Similar species:** Turquoise Parrot, female: has whitish mask; note range. Other female grass-parrots do not have blue face; most have less pale blue on wing, less green–yellow contrast. **Voice:** feeble twittering. **Habitat:** mallee and other eucalypt woodlands; mulga, other acacias; belar, other she oaks; spinifex, saltbush, succulents, e.g. parakeelya. Reported to favour country burned in recent years (Blakers et al, 1984). **Breeds:** Aug.–Dec. **Nest:** in hollow of eucalypt, mulga, up to 8 m, sometimes with some leaves; several pairs nearby. **Eggs:** 3–5; white, rounded. **Range and Status:** s. inland Aust., its heartland being Gt Victoria Desert in SA/WA. In good seasons, numbers increase, and over several years birds may extend to far sw. Q, w. NSW, far nw. Vic., 'Murray Mallee' (SA), w. to Norseman–upper Murchison R. (WA) and n. to near Alice Springs (s. NT). Highly nomadic; irruptive.

BOURKE'S PARROT

♂

♀

TURQUOISE PARROT

♀

♂

♂

SCARLET-CHESTED
PARROT

♀

♂

GROUND PARROT *Pezoporus wallicus* 28–32 cm

Other names: Button-grass or Swamp Parrot.

Slender, long-tailed, grass-green parrot; *streaked, mottled black, barred yellow; small red forehead-patch*; eye pale yellow; tail long, barred. **Immature:** duller, lacks red; eye brown. Singles, pairs, open companies: shy, feeds on ground; climbs low plants. Flushes unexpectedly: *flies fast, low, with snipe-like twists, bursts of wingbeats and glides on depressed wings, showing pale wingbar, long, barred tail*; plunges to cover, runs. **Voice:** mostly dawn, dusk: high-pitched, rapid, morse-code like, ascending notes or beautiful, measured, bell-like notes: 'tee . . . tee . . . stit' (Forshaw, 1981); also clear, sustained, cricket- or budgerigar-like chirrups. **Habitat:** coastal heaths, swampy areas, drier ridges, burned areas in same; nearby grasslands. In Tas., button-grass moorland. **Breeds:** Sept.–Dec.; autumn in ne. NSW. **Nest:** cup of bitten-off stems; in tussock, stunted bush, with entrance-tunnel. **Eggs:** 3–4; white, slightly pointed. **Range and Status:** from ne. of Gympie, and Fraser I. (Q) to e. and s. Vic. (formerly se. SA); widespread w. and sw. Tas. In s. coastal WA, now rare and confined to C. Arid and Fitzgerald R. NPs. (Garnett, 1993). Sedentary, with local seasonal movements. Common Tas.; endangered WA.

NIGHT PARROT *Pezoporus occidentalis* 22–24 cm

Other name: Spinifex Parrot.

Dumpy olive–green parrot with large head and eye, and rounded, wedge-shaped tail; *streaked, mottled dark brown, barred pale yellow, no red on forehead*; yellowish below; outer tail feathers barred black, yellow; pale yellow wingbar in flight. Spends day in cavity in spinifex or low shrub. When disturbed, flies low, fast or 'fluttering' 20–30 m, then drops. Runs, squats, hugs ground, keeps to cover. At dusk, flies to water before moving out to feed on spinifex seeds, chenopods. **Similar species:** Ground Parrot. Caution: Bourke's Parrot also called 'Night' or 'Sundown' Parrot. **Voice:** squeak when flushed; at water, harsh loud double note or croaking alarm-note; also long-drawn whistle of two notes, repeated at 3-second intervals. **Habitat:** seeding spinifex on stony rises, breakaway country, sandy lowlands; shrubby glasswort, chenopods; succulents on flats around salt lakes; flooded claypans, saltbush, bluebush, bassia associations. **Breeds:** July–Aug., or after rain. **Nest:** chamber *c.* 25 cm across in spinifex clump, densely lined with spinifex spines, reached by tunnel; or platform of small sticks in shrubby glasswort. **Eggs:** 4; white, about size of Crested Pigeon's. **Range and Status:** widespread across inland Aust. until *c.* 1900, when it declined from pastoral settlement, drought, fire; introduced camel, rabbit, fox, feral cat. 'Lost' for decades, still subject of sight-records, some no doubt authentic. In Oct. 1990, a dry, feathered body, months dead, was found by museum ornithologists beside Highway 83, n. of Boulia (Q). Highly nomadic: likely to occur anywhere from w. Q to nw. NSW; s. NT; inland SA; inland WA w. to Pilbara, w. coast. Endangered.

BUDGERIGAR *Melopsittacus undulatus* 17–20 cm

Bright green with yellow forehead/throat; upperparts closely barred; cere blue in male, paler in nonbreeding female, brown in breeding female. **Immature:** duller; forehead barred. Parties, flocks: feeds in grass, flushes chattering. Flight swift, showing *yellow wingbar*; at times flies in undulating hordes of many thousands. Rests in foliage during heat; drinks morning and afternoon; often with cockatiels, zebra finches. **Voice:** musical chirrup; zizzing chatter; rasping scolds. **Habitat:** grasslands, spinifex, pastoral country, saltbush, mallee, mulga; eucalypts on watercourses, freshwater lakes; crops, roadsides. **Breeds:** March–Sept., or after rain, in n.; Aug.–Jan. in s.; often many pairs in same hollow tree. **Nest:** in hollow limb, stump, fence-post. **Eggs:** 4–6+; white, rounded. **Range and Status:** inland, more arid Aust.: spring–summer movements (or in drought) to breed in subcoastal s. Aust. In good seasons extends to subcoastal n. Aust. (except C. York Pen.). In drought retreats to e., s. and w. coastal areas, Top End (NT). Abundant; highly nomadic.

GROUND PARROT

NIGHT PARROT

♀

♂

BUDGERIGAR

ORIENTAL CUCKOO *Cuculus saturatus* 28–33 cm

Other name: Himalayan Cuckoo.

Bill part-yellow; *eye, eye-ring and feet yellow; underparts whitish, wavily barred black*. **Female:** similar; upperbreast washed buff. Some ('hepatic') females are red–brown above, whitish below, *barred black on upperparts, rump, tail*; barred finer below, from throat down. **Immature:** barred as female; upperparts grey–brown or red–brown with buff scalloping; bill, legs grey–yellow. Singles, parties: shy; flight swift, falcon-like; underwings barred black and white. **Similar species:** Pallid Cuckoo; Barred Cuckoo-shrike.

Voice: mournful trill on three notes, repeated with rising crescendo; also harsh 'gaak-gaak-gak-ak-ak-ak', like Dollarbird. **Habitat:** monsoon forest, rainforest edges; leafy trees in paddocks; river flats, roadsides, mangroves, islands. **Range and Status:** widespread Asian cuckoo: race *horsfieldi* breeds Mongolia, China, Japan: migrates to Indonesia, PNG, NZ. Regular nonbreeding migrant (Sept.–May) to coastal n. and e. Aust. and islands; from Kimberley (WA), casual Pilbara–w. deserts, to ne. and e. Q, e. NSW, s. to *c*. Shoalhaven R.; also Lord Howe I. Some overwinter. Uncommon.

PALLID CUCKOO *Cuculus pallidus* 28–33 cm

Note *dark bill, dark eye with gold eye-ring; shadowy dark mark down neck from eye; olive–grey feet; white (or buff) mark on nape; prominent white (or buff) toothings to edges of tail*. **Juvenile** (not illustrated): grotesque; bill pale horn; plumage untidily variegated black and white; head huge, tail short, gape yellow. **Immature:** grey–brown above, grey below; head/neck untidily streaked, mottled rich buff, brown, white; triangular buff–white toothings on back/wings/tail; brown bars on upperbreast. Becomes greyer, hindneck mottled buff; wing-feathers finely toothed buff or white; may breed in this plumage. Singles, pairs: calls persistently from high branches, overhead wires, fences; flies down to seize hairy caterpillars in grass. Sustained flight slipping, undulating; note small head, pointed wings; alighting, tail raised and lowered; wings droop. Noisy chases when courting. Often noticed by distinctive call. **Similar species:** Oriental Cuckoo can be confused with barred imm. Pallid, but note other features. **Voice:** male: well-known upward chromatic scale of eight whistled notes, rising in quarter-tones. Pursuing males utter demented, rising 'crookyer'; staccato 'pip-pip-pip-pip'. Female: hoarse brassy whistle. **Habitat:** woodlands, scrublands, mangroves, pastoral country, farmland, golf-courses, roadsides, rail reserves, gardens. **Breeds:** July–Dec. **Egg:** 1; pale pink, spotted deeper; in cup-nest of honeyeater, flycatcher, woodswallow, oriole, cuckoo-shrike; each adult female probably lays numerous eggs each season. **Range and Status:** Aust., Tas.: breeding migrant to coastal se. Aust. and Tas., arriving Sept.–Oct. (sometimes earlier). Mostly breeds s. of Tropic (Blakers et al, 1984). Winters inland and Top End (NT); some migrate to Timor, PNG. Adults mostly leave s. Aust. by Jan., imms later, some overwinter. In s. WA, arrives May, leaves Dec.

LONG-TAILED CUCKOO *Eudynamys taitensis* 40–46 cm

Other names: Long-tailed Koel.

Large, *long-tailed brown cuckoo with white eyebrow; white below with dark brown streaks*; eye yellow; legs greenish yellow. **Female:** smaller, more rufous. **Immature:** *white spots on above; underparts buff with dark streaks*. Shy, skulking; perches lengthways on branches. Flight slipping; note long, barred tail. **Similar species:** Koel, female: *dark bars on breast*. **Voice:** in NZ, when breeding, 'drawn-out . . . screech: *shweesht* . . . also . . . falcon-like "kik-kik-kik-kik". . .' (Soper, 1984). **Habitat:** fringes of scrub, rainforest and mangroves. **Range and Status:** breeds in NZ Oct.–March: migrates to islands off se. PNG; Bismarck Arch. and Pacific. Irregular migrant, Lord Howe I., Norfolk I. and probably outer islands of Gt Barrier Reef.

'hepatic' ♀

♂

imm.

ORIENTAL CUCKOO

imm.-1

adult

PALLID CUCKOO

imm.-2

LONG-TAILED CUCKOO

FAN-TAILED CUCKOO *Cacomantis flabelliformis* 25–27 cm

Slate-grey above; throat and *upperbreast pale to warm cinnamon–buff; underparts paler; tail slim, infrequently fanned; feathers wavily notched white on both edges.* Eye brown; eye-ring yellow; legs/feet olive–yellow. **Female:** duller, greyer below. **Juvenile:** differs — lustrous rufous-brown above; *underparts dull white, finely mottled, barred, black, grey and brown.* Singles, pairs: sits motionless, calling from high branches, stumps, overhead wires; posture upright, tail downpointed. Flight easy, undulating; note pale wingbar; tilts tail on alighting. **Similar species:** Brush Cuckoo: plainer; eye-ring and feet grey; less notching on (squarer) tail-feathers. Brush Cuckoo juvenile: pattern of upperparts more variegated than imm. Fan-tailed; paler below with clearer fine bars. Chestnut-breasted Cuckoo: darker, richer-coloured; note range and calls. **Voice:** sad, leisurely, downward trill, 'pee-eeer'; also slow, rising, quiet, 'get-woorrk'. Female: brisk, shrill 'too-brrreeet'. **Habitat:** denser than Pallid: rainforest, river red gum forests, mangroves, open woodland, paddocks, roadsides, orchards, gardens. **Breeds:** July–Jan. **Egg:** 1; mauve–white with red/brown spots at large end; deposited in domed nest of fairy wren, thornbill, scrubwren; less often in cup-nest of honeyeater, flycatcher. **Range and Status:** e. Aust. and sw. WA, from C. York (Q) to Tas. and s. Eyre Pen. (SA), inland to *c.* Cunnamulla (Q)–Bourke (NSW) (Noske, 1978); also s. WA., e. along Bight coast, and n. to Shark Bay. In se. Aust. and sw. WA, inland autumn migration. Common; part-migratory. Also Fiji, PNG, Aru Is.; vagrant NZ.

CHESTNUT-BREASTED CUCKOO *Cacomantis castaneiventris* 23–25 cm

Like a small, dark, richly coloured Fan-tailed Cuckoo: *lustrous slate–blue above, orange–chestnut below; tail-feathers notched white, more boldly on inner webs, and tipped white;* eye brown; eye-ring and legs yellow. **Female:** duller. **Immature:** plain chestnut–brown above, paler buff–brown below. Quiet, inconspicuous: watches from low perch, flies to ground for prey, showing pale wingbar; hovers low, tail downpointed; picks insects from leaves in rainforest. **Voice:** like descending trill of Fan-tailed Cuckoo; also a brief, grasshopper-like 'chirrip', described by G. Beruldsen (1990) as 'almost impossible to differentiate [from] . . . short trill of . . . Yellow-billed Kingfisher'. **Habitat:** rainforest, monsoon forest; scrub along watercourses; mangroves. **Breeds:** egg and hosts not certainly known; possibly include Tropical Scrubwren. **Range and Status:** e. C. York Pen. (Q), from C. York s. to Bloomfield R. (Cooktown–Mossman), inland to McIlwraith Ra. Probably extends further s., e.g. sight-records Mt Lewis and Julatten (Pavey, 1991). Uncommon; sedentary; possibly part-migratory to PNG, where also resident.

BRUSH CUCKOO *Cacomantis variolosus* 22–26 cm

Plain small cuckoo: grey–brown above; *grey breast washed buff; under tail-coverts buff. Tail squarer than Fan-tailed,* with *white notching on inner webs, white tips;* eye-ring grey; legs grey–pink. **Immature:** more variegated pattern than imm. Fan-tailed: *brown above with plentiful buff streaks and angular feather-margins; wing and tail-feathers deeply notched buff; breast brokenly mottled, white underparts more openly barred dark brown.* Singles, pairs, displaying parties: unobtrusive, *but revealed by distinctive, incessant call.* Perches in leafy trees; flies to take insects in foliage or on ground. Sustained flight swift, undulating, showing pale wingbar. **Similar species:** Fan-tailed Cuckoo: eye-ring, legs yellow; *breast more cinnamon–buff;* tail longer, pointed; *notched white on outer feathers.* **Voice:** 7–8 shrill, *far-carrying, deliberate, descending notes,* 'fear-fear-fear-fear . . . ', widely heard day/night in warmer months. Parties display with wild, shrill, repeated, rising phrases like 'where's-the-pippy?'. **Habitat:** rainforests, forests, woodlands; alpine country in se. Aust. in summer; leafy trees on watercourses; swamp woodlands, mangroves, scrubby roadsides. **Breeds:** Oct.–Feb. in se. Aust.; most months in n. Aust. **Egg:** 1; whitish, with faint purplish brown and lavender markings; deposited in cup nest of robin; flycatcher, fantail, honeyeater; occasionally domed nest of gerygone, fairy wren, scrubwren. **Range and Status:** coastal n. and e. Aust.; regular breeding migrant to se. Aust., mostly in forests of Dividing Ra. in se. Q, NSW and e. Vic., arriving Sept.–Oct., departing Feb.–April; casual nw. Vic. mallee, adjacent SA. In n. Aust., both resident and passage migrant. Some migrate in winter to Solomon Is., PNG, Indonesia. Common in n., uncommon in s. Aust.

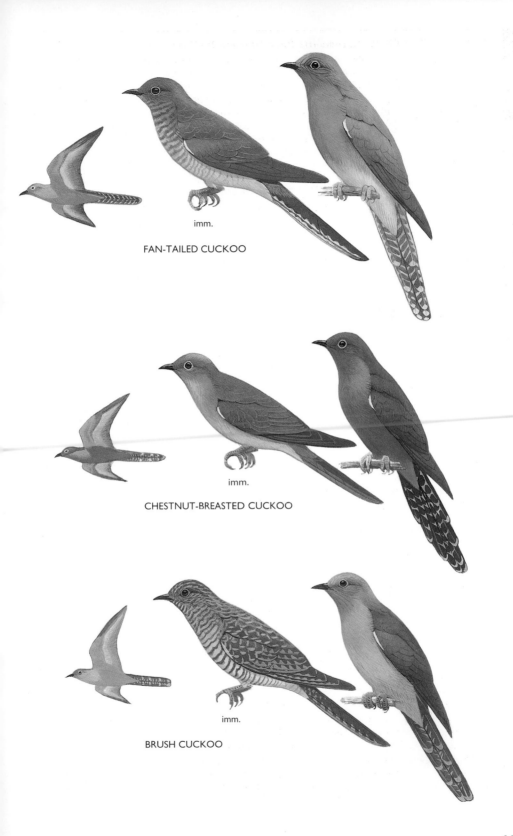

FAN-TAILED CUCKOO

imm.

CHESTNUT-BREASTED CUCKOO

imm.

BRUSH CUCKOO

imm.

HORSFIELD'S BRONZE-CUCKOO *Chrysococcyx basalis* 15–17 cm

Pale brown above, glossed green; *feathers fringed paler; long white eyebrow above brown mark curving down neck; breast-bars broken; bases of outer tail-feathers rufous; eye dark.* **Immature:** grey–brown, whitish below; shadowy bars develop; *tail as adult.* Singles, parties: calls from high branches, wires. Forages low, for hairy caterpillars. Flight swift; pale wingbar. **Similar species:** Shining Bronze-Cuckoo. **Voice:** clear, *descending* 'tseeeeuw'; often kicks up at end; brisk 'chirrup'. **Habitat:** woodlands; mallee, mulga, saltbush, saltmarsh, mangroves, roadsides, golf-courses. **Breeds:** July–Jan. **Egg:** 1; whitish, speckled pink, red; in domed nest of fairy-wren, gerygone, thornbill; cup nest of robin, chat. **Range and Status:** breeding migrant to s. Aust., Tas., June–March; breeds/overwinters inland. Resident n. Aust., breeds summer; winter migrant to w. PNG; Indonesia; Christmas I., Indian Ocean.

SHINING BRONZE-CUCKOO *Chrysococcyx lucidus* 16–18 cm

Aust. race *plagosus:* bronze–green above; head purplish–brown; *face, underparts white, with tidy bronze–brown bars; eye pale brown.* **Immature:** grey–brown, whitish below; shadowy bars develop. Nominate race: *greener; forehead scalloped white.* Singles, parties: courting males chase with staccato calls, spread wings. Flight swift, with pale wingbar. **Similar species:** Horsfield, Little Bronze-Cuckoos. **Voice:** like person whistling dog: 'fwee-fwee-fwee', each note *rising strongly;* descending, staccato 'pee-eeerr'. **Habitat:** rainforest, forest, woodland, gardens. **Breeds:** Aug.–Jan. **Egg:** 1; olive–bronze; in nest of thornbill, fairy-wren, scrubwren; flycatcher, silvereye, honeyeater. **Range and Status:** race *plagosus:* breeding migrant to coastal se. Aust. and sw. WA, Oct.–April. Birds from se. Aust. winter in Q, PNG, e. Indonesia. Birds from sw. WA, in w. Indonesia. Nominate race breeds NZ, migrates to Solomon Is. through Lord Howe, Norfolk Is., casual coastal e. Aust. spring–autumn.

LITTLE BRONZE-CUCKOO *Chrysococcyx minutillus* 14–15 cm

Eye and eye-ring red (male); tan (female): forehead glossy black with white scallops; upperparts pale bronze–green; underparts white with fine black scallops; inner tail-feathers rufous. **Immature:** eye brown; grey–green above, whitish below, part-barred. **Similar species:** Gould's Bronze-Cuckoo. **Voice:** 4–5 quick, clear, descending notes, repeated. **Habitat:** near water: edges of rainforest, monsoon forest, open forest, paperbarks, mangroves, gardens. **Breeds:** Sept.–Jan. **Egg:** 1; buff/greenish olive, freckled red–brown; in domed nest of gerygone, honeyeater. **Range and Status:** Nominate race: Kimberley (WA)–Top End (NT). Race *barnardi:* from *c.* Byfield (Q) to *c.* Kempsey (NSW), inland to Tenterfield. Some migrate in autumn to C. York Pen., s. PNG. Also widespread PNG–se. Asia.

GOULD'S BRONZE-CUCKOO *Chrysococcyx russatus* 14–15 cm

Possibly conspecific with Little Bronze-Cuckoo: *rufous wash on upperparts, neck and tail; breast-bars more bronzed.* Female less rufous. **Voice:** like Little Bronze; also long, descending, grasshopper-like trill. **Habitat:** rainforest, eucalypt forest, woodland, paperbarks, mangroves. **Breeds:** Oct.–Jan. **Egg:** 1; olive–bronze, peppered darker; in nest of gerygone. **Range and Status:** coastal ne. Q, s. to *c.* Bowen. Sedentary. Also s. PNG.

BLACK-EARED CUCKOO *Chrysococcyx osculans* 19–21 cm

Glossy pale brown above; *curving black mask under white eyebrow; breast pale salmon to fawn; rump whitish; tail dark brown, outer feathers barred, tipped white.* **Immature:** duller. Keeps to shrubby vegetation; courting males chase noisily; *note pale wingbar/rump.* **Voice:** plaintive, descending 'feeeeeee'; staccato 'pee-o-wit, pee-o-weer'. **Habitat:** drier woodlands, scrublands: mallee, mulga, lignum, saltmarsh, riverside thickets. **Breeds:** Aug.–Jan. in s. Aust.; March–July inland. **Egg:** 1; chocolate-brown; in nest of Speckled Warbler, Fieldwren, Redthroat; thornbill, scrubwren, heathwren. **Range and Status:** inland, drier coastal Aust. Breeding migrant to subcoastal s. Aust., Aug.–Feb.; vagrant Tas. Winter migrant coastal n. Aust.; sparse C. York Pen.; some to s. PNG, e. Indonesia. Uncommon.

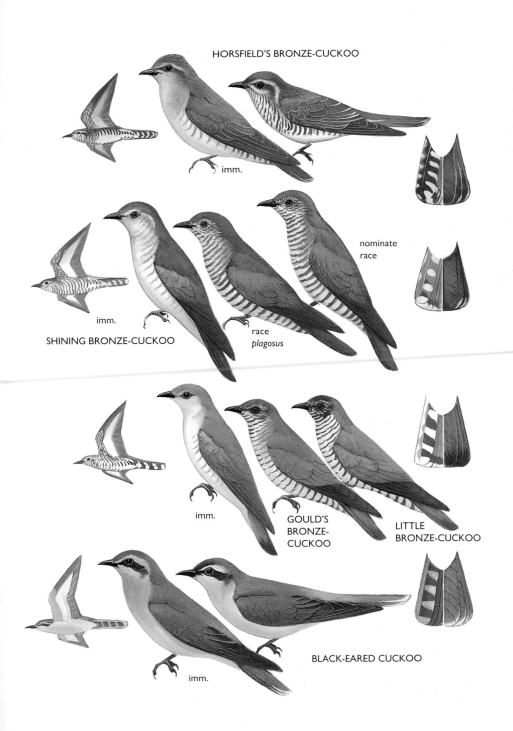

HORSFIELD'S BRONZE-CUCKOO

imm.

SHINING BRONZE-CUCKOO

imm.

nominate
race

race
plagosus

imm.

GOULD'S
BRONZE-
CUCKOO

LITTLE
BRONZE-CUCKOO

imm.

BLACK-EARED CUCKOO

COMMON KOEL *Eudynamys scolopacea* 40–46 cm

Other names: Cooee or Rain Bird.

Large cuckoo, well-known by distinctive call. **Male:** glossy blue–black; *bill whitish horn; tail long, rounded; eye red.* **Female:** crown/nape/face black; upperparts cocoa-brown *with plentiful white spots, bars;* buff–white whisker-mark above black throat-stripe; underparts white to chestnut–buff, *lightly barred darker.* **Immature:** like female, but *head rufous,* mottled; eye brown, later orange. Sub-adult males blackish with traces of rufous-barring. Singles, pairs; parties in leafy, fruiting trees. Wary, elusive: courting males noisy with feverish flight-chases; calls day/night, especially in wet. **Similar species:** Long-tailed Cuckoo, Satin Bowerbird, Spangled Drongo. **Voice:** male: far-carrying, slow 'kooeel'; brisk, rising 'quoy-quoy-quoy-quoy'; 'quodel-quodel-quodel', 'wirra wirra wirra' or rising, demented 'weir-weir-weir-weir!'. Female: shrill, four-note brassy piping. Silent after breeding. **Habitat:** leafy, fruiting trees on fringes of rainforests, woodlands, streams; farmlands, parks, streets. **Breeds:** Sept.–March. **Egg:** 1; salmon–pink, marbled reddish, violet–grey, in nest of friarbird, wattlebird, Blue-faced Honeyeater, White-rumped Miner, Olive-backed Oriole, Figbird, Paradise Riflebird, Magpie-lark. **Range and Status:** winters PNG–Indonesia; breeding migrant (Aug.–May) to n. and e. Aust. from Kimberley (WA) to s. coast, NSW; casual s. WA, e. Vic., NZ. Ranges to India–s. China.

CHANNEL-BILLED CUCKOO *Scythrops novaehollandiae* 58–66 cm

Other names: Flood, Rain or Stormbird; Fig Hawk, Hornbill.

Huge pale grey cuckoo with large, curved, straw-coloured bill, red skin around eye; tail with dark terminal band, tipped white. **Immature:** paler; no red; scalloped buff above. Singles, pairs, small flocks: shy, keeps to heads of leafy figs; harassed by other birds; often first noted by call. Flight strong, hawk-like, with regular beats; often high; *like flying cross.* **Voice:** raucous, repeated, rising shout, 'oik' or 'awk'; flying or perched; often at night. **Habitat:** rainforest, open forest, woodland, swamp woodland, fruiting trees in farmland, roadsides. **Breeds:** Aug.–Dec. **Eggs:** dull white to buff, blotched reddish, purplish brown, below surface. May lay up to 5 eggs in one nest. Hosts include Pied Currawong, Australian Magpie, Torresian Crow. **Range and Status:** summer breeding migrant from Indonesia–PNG to n. and e. Aust.: from Kimberley (WA), where rare (casual s. to Pilbara), to Top End (NT); widespread in Q; NSW, s. to *c.* Sydney, inland to Moree–Warrumbungle NP–Barellan. Arrives Aug.–Sept., departs March–April, earlier (Dec.–Feb.) from NSW. In good seasons extends (and breeds) to Channel Country of sw. Q–ne. SA; also s. NT (Alice Springs). Casual s. NSW, ACT, c. Vic., Tas.

PHEASANT COUCAL *Centropus phasianinus* 50–70 cm. Female larger.

Other names: Cane Pheasant, Swamp Pheasant.

Long-tailed, short-legged, skulking, pheasant-like bird. **Breeding plumage:** *bill black; eye red; head/neck/body blackish, streaked by glossy feather shafts; wings and back chestnut, barred/streaked black, rusty and cream.* **Nonbreeding:** *bill horn-coloured; head/neck/body yellow–buff;* upperparts rufous, streaked paler, richly barred and patterned. **Immature:** bill and eye brown; plumage fawner. Singles, pairs: sits oddly in leafy saplings, fence-posts; runs heavily across roads, clearings; flies clumsily on short wings, flops into cover; ascends saplings, flies from top. Takes eggs, nestlings; mobbed by other birds. **Voice:** deep, hollow accelerating, descending 'coop-coop-coop-coop-coop-coop', like liquid glugging from bottle; quiet scolding. **Habitat:** grassy, swampy flats, wet heathlands; rank growth in clearings, wasteland; scrub on watercourses, lantana thickets, brigalow, pandanus, mangrove-fringes, sugar-cane, roadsides, gardens. **Breeds:** Oct.–April. Builds own nest, incubates eggs, feeds young. **Nest:** saucer-shaped, of grass lined with leaves, in grass clump, bush, pandanus, sugar-cane; drawn together overhead, open each end; up to 2 m from ground. **Eggs:** 3–5 (7); dirty white, chalky; stained brownish, scratched. **Range and Status:** coastal nw., n. and e. Aust., from Pilbara and Kimberley (WA) to Top End (NT), Gulf coast (Q); n. and e. Q, inland to Carnarvon Ras. NP–Mitchell–Warwick; e. NSW s. to near Ulladulla, inland to *c.* Narrabri. Common. Sedentary. Also PNG.

COMMON KOEL

imm.

♀

♂

imm.

CHANNEL-
BILLED
CUCKOO

non-
breeding

PHEASANT COUCAL

breeding

POWERFUL OWL *Ninox strenua* 60–66 cm. Male larger.

Very large owl with large golden eyes: dark grey–brown above, mottled and barred whitish; white or buff–white below, with bold grey–brown V-barring; tail large, dark grey–brown, widely barred white above and below. Legs feathered; feet dull yellow, very powerful, with heavy claws. **Immature:** back, wings paler, more heavily barred white; face white, with dark eyepatches; *underparts white, with sparse fine dark streaks,* faint barring on flanks. By day roosts singly, in pairs or family groups, on branch of densely foliaged to fairly open tree in forest or woodland. Often clutches part-eaten remains of prey, e.g. ringtail possum, glider, flying fox, currawong, magpie, lorikeet. Roosts (and breeding hollows) may be occupied intermittently for years. Some individuals are easily approached by day; shy and difficult to observe by night. Occasionally aggressive to humans at nest. **Similar species:** Barking Owl: white spots on wings; grey or brown streaks below. **Voice:** male: an impressive low, slow, far-carrying 'whoo-hooo', second note usually lower. Female's call higher pitched; second note higher. Also a sheep-like bleating near nest (D. Hollands, pers. comm.). **Habitat:** pairs occupy a large, probably permanent, home range in mountain forests, gullies and forest margins; sparser hilly woodlands; coastal forests, woodlands, scrubs; exotic pine plantations; large trees in private/public gardens, some in cities. **Breeds:** June–Sept. **Nest:** on decayed debris; in hollow trunk or limb 8–20 m or more high in forest tree. **Eggs:** 1–2 (3); dull white, oval. **Range and Status:** suitable habitat in e. and se. Aust., mostly within *c.* 200 km of coast, from Eungella NP (Q) inland to *c.* Carnarvon Ra. NP; exceptionally to e. of Longreach (Q) (Pavey, 1994); e. NSW, inland to *c.* Tenterfield–Coonabarabran; e. Vic. and Central Highlands w. to *c.* Mt Alexander–Stawell–Grampians NP, to far sw. Vic and adjacent far se. SA (Mt Burr); casual to Vic. mallee, near Wyperfeld NP. Sedentary; dispersive when young. Uncommon.

RUFOUS OWL *Ninox rufa* 45–55 cm. Male larger.

Large, richly coloured tropical owl with broad crown; upperparts dark rufous-brown with indistinct paler barrings; *underparts orange–buff with dense, fine, rufous-brown bars;* tail broadly barred above and below; eyes greenish yellow; large feet dull yellow. **Female:** smaller and darker. **Immature:** more broadly barred than adults (Hollands, 1991). By day perches alone or in pairs, on robust branch of leafy tree in rainforest or swamp-woodland. Can be fiercely aggressive when nesting. **Voice:** slow 'woo-hoo!', like Powerful Owl but softer and less far-carrying; an occasional, sharp single note. Female: sheep-like bleating call (Hollands, 1991). **Habitat:** mostly lowland (but also some highland) rainforest; patches of monsoon forest; vine scrub, gallery forest along creeks (Hollands, 1991); swamp-woodland, mangroves; eucalypt woodlands adjacent to above habitats. **Breeds:** June–Aug., NT; July–Nov., e. Q. **Nest:** on debris in large hollow in trunk or large branch; 5–30 m high. **Eggs:** 2 (3); white, glossy. **Range and Status:** broken distribution in suitable habitat from Prince Regent R. in nw. Kimberley (WA) to Top End (NT); and from C. York Pen. (Q), s. to near Byfield (n. of Rockhampton), inland to Atherton Tableland–upper Burdekin R. and Blackdown Tableland NP, sw. of Dingo. Dark race *queenslandica* occurs in ne. Q, s. of *c.* Cooktown. Rare. Sedentary. Also PNG, Aru Is.

POWERFUL OWL

imm. ♀

adult ♂

RUFOUS OWL

typical
adult ♂

♂ dark race
queenslandica

301

BARKING OWL *Ninox connivens* 35–45 cm. Male larger.

Robust owl with piercing yellow eyes *without* surrounding dark eye-patches and 'goggles'. Plumage *smoky brown to grey above, with large white spots on wings; whitish below, with dark grey to rusty streaks*; legs feathered; powerful feet dull yellow. Smaller, darker forms in tropical n. Aust. Roosts by day, often in pairs in leafy trees, often near watercourses. When approached, instantly alert, head snapping in direction of intruder; often clutches remains of prey. At times active, vocal before dark. **Similar species:** Powerful Owl, Southern Boobook. **Voice:** unmistakable, *quick*, dog-like 'wok-wok' or 'wook wook', preceded by growl; soft at first, becoming emphatic, loud and far-carrying; sometimes in duet; male call deeper, female call quicker, sharper (Hollands, 1991). Also, at beginning of breeding, occasional blood-curdling, human-like *wavering, sobbing scream*, sometimes heard by day. **Habitat:** open forests, woodlands, dense scrubs, foothills; river red gums, other large trees near watercourses, penetrating otherwise open country; paperbark woodlands. **Breeds:** July–Nov. **Nest:** on decayed debris; in tree hollow, from low to 10 m+ high; occasionally on ground, at times in rabbit burrow (D. Hollands, pers. comm.). **Eggs:** 2–3; dull white, roundish. **Range and Status:** mainland Aust. and some n. coastal islands. Rare, or absent from, arid, treeless or heavily forested regions. Nowhere common except perhaps in parts of Q, and Kimberley (WA). Sedentary. Also PNG; e. Indonesia.

BROWN HAWK-OWL *Ninox scutulata* 29–30 cm

Other name: Oriental Hawk-Owl.

Small, yellow-eyed, rich-brown Asian owl; note absence of pale 'goggles', small white mark over bill and longish barred tail. *Breast buff–white, broadly streaked rich brown or red–brown; under tail-coverts whitish.* Often active in early evening, hawking for dragonflies (Smythies, 1968). **Voice:** (in Indonesia) 'mellow, rising falsetto whistle *pung-ok*, the second note short with rising inflection, repeated every one or two seconds . . .' (MacKinnon & Phillipps, 1993). **Range and Status:** e. Asia; resident and migratory races in Indonesia. Carcass of a bird of migratory e. Asian race *japonica* collected Ashmore Reef (off nw. WA), Jan. 1973.

Note: **Indonesian Hawk-Owl,** *Ninox squamipila* (26–29 cm). Resembles small, red–brown Boobook, with yellow eyes and whitish breast finely barred rufous. Habits and calls like Boobook. Race *natalis* confined to Christmas I. (Indian Ocean), where vulnerable (Garnett, 1993).

SOUTHERN BOOBOOK *Ninox novaeseelandiae* 25–36 cm. Female larger.

Other names: Mopoke or Morepork.

Widespread small brown owl *with suggestion of large, pale-rimmed 'goggles' bordering dark patch around each eye*; large pale spots on wings; underparts reddish brown, with *thick brown and white streaks or heavy irregular white mottling (or spots)*; legs feathered to 'ankle'. Race *boobook*: dark brown above, with red–brown and white markings below. Race *lurida*: smaller, dark reddish brown; lacks 'goggles'; spotted, not streaked, below. Race *ocellata*: pale cinnamon–brown above, white with buff streaks below. Most mainland races have *grey–green eyes*, but eyes of small, white-spotted migratory Tas. race *leucopsis are yellow*. **Immature:** eyes brown; plumage suffused with buff. Solitary; pairs, family parties; roosts by day in thick foliage. Disturbed, slips silently out, mobbed by small birds. At dusk sits watchfully on exposed branches, fences, telephone poles; street-lights; flies up to capture flying insects. **Similar species:** Barking Owl. **Voice:** well-known: quick, falsetto 'boobook' or 'morepork', oft-repeated; also, seldom heard, falsetto 'yo-yo-yo-yo', mostly in autumn; near nest, drawn-out, rising, cat-like 'brrrwow' and low, monotonous 'mor-mor-mor'. Young birds: cricket-like trills. **Habitat:** rainforests to mallee, dense mulga; margins of almost treeless plains; woodlands; lightly timbered farming country; pine forests, orchards, parks, gardens; street-trees, including leafy, exotic poplars, elms, willows, cypresses. **Breeds:** Aug.–Dec. **Nest:** on decayed wood debris; in tree-hollow. **Eggs:** 2–3; white, rounded. **Range and Status:** widespread in several well-marked races in Aust., islands and Tas. Clockwise from top right figure they are: (1) race *boobook*: coastal e. Aust; (2) race *leucopsis*: Tas., with some winter migration to mainland; (3) typical imm., race *boobook*; (4) race *lurida*: humid coastal ne. Q, in rainforests; (5) race *ocellata*: inland, n. and w. Aust. Common; sedentary, part-migratory or nomadic. During mouse plagues, irrupts into cereal-growing areas. Extinct Lord Howe I., nearly so on Norfolk I. Also resident Indonesia, s. PNG, NZ.

BARKING OWL

♂ small northern form

♂

BROWN HAWK-OWL

race *ocellata*

SOUTHERN BOOBOOK

race *boobook*

race *lurida*

typical imm.

race *leucopsis*

LESSER SOOTY OWL *Tyto multipunctata* 30–38 cm. Female larger.

Smaller, slighter, paler than Sooty Owl; *more plentifully marked with larger silvery spots. Eyes black; facial mask silvery, rounded, with dark outline;* upperparts marbled black and silver, *with large silvery spots on mantle and wing-coverts; underparts silvery grey with mottling of blackish Vs on upper breast,* shadowy bars on surface of underwings and tail; paler below and on feathered legs; feet robust. Reported to use low hunting perches in rainforest; perches on sides of trunks like Yellow Robin; roosts in hollows, also among vines and figs (Hollands, 1991). **Habitat:** tall tropical mountain rainforests; adjacent tall eucalypt forests. **Voice:** 'falling bomb' whistle, higher-pitched and softer than Sooty Owl; also trills, chirrups and screams. **Breeds:** Feb.–July; most records March–May (Hollands, 1991). **Eggs:** 2; dull white, oval. **Range and Status:** rainforests and margins, adjacent tall eucalypt forests of Gt Dividing Ra., from *c.* Cooktown to *c.* Paluma, near Townsville, and Hinchinbrook I. (ne. Q). Sedentary. Also Jobi I. and PNG.

SOOTY OWL *Tyto tenebricosa* 38–50 cm. Female larger.

Robust, *short-tailed, sooty black barn owl with oval grey facial disc outlined in black; eyes black, very large; upperparts sooty, with sparse silvery white spots; underparts sooty dark grey with small silvery spots and Vs;* legs sparsely feathered; *feet massive.* Secretive: roosts by day in hollow of tall forest tree or in heavy vegetation. When disturbed, may blunder out with heavy wingbeats or remain quiet, seemingly drowsy. **Voice:** *weird, far-carrying, descending strident or mellow whistle, like falling bomb,* uttered at intervals; other very loud calls; also descending, rolling, cricket-like, chirruping trills. **Habitat:** tall, wet forests in sheltered e. and se.-facing mountain gullies, with dense understorey layer (Kavanagh & Peake in Olsen, 1993). **Breeds:** April–June, but also autumn, spring (Hollands, 1991). **Nest:** on decayed debris; in hollow trunk of eucalypt; up to over 30 m high; or in high cavity in cave. **Eggs:** 1–2; white, oval. **Range and Status:** coastal e. Aust.: mostly on and e. of Divide from Dandenong Ras., e. of Melbourne–Kinglake NP (Vic.), (possibly further w., but not in Otway Ras.) to Conondale Ra. (se. Q); reported presence on Flinders I., Bass Strait, unconfirmed (Garnett, 1993). Probably commoner than records suggest: until field studies in recent decades, this and Lesser Sooty Owl were among our least-known birds. Also PNG.

LESSER SOOTY OWL

imm.

SOOTY OWL

imm.

BARN OWL *Tyto alba* 30–40 cm. Female larger.

Other names: Delicate, Screech or White Owl.
The 'white owl', known worldwide by white, heart-shaped facial disc; upperparts grey to yellow–buff, with sparse black and white spots; white below, with sparse dark spots; legs slender, feathered white to above 'ankle'. Sexes similar. Sometimes flushed by day from hollow tree, dense foliage, tall grass; harried by other birds. On wing looks white, large-headed, long-winged; *toes protrude just beyond tail.* At night, hunting for mice, flies slowly, head down; hovers, *sits white and upright on fence-posts.* **Similar species:** Grass Owl, male. Masked Owl, pale form: facial disc rounder, with more definite black outline; legs fully-feathered; *feet and talons much heavier.* **Voice:** hoarse, thin, wavering, reedy screech, 'sk-air!' or 'skee-air!'. **Habitat:** open forests, woodlands, grasslands; caves, ledges; offshore rocky islands; farmlands, grain-stubbles, railyards, towns; occasionally roosts, nests in old buildings. **Breeds:** spring, autumn; any month when introduced house mice abundant. **Nest:** usually in large tree-hollow. **Eggs:** 3–4 (6); white, rounded. **Range and Status:** widespread Aust. and coastal islands; rare Tas. Irrupts in response to upsurges of introduced house mice, native rodents. In s. Aust. during colder months, many die from starvation. Common to uncommon; nomadic. Cosmopolitan.

GRASS OWL *Tyto capensis* 33–38 cm. Female larger.

Other name: Eastern Grass Owl.
Male: facial disc/underparts white. **Female:** pale orange–buff, with dark speckles. Both sexes: *upperparts rich yellow–buff, marbled blue–black, dark grey; wings and tail broadly barred dark brown and buff, with silvery spots. Legs long, with sparse feathers, 'shin' bare, pinkish.* Singles, companies: roosts on trampled platform in tussock, tall sedge, sorghum crop, wet heath; when numerous, area intersected with 'runs'. Disturbed, bursts out, flies slowly, sails, before dropping. Looks large-headed; *dark wingtips contrast with pale patch on centre wing.* Sometimes hunts by day; lazy flapping broken by glides, *long rigid legs often held at downward angle clear of tail*, feet protrude well beyond tail (Estbergs et al, 1978). *Standing, posture taller, more upright than Barn Owl*; with longer, bare lower legs. **Voice:** hissing scream, louder than Barn Owl; also soft, high-pitched, cricket-like, chirruping trill. (Captive courting male called in phrases of 5–6 trills, with 2–3 seconds between each (Pettigrew, 1986).) **Habitat:** tall grass; swampy, sometimes tidal, areas; mangrove-fringes, grassy plains, coastal heaths, grassy woodland, cane-grass, lignum, sedges, cumbungi, cultivated sorghum, sugar cane, grain-stubble. **Breeds:** mostly March–June in coastal n. Aust.; any month when food abundant. **Nest:** trampled platform in tussocks, low shrubs (e.g. mangroves), sugar cane, with approach-run. **Eggs:** 4–6; white, smooth, oval-elongate. **Range and Status:** n. Aust. (and inland e. Aust.) from Kimberley (WA) to ne. NSW. Two main population centres: (1) far inland e. Aust., in region of L. Eyre Basin (sw. Q, e. NT, ne. SA). When native Long-haired Rats, *R. villosissimus*, abundant, Grass Owls increase across plains of w. Q–e. NT; (2) coastal heaths, grasslands, canefields, sorghum crops, in e. Q–ne. NSW, from *c.* Port Douglas (Q) to *c.* Kempsey (NSW), inland to *c.* Narrabri. Generally rare, locally common; nomadic, irruptive. Also Fiji to se. Asia, s. China, India; Africa.

MASKED OWL *Tyto novaehollandiae* 33–55 cm. Female larger.

Larger, more robust than Barn Owl, with *rounder, black-bordered facial disc; fully feathered legs, heavier feet/talons.* Size, colour vary: some are white as Barn Owls, others blackish above, buffish chestnut below; females of Tas. race *castanops* largest, darkest (world's largest *Tyto*.) Male: paler. Roosts by day in tree-hollows, thick foliage; hunts by night in woodlands, clearings, open plains. Prey includes possums, rabbits, currawongs. Male has high-circling nocturnal display-flight, uttering continual rattling call (J. Young, pers. comm.). Some roost/nest in caves of Nullarbor Plain, others inhabit nearly treeless plains far inland. **Similar species:** Barn Owl. **Voice:** loud version of Barn Owl: drawn-out, screeching 'cush-cush-sh-sh' or 'quair-sh-sh-sh'; 'very loud, musical shriek' (Ambrose & Debus, 1987). **Habitat:** forests, open woodlands, farmlands with large trees, e.g. river red gums, adjacent cleared country; partly forested coastal plains in Vic.; timbered watercourses, paperbark woodlands, caves. **Breeds:** any month, mostly autumn–winter. **Nest:** on decayed debris in hollow eucalypt 12–20 m high; bare sand or earth of cave. **Eggs:** 2–3; dull white, elongated. **Range and Status:** coastal mainland Aust.: widespread but very sparse. Race *melvillensis* more common on Bathurst I., Melville I. (NT) (Garnett, 1993). Race *castanops* in Tas. fairly common and widespread. Sedentary. Also s. PNG; Manus I., e. Indonesia. Introduced Lord Howe I.

BARN OWL

GRASS OWL

♂

♀

MASKED OWL

♀ race *castanops*

♂ pale morph

♂ typical morph

307

TAWNY FROGMOUTH *Podargus strigoides* 33–50 cm. Male larger.

Other names: 'Frogmouth-Owl', Morepork.
Most widespread frogmouth. *Variable: plumage grey, mottled; marbled paler grey or brown, with dark streaks; tawny shoulders; eye yellow to orange–yellow, with slight pale eyebrow;* underparts paler, *black marks down sides of throat/breast;* tail finely banded dark/light grey. **Male:** darker, greyer; markings bolder, more marbled; bill longer. **Female:** plainer, browner, less marbled; some washed rufous. Small inland and n. race *phalaenoides* has large head/bill: plumage plainer, dusky grey in s. to silver–grey in n. Aust. Birds in coastal n. Aust. *c.* half-size of e. coast *strigoides*. Pairs, family parties: roosts branch-like by day. Active at dusk: eyes large, feathers expand, sits watchfully on branches, fence-posts, glides silently down like Kookaburra to seize prey. **Similar species:** Papuan, Marbled Frogmouths: *note range.* **Voice:** resonant, low, pulsing 'oom-oom-oom-oom', slow or rapid, difficult to locate; grunts, drums when alarmed; growls, cat-like sounds from young. **Habitat:** forest, rainforest margins; tracks, clearings; open woodlands, timbered watercourses; mallee, mulga, myall, belar scrubs, pandanus, coastal tea-tree, banksia-scrubs, alpine woodland, roadsides, golf-courses, parks, well-treed gardens. **Breeds:** Aug.–Dec.; after rain inland. **Nest:** flimsy, of sticks, leaves; on horizontal fork 5–10 m high; or old nest of chough, cuckoo-shrike, magpie. **Eggs:** 2; white, rounded. **Range and Status:** Aust., Tas., coastal islands. Nominate race: coastal e. Aust. to w. slopes of Gt Divide, n. to *c.* Hughenden–Cairns (Q); sw. to se. SA. Race *phalaenoides*: widespread across continent and islands w. of those limits, also C. York Pen. and Torres Strait (Schodde & Mason, 1980). Common. Sedentary. Also s. PNG.

MARBLED FROGMOUTH *Podargus ocellatus* 37–48 cm

Other name: Plumed Frogmouth.
Rainforest frogmouth with two well-separated Aust. races: *small marmoratus* (37–41 cm) of e. C. York Pen. (Q); larger *plumiferus* (44–48 cm) of se. Q–ne. NSW. Note *tuft of buff/barred plumes over bill, pale eyebrow, orange–yellow eyes, shadowy pale barring on flight-feathers, long, jagged tail.* Males slightly larger, shorter tailed, greyer than females, *with marbled blotches on wings, sides of breast;* some male *marmoratus* have sooty upperparts. Females *plainer rufous; tawny, paler below.* Immature: paler bill and feet. Pairs, family parties: *perches high or low on thick vines,* overhead branches; forages along rainforest tracks, streams, into nearby eucalypt woodland. Roosts among vine-tangles; stubs near trunks. Adopts 'frozen' posture (Smith et al, 1994); or flattens against support (Schodde & Mason, 1980). **Voice:** rapid, descending 'coop-coop-coop-gobble-gobble-gobble' (C. Corben, in Schodde & Mason, 1980); deep, pulsing 'kooloo-kooloo-kooloo'. **Habitat:** *marmoratus:* monsoon forest, vine scrub, gallery forest on creeks, nearby eucalypt, other woodlands; *plumiferus:* pockets of closed subtropical rainforest up to *c.* 700 m. **Breeds:** Aug.–Dec. **Nest:** small, cuplike platform of vine tendrils, etc., on fork or (ne. Q) ant house plant, *Myrmecodia;* from ground to 40 m. **Eggs:** 1–2; dull white, rounded, oval. **Range and Status:** race *marmoratus:* C. York (Q) s. on e. coast to McIlwraith Ra.; race *plumiferus:* patchily from Many Peaks Ra., s. of Gladstone (Q), to Lismore (n. NSW), inland to *c.* Kalpowar (Q) (Corben & Roberts, 1993). Local, uncommon. Sedentary. Also Solomons, PNG.

PAPUAN FROGMOUTH *Podargus papuensis* 50–60 cm

Largest frogmouth: *bill bulbous; eye red; tail long; wings darker than Tawny Frogmouth.* **Male:** marbled tawny, rufous and grey above, with underlying pale grey and black barrings, black streaks. *Note cream–white eyebrow, buff bar along shoulder; sides of face, throat, breast greyer, blotched whitish.* **Female:** more rufous; more evenly, finely marked than male, with less blotching; bill smaller, tail shorter. **Immature:** browner, darker. Habits like Tawny Frogmouth; habitat, roosting places often denser. **Voice:** resonant 'oo-oom' like Tawny but deeper, slower; weird ghostly laugh, 'hoo-hoo-hoo'. **Habitat:** margins of rainforests, tracks, clearings, eucalypt woodlands, scrubs, watercourse vegetation, swamp, dune woodland, mangroves, suburban parks with trees; campgrounds. **Breeds:** Aug.–Jan. **Nest:** scanty, of sticks, on base of branch, heavy fork; low to high. **Eggs:** 1–2; white, variable. **Range and Status:** ne. Q, and islands: large, pale race *rogersi:* C. York, s. on Gulf coast to Staaten R., s. on e. coast to *c.* Cooktown; smaller, darker rainforest-dwelling race *baileyi:* s. to *c.* Mt Spec NP, near Townsville. Common in n., scarce, mostly coastal, s. of Cooktown. Sedentary. Also Torres Strait, PNG, Aru, other islands.

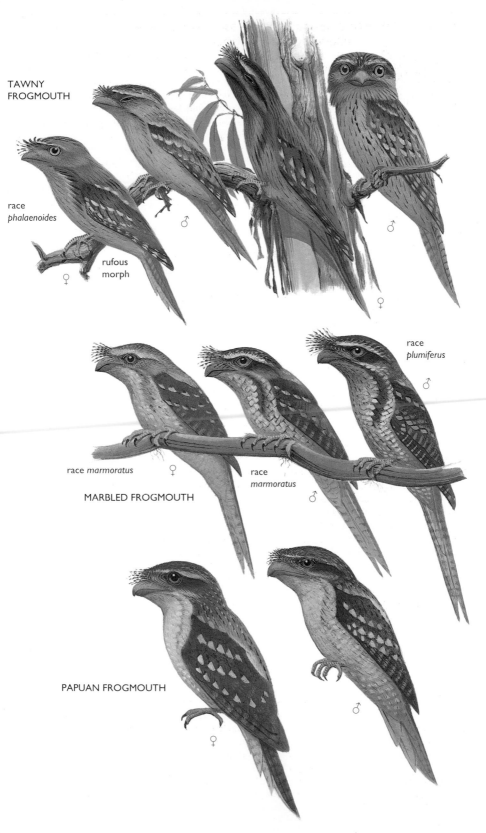

TAWNY
FROGMOUTH

race
phalaenoides

rufous
morph

♀

♂

♂

♀

race
plumiferus

♂

race *marmoratus*

♀

race
marmoratus

♂

MARBLED FROGMOUTH

PAPUAN FROGMOUTH

♀

♂

309

AUSTRALIAN OWLET-NIGHTJAR *Aegotheles cristatus* 20–24 cm

Other name: 'Moth Owl'.

Like a miniature owl with a tiny, broad bill, cat-like whiskers, pink feet, longish tail. Note head-markings. Plumage dark in s. Aust., paler in inland, n. and nw. Aust. Immature, and some females, are rufous, especially in Pilbara region (WA). Roosts by day in tree-hollow; peers curiously from, or suns itself in, entrance. Occasionally in rock-crevice. At night takes insects in flight, on branches and on ground; flight swift, direct or fluttering, acrobatic. Sits *upright, crossways on limbs: unlike true nightjars, eyes do not glow in spotlight.* **Voice:** high-pitched grating 'chirr-chirr-chirr', sometimes by day; somewhat like Brown Falcon. **Habitat:** varied — rainforests, eucalypt forests, woodlands; arid inland scrubs; trees on inland watercourses, billabongs. **Breeds:** Aug.–Dec. **Nest:** hollow in tree, stump, fencepost; lined with green eucalyptus leaves. **Eggs:** 3 (5); white, rounded. **Range and Status:** Aust., Tas., coastal islands. Common and very widespread in suitable habitat. Sedentary. Also PNG.

WHITE-THROATED NIGHTJAR *Eurostopodus mystacalis* 32–37 cm. Female larger.

Other names: Fern or Laughing 'Owl'.

Largest, darkest nightjar: *at rest, long wingtips extend to tail-tips.* No white on tail; *in flight, small white spots on wingtips.* **Immature:** mottled reddish brown, black. Singles, pairs: looks large, dark in flight. **Voice:** rising deep 'kook's accelerate into a weird staccato laugh. **Habitat:** bare ground with leaves, rocks, branches; bracken, on dry ridges, slopes of coastal heath; forests, woodlands, wallum country; in Townsville (Q), up to 15 migrating birds reported to roost in winter on roof-trusses of large rail shed. **Breeds:** Sept.–Feb. **Egg:** 1; cream, blotched, spotted purplish brown, light brown, black spots at large end, light grey lines; laid on leaf litter, bare ground. **Range and Status:** coastal e. Aust.: from C. York (Q) to Otway Ras. (s. Vic.), inland to w. slopes of Divide, overlapping range of Spotted Nightjar. Resident ne. Aust.; breeding migrant Aug.–May in se.; some migrate to PNG, Solomons.

LARGE-TAILED NIGHTJAR *Caprimulgus macrurus* 26–29 cm

Other names: Axe Bird, Carpenter Bird, Hammer Bird, White-tailed Nightjar. Our only nightjar *with prominent white spots on closed wings; white in wing and tail visible in flight.* At rest, wings shorter than tail. Best known by voice. **Voice:** 4 to *c.* 50 monotonous hollow chops, like axe struck against log, mostly in summer; frog-like croaks when disturbed. **Habitat:** open, leafy ground on margins of rainforest; vine scrubs, paperbarks, mangroves, plantations, gardens. **Breeds:** Aug.–Jan. **Eggs:** 2; cream to pinkish stone, underlying fleecy markings of lilac–grey; laid in leaf-litter. **Range and Status:** coastal Top End (NT); coastal n. Q from Bynoe R. on the Gulf (Blakers et al, 1984) to C. York; s. on e. coast to Cooloola NP–Fraser I; coastal islands. Common lowlands, scarce highlands; patchy s. of Ingham. Sedentary. Also Torres Strait, New Britain, PNG to se. Asia, China, w. Pakistan.

SPOTTED NIGHTJAR *Eurostopodus argus* 29–33 cm

Smallish widespread nightjar. At rest, wings shorter than tail. *Plumage scalloped, spotted and barred buff or rufous; underparts plain rufous.* **Immature:** rufous, with rusty pink tone. Singles, pairs, parties: in flight *small white patch on primaries,* none in tail. Flight buoyant, with quick flicks, turns, glides on raised wings — wingspots luminous white in spotlight; eyes glow diamond pink. **Voice:** rising 'caw-caw-caw-tukka-tukka-tukka-tukka-tuk' or 'wokka-wokka-chokka-chokka-chooka-chooka'. **Habitat:** drier eucalypt woodlands; stony, sandy ridges; mallee, mulga, pine scrubs; lignum; spinifex associations. **Breeds:** Sept.–Jan. **Egg:** 1; greenish cream, spotted, dotted black, grey–brown, reddish purple; leaf-litter. **Range and Status:** widespread in mainland Aust. and islands: mostly in drier habitats w. of Divide, and drier coastal regions. Common. Possibly winter migrant within Aust. and to PNG.

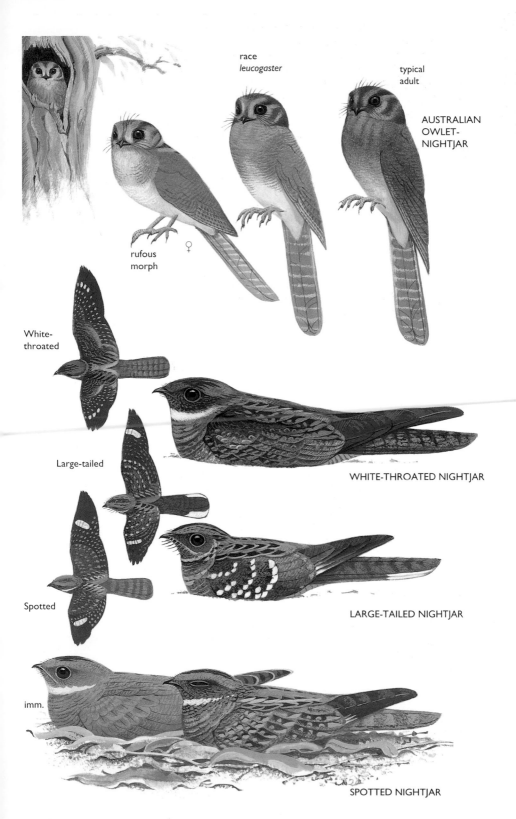

race
leucogaster

typical
adult

AUSTRALIAN
OWLET-
NIGHTJAR

rufous
morph

♀

White-
throated

Large-tailed

WHITE-THROATED NIGHTJAR

Spotted

LARGE-TAILED NIGHTJAR

imm.

SPOTTED NIGHTJAR

GLOSSY SWIFTLET *Collocalia esculenta* 9–11.5 cm

Other name: White-bellied Swiftlet.

Smallest swiftlet: *glossy black with dark hood and contrasting whitish belly*, mottled black at front and rear margins. Underwings dark; tail long, wedge-shaped, with a notch in central tail-feathers (Bartram, 1988). Small parties; flocks alone or with White-rumped Swiftlets: flies rapidly, close to ground, with acrobatic darting, rolling and changes in direction (Webb, 1992); wingbeats shallow, wings depressed. **Similar species:** White-rumped Swiftlet: greyer, with white rump; pale underparts can cause confusion with Glossy.
Small, pale-bellied swiftlets seen over n. Aust. may be this, or Cave Swiftlets, *C. linchi* — both common in nearby Indonesia. **Voice:** 'tight, grating cheeps' (Webb, 1992). **Habitat:** airspace over forests, clearings; gaps, gorges, trails, streams, open country, timbered watercourses. **Range and Status:** breeds Malaysia–Indonesia–PNG; New Cal., New Heb. Irregular summer–autumn visitor to ne. Q from C. York to Finch Hatton Gorge, near Mackay (but see above).

WHITE-RUMPED SWIFTLET *Collocalia spodiopygius* 11–12 cm

Other name: Grey Swiftlet.

Small dark grey–brown swift with narrow grey–white rump and slightly forked tail; belly paler grey–brown. Parties, large flocks are resident in and around breeding caves. Soars, dips like stiff-winged swallow with erratic turns; hawks over pastures, tree-tops with Tree Martins, Welcome Swallows. Flocks soar high in thundery weather. Rests on walls of caves, occasionally tree-trunks. Two races in Aust.: *terraereginae* mostly on Q coasts, islands and coastal ranges; the smaller, paler, whiter-rumped race, *chillagoensis*, is peculiar to Chillagoe district, inland from Cairns. **Similar species:** Glossy, Uniform Swiftlets. **Voice:** overhead, high-pitched cheeps; *in nesting caves, incessant metallic clicking, for echo-location.* **Habitat:** airspace over rainforest, cleared lands, beaches, gorges; breeds in isolated caves, cavities between boulders on coastal islands, mountain gorges, hills. **Breeds:** July–Feb. **Nest:** shallow basket of dried saliva reinforced with dry grass, she oak needles, twigs, feathers; in dense colonies of hundreds on dark walls/roofs of caves, boulders. **Egg:** 1; white, elliptical, slightly glossy. **Range and Status:** coastal ne. Q, continental islands, highland areas to over 1000 m; from Claudie R., s. to Finch Hatton Gorge–Eungella NP, near Mackay. Common below 500 m. Sedentary. Casual se. Q, ne. NSW, SA. Also islands of PNG, w. Pacific.

UNIFORM SWIFTLET *Collocalia vanikorensis* 12.5 cm

Other name: Lowland Swiftlet.

Small, dark swift with slightly forked tail: blackish brown to glossy greenish black above, greyer brown below. In Solomon Is., reported to associate with Glossy Swiftlet; more sluggish than White-rumped Swiftlet, 'a much swifter and more acrobatic flier' (Webb, 1992). **Voice:** 'soft, twittering sounds' (Webb, 1992). **Habitat:** airspace over coastal lowlands; woodlands, settlements, cultivation. **Range and Status:** breeds widely from e. Indonesia to PNG, Solomon Is., New Cal., New Heb. One specimen from Peak Pt
(C. York, Q), Sept. 1913; several possible sight-records, e.g. small dark swifts in flocks of White-throated Needletails, Atherton Tableland, Jan. 1971 (Bravery, 1971); and 'smaller, uniformly coloured swiftlets' in flocks of Fork-tailed Swifts near tip of C. York, 1989 (Beruldsen, 1990). Note: every flock of swifts should be checked for 'strangers', but some *Collocalia* swiftlets of Indonesia–PNG are only doubtfully identifiable in the field.

GLOSSY
SWIFTLET

WHITE-RUMPED
SWIFTLET

UNIFORM
SWIFTLET

313

HOUSE SWIFT *Apus affinis* 13–15 cm; span 34–36 cm

Other name: Little Swift.

Medium-sized, *blue–black, white-throated swift*; wings broad, shortish, paler below. *Clear-cut white rump and upper tail-coverts form a square patch; tail square, only slightly notched, roundish when fanned; paler below.* Flight described as 'steady, even' (MacKinnon & Phillipps, 1993) and 'comparatively slow and bat-like, with series of quick wingbeats alternating with short glides' (Jonsson, 1992). **Similar species:** White-throated Needletail: larger, lacks white rump. Fork-tailed Swift: more slender, with tapering wings; long forked tail; white throat and rump less clear cut. **Voice:** 'shrill rattling trill' (King et al, 1980). **Habitat:** cliffs, caves, open areas, towns, houses. In Sumatra, Java and Bali, common in towns, coastal areas. (MacKinnon & Phillipps, 1993). **Range and Status:** breeds from n. Africa to Japan, se. Asia, Philippines, Indonesia e. to Bali. Live specimen Top End (NT), March 1979 (Robertson, 1980). Recent summer sight-records, Cairns–Mossman region. Likely to occur anywhere in Aust., perhaps 'caught' in flocks of regular migratory species. Casual.

FORK-TAILED SWIFT *Apus pacificus* 16–19 cm; span 38–43 cm

Other names: Pacific or White-rumped Swift.

Wings long, slender and curving; body cigar-shaped; long forked tail often carried closed; throat paler; rump pure white, visible at sides; underparts finely scalloped white. Movements in Aust. influenced by weather-patterns. Open flocks, sometimes immense, precede summer thunderstorms. Mixes with White-throated Needletails, swallows, martins, woodswallows. Flies more buoyantly and slowly than Needletail, with gentle erratic flutters and turns; seems to roll in flight. Reported to roost on cliffs, in large trees, but may spend nights on wing. **Similar species:** White-throated Needletail. White-rumped Swiftlet: smaller; tail less forked; no white throat. **Voice:** long, high-pitched 'dzee, dzee' or 'skree-ee-ee'; twitterings and buzzing notes. **Habitat:** aerial: over open country, from semi-deserts to coasts, islands; sometimes over forests, cities. **Range and Status:** breeds Siberia and Himalayas e. to Japan, se. Asia. Regular summer migrant, arriving nw. Aust. early Oct., extending through WA–SA, locally far outnumbering White throated Needletails. Occasional mass movements, associated with late summer low-pressure systems, into e. Aust. and Tas., where otherwise uncommon. Most leave Aust. by mid-April. Vagrant NZ, Macquarie I. Also PNG.

WHITE-THROATED NEEDLETAIL *Hirundapus caudacutus* 19–21 cm; span *c.* 50 cm

Other name: Spine-tailed Swift.

Large, long-winged, powerful swift, one of world's fastest birds. *Forehead, throat and under tail-coverts white; short dark square tail has small, extended needle-like shafts; brown on mid-back fades to whitish 'bulls-eye' in centre.* Loose parties to large, open flocks appear during humid, unsettled, thundery weather, from near grass-level to high overhead. Feeding on rising insects, the birds streak past in long, curving rushes, with bursts of quick wingbeats or fast raking glides and an audible '*swoosh!*' as they pass. They head in one direction or soar in rising air-columns, wings spread, tails fanned, with occasional upward flutters or downward dives after insects. White-throated Needletails have been observed from aircraft at up to *c.* 2000 m above sea level over Aust. Alps. Air-speed when overtaken at *c.* 1000 m above sea level was *c.* 120–125 km/h (Coventry, 1989). **Similar species:** Fork-tailed Swift: flight less dashing, more rolling: wings slimmer; body, rump white; long forked tail often closed in point. Australian Hobby: at distance has similar speed, shape and wingbeat. **Voice:** high-pitched chitter, usually in aerial chases. **Habitat:** airspace over forests, woodlands, farmlands, plains, lakes, coasts, towns; feeding companies frequently patrol back and forward along favoured hilltops and timbered ranges. **Range and Status:** breeds from w. Siberia, Himalayas, e. to Japan. Regular summer migrant to e. Aust.; arrives from mid-Oct., departs by mid-April. Rare in c. and w. Aust., where outnumbered by Fork-tailed Swift; locally common in e., especially e. Q. Vagrant Macquarie I.; NZ.

HOUSE
SWIFT

FORK-TAILED
SWIFT

WHITE-THROATED NEEDLETAIL

315

LITTLE KINGFISHER *Alcedo pusilla* 11.5–13 cm

Tiny; *glossy dark blue above*, (paler in n. Aust.), *white below; white spot before eyes and on sides of neck; feet black*. **Immature:** paler, scalloped. Perches low, plunges, returns to perch; sometimes hovers. Flight darting, direct, low over water. **Similar species:** Forest Kingfisher. **Voice:** squeaks. **Habitat:** well-vegetated coastal creeks; streams in rainforests; tidal, mangrove-lined creeks, swamps. **Breeds:** Oct.–March. **Nest:** small burrow in creekbank. **Eggs:** 4–5; white, rounded, glossy. **Range and Status:** coastal Top End (NT); coastal n. and ne. Q, from Normanton–C. York to s. of Mackay. Sedentary; with local movements. Also Torres Strait, PNG, Solomon Is.

AZURE KINGFISHER *Alcedo azurea* 17–19 cm

Glossy royal blue above, with whitish rear 'eye-spots'; orange–rufous below; feet red. **Immature:** bill shorter; duller mid-blue on rump; sides blackish. Singles, pairs: perches on logs, roots, low branches or on posts over water. *Bobs head, raises tail*; hovers, makes quick splashing dives; *flies arrowlike low over water*. **Similar species:** Little Kingfisher, Forest Kingfisher. **Voice:** shrill squeak, 'peet peet', in flight. **Habitat:** root-festooned banks of fresh or tidal creeks; rivers, streams in rainforest; lakes, swamps, estuaries, mangroves. **Breeds:** Sept.–Jan. in s. Aust.; Nov.–April in n. **Nest:** small burrow in creek-bank. **Eggs:** 5–7; white, rounded, glossy. **Range and Status:** coastal n., e. and se. Aust.: from w. Kimberley (WA) to sw. Tas; sw. Vic.–far se. SA: inland to *c*. Riversleigh–Longreach (Q); Lachlan, Murrumbidgee Rs. (NSW); downstream on Murray R. to *c*. Darling R. anabranch–Mildura (Vic). Common; mostly sedentary. Also PNG; e. Indonesia.

LAUGHING KOOKABURRA *Dacelo novaeguineae* 41–47 cm

Big bill pale below; *crown brown, dark brown 'ear-patch'; brown eye; brown wing mottled pale blue*; older males have centre-rump blue–green. **Immature:** shorter dark bill; fine brown scallops. Pairs, territorial groups of a dominant pair and subordinate 'helpers'. Perches watchfully, makes sloping glides onto insects, reptiles. Flight level, direct; bill, white wingpatches and white-tipped, barred, red–brown tail. In spring, makes high circular display-flights over 'enemy territory' with deep, stiff wingbeats. **Voice:** famed 'laugh': staccato 'kook-kook-kook' rising to shouted 'kook-kook-kook-ka-ka-ka', slowing to chuckles; taken up by group, answered by others. **Habitat:** woodland, forest clearings, timbered watercourses, farmland, orchards, parks, gardens. **Breeds:** Sept.–Jan. **Nest:** level tree-hollow to 20 m high; hole in bank, tree-termite nest, haystack, wall. **Eggs:** 2–3; white, roundish. **Range and Status:** mainland e. Aust.: from C. York (Q) to Eyre Pen. (SA): inland on watercourses to *c*. Longreach–Cunnamulla (Q); Darling R. (NSW); most Vic.; s. Flinders Ras. (SA). *Introduced:* sw. WA (1897 on), now Geraldton–Esperance; Tas. (1905), mostly in e. and n.; Kangaroo I. (SA) (1926); Flinders I., Bass Strait (*c*. 1940). Common. Sedentary.

BLUE-WINGED KOOKABURRA *Dacelo leachii* 38–40 cm

Other names: Barking, Howling Jackass.

Distinguished from Laughing Kookaburra by streaked white head; 'fishy' white eye; blue wings; uniform pale blue rump; tail deep-blue (male); red–brown, barred darker (female). Plumage more buff in nw. Aust. (race *cliftoni*). **Immature:** paler streaks on head; darker mottlings. Singles, pairs; territorial groups: shy, often quiet in foliage. In flight, note pale head and wingpatch, blue rump. **Voice:** appalling; a guttural 'klock, klock', developing into a cacophony of mechanical squawks, screeches; in chorus. **Habitat:** tropical, subtropical open woodlands; paperbark swamps, timber on watercourses, clearings, canefields, farmlands. **Breeds:** Aug.–Jan. **Nest:** in tree-hollow; tree-termite nest. **Eggs:** 3–4; whitish, rounded. **Range and Status:** coastal nw., n. and ne. Aust. and islands: from Shark Bay–Pilbara (WA) to *c*. 50 km sw. of Brisbane (Q). Uncommon. Sedentary; local seasonal movements. Also Torres Strait, s. PNG.

LITTLE KINGFISHER

AZURE KINGFISHER

imm.

LAUGHING KOOKABURRA

♂ Laughing

♂ Blue-winged

BLUE-WINGED
KOOKABURRA

♀

♂

race
cliftoni

♂

FOREST KINGFISHER *Todiramphus macleayii* 18–23 cm

Deep blue above, pale turquoise on back; underparts white. In flight, *prominent white wing-spot. Male: white collar; female none.* **Immature:** duller; upperparts scalloped buff; white areas washed buff. Singles, pairs: perches on high branches, overhead wires; darts down to seize large insects, small reptiles. **Similar species:** Sacred, Collared Kingfishers: greener; no wing-spot; Sacred often buffer. Little Kingfisher. **Voice:** high-pitched, scratchy 'krree-krree-krree'; loud rattle; scolding screeches, chatterings near nest. **Habitat:** open forest, woodland, timber, watercourse vegetation, farmlands, canefields, beaches, mangroves. **Breeds:** Sept.–Jan. **Eggs:** 3–5; white, rounded; on decayed debris in hollow branch, trunk; tree-termite nest, 3–25 m high. **Range and Status:** nominate race: Top End (NT) to Gulf Coast (Q); race *incincta*: coastal e. Aust. from C. York (Q) to Macleay R. (NSW); occasional Sydney; casual se. NSW; s. Vic.; inland to Mt Surprise–Chinchilla (Q)–Moree (NSW). Breeding migrant to se. Q–ne. NSW, Sept.–March. Common. Also PNG, New Britain, etc.; resident and winter migrant from Aust.

SACRED KINGFISHER *Todiramphus sanctus* 20–23 cm

Male: *crown dark blue–green; mask black; wings/tail peacock blue; back green; collar/underparts variably buff–white.* **Female:** *greener above, collar/underparts whiter.* **Immature:** *duller with buff feather-margins.* Singles, pairs, migratory parties: perches in trees, wires, posts, stumps; darts down to seize large insects, small reptiles. Flight swift, direct, showing warm buff wing-linings. Noisy when breeding. **Similar species:** Forest Kingfisher: in flight, white wing-spot. Collared Kingfisher. **Voice:** high-pitched 'dek dek dek dek' usually of 4–5 notes, oft repeated; peevish, rising 'keer keer keer'; harsh scoldings; rising musical trill. **Habitat:** open forests/woodlands; margins of rivers, lakes; seashores, mangroves, mudflats, islands, golfcourses, parks, garden ponds. **Breeds:** Sept.–March. **Eggs:** 3–4; white, rounded; on debris in tree hollow, tree-termite nest; tunnel in bank. **Range and Status:** resident n. Aust.; regular spring–summer breeding migrant (Sept.–April) to coastal/subcoastal s. Aust., from n. of Brisbane (Q) to sw. WA; casual Bass Strait islands, Tas. Also Norfolk, Lord Howe Is. Winters inland and n. coastal Aust., PNG, Indonesia. Also resident Indonesia, PNG, Solomon Is., New Cal., NZ.

COLLARED KINGFISHER *Todiramphus chloris* 24–29 cm

Other name: Mangrove Kingfisher.
Larger, darker bronze–green and whiter than Sacred Kingfisher. *Bill longer, heavier; crown darker, merging with broad black mask; small white forehead-spot; large white rear collar.* **Male, breeding:** peacock-blue wings/tail. **Female:** more uniformly green, white below. **Immature:** duller, with dark scallops. Note habitat: hunts crabs, large insects, small reptiles. **Similar species:** Sacred, Forest Kingfishers. **Voice:** slower, louder than Sacred: two deliberate 'kek' notes, first slightly higher than second, often preceded by short, preliminary note; also loud, clear 'pukee pukee pukee'; peevish, rising 'keer keer'. **Habitat:** in Aust., mangroves, tidal creeks, nearby beaches, mudflats, jetties, poles, street trees, gardens. **Breeds:** Sept.–March. **Eggs:** 3–4; rounded, whitish; in hollow of mangrove; cavity in tree-termite nest, 10+ m high. **Range and Status:** coastal n. Aust., from ne. NSW (lower Clarence R.) to Shark Bay (WA). Common. Sedentary; s. birds nomadic or migratory. Also Polynesia to Red Sea.

RED-BACKED KINGFISHER *Todiramphus pyrrhopygia* 20–24 cm

Male: *crown streaked grey–green; long black mask; mantle grey–green; wings/tail dusty blue; lower back pale orange–tan.* **Female:** duller, greyer above. Singles, pairs: perches open dead trees; overhead wires; often far from water or cover. Flight swift, direct: hunts large insects, small reptiles, house mice. **Similar species:** Sacred Kingfisher. **Voice:** mournful level whistle, 'peel'; parrot-like chatter and far-carrying 'k-prrr, k-prrr' when courting. **Habitat:** sparse inland woodlands, scrublands; often far from water: gibber, spinifex, other grasslands; tree-lined dry watercourses; grassy tropical woodlands. **Breeds:** Aug.–Feb. **Eggs:** 4–5; white, rounded; in burrow in creek-bank, cliff, road-cutting, sand-dump, termite-mound; occasionally in hollow branch. **Range and Status:** mainland Aust.: spring–summer (Sept.–Feb.) breeding migrant to inland and drier subcoastal se. and sw. Aust.; vagrant s. Vic., Tas. Winters in inland and n. Aust. Uncommon. Migratory; nomadic.

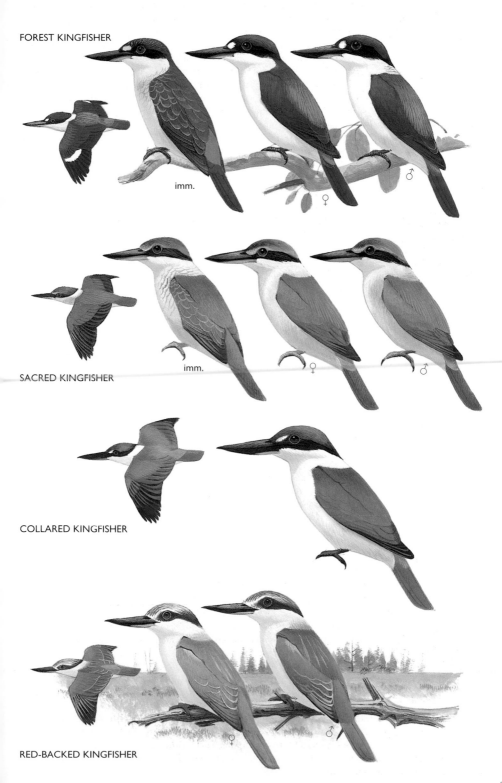

FOREST KINGFISHER

imm.

♀

♂

SACRED KINGFISHER

imm.

♀

♂

COLLARED KINGFISHER

RED-BACKED KINGFISHER

♀

♂

BUFF-BREASTED PARADISE-KINGFISHER *Tanysiptera sylvia* 29–35 cm, incl. tail

Other name: White-tailed Kingfisher.
Bill orange–red; crown/upperparts black and deep blue; underparts yellow–chestnut; back/rump white; two very long, white ribbon-like tail-plumes, abraded when nesting. **Immature:** *bill black;* wings dull blue; *breast dirty cream; lacks tail-plumes.* Singles, pairs: shy; often hard to see in rainforest. Flight floating but rapid; on alighting, raises/lowers tail-plumes. **Voice:** rapid, rising, nightjar-like 'quill-quill-quill-quill'. . . or 'choga-choga-choga', 6–10 times; musical, descending trill; screeching chatters. **Habitat:** rainforest with open ground; scrubby mountain gullies; riverside vine scrub; well-vegetated gardens. **Breeds:** Oct.–Feb. **Eggs:** 3–4; white, rounded; in tunnel in active termite nest, entrance near ground-level. **Range and Status:** summer breeding migrant (Oct.–April) to coastal ne. Q from PNG, from C. York s. to Mt Spec, near Townsville; some overwinter. Sight-records further s., e.g. Finch Hatton Gorge (Nix, 1984), Yeppoon (Britton, 1990). Locally common. Also e. PNG, Bismarck Arch.

YELLOW-BILLED KINGFISHER *Syma torotoro* 18–21 cm

Note range: head rusty orange; throat white; *slim black mark around eye; black patches on hindneck resemble large 'eyes' when head-plumes raised; back/wings blue–green; tail blue.* **Female:** *black crown, broader black neck-marks.* **Immature:** bill black. Singles, pairs, family parties: perches low, dives to ground for prey; aggressive when nesting (Blakers et al, 1984). **Voice:** loud, prolonged, whistling trills, falling then rising; screeching scolds. **Habitat:** lower levels, margins of tropical rainforest; scrubs on watercourses; adjacent eucalypt woodland. **Breeds:** Nov.–Jan. **Eggs:** 3–4; white, rounded; in burrow in tree-termite nest, 3–12 m high, usually at edge of scrub, open forest; or in tree hollow. **Range and Status:** in Aust., confined to n. C. York Pen. (Q), s. to Aurukun on w. coast, Princess Charlotte Bay in e. Common. Sedentary. Also PNG and islands.

RAINBOW BEE-EATER *Merops ornatus* 23–28 cm, incl. tail-points

Other names: Rainbow Bird, Kingfisher.
Gorgeous blue-and-green bird: *bill finely curved; eye red in blue-edged long black eyeline; throat orange–yellow with black crescent.* **Male:** *crown orange–bronze; tail-shafts extend 2.5 cm,* often broken when nesting. **Female:** *crown greener, 'shafts' shorter.* **Immature:** greener, *with dark eye, creamish throat.* Pairs, parties, loose flocks: perches fences, dead branches; dashes into air after bees, wasps, dragonflies. Flight undulating, *soaring, on translucent orange, black-edged wings.* In n. Aust., wintering companies roost in mangroves, rainforest. **Voice:** rolling 'pirr, pirr'; sharp 'pik!'. **Habitat:** open woodlands with sandy, loamy soil; sandridges, sandpits, riverbanks, road-cuttings, beaches, dunes, cliffs, mangroves, rainforest, woodlands, golfcourses. **Breeds:** Oct.–Feb. in s.; Sept.–Oct., May–July in n. Aust., in pairs with helpers, in loose colonies. **Eggs:** 4–5; white, glossy, rounded; in burrow in sandy ground, bank, cutting. **Range and Status:** breeding resident in n. Aust.; summer breeding migrant (Sept.–April) to se.–sw. Aust. In inland and dry w. coast, mostly passage migrant, some breeding. Winters n. Aust., Solomon Is., PNG, e. Indonesia. Common.

DOLLARBIRD *Eurystomus orientalis* 26–30 cm

Stocky upright green bird with *wide red bill, eye-ring and legs; large dark brown head; wings/back greenish blue; flight-feathers deep blue; tail short, black tipped.* **Immature:** duller; bill blackish, then flesh-coloured. Singles, pairs, open companies: sits on powerlines, dead trees over woodland or water; sallies after flying insects with deep, loose wingbeats; *shows blue–white wingspot,* hence 'Dollarbird'. At dusk, dips low, flutters high, like thickset nightjar. **Voice:** harsh, 'kak, kak, kak-kak-kak-kak-kak'. **Habitat:** edges of rainforest, forest, woodland, watercourses, wetlands; country, farmlands, treed outer suburbs. **Breeds:** Oct.–Feb. **Eggs:** 3–5; white, glossy, pointed; on decayed debris in high, level hollow or tree-hole. **Range and Status:** (race *pacificus*) summer breeding migrant (Sept.–April) from PNG and e. Indonesia: to coastal n. Aust. from Kimberley (WA) to C. York (Q), s. in e. Aust. to ne.–c. Vic., inland to *c.* Mt Isa–Blackall–Charleville (Q); Warrumbungle NP–Hay–Barham (NSW). Casual sw. Q; Murray R. w. to Morgan, and Kangaroo I. (SA); s. Vic. Also widespread Indonesia to Asia.

BUFF-BREASTED
PARADISE- KINGFISHER

imm.

♂

♀

YELLOW-BILLED KINGFISHER

RAINBOW BEE-EATER

imm.

♀

♂

DOLLARBIRD

RED-BELLIED PITTA *Pitta erythrogaster* 16–18 cm

Other name: Blue-breasted Pitta.
Note *chestnut–red nape, broad pale blue breastband, wholly red underparts.*
Female: duller; face brownish. **Immature:** like female; wing-feathers fringed buff. Inconspicuous, even when calling. Sits high in canopy, showing red belly and narrow white collar in centre of throat, from white bases of feathers exposed when calling (Beruldsen, 1990). **Voice:** unusual: loud, mellow, tremulous, drawn-out pigeon-like coo or whistle 'whoooo-weeooh', rising, then dropping. **Habitat:** tropical rainforests and scrubs. **Nest:** large, domed, often with substantial landing; on ground by logs or rocks; against root of tree; stumps, in *Pandanus*; vines (usually lawyer), in dimly lit situations (Beruldsen, 1990). **Eggs:** 2–4; cream–white, spotted blue, purplish brown. **Range and Status:** C. York Pen. s. to about Rocky R. (Q). Summer breeding migrant (Nov.–April) from PNG. Occasionally overwinter (Niland, 1986). Casual Weipa (n. Q) (Beruldsen, 1979). Locally common. Also PNG, e. Indonesia to Philippines.

RAINBOW PITTA *Pitta iris* 16–19 cm

Other name: Black-breasted Pitta.
Sole resident pitta in nw. Aust. and our only pitta with black head and breast.
Habits, flight, etc., like Noisy Pitta, incl. electric-blue shoulder-patches and white wingspot. **Voice:** like quicker, shriller Noisy Pitta: brisk, high-pitched 'we-wik-to-wik'; single, high-pitched 'kiew'. **Habitat:** monsoon rainforest, vine scrubs on watercourses, bamboo thickets, mangroves. **Breeds:** Nov.–March. **Nest:** large, domed, with side-entrance; of dead bamboo leaves and other plant material loosely put together; in mangroves or clumps of bamboo 2 m high, sometimes on ground or tussock; lightly roofed over in open situations. **Eggs:** 4; creamy white with sepia blotches, underlying markings of dull purplish grey. **Range and Status:** pockets of suitable habitat from coastal nw. Kimberley and islands (WA) to Top End (NT) e. to Groote Eylandt. Fairly common. Sedentary.

BLUE-WINGED PITTA *Pitta moluccensis* 16–19 cm

Other names: Indian or Moluccan Pitta.
Somewhat like Noisy Pitta but *with whitish throat; buff–brown sides to crown, with black centre streak; more extensive cobalt-blue on shoulders and rump; pinkish red mark in centre of deep buffish underparts,* extending to under tail-coverts. In flight, *shows much larger white 'window' in wings.* **Voice:** loud, clear double whistle (India). **Habitat:** rainforests, mangroves, native gardens (Borneo). **Range and Status:** widespread s. and se. Asia: winter migrant s. to Borneo, Java, Sumatra (Mackinnon & Phillipps, 1993). Four mainland Aust. records, all in nw. WA: Mandora Station, near Eighty Mile Beach, Nov. 1927; Derby, *c.* Nov. 1930; live bird with damaged wing, Burrup Pen., near Dampier, 6 Nov. 1994; one freshly dead, Coconut Well, Broome, summer 1995–1996. Also Christmas I., Indian Ocean. Vagrant.

NOISY PITTA *Pitta versicolor* 18–21 cm

Other name: Buff-breasted Pitta.
Most widespread Aust. pitta: *sides of crown chestnut, face/throat black;* shoulder-patches electric blue; *breast mustard-yellow;* under tail-coverts red (male), pink (female); legs fleshy straw-coloured. **Immature:** duller; dusky fringes to breast-feathers; lacks blue on wing. Singles, pairs: hops on forest floor. Best located by calls, rustling or by bird hammering snails on rock 'anvil'. Flight swift, kingfisher-like: wings blue–green with electric blue shoulder-patches, *white wingspot on black flight-feathers.* **Similar species:** Blue-winged Pitta. **Voice:** high-pitched, rough, three-note whistle, 'walk-to-work' or 'woik-to-woik'; sharp 'keow', single, liquid, mournful note. Calls day/night, from ground or high in forest canopy, mostly in spring/summer, when nesting. **Habitat:** rainforests; tropical/subtropical scrubs; nearby eucalypt forests; when migrating, mangroves, coastal scrubs, well-vegetated gardens. **Breeds:** Oct.–Dec. (ne. NSW–Q); Nov.–Jan. (C. York Pen.). **Nest:** domed, of twigs, leaves, bark, moss; lined with plant-fibre, feathers; between buttress roots, or on stump; ramp of sticks to side-entrance; marsupial dung on ramp and inside. **Eggs:** 2–4; rounded, white or blue–white; spotted, blotched dark purple–brown, shadowy blue–grey. **Range and Status:** coastal e. Aust., from C. York (Q) to lower Hunter R. (NSW); coastal lowlands to 1500 m on Gt Divide. Two races: *simillima*: C. York Pen.; winter migrant to s. PNG. Nominate race: breeds from Cooktown (Q) to lower Hunter R. (NSW): casual Sydney–Illawarra region. Common. Sedentary; autumn–winter movement to coastal lowlands/offshore islands.

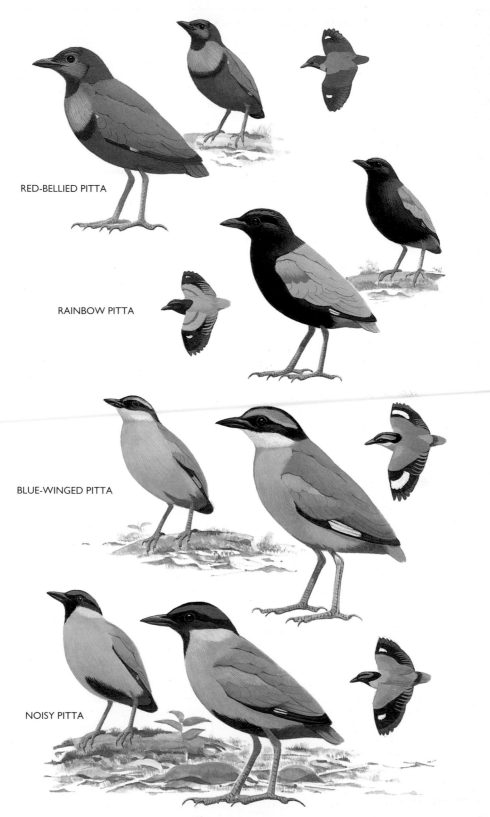

RED-BELLIED PITTA

RAINBOW PITTA

BLUE-WINGED PITTA

NOISY PITTA

ALBERT'S LYREBIRD *Menura alberti* male 90 cm, incl. tail (50 cm); female 76 cm

Richer chestnut than Superb Lyrebird: throat, foreneck and under tail-coverts rich rufous–buff; tail of male slightly upswept; glossy black above, silver–grey below: of two broad, round-tipped 'lyrates', two long, slim central ribbons and ten bushy filamentaries, black above, silvery below. Tail of female (and imm.) of grey–brown, chestnut-washed, broad, pointed, slightly drooped feathers. Singles or pairs: shy; when disturbed, half-runs, half-flies to cover or ascends tree in leaps. Males tread down display platforms of vines; sing and display on these and on ground, logs. **Voice:** male: rough but mellow, far-carrying; 'caw-cree-craw-craw-wheat' or similar phrases; mellow rising 'wooo' like howl of dingo; other deep, liquid calls. Mimics a few other species, incl. whirring of Satin Bowerbird and 'pik!' of Green Catbird; female also mimics. Alarm-call: piercing 'whisk-whisk'. **Habitat:** dense subtropical rainforests and scrubs; look for deep scratchings in leaf-litter. **Breeds:** June–Aug. **Nest:** large, globular, with side-entrance; of sticks, bark, leaves, fern-fronds and rootlets, lined with *rufous flank feathers* (cf. grey flank feathers of Superb); in cleft in rock, between boulders, buttress of tree, on stump. **Egg:** 1; purplish stone to purplish brown, blotched blackish brown in zone around large end; blackish brown streaks, spots. **Range and Status:** Mistake Mts s. of Gatton (Q) (isolated population at Mt Tamborine), s. to Nightcap Ra., near Mullumbimby (ne. NSW). Sedentary. Locally common.

SUPERB LYREBIRD *Menura novaehollandiae* male up to 1 m, incl. tail; female 86 cm

Other name: Native Pheasant.

Plain rich brown above, coppery on wings; deep grey below; legs and feet dark grey, powerful. *Tail of male long and train-like, usually horizontal: of two clubbed 'lyrates' c. 60 cm long; glossy black and rufous above, silvery below, with notched 'windows'; two slender, curved, ribbon-like 'guard-plumes' and 12 lacy filamentaries, black above, silvery below.* Moults annually: full tail acquired at 6–8 years. Tail of female (and imm.): *simpler, drooping and pointed; of 14 broad brown feathers, lyrates smaller, often hidden;* typically looks twisted during incubation. **Immature:** like female; throat rufous; tail shorter. Singles, pairs, parties: mostly seen crossing roads, fleeing in flying bounds. Roosts aloft but feeds entirely on ground; makes extensive scratchings in deep leaf-mould. Flies heavily, downhill or in volplaning descent from trees; occasionally across rivers. In autumn, song and mimicry by each territorial male intensifies; each rakes up numerous low display-mounds or arenas, 1–2 m across, around its territory. Displaying on these and elsewhere, the bird inverts tail over its entire body in a silvery shower, turning slowly about, pouring out a stream of song and mimicry. Display climaxes in a 'dance', when the bird leaps forwards and back in time to a thudding song-phrase 'tuggerah tuggerah tug', repeated. Copulation often follows, on or near mound. Several females may take up separate breeding sites near territory of a successful territorial male, with whom they mate, each building a nest and rearing chick unaided. During spring, song diminishes as males moult tails, renewed by Jan. During summer, forms loose feeding parties of both sexes, females accompanied by young. **Similar species:** Albert's Lyrebird. **Voice:** song, splendid, mellow and far-carrying: stream of mimicked calls of many other birds, interwoven with singer's own repeated phrases. One typical component is a loud, clear 'bilik bilik', and a repeated, seemingly mechanical whirr, running into rhythmical thuds during display. Females sing, and mimic, less powerfully. Adults, large nestlings, have piercing alarm-screech, 'whisk, whisk!'. **Habitat:** temperate, subtropical rainforests, forests, woodlands, from sea-level to above snowline; fern gullies, wooded sandstone gorges, forest plantations, adjacent gardens. **Breeds:** June–Oct. **Nest:** domed, bulky; of sticks, bark, fern-fronds, moss; lined with fibrous rootlets and dense mat of bird's *grey* flank-feathers; on ground, bank, rock-shelf; in stump, log or head of tree-fern or to 25 m in tree fork. **Egg:** 1; stone–grey, deep khaki or purple–brown, spotted, streaked, blotched deep grey and black. **Range and Status:** from Dandenong Ras., Kinglake and Wandong districts e. and ne. of Melbourne (Vic.) (and possibly formerly Lerderderg Gorge near Bacchus Marsh), to highlands in extreme se. Q, n. to c. Stanthorpe. Common. Introduced Tas. 1934–45 in Mt Field NP and near Lune R. in far s.; apparently locally expanding.

ALBERT'S LYREBIRD

SUPERB LYREBIRD

RUFOUS SCRUB-BIRD *Atrichornis rufescens* male 18 cm; female 16.5 cm

Noisy but exceptionally elusive dweller in dense, low, humid growth in openings in mountain rainforests. **Male:** dark rufous-brown above, *finely barred black; throat whitish with black mottlings down centre and onto breast; under tail-coverts rich buff; tail longish, slightly pointed;* cocked in display. Bill like Noisy Scrub-bird. Eye large, dark brown; legs powerful. **Female:** *breast more yellow–buff.* **Immature:** darker above, throat greyer. In winter and spring, territorial males can be located by voice but are seldom seen well.

Scuttles rodent-like through and under fallen leaves; feeds by thrusting leaves aside with bill/head; bounces along logs, hangs momentarily on tree-trunks, rocks. Female shyer; difficult to locate except when nesting. Both sexes hold the longish pointed tail erect over back and slightly droop wings. When pressed, fly feebly a few metres between cover. **Similar species:** Eastern Bristlebird: plainer brown; lacks fine black barrings above, or dark pattern on upperbreast; calls and habitat differ. **Voice:** powerful, loud and very penetrating. Male: 4–12 notes like a sharp, high-pitched 'cheep, cheep, cheep', starting deliberately, falling and accelerating in rapid staccato, almost a crack. Also a repeated ringing note; harsh scoldings. Female usually silent but, when eggs or young approached, sharp 'tick' or feeble squeaks. **Habitat:** isolated pockets of dense, moist tangles of ferns and other undergrowth up to 1 m high; tussocks, fallen logs, etc., with deep leaf-litter in clearings in or near temperate rainforests, incl. Antarctic Beech, *Nothofagus moorei*, to over 1000 m; adjacent wet eucalypt forest. **Breeds:** Sept.–Dec. **Nest:** globular, *c.* 15 cm across, with rounded side-entrance; of broad dry grass with dry leaves, ferns; lined with cardboard-like wood-pulp. **Eggs:** 2; very pale pink, sparsely spotted red–brown, in zone at large end. **Range and Status:** isolated populations above 600 m in highland rainforests from Mistake Mts, s. of Gatton (Q), s. to McPherson Ras. and ranges in ne. NSW, inland to New England Tableland and Gibraltar Ra. NP, s. to Barrington Tops NP (NSW). Rare; sedentary. Range much reduced by logging, clearing and burning of habitat, especially of lowland rainforest.

NOISY SCRUB-BIRD *Atrichornis clamosus* male 21–23 cm; female 20 cm

Local and very elusive; more often heard than seen. *Note restricted range.* Bill dark-horn above, paler below, *strong, pointed, with narrow ridge on top, giving head somewhat triangular appearance.* Wings stubby; *tail longish, flattish, slightly downcurved.* Plumage brown above, finely barred black; throat and breast dull white; under tail-coverts rich yellow–buff; legs and feet powerful. **Male:** *black patch on upperbreast extends in point up centre of throat; white sides of throat form two white streaks* like inverted V when bird raises bill to call.

Female and immature: no black patch on breast. Usually solitary, though single fledged offspring accompanies female for months. Moves rodent-like on or near ground in thickest cover, uses regular tracks but rarely reveals itself; tail often cocked. Flies feebly, probably only when hard-pressed. Female usually silent; seldom seen. **Similar species:** Western Bristlebird: plainer, without fine black barring; breast has paler scallops. Bill/head less triangular. Calls differ. **Voice:** powerful, penetrating and directional; seemingly ventriloquial. Territorial call of male: sweet descending crescendo, 'chip, chip, chip, chip-ip-ip-ip!', at first deliberate, but falling and accelerating into an ear-splitting climax. Also a short song, by male alone, or male and female together; three-note 'zip da dee' repeated once or twice, and 'zit, squeak and chip' calls are described. Female: single calls. **Habitat:** dense thickets of stunted eucalypts; tea-tree, banksia, sheoak, rush, saw-sedge, tall grasses. **Breeds:** May–Nov. **Nest:** domed; of rush, grass or dead leaves, with small side-entrance; lined with thin cardboard-like material. Usually in rushes, tangle of shrubs or clump of *Juncus*, on rough platform 9–70 cm from ground. **Egg:** 1; long oval; dull, very pale buff, with blotched orange–brown, mostly at large end. **Range and Status:** confined to region of Two Peoples Bay Nature Reserve, e. of Albany (WA), where rediscovered in 1961, when long thought extinct. Under careful management, population had increased from a few to *c.* 1000 by 1993. Translocation of birds to nearby areas of suitable habitat, e.g. Mt Manypeaks and Bald I., are seeding additional breeding populations and so reduce risk of annihilation by fire, the probable main cause (with clearing) of near-extinction between 1889 and 1961, when range shrank disastrously. Formerly extended coastally to near Perth. Sedentary. Endangered.

RUFOUS SCRUB-BIRD

imm.

NOISY SCRUB-BIRD

imm.

WHITE-THROATED TREECREEPER *Cormobates leucophaeus* 16–17.5 cm

Other names: Little Treecreeper, 'Woodpecker'.
Dark treecreeper with white throat; no eyebrow. Breast olive–cream, heavily streaked black and white; under tail-coverts barred. **Female:** *ochre spot on neck.* **Immature:** pale freckles on forehead; *female: rump bright chestnut.* Birds in ne. Q smaller, darker. Singles, pairs, family parties: climbs trees briskly, often spiralling; flight between trees fast, swooping, showing pale fawn wing-band. **Similar species:** Red-browed Treecreeper: throat white, eyebrow/eye-ring rich chestnut; parties forage higher. **Voice:** rapid, high-pitched, penetrating piping, beginning with several clear single notes or in a burst; slowing, falling slightly, pausing, continuing *interminably*; rippling mellow trill; musical phrases, subsongs. **Habitat:** rainforests, wetter eucalypt forests, woodlands; coast tea-tree/banksia-scrubs; riverine forests, drier woodlands, sub-inland scrubs — mallee, belar, brigalow. **Breeds:** Aug.–Jan. **Nest:** of bark-shreds; lined with fur, feathers, charcoal; in hollow branch, trunk, 5–15 m high; cavity in building, mine-shaft. **Eggs:** 2–3; white, spotted dark red, purple–brown. **Range and Status:** se. and e. Aust. and islands (except Bass Strait, Tas.). Nominate race: from Mt Lofty Ras./Fleurieu Pen. (SA) (where isolated); lower se. SA, Vic., except drier nw.; e. NSW, to w. slopes of Gt Divide, river red gum forests on Murray R. system; e. Q, n. to c. Rockhampton, inland to Carnarvon Ra. NP. Race *intermedia*: lower ne. Q, incl. Eungella Ra. near Mackay. Race *minor*, 'Little Treecreeper': highlands (300–1200 m) from Mt Spec–Atherton Tableland n. to Mt Amos, near Cooktown (Q). Common. Sedentary.

RED-BROWED TREECREEPER *Climacteris erythrops* 13.5–16 cm

Dark treecreeper with *smaller white throat than White-throated: distinctive rich chestnut eyebrow and eyepatch*; underparts like White-throated *but more darkly patterned with olive–grey and black-bordered white streaks*; under tail-coverts barred black and white. **Female:** *upperbreast streaked chestnut.* **Immature:** grey markings around eye; throat/breast plain grey. Pairs, family parties: more gregarious than White-throated, often forages higher, at heights to c. 40 m; breeds communally. Flight fast, undulating, showing grey–buff wingband. **Similar species:** White-throated Treecreeper. **Voice:** *distinctive quick, explosive, zizzing chatter, almost a buzz*; also single or double contact-note, somewhat like Striated Thornbill. **Habitat:** limbs, loose bark of trunks, upper branches in tall eucalypt forests, mainly in hilly and mountainous country and where these emerge into deep rainforested gullies, to sea-level. **Breeds:** Sept.–Jan. **Nest:** of bark-shreds; lined with fur; in tree-hollow, 6–30 m high. **Eggs:** 2–4; delicate pink–white, finely spotted red and purple–red, mostly at large end. **Range and Status:** se. Aust., from se. Q (Tewantin) s. through forested highlands and coastal NSW, e. and se. Vic. in highlands and coastal forests s. to Wilsons Prom. NP, to ranges e. and n. of Melbourne, w. to Wombat State Forest, but not Otways. Uncommon. Sedentary.

WHITE-BROWED TREECREEPER *Climacteris affinis* 14–15 cm

Bolder white eyebrow than Brown Treecreeper, bolder black and white streaks on ear-coverts; bolder black and white striped underparts; under tail-coverts barred black and white. **Male:** *black streaks in centre of upperbreast.* **Female:** *eyebrow starts with slim orange–rufous streak; broader rufous breast-streaks.* **Immature:** underparts plainer. Singles, pairs, family parties: forages on trunks of rough-barked trees and on ground among fallen trunks, stumps; flies to nearest stump or tree, note broad, pale buff wingband, dark tailband. **Similar species:** Brown Treecreeper: greyer and browner; markings much less contrasting; note that race *melanota*, 'Black Treecreeper', of n. Q has blackish brown upperparts, more contrasting pale eyebrow. Black-tailed Treecreeper: note range; sooty above; no white eyebrow. **Voice:** quiet; sharp, thin 'peep, peep'; scolding chatter; 'peter-peter' like Jacky Winter. **Habitat:** semi-arid, arid inland scrubs; stands of belar in mallee; mulga, native pine, desert-oak, corkwood; black box, lignum, saltbush, includes spinifex; sparsely vegetated dry gravelly ridges. **Breeds:** Aug.–Dec. **Nest:** grass, bark-shreds; lined with fur, hair; in hollow stump or tree, usually near ground. **Eggs:** 2–3; pink, with deep-pink, purplish spots, mostly at large end. **Range and Status:** s. inland Aust., extending to drier w. and Bight coasts: from upper Gascoyne R.–Murchison R.–Mingenew (WA) s. to Southern Cross–Kalgoorlie and e. through n. Nullarbor Plain to Gawler Ras., s. Flinders Ras.–Murray mallee (SA); nw. Vic., s. to Wyperfeld NP; w. NSW e. to Balranald–Hillston–Cobar–Bourke; sw. Q e. to Mitchell, n. to Blackall, thence w. through Channel Country to c. Coniston (NT). Uncommon. Sedentary.

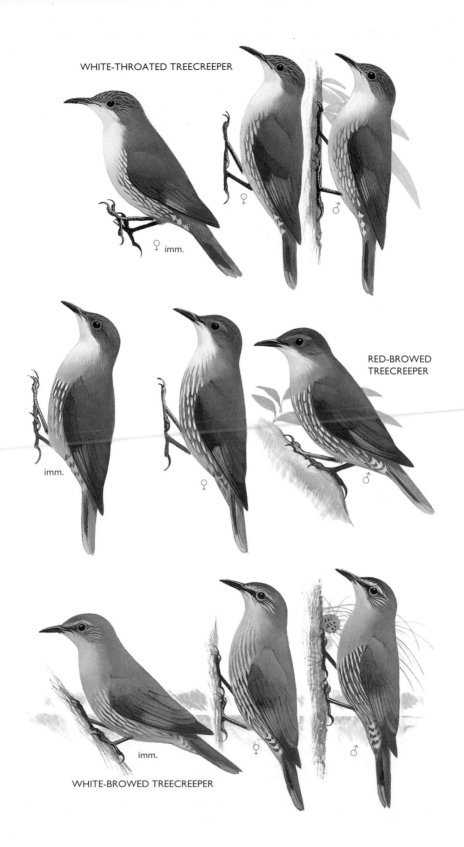

WHITE-THROATED TREECREEPER

♀ imm.

♀

♂

imm.

♀

♂

RED-BROWED
TREECREEPER

imm.

♀

♂

WHITE-BROWED TREECREEPER

329

BROWN TREECREEPER *Climacteris picumnus* 16–18 cm

Other name: 'Woodpecker'.

Head/neck grey, rest of upperparts soft brown; markings subtle — *note short buff eyebrow, slight dark mark through eye; upperbreast plain mouse-grey, cut off by black-edged, pale buff streaks on underparts; under tail-coverts chequered black and white.* **Male:** *cluster of fine black streaks in centre of upperbreast.* **Female:** *cluster of rufous streaks.* **Immature:** greyer, bill paler; breast nearly unstreaked. Singles, pairs, family parties or resident groups. Active: feeds much on ground, at times well out from cover; flight undulating, with fast sailing glides, *showing prominent pale buff wingband, dark tail-band.* Race *melanota,* 'Black Treecreeper', of ne. Q: *uniform blackish brown above, with long cream–white eyebrow.* **Similar species:** White-browed Treecreeper: stronger whitish eyebrow; black/white streaked ear-coverts; note range. Black-tailed Treecreeper: note range. **Voice:** strident 'spink!' singly or explosively rapidly repeated, slowing and descending; harsh sparrow-like rattle; softer contact calls. **Habitat:** drier forests/woodlands/scrubs, with fallen branches: river red gums on watercourses and around lake-shores (especially inland); paddocks with standing dead timber, stumps; margins of denser wooded areas. **Breeds:** May–Dec. **Nest:** of grass; lined with fur; usually in tree-hollow 3–10 m or higher, or in stump or fence-post near ground, base built up with grass or horse, cow, kangaroo dung. **Eggs:** 2–3; pink, thickly freckled, streaked red, purple, mostly at large end. **Range and Status:** suitable habitat in e. Aust.: from Spencer Gulf–L. Frome (SA); most of Vic. *except* wetter forests/woodlands and s. coastal districts; all NSW *except* wetter forests/woodlands in e.; in Q, widespread in drier forests/woodlands w. to Channel Country, n. on e. coast to c. Townsville. Race *melanota:* drier parts of Cardwell Ra.–Conjuboy–Forsayth(Q), w. to s. of Normanton, n. to *c.* Weipa on w. coast C. York Pen.; seldom to e. coastal areas. Common in suitable habitat. Sedentary.

RUFOUS TREECREEPER *Climacteris rufa* 15–17.5 cm

Other name: 'Woodpecker'.

Richest-coloured treecreeper: buff–grey above, with reddish buff face; greyish sides of neck; reddish buff underparts. Centre of breast finely streaked black and buff in male, buff in female. **Immature:** plainer, with distinct rufous rump. Habits like Brown Treecreeper; conspicuous as it spirals up trunks. *In flight, note rufous wingband, dark subterminal tail-band.* **Voice:** single penetrating 'peep'; churring scolds. **Habitat:** wider than other treecreepers: jarrah–karri forests in humid sw. WA; timber on watercourses; golfcourses, parks; wandoo and salmon-gum woodlands further inland; marble gum and mallee–spinifex associations n. of Nullarbor Plain; on Eyre Pen. (SA), mallee–woodland associations. **Breeds:** Aug.–Jan. **Nest:** of soft grasses; lined with plant-down and feathers; base often built up with fur or dung; usually in hollow near ground, but up to 8 m high. **Eggs:** 2–3; whitish, with reddish spots, mostly at large end. **Range and Status:** sw. WA, n. to Shark Bay, inland to Laverton–Vokes Hill, e. to Eyre Pen. (SA), except for unsuitable habitat on Nullarbor Plain; n. to Gawler Ras. (SA). Common in suitable habitat. Sedentary.

BLACK-TAILED TREECREEPER *Climacteris melanura* 17–20 cm

Largest, darkest treecreeper: sooty-brown to blackish above, underparts to under tail-coverts plain earthy rufous-brown; ear-coverts finely streaked black and white; tail black; under tail-coverts dark brown with very indistinct white marks. **Male:** *centre of throat and upperbreast strongly streaked black and white.* **Female:** *throat white, streaking into rich chestnut on upperbreast. In flight, shows broad buff–white wingband, visible as a pale streak when wing closed.* Pairs, resident groups: feeds much on ground, among fallen branches; eats many ants. **Similar species:** Brown Treecreeper race *melanota* in region of possible overlap near Leichhardt–Flinders Rs. (nw. Q); lacks throat-markings of Black-tailed; has chequered under tail-coverts; *in flight away, both look blackish with buff wingband.* **Voice:** clear, strident 'pee, peepeepeepeepeepee, pee, pee'. **Habitat:** open eucalypt forest, grassy woodlands and open scrub in hilly, breakaway country and lowlands; in nw. Aust., large timber, river red gums on watercourses, dead trees. **Breeds:** March–May; Sept.–Nov. **Nest:** of grass; lined with feathers; in hollow 4–10 m high. **Eggs:** 2–3; pink–white, spotted purple and rich purple–red, mostly at large end. **Range and Status:** from Carnarvon (WA), through Hamersley and Kimberley regions into NT, s. to Banka Banka–Alexandria; in nw. Q, e. to lower Leichhardt R.–Cloncurry. Isolated, small, pale race *wellsi* occurs in Pilbara region of c.–w. WA. Common. Sedentary.

imm.

BROWN TREECREEPER

♀

♂

race
melanota

♂

imm.

RUFOUS TREECREEPER

♀

♂

race *wellsi*

♀

♂

♀

♂

BLACK-TAILED TREECREEPER

331

SUPERB FAIRY-WREN *Malurus cyaneus* 13–14 cm

Other names: Blue Wren; Jenny Wren, Superb Blue Wren.
Well-loved 'blue wren' of se. Aust. **Male:** *blue cap and back; blue–black throat and chest; grey–white underparts; tail dark blue.* Male eclipse: *slightly darker olive–brown above than female; bill black; no red–brown around eye; tail deep blue.* **Female:** *mouse-brown; throat/breast whitish;* underparts washed fawn; *bill, lores and eye-ring red–brown; tail brown, washed greenish blue.* **Immature:** like female, with plain brown tail; young males acquire blackish bill and blue tail before first winter, coloured plumage during first breeding season. Pairs, family parties: moves briskly through thickets; hop-searches over short grass; sings briskly from tops of shrubs, thickets, fences. **Similar species:** *other predominantly blue male fairy-wrens have either chestnut shoulder-patch or blue underparts.* **Voice:** accelerating series of 'pips' breaking into loud, brisk merry reel; often like tinny alarm clock. Contact-call and scolding: brisk, splintered 'prip-prip' of varying urgency. Alarm-call: high-pitched 'seee'. **Habitat:** dense low cover with areas of short green grass: coastal heaths, saltmarsh, riverside thickets, bracken, undergrowth of forests, woodlands, blackberry thickets, lantana; margins of roads, tracks, road-reserves, shelterbelts; golf-courses, orchards, parks, gardens. In sub-inland, margins of mallee, bluebush, riverside vegetation, lignum, wetland plants over water. **Breeds:** June–Feb. **Nest:** domed; of grass, moss, rootlets, twigs, spiders' web/egg-sacs; low in tussock, shrub or bracken; occasionally to 6 m in foliage. **Eggs:** 3–4; pink–white, spotted red–brown, mostly at large end. **Range and Status:** se. Aust. and Tas., from Kangaroo I. and s. Eyre Pen. (SA) to Tropic in e. Q. Inland in SA to Mt Lofty Ras.–Murray mallee. Throughout Vic. *except* drier nw. districts; e. NSW; widespread in s. Riverina, in riverside or swampy areas or about homesteads and towns, w. to Balranald–Willandra NP–Nyngan–Walgett. In Q, w. to Mungindi–Morven–Springsure, n. to *c.* the Tropic e. to Eidsvold–Kilcoy–Brisbane suburbs and coast. Common. Sedentary; young females dispersive.

SPLENDID FAIRY-WREN *Malurus splendens* 12–14 cm

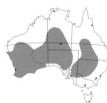

Other names: Banded, Black-backed, Splendid or Turquoise Fairy-wren.
Nominate race: familiar 'blue wren' of sw. WA. **Male:** *glossy violet–blue above and below; crown and especially cheekpatch much paler; black bands around nape and breast; but no black band across lower back (unlike other races); tail short, broad, blue.* **Male eclipse:** bill black; plumage brown, with blackish lores; wings bluish; tail blue. **Female:** *bill, lores and eye-ring pale tan;* upperparts brownish grey; underparts whitish; *tail dull blue.* **Immature:** like female; young males *develop dark bills and blue wings.* **Race callainus,** 'Turquoise Wren', male: *paler than nominate, except for deep violet–blue throat/upperbreast.* Note *black band across lower back,* longer tail. **Race melanotus,** 'Black-backed Wren', male: brilliant glossy cobalt–blue; *cheekpatch paler; black band across lower back broader;* breastband *narrower.* In *callainus* and *melanotus,* female, immature and eclipse male resemble nominate. Family parties, 'brown birds' predominating; in s. WA, reported to forage higher than other fairy-wrens. **Similar species:** Variegated Fairy-wren. Superb Fairy-wren, female: bill, lores, eye-ring red–brown; tail brown, washed blue–green. **Voice:** like Superb, but harder, more metallic; less loud and sharp than chestnut-shouldered wrens. **Habitat:** nominate race: undergrowth on margins, clearings in forests, woodlands; watercourse-vegetation, swamp-margins, golf-courses, orchards; shuns built-up areas. Inland: saltbush, mulga, mallee–spinifex. **Races callainus and melanotus:** mallee–spinifex, dense mulga, saltbush, bluebush; shrubby, grassy gorges in inland ranges; acacia-scrubs; belar with open understorey of smaller shrubs; watercourse-vegetation, including lignum, cumbungi, canegrass. **Breeds:** Sept.–Jan. **Nest:** domed, somewhat untidy; of dry grass, spiders' web, plant-down; low in thicket, tussock, reeds, saltbush, canegrass; spinifex; to 10 m in tree, e.g. paperbark; in mulga-shrub. **Eggs:** 2–4; white, finely spotted red–brown, zone at large end. **Range and Status:** nominate race: s. WA, n. to Shark Bay, inland to upper Ashburton R.–w. Gibson Desert–Wiluna–Laverton, e. coastally to near Eucla. Common, sedentary, local. Race *callainus*: sc. Aust., from Gibson Desert–Gt. Victoria Desert (WA), e. through sw. SA, s. to *c.* Ooldea–n. Eyre Pen.–Port Germein, thence n., mostly w. of Flinders Ras., to Simpson Desert; in s. NT, mostly in deserts circling ranges, e. to Finke, nw. to Tanami desert. Patchy and uncommon; part-nomadic. Race *melanotus*: inland e. Aust.: e. from *c.* Mannum–Annadale (SA), e. fringes of Mt Lofty–s. Flinders Ras. to sw. Q, n. to Thargomindah–Windorah–upper Diamantina R.–Winton, e. to Tambo–Mitchell; e. in NSW to *c.* Moree–Peak Hill–Griffith–Balranald; nw. Vic. from Swan Hill, sw. to Wyperfeld NP; w. to Murray mallee of SA, s. to *c.* Coonalpyn. Patchy; part-nomadic.

SUPERB FAIRY-WREN

♂ eclipse

♂ in moult

♂

♀

SPLENDID FAIRY-WREN

race *melanotus* ♂

race *callainus* ♂

nominate race

♂

♂ eclipse

♀

VARIEGATED FAIRY-WREN *Malurus lamberti* 11–14.5 cm

Other names: Lambert's, Lavender-flanked or Purple-backed Fairy-wren.
The sole chestnut-shouldered fairy-wren across much of eastern, inland and mid-west coastal WA. **Male, breeding:** *crown and large, pointed cheekpatches bright blue; 'shoulder-patch' chestnut; back royal blue to purple, extending to sides of upperbreast; lores, throat and chest jet black, cut off sharply by fawn–white underparts; tail long, blue–black, tipped white.* (Note: male of nominate race *lamberti* of coastal e. Aust. has *nearly uniform rich sky blue crown and cheekpatches;* male of race *assimilis* has *crown richer violet–blue than cheekpatches; purple back.*) **Male, eclipse (all races):** *like female but bill and lores black (not shown on plate); underparts whiter than female.* **Female:** *bill tan; prominent dark chestnut lores and eye-ring. Upperparts pale brown, incl. very long, blue-washed tail; underparts fawn–white, washed buff on flanks.* Note: in nw. Aust., two distinctive races: *dulcis,* of Arnhem Land escarpment (NT), male: *flanks deep-lavender; tail short, blue with white tips;* female: *lores and eye-ring white; upperparts blue–grey; tail blue, tipped white.* Race *rogersi,* ranging w. from Arnhem Land escarpment (NT) into Kimberley region (WA): similar, but females have tan-coloured lores and eye-ring. Both *dulcis* and *rogersi* interbreed with *assimilis* where their ranges overlap. Pairs, parties: 'brown birds' usually predominate; coloured males may forage together, often high in shrubs, trees. **Similar species:** Blue-breasted Fairy-wren in s. WA–Eyre Pen. (SA); Red-winged Wren in s. WA; Lovely Fairy-wren in ne. Q (see p. 336). Female 'blue-wrens' lack distinctive dark-chestnut lores and eye-ring; most have shorter tails. **Voice:** somewhat like Superb, but harder, higher-pitched. **Habitat:** nominate race *lamberti:* shrub associations, undergrowth, margins of clearings in forests, woodlands, heaths, sandplain and dune-vegetation, coastal blackberry thickets, golfcourses, orchards, parks, gardens. Race *assimilis:* mallee, mulga, saltbush, lignum and spinifex; shrubby or rank grassy vegetation on watercourses. Races *dulcis* and *rogersi:* shrubs and spinifex in rugged sandstone hills and gorges; shrubs, grass on watercourses; pandanus, paperbarks by freshwater springs, pools. **Breeds:** July–March. **Nest:** domed, loosely woven; of soft grass, bark-strips, plant-down, spiders' web and egg-sacs; low in undergrowth or low shrub, or tall tuft of grass. **Eggs:** 3–4 (*dulcis* and *rogersi* 2–3); white, finely speckled with reddish purple, mostly at large end. **Range and Status:** nominate race: coastal e. Aust., from c.–e. Q to far s. coastal NSW. Race *assimilis:* widespread in mainland Aust.; *absent from* ne. Q beyond *c.* Georgetown–upper Burdekin R.–Townsville, from s., e. and ne. Vic., from extreme se. SA, Adelaide–Mt Lofty Ras. and Kangaroo I., from s. WA s. and w. of Geraldton–Eucla (but with long coastal extension s. from Geraldton to near Perth). Race *dulcis:* w. Arnhem Land (NT) from King R. w. to near South Alligator R. Race *rogersi:* w: fringes of Arnhem Land escarpment (NT) w. to Kimberley region (WA). Fairly common. Mostly sedentary.

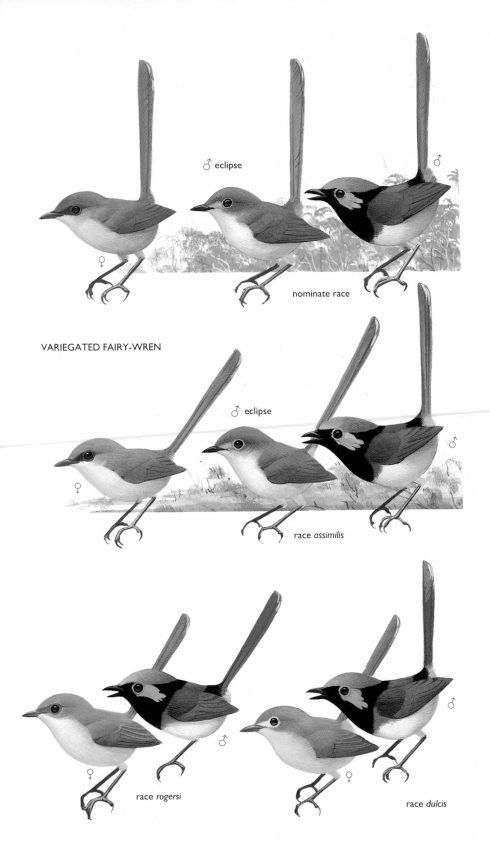

♂ eclipse

♂

♀

nominate race

VARIEGATED FAIRY-WREN

♂ eclipse

♂

♀

race *assimilis*

♂

♀

race *rogersi*

♂

♀

race *dulcis*

335

LOVELY FAIRY-WREN *Malurus amabilis* 11.5–13 cm

Male, breeding: like Variegated Fairy-wren *but with short, rounded tail, broadly tipped white. Crown and cheekpatch notably rounder than Variegated, bright pale blue; breast black; underparts white.* **Male, eclipse:** some males moult into complete female-like plumage, others moult only partially. **Female:** bluest female fairy-wren: *bill black; lores and eye-ring white; ear-coverts and side of neck deep sky–blue; upperparts bright grey–blue; underparts white. Tail short, grey–blue broadly tipped white, outer feathers edged white.* **Immature:** like dull female; bill blackish brown; tail longer. Pairs, family parties: hop-searches in shrubs/trees of scrub, rainforest and swamp-woodland from leaf-litter to 15 m+ high, calling continually, cocking and flirting white-tipped tail (Schodde, 1982). **Similar species:** Variegated Fairy-wren, female: deep chestnut lores and eye-ring; underparts buff–white; both sexes, tails longer. **Voice:** soft, drawn-out 'prip's; brisk single reel. **Habitat:** margins, clearings/tracks in rainforest; vine scrub, swamp-woodland, mangroves; well-vegetated watercourses; wastelands. **Breeds:** any month, but mostly July–Dec. (Schodde, 1982). **Nest:** rough domed structure, of grass, bark, leaf-skeletons, grass-stems, spiders' web; lined with fine grass, paperbark, fur, feathers. **Eggs:** 2–3; creamy white, very finely, sparingly flecked red–brown, in faint zone at large end. **Range and Status:** ne. Q: from Townsville–Atherton Tableland to C. York Pen., s. on w. coast to *c.* Edward R. Common. Sedentary.

BLUE-BREASTED FAIRY-WREN *Malurus pulcherrimus* 13.5–15 cm

Other names: Blue-breasted Superb Warbler or Fairy-wren.
Male, breeding: *crown, eye-ring and cheekpatch deep, uniform lilac–blue; black mask from bill, past eye to partial rear collar; throat and upperbreast black, washed deep, slightly glossy purple–blue; tail large, dusky blue, with faint white tips on outer tail-feathers.* Female, immature and eclipse male not safely distinguished from ditto Variegated, though more uniformly deep grey–brown on upperparts. **Similar species:** Variegated and Red-winged Fairy-wrens. **Voice:** like Variegated. **Habitat:** undergrowth in drier forests, woodlands; sandplain-scrubs, heaths; tea-tree and mallee associations; low dense dune-vegetation, acacia-thickets, saltbush. In SA (Eyre Pen.), heath country, swampy localities. **Breeds:** Aug.–Nov. **Nest and eggs:** like Variegated. **Range and Status:** broken distribution in sw. WA and Eyre Pen. (SA). In sw. WA it occurs between ranges of Variegated and Red-winged Fairy-wrens; absent from wetter parts. The n. and e. limits are *c.* Shark Bay–Mingenew–Bunjil–Wongan Hills–Gibb Rock–Norseman and e. to Bight coast s. of Mundrabilla, coastally e. to Eucla. Approx. s. and w. limits are Moore R., passing inland of Perth to wheatbelt and s. past Katanning to s. coast near Albany. Overlaps Variegated Wren on w. coast, Shark Bay–Moore R. In SA, confined to s. Eyre Pen., n. and e. to Kimba–Whyalla. Common in WA; uncommon SA. Sedentary.

RED-WINGED FAIRY-WREN *Malurus elegans* 14–16 cm

Other name: Marsh Wren.
Largest, most robust fairy-wren. **Male, breeding:** like Blue-breasted *but crown/cheekpatch/mantle pale silvery blue; feathers of back have white bases, making mantle conspicuously blue–white; shoulder-patch pale chestnut, extensive.* **Male, eclipse:** like female but lores *black.* **Female:** like female Blue-breasted *but bill blackish; lores chestnut, giving head a 'different' look* (G. Chapman, pers. comm.); *crown and tail deep grey–brown; mantle washed chestnut.* **Immature:** like dull female. Pairs, resident family groups: forages within low, dense, often marshy vegetation. Sometimes associates with Splendid Fairy-wren. **Similar species:** Variegated Fairy-wren, male: deeper lilac-blue head and back. Female: tan bill, dark chestnut lores and eye-ring; bluish tail. **Voice:** 3 or 4 short clear notes followed by trilling warble; 'pripping' notes sharper and louder. **Habitat:** thick scrub and swamp-vegetation, often with sword-grass and tea-tree, on margins of streams, freshwater swamps; swamp-woodlands; understorey in jarrah–karri forest; moist gullies in ranges; nearby eucalypt woodlands; coastal dune vegetation; well-vegetated gardens, orchards. **Breeds:** Sept.–Dec. **Nest:** large, round, sturdily constructed, of grass, bark-strips, leaves; usually in rush-clump in swampy vegetation; reeds, rushes over water or near ground in base of rush. **Eggs:** 2–3; white, lightly spotted red–brown, mostly at large end. **Range and Status:** confined to far sw. WA, from near Perth s. through Darling Ra., jarrah–karri forests in Busselton–Albany region, s. and e. to Albany–Stirling Ra. NP, e. to near Fitzgerald R. Moderately common; reduced by habitat disturbance. Sedentary.

LOVELY FAIRY-WREN

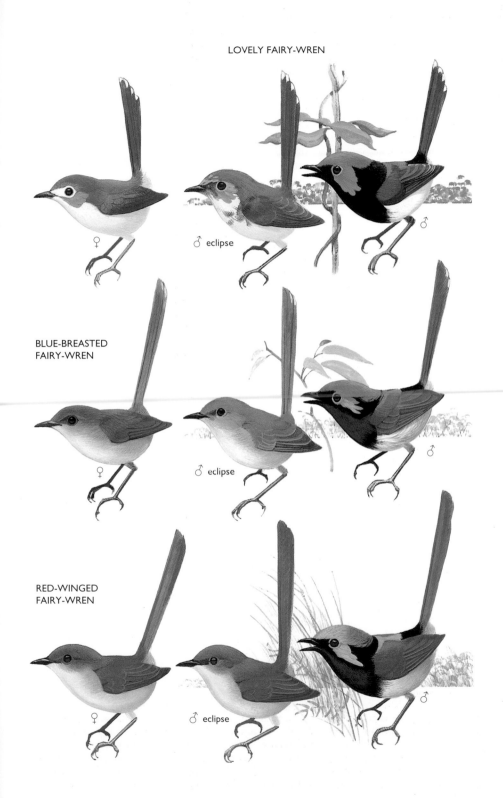

♀ ♂ eclipse ♂

BLUE-BREASTED
FAIRY-WREN

♀ ♂ eclipse ♂

RED-WINGED
FAIRY-WREN

♀ ♂ eclipse ♂

PURPLE-CROWNED FAIRY-WREN *Malurus coronatus* 14–15.5 cm

Other name: Lilac-crowned Wren.

Male: *crown deep lilac with black centre; broad black mask extends around nape*; tail blue; underparts cream, washed buff. **Male, eclipse:** head grey; eyepatch blackish. **Female:** crown blue–grey; fine white eyebrow and eye-ring; *chestnut eyepatch; blue tail.* **Immature:** like female; no white around eye. Pairs, family parties: often high in trees. **Voice:** loud, low-pitched reeling, with elements of scrubwren; high-pitched 'cheepa-cheepa-cheepa'; contact-call short 'drrt' or 'jk' note like Fairy Martin; deep scolds. **Habitat:** pandanus/paperbark thickets, with tall canegrass and other dense low cover, mostly fringing rivers, creeks, lakes; rarely mangroves. **Breeds:** Aug.–Jan.; April–May. **Nest:** domed, bulky; of strips of paperbark, canegrass; in pandanus, near water. **Eggs:** 3; pink–white, with spots, splashes of brownish pink. **Range and Status:** nominate race: n. and e. Kimberley (WA), from Drysdale R. e. to Victoria R. (NT) (Rowley, 1993); s. to upper Fitzroy, Hann and Margaret Rs. (WA); Ord R. on upper L. Argyle (WA). Race *macgillivrayi*: e. NT, from lower Roper, Towns, Limmen Bight, McArthur Rs. e. to Gregory–lower Leichhardt Rs. (nw. Q); s. to Mallapunyah (NT); Lawn Hill NP–Riversleigh–Kamilaroi (Q). Very local; habitat decimated by burning and stock. Sedentary. Nominate race vulnerable (Garnett, 1993).

WHITE-WINGED FAIRY-WREN *Malurus leucopterus* 11.5–13 cm

Other names: Black-and-white, Blue-and-white, White-backed Fairy-wren.

Nominate race, male breeding: *black (often with some blue feathers), with mostly white wings.* **Race *leuconotus*,** 'Blue-and-white Fairy-wren', male breeding: *cobalt-blue (occasionally black) with white wings.* **Male, eclipse:** like female; bill dark horn in older birds; *moulting birds patchy.* **Female and immature:** palest, dullest fairy-wren; no eye-marking; bill sandy-brown; upperparts pale mouse-brown; tail washed grey–blue; underparts off-white; flanks buffish. Parties of 8–12, mostly 'brown birds'. Shy; forages in low vegetation. In flight, male's buzzing white wings show against blue body. **Voice:** rapid, undulating musical reeling, like fishing reel; splintered, insect-like 'prip prip'. **Habitat:** nominate race: low heath, scrub, saltbush. Race *leuconotus*: tall grasses, low dense shrubs; tangled clumps on open, often treeless arid wastes; saltbush, bluebush, roly-poly, spinifex, dead finish, lignum, swamp canegrass; margins of salt lakes, coastal inlets, saltfields. **Breeds:** mostly Aug.–Feb. **Nest:** domed, of grasses, plant-stems, spiders' web, plant-down; low in shrub, grass. **Eggs:** 3–4; white, finely spotted red–brown, purplish. **Range and Status:** nominate race: Dirk Hartog and Barrow Is. (WA). Common. Sedentary. Race *leuconotus*: w. coastal and inland Aust., from Port Hedland–Pilbara region (WA) to Tanami–Banka Banka (NT), s. Barkly Tableland e. to *c.* Mt Isa–Richmond–Roma–Goondiwindi (Q); inland NSW, e. to w. foothills of Divide; nw. Vic., e. to *c.* Kerang; Murray mallee (SA), to coastal areas near Adelaide; coastally w. from Streaky Bay (SA) to Esperance (WA), thence to near Perth. Common. Part-nomadic.

RED-BACKED FAIRY-WREN *Malurus melanocephalus* 10–13 cm

Smallest fairy-wren. **Male, nominate race:** *chocolate–brown, back orange–scarlet.* **Male, race *cruentatus*:** *black, with crimson back*; tail short, blackish. **Male, eclipse:** like female; patchy when moulting. **Female, both races:** bill/legs pinkish brown; no eye-markings; upperparts/tail pale brown washed cinnamon; underparts fawn–white, washed ochre. **Immature:** like female; tail longer. Pairs, family parties, companies of 30–40 (Schodde, 1982); 'brown birds' predominating. Shy; tamer near settlement. **Similar species:** Variegated Wren, female. White-winged Fairy-wren, female. **Voice:** louder, more irregular reel than Variegated; other notes robust. **Habitat:** tall grass, in open woodlands, swamp-woodlands; rainforest fringes; lantana, other scrubby thickets; plantations, gardens. Inland, tall grass on watercourses, foothills; low scrubs, spinifex, plantations, gardens. **Breeds:** Nov.–March; in coastal se. Aust., Aug.–Feb. **Nest:** globular, of grass, bark-strips, leaves; in grass, low shrub, thicket. **Eggs:** 3 (4); white, sparsely, finely spotted light red, mostly at large end. **Range and Status:** race *cruentatus*: coastal n. and e. Aust.: from *c.* Broome (WA), Kimberley and Top End (NT), s. to Tanami–Tennant Creek–Barkly Highway; in Q, e. to C. York Pen. and ne. coast; inland to Mt Isa–Richmond. Nominate race: e. Q, from *c.* Cooktown coastally s. to *c.* Myall Lakes (NSW), inland to Carnarvon Ra. NP–Bunya Mts–Warwick (Q); Casino and *c.* 30 km w. of Gloucester (NSW). Races intergrade between *c.* Cooktown–Burdekin–Gilbert Rs, ne. Q (Schodde, 1982). Common. Sedentary.

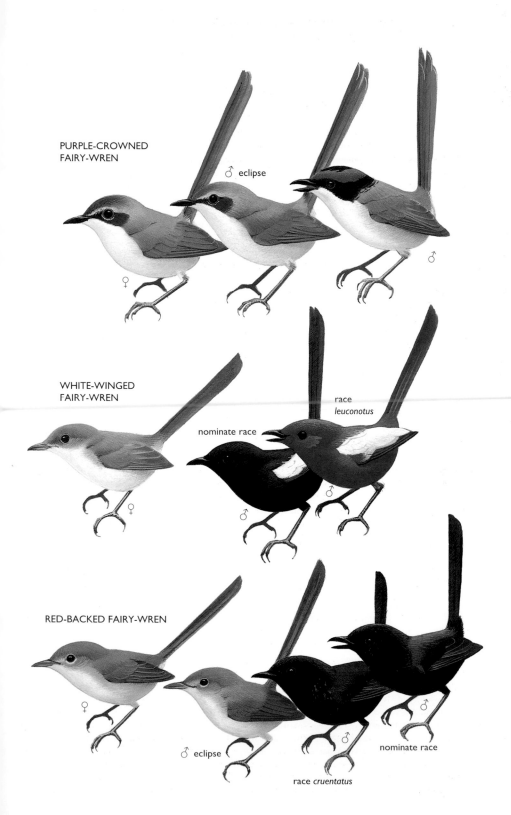

PURPLE-CROWNED
FAIRY-WREN

♂ eclipse

♀

♂

WHITE-WINGED
FAIRY-WREN

nominate race

race
leuconotus

♀

♂

♂

RED-BACKED FAIRY-WREN

♀

♂ eclipse

race *cruentatus*

nominate race

♂

♂

SOUTHERN EMU-WREN *Stipiturus malachurus* 15–19 cm, incl. tail (9–12 cm)

Other names: Button-grass Wren, Sticktail.
Male: *crown tawny-rufous, streaked darker; eyebrow/throat lavender–blue; ear-coverts tawny-grey with fine pale streaks; upperparts grey–brown, strongly streaked black; underparts rich tawny-buff.* Tail long, sparse, nearly twice length of body, erect when excited. **Female:** no blue; throat/underparts rich tawny-buff. **Immature:** male: paler blue throat; no blue eyebrow; tail shorter. Pairs, family parties: shy; moves nimbly through dense low cover, bounces over ground, climbs tussocks, open shrubs. Flight feeble, tail streaming.
Similar species: Mallee and Rufous-crowned Emu-wrens: males have streaked blue ear-coverts; note *range*. Fairy-wrens. **Voice:** male: like fairy-wren but higher-pitched, insect-like; contact call: splintered, 'prip prip' and running high-pitched notes. Alarm-call: high-pitched 'seee'. **Habitat:** heaths with 'grasstrees', banksias, hakeas; rushes, sedges, scrubby thickets; lignum, montane gullies, subalpine grasslands, heathy woodlands. In Tas., button-grass plains, montane moors. On Kangaroo I., marginally in mallee–spinifex. In sw. WA, dune-vegetation, sandplain-heaths, dry eucalyptus, acacia–spinifex.
Breeds: Sept.–Jan. **Nest:** domed, of loose fine grass, rootlets, moss; lined with finer grass; low in tussock or dwarf shrub. **Eggs:** 3; white, tinted pink, minutely dotted, blotched light red–brown at large end.
Range and Status: coastal se. and sw. Aust. and Tas., from sea-level to over 1000 m. In WA, from Shark Bay–Dirk Hartog I., s. and e. to Israelite Bay, inland to Wongan Hills–Hyden–Norseman. In se. Aust., Kangaroo I.–s. Eyre Pen., s. Mt Lofty Ras., s. Fleurieu Pen. and coastal se. SA; in Vic., inland to Grampians–Colac–Yellingbo and s. foothills of Divide in Gippsland; in NSW, inland to S. Tablelands–Blue Mts–Kanangra Boyd NP–Gibraltar Ra. NP.; n. coastally to Cooloola NP–Fraser I. (se. Q). Habitats fragmented; locally common to vulnerable or endangered, according to race. Sedentary.

MALLEE EMU-WREN *Stipiturus mallee* 13–15 cm, incl. tail (8–9 cm)

Male: *crown plain rufous; eyebrow, face, throat and upperbreast deep lilac–blue, paler around eye; ear-coverts blue, finely streaked black and white; underparts tawny-buff. Tail flimsy, c. 1.5 times length of body.* **Female:** lacks blue; *lores whitish; eyebrow, face and ear-coverts tawny, finely streaked dark grey and white; underparts plain buff.* Pairs, family parties, autumn–winter groups. Shy; climbs seeding stems to spy observer, but movement sends it dropping into spinifex, or scurrying, half-flying, tail lowered. Moves quickly through spinifex, low foliage of mallee gums. **Similar species:** Southern Emu-wren: dark-streaked crown; finely streaked tawny-grey ear-coverts. **Voice:** alarm-call: splintered, high-pitched, insect-like 'see see'. **Habitat:** spinifex, with mallee gums, native cypress, on sandhill swales, slopes; also tall heathland with tea-tree, broom, fringe-myrtle, spinifex. **Breeds:** Aug.–Oct. **Nest:** neat, hooded structure of spinifex spines, root fibres, grass, spiders' web and egg-sacs, lined with plant-down, feathers. **Eggs:** 3; finely flecked red–brown, mostly at large end. **Range and Status:** region s. of Murray R. in nw. Vic.–se. SA: from Hattah–Kulkyne NP (Vic.) s. to Wyperfeld NP–Big Desert Wilderness; w. into SA, from c. Nadda–Peebinga s. to Ngarkat Cons. Park, n. of Keith, w. to Carcuma Cons. Park, ne. of Coonalpyn (Carpenter & Matthew, 1992). Abuts range of Southern Emu-wren in se. SA. Rare. Vulnerable.

RUFOUS-CROWNED EMU-WREN *Stipiturus ruficeps* 12–13 cm, incl. tail (6.5–7.5 cm)

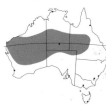

Brightest emu-wren; note range: *crown plain, bright rufous; tail-feathers shorter, less flimsy, c. 1.3 times body length.* **Male:** *deep sky-blue eyebrow, face, throat; ear-coverts blue, finely streaked black and white; underparts rufous–buff.* **Female:** lacks blue; lores whitish; face and ear-coverts tawny cinnamon, finely streaked white; underparts rufous–buff. **Immature:** like pale adults. Pairs, parties: climbs seed-stems of spinifex; crawls mouse-like through clumps. Flies feebly when pressed. **Similar species:** Mallee Emu-wren: note range. See Fairy-wrens. **Voice:** insect-like 'prip, prip'; alarm-call: high-pitched squeak, 'seeeeeeet'. **Habitat:** spinifex, on sides/gullies of rocky ridges, with sparse shrubs. **Breeds:** Aug.–Oct. **Nest:** domed, with side-entrance; of fine grass, bark-shreds, plant-down, spiders' web/egg-sacs; in spinifex-clump, low shrub. **Eggs:** 2–3; white, speckled, blotched brown, red–brown, in zone at large end. **Range and Status:** arid inland, e. to Winton–Fermoy–Opalton (Q), also Buckingham Downs Stn., c. 125 km n. of Boulia; in NT, n. to Frewena–Wauchope, s. to James Ra., Macdonnell Ras., Simpson Desert; in WA, extends to w. coast, near NW Cape, n. to c. 20˚S in Gt Sandy Desert, s. to E. Murchison district–Kathleen Valley–Naretha and n. Gt Victoria Desert (to c. 100 km e. of Neale Junction) and nw. SA. Local, sedentary. Status uncertain.

SOUTHERN EMU-WREN

imm. ♂

♂

♀

MALLEE EMU-WREN

♀

♂

RUFOUS-CROWNED EMU-WREN

♀

♂

341

BLACK GRASSWREN *Amytornis housei* 18–21 cm

Male: *black and rich chestnut, with fine white streaks.* **Female:** *underparts light chestnut.* **Immature:** duller, streaks fainter. Pairs, parties: runs, bounces over rocks; bobs, flicks but seldom cocks ample tail. Makes short downward glides; runs with head/tail lowered into crevices, scuttles rat-like along ledges. **Voice:** strong, reeling, like fairy-wren but harsher, more continuous; 'sharp arresting chirping ticking and grating' (Schodde, 1982). **Habitat:** spinifex in piled red to black sandstone; gullies with tumbled rocks, sparse trees, shrubs. **Breeds:** *c.* Dec.–March. **Nest:** bulky, domed, of spinifex stems, lined with soft grass, in top of spinifex-clump (Schodde, 1982). **Eggs:** not described. **Range and Status:** nw. Kimberley (WA), between Drysdale R. NP in ne. and Isdell R.–Yampi Pen. in sw. Locally common. Sedentary.

WHITE-THROATED GRASSWREN *Amytornis woodwardi* 20–22 cm

Note black, white-streaked upperparts, red–brown rump, black whisker-mark, *white throat separated from rusty underparts by black-and-white streaked breastband.* **Female:** richer rusty underparts. Singles; pairs to parties: leaps to snatch insects from leaves, stems; gleans insects, seeds from rock faces (Noske, 1992). Runs in bursts over rock-faces with head/tail lowered; darts into crevices. **Similar species:** Carpentarian Grasswren: smaller, more rufous; underparts white with no breastband. **Voice:** rich series of rising and falling notes and trills; animated chirping with snatches of song. Alarm, contact calls: strong, sharp 'tzzzt'. **Habitat:** sandstone escarpments, broad valleys, terraced hillsides; narrow rocky gullies; plateaux of gravelly soil with spinifex; sparse eucalypts, low shrubs (Noske, 1992). **Breeds:** Dec.–May. **Nest:** bulky, domed; of grass, leaves, paperbark, in top of spinifex, or other tussock. **Eggs:** 2; slender, oval, off-white, sparsely speckled, blotched red–brown, purple–grey, pale sepia, mostly at large end. **Range and Status:** n. and w. Arnhem Land (NT), from e. of Oenpelli, sw. to El Sharana–upper Mary–S. Alligator–Katherine Rs. Locally common. Sedentary.

CARPENTARIAN GRASSWREN *Amytornis dorotheae* 16–17.5 cm

Other names: Dorothy's or Red-winged Grasswren.

Note slim orange–brown eyebrow, rufous upperparts; throat/breast white with black whisker-mark *but no streaked breastband;* flanks/underparts pale orange–buff (male), chestnut (female). **Immature:** duller, streaks fainter. Pairs, parties: shy, tail erect, bounces with short flights over rocks; shelters in rock-crevices. **Similar species:** White-throated Grasswren. **Voice:** high-pitched, cricket-like chirping 'ssstzz'; harsher in alarm; rich fairy-wren-like trills, churring (Schodde, 1982). **Habitat:** spinifex; sparse shrubs, eucalypts, on sandstone escarpments, gullies. **Breeds:** Nov.–March. **Nest:** bulky, domed, loose; of spinifex seed-stems, leaves, in spinifex. **Eggs:** 2–3; oval, smooth, glossy; pink–white, marked red–brown/mauve, mostly at large end. **Range and Status:** colonies on 'Gulf Fall' escarpments, in e. NT–nw. Q, from Tawalla and Bukalara Ras. near Borroloola (NT) to upper Nicholson R. (NT–Q border); se. to Lawn Hill NP, e. to *c.* Gunpowder–Mt Isa (Q) (Beruldsen, 1992). Sedentary.

STRIATED GRASSWREN *Amytornis striatus* 14.5–19.5 cm.

Soft red–brown above, streaked white; eyebrow orange–buff; throat white, *strong black whisker-mark;* female flanks pale-chestnut. **Immature:** duller. Birds in inland and w. (race *whitei*) brighter; those in se. (race *striatus*) washed grey–brown; race *merrotsyi*, Flinders Ras. (SA) shorter tailed. Pairs, family parties: elusive; forages in spinifex; small shrubs, low mallee; hops/runs; tail cocked; flies feebly. **Similar species:** Thick-billed, Eyrean Grasswrens. **Voice:** sweet, rippling melody, with 'tu-tu-tu' notes. Contact call: thin, very high-pitched 'see'; twittering scolding. **Habitat:** spinifex, with mallee, acacias; other inland scrubs; coastal scrubs in WA. **Breeds:** Aug.–Nov., se. Aust.; Feb.–April, nw./inland. **Nest:** domed, of spinifex spines in spinifex clump; lined with bark-strips, plant-down. **Eggs:** 2 (3); oval, white; finely spotted, streaked red–brown. **Range and Status:** c. and sw. Q, c. and sw. NSW, nw. Vic., e., n. and w. SA, s. NT; widespread in inland WA and Pilbara, reaching coast at Eighty Mile Beach–n. Shark Bay. Locally common; patchy. Sedentary.

BLACK GRASSWREN

♀

♂

WHITE-THROATED GRASSWREN

♀

♂

CARPENTARIAN GRASSWREN

♀

♂

STRIATED GRASSWREN

♀

race *whitei*

♂

race *merrotsyi*

♂

nominate race

♂

EYREAN GRASSWREN *Amytornis goyderi* 14–16.5 cm

Bill silver–grey, sturdy; tail longish. Crown/upperparts rufous, streaked white; face/ear-coverts buff–grey, finely streaked black; underparts whitish. **Female:** *flanks rufous.* Singles, pairs, families: shy; forages around canegrass in hops, bounding runs, wings open, tail cocked. Climbs for quick view, or to sing. **Similar species:** Thick-billed, Striated Grasswrens. **Voice:** faint two-syllable whistle, 'sw-it', 'swi-it'. Alarm-call: high-pitched 'zeeet'. Song: jumbled reel of silvery cadences (Schodde, 1982). **Habitat:** clumps of dune canegrass on dunes. **Breeds:** June–Sept. **Nest:** hooded; of canegrass leaves, stems, rootlets; lined with fine grass, plant-down. **Eggs:** 2–3; small, dull white, finely spotted, blotched purple, red–brown, smudged grey/lavender, in zone at large end. **Range and Status:** Simpson/Strzelecki Deserts in far sw. Q, far se. NT, ne. SA. Locally common. Sedentary; locally nomadic.

DUSKY GRASSWREN *Amytornis purnelli* 15–18 cm

Darker, slimmer, finer-billed than Thick-billed Grasswren: note rufous lores, buff–grey underparts; female's flanks chestnut. Race *ballarae: smaller, brighter.* Small parties: shy, inquisitive; bounces over rock-faces, boulders, longish tail cocked; takes cover in crevices; flies low, straight, frequently downhill. **Similar species:** Striated Grasswren. **Voice:** reeling trill, more sibilant than fairy-wren; 'sree-sreeee-sree-teu-teu'. Alarm-call: harsh 'chip-chip!'; high-pitched 'seet'. **Habitat:** rocky ranges with spinifex; shrubs. **Breeds:** Aug.–Oct. **Nest:** half-domed; loose, of fine soft grass; in spinifex-clump, tussock, dense low bush. **Eggs:** 2–4; oval, glossy; white or pinkish; spotted, blotched light/dark red–brown, lilac–grey; in cap. **Range and Status:** nw. SA–far e. WA, through inland NT; isolate race *ballarae* in Selwyn Ra. (nw. Q). Locally common. Sedentary.

THICK-BILLED GRASSWREN *Amytornis textilis* 15–20 cm

Thickset dull grasswren with stout dark bill. **Nominate race:** *underparts pale grey–buff.* Race *modestus: plain pale-fawn, finely streaked.* Female: chestnut flanks. *Note habitat.* Shy, elusive; bounces between saltbush; hides miraculously. **Similar species:** Dusky, Striated, Eyrean Grasswrens. **Voice:** quiet; clear, silvery song; high-pitched alarm squeaks; low, chirping 'teck-teck' (Schodde, 1982). **Habitat:** *sandy lowlands*; depressions in gibber plains with dense low saltbush, bluebush, cottonbush, nitre-bush; clumps of swamp canegrass on watercourses; flood debris. Near Shark Bay (WA), sandplain vegetation with *acacia* shrubs 1–3 m tall over grasses, herbs (Brooker, 1988). **Breeds:** July–Sept. **Nest:** cup-shaped or half-domed, of loose grass, bark; lined with fine grass, fur, feathers; low in saltbush, bluebush, canegrass, flood debris. **Eggs:** 2–3; white, cream, pink, spotted/blotched red–brown, purplish grey, or speckled red–brown. **Range and Status:** nominate race: coastal sandplain on cw. coast WA, NW Cape–Peron Pen., Shark Bay (Brooker, 1988). Race *modestus*: lowlands of s. NT and Macdonnell Ras., s. to Everard Ras.–Coober Pedy–William Ck–w. side of Flinders Ras. (SA). Possibly extinct e. SA/NSW. Race *myall*: s. inland SA, Nullarbor Plain–Gawler Ras.–Iron Knob. Locally common, generally sparse; extinct in parts of former range.

GREY GRASSWREN *Amytornis barbatus* 18–20 cm

Distinctive grasswren: face/underparts white; black line through eye; black double 'necklace'; flanks pale buff (both sexes). Pairs, parties: perches atop canegrass, lignum-clumps; drops. Flushed, runs, bounces between cover; flies rapidly low to next, tail trailing. **Similar species:** Striated, Eyrean Grasswrens. **Voice:** 3–4 high-pitched, metallic ringing notes, less 'electric' than Striated; rapid 'pit-choo', second syllable descending quickly (Joseph, 1982). Disturbed, prolonged twittering. **Habitat:** tall dense clumps of lignum; swamp canegrass on overflow channels; swamps; rushes, low shrubs; old man saltbush. **Breeds:** July–Sept. **Nest:** bulky, loose, semi-domed, of grass; in lignum, swamp canegrass. **Eggs:** 2 (3); rounded-oval, dull white, tinged pale pink, fine nutmeg-brown markings in zone. **Range and Status:** pockets of suitable habitat in far sw. Q, far nw. NSW and far ne. SA, on overflow systems of Bulloo R., Eyre Ck, lower Diamantina R. Locally nomadic.

EYREAN GRASSWREN

♀

♂

DUSKY GRASSWREN

♀

♂

♀

race
ballarae

♂

THICK-BILLED GRASSWREN

♀

♂

race
modestus

nominate
race

♀

♂

GREY GRASSWREN

SPOTTED PARDALOTE *Pardalotus punctatus* 8–10 cm

Other names: Diamondbird, Yellow-rumped Pardalote.
Male: *upperparts black, prominently spotted white; eyebrow white; rump chestnut/red; throat/under tail-coverts rich yellow.* **Female:** duller; spots cream; no yellow on throat. **Immature:** like female; duller. **Race *xanthopygus*, 'Yellow-rumped Pardalote':** *rump golden.* Singles, pairs, family parties, autumn–winter companies; elusive in foliage; listen for calls, chipping sounds. **Similar species:** Striated and Forty-spotted Pardalotes. **Voice:** plaintive 'deedee' or high-pitched, 'sleep, deedee'; the 'sleep' clear, piping; the 'deedee' higher, descending; often with sharp extra 'peep'. **Habitat:** eucalypt forests, woodlands, scrubs, watercourses, golfcourses, parks, gardens. Race *xanthopygus*: mallee, mulga associations. **Breeds:** Sept.–Dec. **Nest:** globular; of bark-shreds, lined with grass; in burrow near top of bank, road-cutting, garden sandheap, fern-basket, brickwork. **Eggs:** 3–4 (5); oval, white. **Range and Status:** e. Aust. from Atherton Tableland (Q) to Tas., w. to se. SA–Mt Lofty Ras.; coastal sw. WA, w. and s. of Stirling Ra. NP–Northam–Jurien Bay. Race *xanthopygus*: s. inland NSW, c. and nw. Vic., s.–c. SA, Kangaroo I., w. SA and Gt Victoria Desert into WA to Stirling Ra. NP–Tambellup. Common. Migratory; seasonally nomadic.

FORTY-SPOTTED PARDALOTE *Pardalotus quadragintus* 9–10 cm

Plain olive–green above; paler, greyer below. Note *yellow–olive face and under tail-coverts; wing-coverts/flight feathers black, prominently spotted white on tips.* Singles, pairs, parties: feeds on lerps/manna in high foliage, difficult to observe. **Similar species:** Spotted Pardalote. **Voice:** double piping note in monotone, like Spotted, but harsher. **Habitat:** drier eucalypt forests, especially Manna ('White') Gum, *Eucalyptus viminalis*. **Breeds:** Aug.–Dec. **Nest:** shreds, strips of stringy bark; lined with grass, fur, feathers; in tree-hollow, 1–20 m high; sometimes in burrow. **Eggs:** 4; roundish, white. **Range and Status:** now confined to coastal se. Tas.: South Bruny I. n. to Maria I., adjacent Hobart environs, especially Tinderbox Pen., s. of Kingston. Rare, local. Sedentary; young dispersive. Endangered.

RED-BROWED PARDALOTE *Pardalotus rubricatus* 11–12 cm

Pale pardalote with large bill. *Crown black with large white spots; eyebrow orange then deep buff; broad golden-buff wingstreak.* **Immature:** duller. Singles, pairs: tends to feed high. **Voice:** 5 whistled notes: two slow and rising, three quicker and higher; or one slow, followed by five quicker, higher notes. **Habitat:** drier eucalypt woodlands, scrublands; tall mulga and other acacias; gums on watercourses. **Breeds:** July–Sept. in s.; March–April in n. **Nest:** globular or cup-shaped, compact; of bark-strips, lined with grass; in tunnel. **Eggs:** 2–3; rounded, dull white. **Range and Status:** coastal n. and inland Aust., s. on e. coast to c. Rockhampton (Q); s. inland to Mitchell (Q); nw. NSW, s. and e. to Brewarrina–Hillston–Broken Hill; n. SA, s. to Flinders Ras.–Gawler Ras.–Gt Victoria Desert; in WA, to w. coast from Gascoyne R., n. to Kimberley region. Fairly common; scarce in e. Q. Nomadic.

STRIATED PARDALOTE *Pardalotus striatus* 9.5–11.5 cm

Other names: Pickwick, Wittachew, Chip-chip.
Crown plain black or streaked white (see plate for racial differences); white eyebrow starts with bold rich yellow mark; white wing streak starts with red or yellow spot. Females duller. Immature crown plain or lightly scalloped. **Similar species:** Spotted, Red-browed Pardalotes. **Voice:** sharp 'chip-chip', 'pick-it-up', 'wittachew'; stuttered 'pretty-de-Dick' or 'wdididup'. Flat hard trill; soft 'cheeoo' or 'pee-ew, pee-ew'. **Habitat:** eucalypt forests, woodlands, scrublands; river red gums; mallee, mulga, other dry scrubs; rainforests, mangroves, roadsides, golfcourses, parks, gardens. **Breeds:** June–Feb. **Nest:** globular, of bark fibre, rootlets, fine grass; in tree hollow, 3–25 m high; tunnel in creekbank, road-cutting; mid-section of tall bank; cracks in brickwork, weatherboards; disused nest of Fairy Martin. **Eggs:** 2–5; white, oval. **Range and Status:** Aust., Tas., coastal islands. Nominate race: breeds Tas., Bass Strait islands: migrates to mainland se. Aust. (March–Oct.) Race *substriatus*: Aust. mostly w. of Divide; incl. Kangaroo I., SA; to w. coast WA, n. to Pilbara; nomadic inland autumn–winter, except driest deserts. Race *ornatus*: se. Aust.; e. Vic., occasional se. SA; e. NSW; winter migrant to NSW–Q. Race *melanocephalus*: from Hunter R. (NSW) to ne. Q, w. to Barcaldine. Sedentary. Race *uropygialis*: n. Aust., from C. York Pen. (Q) to Kimberley (WA). Common. Sedentary.

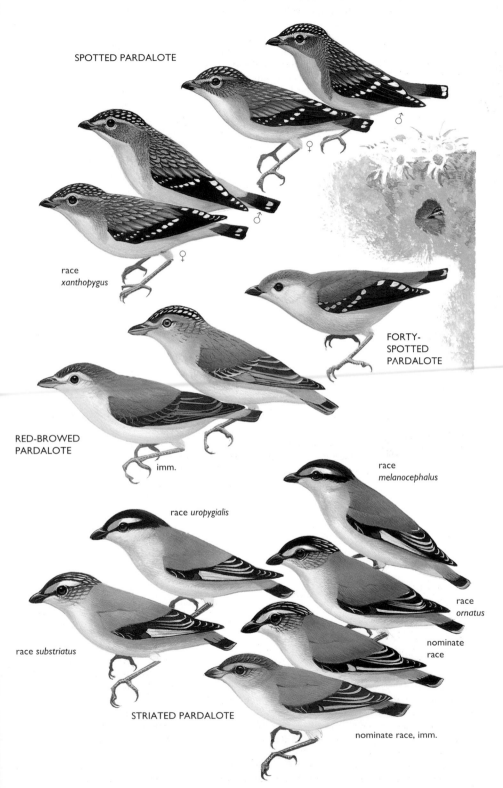

SPOTTED PARDALOTE

♂

♀

♂

race
xanthopygus

♀

FORTY-
SPOTTED
PARDALOTE

RED-BROWED
PARDALOTE

imm.

race
melanocephalus

race *uropygialis*

race
ornatus

race *substriatus*

nominate
race

STRIATED PARDALOTE

nominate race, imm.

EASTERN BRISTLEBIRD *Dasyornis brachypterus* 20–22 cm

Other name: Brown Bristlebird.

Slight pale eyebrow over red eye; *upperparts dark olive–brown; pale chestnut wash on short rounded wings; tail longish, feathers graduated*; throat/underparts pale grey to brown *with indistinct large pale grey spots or scallops on breast*. Heard more often than seen; moves quietly and quickly through dense heath and grass tussocks, along logs, *tail mostly horizontal, or when excited, raised, sometimes fanned*; in spring, calls as it forages. Most flights short and low. **Similar species:** Rufous Bristlebird; Rufous Scrub-bird; Pilotbird. **Voice:** loud, high-pitched, melodious and silvery: common phrase sounds like 'sweet, bijou' repeated at *c.* 5 second intervals for over 1 minute; of sweet but strangely penetrating quality; ends in something of a whipcrack. Also chattering, staccato, squeaky silvery notes, like fairy-wren but brighter, higher pitched. **Habitat:** coastal woodlands, dense scrubs and heathlands, especially where low heathland borders taller woodland or dense tall tea-tree. In McPherson Ras. (Q), heathy country above 600 m and open areas with gullies and ridges vegetated with dense *Poa* tussocks, near tall open eucalypt woodland, rainforest. Fire makes habitat unsuitable in short term but probably necessary for long-term (9+ years) optimal conditions (Bramwell et al, 1992). **Breeds:** Aug.–Oct. **Nest:** domed; of sticks, bark and grass; in low tussock, near ground. **Eggs:** 2; buff–white, with irregular fine blotchings of red–brown to purplish brown, zoned at large end. **Range and Status:** coastal se. Aust.: scattered, isolated populations, from *c.* Marlo (e. Vic.) (and possibly w. Gippsland) to Cooloola NP and Conondale Ra., *c.* 100 km n. of Brisbane (Q). Rare, local. Sedentary. Vulnerable.

WESTERN BRISTLEBIRD *Dasyornis longirostris* 17–20 cm

Other name: Brown Bristlebird.

Like a small Eastern Bristlebird but *more scalloped or dappled pale grey*. Usually in pairs: walks or hops slowly, with short, fast dashes; active, pecks at ground, digs with bill. Pokes under leaves, sweeps leaves aside with bill. Tail mostly horizontal; elevated in alarm. When running, wings droop. Usually flies only in response to sudden disturbance, rarely more than 10–20 m, skimming vegetation, tail partly or fully fanned (Smith, 1987). **Similar species:** Noisy Scrub-bird. **Voice:** quick, clear, silvery 'chip-pee-tee-peetle-pet'; differing between individuals, sex, location. Contact call: soft 'chip'; louder 'zit'. When flushed, high-pitched alarm-call: 'zeeat' (Smith, 1987). **Habitat:** dense, low, closed coastal heaths; open heaths with dense clumps of shrubs, eucalypt thickets; tall swampy heaths. Much reduced by fire, draining for agriculture, but may need fire for optimal status over 5–10+ years. **Breeds:** Aug.–Oct. **Nest:** large, loose, globular, with side-entrance; of twigs, wiry grass, leaves; low in grass, shrub, under cover. **Eggs:** 2; dull brownish white, blotched, freckled purplish brown, most at large end. **Range and Status:** s. WA: formerly from Albany coastally n. to near Perth. Now confined to Two Peoples Bay NR–Waychinnicup R., e. of Albany; Fitzgerald R. NP near Hopetoun (WA). Sedentary. Endangered.

RUFOUS BRISTLEBIRD *Dasyornis broadbenti* 24–27 cm

Largest bristlebird: *rich rufous cap and 'ear-mufflers'* contrast with olive–grey upperparts; wings washed rufous; underparts *distinctly scalloped pale grey*. Shy, elusive, inquisitive; more often heard than seen; *runs swiftly; alarmed, raises, spreads longish full tail*. **Similar species:** Eastern Bristlebird; female Common Blackbird. **Voice:** 3 or 4 clear, penetrating, silvery notes rising in quick succession, ending with double whip-like crack; last 3 often echoed by female: 'chip, chip, chip, chewee', or with softer 'chew-a'. Variations: 'chip, chip, chip, chip-choowee' or 'chit, chit, chit, chit, chewee-wit'; short, sharp alarm-call. **Habitat:** coastal scrubs and thickets; gullies with rank growth of sword-grass, blackberries, etc.; undergrowth in gullies in temperate rainforest. **Breeds:** Aug.–Oct. **Nest:** largish, untidy, domed; of thin twigs; usually in small tea-tree, clump of sword-grass 0.5–2 m high. **Eggs:** 2; whitish, heavily, uniformly freckled red and purplish. **Range and Status:** from mouth of Murray R. (SA), e. along coast to Ironbark Basin near Torquay (Vic.); ranges varying distances inland in suitable habitat, e.g. Terang–Colac (Vic.). Fairly common. Local. Sedentary. Until recent decades, w. race *litoralis* was found from C. Naturaliste–C. Leeuwin (far sw. WA); possibly now extinct.

EASTERN
BRISTLEBIRD

WESTERN
BRISTLEBIRD

RUFOUS
BRISTLEBIRD

ROCK WARBLER *Origma solitaria* 12–14 cm

Other names: Cataract-bird, Cavebird, Hanging Dick, Origma.

The only bird confined to NSW. Somewhat like a scrubwren; *olive–grey–brown above, washed rufous, especially on rump*; tail black; *throat grey; breast and underparts plain rich reddish rufous.* **Immature:** throat tinged tawny. Solitary pairs, family parties: active, restless; flicks tail sideways; hops swiftly over rocks; creeps mouse-like into crevices. **Similar species:** Pilotbird. **Voice:** highly vocal; shrill, melancholy call described as 'good-bye', uttered three or four times; shorter, high-pitched variation of this, uttered intermittently; rasping but slightly liquid note; harsh scolding. **Habitat:** wooded, rocky hillsides; gullies; cliffs and caves in weatherbeaten sandstone and limestone; usually near water; sometimes suburban gardens. **Breeds:** Aug.–Dec. **Nest:** bulky ragged hanging mass, tapered at both ends; with side-entrance; of root and bark fibre, moss and grasses bound with spiders' web; suspended from sloping wall or roof of shaded cave, overhanging rock, stalactite; or in road culvert, mineshaft, house verandah, shed, wire-mattress. **Eggs:** 3; glossy, usually pure white. **Range and Status:** confined to Hawkesbury sandstone and adjoining limestone areas in se. NSW, from *c.* Budawang NP near Milton on s. coast to Sydney region, n. to Upper Hunter R., inland in Blue Mts to Kanangra Boyd NP, w. to Wombeyan Caves–Tuglow–Bungonia, and nw. to Denman–Merriwa, inland to Munghorn Gap NR, near Mudgee. Fairly common. Sedentary.

PILOTBIRD *Pycnoptilus floccosus* 16.5–17.5 cm

Forehead to breast rich buff with slight scaly pattern; eye red; *tail usually carried high, flicked up and down.* Feeds mostly on ground; hopping briskly; when disturbed, moves quickly, rat-like, through dense undergrowth. Flight not strong but at times forages up into trees. Unusual name arises from habit, regular at least in Sherbrooke Forest (Vic.), of accompanying foraging Superb Lyrebirds, like pilotfish with shark, snapping up soil-invertebrates they uncover. **Similar species:** Rock Warbler. **Voice:** piercing and sweet, not unlike a bristlebird. Male: silvery, far-carrying 'ee-see-a-week', and similar notes; answered by female: 'whit-a, whit-ee' or 'qui-wit-tui-wit-tee'; often imitated by Superb Lyrebird; also softer notes, 'tui-wit', etc. **Habitat:** leaf-litter, ferns, sword-grass, wire-grass, fallen logs of temperate rainforest, wet eucalypt forest, and alpine and drier coastal woodland; gardens adjacent to forests. **Breeds:** Aug.–Dec. **Nest:** like miniature lyrebird's; untidy, globular with side-entrance; of strips of bark, dead leaves, rootlets; on or near ground among fallen branches, sword-grass, ferns. **Eggs:** 2; largish, short and swollen; green to dark grey, smoky brown or rich purple–brown, with darker zone at large end. **Range and Status:** patchily distributed in forests and dense scrubs in coastal and highland areas of Gt Dividing Ra. from Dandenong Ras.–Wilsons Prom. (Vic.) inland to Brindabella Ra. (ACT); n. to n. Blue Mts, Heathcote NP and Royal NP, s. of Sydney (NSW). Mostly on ranges and in denser coastal forests from sea-level to *c.* 500 m, but one record at 1550 m in Kosciusko NP (Cooper, 1990). Fairly common. Sedentary.

ROCK WARBLER

PILOTBIRD

SCRUBTIT *Acanthornis magnus* 11–11.5 cm

Slightly curved bill, grey–brown face/ear-coverts, pale eye, pale eye-ring; white tips to secondaries; white throat/upperbreast. Shy, inconspicuous; moves mouse-like, hops up tree-trunks, like treecreeper. **Similar species:** Tasmanian Scrubwren. **Voice:** 'to-wee-to'; pleasant whistling. **Habitat:** undergrowth of temperate rainforests, fern-gullies; on King I., paperbarks. **Breeds:** Sept.–Dec. **Nest:** domed; of bark-strips, grass, leaves, treefern fibre, green moss, lichen; among ferns, low shrub, blackberries. **Eggs:** 3–4; white, finely freckled dull red, red–brown. **Range and Status:** Tas.; widespread except drier e. coast; on King I., sparse in suitable habitat. Fairly common. Sedentary.

WHITE-BROWED SCRUBWREN *Sericornis frontalis* 11–13 cm

Other name: Spotted Scrubwren.

Male: *blackish mask; cream eye; white eyebrow and bold curving silver–white whisker-mark; rufous rump; variable dark tail-band.* **Female:** duller, mask browner. **Immature:** duller. Pairs, parties: fussy; hops briskly on ground, logs, undergrowth; scolds intruders; tame in gardens. **Similar species:** Tasmanian, Tropical Scrubwrens; Thornbills. **Voice:** clear, sustained 'tseer-tseer-tseer', or 'seat-you, seat-you', etc.; deep zizzing scolding, at intruders, cuckoos, snakes. **Habitat:** undergrowth of forests, woodlands, scrubs, from sea-level to above snowline: riverside thickets; heaths; bracken, saltmarsh, mangroves; parks, gardens. Race *maculatus*: mallee, mulga, saltbush. **Breeds:** June–Dec.; communally. **Nest:** domed of loose grass, twigs, fine roots, leaves; in bank; roots; undergrowth, sword-grass, tussock; hanging tin, coat in outhouse. **Eggs:** 2–3; stout oval; grey–white to pale buff; blotched, spotted dull brown/purplish brown. **Range and Status:** coastal e., s., sw. Aust. Race *laevigaster*: coastal ne. Aust., from Cairns–Atherton Tableland (Q) to ne. NSW. Nominate race: mainland se. Aust., w. to Adelaide region (SA). Race *maculatus*: coastally w. from Kangaroo Is. and Spencer Gulf (SA), to s. WA, inland to *c.* L. Grace–Narrogin–Moora. Common. Sedentary.

TASMANIAN SCRUBWREN *Sericornis humilis* 12–14 cm

Other name: Brown Scrubwren.

Like White-browed Scrubwren but larger, plainer, browner below. **Range and Status:** Tas.; Flinders, King and other islands in Tas. region. Common. Sedentary.

YELLOW-THROATED SCRUBWREN *Sericornis citreogularis* 12–15 cm

Male: *eye red–brown in black mask; long white-to-yellow eyebrow; prominent yellow throat; legs pink, longish.* **Female:** duller; mask brown. Singles, pairs: hops briskly on leaf mould, tracks. **Voice:** strong sweet song, includes mimicry; alarm call: sharp 'tick'. **Habitat:** gloomy understorey of coastal/mountain rainforests, woodlands, vegetated gullies; often near water. **Breeds:** July–March. **Nest:** domed, pendulous; of blackish rootlets, palm-fibre, skeleton-leaves, twigs, ferns, mosses, lichen. Hung from twig, vine in dark place, over water, track. **Eggs:** 2–3; glossy, pink to chocolate–brown, with shadowy zones. **Range and Status:** (1) highlands between Cooktown–Townsville (ne. Q), inland to Atherton–Ravenshoe. (2) coastal se. Q–NSW, from Cooroy–Bunya Mts (Q) s. to Illawarra region. Common. Sedentary.

FERNWREN *Oreoscopus gutturalis* 13–15 cm

Note distinctive white eyebrow/throat, separated by brown mask, margined below by black 'bib'. **Immature:** plainer, browner. Pairs hop, bow, elevate short tails, flick leaves with bills. **Voice:** penetrating whistle; harsh scolding; high 'chips'. **Habitat:** leaf-litter under ferns, undergrowth in mountain rainforests. **Breeds:** June–Nov. **Nest:** large, domed; of rootlets, twigs, skeleton leaves, moss, lichen; under overhanging bank, cave amid ferns, mosses; in dark place. **Eggs:** 2; oval, white, finely spotted chestnut, tan. **Range and Status:** highlands of ne. Q above *c.* 600 m (Blakers et al, 1984), from *c.* Cooktown s. to Mt Spec. Fairly common. Sedentary.

SCRUBTIT

WHITE-BROWED SCRUBWREN

race
laevigaster

♂ nominate
race

race
maculatus

♀

TASMANIAN
SCRUBWREN

YELLOW-THROATED
SCRUBWREN

♀

♂

FERN WREN

imm.

♂

♀

LARGE-BILLED SCRUBWREN *Sericornis magnirostris* 11.5–13 cm

Longish straight bill seemingly inclined upwards; large, dark red eye stands out in plain, pale buff face; rump/base of tail washed rufous. Pairs, parties; behaves like thornbill: climbs acrobatically on vines, trunks, branches; flutters high in foliage, infrequently descends to forest-floor. **Similar species:** Atherton Scrubwren: face less buff; habits more terrestrial. **Voice:** penetrating scrubwren call: 's-cheer, s-cheer, s-cheer, s-cheer'; mimics White-browed, Yellow-throated, Brown Thornbill, etc. Foraging parties utter fussy, zigzag, thornbill-like chittering. **Habitat:** tropical, temperate rainforests, from sea level to *c.* 1500 m. **Breeds:** July–Jan. **Nest:** domed; loose, of bark-fibre, grass, moss; in creeper, among twigs; usurps nests of Yellow-throated Scrubwren, Brown Gerygone. **Eggs:** 3–4; dull white to pale purplish brown with pale streaks, fine spots, in cap at large end. **Range and Status:** coastal e. Aust., from Kinglake NP, ne. of Melbourne (Vic.) to near Cooktown (Q); inland to *c.* Tenterfield (NSW)–Chinchilla (Q). In se. Aust., n. to *c.* Shoalwater Bay (Q) from sea-level to *c.* 1000 m. From *c.* Eungella NP n. to near Cooktown, mostly in highland rainforests (Blakers et al, 1984). Sedentary.

ATHERTON SCRUBWREN *Sericornis keri* 13.5 cm

Larger and *greyer* than Large-billed Scrubwren: *olive–brown of upperparts extends over forehead and face; tail more reddish brown at base;* darker below; central breast and belly *yellowish*. Forages lower in trees and on ground, in contrast to fluttering arboreal behaviour of Large-billed. **Voice:** quiet 'sip sip sip'; small chatterings. **Habitat:** understorey of mountain rainforests. **Breeds:** Oct.–Dec. **Nest:** domed; of dried plant material, skeleton leaves; lined with feathers; in bank among grass, ferns. **Eggs:** 2; like White-browed Scrubwren. **Range and Status:** rainforests of Atherton Tableland (Q) above 600 m. Uncommon. Sedentary.

TROPICAL SCRUBWREN *Sericornis beccarii* 11.5 cm

Other name: Little Scrubwren.

Note range; orange–scarlet eye: eyebrow broken; blackish mask reduced to 'scorched' area before eye; black-and-white chevrons on wing; white tips to wing-coverts form two lines; rump cinnamon, no tail-band; legs long, pink. **Female:** duller. Race *dubius:* plainer; cinnamon–buff, with fainter facial markings. Pairs, parties: fossicks among dead leaves/debris on ground or high among vines, leaf-masses. **Voice:** like White-browed Scrubwren, contact call 'wit-wit'; small chatterings. **Habitat:** rainforests, monsoon forests, vine-scrubs on watercourses. **Breeds:** Oct.–Jan. **Nest:** domed; of leaves, rootlets, lined with feathers; suspended in hanging roots on creekbanks, dead leaves in bushes, vines. **Eggs:** 2–3; faint reddish brown, with light brown fleecy markings on large end. **Range and Status:** C. York Pen. (Q), s. to Archer R., Coen and Rocky R. Race *minimus* occupies n. part of the range; merges with *dubius c.* Iron Ra.–Lockhart R. on e. coast and Wenlock–Watson–Archer Rs. in w. Common. Sedentary. Also PNG.

REDTHROAT *Pyrrholaemus brunneus* 11.5 cm

Soberly coloured; *face/underparts plain grey.* **Male:** *small rusty throat-mark.* **Female:** whitish from bill to eye; grey–white throat. Usually in pairs: shy; forages on ground; disappears hopping mouse-like into cover; emerges to inspect intruder, or flies, *showing largish black, white-tipped tail.* Breeding males sing conspicuously; this and Shy Heathwren are the sweetest singers of inland scrubs. **Similar species:** Inland Thornbill: streaked breast; reddish rump. Slaty-backed Thornbill: dark-streaked crown; pale chestnut rump. **Voice:** rich, canary-like song, 'jur-jerrig-jerriganee, a pitta-pitta-pit'; from top of cypress pine, mulga, mallee; mimics. **Habitat:** inland scrubs, mulga, other acacias; mallee-associations, with spinifex; eucalypt regrowth; tea-tree, saltbush, bluebush. **Breeds:** Aug.–Nov. **Nest:** globular; of bark-strips, grass; in low shrub, spinifex, occasionally in tree hollow, lizard-burrow. **Eggs:** 3–4; purplish brown, darker at large end. **Range and Status:** inland Aust. from near Winton (Q), w. across s. NT and s. to Balranald (NSW)–nw. Vic.–Murray mallee (SA); w. to L. Grace–Moora (WA), thence coastally n. to Pilbara. Uncommon. Sedentary.

LARGE-BILLED
SCRUBWREN

ATHERTON
SCRUBWREN

TROPICAL
SCRUBWREN

nominate
race

♀

♂

race *dubius*

♀

♂

REDTHROAT

CHESTNUT-RUMPED HEATHWREN *Hylacola pyrrhopygia* 13.5–14 cm

Dark, cock-tailed: *unstreaked grey–brown above with pale eyebrow, chestnut rump; black band on outer tail-feathers, white tips.* **Female:** duller. **Immature:** buffer. Singles, pairs: shy; hops briskly. In flight, note rump/tail markings. **Similar species:** Shy Heathwren, Striated Fieldwren. **Voice:** melodious song; swells until air rings; skilled mimic; duets; harsh 'zeet'. **Habitat:** heathy woodlands, scrublands; box/ironbark forests. **Breeds:** July–Nov. **Nest:** globular, untidy; of grass, rootlets, bark-strips; on ground, in grass, low shrub. **Eggs:** 3; salmon-pink, freckled, blotched brown. **Range and Status:** coastal se. Aust., from se. Q to se. SA; inland to Warrumbungle NP–Narrandera (NSW), Rutherglen–Inglewood–n. Grampians NP (Vic.); in SA isolate population, s. Flinders Ras.–Mt Lofty Ras.–Fleurieu Pen. Uncommon. Sedentary.

SHY HEATHWREN *Hylacola cauta* 11.5–14 cm

Other names: Mallee Heathwren.
Paler, *with bold white eyebrow; black-and-white chevron on wing; rump fiery-chestnut; tail boldly black/white; underparts whiter with conspicuous black streaks.* **Immature:** plainer; fawn below. Pairs, parties: bounces over ground, tail cocked. **Voice:** sweet 'chee-chee-chick-a-dee'; mimics. **Habitat:** mallee, cypress pine, heathy banksia/tea-tree. **Breeds:** July–Nov. **Nest:** like Chestnut-rumped; at foot of mallee, shrub, tussock. **Eggs:** 3; oval; olive–grey with underlying dark spots in zone. **Range and Status:** mallee areas of w. NSW–nw. Vic.–se. SA (and Kangaroo I.), n. to s. Flinders Ras.–Gawler Ras.; in s. WA, n. to Kalgoorlie–Murchison R.; *except* w. of Dongara–Stirling Ras. NP. Uncommon. Sedentary.

STRIATED FIELDWREN *Calamanthus fuliginosus* 12.5–14 cm

Other names: Cocktail, Fieldlark, Reedlark, Sandplain-Wren.
Greenish buff with paler eybrow and throat, buff lores, face and flanks; bold dark streaks above/below; cocks short, dark-banded, pale-tipped tail. Shy: hops, runs on ground. Sings from shrubs, tussocks, fence-wires; dives to cover. **Similar species:** Chestnut-rumped Heathwren. **Voice:** spirited 'whirr-whirr-chick-chick-whirr-ree-ree'. **Habitat:** low shrubs, tussocks, swamp-fringes, saltmarsh; alpine, coastal heaths; dune-vegetation. **Breeds:** July–Dec. **Nest:** domed; of grass, plant-stems; on/near ground, in tussock, sedge, shrub. **Eggs:** 3–4; buff/light chestnut; freckled darker, blotched rufous, chestnut. **Range and Status:** coastal se. Aust. and Tas.: from nw. of Sydney, through s. coast NSW, e. and s. Vic., inland to Gt Divide–Grampians NP, w. to *c.* L. Alexandrina (SA). Also Tas., Flinders I., King I. Uncommon. Sedentary.

RUFOUS FIELDWREN *Calamanthus campestris* 13 cm

Like Striated but *grey–brown above, washed buff on forehead/face; off-white below, with finer dark streaks; some w. populations nearly fox-red on crown/rump.* **Similar species:** Shy Heathwren, Grasswrens. **Voice:** like Striated. **Habitat:** inland/saltmarsh vegetation: saltbush, bluebush, spinifex, roly-poly; low shrubs in depressions in gibber plains. **Breeds:** July–Nov. **Nest:** globular, of grass, lined with feathers, plant-down; in tussock, shrub, spinifex. **Eggs:** 3–4; buff to brown, freckled chestnut/dark brown. **Range and Status:** populations from sw. Q–far w. NSW–far nw. Vic., w. through SA to s. WA, n. to NW Cape and Gt Sandy Desert, *except* sw. corner. Uncommon, patchy. Sedentary.

SPECKLED WARBLER *Chthonicola sagittata* 11.5–12.5 cm

Male: *crown black, streaked buff; black line over long whitish eyebrow; dark red eye stands out in pale face; underparts cream with bold black streaks.* **Female:** chestnut streak in eyebrow. Pairs, with thornbills, etc.: hops over ground, logs, trunks; 'freezes'. Flies showing black tail-band, white tip. **Voice:** sweet song with mimicry; rasping scolding. **Habitat:** drier woodlands with tussocks, branches, rocks; in Q, mulga, brigalow, vine scrubs. **Breeds:** Aug.–Jan. **Nest:** domed, of grass, bark-shreds, moss, lined with fur; on ground, low shrub, tree-trunk. **Eggs:** 3–4; chocolate–red; with shadowy zone. **Range and Status:** se. Aust., on and inland of Divide e. to Brisbane; from inland of Mackay (Q), to w. Vic., *c.* Grampians NP–Harrow. Uncommon; patchy. Sedentary.

CHESTNUT-RUMPED
HEATHWREN

SHY HEATHWREN

STRIATED FIELDWREN

RUFOUS FIELDWREN

SPECKLED WARBLER

357

BROWN GERYGONE *Gerygone mouki* 9–11 cm

Other name: Brown Warbler.

Widespread se. race *richmondi: long grey–white eyebrow, pale grey face/breast; buff-washed flanks;* eye red–brown. Nominate race (ne. Q): browner, foreneck buffer. Pairs, parties: incessantly active, vocal; flutters around foliage high to low; snaps flying insects, *shows broad blackish subterminal tail-band, with large white spots near tips.* **Voice:** atypical: brisk, incessant 'which-is-it'; 'diddle-it-did-it'. **Habitat:** wet coastal/mountain rainforests, vegetated gullies, mangroves. **Breeds:** Aug.–Feb. **Nest:** hooded, with tapering tail; of rootlets, bark-fibre, spiders' web, moss, lichens; suspended from low twig, vine. **Eggs:** 3; whitish, speckled red–brown. **Range and Status:** coastal e. Aust., from *c.* Sale (Vic.) to near Cooktown (Q); n. from Tully (Q) above *c.* 250 m. Canberra, Sydney Botanic Gardens (Blakers et al, 1984). Common. Sedentary.

LARGE-BILLED GERYGONE *Gerygone magnirostris* 10.5–11.5 cm

Other names: Floodbird, Large-billed Warbler.

Heavy bill; red–brown eye; white spot at bill; fine white eyelids; olive–brown above; buff sides to breast; dark subterminal tail-band with faint white spots. Singles, pairs: climbs in, flutters around foliage. **Voice:** descending, lilting reel; each set of 3–4 notes flicks up at end, falls again. **Habitat:** rainforest, paperbarks on streams; eucalypt woodlands, mangroves, gardens. **Breeds:** Sept.–April. **Nest:** hooded, with ragged tail (like flood-debris); of grass, rootlets, leaves, plant-fibre, spiders' web; hung from vine, branch over stream, swamp; often near paper wasp nest. **Eggs:** 2–3; whitish, freckled red–brown. **Range and Status:** coastal n. Aust., and islands, from *c.* Mackay (Q) to w. Kimberley (WA). Common. Sedentary. Also PNG.

MANGROVE GERYGONE *Gerygone levigaster* 11 cm

White line from bill curves over reddish eye; blackish lower half of tail with large white spot near tips of outer feathers. **Immature:** yellowish eyelids, wash on throat. Singles, pairs, parties: forages in mangrove foliage; hovers. **Similar species:** Brown Gerygone, Western Gerygone. **Voice:** sweet, fugitive 'falling-leaf'; more declamatory than Western. **Habitat:** mangroves, coastal woodlands, gardens. **Breeds:** Sept.–March in se.; most months in n. **Nest:** globular, hooded, wispy tail; of grass, bark-fibre, spiders' web, in mangrove to 5 m high. **Eggs:** 3; pink–white, freckled red–brown. **Range and Status:** coastal n. and e. Aust. from Derby (WA) to *c.* Newcastle (NSW). Casual Botany Bay (Hoskin, 1991). Common. Sedentary.

DUSKY GERYGONE *Gerygone tenebrosa* 11–13 cm

Largest gerygone: eyes straw–white; curving white line from bill over eye; white eyelids; no obvious tail-marks. **Immature:** eye honey-coloured; throat/flanks washed yellow. Elusive in mangroves. **Similar species:** Mangrove Gerygone, Western Gerygone. **Voice:** slow, thoughtful 'chew chew chew wee'; 'chif chif choowet', like whistler. **Habitat:** mangroves, nearby swampland, creekside scrub. **Breeds:** Sept.–March. **Nest:** domed; of bark-fibre, spiders' web; in mangrove. **Eggs:** 2; white, spotted red–brown. **Range and Status:** coastal nw. WA, from nw. Kimberley to Shark Bay, *except* where mangroves absent. Present L. Macleod, n. of Carnarvon (Smith & Johnstone, 1985). Common. Sedentary.

WESTERN GERYGONE *Gerygone fusca* 10–11 cm

Note faint white eyebrow, whitish underparts; tail white at base with broad blackish subterminal tail-band, white spots near tips. **Immature:** eye cream to brown; *yellow wash on throat, breast.* **Similar species:** Brown, Dusky, Mangrove Gerygones. **Habitat:** drier open forests, woodlands; coastal inland eucalypt; mulga, other acacia scrubs. **Voice:** sweet, elfin, silvery 'falling leaf melody' that seems to finish before end. **Breeds:** Aug.–Nov. **Nest:** globular, hooded, tail wispy; of fine grass, bark-fibre, spiders' web; in outer foliage up to 10 m. **Eggs:** 2–3; pink–white, blotched, speckled red–brown. **Range and Status:** three discrete populations across e., c. and w. Aust.: e. to near coast between *c.* Rockhampton (Q) and Sydney (NSW); s. coast (Vic.); w. coast from *c.* Esperance–NW Cape (WA). Common s. WA; sparse elsewhere. Sedentary; nomadic; often far beyond stated limits, e.g. Broome (WA). Also s. PNG.

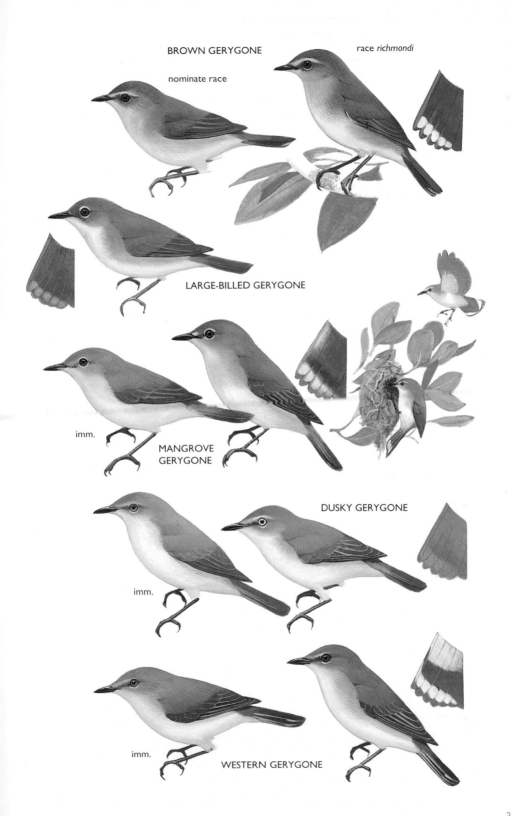

BROWN GERYGONE

nominate race

race *richmondi*

LARGE-BILLED GERYGONE

imm.

MANGROVE
GERYGONE

DUSKY GERYGONE

imm.

imm.　WESTERN GERYGONE

GREEN-BACKED GERYGONE *Gerygone chloronotus* 9–10 cm

Crown/cheeks grey with no eyebrow; eye red; upperparts/rump greyish olive–green; underparts white with lemon wash on flanks; tail plain grey–brown. Singles, pairs: shy, but present in gardens in Darwin and elsewhere. Actions like other gerygones; forages in middle canopy; hovers around outer foliage. **Similar species:** White-throated Gerygone: yellow breast. Lemon-bellied Flycatcher: bill shorter, broader; underparts yellower; song differs. **Voice:** slighter than other gerygone-songs. **Habitat:** tall dense vegetation, especially near water and on scrubby escarpments: monsoon and heavy mixed forests; bamboo-thickets, paperbark-swamps, mangroves, eucalypt forest; large fig trees, gardens. **Breeds:** Oct.–April. **Nest:** domed, globular, with side-entrance; suspended from leafy branch. **Eggs:** 2–3; whitish with fine red–brown freckles. **Range and Status:** coastal, subcoastal nw. Aust., from Top End (NT), incl. Groote Eylandt–Melville I. and other islands, to w. Kimberley–Broome (WA). Common. Sedentary. Also PNG, Aru Is.

FAIRY GERYGONE *Gerygone palpebrosa* 10–11.5 cm

Two distinctive Aust. races overlap and interbreed in ne. Q between *c.* Cooktown and Innisfail, becoming paler southwards. **Race** *personata*, '**Black-throated Warbler**': male: white spot before eye; *dull blackish throat/upperbreast; prominent white whisker-mark;* underparts fawn to lemon; little white in tail. Female: whitish throat merges into pale lemon breast; tail as above. Immature (both races): throat washed yellow. In overlap zone, some males have dull black throats. **Race** *flavida*: male: whitish spot on forehead; white whisker-mark; *black mark under chin;* centre of throat and underparts pale lemon; blackish subterminal tail-band, with *slight white tips*. Female: no dark mark under chin; indistinct whitish whisker-mark. Singles, pairs, parties: forages in outer foliage; hovers like other gerygones. **Similar species:** White-throated Gerygone: white throat; yellow breast; white spots in tail. Imm.: easily confused; look for adults. See also Green-backed Honeyeater. **Voice:** simple, animated undulating warble: less developed than White-throated. **Habitat:** edges of lowland rainforest, vine forest, leafy trees on watercourses; eucalypt woodland, scrubland; mangroves. **Breeds:** Sept.–March. **Nest:** globular, hooded, with wispy tail; of bark, plant-fibre, spiders' web; suspended from branch near, over water; often near paper wasp nest. **Eggs:** 2–3; pink–white, finely freckled, spotted red–brown. **Range and Status:** ne. Q and islands. Race *personata*: C. York Pen., s. to *c.* Atherton Tableland–Hartleys Creek on e. coast and Staaten R. on w. coast. Race *flavida*: coastally s. from *c.* Cairns–Atherton Tableland to near Rockhampton. Fairly common. Sedentary. Also PNG, Aru Is.

WHITE-THROATED GERYGONE *Gerygone olivacea* 10–11.5 cm

Other names: Bush or Native Canary.
Note white throat/clear yellow breast; red eye; upperparts buff–grey, tinged olive; tail blackish, *outer feathers white near base and with bold white spots near tips;* n. forms have less or no white in tail. **Immature:** throat *yellowish*. Singles, pairs: active in branchlets; switches body about, flirts tail; hovers outside foliage, *showing white in tail*. Usually discovered by charming song, especially when nesting. **Similar species:** Fairy Gerygone. **Voice:** oft-repeated beautiful, silvery 'falling-leaf' of song in minor key, with upward recovery towards end, tailing off. **Habitat:** trees, saplings in open forest, woodlands, lightly timbered hills; scrub, regrowth; trees on watercourses. **Breeds:** Sept.–Nov. **Nest:** globular, hooded, with wispy tail; of bark-fibre, grass, spider's web; hung in sapling, low to 15 m high. **Eggs:** 2–3; white, pink–white, heavily spotted, blotched, freckled red, red–purple; zone at large end. **Range and Status:** e. and n. Aust. Nominate race: C. York Pen. (Q) to w. Vic., inland to Augathella–Richmond (Q); Narrabri–Warrumbungle NP (NSW); sparse w. to Adelaide region (SA), with some breeding. Spring–summer breeding migrant (Sept.–April) to se. Aust.; winters mostly in Q. Race *rogersi*: Gulf lowlands (coastal nw. Q) through Top End (NT) to w. Kimberley (WA). Common to uncommon; patchy. Sedentary and/or migratory.

GREEN-BACKED GERYGONE

imm.

FAIRY GERYGONE

race
personata

imm.

♀

♂

race
flavida

imm.

♀

♂

WHITE-THROATED GERYGONE

imm.

MOUNTAIN THORNBILL *Acanthiza katherina* 10 cm

Bill large; eye yellow–white; indistinct fawn scalloping on forehead; upperparts grey–green; rump tawny; tail with dark outer band, pale tips. Underparts whitish; flanks yellow–buff. **Immature:** *duller; eye brown.* Pairs, parties: forages actively in rainforest foliage, paleness suggests a Gerygone. **Similar species:** no Gerygone in Q has pale eyes; calls differ. **Voice:** like Brown Thornbill's trill, 'drrrrrr', more musical, stronger, louder, clearer; common call is a descending 'tschewtschewtschew'. **Habitat:** mountain rainforests, wooded streams, above 450 m. **Breeds:** Sept.–Jan. **Nest:** bulky, domed; externally of green moss. **Eggs:** 2; white, finely spotted, blotched red–brown. **Range and Status:** highlands of ne. Q, from s. of Cooktown to Mt Spec near Townsville. Common. Sedentary.

TASMANIAN THORNBILL *Acanthiza ewingii* 10 cm

Like Brown Thornbill: bill shorter; forehead pale tan; *wing-feathers edged orange–chestnut; breast greyer, less streaked; underparts whiter; tail longer.* Habits like Brown Thornbill, but habitats denser, wetter. **Similar species:** Tasmanian Scrubwren; Scrubtit. **Voice:** like Brown Thornbill; typical call 'zit zit zit whoorl'. **Habitat:** forests, woodlands, scrubs. **Breeds:** Sept.–Jan. **Nest:** like Brown Thornbill, neater, more compact, with green moss. **Eggs:** 3–4; pinkish white, lightly freckled red–brown. **Range and Status:** Tas., coastal islands, King I. and Furneaux Group, Bass Strait. Common. Sedentary.

BROWN THORNBILL *Acanthiza pusilla* 10 cm

Varies geographically; warm brown to olive–brown above, flanks olive–buff to yellowish white. *All have buff scallops on forehead; large dark red eye; blackish arrow-streaks on grey throat/breast; rump/tail-base tawny; tail grey–brown with blackish subterminal band, paler tips.* Singles, pairs, family parties: fussily active; forages in lower branchlets, undergrowth; hangs, flutters. In flight, flirts tail. **Similar species:** Striated, Inland, Tasmanian Thornbills. **Voice:** deep, rolling 'pee-orr'; fussy squeaks, churrs; deep, zizzing scolding; alarm-call: high-pitched 'seee'. **Habitat:** understorey in rainforest; eucalypt forests, woodlands, scrubs; watercourse vegetation, bracken, wetland plants; dune-vegetation, mallee fringes, saltmarsh, mangroves, parks, gardens. **Breeds:** June–Dec. **Nest:** domed; of bark-shreds, grass, spiders' web and egg-sacs; low in undergrowth. **Eggs:** 3; whitish; blotched, freckled red–brown. **Range and Status:** se. Aust.: from Proserpine (Q) to Yorke Pen.–Kangaroo I. (SA). In Q, w. to *c.* Cracow–Toowoomba; in NSW, w. to *c.* Inverell–Warrumbungle NP–The Rock, w. in Murray Valley to *c.* Barham; all Vic., *except* nw. mallee; w. to se. SA–Mt Lofty Ras.; King I. and Tas. Common. Sedentary.

INLAND THORNBILL *Acanthiza apicalis* 9.5–11.5 cm

Greyer above, whiter below than Brown; forehead scalloped whitish; rump red–brown; tail-band wider, outer tail-feathers tipped white; often carries tail cocked. Inland birds pale; bill longer. In wetter sw. WA, darker, richer, like Brown. **Similar species:** Chestnut-rumped, Slaty-backed Thornbills. **Voice:** like Brown, but harsher; spirited territorial song; high-pitched 'see-see' contact-call. **Habitat:** dry scrubs, woodlands. In sw. WA, wetter forests, coastal scrubs, heaths, mangroves. **Breeds:** July–Dec. **Nest and Eggs:** like Brown Thornbill. **Range and Status:** complements Brown Thornbill: widespread inland Aust. nw. Vic., w. NSW; w. Q; w. to *c.* Mt Isa (Q)–Barkly Tableland (NT)–Gt Sandy Desert (WA); all WA s. of *c.* Tropic; all SA *except* se. Common. Sedentary, locally nomadic.

SLATY-BACKED THORNBILL *Acanthiza robustirostris* 9.5 cm

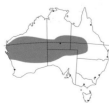

Dusky blue–grey above, crown streaked black; bill robust; eye red; underparts whitish, washed buff; rump tawny; tail blackish with pale tips. Pairs: forage in mulga foliage; mix with Inland Thornbills. **Similar species:** Inland, Chestnut-rumped Thornbills. **Voice:** 'see-see' contact-call; harsh 'thrip thrip' alarm-call. **Habitat:** dense mulga; herbage near salt lakes. **Breeds:** Aug.–Nov. **Nest:** domed, of grass, spiders' web; in mulga. **Eggs:** 3; white, faintly pink; finely speckled red–brown, in cap. **Range and Status:** w. inland Aust.: from *c.* Charleville (Q), w. through s. NT, s. to Everard–Musgrave Ras. (SA); to w. coast *c.* Geraldton–Carnarvon, n. inland to Peak Hill–Ophthalmia R., s. to Yalgoo–Broad Arrow. Uncommon. Sedentary.

MOUNTAIN THORNBILL

TASMANIAN THORNBILL

BROWN THORNBILL, pale

BROWN THORNBILL, dark

INLAND
THORNBILL

SLATY-BACKED THORNBILL

imm.

BUFF-RUMPED THORNBILL *Acanthiza reguloides* 11cm

Other names: Bark or Buff-rumped Tit, Varied Thornbill.

Plain olive–grey above, yellow–fawn below. *Note fine tan scallops on forehead, pale eye, caramel–buff rump, blackish, pale-tipped tail.* **Immature:** plainer; eye dark. Pairs, parties, autumn–winter companies: hops over ground, trunks, branches, foliage; flies bouncingly, flashing buff rumps. **Race** *squamata,* 'Varied Thornbill' (e. Q): *greener, rump/underparts yellower.* **Similar species:** Yellow-rumped, Slender-billed Thornbills. **Voice:** rapid musical tinkling on two levels: 'pitta-pitta-pit'; harder, higher-pitched than Yellow-rumped.

Habitat: untidy open stringybark forest, woodland, scrub, with fallen branches, tussocks, rocks; golfcourses. **Breeds:** communally, Aug.–Jan. **Nest:** untidy, domed; of grass, bark-fibre, spiders' web; under bark, debris in fork, fallen limbs, base of tree, tussock. **Eggs:** 4; whitish, freckled, streaked red–brown, spotted purplish lilac; in zone. **Range and Status:** e. and se. Aust.: race *squamata* e. Q from *c.* Atherton Tableland s. to *c.* Eungella NP; nominate race widespread in e. Aust. w. to Fleurieu Pen.–Mt Lofty Ras.–s. Flinders Ras. (SA). Uncommon; patchy. Sedentary.

WESTERN THORNBILL *Acanthiza inornata* 10 cm

Plainest thornbill: *note fine pale scallops on forehead/face and slightly warmer buff rump;* tail buff–brown with broad blackish subterminal band. Pairs, parties: forages in foliage, lower bushes and ground. **Similar species:** Slender-billed Thornbill: note habitat. **Voice:** quiet tinkling twitter; mimicry. **Habitat:** tall forests to open woodlands; coastal scrubs. **Breeds:** Sept.–Dec. **Nest:** domed; of grass, plant-stems/fibre, spiders' web; in bushy tree against trunk, tree-hollow, upright small branches of shrub, tree; under bark. **Eggs:** 3; flesh–white, freckled red–brown, zoned. **Range and Status:** sw. WA: from *c.* Hill R.–Moora s. and e. to Stirling Ras. NP. Common. Sedentary.

SLENDER-BILLED THORNBILL *Acanthiza iredalei* 9–10 cm

Other names: Dark or Samphire Thornbill.

Small variable thornbill: *bill small, black; eyes pale; fine black-and-white scalloping on forehead; tail blackish, with paler tips.* Birds w. of *c.* Port Augusta (SA): *palest; rumps off-white to pale yellow; underparts off-white; flanks tinged lemon; faint mottling on throat* (J. Matthew, 1994). Birds n. of Adelaide, around heads of Spencer/St Vincent Gulfs: *darker olive–grey; small buff rump; underparts grey–white; flanks washed olive–buff.* Birds in se. SA–w. Vic. heathlands: paler grey, flanks paler. Pairs, parties, autumn–winter companies: feeds on ground, low shrubs; flight low, bouncing; *rump contrasts with blackish tail.* **Similar species:** Buff-rumped Thornbill. **Voice:** tinny, rattling 'tsip tsip'. **Habitat:** low, dense saltbush, bluebush; cotton-bush (*Mairena* spp.); samphire on salt lakes, saltmarshes; low banksia, tea-tree, casuarina scrubs, sandplain-heaths; mulga, other acacias; mangroves. **Breeds:** Aug.–Nov. **Nest:** domed; of grass, plant-down; in low shrub. **Eggs:** 3; white, speckled red–brown, at large end. **Range and Status:** populations from Big/Little Deserts (w. Vic.); se. SA (n. to *c.* Pinnaroo–Tailem Bend); coastally n. from Adelaide to Port Augusta–Whyalla; w. through n. Eyre Pen.–Gawler Ras.; scattered in n. SA; w. through Nullarbor Plain s. of Transcontinental Railway; s. inland WA to w. coast *c.* Carnarvon–Shark Bay, avoids humid sw. WA. Local; uncommon. Sedentary, nomadic.

CHESTNUT-RUMPED THORNBILL *Acanthiza uropygialis* 10–11.5 cm

Plain, pale thornbill: *upperparts mouse-grey; forehead finely scalloped black and white; eye whitish; underparts whitish; rump pale chestnut; tail black with pale tips.* Pairs, small flocks: forages on ground, shrubs, low trees; flies bouncingly, *showing contrasting rump/tail.* Often with other thornbills, whitefaces. **Similar species:** Slate-backed Thornbill: bluer grey with fine dark streaks on crown; eye red. Brown/Inland Thornbills: dark eyes, streaked breasts. **Voice:** penetrating 'see-see'; far-carrying song of similar phrases, from tops of mulgas; double buzzing scold; 'tchik, tchik' flight-call. **Habitat:** drier woodlands, scrubs, thickets; saltbush, bluebush, lignum; open pastoral country; among dead trees, stumps. **Breeds:** July–Dec. **Nest:** domed; of grass, fur, feathers; in hollow stump, fence-post, tree-hollow; 1–15 m high. **Eggs:** 2–4; white, spotted red–brown. **Range and Status:** widespread s. inland and w. Aust., to s. coast w. from Yorke and Eyre Pens (SA); *absent from* humid sw. WA. Common. Sedentary.

BUFF-RUMPED THORNBILL

nominate race

imm.

imm.

race
squamata

WESTERN THORNBILL

SLENDER-BILLED THORNBILL

SA Gulf
form

imm.

CHESTNUT-RUMPED THORNBILL

YELLOW-RUMPED THORNBILL *Acanthiza chrysorrhoa* 11–13 cm

Largest thornbill: *eyebrow white; crown black, spotted white; eye pale; rump bright yellow.* Inland, nw. Q birds paler, greener; whiter below, washed yellow. Pairs, companies: hops on open ground, branches; teeters. Flies bouncingly, *yellow rump contrasting with black, white-tipped tail.* **Similar species:** Buff-rumped Thornbill. **Voice:** pretty tinkling, cyclic song; flight-call 'check-check'. **Habitat:** short grass on edges of woodlands, scrublands; paddocks, plantations, golfcourses, farms, parks, lawns. **Breeds:** July–Dec. **Nest:** untidy, domed, with hidden side-entrance, capped with rudimentary false cup 'nest'; of grass, plant-fibre, spiders' web, egg-sacs; in outer foliage of shrub, tree eucalypt, acacia, introduced conifer, low to 8 m; or in stick nest of raptor, babbler. **Eggs:** 3–4; dull white, lightly spotted red–brown. **Range and Status:** e. Aust. and Tas. (*except* coastal ne. Q n. of Rockhampton); w. through c. Aust., n. to *c.* Tennant Ck; widespread s. WA, n. to *c.* Wiluna–Port Hedland; absent driest deserts. Common. Sedentary.

STRIATED THORNBILL *Acanthiza lineata* 10 cm

Often confused with Brown Thornbill: *note pale brown eye, dense white streaks on tan crown, face/ear-coverts;* back greenish; rump/tail warm-brown; underparts yellow–white, streaked blackish. **Immature:** more fawn. Groups, autumn–winter flocks: forages in foliage; hovers, showing *dark tailband.* **Similar species:** Weebill; Brown, Yellow Thornbills. **Voice:** insect-like 'tiz, tiz', with an incisive chipping quality; other high-pitched notes, sharper, more splintered than Brown. **Habitat:** wetter eucalypt forests/woodlands to mallee, mangroves; parks, gardens. **Breeds:** July–Dec. **Nest:** neat, hooded, of bark-fibre, grass, spiders' web; suspended in foliage, 1–20 m high. **Eggs:** 2–4; pink–white, freckled red–brown, in zone. **Range and Status:** coastal se. Aust.: from e. of Biloela (Q), s. and w. to Bunya NP–Warwick; in NSW, inland on w. slopes to *c.* Inverell–Warrumbungle NP–Cocoparra NP; w. in river red gum forests to *c.* Gunbower–Barham; in Vic., n. to Bendigo–Little Desert; w. in coastal se. SA to Fleurieu Pen.–Mt Lofty Ras.; Kangaroo I. Common. Sedentary.

YELLOW THORNBILL *Acanthiza nana* 10 cm

Other name: Little Thornbill.

Yellowest thornbill, richer in coastal se. Aust., paler inland. *Note ochre wash on chin/throat, red eye;* ear-coverts olive–grey with *dense pale 'shaving brush' streaks.* Singles, pairs, parties: hovers, shows dark tail, pale tips; *always seems to be moving somewhere.* **Similar species:** Weebill, Striated Thornbill, Fairy Warbler, White-throated Warbler, imm. **Voice:** brisk, deep 'chidid' or 'chidid-tiz-tiz'; less insect-like than Striated, more like Weebill. **Habitat:** drier woodlands, coastal, inland scrubs, riverine forests, trees in paddocks, mangroves, golfcourses, orchards, parks, gardens; often in bifurcated ('feathery') foliage, e.g. of acacias; some paperbarks; hoop pines, *Araucaria,* in rainforest. **Breeds:** Aug.–Dec. **Nest:** domed, untidy; of bark-shreds, grass, tendrils, moss, lichen, spiders' web; high in foliage. **Eggs:** 2–4; whitish; blotched, freckled red–brown, chocolate, lilac. **Range and Status:** e., se. Aust.: highland population Atherton Tableland (ne. Q), otherwise n. to *c.* Mackay, w. to Blackall–Cunnamulla; in NSW, w. to Cobar–Ivanhoe; widespread Vic., s. and w. to Goolwa–Adelaide (SA), n. to Flinders Ras. Common; patchy. Sedentary.

WEEBILL *Smicrornis brevirostris* 8–9 cm

Tiny, with *short horn-coloured bill, cream–buff eyebrow, whitish eye, dark-streaked ear-coverts.* S. and e. races olive–green above, cream–buff below, with slight dark streaks; inland and n. birds smaller, paler, yellower — smallest Aust. bird. Pairs, family parties: flutters outside foliage, showing dark-banded, pale-tipped tail. Often heard before seen. **Similar species:** Yellow Thornbill. **Voice:** robust: deep, far-carrying 'weebit, weebee!' or 'willy-weet, willy-weetee!'; quick, deep 'tidid tidid'. **Habitat:** drier woodlands: river red gum/black box saplings; mallee, mulga, other acacias. **Breeds:** Aug.–Feb. **Nest:** hooded like baby's woollen bootee, of plant-down, leaves, grass, spiders' web; in outer foliage, 1–10 m high. **Eggs:** 2–3; white, buff–white, grey–brown, freckled brown. **Range and Status:** mainland Aust., *except* treeless deserts, wettest forests, agricultural areas. Common. Sedentary; locally nomadic.

YELLOW-RUMPED THORNBILL

STRIATED THORNBILL

YELLOW THORNBILL

inland form

Coastal se. form

inland form

WEEBILL

se. form

SOUTHERN WHITEFACE *Aphelocephala leucopsis* 10–12.5 cm

Other names: Eastern, Western Whiteface, Squeaker.
Sturdy small grey–brown bird, usually first noticed by calls. *Note stubby bill, white forehead with black margin, pale eye.* Underparts pale grey; *flank-mark olive–buff to rich pale chestnut in WA race* castaneiventris *'Western Whiteface'.* Pairs, small flocks: forages mostly on ground, with much squeaky twittering, often with thornbills and (inland) with other whitefaces; investigates stumps, fence-posts; flirts tail in flight, *broad black tail-band, tipped white.* **Similar species:** Chestnut-breasted, Banded Whiteface. Zebra Finch, imm.: greyer; black tail with white ladder-pattern. **Voice:** continual twittering, 'tweet-tweeter' on one note; flight-call, brisk 'wit, wit-awit'. **Habitat:** dry, sparse open forest/woodland; inland scrubs e.g. mallee, mulga, cypress pine; saltbush, dead trees, stumps, black box/lignum flats. **Breeds:** June–Dec. **Nest:** large, untidy, domed; of grass, rootlets, bark; in hollow limb, stump, fence-post, foliage of shrub, low tree, or sheds, nest-boxes. **Eggs:** 2–5; whitish to buff, purplish grey, freckled, blotched brown to reddish; zone at large end. **Range and Status:** drier habitats of s. Aust.: in Q, n. to Birdsville–McGregor Ra.–Chinchilla, e. to Darling Downs; in NSW, e. to c. Tenterfield, Scone–Stroud–sw. shale areas in Sydney region–Bundanoon–Cooma; in Vic., Bendoc area in far e., but mostly drier foothills n. of Divide, w. and n. of Hume Dam–Fraser NP–Wandong–You Yangs–Castlemaine–Grampians NP; in SA, s. to Joanna–Adelaide region–Eyre Pen.; all s. WA *except* sw. corner w. of Eucla-Mullewa; n. to beyond Tropic in WA and NT e. to Jervois Ra. Locally common; patchy. Sedentary.

CHESTNUT-BREASTED WHITEFACE *Aphelocephala pectoralis* 10 cm

Seldom observed: like Banded Whiteface *but richer in colour, made unmistakable by its broad, rusty breastband.* **Immature:** paler breastband, with a few dark spots. Pairs, small flocks: hops on ground; shy; when approached flies to take cover in low bushes. Mixes with both other Whitefaces. Call, once learned, should alert observer to its presence. **Similar species:** Banded Whiteface. **Voice:** silvery tinkling trill; weaker, softer than Banded. **Habitat:** semi-desert tablelands with bare ground and gibber, sparsely vegetated with bluebush, saltbush, black oak, mulga, etc., with sparse grass, 'dead finish', *Acacia tetragonophylla,* and *Eremophila* spp. **Breeds:** probably c. Aug.–Nov. **Nest:** globular with side-entrance near top but no entrance-spout; loosely constructed of dead twigs; lined with wool, feathers; one in bluebush 30 cm from ground. **Eggs:** 3; oval, pale pink, with purplish grey markings, densest on large end. **Range and Status:** confined to nc. and ne. SA, from c. se. of Tarcoola, in Gawler Ras., n. to Wellbourn Hill–Todmorden; ne. to region of Goyders Lagoon; s. to lower Strzelecki Track–Leigh Ck–Myrtle Springs. Rare; elusive; locally nomadic (?).

BANDED WHITEFACE *Aphelocephala nigricincta* 11–12.5 cm

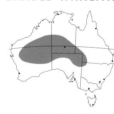

An obvious whiteface with *distinct black band across whitish breast; sandy–buff above, richer on rump*; tail blackish, tipped buff–white. Pairs, small flocks: often with other whitefaces and/or thornbills. Feeds mostly on ground, hops actively; takes cover in low bushes. Male has distinctive song-flight; rising high at an angle, flutters momentarily, singing, before dropping back to cover (other whitefaces may behave similarly). **Similar species:** Southern Whiteface, Chestnut-breasted Whiteface, Double-barred Finch, White-fronted Chat. **Voice:** song, musical trill or tinkle, sometimes in flight; somewhat like 'alarm-clock' note of White-plumed Honeyeater; alarm-call, harsh cricket-like 'bzz-bzz'. **Habitat:** open mulga and other inland scrubs; vegetation on watercourses; saltbush, bluebush, grassland, gibber; sandhills with sparse low shrubs. **Breeds:** June–Oct., and after rain. **Nest:** domed; of sticks, with spoutlike entrance; in open bush; or of grass, bark, in hollow spout. **Eggs:** 2–4; oval, whitish to buff; with plentiful pale red–brown blotches, forming zone at large end. **Range and Status:** inland and cw. Aust., e. to far sw. Q (e. and n. to Betoota–Bedourie); n. in NT to Tarlton Downs–Barrow Ck–Tanami; n. in WA to Gt Sandy Desert and s. to middle Gascoyne R.–Cue; n. SA, s. to Musgrave Ras.–L. Eyre Basin. Casual marginally into extreme w. NSW, from Sturt NP s. to region of Broken Hill. Fairly common. Sedentary or locally nomadic.

race
castaneiventris

SOUTHERN WHITEFACE

CHESTNUT-BREASTED WHITEFACE

BANDED WHITEFACE

LITTLE WATTLEBIRD *Anthochaera chrysoptera* 26–31 cm

Other name: Brush Wattlebird.

Dull brown, longish honeyeater, *with fine silvery streaks above and below; lacks wattles; darker down chin/throat;* eye blue–grey to brown; legs dark grey. In flight, *rufous wingpatch,* white tips to wing and tail-feathers. **Immature:** eye brown; streaks less distinct. **Race lunulata** (sw. WA): *bill longer; eye red; silvery patch of streaks on sides of throat.* Singles, pairs, loose companies: active, noisy, aggressive; postures jerkily with bill/tail raised, rattling bill. Tame resident in gardens. **Similar species:** Striped Honeyeater: whitish head/upperparts streaked black; rump paler; calls differ. Red Wattlebird. Yellow Wattlebird, (Tas. only). **Voice:** many squeaky, musical lilting notes: strident 'cookay-cock'; raucous 'fetch the gun'; mellow, guttural 'yekkop, yekkop'. Alarm-call: emphatic 'kwock!'; nasal 'shnairt!'. **Habitat:** banksia/eucalypt woodlands; heathlands, tea-tree scrub, sandplain-heaths; in se. Q, lantana thickets, wild tobacco, parks, gardens. **Breeds:** June–Dec. **Nest:** loose, untidy cup of twigs; lined with shredded bark, plant-down; 1–10 m in fork of banksia, tea-tree, eucalypt sapling. **Eggs:** 1–2; salmon-pink/red, spotted red–brown to purplish red. **Range and Status:** coastal se. Aust., Tas. (but not Bass Strait islands) and sw. WA. In Q, from *c.* Cooloola NP–Fraser I. (Q) inland to Toowoomba. Coastal NSW, breeding to *c.* 600 m in Blue Mts, inland to ACT (irregular) and Kosciusko NP. In Vic., mostly s. of Divide, in w., n. to Little Desert–Wyperfeld NPs; casual Swan Hill. In SA, w. coastally to Mt Lofty Ras., Yorke and s. Eyre Pen.; Kangaroo I. In Tas., coastal e. and n., sparse inland; rare w. coast. In sw. WA, race *lunulata,* w. and s. of Israelite Bay–Stirling Ras. NP–L. Grace–Northam–Geraldton. Common. Sedentary; locally nomadic.

RED WATTLEBIRD *Anthochaera carunculata* 33–36 cm

Crown black; face white below red eye; fleshy red neck-wattles (longer, redder with age); centre of belly lemon–yellow; legs pink. **Female:** smaller, tail shorter. **Immature:** paler, plainer; wattle small, pink. Singles, pairs, nomadic flocks: noisy, aggressive; acrobatic at blossoms; takes flying insects, hops on ground. Flight strong, direct, undulating, showing white tips to wing/tail feathers; often settles on high bare branches. Attracted to gardens, nectar-feeders, vineyards. **Similar species:** Little Wattlebird: fine silvery streaks; lacks wattles; yellow belly; note chestnut wingpatches in flight. Yellow Wattlebird (Tas.): larger, paler streaked; long yellow wattles. **Voice:** hacking cough 'yak', 'yakayak' or 'yaak, yakyak'; deep, mellow, ringing 'tew-tew-tew-tew'. Alarm-call: single emphatic 'chock!'; many others. **Habitat:** eucalypt forests, woodlands, scrubs: mallee, coastal scrubs, heaths; orchards, golfcourses, parks, gardens. **Breeds:** July–Nov. **Nest:** untidy saucer of sticks, leaves, grass; lined with bark-strips, fur, hair; 2–16 m high in fork, or on bark against trunk. **Eggs:** 2–3; pale pink/red-buff, spotted red–brown, reddish purple. **Range and Status:** se., s. and sw. mainland Aust. and islands: in Q, n. to Darling Downs–Brisbane; in NSW, inland to Inverell–Warrumbungle NP–Hillston–mallee areas of sw.; throughout Vic.; s. SA and Kangaroo I., n. to Flinders Ras.–Gawler Ras., coastally w. along Bight; widespread sw. WA, n. to Gt Victoria Desert–Kalgoorlie–Paynes Find–Shark Bay. Common. Blossom nomad, with contradictory seasonal movements. In summer, ranges up to 2000 m in NSW and Vic. Alps; large autumn movement from Gt Dividing Ra. to coastal lowlands/sub-inland plains. In s. WA, moves to coastal and n. areas in autumn.

YELLOW WATTLEBIRD *Anthochaera paradoxa* 37–45 cm

Largest honeyeater: *head/body whitish with prominent dark streaks; eye brown; note long pendulous yellow to orange wattles;* centre of lower breast/abdomen rich yellow; *tail long,* tipped white; legs pink. **Immature:** no wattle. Singles, pairs, seasonal flocks; open companies when blossoms abundant. Active, acrobatic; flight strong, direct, undulating. Tame where fed; at times pest in orchards. **Similar species:** Little/Red Wattlebirds: *note range.* **Voice:** harsh, gurgling, guttural, like coughing/vomiting. **Habitat:** mountain shrubberies/sub-alpine forest to lowland forests; open woodlands; coastal scrubs, especially with banksias; golfcourses, orchards, parks, gardens. **Breeds:** July–Jan. **Nest:** large open saucer of twigs, bark-strips; wool; lined with grass, wool; low to *c.* 20 m high in fork. **Eggs:** 2–3; salmon–red, spotted, blotched red–brown, purplish red, blue–grey. **Range and Status:** Tas. and King I.: common e. and c. Tas., uncommon n. coast w. of Tamar R., rare w. coast. Uncommon King I. Resident, altitudinal migrant or nomad; extends to above snowline in late summer.

LITTLE
WATTLEBIRD

race *lunulata*

RED
WATTLEBIRD

imm.

imm.

YELLOW WATTLEBIRD

LITTLE FRIARBIRD *Philemon citreogularis* 25–29 cm

Smallest friarbird, *no bill-knob: bare blue–grey skin under eye widens over cheeks*. **Female:** smaller. **Immature:** throat washed yellow. Singles, pairs, flocks: feeds on nectar, fruit; hawks flying insects. Wingbeats shallow, quivering; tail square-cut, with pale tips. **Similar species:** see other friarbirds. **Voice:** mellow 'gee-wit' or 'chewip', extended into song; falsetto phrases like 'I've-got-red-hair-air'; chattering scoldings. **Habitat:** open forests/woodlands/ rivers; swamp-woodlands, mangroves, orchards, vineyards, parks, gardens. **Breeds:** July–Nov. **Nest:** deep, flimsy cup of grass, bark-fibre, twigs, rootlets; spiders' web; 2–10 m high in drooping foliage. **Eggs:** 2–3(4); whitish pink to salmon–red, spotted purplish red, purple, chestnut. **Range and Status:** n. and e. Aust. and islands; inland on watercourses. Blossom nomad in n.; summer breeding migrant to se. Aust. (Sept.–April). Common. Also s. PNG.

NOISY FRIARBIRD *Philemon corniculatus* 31–35 cm

Other name: Leatherhead.

Bare black head with angular bill-knob; eye red; long, curving silver–white plumes on 'cowl' and upperbreast. **Immature:** no knob; eye brown; coarse pale scallops; throat washed yellow. Singles, parties, flocks: white tail-tips prominent. Noisy, aggressive in blossoms, hawks flying insects; eats grapes, soft fruit, blackberries. **Voice:** harsh, repeated 'tobacco'; 'keyhole'; 'poor soldier'; 'yakob'; mellow, ringing 'chog!-'eeyit' or 'ch-will'; mellow 'chew, chewip' like Little Friarbird. **Habitat:** open forests, woodlands; watercourses, swamp-woodland; coastal, sub-inland scrubs; orchards, vineyards, parks, gardens. **Breeds:** July–Jan. **Nest:** large, deep, untidy cup of wool, stringy bark, leaves, rootlets; in leafy branch, 3–10 m high. **Eggs:** 2–4; deep pink, spotted, blotched chestnut–red, purplish grey. **Range and Status:** e. Aust. and islands: from C. York Pen. (Q) to n.–c. Vic., w. along Murray R. into e. SA. Blossom-nomad in Q; summer breeding migrant in se. Aust. (Sept.–April); some overwinter. Conspicuous autumn migration in coastal e. NSW–se. Q. Also s. PNG.

SILVER-CROWNED FRIARBIRD *Philemon argenticeps* 27–32 cm

Small friarbird: distinguished from Helmeted by (1) *more prominent bill-knob;* (2) *black facial skin forms angular point behind eye;* (3) *underparts whitish.* **Immature:** no knob; eye brown; throat washed yellow. Pairs, parties, flocks: acrobatic, noisy when feeding. **Similar species:** Helmeted, Noisy Friarbirds. **Voice:** nasal, cat-like calls, e.g. 'more tobacco, uh'; repeated. **Habitat:** tropical open forests, woodlands, watercourses, mangroves, gardens, towns. **Breeds:** Sept.–Dec. **Nest:** suspended cup of bark-fibre, grass, spiders' web; from fork in foliage, 3–13 m high. **Eggs:** 1–2; pale salmon–pink to pinkish buff; spotted, freckled red–brown, purplish brown/grey. **Range and Status:** coastal n. Aust.: from Derby (WA), e. through Kimberley and Top End (NT), e. and s. to Larrimah–Mallapunyah, Groote Eylandt; in Q, s. to Cloncurry–Flinders R. on Gulf coast, and from C. York–Weipa s. on e. coast to c. Townsville–Magnetic I.; casual further s. Common. Blossom nomad, with regular local movements.

HELMETED FRIARBIRD *Philemon buceroides* 32.5–37 cm

Other name: Sandstone Friarbird.

Largest mainland honeyeater: *browner than Silver-crowned, with lower, rounded 'bill-knob'* (absent in Arnhem Land escarpment (NT)); *eye red; grey facial skin has rounded contour behind eye.* **Immature:** no knob; eye brown; pale scalloping on upperparts. Singles, pairs, small flocks: noisy, aggressive. **Voice:** loud, varied: 'poor-devil', repeated; many complex calls; in Arnhem Land escarpments, repeated metallic 'chillanc'; 'chank'; 'whack-a-where'. **Habitat:** rainforest, monsoon forest, eucalypt forests/woodlands; paperbarks, mangroves, pandanus, blossom, fruit trees in gardens, towns. **Breeds:** Aug.–March. **Nest:** deep cup of bark-strips, stems, rootlets; slung from horizontal fork in high foliage. **Eggs:** 3–4; pale pink, spotted brown, dark red, purple. **Range and Status:** (1) ne. Q and islands: from C. York s. to Weipa on w. coast and to c. Rockhampton on e. coast; (2) coastal Top End NT and islands; (3) Arnhem Land escarpment (NT). Common to uncommon. Seasonally nomadic. Also Torres Strait, New Britain, PNG, e. Indonesia.

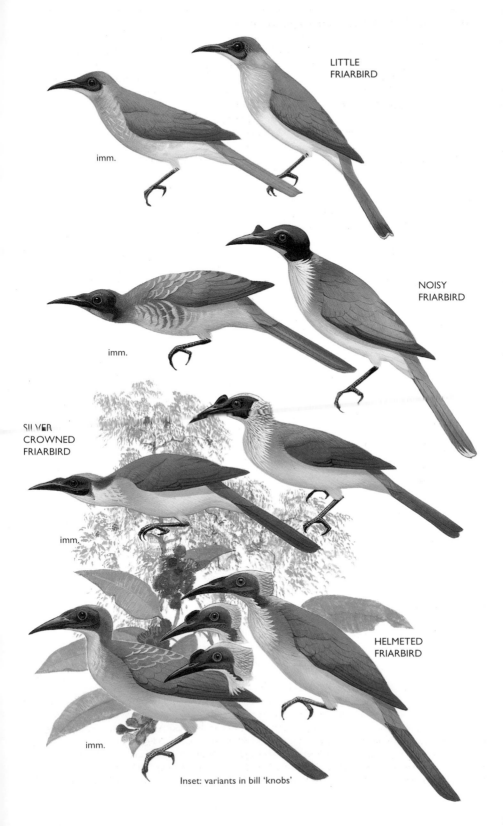

LITTLE
FRIARBIRD

imm.

NOISY
FRIARBIRD

imm.

SILVER
CROWNED
FRIARBIRD

imm.

HELMETED
FRIARBIRD

imm.

Inset: variants in bill 'knobs'

SPINY-CHEEKED HONEYEATER *Acanthagenys rufogularis* 22–26 cm

Dark-tipped deep pink bill; pink gape; eye blue; long dark mask; white/yellow brush-streak down neck; throat/upperbreast apricot–buff. Inland birds paler. **Immature:** cheek-stripe yellow. Singles, pairs, parties: calls from dead branches, wires. Flight undulating, shows *whitish rump/tail-tip.* Makes steep high song-flight. **Voice:** gurgling; 'widit, widit-ear, peer-peer, peer-peer', etc., or 'wee-ear, chonk-chonk'. Song-flight: 'give-the-boy-a-go', repeated. Alarm-call, 'tok!'; mimics. **Habitat:** drier inland/coastal woodlands, scrubs; fruiting plants, incl. mistletoe; gardens. **Breeds:** June–Jan. **Nest:** flimsy cup of grass, she oak needles, spiders' web; lined with fur, grass, wool; in hanging foliage, 2–3 m high. **Eggs:** 2–3; white to cream–buff, spotted, blotched dark brown, in cap. **Range and Status:** mainland Aust., *except* (1) tropical n. Aust. (but n. to Gulf lowlands); (2) coastal se. and far sw. Aust. Reaches e. coast at points n. to Townsville (Q); extends coastally e. to Port Phillip region, casual Gippsland Lakes (Vic.); Kangaroo I. (SA). Uncommon. Sedentary; nomadic.

STRIPED HONEYEATER *Plectorhyncha lanceolata* 21–23 cm

Bill blue-grey, finely dark-pointed; head/nape whitish, streaked black. **Immature:** whiter, less streaked. Singles, pairs, parties. In flight, rump/wings plain brown; *tail longish, slightly forked, square at corners.* **Voice:** mellow, rolling 'cherree-cherree-chirrarip'; or 'free-wheat-peeler-peeler', rising, falling; male performs song-flight. **Habitat:** drier scrubs, woodlands, she oaks, mulga, cypress pine, mallee, saltbush, coastal banksia, paperbarks, tea-tree; swamp/savannah woodlands; mangroves, orchards, gardens. **Breeds:** communally Aug.–Jan. **Nest:** deep cup of rootlets, plant-down, feathers, wool, spiders' web; in drooping foliage 1–6 m high. **Eggs:** 2–4; flesh-pink, sprinkled red–buff, blue–grey. **Range and Status:** inland e. Aust. s. of Tropic, w. to Spencer Gulf (SA); patchily to e. coast from n. of Sydney (NSW) to near Cooktown (Q). Uncommon. Sedentary on coast; seasonal nomad inland.

REGENT HONEYEATER *Xanthomyza phrygia* 20–23 cm

Other names: Warty-faced Honeyeater, Flying Coachman.
Striking: *head/neck black; warty pink or yellow facial skin; bold scaly plumage pattern; broad yellow edges to black wing/tail-feathers.* **Female:** smaller. **Immature:** browner; bill yellowish. Pairs, parties, flocks: aggressive, with fluttering display-flights; forages in blossoms, foliage, trunks; takes nectar, insects. **Voice:** anvil-like 'chink-chink'; slow, mellow 'quippa-plonk-quip', 'quip kik'; liquid 'cloop'; mewing, turkey-like calls. Mimics. **Habitat:** dry open forests, woodlands, especially red ironbark, yellow box, yellow gum (Franklin et al, 1989); mistletoe on river oaks; trees in farmlands; streets, gardens. **Breeds:** mostly Aug.–Jan. **Nest:** large cup of grass, bark-strips; lined with hair, plant-down; 2–10 m in upright fork, mistletoe. **Eggs:** 2–3; salmon–buff, spotted, zoned red–brown, purplish red. **Range and Status:** seriously reduced in range/numbers by habitat clearance and alteration. Patchy, irregular spring–summer breeding migrant to Dubbo–Warrumbungle NP, Munghorn Gap NR–Hunter R. and Windsor regions (NSW); Wangaratta–Chiltern–Bendigo regions (Vic.). In se. Q, mostly autumn–winter migrant, n. to *c.* Rockhampton. Endangered.

BLUE-FACED HONEYEATER *Entomyzon cyanotis* 30–32 cm

Note striking two-tone blue facial skin, yellow–white eye; crown/nape black, with white nape-band; upperparts olive–green; underparts white, with dusky black bib. Birds from ne. Q to n. WA, incl. race *albipennis*, show white on base of primaries in flight. **Immature:** face olive–green; bib grey. Pairs, parties, flocks: aggressive; forages in foliage, blossoms, fruit; flight undulating. **Voice:** repeated 'woik', or 'queet?'; softer 'hwit, hwit'. **Habitat:** open forests, woodlands, scrubs; pandanus, paperbarks, watercourses, farmlands, roadsides, bananas, orchards, golfcourses, parks, gardens. **Breeds:** June–Jan. **Nest:** deep cup of bark, rootlets, grass, spiders' web; lined with plant-down, hair; or bulky twigs; in bark debris, fork, 3–10 m high; or old nest of babbler, Magpie-Lark, Apostlebird, or in hole in nest of tree-termites. **Eggs:** 2–3; buff-pink/salmon-pink, spotted red–brown, purplish red. **Range and Status:** coastal n. and e. Aust.: from Kimberley (WA) to Myall Lakes (NSW); inland se. Aust. w. to *c.* Morgan (SA); s. to *c.* Bendigo (Vic.), sw. to *c.* Naracoorte (SA); casual w. to Langhorne Ck. Common n. Aust., patchy in se. Sedentary; locally migratory. Also s. PNG.

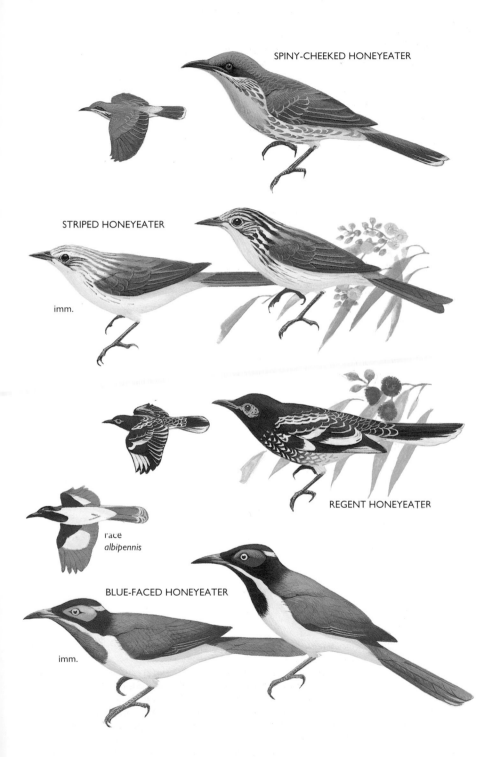

SPINY-CHEEKED HONEYEATER

STRIPED HONEYEATER

imm.

REGENT HONEYEATER

race
albipennis

BLUE-FACED HONEYEATER

imm.

BELL MINER *Manorina melanophrys* 19 cm

Other name: Bellbird.

Bill/legs deep yellow; red triangle behind eye; plumage olive–green with slight dark facial marks. **Immature:** mark behind eye olive, becoming orange. Pairs, family parties in colonies of hundreds. Inconspicuous in foliage, blossoms; demonstrative; glides with wings in V when joining group-displays. **Voice:** bell-like 'tink'; harsh 'kweek'; sharp 'jak jak jak'; complaining 'kwee-kwee'. **Habitat:** temperate rainforest; eucalypt/angophora woodland with dense shrubby understorey; in gullies near rivers, creeks; swamp gum woodland; well-treed suburbs; gardens. **Breeds:** communally: June–Dec. **Nest:** large cup of grass, leaves, plant-down, spiders' web; in upright fork, 1–4 m high. **Eggs:** 1–2 (3); white, pale pink, spotted purplish, red–brown. **Range and Status:** coastal se. mainland Aust. and Gt Divide: from e. of Melbourne to c. Gympie (Q); casual ACT, c. and w. Vic. Common. Sedentary, with re-locations; recent expansion.

YELLOW-THROATED MINER *Manorina flavigula* 25–27.5 cm

Other names: White-rumped Miner; 'Dusky Miner' (s. WA).

Paler than Noisy Miner, with whitish rump. Crown grey; black mask extends to silver-tipped ear-coverts, with whitish, yellow-fringed spot behind; forehead, chin and foreneck often washed yellow; yellow gape extends under eye beside white whisker-mark (McLaughlin, 1993). Dark race *obscura* 'Dusky Miner' in s. WA has sooty mask. **Immature:** markings softer; throat yellower. Companies larger than Noisy Miners; ventures farther from woodland. **Voice:** keener, higher-pitched than Noisy. **Habitat:** drier woodlands, scrublands; grasslands with flowering shrubs; drier coastal scrubs, banksia-woodlands, heaths; golfcourses, gardens. In inland and WA, occupies river red gums on watercourses. **Breeds:** July–Dec., or after rains. **Nest:** like Noisy Miner; often lower. **Eggs:** 3–4; salmon-pink/salmon-red; spotted, blotched darker. **Range and Status:** widespread mainland Aust., *except* coastal e. and se. Aust., C. York Pen. (Q), e. coastal NT, driest deserts. Common; patchy. Sedentary; local nomadic movements.

BLACK-EARED MINER *Manorina melanotis* 25 cm

More uniformly grey from crown to rump than Noisy Miner. Absence of pale rump separates it from Yellow-throated; absence of pale tail-tips helps separate it from both Yellow-throated and Noisy Miners. Pure Black-eared differs from Yellow-throated in se. Aust. as follows: black mask starts at bill, extends back under *and over* eye, and uniformly over ear-coverts; there is an obscure grey 'moustache-streak' (McLaughlin, 1993). Small parties: fugitive; inspects intruder, calls complainingly, vanishes. Note range, habitat. **Voice:** like Noisy Miner. **Habitat:** dense, tall mallee formations probably with understorey of spinifex; low flowering shrubs. **Breeds:** Sept.–Oct. **Nest and eggs:** like Noisy/Yellow-throated. **Range and Status:** small, local colonies in mallee region of nw. Vic., e. to Hattah–Kulkyne NP–Annuello; Murray mallee of SA, n. to Murray R.; reported in far sw. NSW. Sedentary; locally nomadic. Interbreeding with invasive Yellow-throated Miner is thought to have reduced pure-bred population, threatening the species' survival. Very rare. Endangered.

NOISY MINER *Manorina melanocephala* 24–27 cm

Other names: Micky, Soldierbird.

Immediately separated from other miners *by whitish forehead, black crown and cheeks. In flight, rump grey, dark tail tipped whitish.* Colonial, aggressive, with noisy group displays; forages in foliage, blossoms; probes bark; often on ground. Male has steep song-flight. Normal flight level, glides on upraised wings. Nesting females fly with heads raised. **Similar species:** Yellow-throated, Black-eared Miners. **Voice:** complaining 'pwee pwee pwee'; chuckling 'weedidit'; liquid notes. Alarm-call: strident 'pee, pee, pee'. **Habitat:** grassy open forests, woodlands, without shrub-layer; large trees on inland watercourses; coastal banksias, paperbarks, heaths, shelterbelts, roadside timber, golfcourses, outer suburbs, parks, gardens. **Breeds:** communally, June–Dec. **Nest:** untidy cup of twigs, grass, spiders' web, wool; in fork of leafy branch, 2–13 m high. **Eggs:** 2–4; buff–white, pink; freckled, spotted, blotched red–brown, blue–grey, lilac. **Range and Status:** e. Aust. and ce. Tas.: n. to c. Musgrave (e. C. York Pen., (Q)); w. to Mt Lofty Ras.–Adelaide, Yorke Pen. (SA). Common. Sedentary, with local movements.

BELL MINER

race
obscura

YELLOW-THROATED MINER

imm.

yellow-
throated

BLACK-EARED MINER

black-
eared

noisy

NOISY MINER

imm.

LEWIN'S HONEYEATER *Meliphaga lewinii* 19–21.5 cm

Largest, darkest, member of *look-alike* trio. Bill black, strong; eye grey: *wide, whitish gape-streak to below eye; pale yellow 'half moon' earmark.* Colour varies; shade and shape of earmark vary. Singles, pairs: bold; probes blossoms, raids cultivated fruit; sweet food in houses, picnic tables. Flight strong, irregular, with 'flop-flop' of wings. **Voice:** long, tremulous machinegun-rattle, peevish scolds. **Habitat:** rainforests, from coast to over 1000 m in summer in se. Aust.; above 200 m n. of Townsville (Q); in s. Q–n. NSW, sub-inland lowland forests/woodlands, brigalow/belar scrubs, coastal scrubs/heaths, mangroves, cultivation, canefields, orchards, blackberries, lantana, gardens. **Breeds:** Aug.–Jan. **Nest:** untidy, strong cup of bark, grass, moss, lichen; spiders' web; leaves, paper; fabric; lined with plant-down; 1–6 m in foliage of leafy shrub/tree. **Eggs:** 2 (3); white, spotted deep red. **Range and Status:** coastal e. Aust. and islands: from McIlwraith Ra., e. C. York Pen.(Q) and Cooktown (Q) to near Melbourne (Vic.); inland to Carnarvon Ras. NP (Q); Mt Kaputar NP–Rylstone–Mt Kosciusko NP (NSW); e. Vic., w. to Toolangi–Gembrook; casual Dandenong Ras., s. to Strzelecki Ras.–Gippsland Lakes (Emison et al, 1987). Common in n., uncommon in s.; migrates from highlands to lowlands in autumn–winter.

YELLOW-SPOTTED HONEYEATER *Meliphaga notata* 17.5 cm

Other name: Lesser Lewin Honeyeater.

Smaller then Lewin's: bill finer, comparatively longer; plumage brighter; eye brown; *gape-streak yellow; yellow earmark forms rounded triangle.* C. York birds paler, brighter. Singles, pairs: aggressive; flight swift, undulating; feeds acrobatically; tame around habitation. Note range. **Voice:** loud; high-pitched metallic, descending, 'keah-keah-keah-keah!'; machinegun rattle like Lewin's, inferior in tone, volume; speed varying; loud scolding. **Habitat:** rainforests, monsoon forests, vine scrubs, eucalypt woodlands, watercourses, mangroves, bananas, cultivation, lantana, gardens; mostly below *c.* 400 m. **Breeds:** Aug.–Feb. **Nest:** cup of bark-shreds, palm fibre, spiders' web, lichen; lined with plant-down; 1–3 m high in low shrub, mangrove. **Eggs:** 2; pink–white, spotted reddish, purple. **Range and Status:** ne. Q: from C. York s. to Aurukun R. on w. coast; Townsville on e. coast in lower foothills, coastal islands. Common. Sedentary, nomadic. Also Torres Strait, PNG.

GRACEFUL HONEYEATER *Meliphaga gracilis* 14–16.5 cm

Smallest of trio; bill proportionately longer, slimmer; *thin yellow gape-streak; rounded cream earmark; paler olive–brown, cheeks/underparts greyer;* plumage softer, contours rounder. Singles, pairs: unobtrusive; feeds among foliage, blossoms; takes flying insects. **Voice:** sharp 'tuck', or 'pick'; differs from Lewin's, Yellow-spotted. **Habitat:** rainforest, vine scrubs, eucalypt woodlands, coastal scrubs, stream-vegetation, lantana, orchards, gardens. **Breeds:** Oct.–Feb. **Nest:** cup of grass, moss, lichen, spiders' web; lined with plant-down; usually low, sometimes over water. **Eggs:** 2; rich salmon-pink, dotted, spotted red, chestnut, purple–grey. **Range and Status:** ne. Q: coastal lowlands from C. York s. to Edward R. on w. coast and to Ingham–Hinchinbrook I. on e. coast; to above 600 m in Atherton region (Blakers et al, 1984). Sedentary. Also s. PNG, Aru Is.

WHITE-GAPED HONEYEATER *Lichenostomus unicolor* 18–21.5 cm

Other name: River Honeyeater.

Plain grey–brown with olive wash on primaries; *cream–white to yellow horizontal half-moon on gape.* Pairs, parties: noisy, aggressive, with group-chases, displays. **Similar species:** Lewin's Honeyeater: half-moon earmark. **Voice:** rollicking calls, choruses: 'whit whit, awhit-whit, awhit-whit'; explosive 'chiew' or 'chop'. **Habitat:** near water in pandanus; mangroves, paperbarks, woodlands, homestead environs, streets, gardens. **Breeds:** Sept.–May. **Nest:** cup of fine grass, rootlets, hair, plant/bark-fibre, spiders' web; in horizontal fork of leafy tree, shrub, 2–16 m high. **Eggs:** 2; whitish pink, spotted, blotched red, purple. **Range and Status:** tropical n. Aust. and islands: from Broome (WA) through Kimberley, Top End (NT), e. on Gulf coast, n. to Archer R. on w. coast C. York Pen. (Q); s. on e. coast from *c.* Lakefield NP, to upper Burdekin R.–Proserpine. Inland to Fitzroy R. (WA)–Newcastle Waters (NT); Mt Isa–Georgetown–Atherton Tableland (Q). Common n. Aust.; uncommon e. coast. Sedentary.

LEWIN'S
HONEYEATER

YELLOW-SPOTTED
HONEYEATER

GRACEFUL HONEYEATER

WHITE-GAPED HONEYEATER

WHITE-LINED HONEYEATER *Meliphaga albilineata* 19 cm

Dark grey–brown above, whitish below; breast mottled; eye grey; *black mask split by silvery white line from yellow gape that swings up behind eye; ear-coverts black, tipped white.* **Immature:** no white stripe; ear-coverts tipped yellow. Singles, pairs: flight quick, undulating, with 'flop flop' of wings. Shy, solitary, heard more than seen; mixes with other honeyeaters in blossoming trees. **Voice:** wild, melodious: whistling double call, a rising, repeated '*tue-ee-ee, tue-i-in*', amplified by rocky gorges. **Habitat:** rainforest, paperbarks; eucalypt woodlands on sandstone escarpments; hills. **Breeds:** Aug.–Jan. **Nest:** deep cup, of creepers, spiders' web, fibre; lined with plant-fibre; slung 1–5 m in outer branchlets. **Eggs:** 2; pink–white, washed, spotted red–brown. **Range and Status:** nominate race: n. and w. escarpments of Arnhem Land Plateau (NT). Race *fordiana*: nw. Kimberley (WA), and islands, from *c.* King Leopold Ras. to Drysdale R. NP (Blakers et al, 1984). Locally common.

EUNGELLA HONEYEATER *Lichenostomus hindwoodi* 16–18 cm. (Pronounced 'Youngulla'.)

Recently described: dark grey–brown with *slightly scalloped crown, pale shaft-streaks on underparts.* Note: (1) *black bill, blue–grey eyes;* (2) *whitish streak from bill passes under eye, swings up and broadens;* (3) *white spot above, behind eye;* (4) *swept up white/yellow ear-coverts.* Noisy: wary, aggressive but elusive; eats fruit, nectar of eucalypts, mistletoes; hawks insects. **Similar species:** Bridled Honeyeater. **Voice:** 'loud, imperious . . . reminiscent of the [Spangled] Drongo's opening harsh rattle, and the latter part of . . . Willie Wagtail's "sweet pretty creature"'(Robertson, 1961). **Habitat:** rainforest above *c.* 600 m; lower eucalypt woodlands in winter. **Breeds:** Oct. **Nest:** deep cup of green–grey moss; lined with plant-fibre; in leafy branch *c.* 4 m high. **Eggs:** 2; buff–cream, blotched brown at large end (Robertson, 1961). **Range and Status:** Eungella NP–Mt Dalrymple State Forest on Clarke Ra., 80 km w. of Mackay (Q). Probable winter movement to coastal lowlands.

BRIDLED HONEYEATER *Lichenostomus frenatus* 20–22 cm

Other name: Mountain Honeyeater.
Distinctive dark honeyeater: *bill black with yellow base; eye grey; yellowish/pink line curves from gape under eye in small fleshy patch. Forehead/face, throat and ear-coverts black; white scalloping behind eye; yellow tip on ear-coverts; pale grey patch on side of neck.* Singles, pairs, small flocks: active, pugnacious; tame in rainforest parks. **Similar species:** Eungella Honeyeater. **Voice:** clear, imperious 'we-are' or 'wachita-wachita'. **Habitat:** highland rainforests, watercourse vegetation, wetter eucalypt woodlands; in winter, paperbarks, eucalypt woodlands. **Breeds:** Sept.–Dec. **Nest:** cup of fine twigs, stems; lined with plant-fibre; in leafy twigs, vine, usually low. **Eggs:** 2; whitish, spotted red–brown, grey–brown, purplish grey. **Range and Status:** ne. Q: from near Cooktown (Mt Amos), s. on highlands to Paluma Ra., near Townsville. Common. Sedentary, winter movement to coastal lowlands.

YELLOW-FACED HONEYEATER *Lichenostomus chrysops* 16–18 cm

Charming olive grey–brown honeyeater with *curving yellow streak back from bill below eye, splitting narrow black 'mask'; slight yellowish mark behind eye;* flanks buffish. Singles, pairs: active in foliage; hovers, often low. **Similar species:** Eungella, Bridled, Singing Honeyeaters. **Voice:** brisk 'chickup'; clear, descending 'calip, calip, calip'; flight-call: 'dep'. **Habitat:** forests, woodlands, coastal scrubs, heaths, mangroves; alpine regions over 1800 m; blackberries, lantana, golfcourses, orchards, parks, gardens. **Breeds:** July–Jan. **Nest:** cup of grass, bark-fibre, moss, lichen; slung in foliage 1–6 m high. **Eggs:** 2–3; pink to red–buff; spotted, blotched chestnut–red, purplish grey. **Range and Status:** e. and se. Aust.; highland population in ne. Q, from *c.* Cooktown (Mt Finnigan) s. to Mt Elliott, near Townsville. Main population breeds from se. Q through se. Aust. to Fleurieu Pen.–Mt Lofty Ras.; casual Kangaroo I. (SA); resident King I. (Bass Strait); vagrant Tas. Part-migratory: autumn movement down from high country; large autumn northward migration with White-naped Honeyeaters to coastal NSW–Q, through Gippsland Lakes, ACT, Blue Mts. Disperses w. to inland NSW–Q, n. to *c.* Iron Ra., C. York Pen. (Q). Common.

WHITE-LINED
HONEYEATER

EUNGELLA
HONEYEATER

BRIDLED HONEYEATER

imm.

YELLOW-FACED
HONEYEATER

YELLOW HONEYEATER *Lichenostomus flavus* 17.5 cm

Plump yellow–green honeyeater with slight dark line through eye; yellowish eyebrow and facial stripe. **Immature:** greener. Singles, pairs: placid; movements jerky. Feeds in blossoms, foliage; orchards, gardens for soft fruits. Flight undulating, with distinctive 'flop-flop' of wings. **Voice:** clear, emphatic 'whee-a, whee-a, whee-a', with a short rattle; metallic 'tut-tut-tut'; scolding rattle, like House Sparrow; peevish, scratchy 'jab!'. **Habitat:** watercourse vegetation, pandanus, paperbarks, eucalypt woodlands, rainforest margins, tropical scrubs, mangroves, orchards, gardens, urban areas. **Breeds:** Sept.–Feb. **Nest:** shallow cup of bark, grass, palm-fibre, spiders' web; 1–10 m high in leafy shrub or tree; in orchard, garden. **Eggs:** 2; pale to deep pink, spotted, blotched red–brown, chestnut, purplish grey. **Range and Status:** ne. Q: from Flinders R. on Gulf coast s. to Mt Isa, n. to C. York (Jardine R.); s. on e. coast to *c.* Broad Sound; inland on Tablelands, mostly below 450 m. Patchy; fairly common. Sedentary.

SINGING HONEYEATER *Lichenostomus virescens* 18–22 cm

Other names: Grape-eater or Grey Peter.
Fawn–grey: bold black mask runs down neck; thinner line of yellow below ends in broad silvery white mark. Solitary, pugnacious: feeds in low, often isolated, flowering, berried shrubs; raids soft fruits, grapes. **Similar species:** Yellow-faced; Varied, Mangrove Honeyeaters. **Voice:** dry 'prrit prrit prrit', running, machinegun-like 'crik-crikit-crikit-crikit'; scratchy, peevish 'scree'. **Habitat:** coastal dune vegetation; inland mulga, mallee scrubs; isolated shrubs, thickets on watercourses; orchards, vineyards, gardens. **Breeds:** July–Feb., or after rain in n. **Nest:** untidy cup of grass, plant-stems, spiders' web; lined with hair, fur, plant-down; in shrub 1–4 m high. **Eggs:** 2–3; pink–white to yellow–buff, sparsely to thickly spotted red–brown. **Range and Status:** Aust. mainland and drier islands. Absent from, or sparse on, e. coast *except* c. Rockhampton–Townsville (Q). Sparse C. York Pen. (Q), Top End (NT), Kimberley (WA). Extends e. along Vic. coast to *c.* Westernport–Gippsland Lakes. Common in suitable habitat. Sedentary.

VARIED HONEYEATER *Lichenostomus versicolor* 18–21 cm

Bill black; *long black mask extends down side of neck above broad yellow streak; white patch on side of neck; throat/breast yellow with brown streaks.* Singles, pairs, parties: noisy, conspicuous in foliage, blossoms. **Similar species:** Singing, Mangrove Honeyeaters. **Voice:** loud, rollicking: 'which-way, which-way-you-go'; 'get-your-whip' or 'hear-hear'; 'Peacock beware!'. **Habitat:** coastal scrubs, adjacent woodlands; mangroves; trees on suburban waterfronts; streets, gardens of coastal towns. **Breeds:** Aug.–Nov. **Nest:** flimsy cup of plant-stems, leaves, sea-grass, rootlets, plant-fibre, spiders' web; lined with plant-down; in mangrove, introduced mango, up to 4 m. **Eggs:** 2; pale pink, deeper at large end, finely spotted red–brown. **Range and Status:** coastal ne. Q and islands, from C. York s. to Halifax Bay. In Townsville–Cardwell region (Q), interbreeds with Mangrove Honeyeater. Locally common, sedentary. Also Torres Strait, PNG and islands.

MANGROVE HONEYEATER *Lichenostomus fasciogularis* 18–21 cm

Like Varied Honeyeater, with *brown barred pattern on yellow throat; grey–brown zone across upperbreast.* Pairs, parties: noisy, aggressive; feeds in outer foliage of mangroves; forages over lower trunks, roots. **Similar species:** Varied, Singing Honeyeaters. **Voice:** calls strong, clear; some like Varied Honeyeater; once learned, difference recognisable; alarm-rattle somewhat like Lewin's. **Habitat:** mangroves, nearby eucalypt woodlands; trees in coastal towns. **Breeds:** Aug.–Nov. **Nest:** deep cup of fine dry grass, sea-grass, spiders' web, egg-sacs; lined with fine rootlets; in mangrove-fork to 60 cm above high water. **Eggs:** 2; pale salmon–pink, spotted red–brown. **Range and Status:** coastal e. Aust. and islands, incl. Capricorn Group; from *c.* Townsville (Q), s. to *c.* Macksville (NSW). Common in n., rare in s. Sedentary. Interbreeds with Varied in Townsville–Cardwell region (Blakers et al, 1984).

YELLOW HONEYEATER

SINGING HONEYEATER

VARIED
HONEYEATER

MANGROVE
HONEYEATER

WHITE-EARED HONEYEATER *Lichenostomus leucotis* 20–22 cm

Black from face to upperbreast, with large white earpatch; crown grey; upperparts olive–green; underparts yellow–olive. **Immature:** duller; crown olive–green. Singles, pairs: nervously active; probes noisily under loose bark; makes 'flop-flop' of wings in flight; attacks fruit in orchards. Near nest, performs distraction display. **Similar species:** Yellow-throated Honeyeater: Tas. region only. **Voice:** jarring, descending 'chung-chung-chung'; mellow 'chockup, chockup', or 'beer-brick, beer-brick'. Inland populations: lighter calls of more syllables, e.g. mellow 'cherrywheet, cherrywheet', or quick 'chittagong'; also rapid machinegun-like 'chock-chock-chock-chock-chock'; other calls when breeding. **Habitat:** wet forests, woodlands, bracken, vegetation on streams, coastal heathlands/scrubs. In sub-inland: mallee, brigalow, belar. In s. WA: salmon-gum woodlands, tea-tree thickets around salt lakes. **Breeds:** Aug.–Dec. **Nest:** deep cup of bark-shreds, grass, spiders' web; lined with wool, fur, hair; 1–3 m high, or low in bracken. **Eggs:** 2–3; whitish to pale cream, sparingly spotted, blotched red, red–brown. **Range and Status:** widespread but patchy, *in suitable habitat*, s. from Hughenden–Charters Towers (Q), inland to Blackall–Carnarvon Ras NP; e. NSW, inland to Pilliga Scrub, c. and sw. mallee areas; all Vic.; s. SA and Kangaroo I.; s. WA n. to Murchison R., *except* wetter sw. corner. Fairly common except in n. Sedentary; nomadic; in se. Aust., regular autumn–winter movement to coastal lowlands.

YELLOW-THROATED HONEYEATER *Lichenostomus flavicollis* 20 cm

Blackish face/upperbreast offset by bright yellow throat and small cream–white mark behind eye; crown/underparts grey. Behaviour like White-eared Honeyeater. **Voice:** common calls: 'tonk, tonk, tonk', 'tchook, tchook' or 'chur-uk, chur-uk'; also 'pick-em-up'. **Habitat:** forests, woodlands, except rainforest; coastal scrub and heath; golfcourses, orchards, parks, gardens. **Breeds:** Aug.–Jan. **Nest:** small cup of grass, bark-shreds, leaves, spiders' web; lined with fur, treefern fibres; wool; often within 1 m of ground in low bush, tussock; occasionally to 10 m in foliage. **Eggs:** 2–3; pale pink or fleshy buff, with dots of chestnut–red, purplish grey. **Range and Status:** Tas., King I. and Furneaux Group, Bass Strait. Common; widespread. Sedentary.

YELLOW-TUFTED HONEYEATER *Lichenostomus melanops* 17–22 cm

Other name: Helmeted Honeyeater.

Striking: *broad glossy black mask ends in bright golden, pointed ear-tufts; throat clear golden yellow, with smutty central stripe.* This guide recognises two races: (1) Nominate race; widespread in se. Aust.: erectile plushlike golden feathers of forehead; crown olive–yellow to dull gold, *merging into* pale olive–fawn/darker olive–grey upperparts; tail tipped paler. Gippsland form larger, darker. (2) Race *cassidix* 'Helmeted Honeyeater', the Vic. bird emblem, found only in this State: larger, with fixed 'helmet' of golden, plushlike feathers on forehead and *dull golden crown/nape cut off by blackish olive–brown back*; tail longer, tipped white. Singles, pairs, parties, in local colonies. Active, aggressive; feeds on blossom-nectar, lerps, 'honeydew', manna, *sap exuding from bark*; insects, berries. Parties skirmish and display, chattering, wings drooping, tails raised. **Voice:** contact call: scratchy 'jeow!', sharp 'yip'; sharp 'querk' in chorus. **Habitat:** nominate race: eucalypt forest/woodland with dense undergrowth of tea-tree, to drier woodlands/scrublands with low, open shrub-layer; mallee, cypress pine, belar, brigalow. Race *cassidix*: streamside/swamp-woodlands of Mountain Swamp Gum; Swamp Gum; with Scented Paperbark, Woolly and Prickly Tea-tree understorey, and sedges (Garnett, 1993). **Breeds:** June–March. **Nest:** substantial cup of grass, bark-strips, spiders' web, egg-sacs, often with paper, wool, leaves, etc.; lined with plant-down, fine grass, feathers; slung in slender fork in shrub, sapling; foliage or hanging bark to 20 m; fallen branches near ground; tussock, mine-shaft. **Eggs:** 2–3; pink-buff; spotted, blotched red–brown, purplish grey. **Range and Status:** nominate race: coastal and inland se. Aust.: n. in brigalow belt to near Clermont (Q), coastally n. to c. Cooloola NP–Noosa (Q) and s. through coastal NSW–Vic. to c. Noojee (Vic.); w. to Carnarvon Ra. NP–Goondiwindi (Q); Moree–Warrumbungle NP–Jerilderie (NSW); e. and n. Vic., w. through ne. c.–w. Vic. to Grampians NP–L. Desert NP, just to se. SA (Naracoorte region). Common. Seasonally nomadic, irruptive. Race *cassidix*: mostly confined to Yellingbo State Faunal Reserve, 50 km e. of Melbourne (Vic.). In 1996, total population of *cassidix*, wild and captive, was *c.* 100 birds. Very rare. Sedentary. Endangered.

WHITE-EARED
HONEYEATER

imm.

YELLOW-THROATED HONEYEATER

♀

♂

YELLOW-TUFTED
HONEYEATER

nominate
race

Gippsland form

race *cassidix* 'Helmeted Honeyeater'

PURPLE-GAPED HONEYEATER *Lichenostomus cratitius* 16–19 cm

Crown grey; mask blackish; note line of lilac gape-skin above yellow throat-streak; pointed yellow ear-coverts. Singles to companies at blossoms: shy; *climbs* through foliage (T. Garnett, pers. comm.). **Similar species:** Grey-headed, Yellow-plumed, Grey-fronted Honeyeaters. **Voice:** clicking notes; harsh chirp; whiplike whistle; in flight, sharp 'twit-twit'; chatterings. **Habitat:** mallee, broombush, banksia/heathland, eucalypt woodlands, scrub on watercourses, blossoming street trees. **Breeds:** July–Dec. **Nest:** cup of bark-strips, grass, spiders' web, egg-sacs; lined with fine grass, plant-down; low in leafy branchlets. **Eggs:** 2; white, tinged pink, spotted, speckled red–brown, in zone. **Range and Status:** patchy across semi-arid s. Aust.: mallee areas of sw. NSW, c. and nw. Vic., s. to Little Desert–Bendigo; w. to s. Flinders Ras. (SA), s. to Coorong, Kangaroo I.; York, Eyre Pens., w. coastally to c. Fowlers Bay. In WA, w. coastally from c. Eyre–Israelite Bay, to Stirling Ra. NP, n. to Northam–Wongan Hills; casual beyond those limits. Uncommon. Sedentary, nomadic.

GREY-HEADED HONEYEATER *Lichenostomus keartlandi* 15–16 cm

Crown clear-grey; underparts pale lemon, lightly streaked fawn; blackish mask broadens to dusky-grey patch on ear-coverts, margined below by broad, upswept yellow neck-plume. Pairs, parties; colonial; sedate. **Voice:** 'chee-toyt, chee-toyt'; mellow 'chickowee'; in flight, peevish 'check, check, check'. Alarm-call: weak alarm-clock trill. **Habitat:** rugged, lightly wooded hillsides/gorges above watercourses; often with spinifex. In parts, e.g. Mt Olga (NT) and Gregory R. (Q), occupies watercourse habitat. Also lowland woodlands, mallee, mulga, desert oaks; blossoming grevilleas, hakeas, eremophilas. **Breeds:** July–Oct. **Nest:** cup of fine bark-strips, plant-down, spiders' web; in slender fork, low shrub. **Eggs:** 2; whitish, pale pink, spotted, blotched pale brown to reddish. **Range and Status:** n. inland Aust.: e. to c. Opalton (Q), n. to c. Burketown (Q), Borroloola–Roper R. (NT), s. Kimberley (WA), s. to c. Cunnamulla (Q), Oodnadatta–Musgrave Ras. (SA), Giles–Carnarvon (WA). Sedentary; seasonally nomadic.

GREY-FRONTED HONEYEATER *Lichenostomus plumulus* 13–16 cm

Other name: Yellow-fronted Honeyeater.

Forehead pale grey; small black mask; crown/upperparts olive–fawn; underparts pale fawn, with darker streaks. Conspicuous yellow neck-plume, finely edged black above. Solitary pairs; companies at blossoms. Wary; flies far; note longish, square-cut tail. **Similar species:** Yellow-tinted, Grey-headed, Yellow-plumed Honeyeaters. **Voice:** in song-flight, 'it-wirt, wirt, wirt'. Alarm-call: single sharp 'boink'. **Habitat:** grassy eucalypt woodlands; timbered rocky hills/gorges above watercourses; inland mallee; mulga; banksia/heath associations. **Breeds:** July–Jan. **Nest:** cup of bark-fibre, spiders' web, egg-sacs; lined with plant-down; low in foliage. **Eggs:** 2 (3); pale salmon-pink, freckled pale red–brown, in zone. **Range and Status:** scattered, *in suitable habitat*, over much of continent w. of Gt Divide; absent from driest deserts and humid coastal regions. Patchy. Sedentary; nomadic.

YELLOW-PLUMED HONEYEATER *Lichenostomus ornatus* 13–16 cm

Other name: Mallee Honeyeater.

Olive–green above with upswept, bright yellow neck-plume; breast whitish, strongly streaked grey–brown. Singles, pairs, parties in colony: vivacious; male has steep song-flight. **Similar species:** Purple-gaped, Grey-fronted Honeyeaters. **Voice:** flatter, harder than White-plumed; liquid 'joe-joe-*hik*'; brisk 'chickwididee'; in song-flight, 'hit joe-joe, 'hit joe-joe, hit'. Alarm-call: flat, machinegun-like trill. **Habitat:** mallee, often far from water; eucalypt woodlands/forests; cypress-pine, belar; coastal heaths with banksias, sheoaks, tea-tree thickets; when travelling, river red gums on watercourses; coastal forests in sw. WA. **Breeds:** July–Jan. **Nest:** cup of dry grass, plant-down, spiders' web; in foliage 1–12 m. **Eggs:** 2; whitish/pale red–buff, deepening at large end; freckled, spotted red–brown. **Range and Status:** s. inland Aust.: mallee areas of c. NSW, e. to Gilgandra–Orange–Temora; mallee of c. and nw. Vic., s. to Tarnagulla; Murray mallee of SA, w. to York–Eyre Pens.; n. to s. Flinders Ras.–L. Frome–Ooldea (SA); w. to Coolgardie (WA); n. to c. Shark Bay. Common locally; at times casual far from 'normal' range.

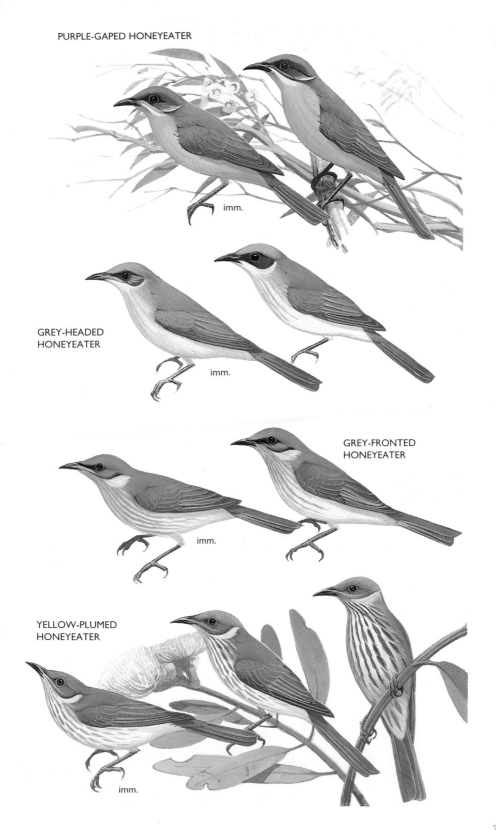

PURPLE-GAPED HONEYEATER

imm.

GREY-HEADED
HONEYEATER

imm.

GREY-FRONTED
HONEYEATER

YELLOW-PLUMED
HONEYEATER

imm.

YELLOW-TINTED HONEYEATER *Lichenostomus flavescens* 14–16 cm

Other name: Pale-yellow Honeyeater.
Bill black; face yellowish with fine, curved black neck-plume. **Immature:** base of bill yellow. Brisk, active; in small resident colonies, nomadic flocks. **Similar species:** in region of Townsville–w. Atherton Tableland, where Fuscous Honeyeater is yellower, it may be confused. **Voice:** sharp little 'jer', 'jer-jer' or harsh descending 'tew, tew, tew' almost continuously. Alarm-call: feeble trilled 'weeweeweewee'. **Habitat:** grassy tropical woodland; thickets on watercourses; river red gums; occasionally mangroves. **Breeds:** July–March. **Nest:** cup of bark-shreds, grass, spiders' web, egg-sacs, lined with fine bark; in shrubby tree, 2–3 m high. **Eggs:** 2; pink, lightly spotted red–brown. **Range and Status:** n. Aust. and coastal islands: from Broome (WA), through Kimberley, across Top End (NT), s. to Larrimah–McArthur R.; nw. Q s. to Mt Isa, e. to Mitchell R., s. C. York Pen. (casual n. on w. coast to Weipa); e. to Atherton Tableland (w. of Herberton)–Innisfail–Hervey Ra., nw. of Townsville. Common. Sedentary; blossom nomad. Also PNG.

FUSCOUS HONEYEATER *Lichenostomus fuscus* 15–16 cm

Plain honeyeater *with dark 'bruised' shading around eye; small black-edged yellow plume on neck. Bill/eye-ring black when breeding, but base of bill/eye-ring yellow in nonbreeding adults and especially imms.* Pairs, family parties in colony; nomadic flocks. Feeds high, inconspicuously, or low in heath in winter. Distinctive calls enliven woodlands. **Similar species:** Grey-fronted, Yellow-tinted, White-plumed Honeyeaters. **Voice:** common call in Vic. is guttural 'pitt-quoll, pitty-quoll'. In song-flight, deep metallic twanging 'tew-tew-tew-tew' or 'clitchit-clee-you', repeated. Contact-call, short 'jeow'. **Habitat:** open forests/woodlands; river red gums on watercourses, rainforest margins; inland scrubs — belar, brigalow; tall mallee, coastal banksia-scrubs, heathlands; gardens. **Breeds:** Aug.–Dec. **Nest:** cup of fine bark-strips, grass, spiders' web; lined with hair, wool, plant-down; in leafy outer branchlets 1–20 m high. **Eggs:** 2–3; yellowish to buff–pink with faint red–brown, pale lilac spots. **Range and Status:** e. and se. Aust.: from Cooktown–Atherton Tableland (Q) to e. SA. In Q, inland to upper Mt Garnet–Charters Towers–Chinchilla–Wallangarra; in NSW, inland to Bingara–Warrumbungle NP–L. Cargelligo–s. Riverina, in river red gum forests; in Vic., widespread in ne. and central woodlands, s. to Melbourne, w. through Grampians NP; *absent from* coastal areas (*except* Gippsland Lakes) and mostly from nw. Vic.; in se. SA, n. to Sutherlands–s. Flinders Ras. Common. Sedentary; blossom nomad; seasonal altitudinal migrations in se. Aust.

WHITE-PLUMED HONEYEATER *Lichenostomus penicillatus* 15–17 cm

Other names: Chickowee, Greenie, Native Canary.
Pale olive–grey with clear-cut white neck-plume, some margined blackish above. In inland, n. Aust. and WA, head yellow; body paler. **Immature:** *rich yellow base to bill; neck-plume less distinct.* Singles, pairs, parties, in colony: feeds low to tops of tallest trees; nervously active. **Similar species:** Yellow-plumed Honeyeater. **Voice:** contact call 'due-wheat!'; brisk 'chickowee' or 'chickabiddy' (local dialects); in song-flight, repeated 'chickowee, chickowee', 'chick-wert, chick-wert'; alarm-call: high-pitched strident trill, like alarm-clock. **Habitat:** seldom far from water in open forests, woodlands; mostly in river red gums on watercourses; but also mallee, blossoming woodlands/heaths, shelterbelts, road reserves, golfcourses, orchards, town/inner city parks, gardens. **Breeds:** July–Jan; inland, any month after rain. **Nest:** deep cup of grass, spiders' web; lined with plant-down, horsehair; slung from outer leafy branchlets 1–25 m high. **Eggs:** 2–3; white, pale buff–deep pink, minutely spotted chestnut–red toward large end; purple–red, deep-lilac spots below surface. **Range and Status:** widespread in e. and se. Aust. and mostly in river red gums on watercourses throughout interior. *Absent from* coastal n. NSW, coastal Q and tropical coastal n. Aust., driest w. deserts, sw. WA (but with local extension coastally s. to c. Perth); *absent from* Bight coast–Nullarbor–Gt Victoria Desert region. Otherwise widespread; common; colonial. Sedentary, with local nomadism.

YELLOW-TINTED HONEYEATER

imm.

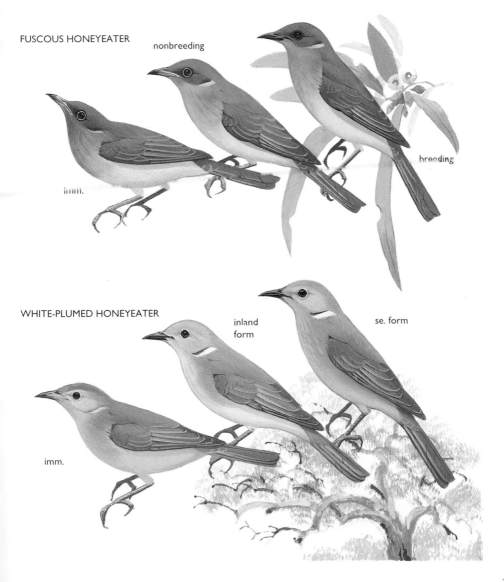

FUSCOUS HONEYEATER

nonbreeding

imm.

breeding

WHITE-PLUMED HONEYEATER

inland
form

se. form

imm.

BLACK-CHINNED HONEYEATER *Melithreptus gularis* 16–17 cm

Note *blue eye-crescent and large creamy nape-band; blackish chin and centre of throat; underparts white, washed grey–buff; legs yellowish.* **Immature:** duller, more fawn; bill orange, tipped brown; *legs orange.* Pairs or small parties: active, demonstrative; forages on limbs, trunks and in foliage, usually fairly high; always travelling 'somewhere else'. Often noted by unusual calls/song. N. race *laetior* ('Golden-backed Honeyeater') has yellow–green eye-crescent; golden olive back; note range. **Similar species:** White-throated Honeyeater: pure white throat/underparts; calls differ. **Voice:** curious, high-pitched, grating, croaking notes, often in flight; developed into song; often in concert. **Habitat:** drier eucalypt forests, woodlands, timber on watercourses, often no understorey; scrubs. Ironbark forests on w. slopes, NSW; n. and c. Vic. **Breeds:** July–Dec. **Nest:** fragile cup of bark-shreds, grass, plant-fibre, wool, spiders' web; slung high in outer foliage. **Eggs:** 2; pale salmon-pink, reddish yellow spots at large end. **Range and Status:** widespread but patchy: from s. C. York Pen. (Q), s. and w. to Victor Harbour–Mt Lofty Ras.–s. Flinders Ras. (SA); in e. Aust., mostly on and w. of Gt Divide, patchily to e. coast from Lakefield NP (ne. Q) to Illawarra region (s. NSW). West from C. York Pen.–se. Gulf lowlands–Mt Isa–Opalton (Q), nominate race replaced by distinctive race *laetior*, extending almost throughout NT, *except* ne. Top End, s. to c. Alice Springs, possibly ne. SA; in n. WA, widespread in Kimberley–Pilbara–w. Gt Sandy Desert region, s. to Newman–NW Cape. Uncommon. Seasonally nomadic.

STRONG-BILLED HONEYEATER *Melithreptus validirostris* 15–17 cm

Other names: Barkbird, Blackcap, Black-capped Honeyeater.
The only Tasmanian honeyeater with a white nape-band; eye-crescent blue; whitish below with blackish mark down from chin; underparts washed grey–brown. **Immature:** bill, eye-ring, legs pale yellow. Pairs, flocks: in absence of treecreepers in Tas., works over limbs, trunks, noisily probing bark with robust bill; occasionally feeds on ground. Mixes with Black-headed Honeyeater outside breeding season. **Similar species:** Black-headed Honeyeater: head/throat black; eye-crescent white. **Voice:** short sharp 'cheep', cheep'. **Habitat:** forests to coastal scrubs with heavy undergrowth. **Breeds:** Aug.–Dec. **Nest:** deep cup of bark-shreds, grass, fur, hair, wool; slung from twigs in top of sapling or outer foliage. **Eggs:** 2–3; pinkish buff, spotted dark red–brown, purplish grey. **Range and Status:** confined to Tas., King I. and Furneaux Group, Bass Strait; more generally distributed in Tas. than Black-headed. Common. Sedentary.

BROWN-HEADED HONEYEATER *Melithreptus brevirostris* 11–14 cm

Duller than rest of group: *crown brownish; ear-coverts darker brown; skin around eye buff to pale cream; nape-band dull cream;* upperparts washed olive–green; underparts pale fawn. **Race *leucogenys*** (sw. WA): head darker, cheeks whiter; eye-ring orange–buff. **Immature:** washed olive–green on crown/wings; *eye-skin pale blue.* Singles, small flocks, especially in autumn: conspicuous by calls, bouncing flight between trees. Works sittella-like over limbs, foliage, hanging acrobatically, fluttering, always moving. Gathers fibre for nest from cattle, koalas, human heads and garments. **Similar species:** imms. of White-throated, White-naped Honeyeaters: patchy brown–orange and blackish heads; check for nearby adults. **Voice:** contact-call: sweet 'yet' or 'yet yet'; loud 'chips'. Song: animated staccato 'chip-chip-chip-chip-chip' starting with separate notes, accelerating, splintering, ending with separate 'chip's. Alarm-call: flat hard trill. **Habitat:** rainforests, eucalypt forests, woodlands, swamp-woodlands; scrublands — mallee, belar; coastal tea-tree, banksia-scrubs. **Breeds:** Aug.–Jan. **Nest:** firmly woven, deep cup of bark-shreds, grass, hair; lined with fur; slung from branchlets in leafy sapling or tree, 3–15 m high. **Eggs:** 2–3; whitish pink, pale salmon; lined, dotted, spotted chestnut–red with similar markings below surface, mostly at large end. **Range and Status:** widespread coastal se. Aust. and islands; s. WA. In e. Q, ranges n. to (? hinterland of) Bowen, inland to Idalia NP, 100 km n. of Tambo–Cunnamulla; e. to Rockhampton–Chinchilla–Cunninghams Gap; sparse ne. NSW, s. to Clarence R.; otherwise widespread e. and s. NSW, inland to Bourke–Ivanhoe–mallee areas of far sw.; nearly throughout Vic.; in s. SA, n. to L. Frome–Flinders Ras.–L. Torrens–Gawler Ras.–Ooldea–Yalata; in s. WA, w. along Bight coast, from Mundrabilla–Zanthus, inland to Leonora (race *leucogenys*, coastal sw. WA, n. to Shark Bay). Common. Sedentary; nomadic or part-migratory.

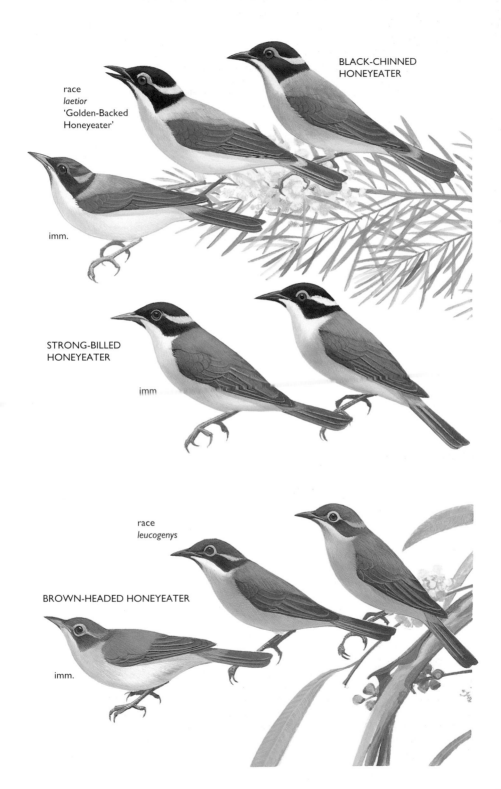

race
laetior
'Golden-Backed
Honeyeater'

imm.

BLACK-CHINNED
HONEYEATER

STRONG-BILLED
HONEYEATER

imm

race
leucogenys

BROWN-HEADED HONEYEATER

imm.

WHITE-THROATED HONEYEATER *Melithreptus albogularis* 12.5–14.5 cm

Like White-naped Honeyeater; *eye-crescent whitish to pale blue; nape-band bold, nearly reaching eye; chin, entire underparts white.* **Immature:** duller; crown patchy tawny black; eye-crescent dull blue–white; fainter nape-mark. Behaves like White-naped, but not strongly migratory. **Similar species:** White-naped Honeyeater: red eye-crescent in e. Aust.; slight black chin; calls differ. In WA, where White-naped has white or greenish eye-crescent, White-throated absent. **Voice:** sharper than White-naped: peevish 'psee'; a repeated 'T-tee, T-tee, t-tee' or 'georgee, georgee' somewhat like double note of Leaden Flycatcher. Flight-call: explosive 'dip'. Song: ringing 'chick, chick-chick, chick-chick, chick', usually from treetop. Alarm-call: flat hard trill, like Brown-headed. **Habitat:** forests, woodlands; paperbark woodlands, timber on watercourses, occasionally mangroves; adjacent parks, gardens. **Breeds:** most months, according to rainfall. **Nest:** delicate cup of bark or other soft material, spiders' web; slung from slender fork in outer foliage, 5–16 m high. **Eggs:** 2; light pink, blotched, freckled red–brown. **Range and Status:** n. and e. Aust. and islands: from Broome (WA), Top End (NT), s. to Victoria R. Downs–Renner Springs; Gulf coast of Q, s. to Mt Isa–Gregory R.; n. to C. York, s. through e. Q, inland to Glendower–Carnarvon Ra. NP–Ipswich; s. coastally to Stuarts Point, *c.* 20 km s. of Nambucca Heads (ne. NSW). Common. Sedentary; part migratory or nomadic. Also s., se. PNG.

WHITE-NAPED HONEYEATER *Melithreptus lunatus* 13–15 cm

Other name: Black-cap.

Small, neat; crown/nape black, *nape-band stops short of eye and in se. Aust. is slender; eye-crescent orange–red; chin blackish.* Upperparts olive–green; underparts white. **Immature:** duller; crown patchily tawny brown/black; eye-crescent orange; face black; slight nape-band, or none. Forms in sw. WA somewhat larger, bill longer, chin darker; eye-crescent *whitish* in sw. coastal areas (race *whitlocki*); greenish n. from Perth and in drier sw. Aust. (race *chloropsis*); *nape-band bolder.* Small open companies, as part of colony: active in higher foliage, hanging bark; flocks chase through treetops, chittering. **Similar species:** Brown-headed Honeyeater for imm. White-naped. White-throated Honeyeater: bolder nape-band; eye-crescent pale blue; chin/throat white; note range. **Voice:** thin, scratchy 'shirp, shirp, shirp'; constant cheeps and chitterings; liquid, mellow 'tsew-tsew-tsew'. Alarm-call, taken up by many birds when flying raptor appears: tense, quiet 'pew, pew, pew'. **Habitat:** forests, woodlands; in se. Aust. prefers smooth-barked eucalypts such as manna gums; also stringybarks, ironbarks, coastal scrubs, adjacent parks, gardens. **Breeds:** communally, Aug.–Dec. **Nest:** delicate hanging cup of fine grass, bark-shreds, plant-down, spiders' web; slung from slender fork, 5–20 m high. **Eggs:** 2–3; pink, buff, finely spotted red–brown, grey, mostly at large end. **Range and Status:** coastal e. Aust. and sw. WA: from highlands of ne. Q (Atherton Tableland–Mt Spec) to Yorke Pen. and Kangaroo I. (SA). In Q, ranges inland to Duaringa–Carnarvon Ras. NP–Warwick; in NSW, inland to Mt Kaputar NP–Warrumbungle NP–Cowra–Moulamein; widespread in e. and s. Vic.; winter visitor Kiata, Swan Hill; in se. SA, n. to Morgan–Clare, w. to Yorke Pen. In sw. WA, widespread s. and w. of a line connecting Esperance and Moora. Common; migratory. Part of se. Aust. population migrates coastally n. April–May, to ne. NSW–se. Q, returning in Aug.–Oct. At Mallacoota (e. Vic.), Blue Mts, Tuggerah Lakes (NSW), etc., conspicuous north-bound autumn flocks, with Yellow-faced Honeyeaters, etc., may number thousands per day. Spring return less conspicuous.

BLACK-HEADED HONEYEATER *Melithreptus affinis* 12.5–14.5 cm

Other name: Black-cap.

Note range; distinguished by *short bill, black head/throat, with small whitish eye-crescent; no nape-band;* olive–green above, white below, with *black mark on side of breast.* **Immature:** head patchy dun–brown. Usually in flocks, larger in autumn–winter. Active, pugnacious; mixes with Strong-billed Honeyeaters; raids fruit. **Voice:** distinctive sharp whistle; also harsh 'shirp shirp', like White-naped. **Habitat:** drier eucalypt forests, woodlands; coastal heaths, orchards, gardens. **Breeds:** Oct.–Jan. **Nest:** deep cup of fibrous bark, fine grass, plant-down, hair, fur, spiders' web; slung in foliage often at considerable height. **Eggs:** 2–3; pale pink, spotted red–brown, purple–grey. **Range and Status:** confined to Tas., King I. and Furneaux Group, Bass Strait; well-distributed in n. and e. Tas., up to *c.* 900 m, but straggler to suitable pockets of habitat on w. coast. Common. Sedentary.

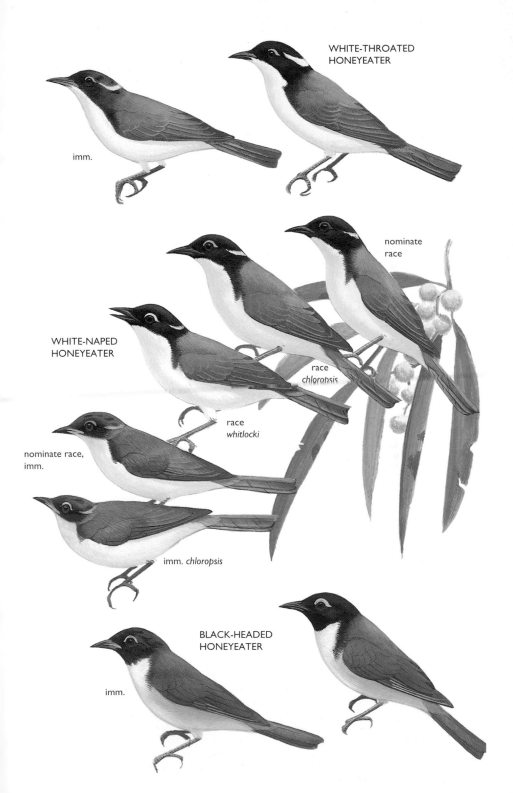

WHITE-THROATED
HONEYEATER

imm.

nominate
race

WHITE-NAPED
HONEYEATER

race
chloropsis

race
whitlocki

nominate race,
imm.

imm. chloropsis

BLACK-HEADED
HONEYEATER

imm.

NEW HOLLAND HONEYEATER *Phylidonyris novaehollandiae* 17–18cm

Other name: Yellow-winged Honeyeater.

Bill black, longish; *face black, with white eye, white rear eyebrow, whisker-tuft and ear-tuft*; sparse spiky 'beard'; *bold yellow wing-panels; white tips to outer tail-feathers visible in flight.* **Immature:** browner; gape yellow; eye grey; ear-tuft smaller. Singles, parties, in local colony: active at blossoms; with fights, chases, noisy 'corroborees'. **Similar species:** White-cheeked Honeyeater. **Voice:** sharp 'jik'; squeaky 'phsee'; high-pitched alarm-rattle, jigging scolding. **Habitat:** eucalypt forests/woodlands with scrubby understorey; creekside, coastal scrubs, heathlands; mallee-spinifex, golfcourses, orchards, parks, gardens. **Breeds:** mostly July–Jan. **Nest:** rough small cup of twigs, grass, stems, spiders' web, plant-down; in fork of low dense shrub, bracken, 1–3 m high. **Eggs:** 2–3; buff–white to pink; spotted, blotched chestnut–red, slate-grey. **Range and Status:** coastal se. Aust.; from *c.* Gympie (Q) to s. Eyre Pen.–Kangaroo I. (SA), Tas., Bass Strait islands. In s. WA, widespread s. of Cocklebiddy–L. King–Eneabba. Common (except coastally n. of Sydney). Sedentary; autumn–winter dispersal in WA.

WHITE-CHEEKED HONEYEATER *Phylidonyris nigra* 16–18 cm

Differs from New Holland in *dark-brown eye, larger white cheekpatch; no white tips to outer tail-feathers.* Pairs, parties: active, with group-displays. **Voice:** squeaky 'chip-chew, chippy-chew'; quick 'chip' or 'hiccup'. Flight-song: 'twee-ee-twee-ee'. Alarm-call: rapid 'hee-hee-hee', etc. **Habitat:** rainforest margins, eucalypt forests, watercourse-vegetation; coastal scrubs, paperbarks, wet heaths. In sw. WA: coastal thickets, sandplain-heaths, woodland understorey. **Breeds:** April–Nov. (ne. Q); Aug.–Nov.(NSW, s. WA). **Nest:** rough cup of twigs, bark, grass, rootlets, spiders' web, plant-down; low in shrub, heath, tall grass. **Eggs:** 2–3; like New Holland. **Range and Status:** coastal e. Aust. (and highlands); and sw. WA. Nominate race: highlands of ne. Q, from Atherton Tableland s. to Eungella NP, near Mackay. Main population from *c.* Tropic in Q, s. on coast and highlands to *c.* Bermagui (NSW); casual inland, far e. Vic.; vagrant e. Tas. Common n. of Sydney, scarce s. coast. In s. WA, race *gouldi* widespread Israelite Bay–Murchison R. (w. coast); sparse n. of Perth, *absent* sw. forest zone. Common. Sedentary; local seasonal movements.

WHITE-FRONTED HONEYEATER *Phylidonyris albifrons* 16–18 cm

Unusual: *white mask from forehead to eye; small red spot behind eye; blackish, scaly head; black throat/breast*; underparts white. **Female:** browner. **Immature:** browner; face dusky; no red spot. Singles, pairs, flocks: shy, elusive; often first noted by calls from shrub-top. **Voice:** metallic, scratchy, in minor key: 'pert-pertoo-peet'; 'quack-peter-peter-peter'; 'peter-peet-peet'; 'tsing tsing tsing'; peevish, canary-like 'tweet'; scolding 'tuck, tuck', with click. **Habitat:** drier inland and coastal scrubs, heaths; mulga, mallee, blossoming shrubs, timber on watercourses, eucalypt woodlands. **Breeds:** Aug.–Dec., or after rain. **Nest:** cup of grass, bark-shreds, spiders' web, plant-down; in small low shrub or on ground. **Eggs:** 2–3; pale buff, clouded reddish, spotted chestnut, purplish grey. **Range and Status:** widespread across Aust. mainland w. of Divide and s. of tropical n. Aust. Resident coastal WA: Broome–Perth and s. coast Albany (WA)–Coorong (SA). Moves to coastal s. Aust. in summer; n. to Kimberley and n. coast in winter; generally coastwards in droughts. Blossom nomad/migrant. Locally common; at times migrates in large numbers.

WHITE-STREAKED HONEYEATER *Trichodere cockerelli* 16–18 cm

Other name: Brush-throated Honeyeater.

Bill *tipped black, blue–grey at base; head/face dark grey; eye red; yellow line from bill below eye; golden yellow tuft behind ear-coverts; bristle-like whitish plumes on throat/breast.* **Immature:** gape yellow; eye brown; head markings simpler, browner above, off-white below, without plumes. Singles, pairs, small parties: aggressive; forages in blossoming banksias, eucalypts, paperbarks with other honeyeaters, sunbirds. **Voice:** loud scolding; sweet, liquid, high-pitched, four-note whistle like Brown Honeyeater: 'blink blink blink', etc. **Habitat:** paperbarks, tropical heathlands, vine scrub, nearby eucalypt woodlands. **Breeds:** Jan.; April–June. **Nest:** cup of fine rootlets, grass, spiders' web; lined with grass; in low fork *c.* 1 m+ high. **Eggs:** 2; salmon–pink, spotted, blotched darker. **Range and Status:** C. York Pen. (Q), s. to Archer R. on w. coast, Helenvale on e. coast. Fairly common. Locally nomadic.

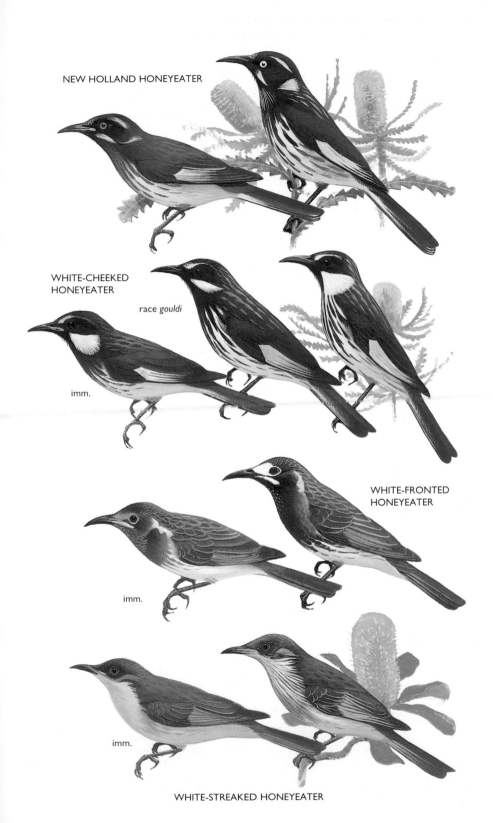

NEW HOLLAND HONEYEATER

WHITE-CHEEKED
HONEYEATER

race *gouldi*

imm.

WHITE-FRONTED
HONEYEATER

imm.

imm.

WHITE-STREAKED HONEYEATER

CRESCENT HONEYEATER *Phylidonyris pyrrhoptera* 15–16 cm

Bill longish, curved. **Male:** *dark grey with fine black/white eyebrow; black 'wishbone' on whitish breast; bold yellow panel on wing/tail.* **Female:** *browner; 'wishbone' less distinct.* **Immature:** like dull adults. Singles, pairs; autumn–winter companies in blossoming eucalypts, banksias, heath, correas, mistletoes; heard afar. Shy; tamer in gardens. **Similar species:** Tawny-crowned Honeyeater, Eastern Spinebill. **Voice:** high-pitched, jagged 'eejik!'; in winter, simple 'jik'. **Habitat:** alpine woodlands; wetter eucalypt forests/woodlands; understorey on creeks, gullies; coastal scrubs, tall heaths, mallee, orchards, gardens. **Breeds:** July–Jan. **Nest:** bulky cup of stringy bark, spiders' web, grass, plant-down, hair, feathers; in low dense shrub, swordgrass, fern, 1–2 m high. **Eggs:** 3; pale pink, red–buff, deeper at large end; spotted pink, red, chestnut, purplish brown. **Range and Status:** coastal se. Aust.; Bass Strait islands and Tas., where abundant; from Barrington Tops NP–Hunter R. region (NSW) to (isolate population) Mt Lofty Ras.–Kangaroo I. (SA). Widespread breeding in high country in summer; disperses to lowlands in autumn–winter; casual lower Murray R. (SA). Common. Seasonally dispersive.

TAWNY-CROWNED HONEYEATER *Phylidonyris melanops* 16–17 cm

Slender, graceful, long-billed *pale brown and white* honeyeater: *crown creamy-buff, separated by white eyebrow from black mask curving in 'wishbone' down sides of white breast.* **Immature:** *brownish with buff streaks; throat yellow.* Singles, pairs, open companies: sits atop shrubs, dead branches, to watch, sing. Flies pipit-like, low to cover or gracefully far/high, showing cinnamon wing-linings. **Similar species:** Crescent Honeyeater, Eastern/Western Spinebills. **Voice:** liquid, fluty, ascending 'a-peer-peer-pee-pee'; shorter, beautiful, liquid, metallic phrases. **Habitat:** heathlands; stunted banksia, sandplain vegetation; mallee, 'grass-tree country', blossoming eucalypt woodlands, regrowth, button-grass woodlands, street trees. **Breeds:** June–Jan. **Nest:** untidy cup of grass, bark-strips, spiders' web, plant-down, wool; near ground in dense low vegetation. **Eggs:** 2 (1–4); large, pointed, whitish, blotched chestnut–red at large end. **Range and Status:** from ne. NSW (Evans Head) to Eyre Pen.–Kangaroo I. (SA), inland to Blue Mts (NSW); coastal e. Vic. to Big Desert NP. Autumn–winter dispersal to w. slopes–Murray Valley–s. Flinders Ras. Resident coastal Tas. In s. WA, widespread w. and s. of Israelite Bay–Norseman–Southern Cross–Murchison R., disperses inland in winter. Fairly common. Sedentary; seasonally nomadic.

EASTERN SPINEBILL *Acanthorhynchus tenuirostris* 15–16.5 cm

Unmistakable fine, curved bill. **Male:** *crown and 'wishbone' black; rufous/black patch on white throat; wings gunmetal; underparts rufous–buff; tail black, prominently edged white.* **Female:** *crown grey.* **Immature:** *olive–grey above, plain yellow–buff below.* Singles, pairs: flight erratic, with quick 'flip flop'; flashes white outer tail-feathers; hovers. **Similar species:** Crescent, Tawny-crowned Honeyeaters. **Voice:** long, tinkling, staccato piping; explosive twittering rondos; twittering flight-song. **Habitat:** forests, woodlands, heathlands, flowering shrubs, thickets, gardens. **Breeds:** Aug.–Dec. **Nest:** cup of grass, moss, hair, spiders' web, feathers; slung in foliage 1–5 m+ high. **Eggs:** 2–3; whitish, pink–buff, spotted chestnut, brown. **Range and Status:** coastal e., se. Aust. and Tas.: ne. Q highlands above 500 m, from near Cooktown to Eungella NP, n. of Mackay. Coastal se. Aust., from Cooloola NP–Fraser I. (Q) to s. Vic., Tas., Bass Strait islands, w. to Mt Lofty Ras., Kangaroo I. (SA). Extends well inland in Q–NSW. Autumn–winter dispersal from highlands to lowlands. Common. Sedentary; dispersive.

WESTERN SPINEBILL *Acanthorhynchus superciliosus* 12–15 cm

Unmistakable fine, curved bill. **Male:** *black crown; white eyebrow; black mask; white throat; orange–chestnut collar, bordered below by white/black bands; outer tail-feathers white, flirted in flight.* **Female:** *plainer; nape rufous; breast rufous–buff, without bands.* **Immature:** like plainer female. Behaviour like Eastern; less adapted to urban encroachment. **Voice:** high, staccato piping. **Habitat:** understorey of forests/woodlands; sandplain heaths, coastal scrubs; thickets of banksias/dryandras. **Breeds:** Sept.–Jan. **Nest:** cup of bark-shreds, plant-stems, spiders' web, plant-down; 1–5 m in shrub, low tree. **Eggs:** 1–2; blue–white, pink–white, spotted, blotched chestnut, purple–brown, in zone. **Range and Status:** sw. WA: from n. of Jurien Bay to Israelite Bay inland to Moora–Corrigin–L. Grace. Common. Locally nomadic.

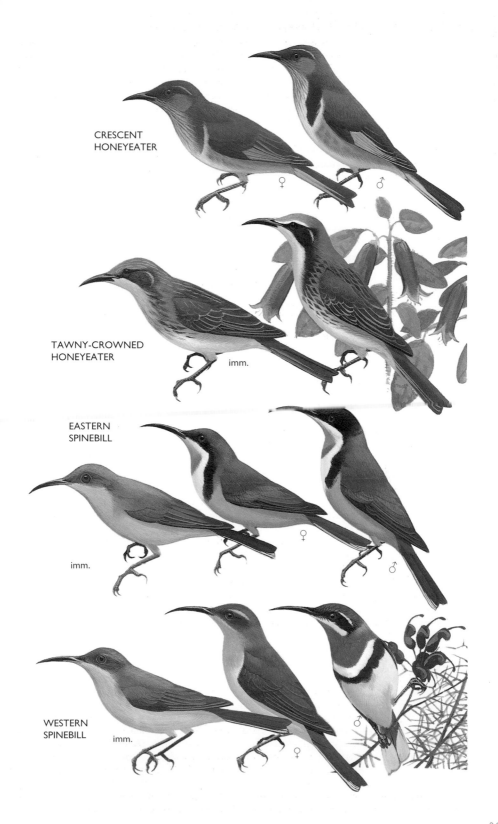

CRESCENT
HONEYEATER

♀   ♂

TAWNY-CROWNED
HONEYEATER

imm.

EASTERN
SPINEBILL

imm.

♀   ♂

WESTERN
SPINEBILL

imm.   ♀   ♂

BROWN-BACKED HONEYEATER *Ramsayornis modestus* 11–13 cm

Note pinkish brown bill and legs; olive–brown above and on ear-coverts; throat/underparts white, with *sparse brownish scallops. Thin white line from bill under eye, above a thinner dark brown streak.* **Immature:** gape-streak washed yellow; breast *streaked* brown; rump rufous. Pairs, small colonies: lively; with other honeyeaters at blossom. **Similar species:** Bar-breasted; imm. Rufous-banded, Rufous-throated Honeyeaters. **Voice:** fussy, chattering 'shee-shee-shee'; sharper 'chit' rapidly repeated. Flight-call: 'mick-mick-mick'. **Habitat:** paperbark woodlands, waterside thickets, blossoming eucalypt woodlands, mangroves; ventures far from cover; perches dead trees. **Breeds:** Oct.–March. **Nest:** *domed,* hanging, of paperbark strips, spiders' web, egg-sacs; suspended from branchlets, 1–16 m high, near or over water, in loose colony in paperbarks, eucalypts, mangroves. **Eggs:** 2; white, dotted purplish black. Parasitised by Brush Cuckoo. **Range and Status:** coastal ne. Q and islands: from C. York (Q), s. on w. coast to Archer R.; on e. coast s. to *c.* Bowen; inland to Coen–Atherton Tableland. Common; patchier in higher, drier parts of range. Migratory, or seasonally nomadic. Also Torres Strait Is., PNG.

BAR-BREASTED HONEYEATER *Ramsayornis fasciatus* 13–15 cm

Crown scalloped black and white; black line from bill down throat; underparts white, scalloped black. **Immature:** *breast streaked; primaries edged yellow–buff.* Singles, pairs: often with other honeyeaters at blossoms; inconspicuous. **Similar species:** Brown-backed Honeyeater. **Voice:** soft, purring 'mew'; shrill quick piping. **Habitat:** paperbarks; eucalypt woodland, blossoming grevilleas, etc.; mangroves, monsoon forest, montane heathland. **Breeds:** Dec.–April. **Nest:** *domed,* hooded; of paperbark, rootlets, spiders' web, hanging bark-strips; in paperbark over water, *c.* 1 m high. **Eggs:** 2–3; white, freckled, dotted light red–brown, zoned at large end. **Range and Status:** coastal tropical n. Aust. and islands: from Broome–Fitzroy R. (WA) through Kimberley; Top End (NT), s. to Mataranka–McArthur R.; e. on rivers of Gulf to C. York Pen. (Q); s. on e. coast to *c.* Rockhampton (Q). Mostly common; scarce in e. Q. Blossom nomad.

MACLEAY'S HONEYEATER *Xanthotis macleayana* 20 cm

Unusual stocky, slightly scruffy honeyeater with largish bill, short tail: *patch of bare buff skin around eye, yellowish at distance. Cap black, plumage grey and ochre, with plentiful yellow–white streaks; under tail-coverts deep grey; legs blue–grey.* **Immature:** duller. Singles, pairs: movements deliberate; climbs trunks, vine-tangles; acrobatic at blossoming eucalypts, umbrella trees; feeds on insects, oranges, mandarins, berries in orchards, gardens, bird-tables. **Similar species:** Tawny-breasted Honeyeater. **Voice:** brisk, rollicking 'pchee, cherreep, pchee cherreep' or 'a free TV, a free TV', differing locally. **Habitat:** rainforest margins; vegetation on watercourses; paperbarks; blossoming eucalypt forests, woodlands; orchards, gardens. **Breeds:** Oct.–Jan. **Nest:** cup of palm-fibre, leaves, bark-shreds, spiders' web; low to high in canopy. **Eggs:** 2; pinkish buff, spotted red, chestnut with lilac, dark-grey markings. **Range and Status:** ne. Q: from Cooktown coastally s. to Mt Spec NP near Townsville; lowlands to highland rainforests, incl. Atherton Tableland. Common. Probably sedentary.

TAWNY-BREASTED HONEYEATER *Xanthotis flaviventer* 18–20 cm

Other name: Buff-breasted Honeyeater.
More softly marked, less streaked than Macleay's. Note *bare pale buff skin around eye, pale grey throat/neck, buff tips to wing-coverts, tawny, softly streaked underparts, brownish white under tail-coverts; legs blue–grey.* **Immature:** plainer; mantle scalloped. Singles, pairs, parties: active, pugnacious, noisy; feeds in high foliage, blossoms; lower at edge of scrub. **Similar species:** Macleay's Honeyeater. Magnificent Riflebird, female. **Voice:** 'which-witch-is-which'; loud whistled song. **Habitat:** vine scrub; edges of rainforests; eucalypt woodlands; heathlands, mangroves. **Breeds:** Nov.–March. **Nest:** cup of bark-shreds, paperbark; lined with rootlets, bark-strips; in shrub, leafy tree, incl. mangrove, 3–16 m high. **Eggs:** 2; whitish pink with small red–brown, grey spots; glossy. **Range and Status:** n. C. York Pen. (Q): s. to Aurukun on w. coast; Rocky R. on e. coast. Uncommon. Sedentary. Also PNG and islands.

BROWN-BACKED HONEYEATER

imm.

BAR-BREASTED
HONEYEATER

imm.

MACLEAY'S
HONEYEATER

imm.

TAWNY-BREASTED
HONEYEATER

imm.

RUFOUS-THROATED HONEYEATER *Conopophila rufogularis* 13–14 cm

Grey–brown honeyeater with distinctive rufous throat; bold yellow edges to flight/tail feathers. **Immature:** throat fawn–white. Parties, flocks: demonstrative, with noisy, wing-fluttering displays; joins other honeyeaters at blossoms. **Similar species:** Rufous-banded Honeyeater: head greyer; breastband rufous. **Voice:** sharp 'zit-zit'; chatters like House Sparrow, tone sweet or scratchy, peevish. **Habitat:** near water; paperbarks, mangroves, scrublands, grassed woodlands; river red gum thickets; gardens, street trees. **Breeds:** Sept.–April. **Nest:** deep cup of paperbark-strips, grass, spiders' web; lined with plant-down; in foliage, 1–6 m. **Eggs:** 2–3; white with pink, red spots. **Range and Status:** coastal n. Aust.: from *c.* Broome (WA) to C. York Pen. (n. to Embley Ra., *c.* 80 km inland of Weipa); inland parts of Atherton Tableland, s. to Ayr (Q); casual s. to Gympie–Fraser I. In summer, further inland. Common in n., patchy e. coast. Blossom nomad.

RUFOUS-BANDED HONEYEATER *Conopophila albogularis* 12–13 cm

Head greyer than Rufous-throated; white throat cut off by broad rufous breastband; bold yellow edges to flight/tail-feathers. **Immature:** *breastband partial or absent.* Pairs, parties: noisy, aggressive with other honeyeaters at blossoms. **Similar species:** Rufous-throated, imm. **Voice:** repeated, rising 'zzheep', like young cuckoo. In group-display, brisk, silvery 'sweeta-swee, sweeta-swee'. **Habitat:** watercourse vegetation, mangroves, paperbarks, monsoon forest, eucalypt woodland, coastal scrubs, cultivation, gardens. **Breeds:** Sept.–April. **Nest:** deep hammock of paperbark-strips, plant-fibres, spiders' web; lined with grass; 1–3 m among leaves, often over water. **Eggs:** 2–3; white, spotted, dotted red–brown, in cap. **Range and Status:** coastal n. Aust. and islands: from Top End (NT), s. to Victoria R. Downs–Katherine–Roper R.; e. on Gulf coast to w. and ne. coast C. York Pen. (Q), s. to *c.* Lakefield NP (Stewart, 1984). Common. Also Torres Strait, PNG, Aru Is.

GREY HONEYEATER *Conopophila whitei* 10.5–12 cm

Tiny honeyeater with nearly straight, grey bill, blackish at tip; slight dark mark from bill to eye; faint pale eye-ring. Upperparts/breast cold grey; throat/underparts paler; flight/tail-feathers blackish brown; tail faintly tipped white. Worn plumage browner; tail-tips buffish. **Immature:** *thin yellowish eye-ring; yellow–green wash on flight-feathers; faint yellow wash on throat; hint of rufous–grey breastband.* Unobtrusive: searches mulga foliage for insects, flies tree to tree; pierces red *Eremophila* blossoms for nectar (Roberts, 1980–81); takes mistletoe berries. **Similar species:** Western Gerygone; Thornbills. **Voice:** 'slightly harsh . . . quite loud, "cre-seek" . . . last note higher . . . like rapid version of . . . "kisseek" of White-Bellied Cuckoo Shrike' (Roberts, 1981). Also 'short . . . reel not unlike . . . Fairy-wren [and] short, high-pitched jingling song' (Curry, 1979). **Habitat:** mature mulga, *Acacia aneura*, woodland; open mulga with spinifex; tall open scrub dominated by other acacias, eremophilas; sandhills with red mulga, *A. cyperophylla*; canegrass, beefwood, desert bloodwood. **Breeds:** Aug.–Sept. (Nov.) and May in Pilbara (WA); (after rain?) (Start & Fuller, 1995). **Nest:** fragile hammock of plant-fibre, spiders' web; in outer foliage *c.* 2 m high. **Eggs:** 1 (2); white, pink–white, mid-zone of red–brown markings. **Range and Status:** inland Aust., from ne. SA (possibly sw. Q) to Pilbara (WA); n. to *c.* Frewena–Wave Hill (NT); s. through nw. SA (Musgrave Ras.–Granite Downs) to Gt Victoria Desert–Wanjarri–Yalgoo (WA), (Paton, 1981). Regular in mulga belt n. of Alice Springs (NT). Rare, little known; nomadic.

GREEN-BACKED HONEYEATER *Glycichaera fallax* 11–12 cm

Grey bill nearly as long as head; eye grey–white, with narrow whitish eye-ring; back olive–green, wings browner; tail blackish brown; underparts fawn, washed yellow; legs blue–grey. **Immature:** duller; gape pale fleshy yellow; eye brown with *slight* pale grey eye-ring. Singles, pairs, small winter flocks (Pavey, 1991). Movements rapid; gleans insects in rainforest foliage. Hops on limbs, hangs head-down, flutters, hovers to take insects; chases, twists through trees. **Similar species:** Fairy Warbler, female: similar, but *bill shorter*; eye red. **Voice:** thin, insect-like 'peep'; soft twitter; aggressive, rapid 'twit' or 'twee-twee-twit-twit'. **Habitat:** rainforest, vine forest, blossoming eucalypt woodlands. **Breeding:** nesting not recorded; possibly winter. **Range and Status:** e. C. York Pen. (Q), from Iron Ra s. to McIlwraith Ra., w. to near Weipa. Fairly common. Sedentary. Also PNG and islands.

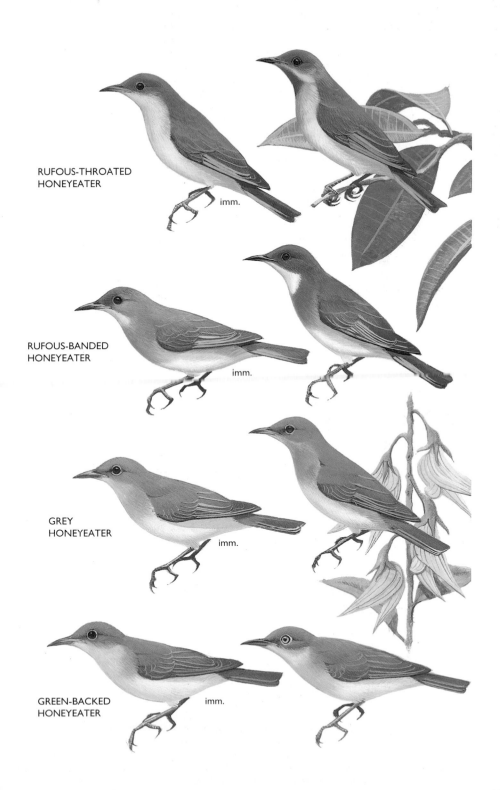

RUFOUS-THROATED
HONEYEATER

imm.

RUFOUS-BANDED
HONEYEATER

imm.

GREY
HONEYEATER

imm.

GREEN-BACKED
HONEYEATER

imm.

BANDED HONEYEATER *Certhionyx pectoralis* 11.5–13.5 cm

Note black upperparts and breastband, white underparts and rump. **Immature:** *gape/face yellow; crown/back tawny, mottled;* breastband absent or brownish. Pairs, small flocks: active, noisy in blossoms. **Similar species:** Black, Pied Honeyeaters. **Voice:** throaty 'dup'; scratchy 'jap'; peevish, finch-like 'tweet'; clear, cheerful song. **Habitat:** grassy woodlands; paperbarks, coastal scrubs, mangroves, watercourse vegetation; drier habitats when bauhinias, etc., blossom. **Breeds:** Oct.-April. **Nest:** flimsy cup of grass, bark, spiders' web; in foliage of tea-tree, paperbark, low to 6 m. **Eggs:** 2; cream–buff, with band of deeper buff. **Range and Status:** tropical n. and ne. Aust.: from w. Kimberley (WA), through Top End (NT), Gulf coast and C. York Pen. (Q), s. to *c.* Cooktown; inland to Victoria R. Downs (NT)–Mt Isa–Charters Towers (Q). Common. Blossom nomad.

BLACK HONEYEATER *Certhionyx niger* 10–12 cm

Bill longish, curved. **Male:** *black upperparts and wedge down centre of white underparts.* **Female:** *grey–brown; obscure whitish rear-eyebrow; underparts whitish, mottled grey–brown; legs blackish.* **Immature:** like smutty female. Pairs, parties: perches dead limbs, blossoms; hawks flying insects. Male flies steeply up *c.* 15 m, descends on quivering, down-arched wings, calling. Females gather campfire ashes (for calcium?). **Similar species:** Pied Honeyeater. **Voice:** clear, 'seep' or 'see-see', from top of twig, and in song-flight; sparrow-like chirp; chatter. **Habitat:** blossoming eremophilas, desert bloodwoods; regrowth with dead, fire-blackened branches. **Breeds:** Aug.–Dec., and after rain. **Nest:** frail cup of grass, twigs, rootlets, spiders' web; in low fork of live, dead or burned mallee, acacia; fallen branch. **Eggs:** 2; buff; spotted, zoned olive–grey. **Range and Status:** arid inland Aust., w. to Broome–Geraldton (WA): patchy; moves toward s. coasts spring/summer; n. coasts autumn/winter. In drought irrupts coastwards in all States; may breed. Locally common. Blossom nomad.

PIED HONEYEATER *Certhionyx variegatus* 15–18 cm

Male: *note arched blue–grey bill, blue–grey wattle under eye, black throat; white wingbar, rump, tail-panels and underparts.* **Female:** grey–brown above with faint pale eyebrow; *smaller wattle; strong 'netted' pattern on wings;* whitish underparts streaked darker. Pairs, parties: in blossoming eremophilas, hakeas, grevilleas, mistletoes, eucalypts; nervous, flicks tail. Courting males call incessantly; fly with quivering wings; rise steeply, dive bomblike, tail fanned. **Similar species:** Black Honeyeater. White-winged Triller. **Voice:** courting males emit incessant high-pitched, morse code-like 'peepee-pee-pee' or 'pee-peepee-pee'. **Habitat:** arid scrublands, mulga, mallee-spinifex, flowering shrubs/trees, eucalypt woodlands. **Breeds:** Sept.–Nov., or after rain. **Nest:** untidy cup of grass, twigs, spiders' web; in fork of shrub, tree to 5 m. **Eggs:** 2–3 (4); pale fawn, blotched pale grey; clustered blackish spots. **Range and Status:** arid interior, e. to c. Q–NSW, to w. coast *c.* Port Hedland–Geraldton (WA); s. to Nullarbor Plain–Murray mallee (SA); casual nw. Vic. Patchy, irregular. Locally common; highly nomadic.

PAINTED HONEYEATER *Grantiella picta* 16 cm

Male: *bill deep pink; eye red; upperparts black; golden edges to flight/tail-feathers;* underparts white; black spots on flanks. **Female:** smaller, browner, fewer spots. **Immature:** like female; more spotted. Singles, colonies of mated pairs, nomadic parties. Elusive: eats mistletoe berries, nectar, insects. Courting males call from treetops, and in song-flight; chase in dipping, weaving pursuits. **Voice:** clear, sing-song: 'Sue-see, Sue-see', or reverse, 'see-Sue', etc., second syllable higher. **Habitat:** mistletoes in eucalypt forests/woodlands; black box on watercourses; box–ironbark–yellow gum woodlands; paperbarks, casuarinas; mulga, other acacias; trees on farmland; gardens. **Breeds:** Oct.–March. **Nest:** flimsy cup of plant-fibre, spiders' web, rootlets; in foliage 3–20 m high. **Eggs:** 2–3; oval, salmon-pink; spotted, speckled red–brown, lilac. **Range and Status:** e. and n. Aust.: spring–summer (Sept.–Feb.) breeding migrant to se. Aust., e. to *c.* Brisbane (Q), Hunter R.–Sydney shale (NSW), w. slopes–Riverina, c. Vic., s. to *c.* Wangaratta–Lower Plenty–You Yangs–Grampians NP–Edenhope. Winter dispersal n. into Q (C. York Pen.), far e. SA–e. NT, n. to *c.* McArthur R.–lower Top End. Movements influenced by rainfall, fruiting of mistletoes. Rare. Migratory; nomadic. Threatened.

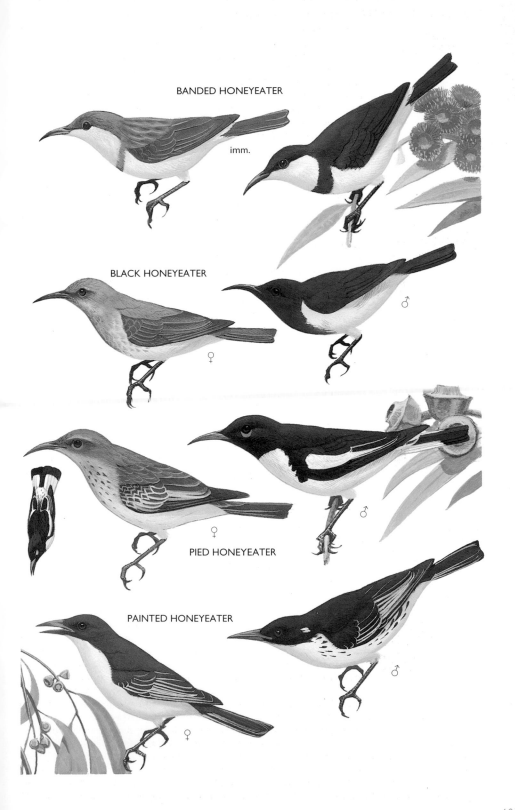

BANDED HONEYEATER

imm.

BLACK HONEYEATER

♀

♂

♂

♀

PIED HONEYEATER

♂

PAINTED HONEYEATER

♂

♀

DUSKY HONEYEATER *Myzomela obscura* 12–15 cm

Distinctive rich coppery grey–brown, darker on throat. Some paler or *have faint rusty wash on head/neck.* **Immature:** gape yellow. Pairs, parties: pugnacious; hangs, hovers at blossoms with other honeyeaters. **Similar species:** Brown; Red-headed, Scarlet Honeyeaters (females). **Voice:** obscure squeak: 'see see'; mournful whistle; high-pitched, trilling, tzizzing chatterings; winnowing scoldings. **Habitat:** vine scrubs, rainforests, watercourse-vegetation, blossoming eucalypt woodlands; mangroves, paperbarks, lantana thickets, gardens. **Breeds:** Aug.–Dec. **Nest:** cup of rootlets, grass, spiders' web; in outer foliage, to 5 m. **Eggs:** 2; pink–white, finely spotted red–brown, dark grey. **Range and Status:** tropical coastal n. Aust. and islands: from Victoria R.–Top End (NT) e. to Gulf coast, s. to Katherine Gorge; in Q, from Edward R., n. around C. York, coastally s. to *c.* Southport, inland to *c.* Kenilworth. Common, *except* s. of Rockhampton. Also Torres Strait, PNG, Aru Is., Moluccas. Sedentary; locally nomadic.

RED-HEADED HONEYEATER *Myzomela erythrocephala* 11–13 cm

Male: *red head/neck/rump cut off by dark brown wings/back and dark grey underparts.* **Female and immature:** *brown, washed red on forehead/throat.* Pairs, companies at blossoms: darting, flicks tail, sallies after insects. **Similar species:** Dusky, Brown, Scarlet Honeyeaters. **Voice:** repetitive, metallic, jingling song (Hall, 1974). Contact-call: harsh 'chiew-chiew'; female, sibilant squeak. **Habitat:** mangroves, monsoon forests, vine scrubs, blossoming eucalypt woodlands; paperbarks, watercourse-vegetation, parks, gardens. **Breeds:** March–Sept. **Nest:** cup of fine bark-strips, spiders' web, leaves; lined with bark, rootlets; in leafy branch of mangrove to 12 m over water. **Eggs:** 2; whitish, with fine red spots, blotches. **Range and Status:** coastal tropical nw. and n. Aust. and islands: from Broome (WA) to C. Melville, e. C. York Pen. (Q); inland to *c.* Katherine Gorge (NT). Common. Sedentary; local nomadic movements. Also w. Torres Strait, PNG, e. Indonesia.

SCARLET HONEYEATER *Myzomela sanguinolenta* 10–11 cm

Male: *head/breast/back and rump bright scarlet; wings/tail blackish; underparts whitish.* **Female:** *tawny brown; slight reddish wash on chin.* **Immature:** like female; gape yellow. Singles, pairs, companies at blossoms: aggressive, chases in bouncing flight. Males call from treetops, high branches. **Similar species:** Red-headed, Brown, Dusky Honeyeaters; Crimson Chat. **Voice:** male: quick, explosive, silvery, 'falling leaf' song; squeaks, twitterings. Both sexes: brisk 'chiew-chiew'. **Habitat:** rainforests; blossoming eucalypt forests; woodlands, paperbarks, heaths, coastal scrubs, watercourse-vegetation, mistletoes, street/garden trees/shrubs. **Breeds:** June–Jan. **Nest:** delicate cup of bark-shreds, spiders' web; in foliage to 10 m. **Eggs:** 2 (3); whitish; spotted, blotched red–brown, brown–yellow, pale mauve. **Range and Status:** coastal e. Aust. and islands: from *c.* Cooktown (Q) to Gippsland (Vic.), w. inland to Mt Surprise–Carnarvon Ras. NP (Q), Inverell–Mudgee (NSW), shale areas, sandstone heaths, Sydney region (Hoskin, 1991). Summer migrant s. coast NSW–e. Vic., w. to *c.* Gippsland Lakes; casual ACT, ne. Vic., Melbourne. Part-migratory. Also New Cal., e. Indonesia.

BROWN HONEYEATER *Lichmera indistincta* 11–15 cm. Male much larger.

Plain brown honeyeater *with longish curved bill; yellowish/silvery white spot behind eye;* flight/tail-feathers edged yellowish. Gape yellow; black in breeding males. **Immature:** yellow–white mark near gape, no yellowish, silvery spot. Singles, pairs, flocks: demonstrative, aerobatic; song distinctive. **Similar species:** Dusky Honeyeater; Red-headed, Scarlet Honeyeaters, females. **Voice:** strong, varied, like Clamorous Reed-Warbler; 'sweet-sweet-quarty-quarty'; grating 'kreee?'; throaty 'dup'. **Habitat:** eucalypt forests, inland scrubs and watercourses, subtropical/tropical woodlands, rainforest-margins, coastal scrubs, paperbarks, mangroves, inland watercourse-vegetation, golfcourses, parks, gardens. **Breeds:** June–Jan. **Nest:** deep cup of grass, bark-shreds, leaves, palm-fibre, spiders' web; in foliage 1–6 m high. **Eggs:** 2–3; white with red–brown spots. **Range and Status:** widespread mainland Aust. *except* Western and Simpson Deserts, Nullarbor and sse. Aust. In nw. SA, extends s. into Gt Victoria Desert. In NSW, extends w. to Wanaaring, s. to Hillston–Dubbo–Hunter R., coastally s. to Cronulla–Port Hacking. Casual w. of Coober Pedy (SA); Red Cliffs (Vic.). Common. Sedentary; locally nomadic.

DUSKY HONEYEATER

RED-HEADED HONEYEATER

♀

♂

SCARLET
HONEYEATER

♀

♂

BROWN HONEYEATER

♂ breeding

CRIMSON CHAT *Epthianura tricolor* 10–12 cm

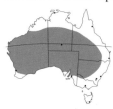

Male: *crimson crown/breast/rump with blackish mask, white throat; eye yellow–white.* **Male eclipse (May–Aug.); female and immature:** brownish above, *patchy red on breast/rump.* Pairs, flocks with other chats: forages on ground; flies bouncing; note *scarlet/pink rump; white-tipped black tail.* Courting males hover butterfly-like. **Voice:** Red-capped Robin. **Voice:** high-pitched 'seee'; soft 'dik-it, dik-it', brisk 'check check'; rattles, trills. **Habitat:** open woodlands, plains, scrubs, grasslands. **Breeds:** June–Oct., or after rain. **Nest:** deep cup; of grass, twigs, stems; low in shrub, grass. **Eggs:** 3–4; white, spotted red–purple. **Range and Status:** inland Aust., to. coast s in WA–SA. Common. Nomadic, irruptive in response to rainfall, drought; moves s. in spring, n. in autumn; irregularly reaches e., n. coasts.

ORANGE CHAT *Epthianura aurifrons* 10–11.5 cm

Male: *face/throat black; body/rump orange–yellow; eye red–brown.* **Female and immature:** mottled sandy brown above with *yellow rump; yellow–fawn below; eye red–brown.* Pairs, loose companies: on ground; often with Crimson Chats. Flies high; note *yellow rump, blackish pale-tipped tail.* **Similar species:** Yellow Chat, female. Gibberbird. **Voice:** canary-like 'chee-chee-chee'. **Habitat:** sparse grasslands, gibber; saltbush, bluebush, samphire, salt lakes. **Breeds:** Aug.–Feb. **Nest:** cup of grass, rootlets; low in shrub. **Eggs:** 3; white, sprinkled purplish red. **Range and Status:** inland e. Aust., sparsely to w. and s. coast, WA e. to Coorong (SA). Locally nomadic; less irruptive than Crimson; casual nw. Q, c. Vic.

YELLOW CHAT *Epthianura crocea* 10–11.5 cm

Male: *eye cream–white; head/body gold to yellow–white; variable black crescent on breast.* **Female:** eye cream–white; *eyebrow yellowish; no breastband.* **Immature:** greyer; eye *tan.* Pairs; local populations; sometimes with other chats. Forages waterside vegetation, mud, low green growth. In flight, *golden rump, blackish, white-tipped tail.* **Similar species:** Orange Chat, female: eye red–brown; upperparts browner. **Voice:** piping 'te-tsu-te'; strident churring; sparrow-like 'chirp' (Black et al, 1985). **Habitat:** bullrushes, pencil rush, sedges, swamp canegrass, lignum on seasonal wetlands; artesian bore-drains; saltbush, bluebush on plains. **Breeds:** Sept.–Nov., March–June, after rain. **Nest:** cup of stems, grass, feathers; in shrub, sedge, canegrass; over water. **Eggs:** 2 (3); white, dotted blackish red. **Range and Status:** from Roebuck Plains, near Broome (WA), to Barkly Tablelands (NT)–Gulf lowlands (Q), e. to *c.* Hughenden; *also Curtis I., off Rockhampton (Q)* (Arnold et al, 1993). Inland s. on bore drains to *c.* Windorah (sw. Q), Pandiburra Bore (ne. SA). Casual Broken Hill–Kinchega NP (NSW). Rare. Sedentary; nomadic.

WHITE-FRONTED CHAT *Epthianura albifrons* 11–13 cm

Male: *forehead/face/underparts white, black cowl joins black breastband; eye yellow–white.* **Female:** eye yellow–brown; *face/upperparts grey–brown; thin breastband.* **Immature:** duller; lacks breastband. Pairs, parties; walks with swagger; perches tussocks, fences. Flight bouncing. **Similar species:** Double-barred Finch, Banded Whiteface. **Voice:** metallic 'tang'. **Habitat:** open damp ground, grass clumps, fencelines, heath, samphire saltmarshes, mangroves, dunes, saltbush-plains. **Breeds:** July–Jan. **Nest:** cup of grass, twigs; deep in tussock, low shrub. **Eggs:** 3–4; white; spotted reddish; purplish brown. **Range and Status:** s. Aust.: n. to Shark Bay (WA)–s. Q; Tas. Common. Sedentary; nomadic in n.

GIBBERBIRD *Ashbyia lovensis* 12.5 cm

Other names: Desert or Gibber Chat.

Long-legged, pipit-like: *mottled sandy above with pale yellowish face/breast, whitish-yellow eyes.* **Female:** duller, breast sandier. Pairs: runs with swagger; stands on stones. Flies tail-down, fluttering; flies high, strongly, *showing yellow-edged sandy rump, black tail.* **Similar species:** Orange Chat, female. **Voice:** squeaky 'dip dip'. **Habitat:** open gibber, with sparse dwarf bushes, grass-tufts; wind-scalded, bare earth in saltbush-bluebush. **Breeds:** June–Dec., or after rain. **Nest:** cup of grass, twigs; in depression. **Eggs:** 3; white, spotted red–brown. **Range and Status:** inland e. Aust.: far s. NT, far w. Q, far nw. NSW (formerly s. to Ivanhoe–Mossgiel); ne. SA, s. to *c.* Quorn, w. to *c.* Stuart Hwy; vagrant s. inland WA. Uncommon. Nomadic.

CRIMSON CHAT

♀

♂

ORANGE CHAT

♀

♀

YELLOW CHAT

♀

♂

WHITE-FRONTED CHAT

♀

♂

GIBBERBIRD

♀

♂

YELLOW-LEGGED FLYCATCHER *Microeca griseoceps* 12 cm

Similar to Lemon-bellied: *head large; bill cream below; legs bright orange–yellow; tail squarish at end.* Singles, small parties: cocks tail, forages thornbill-like high or low in canopy, flies to pick insects from leaves, and on wing. **Similar species:** Grey Whistler, race *peninsulae.* **Voice:** subdued piping, 'zzt, zzt, zzt'; repeated clear whistle; song like Yellow-breasted Boatbill. **Habitat:** edges of lowland rainforest; vine scrub, eucalypt woodland, paperbarks. **Breeds:** Oct.–Feb. **Nest:** small broad cup of fine rootlets, lichen, paperbark, spiders' web; on high horizontal dead branch. **Eggs:** 2; pale blue with dark brown, grey specks, heaviest at large end (Noske & Sticklen, 1979). **Range and Status:** ne. C. York Pen. (Q), s. to Claudie R. (possibly also Atherton Tableland (Nagle, 1987)). Local; uncommon; little known. Also PNG.

LEMON-BELLIED FLYCATCHER *Microeca flavigaster* 12.5–14 cm

Other names: Lemon-breasted Flycatcher, Kimberley Flycatcher.
Bill dark grey; lores, slight eye-ring and throat whitish; *upperparts dull olive; underparts washed lemon; tail lightly forked; legs dark grey.* **Immature:** browner, streaked paler, mottled darker. Singles, pairs: perches on dead trees, phone wires; sallies high after insects; forages in canopy, flirts tail; hovers over foliage, grasses. High, circling song-flight. **Race *tormenti*** 'Kimberley' or 'Brown-tailed Flycatcher': grey–brown; *wing-coverts/rump washed olive–green;* underparts grey–white, washed buff–grey; *tail brown,* white spot on each outer tail-feather.
Similar species: Yellow-legged Flycatcher, Grey Whistler. **Voice:** sweet, clear; loudest at dawn: brisk 'quick, quick, come with me, Tito', or 'Do be sweet, to Cynthia'; bouncing 'chauncey-chauncey *chew!*' **Habitat:** eucalypt woodland, pandanus, by water; edges of rainforest, monsoon forest; mangroves, watercourse-vegetation, parks, gardens. **Breeds:** Aug.–March. **Nest:** smallest Aust. nest; tiny shallow cup of bark-fibre, spiders' web. **Egg:** 1; pale blue, finely spotted purplish red. **Range and Status:** coastal n. Aust. and islands, from w. Kimberley (WA) to ce. Q. Race *tormenti:* w. Kimberley. Race *flavigaster:* e. from c. Ord R. (WA), Top End (NT), s. to *c.* Elsey–Gulf coast (NT/Q). Race *terrareginae:* C. York Pen. (Q), s. on e. coast to *c.* Broad Sound (Q). Locally common; scarce above 550 m. Sedentary. Also PNG.

JACKY WINTER *Microeca fascinans* 12–14 cm

Other names: Brown Flycatcher, Peter Peter, Stumpbird.
Small confiding grey–brown bird of much charm: slight white eyebrow; dark eyemark; breast white, washed grey–brown; *blackish brown tail has prominent white outer feathers.* **Immature:** streaked paler above, mottled below. Singles, pairs: watches from dead trees, stumps, fence-posts; wags tail. Sallies high after insects, hovers over grass; white tail-edges prominent. Sings loudly from high branches; makes high, wavering song-flights. **Similar species:** Lemon-bellied Flycatcher, race *tormenti.* 'Brown' red robins. **Voice:** sustained, high, clear phrases: 'peter-peter-peter', 'plicky-plicky-plicky'; mimics. **Habitat:** open woodlands, scrublands; paddocks with live/dead trees; stumps, fences, timber on dams, watercourses, country roadsides, golfcourses, orchards. **Breeds:** July–Dec. in s.; after rain in n. and inland. **Nest:** tiny shallow cup of grass, spiders' web, bark, lichen; on horizontal, often dead, branch or fork, 1–20 m high. **Eggs:** 2; pale green–blue, spotted purplish brown, lilac. **Range and Status:** mainland Aust.: sparse n. C. York Pen., driest deserts; scarce seasonal visitor c. Aust. Common; patchy in settled areas. Sedentary; dispersive in winter. Also PNG.

YELLOW-BREASTED BOATBILL *Machaerirhynchus flaviventer* 11–12.5 cm

Small, boldly marked, cock-tailed flycatcher with *grotesquely large, flat bill.* **Male:** blackish above. **Female:** olive–grey above, markings less bold; throat whitish. **Immature:** like dull female. Pairs, parties; vivacious; forages through canopy, branchlets; sallies after flying insects; often in mixed feeding associations. **Voice:** constant soft, insect-like trilling, 'wit, see-ee-ee, wit'; other wheezing notes, pretty warbles. **Habitat:** rainforest, vine scrub, creekside vegetation, eucalypt woodland, lantana. **Breeds:** Sept.–Feb. **Nest:** hammock of fine twigs, stalks, spiders' web; in slender horizontal fork among leaves, 4–20 m high. **Eggs:** 2; white; spotted red–purple, yellow–red. **Range and Status:** from C. York (Q), s. to Archer R. on w. coast; s. to Ingham on e. coast. Locally common. Sedentary. Also PNG.

YELLOW-LEGGED
FLYCATCHER

race
tormenti

LEMON-BELLIED
FLYCATCHER

JACKY WINTER

YELLOW-BREASTED BOATBILL

♀

♂

FLAME ROBIN *Petroica phoenicea* 12.5–14 cm

Male: differs from male Scarlet Robin in *dark grey upperparts with small white mark over bill; flame-red underparts start at throat*. **Female:** pale brown above, *small white mark over bill; buff–white broken-arrow wingmark*; breast buff–brown; *outer tail-feathers white*. **Immature:** like female; some are washed yellow–orange on breast. Pairs in spring–summer; open companies in autumn–winter; perches upright on thistles, stumps, fence posts; bright males conspicuous; roosts communally in thickets, orchards. **Similar species:** Scarlet Robin, female: large white forehead-patch; breast pale red. **Voice:** high-pitched, lilting 'you may come, if you will, to the sea'. 'Brown birds': brief 'peep'. **Habitat:** summer: forests, woodlands, scrubs, from sea-level to *c.* 1800 m. Autumn–winter: open woodlands, plains, paddocks, golfcourses, orchards, parks. **Breeds:** Aug.–Jan. **Nest:** bulky rough cup of bark, grass, spiders' web, moss, lichen or hanging bark-strips; lined with fur, hair, plant-down; in tree cavity, often charred; broken tree-fork to 20 m; behind bark, overhung bank, rock fissure, upturned roots, woodpile, shed, mine-shaft. **Eggs:** 3–4; green–white; freckled, spotted yellow–chestnut, lilac, in zone. **Range and Status:** se. Aust. and Tas.: breeds timbered foothills to high country of Gt Divide, from n. NSW tablelands to Vic., islands of Bass Strait, Tas., possibly se. SA. Widespread autumn–winter dispersal, w. to Kangaroo I. (SA), n. to Balranald–Hay (NSW); Chinchilla (Q). Sedentary in high country n. of Blue Mts (NSW). Some Tas. birds annually migrate across Bass Strait. Sedentary, dispersive, migratory.

SCARLET ROBIN *Petroica multicolor* 12–14 cm

Male: *black above with large white forehead-patch, bold white mark on wing*, white edges to tail; *upperbreast black; breast scarlet to orange–red; underparts white.* **Female:** *pink or red wash on breast; large whitish forehead-patch; buff–white broken-arrow wingmark*; tail edged white. **Immature:** like dark female; no red breast. Singles, pairs: in summer, forages in stringybark, other eucalypt woodland; from stumps, low branches, darts to seize prey on ground; in autumn/winter moves locally to more open habitats. **Similar species:** Flame Robin, male: grey above, flame-red breast starts at *throat*; female paler, forehead-mark smaller; breast brown. **Voice:** pretty, lilting, 'wee-cheedalee-dalee'; quiet 'tick'; scolding chatter. **Habitat:** foothill forests, woodlands, watercourses; in autumn–winter, more open habitats: river red gum woodlands, golfcourses, parks, orchards, gardens. **Breeds:** Aug.–Jan. **Nest:** untidy cup of bark-strips, moss, grass, spiders' web, with strips of bark, lichen; lined with hair, fur, feathers; 1–3 m (sometimes to 16 m), in fork, horizontal branch; loose bark, tree cavity, often charred; in sw. Aust., fork in grasstree. **Eggs:** 3; pale green/blue, dull white; spotted brown, purplish brown, blue–grey in zone. **Range and Status:** se. Aust., Tas., sw. WA. In Q, from granite belt n. to *c.* Chinchilla, casual e. to near Brisbane; in NSW, w. to Moree–Warrumbungle NP (winter visitor to Riverina, w. to *c.* Moulamein–Barham); in Vic., widespread *except* nw. mallee; in SA, from se. to Mt Lofty Ras.–s. Flinders Ras., s. Eyre Pen., Kangaroo I.; in WA, w. and s. of Esperance–L. Grace–Lancelin. Fairly common. Seasonally dispersive. Also Norfolk I., Solomon Is., Fiji–Samoa.

RED-CAPPED ROBIN *Petroica goodenovii* 11–12 cm

Male: brilliant tiny robin *with scarlet cap and breast, white flanks/underparts*; black above with bold white wing-mark; white edges to tail. **Female:** smallest, palest red robin; *pale buff–grey, with pale brick-red cap; whitish broken-arrow wingmark*; underparts whitish, washed buff–grey; *some have pinkish breast*. **Immature:** lacks rusty cap; young males develop rusty breast. Singles, pairs: perches low; darts to take insect-prey on ground; disturbs it with shuffling foot, waving wings; snaps flying insects. **Similar species:** Crimson Chat, Jacky Winter. **Voice:** running, insect-like trill, 'dit-dit-drrrr-it'; sparrow-like scold; sharp 'tick'. **Habitat:** drier scrubs/woodlands: cypress pine, mulga, sheoak, mallee; open eucalypt forests, woodlands, coastal scrubs; shelterbelts in winter; golfcourses, orchards, country gardens. **Breeds:** July–Jan. **Nest:** tiny cup of soft, shredded bark, grass, spiders' web, lichen; on fork, horizontal branch, 1–3 m high. **Eggs:** 2–4; blue–green, grey–green; plentiful purple–brown flecks around middle. **Range and Status:** mainland Aust., mostly s. of Tropic and inland of Gt Divide; casual coastwards of Divide in e. Q, e. NSW, far e. Vic.; absent wetter ne. NSW, s. Vic. Common; dispersive in nonbreeding season; in winter some inland birds move into tropical n. Aust.; w. to Broome (WA); n. to *c.* Tennant Ck (NT), Camooweal–Charters Towers (Q). In s. WA, moves coastward in winter. Resident Rottnest I.

FLAME ROBIN

imm.

♀

♂

SCARLET ROBIN

imm.

♂

♀

RED-CAPPED ROBIN

imm.

♀

♂

ROSE ROBIN *Petroica rosea* 11–12.5 cm

Most arboreal red robin: *small, longish tailed,* flycatcher-like. **Male:** *upperparts/throat deep grey; breast rose-red; underparts white; outer tail-feathers mainly white.* Young males have faint buff–white wingbar. **Female:** grey–brown above with *whitish broken-arrow wingmark;* grey–white below, with grey breast, some washed rose; *longish tail dark brown, edged white.* **Immature:** like female; without pink breast. Singles, pairs: graceful, active; often high in forest canopy. Droops wings, cocks tail; takes insects from leaves; sallies in tumbling pursuit. **Similar species:** Pink Robin, 'brown birds': rich olive–brown with tan broken-arrow wingmark; tail shorter, no white. **Voice:** male: pretty, insect-like, 'dick, dick; dick-didit, *dzeer-dzeer*', last notes stronger, rising. Contact note: short, scratchy 'skay'; sharp 'tick!' **Habitat:** ferntree, beech, other dense, moist gullies; wetter eucalypt forests/rainforests, from near sea-level in NSW and Vic. to 1000 m. In Q, breeds mostly in mountain rainforests above 500 m. Wide autumn–winter dispersal to lowland woodlands, sub-inland, coastal scrubs, riverside vegetation. **Breeds:** Sept.–Jan. **Nest:** beautiful small deep cup of green moss, spiders' web, lichen; lined with fur, plant-down; on horizontal lichen-covered fork or branch, low to 18 m. **Eggs:** 2–3; pale green, blue–grey; freckled brown, purple, at large end. **Range and Status:** breeds in wetter coastal and mountain forests and rainforests, on and coastwards of Divide, from sea-level to *c.* 1000 m, from sw. Vic. to se. Q. Disperses in autumn–winter w. to Adelaide–s. Flinders Ras. (SA); Murray Valley (Vic.–NSW); coastwards and on w. slopes of Divide (NSW–Q); w. to Carnarvon Ra. NP, coastally n. to Rockhampton (Q). Ranges n. on highlands at least to Eungella NP (Q). Uncommon. Dispersive.

PINK ROBIN *Petroica rodinogaster* 11.5–13 cm

Male: *sooty black above and on upperbreast; no white in wings/tail; breast/belly dusky rose-pink;* some show faint tan wingmark. **Female:** darkest female 'red-breast': *deep olive–brown above with rich-tan broken-arrow wingmark;* slight pale buff mark over bill and on edges to tail *but no white;* some have pink wash on breast. Singles, pairs: quiet; in dim cover perches low, darts to seize insect on ground; flicks wings, tail. **Similar species:** Rose Robin: tail longer; underparts/edge of tail white; female often has pink-washed breast, whitish wingmark. **Voice:** subdued warble; sharp 'tick', like snapping twig; scolding 'chur-r-r-r-'. **Habitat:** dense, dank forest/treefern gullies; disperses in autumn–winter to open forests, woodlands, scrublands — belar, cypress pine, coast tea-tree; gardens, plantations, golfcourses. **Breeds:** Sept.–Jan. **Nest:** larger than Rose; rounded cup of fine bark strips, green moss, spiders' web, grey-green lichen; lined with fern-fibre, hair, grass; in tree-fern, leafy shrub or tree, 1–6 m high. **Eggs:** 3–4; greenish white, thickly sprinkled light chestnut, purple–brown. **Range and Status:** stronghold is Tas., where widespread (incl. some Bass Strait islands); mountain/coastal forests of se. Vic. and far se. NSW (Tennyson Ck Forest Reserve, 40 km s. of Bombala) (Shields & Boles, 1980). Wide autumn–winter dispersal largely by 'brown birds' to coastal tea-tree scrubs/sub-inland lowlands, w. to coastal se. SA, inland to Murray Valley, ACT–L.George, casual n. to near Sydney. Uncommon. Migratory or dispersive.

DUSKY ROBIN *Melanodryas vittata* 16–17 cm

Other names: Dozey; Stump, Tasmanian or Sleepy Robin.
Plainest olive–brown robin; sexes similar. Note slight dark eyeline, *whitish mark at bend of wing, fine white bar across secondaries, tail finely edged buff–white.* **Juvenile:** streaked paler above, wing-feathers edged paler; mottled below. Singles, pairs, small winter flocks: sits watchfully on stumps, posts, darts to ground for prey. Does not flick wings or tail, often seems part of stump. In flight, note *irregular white wingbar.* **Similar species:** female red robins: smaller; pale spot over bill; larger whitish, buff or tan broken-arrow wingmark; pale tail-edges; some have pink on breast. **Voice:** far-carrying 'choo-wee; choo-wee-er', repeated. **Habitat:** rainforest margins; tracks, up to 1200 m; open forests/woodlands, scrubs, newly cleared areas, regrowth, country gardens. **Breeds:** Aug.–Dec. **Nest:** untidy cup of grass, bark, rootlets; lined with hair, wool; in cavity of stump, bole of eucalypt, tree-fork, crevice in bark, low to 6 m high. **Eggs:** 3–4; pale apple–green/olive–green, tinged brown on large end, in zone. **Range and Status:** Tas., Bass Strait islands. Common. Sedentary.

ROSE ROBIN

imm. ♂

♂

♀

PINK ROBIN

imm.

♂

♀

DUSKY ROBIN

juv.

EASTERN YELLOW ROBIN *Eopsaltria australis* 15–16 cm

Grey above, washed olive on lower back/rump; breast clear yellow; legs blackish. **Race** *chrysorrhoa: bright yellow rump.* **Juvenile:** rich brown, streaked paler. **Immature:** like patchy adult; buffish wingmark. Singles, pairs, parties: confiding; flirts wings, cocks tail. Hangs sideways on trunks; pounces on prey. In flight, pale wingbar; *bright yellow rump in race* chrysorrhoa. **Similar species:** Pale-yellow Robin, Golden Whistler. **Voice:** explosive 'chyop-chyop!'; monotonous piping; scolding 'k-k-kair'; soft, squealing whistles. **Habitat:** rainforest, vine forest, scrubby eucalypt woodland/forest; timbered gullies, swamp-woodlands, coast tea-tree/banksia scrubs, mallee, broombush, cypress-pine thickets; mulga, brigalow, other acacia scrubs; snow gum woodlands in summer; orchards, golfcourses, gardens. **Breeds:** communally, June–Dec. **Nest:** substantial cup of bark shreds, spiders' web, lined with grass, leaves; decorated with bark, lichen, moss; in fork to 1–7+m. **Eggs:** 2–3; apple–green/blue–green, dotted, blotched, brownish red, yellow–brown, lilac. **Range and Status:** e. Aust. Nominate race: far se. SA, coastally n. to Hunter R. (NSW), n. inland to Upper Dawson R. (Q). Extends w. to Naracoorte–Murray mallee (SA); Little Desert–Echuca (Vic.); Deniliquin–Roto–Cobar (NSW); Idalia NP (Q). Race *chrysorrhoa:* coastal/mountain forests from ne. NSW to Cooktown (Q). Common. Sedentary; altitudinal migrant; quits highlands in autumn–winter.

WESTERN YELLOW ROBIN *Eopsaltria griseogularis* 15–16 cm

Like Eastern, but with grey upperbreast; rump yellow in coastal s. WA; olive–green inland s. WA and e. to Eyre Pen. (SA). Behaves like Eastern, but forages/nests higher in woodland trees. **Voice:** harsh, explosive 'chip chip', or 'chip chair', lower in pitch, differing in tone, from White-breasted Robin. **Habitat:** open forests, woodlands, with 2–3 m shrub layer; coastal and acacia scrubs; dense mallee; woodland-saltbush associations; mostly avoids dense wet thickets favoured by White-breasted Robin. **Breeds:** July–Dec. **Nest:** robust cup of bark-shreds, spiders' web; lined with dry leaves; decorated with bark-strips, in fork, 1–6 m high. **Eggs:** 2; oval; cream, buff or olive; blotched brownish, red–brown, in zone. **Range and Status:** nominate race: sw. WA, n. and e. to Shark Bay–Kalgoorlie–Eucla. Race *rosinae:* s. SA, from Nullarbor NP at head of Bight, coastally e. to Ceduna–Wynbring, Eyre Pen. and Gawler Ras. (SA); casual Aldinga Scrub, near Adelaide. Common. Sedentary; seasonal movements.

PALE-YELLOW ROBIN *Tregellasia capito* 13 cm

Whitish grey from above bill to below eye; legs yellowish. Race *nana: lores pale orange–buff.* Quieter than Eastern: less tail-cocking/wing-flirting. Tame; hangs sideways on low prickly vines. Seldom leaves gloom of habitat. **Similar species:** Eastern Yellow Robin, race *chrysorrhoa.* White-faced Robin. **Voice:** single/double squeak like Rufous Fantail; harder, peevish notes; soft churring trill; harsh, scolding 'scairr'. **Habitat:** tropical, subtropical rainforests; tangles of lawyer-vine; dense creekside vegetation. **Breeds:** Sept.–Dec. (NSW–Q); July–Dec. (ne. Q). **Nest:** neat cup of grass, rootlets, spiders' web, decorated with moss, bark, lichen, leaves; at junction of stem/leaves of lawyer-vine, or fork in low sapling, to 1–6 m. **Eggs:** 2; green–white with yellowish, brown, chestnut markings. **Range and Status:** nominate race: lowland rainforests, on and coastward of Divide, from *c.* Dungog (NSW), inland to Walcha–Tenterfield, n. to Conondale Ra.–Cooloola NP–Byfield (Q); inland to *c.* Warwick; Fraser and other coastal islands (Q). Race *nana:* mostly highland rainforests up to 1500 m, from Paluma, near Townsville (Q), to near Cooktown, inland on Atherton Tableland and other ranges. Common. Sedentary.

WHITE-FACED ROBIN *Tregellasia leucops* 12–13 cm

Small yellow robin with black head, clownlike white face/chin; upperparts olive–green; *legs pale yellow.* Behaves like Pale-yellow Robin; tame, settles close to inspect observer. **Voice:** rapid, harsh, grating 'chee-chee'; musical five-note song. **Habitat:** tropical rainforests, vine-scrubs, especially lawyer-vine near watercourses. **Breeds:** Oct.–March. **Nest:** neat cup of bark, lawyer-vine fibre, spiders' web; decorated with moss, bark-strips; in lawyer-vine or fork of slender sapling, 1–10 m high. **Eggs:** 2; green–white, spotted red–brown. **Range and Status:** Aust. race, *albigularis:* far ne. Q, patchily from C. York s. to Rocky R. Locally common. Sedentary. Also PNG.

EASTERN YELLOW ROBIN

juv.

race
chrysorrhoa

WESTERN
YELLOW ROBIN

juv.

race
rosinae

PALE-YELLOW ROBIN

juv.

race
nana

WHITE-FACED ROBIN

juv.

HOODED ROBIN *Melanodryas cucullata* 14–17 cm. N. birds smaller.

Male: *bold black hood points down white breast; note white shoulder/wingbar;* black tail, with *prominent white side-panels.* **Female:** grey–brown where male black, grey–white below, some buffish; *white wingbar/tail-panels.* **Immature:** like shadowy adults. Pairs, family groups: shy; sits watchfully on dead branches, stumps; flies to take prey on ground. *Flight strongly undulating, note white wingbar, prominent hour-glass tail-pattern.* **Similar species:** White-winged Triller, male: throat/underparts wholly white. Pied Honeyeater, male: bill blue–grey, arched; blue–grey eye-wattle; more white on shoulder; pale rump. **Voice:** quiet, male's song prominent before dawn: clear 'whee yew, whee yew yew'. **Habitat:** drier eucalypt forests, woodlands, scrubs; with fallen logs, debris; mallee, casuarinas, cypress pine, mulga; cleared paddocks with stumps/dead trees or regrowth; banksia-dominated coastal scrubs. **Breeds:** July–Dec. Communally: three or more may attend nest. **Nest:** open cup of bark-strips, rootlets, grass, spiders' web; on stump, cavity in broken trunk, horizontal fork/branch, stunted eucalypt, on or near dead wood, 1–6 m high. **Eggs:** 2–3; apple–green/pale olive, faint red–brown tint on large end, or clouded rich brown. **Range and Status:** drier woodland/forest habitats in mainland Aust., *except* C. York Pen., driest deserts, wetter coastal areas. Declining in settled areas. Adults sedentary; young dispersive.

WHITE-BREASTED ROBIN *Eopsaltria georgiana* 14.5–16 cm

Distinctive non yellow member of yellow robin group, confined to sw. WA. *Dark blue–grey above, pure white below; narrow white bend of wing; white wingbar in flight.* **Immature:** mottled browner. Coastal n. population between Geraldton–Lancelin paler blue–grey above. Behaves somewhat like Eastern Yellow Robin: note habitat. **Voice:** liquid 'chee-op' ending in a slight whipcrack; a loud 'zhip', repeated. Alarm-call: harsh 'chit'; in aggression, harsh 'zhzhurr'. Male: quiet, animated, chirruping song. **Habitat:** lower, denser, more humid than Western Yellow Robin: well-vegetated creekbeds, gullies; understorey of dense forest, e.g. karri; thickets of acacia, melaleuca, etc., with well-developed canopy, little under-shrubbery and much litter; forest margins with bracken, etc.; coastal dune-thickets; tall coastal heaths. **Breeds:** July–Dec. **Nest:** loose, inconspicuous cup of dry grass, rootlets, spiders' web; decorated with lichen, bark-strips; in low cover, e.g. bracken, 1–2 m high; occasionally to 6 m, in fork of paperbark, etc. **Eggs:** 2; olive, light brown to pale blue, with very fine red–brown specks, streaks. **Range and Status:** sw. WA, from n. of Geraldton s. to *c.* Albany, with coastal gap in Perth region. (Blakers et al, 1984); well-vegetated offshore s. islands. Common. Sedentary.

MANGROVE ROBIN *Eopsaltria pulverulenta* 14.5–16.5 cm

Robust black bill joins broad blackish mask; upperparts metallic blue–grey; underparts whitish, washed grey on sides of upperbreast; tail blackish, outer feathers white at base, forming broad side-panels when spread. **Immature:** patchily brown/rufous above. Pairs, parties: tame but often hard to see in gloomy denseness of habitat; often heard before seen. Flies silently, showing pale wingbar. Sits motionless on branches, roots of mangroves; flutters. Takes food among leaves, branches and on exposed mud; seldom leaves cover. Note range. **Voice:** loud, long, mournful double whistle, 'tew-tee', sounding both near and far; repeated 'chig'; single soft chirring note; excited musical song. **Habitat:** dense, low thickets of coastal mangroves; on coasts, tidal creeks, river mouths. **Breeds:** Aug.–March. **Nest:** small compact cup of bark-strips, plant-fibre, spiders' web; decorated with long strips of dry bark; lined with roots, grass; in fork of dead or living mangrove, 1–5 m high. **Eggs:** 2; light green/dark olive–green, with small spots of red–brown, lilac, below surface. **Range and Status:** coastal tropical Aust., from *c.* NW Cape (WA) to *c.* Proserpine (Q), with breaks where mangroves absent, e.g. Eighty Mile Beach (WA); points on Gulf coast (Q) (Blakers et al, 1984). Locally common. Sedentary. Also PNG, Aru Is.

HOODED ROBIN

imm.

♂

♀

WHITE-BREASTED
ROBIN

MANGROVE ROBIN

WHITE-BROWED ROBIN *Poecilodryas superciliosa* 14–17 cm

Handsome dark brown and buff–white robin with *long white eyebrow, white throat and whisker-mark, double white bar across flight-feathers, white wingtips and tailtips*; white upperbreast washed grey. Larger nw. race *cerviniventris*, 'Buff-sided Robin', has dark brown face, *rich buff or tan flanks and under tail-coverts*. Singles, pairs or trios: quiet, sprightly; cocks, raises and lowers tail; droops wings; hops actively through lower branches and vines. Feeds on ground and mud under cover; tree-trunks; takes flying insects. **Voice:** piping whistle repeated 4 times very loudly, somewhat like a rosella. **Habitat:** in n. Q, rainforests, vine scrub, vegetation along watercourses; coastal scrubs, nearby eucalypt woodlands, especially in wet season. In nw. Aust., pockets of monsoon rainforest, swamp woodlands, bamboo and pandanus thickets by watercourses and springs; mangroves. **Breeds:** Aug.–March. **Nest:** frail cup of twigs lined with rootlets, with pieces of paperbark or patches of lichen loosely attached to outside; in shrub, vine or tree 1–10 m high. **Eggs:** 2; variable; rich apple-green to bluish, spotted with chestnut or purple, some with zone around large end. **Range and Status:** nominate race: coastal ne. Q, vegetation on rivers and streams; highland rainforests n. from Rockhampton to C. York, s. to Mitchell R. on w. Pen. coast. Race *cerviniventris*: from Gregory R. in Gulf lowlands (Q), w. on streams, rivers, marginally to mangroves, to w. Kimberley region and upper Fitzroy R. (WA) (Blakers et al, 1984). Range and available habitat has shrunk in Kimberley region from destruction of waterside thickets by cattle, and by burning. Local; patchy; generally uncommon. Sedentary.

GREY-HEADED ROBIN *Heteromyias albispecularis* 16–18 cm

Large-headed, short-tailed, upstanding, robust robin; note black bill with pale tip, long pinkish flesh legs. Slight dark mark around eye separated by white mark down through eye to white throat. Upperparts deep olive–brown with rufous rump; bold Z-shaped white mark on black wing; breast grey; flanks and underparts buff to olive–buff. Singles, pairs, family parties: unobtrusive; feeds much on ground in leaf-litter; hops briskly upright. Perches motionless, often sideways, on trunk or vine; darts to ground with strange jerking of short tail. In flight, shows black-and-white wingflash and rufous–yellow rump. Sometimes flies high into canopy. **Similar species:** White-browed Robin: browner above, paler below; white eyebrow and tail tips. **Voice:** characteristic sound of ne. Q mountain rainforests: persistent, leisurely, ringing 'pee, pee, pee', or 'bink, bink, bink, bink, brr' with an irregular break, resuming on one level, like Crested Bellbird; heard all months. Also scrubwren-like chattering, chirping. **Habitat:** mostly highland rainforests and margins of tracks, roads, lawns in rainforest parks; but to near sea-level where habitat runs unbroken down from highlands. **Breeds:** Aug.–Jan. **Nest:** flattish untidy cup of rootlets, twigs, lawyer-vine fibre and leaves, decorated with lichen and green moss; in lawyer-vine, at base of leaf in small palm, fork of slender sapling, 1–2 m high. **Eggs:** 1 or 2; cream, brownish, pale green, freckled and blotched dark brown and purplish grey, especially at large end. **Range and Status:** ne. Q: coastal highlands (and some lowlands) from near Cooktown to Mt Spec, near Townsville. Common. Sedentary. Also PNG.

race *cerviniventris*

WHITE-BROWED ROBIN

GREY-HEADED ROBIN

LOGRUNNER *Orthonyx temminckii* 18–20 cm

Other names: Spinetail, Southern or Spinetailed Logrunner.
Small chunky ground-dweller of distinctive habits. **Male:** *face pale grey; throat white with black 'wishbone'; upperparts olive–rufous, boldly mottled black; black wings crossed by curving grey bars;* rump rufous; tail dark brown, spines not prominent. **Female:** *throat orange–rufous.* **Immature:** dense, scalloped pattern; buff wing bars. Pairs, family parties: throws leaf-debris aside with feet, sometimes props on tail; leaves 'soup-plate' depressions. Hops, runs; flies with quail-like whirr on short rounded wings. Noisy parties chase, chatter; wings drooped, tails spread. **Voice:** far-carrying 'be-kweek-kweek-kweek-kweek', oft-repeated; short, throaty, piercing 'quick!' or 'kweek'. **Habitat:** leafy floor of rainforests, with logs, debris, ferns, vines; saplings, blackberries, lantana. **Breeds:** April–Oct. **Nest:** large, domed, with ramp; of sticks, ferns, leaves, treefern fibres, covered with green moss; base reinforced with wood-pulp, lined with rootlets, skeletal leaves; on bank, against stone or log, in tree buttress, ferns, vines. **Eggs:** 2; large, white, oval. **Range and Status:** from Blackall Ras/Bunya Ras. (se. Q) to Illawarra district (s. coast NSW), w. to near ACT. Common in Q, uncommon to rare s. NSW. Sedentary. Also PNG.

CHOWCHILLA *Orthonyx spaldingii* 26–28 cm

Other names: Auctioneer-bird, Northern Logrunner.
Male: *head black, with bare blue–grey eye-ring;* upperparts dark brown; *throat/breast white; legs, feet powerful.* **Female:** *throat/upperbreast rich rufous; underparts white.* **Immature:** fine orange–buff mottlings; barrings. Pairs, parties: hops or runs on forest-floor; scratches among debris. Makes occasional short, whirring flights. **Voice:** chanting choruses at dawn drown out most other voices; quieter later. Typical call deafening 'chow, chowchilla' with variations; other strange, raucous notes; mimics. **Habitat:** debris-strewn floor of rainforests. **Breeds:** April–Oct. **Nest:** large, loose, bulky, domed, of twigs, roots, mosses; among roots, vines; on stump or elk-horn fern, to 4 m high. **Egg:** 1; oval, white. **Range and Status:** coastal ranges of ne. Q, from near Cooktown s. to Mt Spec, near Townsville. Common. Sedentary.

SOUTHERN SCRUB-ROBIN *Drymodes brunneopygia* 20–23 cm

Spirited ground-dweller: large dark eye has *pale rear eye-ring, vertical blackish eyemark; double pale bar across wing-coverts; long, rufous-based, white-tipped tail raised, lowered, flicked rudderlike.* **Immature:** darker, with pale buff streaks, feather-margins. Singles, pairs: forages in ground-debris; flips leaves, flies to snap insects. Runs; scolds from cover but will inquisitively approach quiet observer. **Voice:** sweet musical 'chee-too-kwee?'; 'whip-whip, paree?', while perched on stick, leafy bush, dead tree. Contact-call: long, high-pitched 'seeep'; dry rattling scolds. **Habitat:** mallee, broombush, other dry scrubs; lignum on claypans; heaths, coast tea-tree thickets. **Breeds:** July–Jan. **Nest:** cup in ground-litter; lined with fine twigs, rootlets, strips of bark; with criss-cross barricade of heavy twigs. In open, at base of tree, beside fallen branch. **Egg:** 1; green–grey, spotted, blotched brown. **Range and Status:** mallee of c./sw. NSW, n. and e. to *c.* Condobolin; nw. Vic., e. to *c.* Wedderburn, s. to Little Desert NP; se. SA and Murray mallee, n. to s. Flinders Ras. NP, w. to Eyre Pen.–Kangaroo I. In WA, w. from *c.* Madura, nw. to Shark Bay, inland to *c.* Norseman–Southern Cross–Perenjori; absent from forested far sw. Uncommon. Sedentary.

NORTHERN SCRUB-ROBIN *Drymodes superciliaris* 21–22 cm

Boldly marked, long-tailed scrub-robin *with long flesh-pink legs:* upperparts rufous–buff, *with fiery chestnut rump/base of tail; face/underparts fawn–white, washed tawny; vertical black eyemark; wings black, broad white tips to wing-coverts form prominent double wingbar; white tips to black outer tail-feathers.* Hops, runs briskly over leaf-litter; cocks, fans, raises/lowers tail; tame, inquisitive. **Voice:** long, high-pitched whistle, like quail-thrush; hissing scolds. **Habitat:** leaf-litter of tropical rainforests, vine-scrubs. **Breeds:** Oct.–Feb. **Nest:** depression lined with leaves, plant-fibres; thick outer wall of twigs. **Eggs:** 2; oval; light stone-grey, thickly but finely blotched umber. **Range and Status:** n. C. York Pen. (Q), s. to lower Archer R. on w. coast and to Rocky R. on e. coast. Locally common. Sedentary. Probably extinct in region of Roper R. (NT). Also PNG, Aru Is.

LOGRUNNER

♂

♀

imm.

imm.

CHOWCHILLA

♂

♀

NORTHERN
SCRUB-ROBIN

SOUTHERN
SCRUB-ROBIN

GREY-CROWNED BABBLER *Pomatostomus temporalis* 29 cm

Other names: Happy Family, Red-breasted Babbler, Yahoo.
Largest babbler: *eye pale yellow; crown/nape pale grey; broad white eyebrow over black mask;* upperparts brown–black; underparts warm brown in nominate race, rich rufous–chestnut in race *rubecula* ('Red-breasted Babbler'). Habits like other babblers; feeds higher, in larger trees. *In flight, note chestnut wingpatch.* **Similar species:** White-browed Babbler. **Voice:** clear 'yahoo', sometimes in chorus; brisk 'go-*wah*-hee, go-*wah*-hee'; strident 'peeoo peeoo'; falsetto 'put-yair, put-yair'. **Habitat:** open forests, woodlands, scrublands; farmlands, outer suburbs. **Breeds:** June–Oct.; March–June in WA. **Nest:** large, domed, of sticks, with spout-like entrance; lined with grass, bark-fibre, rootlets, feathers, wool; 3–6 m in shrub, sapling. Extra nests serve as communal roosts. **Eggs:** 2–6; buff to purple–brown, dark grey; with dark brown scribbles. **Range and Status:** nominate race: from extreme se. SA, through n. Vic., s. to Mornington Pen., but mostly n. of Divide; in NSW, e. to Hunter Valley region but mostly w. of Divide, inland to *c.* Balranald–Ivanhoe–Yantabulla; in Q, widespread *except* far sw. corner. Race *rubecula*: from w. of Winton–Normanton (Q) to s. NT–ne. SA (to *c.* Oodnadatta, but absent from Simpson and W. Deserts); w. to Pilbara (WA), coastally s. to Wooramel R., s. inland to *c.* upper Murchison R.–Wiluna. Sedentary. Seriously declining in settled se. Aust.

WHITE-BROWED BABBLER *Pomatostomus superciliosus* 18–22 cm

Other names: Happy Family, Stickbirds, Cackler, Twelve Apostles, Jumper.
Dullest brown babbler, with dark eye; white eyebrow smaller than Grey-crowned Babbler; crown dark brown; white throat shades into brown lower underparts. **Similar species:** Hall's Babbler. **Voice:** chattering, miaowing notes; whistled rising 'sweet-sweet-sweet-miaow'. Alarm-call: brisk 'wit-wit'; rapid, tearing 'chiew-chiew'. **Habitat:** drier scrubby woodlands; mulga, other acacias; mallee, cypress pine scrubs; timber, scrub along watercourses; saltbush. **Breeds:** June–Nov. **Nest:** smaller than Grey-crowned. **Eggs:** 2–3 (5); buff–grey, glossy, with black, hairlike scribbles. **Range and Status:** mainland Aust., mostly s. of Tropic and mostly w. of Gt Divide: n. to Charleville–Chinchilla–Warwick (Q); e. to Hunter Valley (NSW), occasional Yass/ACT; mostly *absent* s. of Divide in Vic.; throughout SA, s. NT and s. WA *except* driest deserts and humid sw. WA. Common. Sedentary.

HALL'S BABBLER *Pomatostomus halli* 23–25 cm

Like a sooty brown White-browed Babbler *with shorter white bib; cut off more abruptly on mid-breast by dark underparts.* **Voice:** squeaky chatterings; frequent liquid note; calls more like Grey-crowned than White-browed; lacks 'yahoo' of former and madder staccato outbursts of latter. **Habitat:** tall mulga and other acacia scrubs; cypress pines; open eucalypt woodlands; spinifex associations. **Breeds:** June–Oct. **Nest:** smaller, neater than Grey-crowned. **Eggs:** 1–2; cream–brown, glossy, with black hairlike scribbles. **Range and Status:** large range in w. Q–far w. NSW; n. to Winton–Boulia (Q); w. at least to McGregor and Grey Ras; e. to *c.* Longreach–Idalia NP–Cunnamulla; s. to *c.* Barrier Ra.–Mootwingee–Brewarrina (NSW). Common in suitable habitat. Sedentary; locally nomadic.

CHESTNUT-CROWNED BABBLER *Pomatostomus ruficeps* 21–23 cm

Note dark eye, chestnut crown bordered by long white eyebrows; double white wingbar; white of throat/breast narrower than White-browed, bordered by dark sides of breast. In flight, shows *two fine, curved white wingbars.* Habits like other babblers, but often seems shyer. **Similar species:** White-browed Babbler. **Voice:** 'we-chee chee chee'; strident, irregular but melodious territorial song from top of tall mulga or similar vantage-point, like piping of Little Eagle. Approached, flocks utter loud 'chack-a-chack'. **Habitat:** drier inland scrubs/woodlands: mallee, mulga, other acacias; cypress pine, belar; on stony ground, sandhills; lignum, Old Man saltbush, samphire. **Breeds:** June–Oct. **Nest:** larger, often higher than White-browed. **Eggs:** 3–5; like White-browed. **Range and Status:** se. inland Aust.: from sw. Q n. to Windorah, e. to Mitchell–Dirranbandi; w. NSW, e. to Lightning Ridge–Nyngan–Condobolin–Moulamein; far nw. Vic., e. to *c.* Swan Hill; e. SA, s. to *c.* Swan Reach; w. to Quorn–w. of Flinders Ras.–Marree–e. of L. Eyre to *c.* Innamincka. Scarce to locally common. Sedentary.

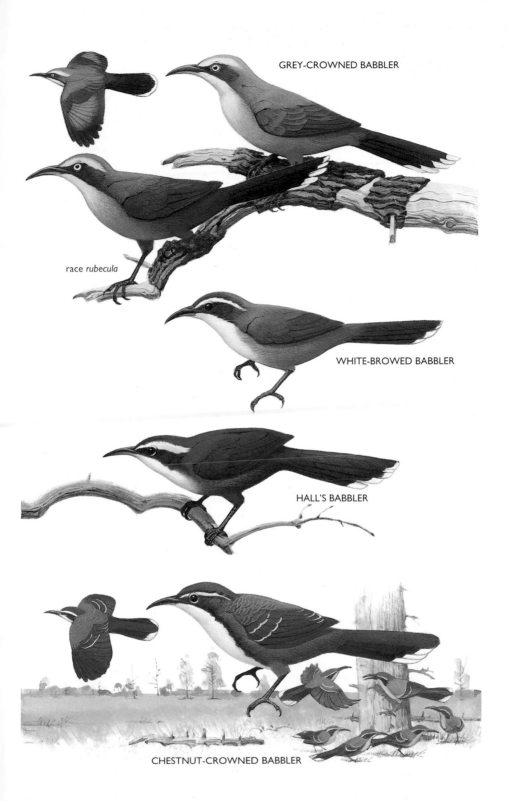

GREY-CROWNED BABBLER

race *rubecula*

WHITE-BROWED BABBLER

HALL'S BABBLER

CHESTNUT-CROWNED BABBLER

423

EASTERN WHIPBIRD *Psophodes olivaceus* 25–31 cm. Male larger.

Male: *black and olive–green crested bird with white patch on side of throat; longish white-tipped fan-tail.* **Female:** *browner; throat mottled whitish.* **Immature:** dull olive–brown; no white on throat. Pairs, family parties: *well-known by whipcrack call.* Hops briskly through undergrowth; probes rotten wood, throws leaves aside. Flight not strong; rarely sustained. **Voice:** *male's long, explosive whipcrack instantly answered by female with 'choo-choo', 'weece-weece', 'awee-awee' or 'witch-a-wee',* differing locally; scolding chuckles; clucks, croaks. **Habitat:** rainforests; wetter eucalypt forests/woodlands; coastal scrubs; blackberries, bracken, lantana, overgrown gardens. **Breeds:** Aug.–Dec. **Nest:** flattish cup of sticks, grass, bracken; lined with rootlets; 1–2 m+ in undergrowth, bracken. **Eggs:** 2–3; blue–white/green; with black/blue–grey hieroglyphic markings. **Range and Status:** coastal e. Aust., from n. and e. of Melbourne through e. and ne. Vic.; in NSW on and e. of Divide; in se. Q, inland to Bunya Mts NP–Toowoomba, n. to *c.* Byfield; coastal islands. Race *lateralis*: ne. Q, from Mt Spec to near Cooktown, inland to Atherton Tableland; mostly above 300 m, but to coast in parts. Common. Sedentary.

WESTERN WHIPBIRD *Psophodes nigrogularis* 20–26 cm

Other names: Black-throated or Mallee Whipbird.
Greyish olive–green, with slight crest; black throat bordered by white whisker; outer tail-feathers with subterminal black band, tipped white. **Immature:** tinged yellow–olive; throat grey–brown. **Race *leucogaster*,** 'Mallee Whipbird': *paler; underparts whiter.* **Nominate race:** darker. Singles, pairs: in undergrowth, bare ground under scrub. Runs swiftly; flies fast, low, direct, showing tail-markings. **Similar species:** Crested Bellbird, Wedgebill. **Voice:** peculiar, grating, of *4 slow notes, like creaking cartwheel:* 'Let's scratch, teach-er', beginning softly, swelling. Female answers 'pick it up'; chittering alarm-call. **Habitat:** dense unburned thickets of low eucalypts: mallee, banksia, acacias, tea-tree, coastal heath; broome honeymyrtle, tall spinifex. **Breeds:** July–Nov. **Nest:** cup of twigs, bark-strips, grass, green sprigs; to 2 m in spinifex under mallee; banksia, swordgrass. **Eggs:** 2; blue, with fine black, brown, grey spots, as though below surface; scrawls, hieroglyphs. **Range and Status:** four races in small, fragmented populations, from s. WA to s. SA–w. Vic., reduced by clearing, burning (Garnett, 1993). Locally common to rare and endangered.

CHIMING WEDGEBILL *Psophodes occidentalis* 19–22 cm

Like Chirruping Wedgebill; breast plainer; *shyer,* less gregarious, more skulking; *calls differ:* approached when singing on shrub-top, drops, falls silent. **Voice:** 4 or 5 quick, peculiar, metallic, ringing notes (or 3, or 2) in descending chime, 'but-did-you-get-drunk' with cyclic pattern; metallic plonk on 'drunk'. Monotonously repeated. **Habitat:** arid acacia scrubs on stony country; mallee-spinifex; broombush on sandhills. **Breeding:** as for Chirruping Wedgebill. **Range and Status:** w. interior Aust.: from Toomba Ras.–Glenormiston–Urandangi (far w. Q), across s. NT, n. to Tanami; to w. coast (WA) from *c.* Onslow s. to Murchison R.; s. inland to *c.* Payne's Find–Leonora, e. through Gt Victoria Desert to Tarcoola–Coober Pedy (SA). Locally common. Sedentary; nomadic.

CHIRRUPING WEDGEBILL *Psophodes cristatus* 19–21 cm

Bill dark, wedge-shaped, brown; plumage pale brown, slim upright crest, slight dark breast-streaks; flight-feathers edged white; tail longish, rounded, blackish brown, tipped white; legs/feet strong. **Immature:** bill horn-coloured, wing-feathers edged buff. Pairs, parties, loose flocks: runs rather than hops. Parties follow-the-leader, with long flat glides, tails part-spread. Often remains calling on shrub-top when approached. **Voice:** duet: one bird calls 'sitzi-cheeri', like budgerigars' rolling chirrup; female(?) answers with upward-rolling 'r-e-e-e-t CHEER!'; combined in endless rondo, echoed by others, effect unusual. **Habitat:** arid country with low saltbush, bluebush, emu bush; acacia scrubs; lignum–canegrass on watercourses. **Breeds:** Aug.–Nov., and after rains. **Nest:** loose cup of twigs; 1–3 m in low shrub. **Eggs:** 2–3; pale green–blue, with grey, purplish, black spots, hieroglyphs. **Range and Status:** e. inland Aust.: from near Port Augusta (SA), n. to *c.* Oodnadatta, w. of L. Eyre, to Simpson Desert in ne. SA–se. NT; e. through s. Flinders Ras. (SA); occasional far nw. Vic.; widespread NSW w. of Darling R.; in Q, e. to Cunnamulla, n. to Charleville–lower Diamantina R. Locally common.

EASTERN WHIPBIRD

imm.

♀

♂

WESTERN WHIPBIRD

imm.

imm.

CHIMING WEDGEBILL

CHIRRUPING WEDGEBILL

imm.

425

SPOTTED QUAIL-THRUSH *Cinclosoma punctatum* 25–28 cm

Sole quail-thrush in coastal se. Aust., Tas. **Male:** *face/throat black; eyebrow/throat-patch white; upperparts streaked/mottled black; breast grey;* underparts white, washed buff; *flanks boldly spotted/streaked black; legs pink.* **Female and Immature:** *eyebrow/throat buff–white, throat-patch yellow–ochre.* Pairs, family parties: shy; walks with backward/forward head movement; flicks tail. Runs, flies in rocketing bursts, flirting white-tipped tail. **Voice:** high-pitched 'seep'. Song, from bare stick: 10–12 soft, far-carrying fluty notes; low, harsh alarm-chatter. **Habitat:** drier forests/woodlands/scrubs with leaf-litter, branches, rocks, tussocks, on sunny side of dry ridges. **Breeds:** June–Nov. **Nest:** loose cup of bark, grass, leaves, rootlets; beside rock, tree, stump, tussock. **Eggs:** 2–3; dull cream/white, marked dark brown, purplish grey. **Range and Status:** se. Aust., from s. of Rockhampton (Q) to e. Tas. and se. SA; inland to Carnarvon Ra. NP (Q); Mt Kaputar–Warrumbungle NPs–Grenfell (NSW); inland to nc. Vic., w. to Grampians NP; also Fleurieu Pen.–s. Mt Lofty Ras. (SA). Sedentary.

CHESTNUT QUAIL-THRUSH *Cinclosoma castanotus* 20–26 cm

Plain olive–brown above, lower back/rump deep chestnut. **Male:** *eyebrow, throat-patch white; throat/breast glossy black.* **Female and Immature:** *eyebrow, throat-mark yellow–buff;* throat/breast grey, cut off sharply by white underparts. *Inland forms: brighter chestnut on back/rump.* Pairs, family parties: walks quietly, unless startled. **Voice:** high-pitched 'seep'; song soft, tremulous, ventriloquial; at dawn from song-perch. **Habitat:** mallee-spinifex; mulga, cypress-pine, with shrub layer; desert eucalypt woodlands; saltbush, desert-heaths, coastal tea-tree. **Breeds:** Aug.–Nov., or after rains. **Nest:** deep cup of bark-strips, sticks; by mallee-trunk, fallen branch, low bush; grass-tuft. **Eggs:** 2 (3); white, spotted, blotched brown. **Range and Status:** s. Aust.: from Round Hill NR (NSW), s. to Cocoparra NP, n. to *c.* Roto; mallee areas of sw. NSW–nw. Vic., s. to ne. Little Desert NP; s. SA *except* se., ne., Bight coast and Nullarbor P.; sw. NT to *c.* 90 km n. of Alice Springs–Kintore Ras.; across s. WA, coastally n. to *c.* Shark Bay; absent wetter sw. WA, but to s. coast. Patchy. Sedentary. Locally nomadic.

CINNAMON QUAIL-THRUSH *Cinclosoma cinnamomeum* 17–24 cm

Nominate race, male: *upperparts cream–buff;* shoulder-patch black, spotted white; flight feathers black with rufous edges. *Eyebrow/throat-patch white; face/throat black; breastband white to cinnamon, margined black below; underparts white.* **Female:** creamy-white eyebrow/throat-patch; throat/upperbreast buff–grey. Race *alisteri*, 'Nullarbor Quail-thrush': smaller (17–19 cm). Male: rich cinnamon–brown; *breast black, cut off by white underparts.* Female: like nominate, but brighter. Pairs, family parties: walks slowly, flicks tail; uses tiny bushes for concealment, shade, lookouts, song-perches. Runs swiftly, flies in rocketing bursts. **Voice:** insect-like 'see see see' or 'sisisisi'. **Habitat:** stony plains/tablelands; ridges; gravelly flats with sparse, low saltbush, bluebush, shrub-grown gullies. Race *alisteri*: sparse, shrub-cover of Nullarbor Plain: bluebush, saltbush; dead finish, etc. (Garnett, 1993). **Breeds:** June–Nov., and after rains. **Nest:** shallow cup of leaves, bark; near low shrub. **Eggs:** 2–3; cream/buff–white, spotted blackish brown, blue–grey. **Range and Status:** nominate race: arid inland s. Aust. Race *alisteri*: Nullarbor Plain, from *c.* Ooldea (SA) to w. of Naretha (WA); s. to Bight coast. Rare. Sedentary; locally nomadic.

CHESTNUT-BREASTED QUAIL-THRUSH *Cinclosoma castaneothorax* 18–24 cm

Markings like Cinnamon, colours richer: *male breastband yellow–chestnut to rich rusty; flanks yellow–chestnut, separated by thin black band from white underparts; back/rump/tail pale yellow–chestnut.* **Female:** throat deeper; *broad rufous–buff zone across breast.* **Race *marginatum*, 'Western Quail-thrush', male:** upperparts rich chestnut; *breastband/flanks bright rich chestnut, cut off below by broad black band;* underparts white. Habits, voice like Cinnamon. **Habitat:** mulga–eucalypts, other acacia scrubs, on stony ground; tea-tree/mallee/grevillea on rocky hillocks. **Breeds:** July–Sept. Nest and eggs like Cinnamon. **Range and Status:** nominate race: sw. Q, s. to *c.* White Cliffs–Cobar (NSW). Race *marginatum*: far sw. NT, n. to Kintore, w. to coast at Shark Bay (WA); s. inland to *c.* Kalgoorlie–Gt Victoria Desert, e. to Everard Ras (SA). Uncommon. Locally nomadic.

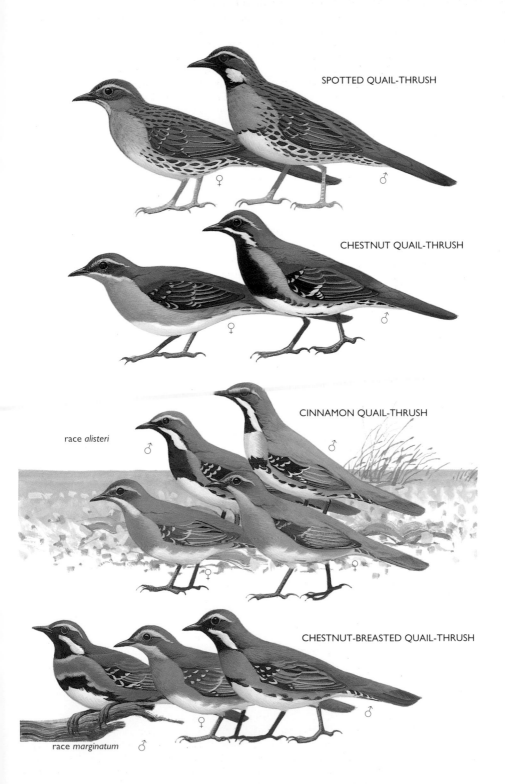

SPOTTED QUAIL-THRUSH

♀ ♂

CHESTNUT QUAIL-THRUSH

♀ ♂

CINNAMON QUAIL-THRUSH

race *alisteri*

♂ ♂

♀ ♀

CHESTNUT-BREASTED QUAIL-THRUSH

♂ ♀

race *marginatum* ♂

VARIED SITTELLA *Daphoenositta chrysoptera* 11–12.5 cm

Other names: Barkpecker, Treerunner, 'Woodpecker'.
A species of five (or six) distinctive geographic races around the continent, hybridising freely where ranges overlap (see map). ■ **Nominate race**,'Orange-winged Sittella' (se. Aust.): *bill longer in male than female; yellowish at base, with long, dark tip; legs/feet orange–yellow, robust; head grey or blackish; throat white (male); blackish grey (female).* Back paler grey–brown with broad dark streaks; rump whitish; *tail short, black with white tips; flight-feathers black with broad, pale orange band, conspicuous in flight; underparts white, lightly streaked darker in Vic., streaking increasing through n. NSW–inland s. Q.* **Immature:** paler; wing-coverts tipped buff; underparts whitish. In flight, wings seem too large for bird; *broad, pale orange wingband, white rump and white tail-tips, conspicuous.* Highly social: breeding groups of 5–7 in spring–summer (or autumn in n.), larger winter companies. Groups forage together, flying into heads of trees, *typically working down branches and trunk with constant rocking-horse motion,* probing and levering bark-flakes with longish, slightly upturned bills, maintaining contact with constant chitterings, before flying on to next tree. When breeding, one female appears to lay, but all members of group feed the young. Roost comunally. **Voice:** high-pitched, thin 'seewit-seewee'; 'chip chip'; constant chittering. Alarm-call: rapid, high-pitched 'didididit'. **Habitat:** open eucalypt woodlands/forests (except heavier rainforests); mallee, inland acacia, coastal tea-tree scrubs; golfcourses, shelterbelts, orchards, parks, scrubby gardens. **Breeds:** July–Dec.; March–April. **Nest:** beautiful, well-camouflaged deep cup of bark-flakes, lichens, spiders' web, moulded to resemble bulge in upright fork of eucalypt, she oak, paperbark, tea-tree; 5–20 m high. **Eggs:** 2–3; blue–white/grey–white, speckled, blotched glossy black, olive–brown; faint grey markings in zone. **Range and Status:** c. and e. Vic.; e. NSW–inland s. Q, merging there with race *leucocephala*. Merges with race *pileata* in w. Vic.–cw. NSW. Common. Sedentary or nomadic.

■ **Race *leucocephala*,** 'White-headed Sittella': *head/neck white in both sexes; wingband orange; upperparts/flanks streaked dark grey.* **Immature:** head mostly grey. **Habitat:** forests/woodlands of Divide/coastal plain; in n. parts, open grassy woodlands. **Range:** from Clarence R. (ne. NSW), to Darling Downs–Mitchell–Blackall–Suttor Ck (Q), to coast near Mackay. Merges with nominate race in ne. NSW–se. Q , and with *striatus* in zone n. to Townsville–Charters Towers.
(Race *albata*, 'Pied Sittella', 'lost' since collected near Bowen (Q), late in 19th century. Probably an intergrade between *leucocephala* and *striatus*; had *unique combination of creamy white head/white wingpatches*.)

■ **Race *striatus*,** 'Striated Sittella': *darkest-headed, most streaked sittella.* **Male:** crown black. **Female:** *head/throat and sometimes upperbreast black.* Both sexes grey–white above, *streaked brownish black; whitish underparts finely streaked blackish; wingband white.* **Immature:** no streaks on breast. **Habitat:** eucalypt forests, grassy woodlands/scrublands. **Range:** ne. Q; Townsville–C. York, w. to Normanton. Merges with *leucocephala* in region of Charters Towers–Townsville and with *leucoptera* in region of lower Flinders R.–Cloncurry.

■ **Race *leucoptera*,** 'White-winged Sittella': like *pileata*, but smaller; wingband white, conspicuous in flight. **Immature:** head greyish. **Habitat:** grassy woodlands, timber on watercourses, scrubby timber on ranges. **Range:** from Opalton–Winton–Cloncurry (Q) n. to Gulf lowlands, w. through Top End (NT) to Kimberley (WA), s. to about Tropic in Q and NT, and to about Broome (WA). Merges with *striatus* in region of lower Flinders R.–Cloncurry (nw. Q) and with *pileata* in s. NT and mid nw. WA.

■ **Race *pileata*,** 'Black-capped Sittella': more boldly marked/clean-cut than nominate race. **Male:** crown black; forehead/sides of face white. **Female:** crown/forehead/cheeks glossy black. *Back plain grey–brown or with slight dark streaks; underparts pure white, unstreaked.* **Immature:** crown greyish black, streaked whitish in juvs. In flight, *orange wingband, white rump, white tips to black tail conspicuous.* **Habitat:** coastal eucalypt forests; woodlands to inland woodlands/scrubs–mallee, mulga, cypress-pine; timber on watercourses; gullies, gorges of ranges; also golfcourses, orchards, parks, gardens. **Range:** WA s. of Tropic; s. NT; most of SA; w. Vic. (occasional to inland e. Vic.); w. NSW and sw. Q. Merges with nominate race in c. Vic. and c. NSW and with *leucoptera* in w. Q–s. NT–mid nw. WA.

VARIED SITTELLA

race
striatus

race
leucoptera

♀

♂

♀

race
leucocephala

race
pileata

♂

♀

imm.

♀

♂

nominate race

429

RED-WHISKERED BULBUL *Pycnonotus jocosus* 20–23 cm

Jaunty, distinctive, with erect black crest, white cheek; red earmark; pink under tail-coverts; white corners to black tail. **Immature:** browner; lacks red earmark. Singles, pairs in local colonies; gregarious in winter. Restless, quick; perches on wires, other high points, sallies after insects. Destructive of berries, flower buds, soft fruits; spreads seeds of privet. **Similar species:** Eastern Whipbird: darker; breast black; no red. **Voice:** pleasant, liquid call described as 'queep-quillya'. **Habitat:** gardens, suburban trees, public parks, wasteland, thickets; marginally into native woodland, scrubland. **Breeds:** Aug.–Feb. **Nest:** shallow, untidy, open cup of bark-fibre, leaves, rootlets; lined with fine twigs, rootlets; to 3 m high in thick cover. **Eggs:** 2–4; glossy, whitish, heavily but finely spotted, some blotched, reddish/purplish brown. **Range and Status:** India, s. China, parts of se. Asia. Introduced Aust. *c.* 1880, later escaped from aviaries. Common, widespread in Sydney region (NSW) w. to Blue Mts, n. to lower Hunter Valley, s. to Shoalhaven R.; separate population Coffs Harbour. In Vic., small colony in South Yarra. Casual elsewhere NSW, Vic., but very uncommon.

CRESTED SHRIKE-TIT *Falcunculus frontatus* 15–19 cm

Bold black-and-white head/crest and yellow breast unmistakeable. Male, black throat, female olive–green. **Immature:** browner above; throat/breast whitish. Race *leucogaster* (s. WA): *white abdomen separates yellow breast and under tail-coverts; wings/tail washed yellow–green.* Race *whitei* (nw. Aust.): smaller; wings/tail washed yellow; rump yellow–green; underparts brighter yellow. Pairs, family parties: often noticed by calls or vigorous tearing of loose bark with strong, hooked bill in search of insects. Opens leaf-galls, seed-cases, dismembers hard-shelled insects held under foot. Flight swift, swooping between trees. **Similar species:** Golden Whistler. **Voice:** slow, sad, descending whistle 'peeer, peeer'; call of race *whitei* described to rise after first descending (Rix, 1970); distinctive chuckle or stutter, 'knock-at-the-door'. Clear, animated song includes mimicry. **Habitat:** rainforests, eucalypt forests/woodlands; in inland se. Aust., river red gums on watercourses, especially saplings, young trees; also acacias, coastal tea-tree, banksia or cypress pine scrubs; golfcourses, orchards, parks, gardens. **Breeds:** Sept.–Jan.; cooperatively, with 'helpers'. **Nest:** deep cup of bark-fibre, spiders' web; decorated with lichen, lined with grass; built around vertical stems in eucalypt foliage 5–25 m high; twigs, leaves, buds nipped off above nest. **Eggs:** 2–3; grey–white, dotted, spotted brown, slate-grey, black. **Range and Status:** nominate race: e. and se. Aust.: highlands of ne. Q; se. Aust., from *c.* Rockhampton to Mt Lofty Ras–Fleurieu Pen. (SA) (where isolated). Mostly on and coastward of Divide; inland to Charleville (Q); Darling R. (NSW). Common. Sedentary. Race *leucogaster*: sw. WA, from *c.* Geraldton e. to *c.* Norseman. Uncommon. Race *whitei*: Top End (NT); most recent records in region of Larrimah–Katherine; records e. of Arnhem Land escarpment and n. to Kapalga, near Darwin; w. through Willaroo–Timber Ck (NT) to Beverley Springs, Kimberley (WA), (Robinson & Woinarski, 1992). Rare. Mostly sedentary.

CRESTED BELLBIRD *Oreoica gutturalis* 20–23 cm

Distinctive inland vocalist. **Male:** *forehead/throat white, bordered by black band from slender erectile black crest to broad black breastpatch;* rest of head grey; eye orange–red; upperparts grey–brown; rump tinged chestnut; underparts whitish; *under tail-coverts buffish.* **Female and Immature:** browner: no breastpatch; eye yellowish. Singles, pairs, family parties, small companies: forages on ground, stumps, low branches; hops briskly. Flight strong, undulating: lacks white tail-tips. Calling, perches high, on exposed dead branch, turning left and right, hence 'ventriloquial' quality. **Similar species:** Wedgebills, Western Whipbird. **Voice:** celebrated, unusual, liquid; starts softly, intensifies: 'did-did-did, didee-dit', 'pan-pan, panella', or mellow 'plunk plunk' or 'plunka-plunka-plunka', last syllable dropping in liquid plonk or like mellow cow-bell; from distance, only this may be heard. Contact-call: thin 'seep', like quail-thrush. Alarm-call: harsh 'chuck-a-chuck-chuck'. **Habitat:** arid scrublands — mulga, other acacias; saltbush, belar, mallee/spinifex; eucalypt woodlands. **Breeds:** Aug.–Dec., or after rain. **Nest:** untidy cup of bark-strips, leaves, twigs; lined with grass, rootlets; 1–3 m high on stump, fork of shrub, tree. Places immobilised live caterpillars around rim. **Eggs:** 3–4; white, blotched dark brown, grey. **Range and Status:** widespread mainland Aust., mostly w. of Gt Divide and s. of tropical coastal n. Aust. Extends to w. coast s. of NW Cape (WA); s. coast of WA/SA, e. to se. SA; *mostly absent from* far sw. WA, s. coastal and e. Vic.; coastal e. NSW–e. Q. Sedentary; locally nomadic.

RED-WHISKERED
BULBUL

imm.

CRESTED SHRIKE-TIT

imm.

♀

♂

race
whitei

♀

♂

race
leucogaster

♀

♂

CRESTED BELLBIRD

♂

♀

♂

imm.

OLIVE WHISTLER *Pachycephala olivacea* 20–22 cm

Large, plain whistler. **Male:** bill blackish; *head grey; upperparts ochre–grey; throat with fine whitish scallops;* grey zone across upperbreast; underparts ochre–buff. **Female:** bill dark brown above, paler below; throat plain grey; breastband less definite. **Immature:** rufous on wings. Singles, pairs: forages on or near ground; mixes with scrubwrens, robins. Elusive; moves away in short low flights between thickets. **Similar species:** Golden Whistler, female. **Voice:** sweet, pensive; some notes powerful: swelling 'cho cho cho cho', or 'jiff, jiff, jiff' repeated monotonously; long, ringing 'peeee' — still, small voice. Common call of s. birds syllabised 'tew-wit-tew' or 'tu-wee-tchow', with whipcrack on second or third syllable; slow, rising, ringing 'cheer, *ritty*', with slight whipcrack. In ne. NSW/se. Q, thoughtful 'peee-pooo'; or 'pooo-peee'. **Habitat:** alpine thickets; wetter rainforests/forests/woodlands; watercourse-vegetation; coastal tea-tree/paperbark scrubs, heaths; blackberries, gardens. More open habitats autumn–winter. In ne. NSW–se. Q, beech forest above *c.* 500 m. **Breeds:** Sept.–Jan. **Nest:** cup of twigs, bark, leaves; lined with grass, rootlets; 1–3 m in dense shrub, tree, bracken, sword-grass. **Eggs:** 2–3; tapering; yellow–white/buff–white; irregular dots, spots; small blotches of brown, underlying lavender, grey. **Range and Status:** coastal se. Aust: from far se. SA–sw. Vic. patchily to Otway Ras. (Vic.), n. coastally to se. Q in wetter forests/alpine woodlands of Gt Divide, to *c.* 1500 m; inland to *c.* Ballarat–Victorian Alps–Snowy Mts–Brindabella Ra. (ACT)–Blue Mts (NSW), dispersing to lowlands, e.g. Canberra, in autumn–winter. From Barrington Tops NP–Gloucester Tops (NSW), n. to McPherson Ras. (se. Q), mostly sedentary in mountain rainforests, incl. Antarctic beech forests above *c.* 500 m. Widespread Tas., Bass Strait islands. Uncommon. Sedentary; altitudinal migrant.

RED-LORED WHISTLER *Pachycephala rufogularis* 19–22 cm

Other name: Buff-breasted Whistler.
Male: *orange–buff face/throat; grey breastband; orange–buff underparts,* some have buff rear collar; flight-feathers edged yellow–buff. **Female:** paler; underparts paler grey. Both sexes: eye red. **Immature:** eye brown; rufous eyebrow, flight feathers edged rufous. Behaves like Gilbert's, but seldom forages high. **Similar species:** Gilbert's Whistler. **Voice:** slow, sweet, wistful, swelling 'see-saw', or 'see-saw-sik', dipping on second syllable, rising on last. **Habitat:** low, patchy mallee/heath/spinifex; stunted mallee on sandhills; cypress pine, broombush. **Breeds:** Sept.–Dec. **Nest:** substantial cup of bark, twigs, leaves, vine tendrils, rootlets; lined with grass; in spinifex, under foliage. **Eggs:** 2–3; buff–white/pink, freckled brown, purple, lavender. **Range and Status:** inland se. Aust.: from Round Hill NR (Roto–Condobolin), Cocoparra NP (NSW), to nw. Vic., Big Desert NP–Sunset Country, occasional to Hattah/Kulkyne NP; w. to Murray mallee of e. SA, occasional (winter visitor?) Mt Lofty Ras–Adelaide Plains; casual L. Alexandrina. In March 1995, isolate population located near Wudinna, c. Eyre Pen. (SA) (Matthew, Croft & Carpenter, 1995). Rare; local. Sedentary; autumn–winter dispersal often beyond 'normal' range.

GILBERT'S WHISTLER *Pachycephala inornata* 19–20 cm

Male: *blackish mask and rich orange–buff throat;* centre of lower breast washed orange–buff. **Female:** *uniform grey; pale eye-ring; throat paler, with slight dark streaks; buff wash on centre of breast/under tail-coverts.* Both sexes: eyes red. **Immature:** similar to female; eyes brown, flight-feathers edged buff. Heard before seen; forages in tops of shrubs/trees, or on ground under cover; moves ahead in strong, undulating flight. **Similar species:** Red-lored Whistler. Golden Whistler, female. **Voice:** far-carrying, sweet, 'jock-jock-jock-jock' or 'pew, pew-pew-PEW-PEW-PEW', swelling, in sequence of 11–18+; breaking into wheezy, explosive 'ee-cha, ee-ch' or 'EE-chop'; soft, in-drawn 'whistler' calls; slow, descending 'wee-e-e-woo' or 'persweee?', rising at end. **Habitat:** tall drier scrubs; woodland with dense understorey; mallee-spinifex, cypress-pine, mulga, belar, buloke, coastal tea-tree; black box/lignum, broom honeymyrtle. **Breeds:** Aug.–Dec. **Nest:** cup of twigs, leaves, grass, wool; lined with grass, plant-fibre; in low fork in shrub; vine, mistletoe, stump; old nest of babbler, butcherbird. **Eggs:** 2–3 (4); whitish/light buff, spotted brown, black, underlying lilac. **Range and Status:** from Warrumbungle NP–Cowra–Tocumwal (NSW), s. to upper Murray R. (Vic.)–Chiltern-Nagambie (casual You Yangs), w. to Wimmera and mallee areas of nw. Vic.; in SA, Murray mallee–Flinders Ras. to n. Yorke Pen.–Eyre Pen., w. to Gawler Ras–Gt Victoria Desert; in s. WA, through s. W. Deserts, w. and n. to Menzies–Paynes Find–Yalgoo, s. to *c.* Northam–Narrogin–Albany. Uncommon. Sedentary or nomadic.

OLIVE WHISTLER

imm.

♀

♂

RED-LORED WHISTLER

imm.

♀

♂

GILBERT'S WHISTLER

imm.

♀

♂

GREY WHISTLER *Pachycephala simplex* 14–15 cm

Other name: Brown Whistler.
Small, whistler with glossy black, longish, slightly hooked bill; large head; dark eye. Two populations in n. Aust.: (1) race *peninsulae,* 'Grey Whistler' (ne. Q): *head grey; faint white eyebrows meet over bill; faint whitish eyelids; shadowy eyeline; large, dark eye. Upperparts washed olive; bend of wing cream; throat white; breast washed olive–grey; underparts lemon; legs/feet blackish.* **Female:** *whitish below; under tail-coverts lemon.* (2) Nominate race, 'Brown Whistler' (Top End, NT): *browner above, white below, buff–grey breastband; white bend of wing.* Singles, pairs: quiet; searches foliage, often high. **Similar species:** Fairy Gerygone, female. Yellow-legged, Lemon-bellied Flycatcher. **Voice:** clear, slow, descending call, 'eee-see-wee-*weekyou*', or only 'eee-see'; lacks whipcrack. Contact-call: 'zuity-beaut'. **Habitat:** rainforests, monsoon forests, vine and coastal scrubs; mangroves, paperbarks. **Breeds:** Sept.–March. **Nest:** cup of grass, leaves, vine tendrils, rootlets, spider's web. **Eggs:** 2; whitish/pale buff, spotted dull brown, lavender. **Range and Status:** Race *peninsulae*: from C. York (Q) s. to *c.* Ingham on e. coast; up to *c.* 900 m in mountain rainforests. Nominate race: Top End (NT), coastal islands; from *c.* Port Keats e. to Groote Eylandt. Uncommon. Sedentary; seasonally nomadic. Also PNG, e. Indonesia.

GOLDEN WHISTLER *Pachycephala pectoralis* 16.5–18.5 cm

Male: *head/breastband black, separating white throat from rich golden yellow nape-band and underparts;* tail grey with black tip. **Female:** grey–brown above, progressively washed deeper olive–green from se. Aust. to Q; *pale tips to wing-coverts form subtle single or double line across wing.* Underparts grey–buff; females from coastal n. NSW–Q have *lemon wash on vent/under tail-coverts.* Bill black, stubby (Tas.) to longish (Q). **Juvenile:** rich rufous. **Immature:** like female; pale base to bill; *rufous margins to wing-feathers.* Pairs when breeding, otherwise solitary, or in mixed-species companies. In spring, both sexes display, duet, sing vivaciously, with see-saw posturing. **Similar species:** Mangrove Golden, Gilbert's, Grey Whistlers. **Voice:** many sweet notes; brisk 'sweetawit, sweetawit'; rising 'wheat-wheat-wheat-WHITTLE!', brisk 'dee-dee-dee-ah-WHIT!'. Contact-call: single, rising 'seeep'. Calls after sudden loud noise. **Habitat:** rainforests, eucalypt forests/woodlands, waterside vegetation, coastal/inland scrubs, mallee/spinifex; brigalow, other dense acacia scrubs; mangroves, orchards, shelterbelts, golf-courses, parks, gardens. **Breeds:** Aug.–Jan. **Nest:** rough cup of bark-strips, spider's web, stems, rootlets, skeleton leaves, fern-fronds, grass, twigs; low in blackberries, treeferns, long grass, upright fork 1–4 m high. **Eggs:** 2–3; oval; white/cream/salmon-pink; freckled, dotted, blotched red–brown, grey, dark brown, black; underlying spots of lavender/dark grey. **Range and Status:** in e. Aust., mountain rainforests above 300 m in ne. Q, s. near Cooktown s. to Eyre Pen.–Yalata (SA), inland to *c.* Carnarvon Ra. NP–St George (Q); Brewarrina–Cobar–Mootwingee (NSW); Flinders Ras.–Gawler Ras. (SA). In WA, ranges w. from *c.* Eucla to s. of Shark Bay; inland to Yalgoo–Bonnie Rock–Coolgardie–Karonie. Also many coastal islands s. from Cairns (Q); widespread Tas.; also Norfolk, Lord Howe Is. Populations both sedentary and migratory: in e. Aust. there is autumn–winter migration from highlands to lowlands; elsewhere, north–south or coastal–inland movements in autumn–winter. Also Fiji to Indonesia.

MANGROVE GOLDEN WHISTLER *Pachycephala melanura* 15–17 cm

Other name: Black-tailed Whistler.
Male: *smaller than Golden Whistler; bill longer, slightly hooked; underparts brighter orange–yellow, extending in broader rear collar and across rump; tail shorter, jet-black.* **Female:** *underparts yellow, varying racially:* female of nominate race *melanura* (nw. WA) *has cream–white breast, yellow lower belly and under tail-coverts;* female of race *robusta* (Kimberley (WA)–Q) *has more greenish upperparts, whitish throat, mostly yellow underparts.* **Immature:** like respective female; rufous edges to secondaries; base of bill straw-colored. Singles, pairs: habits like Golden Whistler, but feeds among tidal debris; diet includes crabs (Blakers et al, 1984). **Similar species:** Grey Whistler. **Voice:** like Golden Whistler but richer, more rollicking, like Rufous Whistler (D. Robinson, pers. comm.). **Habitat:** mangroves, coastal rainforest or monsoon forest; riverside thickets, eucalypt woodlands, coastal scrubs/heath. **Breeds:** Oct.–March. **Nest and eggs:** like Golden Whistler, smaller. **Range and Status:** coastal n. Aust., many coastal islands: from Carnarvon mangroves (WA) to near Mackay (Q). Sight-records in mangroves, Shoalwater Bay (Q). Fairly common. Sedentary. Casual Torres Strait. Related forms from Indonesia to PNG, Pacific islands.

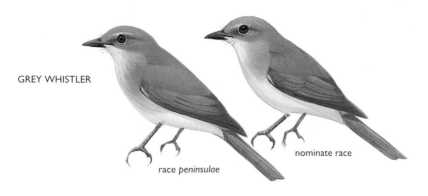

GREY WHISTLER

race *peninsulae*

nominate race

GOLDEN WHISTLER

Queensland ♀

imm.

southern ♀

♂

MANGROVE GOLDEN WHISTLER

♀ nominate race

imm.

♀ race *robusta*

♂

RUFOUS WHISTLER *Pachycephala rufiventris* 16.5–17.5 cm

Male: *crown/upperparts clear grey; strong black mask extends in broad black breast-band, separating white throat from rufous underparts.* **Female:** *brownish grey above, with touch of olive; throat whitish, breast/underparts washed buff, with plentiful dark vertical streaks.* **Immature:** like female; bill pale at base; upperparts more olive; rufous margins to flight-feathers. Young males may breed in imm. plumage. Some adult males are very pale sandy below, with ill-defined masks; some females whitish below, streaked blackish; n. Aust. birds noticeably small. Usually solitary, or in mixed feeding associations in nonbreeding season. In breeding season, both sexes display in typical see-saw, whistler fashion, heads/tails skyward, males conspicuously vocal. **Similar species:** White-breasted Whistler, female. **Voice:** impetuous, spirited spring song; the most 'Australian' of spring sounds: components include a sharp, declamatory 'pllik, chik!' and a ringing, almost explosive 'eee-chong!', uttered singly several times, followed by loud, rippling bursts of melody. Also clear, level, penetrating 'joey-joey-joey', rapidly, monotonously repeated 30+ times. In autumn, both sexes have a beautiful, subdued sub-song. **Habitat:** open forests/woodlands/scrubs, from coasts to arid, inland mallee, mulga; also in taller denser, humid forests of Gt Divide; exotic pine plantations, etc. **Breeds:** Sept.–Feb. **Nest:** fragile cup of twigs, grass; lined with finer material; in upright slender fork, 1–5 m high, in cover; occasionally to 15 m. **Eggs:** 2–4; variable; pale olive–green/olive–brown; freckled, spotted pale red–brown/dark brown, evenly or in zone at large end. **Range and Status:** summer breeding migrant in se. Aust. (less so in sw. WA), arriving Aug.–Sept., departing March–April; many moving into inland and to n. Aust. in autumn–winter. Common; widespread. Vagrant Tas., King I. Also e. Indonesia, PNG, New Cal.

WHITE-BREASTED WHISTLER *Pachycephala lanioides* 19–21 cm

Big striking whistler, *with robust, hooked, shrike-thrush like bill.* **Male:** *crown/nape black, extending in broad black breastband, bordered chestnut; upperparts grey; throat white; underparts buff–white; tail tipped grey.* **Female:** varies racially; *brownish to grey above, sometimes washed olive, wings/tail browner; fawn–white below, washed grey–buff on sides of neck/breast, finely streaked dark brown.* **Immature:** like female, wing-feathers edged rufous; underparts buffer, with heavier streaks. Singles, pairs: forages in foliage and on tidal mud under mangroves, on small crabs, etc. Often first located by ringing calls. **Similar species:** Rufous Whistler, female. Grey Shrike-thrush. **Voice:** loud, clear, deep, musical whistle of 4–6 notes, pausing between each, somewhat like Rufous Whistler; soft, clear whistle falling slightly at end; harsh, sharp alarm-call. **Habitat:** low, dense mangroves; rainforest fringing coastal streams, springs. **Breeds:** March–Oct. **Nest:** scanty large cup of twigs, rootlets, spiders' web; lined with finer rootlets; in mangrove fork 1–3 m high. **Eggs:** 2; buffish, with zone of brown/lavender spots at large end. **Range and Status:** discontinuous distribution in suitable mangrove habitat around coastal n. Aust., from n. of Carnarvon (WA) to Edward R., w. C. York Pen. (Q). Fairly common. Sedentary.

RUFOUS WHISTLER

imm.

♀

pale inland ♂

♂

WHITE-BREASTED WHISTLER

♀

imm.

♂

GREY SHRIKE-THRUSH *Colluricincla harmonica* 22–26 cm

Male: *bill black; lores whitish; back olive–brown.* **Female:** *bill pale grey on sides; lores greyish; faint white eye-ring; back paler; rufous or blackish streaks on face/throat/breast.* In nw. Aust./Top End: *larger, browner, incl. bill.* **Immature:** *tan eyebrow and/or eye-ring; rufous margins to wing-coverts.* **Race *rufiventris*, 'Western Shrike-thrush':** *pale brownish grey; underparts grey–white, belly/under tail-coverts yellow–buff.* Singles, pairs, family parties: forages on branches, trunks, ground/logs. In e. Aust. tame around habitation. Flight undulating. **Similar species:** female whistlers, especially Gilbert's. **Voice:** ringing 'purr-purr, *quee yule!*', '*pip-pip-pip-ho-ee!*', 'ee-all, ee-all, *queel*'. In winter, ringing 'dite!', 'yorrick!' or 'ching'. **Habitat:** eucalypt forests/woodlands; coastal scrubs; mallee, mulga, saltbush; watercourses; homesteads, golf-courses, parks, gardens. **Breeds:** July–Feb. **Nest:** large bowl of bark-strips, grass, rootlets; 2–6 m in fork, tree-cavity, grasstree; coppice-growth; vine against house, down-pipe; tin, basket, shed. **Eggs:** 2–4; white, finely freckled red–brown, blue–grey. **Range and Status:** Nominate race: widespread se. Aust. to coastal n. Aust. Race *rufiventris*: c., sc., and w. Aust.; intergrades with nominate in Flinders Ras. (SA), and far w. Q–NT. Race *strigata*: Tas., Bass Strait islands. Common. Sedentary. Also PNG.

LITTLE SHRIKE-THRUSH *Colluricincla megarhyncha* 17–19 cm

Other name: Rufous Shrike-thrush.
Small, large-billed shrike-thrush: *bill silvery brown above, pinkish on sides. Upperparts olive–grey–brown, crown/nape greyer; throat whitish; underparts rufous–buff, with fine dark streaks; legs pink–brown.* Birds in ne. Q more cinnamon–rufous: in Top End (NT) to w. Kimberley (WA) *bill blackish; eyebrow pale; face/throat whitish; underparts pale rufous.* Singles, pairs: forages on tree-trunks; tangles of vines/leaves; located by calls, rustling bark. **Voice:** deep 'shee-ee, wot wot wot'; or 'wot, wot, shee?'; 'eeee, butch-butch-butcher'; in alarm, loud, sparrow-like 'charip', harsh wheezes. **Habitat:** rainforest (mostly lowland in ne. NSW–se. Q); watercourse vegetation; paperbarks; coastal open forest; mangroves, lantana thickets. **Breeds:** Sept.–March. **Nest:** deep cup of plant-fibre, leaves, rootlets, stems, spider's web; in fork, vine-tangle, low to 10 m. **Eggs:** 2–3; pearly white/pale pink; spotted, blotched brown, with underlying lilac. **Range and Status:** coastal e. and n. Aust., from *c.* Nambucca Heads–Coutts Crossing (NSW) to w. coast, C. York Pen. (Q). Mangroves of sw. Gulf (NT); Top End to w. Kimberley (WA). Common. Sedentary.

BOWER'S SHRIKE-THRUSH *Colluricincla boweri* 21 cm

Small, large-headed, short-tailed shrike-thrush with slaty, olive–brown back, grey-streaked rufous breast. **Male:** *bill black; lores/eye-ring grey; lacks rufous eyebrow.* **Female:** *bill dark grey with pinkish tinge; lores/eyebrow and eye-ring rufous; upperparts slightly paler, greyer.* **Immature:** like female, with rufous on wing-coverts. Singles, pairs: quiet, watches from low perch; forages on lawns near rainforest. **Similar species:** Little Shrike-thrush. **Voice:** quiet: mellow, high, rising 'sheee', followed by lower 'wot, wot, wot, wot'; loud 'tuck'; honeyeater-like 'click'; in alarm, harsh gratings. **Habitat:** rainforests in coastal ranges of ne. Q; lawns near same. **Breeds:** Oct.–Jan. **Nest:** open cup of leaves, skeleton leaves, bark; rootlets; 1–8 m in lawyer-vine, tree-fork. **Eggs:** 2 (3); pearly/pinky white, sparsely blotched red–brown, underlying grey. **Range and Status:** mostly above 400 m in highland rainforests of ne. Q, from Mt Amos, near Cooktown, to Mt Spec, near Townsville; inland to Herberton Ra., but to sea-level where habitat continuous (Blakers et al, 1984). Common. Winter movement to lowlands is reported.

SANDSTONE SHRIKE-THRUSH *Colluricincla woodwardi* 24–26 cm

Rock-dwelling, long, slender shrike-thrush: bill black; head greyish, merging into olive–brown upperparts; lores/throat pale buff; underparts rich olive–buff. **Immature:** wing feathers edged rufous. Singles, pairs: shy; flicks wings, longish rounded tail; throws head back when calling. Makes short flights, hops up rock-faces. Mostly located by splendid echoing call. **Voice:** clear strong notes, gloriously amplified by rocks, cliffs. Contact-call: strident 'peter!'. **Habitat:** sandstone escarpments/gorges. **Breeds:** Oct.–Jan. **Nest:** large untidy cup of bark, spinifex, rootlets; in rock-crevice or ledge. **Eggs:** 2–3; creamy white, blotched brown about large end. **Range and Status:** from escarpments of 'Gulf fall' in far nw. Q to w. Kimberley (WA), s. to region of Fitzroy Crossing. Common in suitable habitat. Sedentary.

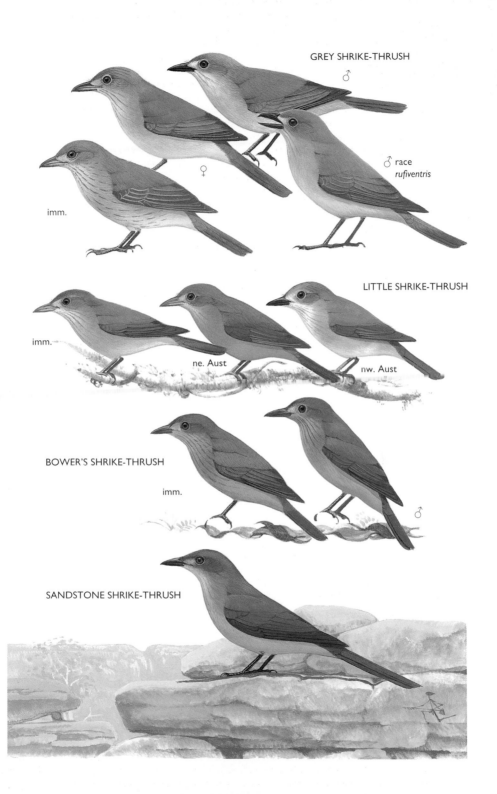

GREY SHRIKE-THRUSH

♂

♀

imm.

♂ race
rufiventris

LITTLE SHRIKE-THRUSH

imm.

ne. Aust

nw. Aust

BOWER'S SHRIKE-THRUSH

imm.

♂

SANDSTONE SHRIKE-THRUSH

BLACK-FACED MONARCH *Monarcha melanopsis* 16–19 cm

Pale grey bill *surrounded by distinctive black forehead and throat patch; grey upperparts/upperbreast contrast with rich rufous underparts; dark grey tail lacks white tips.* **Immature:** bill blackish; head wholly grey. Singles, pairs: movements deliberate; forages in foliage high and low; sallies after flying insects. When breeding, vivacious; often first noted by call. **Similar species:** Black-winged, Spectacled Monarchs. **Voice:** fussy, wheezy chatterings, deep scolds; main call rich, clear 'Why-you, which-you'; harsher 'which-a-where'; clear, mellow drawn-out 'wheech you', repeated; down-slurred 'r,r,rerr' or 'shsh-shsh-shirr', like bowerbird, babbler. **Habitat:** rainforests, eucalypt woodlands; coastal scrubs; damp gullies in rainforest, eucalypt forest; when migrating, more open woodland. **Breeds:** Oct.–Jan. **Nest:** deep cup of bark-strips, rootlets, green moss, spiders' web; in fork of slender sapling, 1–12 m or more high. **Eggs:** 2–3; white, minutely dotted, spotted reddish/red–brown, sparse underlying pale purplish blotches. **Range and Status:** coastal e. Aust. and islands; mostly on and coastwards of Gt Divide: from C. York (Q) to far e. Vic., w. to c. Glenaladale NP (Emison et al, 1987); uncommon, irregular w. to Dandenong Ras.–Kinglake (Vic.); casual w. of Melbourne; rare in ACT; winter vagrant, Kimberley (WA) (Johnstone, 1991). Resident in ne. Q; summer breeding migrant to coastal se. Aust., from Aug.–Sept., to March–April. Many migrate to PNG in autumn–winter. Common in n., uncommon in s.

BLACK-WINGED MONARCH *Monarcha frater* 18–19 cm

Other name: Pearly Flycatcher.
Paler grey than Black-faced Monarch, with contrasting, mostly black, wings and tail. **Immature:** bill darker; head wholly pale grey; wing-feathers edged buff-brown. Singles, pairs. Voice and behaviour like Black-faced Monarch. **Habitat:** rainforests; nearby eucalypt woodlands; mangroves. **Breeds:** Oct.–Feb. **Nest:** compact small cup, of green moss, strips/flakes of paperbark, spiders' web; lined with vegetable-fibre; in upright fork, to 6 m. **Eggs:** 3; creamy white, with scattered irregular spots of red–brown, pale purple, in zone at large end. **Range and Status:** summer breeding migrant (Oct.–March) from PNG to C. York Pen. (Q), s. to McIlwraith Ra., n. of Coen on e. coast. Casual s. to Cooktown, Cairns region (Edmonton), possibly Atherton Tableland. Migrates n. in autumn–winter through w. Torres Strait to PNG (Blakers et al, 1984). Some overwinter locally. Rare.

SPECTACLED MONARCH *Monarcha trivirgatus* 14–16 cm

Slender, active flycatcher: *bill blue–grey; upperparts deep blue–grey; black cloverleaf pattern on face/throat; lower sides of face to breast orange–buff; underparts white; tail black, outer feathers prominently tipped white.* Race *albiventris* of n. Q: upperbreast *orange–buff; most of underparts white.* **Immature:** no black on head; centre of throat greyish; outer tail-feathers tipped buff–white. Singles, pairs, parties: vivacious; flutters, hovers, dodges in foliage; works industriously over trunks, vines, *longish tail fanned, white tips prominent.* Often first located by chatterings. **Similar species:** Black-faced, Black-winged Monarchs. **Voice:** scratchy chatterings; fussy, deep, jigging scoldings, somewhat like rosellas; also quiet, drawn-out 'breer, breer, breer', like Varied Triller. **Habitat:** understorey of mountain/lowland rainforests; thickly wooded gullies; waterside vegetation; mostly well below canopy. **Breeds:** Oct.–Feb. **Nest:** pretty cup of fine bark, plant-fibre, leaf-skeletons, green moss, spiders' web/cocoons; in fork of open shrub, low tree, hanging vine, 1–6 m high, often near water. **Eggs:** 2; oval; pink/creamy white, minutely freckled rich-pink, red–brown, dull purple, mostly on large end. **Range and Status:** coastal ne. and e. Aust. and coastal islands, from C. York (Q) s. to Watson R. on w. coast and to Port Stephens (NSW) on e. coast. Resident s. to Rockhampton; summer breeding migrant to se. Q–ne. NSW, from Sept.–Oct., to May. Common humid ne. Q; elsewhere uncommon in suitable habitat. Also s. PNG, Moluccas, Timor.

BLACK-FACED MONARCH

imm.

BLACK-WINGED MONARCH

imm.

SPECTACLED MONARCH

race *albiventris*

imm.

WHITE-EARED MONARCH *Monarcha leucotis* 13–14 cm

Very distinctive; has been likened to miniature Magpie Lark (see p. 462). *Note bold white marks above/below eyes, sides of head and wing; rump white, outer tail-feathers broadly tipped white;* throat white, more or less flecked black; underparts washed grey. **Female:** duller. **Immature:** black areas browner, white areas washed buff. Singles, isolated pairs: very active; snaps up insects as it flutters among leaves in outer canopy; active during heat of day; calls often. Raises crown feathers, cocks tail when agitated; shows white rump. **Similar species:** Pied, Frilled Monarchs. **Voice:** vivacious; calls freely, chatters incessantly near nest; common phrase is distinctive, clear, far-carrying 'beetaloo, beetaloo'. **Habitat:** rainforest margins/regrowth; dense scrubs on streams; paperbarks; mangroves, adjacent eucalypt forest. **Breeds:** Aug.–Jan. **Nest:** deep cup or goblet of moss, rootlets, spiders' web/cocoons; lined with palm-fibre; in upright fork of tree 10–20 m+ high. **Eggs:** 2; blunt oval; whitish, with small uneven red–brown/lavender spots, mostly large end. **Range and Status:** coastal e. Aust. and mountains of Gt Divide; forested coastal islands: from C. York (Q), s. to *c.* Iluka (ne. NSW); casual Crowdy Bay NP (n. of Harrington, NSW). Uncommon to rare in s.; more common coastally than on highlands. Probable autumn–winter migration from highlands to coastal lowlands.

FRILLED MONARCH *Arses telescophthalmus* 14–15 cm

Two small blue–black and white flycatchers *with erectile neck frills* inhabit ne. Q. This is the n. form; note range. Very like Pied Monarch, *but bare, flanged, bright blue eye-ring broader; underparts of both sexes wholly white; rear collar more extensive/conspicuous.* Tail wholly black. **Male:** black chin. **Female:** white lores. **Immature:** bill dull cream; eye-ring dark grey; white areas dingy. Habits like Pied; when singing, reported to make short whirring flights from twig to twig; chases in parties through rainforest, fluffing feathers, displaying. **Voice:** noisy; harsh scolding calls and trilled song. **Habitat:** rainforest, chiefly in middle spaces/lower canopy. **Breeding:** as for Pied Monarch. **Range and Status:** confined to n. C. York Pen. (Q): s. to McIwraith Ra. on e. coast and to Archer R. on w. coast. Fairly common. Sedentary. Also PNG, Aru Is.

PIED MONARCH *Arses kaupi* 15–16 cm

Immediately distinguished from Frilled Monarch by *broad black breastband.* Note *narrower pale blue eye-ring; chin/throat white; tail wholly black.* **Female:** duller; *white collar incomplete.* **Immature:** bill dull cream; white areas heavily flecked black; mantle grey–brown; throat greyish; breastband grey–brown. Pairs, parties: vivacious; *raises collar in slight frill;* creeps, hops up or down tree trunks somewhat like treecreeper, wings half-open; jerks tail downward; darts after flying insects, tail fanned. **Similar species:** Frilled Monarch. **Voice:** quaint soft 'quacking' notes. **Habitat:** rainforests, palm/vine-scrubs, especially near running water; adjacent eucalypt woodlands. **Breeds:** Oct.–Jan. **Nest:** miniature hanging basket, openly woven of fine twigs, tendrils, spiders' web; decorated externally with lichen; slung between hanging creepers or branches, 6–10 m high. **Eggs:** 2; nearly elliptical; glossy; pink–white, finely spotted/freckled red–brown, reddish chestnut, purple–grey, mostly at large end. **Range and Status:** coastal ne. Q, from Cooktown s. to *c.* Ingham, in rainforests up to 700 m. Fairly common. Sedentary.

WHITE-EARED MONARCH

imm.

FRILLED MONARCH

♂

♀

imm.

PIED MONARCH

♂

♀

imm.

BROAD-BILLED FLYCATCHER *Myiagra ruficollis* 14–16 cm

Male: *bill large/broad, outer edges distinctly bowed outwards, more so than Leaden Flycatcher; head large, somewhat angular; neck slender. Upperparts deep glossy blue–grey, somewhat darker than female Leaden; upperbreast uniform rich buff, deeper/brighter than female Leaden; underparts whitish.* **Female:** *less glossy above, paler below; lores and eye-ring whitish; underparts whitish, lightly washed buff.* **Immature:** like female; wing-feathers margined buffish. Singles, pairs: *larger* than small nw. race *concinna* of Leaden Flycatcher. Quiet; seeks insects in heads of mangroves, leafy trees; quivers tail less than Leaden/Satin Flycatchers. **Habitat:** mangroves, monsoon forest, paperbarks, riverside vegetation, coastal woodlands. **Voice:** clear, far-carrying calls; soft churring. **Breeds:** Oct.–Feb. **Nest:** shallow cup of bark-strips, plant-fibre, spiders' web; decorated with lichen; in dead or living mangrove 1–3 m above high-tide, or over stream. **Eggs:** 2–3; round–oval, glossy; whitish; spotted, blotched dark brown, grey in mid-zone; large end bald. **Range and Status:** coastal n. Aust. and islands: from Fitzroy R., Kimberley region (WA), to Cairns (Q); casual s. to Keppell Bay. Common. Also s. PNG and Timor.

LEADEN FLYCATCHER *Myiagra rubecula* 14–16 cm

Other names: Blue Flycatcher, Frogbird.

Male: *glossy blue–grey above and on upperbreast; lores/face/throat dark grey to blackish, contrasting with grey of upperparts; dark upperbreast cut off sharply by white underparts.* **Female:** *dull lead-grey above, throat pale orange–buff; paler on breast; underparts off-white.* **Immature:** like female, wing-feathers/tail edged buff, mottled across upperbreast. Singles, pairs: alert, active; sits watchfully upright; darts into foliage or air after insects; raises crown-feathers in slight peak when calling; *rapidly quivers tail up/down.* The small race *concinna* (nw. Aust.) has narrower bill. **Similar species:** Satin, Broad-billed Flycatchers. **Voice:** deep, slightly harsh, guttural 'zhirrp', singly or repeated; strident, far-carrying 'see-hear, see-hear'; 'see-kew, see-kew', or 'liprick, liprick'. Vivacious little song when breeding. **Habitat:** coastal woodlands/scrubs to drier, more open eucalypt forests/woodlands; paperbarks, riverside vegetation, mangroves. More likely than Satin to occur in sandy coastal scrubs; avoids dense forest gullies. **Breeds:** Sept.–Feb. **Nest:** neat cup of fine bark, spiders' web; decorated with lichen, bark; on slender dead branch under leafy branch, in woodland, river red gum forest, 5–25 m high. **Eggs:** 2–3; oval; blue–white, spotted in zone with brown, purple–brown, underlying violet; large end bald. **Range and Status:** n. and e. Aust. and coastal islands: from Fitzroy R., Kimberley (WA), to *c.* Ballarat (Vic.). Resident in n. Aust., summer breeding migrant to se. Aust. Sept.–April, wintering in ne. Q and PNG. Mostly coastal, but occurs well inland, especially on watercourses. In NT, ranges s. to Katherine; in Q, inland to Blackall–Mitchell; in NSW, to Moree–Hillston–Barham; in Vic., w. to c. Vic.; rare (breeding) visitor Tas.; casual Portland (Vic.), Mt Lofty Ras. (SA). Common n. and e. coasts; uncommon elsewhere. Also PNG.

SATIN FLYCATCHER *Myiagra cyanoleuca* 15–17 cm

Male: *uniform glossy blue–black, cut off sharply across breast by white underparts.* **Female:** *slightly glossy dusky blue–grey above, throat/upperbreast rich orange–buff; underparts white.* **Immature:** like female; buff edges to wing-feathers. Singles, pairs: active, showy, usually high in trees; darts from branch to branch, sallies after flying insects. Raises crown feathers in angled peak; *quivers tail rapidly, usually up/down, sometimes sideways.* **Similar species:** Willie Wagtail; Restless, Leaden, Broad-billed Flycatchers. **Voice:** more strident than Leaden; guttural 'zhurp!' or 'bzzurt', oft-repeated; strident, clear, carrying 'wu-*chee*-wu-*chee*-wu-*chee*' or 'chell*ee* chell*ee* chell*ee*'; clear, high-pitched 'weir-to-weir-to-weir', or liquid 'thurp, pew-it, pew-it'. **Habitat:** heavily vegetated gullies in forests, taller woodlands, usually above shrub-layer; during migration, coastal forests, woodlands, mangroves, trees in open country, gardens. **Breeds:** Oct.–Feb. **Nest:** neat cup of bark-strips, moss, spiders' web; on horizontal dead branch 5–25 m high, under live foliage. **Eggs:** 2–3; rounded; bluish/greenish white; spotted, blotched dark brown, purple–grey, with zone of dull purple–grey spots; large end bald. **Range and Status:** e. Aust. and islands: from C. York (Q) to Tas., far w. Vic.–far se. SA; casual s. SA, Kangaroo I.; s. WA. Breeds mostly se. Aust./Tas.; arrives Aug.–Oct., regularly returning to same locality; departs Feb.–April; winters in ne. Q, n. from *c.* Rockhampton (Blakers et al, 1984), and in PNG, via Torres Strait islands. Vagrant NZ. Uncommon.

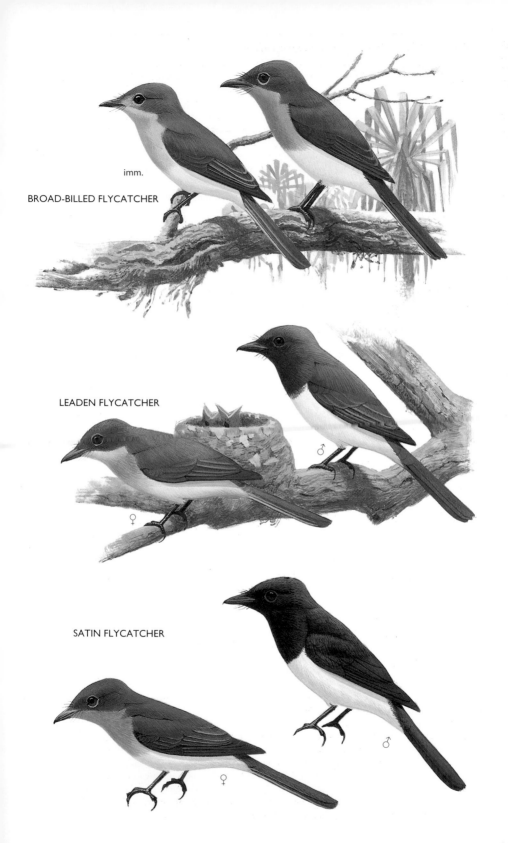

imm.

BROAD-BILLED FLYCATCHER

LEADEN FLYCATCHER

♂

♀

SATIN FLYCATCHER

♂

♀

445

SHINING FLYCATCHER *Myiagra alecto* 17–19 cm

Male: *entirely glossy jet-black.* **Female:** *crown/nape glossy black, rest of upperparts rich chestnut; underparts white.* **Immature:** like dull female. Singles, pairs, small autumn–winter flocks: vivacious, raises crown-feathers in low crest, flicks tail upward. Moves very fast, darts at prey on leaves or mud. Male shyer than female; quickly vanishes. **Voice:** amazing repertoire, from pretty whistlings to croakings: deep, froglike 'zhip, zhip, zhipipipip'; soft, rippling, Whimbrel-like trill and shrill, rising trill. **Habitat:** dense mangroves, pockets of rainforest, paperbarks, pandanus, adjacent eucalypt woodlands, usually near/over water. **Breeds:** Aug.–March. **Nest:** deep, closely woven cup of strips or rough pieces of bark, spiders' web; deep in fork, over water, sheltered by leaves; 1–6 m high. **Eggs:** 2–3; glossy, blue–white/green–white, with minute spots, blotched brown, underlying lilac–grey in zone around large end. **Range and Status:** coastal n. and ne. Aust. and islands: from Broome (WA) (with possibly gap on Gulf coast) to C. York Pen. (Q), s. to Fraser I.–Noosa R.; casual s. to Tweed R. and nearby tidal areas (NSW). Extends inland on watercourses, e.g. S. Alligator R. near El Sherana (NT). Common in n. Aust., scarce to rare s. of Herbert R. (Q). Also Bismarck Arch., PNG and islands, Aru Is., e. Indonesia.

RESTLESS FLYCATCHER *Myiagra inquieta* 16–21 cm

Other names: Dishlick, Dish Washer, Scissors Grinder.

Bill longish; upperparts glossy blue–black; entire underparts silky white, often washed yellow–buff across breast. **Immature:** dull grey–blackish above, wing-coverts edged buff–white. The n. race *nana* is smaller, blacker. Singles, pairs, trios: active, restless; raises crown-feathers in slight crest; *gracefully sweeps ample tail,* but lacks constant switching/sudden movements of Willie Wagtail. Flight swooping, graceful, with deep wingbeats. *Hovers over grasses, branches, foliage with bill open, pouring out stream of grinding, churring sounds which appear to disturb insects into movement.* Perches on stumps, takes spiders, insects, under house eaves, windows. **Similar species:** Satin Flycatcher, male. Willie Wagtail. **Voice:** apart from grinding sounds, a rasping 'zhap', singly or repeated, 'zhap-zhapzhapzhapzhap'; also clear whistle, 'chewee, chewee, chewee', each phrase rising at end; other distinctive calls. **Habitat:** open forests/woodlands; river red gums near water; inland/coastal scrubs; golfcourses, orchards, roadside timber, parks, gardens. **Breeds:** July–Jan. in s. Aust.; Aug.–March in n. **Nest:** large squat cup of bark-shreds, fine grass, spiders' web; beautifully crusted with lichens; on horizontal branch 1–20 m high. **Eggs:** 3; oval, off-white/glossy; with zone of dark brown, grey spots at larger end. **Range and Status:** n., e., se. and sw. Aust. and coastal islands: race *nana* from Broome (WA) through Kimberley and Top End (NT), s. to Morphett Ck–Alexandria; e. along Gulf to *c.* Edward R., w. C. York Pen. (Q). Nominate race: se. C. York Pen. and most Q, scarce in far w.; most NSW *except* far nw.; all Vic.; s. SA and s. WA n. to Gt Victoria Desert–Kalgoorlie–Moora. Fairly common. Sedentary to locally nomadic or part-migratory.

WILLIE WAGTAIL *Rhipidura leucophrys* 19–22 cm

Widespread, well-loved. Black, fan-tailed; *white underparts sharply cut off by black upperbreast. Erectile white eyebrow changes with bird's sex/status/emotional condition from near-invisible to flaring/conspicuous; also slim white whisker-mark.* **Immature:** duller; buffish eyebrow; margins to wing-feathers. Singles, pairs, family parties: bold, perky; watches from low branches, fence-posts, stumps, rocks, backs of farm-animals. Takes insects in twisting flight, in foliage, on ground or floating vegetation, seemingly disturbing them by jerky sweeps of tail, sudden wing-flaring. Large butterflies transferred to feet for carriage to 'de-winging' stations. Skirmishes with larger birds, especially other black-and-white species, e.g. Australian Magpie, Magpie-lark. **Similar species:** Satin, Restless Flycatchers. **Voice:** spirited, sweet: characterised as 'sweet-pretty-creature', but varies much; calls day/night in breeding season; rattling 'rikka-tikka-tikka-tik'. **Habitat:** *most habitats,* except dense forests. **Breeds:** Aug.–Jan. **Nest:** shallow grey cup of fine grass, bark-shreds, rootlets, felted with spiders' web; lined with hair, wool, feathers, plant-down; on horizontal branch, 1–15 m high, often over water, or near nest of Magpie-lark, White-winged Triller; also on fallen branches, orchard/garden trees, clothes hoists, rafters, street-lamps, buildings, boats. **Eggs:** 2–4; creamy buff/yellowish white; spotted, marked light red–brown, wood-brown, olive, grey, in zone. **Range and Status:** mainland Aust., n. Tas. and islands, including Kangaroo I. (SA); Flinders, King Is. Common; widespread. Sedentary; dispersive. Also Solomon Is., Bismarck Arch., PNG, e. Indonesia.

SHINING FLYCATCHER

imm.

♀

♂

race
nana

RESTLESS
FLYCATCHER

imm.

WILLIE WAGTAIL

imm.

447

RUFOUS FANTAIL *Rhipidura rufifrons* 15–16.5 cm

Looks like darting flame with its *fiery rufous rump/tail. Forehead/eyebrow orange–rufous; white breast crossed by band of blackish spots.* **Immature:** duller; wing-feathers edged rufous. Singles, pairs, migrant parties: less active than Grey Fantail, forages lower in undergrowth. Foraging flights quick, jerky; gleans from leaves, branches, ground, logs. **Voice:** squeak, accelerating into brisk, *descending* squeaky song, higher-pitched than Grey. **Habitat:** undergrowth of rainforests/wetter eucalypt forests/gullies; monsoon forests, paperbarks, sub-inland and coastal scrubs; mangroves, watercourses; parks, gardens. On migration, farms, streets, buildings. **Breeds:** Oct.–Feb. **Nest:** neat, fawn-coloured, tailed cup of bark-strips, moss, grass, spiders' web; in shaded fork, low to 5 m+. **Eggs:** 2–3; glossy; stone-coloured, speckled brown, lavender–grey. **Range and Status:** coastal n. and e. Aust., and islands. Breeding migrant (Oct–April) to se. Aust., mostly on and coastward of Gt Divide, w. to Grampians NP–sw. Vic.; casual w. to Mt Lofty Ras.; vagrant Tas. Extends well inland in river red gum forests of Murray Valley/Riverina–Hay–Dubbo (NSW); Darling Downs (Q). Altitudinal migrant in ne. NSW–e. Q, leaving mountain rainforests March–April, returning Sept.–Oct. Regular autumn–winter migrant to PNG across Torres Strait. Also resident Solomon Is., PNG, e. Indonesia, Guam.

GREY FANTAIL *Rhipidura fuliginosa* 14–17 cm

Grey with short white eyebrow; white mark behind eye; white tips to wing-coverts; white throat and whisker-mark; dark breast-band; underparts white, fawn or buffish. Outer feathers of dark grey fan-tail have white shafts and are edged/broadly tipped white, or wholly white, according to race (see plate). **Immature** (all races): browner; head-markings buffish; wing-coverts tipped buff. Singles, pairs, open companies: *switches spread tail; stunts, loops, dives after flying insects.* Forages in foliage to 30 m+; joins feeding-associations. **Similar species:** Mangrove Grey Fantail, Northern Fantail. **Voice:** sharp 'dek'; sweet, tinny, animated fiddle-like song, *ascending,* ending in drawn-out, rising, silvery notes. **Habitat:** coastal/inland scrubs, mangroves, rainforests, eucalypt forests/woodlands; watercourses, golfcourses, orchards, parks, gardens. **Breeds:** July–Dec. **Nest:** beautiful small grey cup, tailed like wineglass without a base, of fine grass, bark-strips, plant-fibre, spiders' web; in slender horizontal fork of shrub, tree, low to 12 m. **Eggs:** 2–3 (4); yellowish or fawn–white, spotted light brown, rufous, grey. **Range and Status:** Aust., Tas., coastal islands: widespread *except* driest deserts. Race *keasti:* highlands of ne. Q; *alisteri:* e. and se. Aust.; *albiscapa:* Tas./Bass Strait Is.; *albicauda:* w. inland Aust.; *preissi:* sw. WA (not illustrated). In se. Aust., Tas. and sw. WA, regular migrant, birds return Sept.–Oct. to breed, move n., inland and down from mountain forests in March–April. Also PNG, Solomon Is., New Heb., New Cal.

MANGROVE GREY FANTAIL *Rhipidura phasiana* 14.5–16 cm

Smaller than Grey Fantail, with longer bill, *large white eyebrow, paler grey upperparts; white spots on wing-coverts; tail shorter, rounder,* outer feathers with broad white edges/tips, white shafts. **Immature:** markings buff–brown. **Voice:** like Grey Fantail but less developed, more twittering; thin 'chip'; high-pitched tinkling song. **Breeds:** Oct.–Feb. **Nest:** smaller than Grey Fantail. **Eggs:** 2; fawn–white; finely freckled light brown, rufous in zone. **Range and Status:** resident in n. coastal mangroves from Shark Bay (WA) to Norman R., (Q). Sedentary; locally nomadic. Also s. PNG.

NORTHERN FANTAIL *Rhipidura rufiventris* 16–5–18.5 cm

Flycatcher-like: *head larger, bill longer, broader than Grey Fantail; tail shorter, less fanned, edged/tipped white; lacks white shafts. Broad grey breastband streaked paler.* **Immature:** browner, with buffish tips to feathers. Singles, pairs: actions subdued; watches from exposed branches, sallies after flying insects. **Voice:** short, metallic 'chip'; tinkling song. **Habitat:** margins of rainforest, vine scrub, monsoon forest; paperbarks, riverside vegetation, mangroves, open eucalypt forest/woodland. **Breeds:** Aug.–Dec. **Nest:** larger, untidier than Grey; on slender fork, 1–6 m, occasionally 20 m high. **Eggs:** 1–2; creamy-white; with zone of brown, underlying blue–grey spots. **Range and Status:** from *c.* Broome (WA) to *c.* Proserpine–Eungella NP (Q). Inland to *c.* Larrimah (NT), Riversleigh (Q). Sedentary; local nomad. Also Solomon Is., Bismarck Arch., PNG, e. Indonesia.

RUFOUS FANTAIL

imm.

race alisteri

race keasti

GREY FANTAIL

race albiscapa

race albicauda

MANGROVE GREY FANTAIL

NORTHERN FANTAIL

BLACK-FACED CUCKOO-SHRIKE *Coracina novaehollandiae* 30–36 cm

Other names: Blue or Grey Jay, Cherry Hawk, Shufflewing, Summerbird. Familiar; *blue–grey with jet black face/throat; underparts white, washed grey; tail broadly margined black, tipped white.* Race *subpallidus* (coastal c. WA): very pale grey, white below. **Immature:** smutty black mask from bill through eye to ear-coverts; crown/throat/breast finely barred greyish. Singles, pairs, parties; large migratory companies. Flight easy, undulating, with wing-closed 'shooting'; on alighting (and when courting), *repeatedly shuffles wings.* Forages in foliage; hovers over canopy, low over grass in breezes. **Similar species:** White-bellied Cuckoo-shrike, race *robusta*. **Voice:** musical, rolling, churring; also 'chereer, chereer', while shuffling wings; harsh 'skair' in aggression. **Habitat:** rainforests, forests, woodlands, scrublands; timber on watercourses; orchards, parks, gardens. **Breeds:** Aug.–Feb. **Nest:** shallow cup of fine twigs, spiders' web; on horizontal limb or fork 6–20 m high. **Eggs:** 2–3; blue–green/olive–green/olive–brown, blotched, spotted brown/red–brown/grey, below surface. **Range and Status:** widespread Aust. and Tas.: regular autumn–winter migration to inland/coastal n. Aust., where large winter companies occur; many cross to PNG/Indonesia. But some regularly overwinter in s. Also resident Indonesia, PNG and Solomon Is. Common. Migratory and sedentary.

WHITE-BELLIED CUCKOO-SHRIKE *Coracina papuensis* 26–28 cm

Other names: Little, Papuan or White-breasted Cuckoo-shrike. Noticeably smaller than Black-faced Cuckoo-shrike. Note *short black mask joining dark eye, margined by fine, white, rear eye-ring. Upperparts blue–grey with darker flight/tail-feathers; underparts white in n. Aust., greyer southward in e. Aust.* **Immature:** dark mask extends to ear-coverts; underparts lightly barred. Race *robusta* (s. Q–Vic.) greyer below; has *widespread dark morph with extensive black in plumage. Males have smutty black head/throat/breast; females retain grey crowns but have smutty side of head/nape, heavy black barring on breast/flanks.* Dark morph immatures mostly resemble females. Habits: like Black-faced Cuckoo-shrike, with less wing-shuffling. Singles, pairs; small autumn–winter companies in treetops, over grasslands. **Similar species:** Black-faced Cuckoo-shrike, imm.: larger; black mask extends further over ear-coverts; faint grey barring on breast; call differs. Adult Black-faced from dark morph *robusta* by size, grey crown and nape, purer, smaller area of black; call differs. **Voice:** *distinctive*, peevish 'kissik, kissik' or 'quiseek'. **Habitat:** forests/woodlands, river red gums; open grasslands; mangroves, plantations, gardens. **Breeds:** Aug.–March. **Nest and eggs:** like Black-faced, but smaller. **Range and Status:** tropical n. Aust., from Kimberley (WA) to C. York Pen. (Q); larger, greyer breasted, migratory race *robusta* widespread but patchy in e. Aust. from c. Cooktown (Q), s. to Vic., w. to Grampians NP/se. SA; w. in river red gum woodlands on Murray R. to c. Berri (SA). Sedentary; migratory; nomadic. Also e. Indonesia, PNG, Solomon Is.

GROUND CUCKOO-SHRIKE *Coracina maxima* 33–36 cm

Graceful, slender, long-legged: the only cuckoo-shrike adapted to foraging mostly on ground. *Head/upper body pale grey; black mask; pale yellow eye; wings and long, slightly forked tail black, contrasting with finely barred white lower back, rump and underparts.* **Immature:** dark eyeline; fine broken barrings on upperparts and throat; eye dark. Pairs, family parties: walks, runs with back-and-forward head-motion. Shy; flight strong, undulating, easy; fluttering wingbeats interspersed with glides on depressed wings, *white back/rump contrasting with black wings/tail.* Perches on stumps, fence posts, hawks flying insects. **Voice:** flight-call, distinctive far-carrying 'pee-ew', pee-ew'; also 'chill-chill . . . kee-lik, keelick'. **Habitat:** open grasslands with dead trees and belts of live trees; timber on watercourses; mallee–spinifex; mulga and other acacias; cypress pine scrubs; claypans, pastures, vineyards. **Breeds:** Aug.–Nov., or after rains. **Nest:** shallow cup of stems, bark, grass, spiders' web/egg-sacs, sometimes wool; on horizontal branch or fork 3–15 m high. Occasionally on old nest of Magpie-lark, White-winged Chough. **Eggs:** 2–3; glossy; olive with brown, red–brown markings toward larger end, irregular black spots. Small groups nest communally, two females sometimes lay eggs in one nest. **Range and Status:** widespread across mainland, mostly inland of Gt Divide, but to near e. coast in lower Hunter Valley (NSW) and from near Brisbane to near Townsville (Q); *sparse or absent* from C. York Pen. (Q) n. of Georgetown–Cunjuvoy; Top End (NT); n. Kimberley (WA); driest deserts and arid coastal areas; Nullarbor Plain and wetter forested areas in se. Aust. and sw. WA. Uncommon; nomadic in response to rainfall.

BLACK-FACED CUCKOO-SHRIKE

race
subpallidus

imm.

race
robusta

imm.

n. Aust
form

race
robusta
dark
morph

WHITE-BELLIED CUCKOO-SHRIKE

GROUND CUCKOO-SHRIKE   imm.

BARRED CUCKOO-SHRIKE *Coracina lineata* 24–26 cm

Other name: Yellow-eyed Cuckoo-shrike.

Small, neat, dark cuckoo-shrike with *black mask, pale yellow eye, finely black/white barred underparts*; bill/legs black. **Immature:** dark eye; scalloped on head/body; underparts whitish. Pairs, parties: makes short flights in canopy to seize fruit; actions quick, precise; flicks wings. Roosts communally. **Similar species:** Oriental Cuckoo. **Voice:** pleasant musical chatter, like toy mouth-organ. **Habitat:** rainforest; vine scrub and margins; eucalypt forests/woodlands; clearings in secondary growth; paperbarks; timber on watercourses; native figs, other trees with fruits; plantations, gardens. **Breeds:** Oct.–Jan. **Nest:** saucer of fine twigs, spider's web; on horizontal fork or branch, to 20 m. **Eggs:** 2; white, spotted brown, purplish grey. **Range and Status:** coastal e. Aust.: breeds s. to Nambucca Heads–Port Macquarie (NSW); casual Hunter Valley. Summer breeding migrant in se. Q–ne. NSW; nomadic in response to ripening of rainforest fruit. Uncommon Q; rare NSW. Also PNG, islands.

CICADABIRD *Coracina tenuirostris* 24–26 cm

Small dark cuckoo-shrike, heard more than seen. **Male:** *dark blue–grey; blackish from bill to cheeks; black wing-feathers edged grey in strong pattern; tail black, central feathers grey; bill/legs black.* **Female:** bill dark brown; *fawn eyebrow over dark eyeline; upperparts grey–brown; underparts cream–buff, with dark brown barrings; tail brown with buff edges/tips.* **Immature:** like scalloped female. Singles, pairs: wary; forages in canopy; movements quick; flight swiftly undulating. **Similar species:** female Trillers. **Voice:** male: harsh, descending, cicada-like buzz repeated 8–20+ times, slowing; soft, explosive 'twik!' or 'twok!'. Female: quick, rolling 'choik', or 'chuit', like young rosella. Breeding population in far ne. Q has different call: loud, ringing 'cree, cree'. **Habitat:** canopy of rainforests, eucalypt forests, woodlands; paperbarks, mangroves. **Breeds:** Oct.–Jan. in s., Jan.–March in n. Aust. **Nest:** shallow cup of twigs, spider's web, lichen; on horizontal branch, 10–25 m high. **Egg:** 1; pale blue–grey/green–grey, marked dull brown, grey–brown, lavender. **Range and Status:** coastal n. Aust.: from Kimberley (WA) to C. York (Q); e. Aust., s. to e. of Melbourne (Vic.); casual s. SA. Breeding migrant in se. Aust., (Oct.–March); winters in n. Aust., PNG. Uncommon. Also e. Indonesia, PNG, Solomon Is.

WHITE-WINGED TRILLER *Lalage sueurii* 16–18.5 cm

Male: glossy black to below eye; pure white below; *white shoulders, white edges to wing-coverts form netted pattern; lower back/rump grey; tail black with white corners.* Male eclipse (March–Aug.): like greyish female with *black wings/tail, grey rump.* **Female:** pale brown above, *dark line through eye, slight pale eyebrow;* buff edges to wing-feathers form *netted pattern;* underparts washed brown. **Immature:** buffer, with scaled pattern. Singles, pairs, small flocks: flight graceful, undulating. Courting males fly slowly over territory, singing, with spread wings/tails. Forages in foliage, ground; hovers; takes nectar. **Similar species:** Varied Triller, Rufous Songlark. **Voice:** clear, descending 'chiff-chiff-joey-joey-joey'; canary-like trill. **Habitat:** open forests/woodlands/scrublands; watercourses. **Breeds:** Aug.–March. **Nest:** shallow cup of grass, rootlets, bark, spider's web; on horizontal branch/fork, 1–20 m high; near nests of other black/white birds. **Eggs:** 2–3; green, streaked/blotched brown. **Range and Status:** nomadic resident in n. and inland Aust.; breeding migrant to s. Aust. (Aug.–March) wintering in inland, n. Aust., perhaps PNG. Casual n. Tas. Fairly common. Also e. Indonesia, PNG.

VARIED TRILLER *Lalage leucomela* 17.5 cm

Note white eyebrow, black eyeline, bold white wingbars, finely barred underparts, yellow–buff belly/under tail-coverts. **Female:** greyer; barred. **Immature:** streaked/scalloped. Singles, pairs, trios: forages quietly in foliage; noticed by call. **Voice:** rolling 'brreeer', 4–8+ times, swelling, falling away; taken up by others. **Habitat:** rainforests, monsoon/vine forests, eucalypt forests/woodlands, paperbarks, watercourses, lantana, gardens. **Breeds:** Aug.–April. **Nest:** shallow cup of twigs, rootlets, grass, spider's web; on horizontal branch/fork, 1–20 m. **Egg:** 1; large, pale greenish, freckled red–brown. **Range and Status:** from n. Kimberley (WA) to Top End (NT); C. York Pen. (Q) to ne. NSW, casual s. to Kuringai Chase NP; mostly below 850 m. Uncommon in s. Sedentary. Also PNG, Bismarck Arch.

BARRED CUCKOO-SHRIKE

imm.

imm.

CIGADABIRD

♀

♂

WHITE-WINGED TRILLER

♀

♂

eclipse

♂

VARIED TRILLER

imm.

♀

♂

453

OLIVE-BACKED ORIOLE *Oriolus sagittatus* 26–28 cm

Graceful thrush-like bird of treetops: *bill deep-pink, slightly arched; eye red; upperparts olive–green, finely streaked black; underparts creamy white with bold dark teardrop streaks; tail grey–green, tipped white.* **Male:** throat/breast washed olive–green. **Female:** bill dull pink. **Immature:** bill/eye blackish; upperparts greyish brown, feathers edged rufous; white below, boldly streaked black. Singles, pairs, small autumn/winter flocks. Often heard first: feeds in canopy; raids gardens, orchards; associates with figbirds. Flight undulating. **Similar species:** Yellow Oriole. Figbird, female. **Voice:** rolling, mellow, oft-repeated 'orry, orry-ole', or 'olly-ole'; harsh scolds; scratchy warbling song. Subsong includes mimicry. **Habitat:** rainforests, eucalypt forests/woodlands, paperbarks; timber on watercourses; taller inland scrubs, incl. mallee; orchards, golfcourses, parks, gardens. **Breeds:** Sept.–Jan. **Nest:** deep, untidy cup of bark-strips, leaves, grass, moss, spiders' web/egg-sacs; wool, string; lined with grass, hair; slung from horizontal fork in foliage 7–20 m high. **Eggs:** 2–4; pale cream; spotted, blotched brown, red–brown, grey. **Range and Status:** n., e. and se. Aust., from Kimberley (WA) to far sw. Vic, far se. SA. Race *affinus*: from Kimberley (WA) to Leichhardt–Norman Rs. (nw. Q). Race *magnirostris*: C. York region (Q). Part-migratory nominate race: remainder of e. Aust. (Blakers et al, 1984). Summer breeding migrant to se. Aust. (Sept.–April), casual w. to Morgan/Mt Lofty Ras.–Adelaide region (SA): winters in n. Aust., far inland in good seasons, mostly on river systems, to far sw. Q, Riverina–Murray Valley. Uncommon. Also PNG.

YELLOW ORIOLE *Oriolus flavocinctus* 26–30 cm

Bill longish, slightly arched, reddish pink; eye red; *plumage dense mustard yellow–green above/below; finely streaked black; flight-feathers/tail blackish, broadly tipped pale yellow.* **Immature:** bill browner; plumage more boldly streaked, with yellow feather-margins. Singles, pairs, small flocks: forages in foliage with figbirds and other fruit-eaters. **Similar species:** Olive-backed Oriole. **Voice:** loud, bubbling call of 3–4 notes: liquid 'yok-yok-yol', characteristic sound near water in coastal n. Aust.; also clear 'pee-kweek'; in aggression, harsh 'scarab!'; soft, warbling, sub-song. **Habitat:** rainforests; dense vegetation on watercourses; woodlands, paperbarks, mangroves, plantations, orchards, gardens. **Breeds:** Oct.–March. **Nest:** deep hammock of bark-strips, vine-tendrils; lined with rootlets; slung in leafy outer branches, 5–16 m high. **Eggs:** 2; cream; spotted, blotched brown, grey. **Range and Status:** from w. Kimberley (WA) to Top End (NT) and coastal islands; in Q, from Cape York Pen., s. on e. coast to *c.* Ingham. Common in suitable habitat. Sedentary. Also PNG.

FIGBIRD *Sphecotheres viridis* 27–30 cm

Other names: Green or Yellow Figbird, Banana-bird, Mulberry-bird.
Two Aust. races: males differ, females similar. Race *flaviventris* 'Yellow Figbird' (tropical n. Aust): male: bright yellow throat/breast; white underparts. Race *vieilloti* 'Green Figbird' (coastal e. Aust.); male: throat/upperbreast/collar mid-grey; flanks green; underparts white. Races interbreed freely in broad zone between *c.* Normanton/Proserpine (Q). *Note male's black head/cheeks, patch of bare red skin around eye, olive–green upperparts and black tail with prominent white edges/corners.* **Female:** *bill dark brown; upperparts dull brown with bare grey–brown skin around eye; underparts whitish, heavily streaked dark brown, so heavily on throat as to appear dark brown.* **Immature:** pale scallops on wing-feathers; young males show shadowy adult markings. Pairs, parties; flocks of 10-*c.*50+: forages in foliage, mostly on fruits, incl. introduced camphor laurel; acrobatic, flutters, hangs head down; often noticed by call. Associates with other fruit-eaters, e.g. orioles; raids garden fruit. Perches overhead wires; flocks trail over rainforest, cross cleared country to fruiting trees. Flight undulating; note prominent white corners to black tail. **Similar species:** Olive-backed Oriole, imm. Yellow Oriole. **Voice:** squeaky, emphatic 'chyer!' or 'jokyer!'; squeaky 'see-kew, see-kew'; other squeaky notes. Song: strong, mellow 'tu-tu heer, tu-heer', etc. **Habitat:** edges of rainforests, eucalypt forests/woodlands; paperbarks, watercourses, mangroves; leafy, fruiting trees in orchards; parks, streets, gardens. **Breeds:** Oct.–Feb. **Nest:** hammock of vines, stems, twigs, rootlets; slung in horizontal fork among foliage, 6–20 m high; several nearby. **Eggs:** 2–3; apple-green/olive–brown; spotted, blotched red–brown. **Range and Status:** race *flaviventris*: n. Kimberley (WA), Top End/Gulf coast (NT), C. York Pen. (Q). Race *vieilloti*: from *c.* Proserpine (Q) s. to *c.* Nowra on s. coast (NSW). Vagrant Vic. Common. Locally nomadic. Also Torres Strait, PNG, e. Indonesia.

OLIVE-BACKED ORIOLE

imm.

YELLOW ORIOLE

imm.

FIGBIRD

♂ race *vieilloti*

♂ race *flaviventris*

♀

WHITE-BREASTED WOODSWALLOW *Artamus leucorynchus* 16–18 cm

Upperparts/upperbreast brownish slate-grey; cut off sharply by pure white underparts; rump white; tail wholly dark grey — unique combination, prominent in flight. Pairs, small flocks, often over water. **Similar species:** Masked Woodswallow. **Voice:** brisk 'pert pert', somewhat like toy trumpet; pleasant song includes mimicry. **Habitat:** dead or live trees beside/over rivers, lakes, wetlands, coasts; islands; mangroves, paperbarks, river red gum forests; jetties, channel-piles. **Breeds:** Aug.–Jan., in loose colony. **Nest:** cup of twigs, grass; to 25 m in fork, branch, broken trunk/spar; protruding bark, mistletoe-clump, tree in water, street-tree, palm, mangrove, artificial structure. May use old nest of Magpie-lark, Welcome Swallow. **Eggs:** 3–4; pink–white to cream; freckled, spotted, red–brown, dark grey. **Range and Status:** from Shark Bay (WA), around coastal n. Aust. to Hunter Valley–Sydney (NSW) and widely through e. inland, s. to nw. SA and s. through L. Eyre Basin to Murray mallee (SA)–Murray Valley/n. Vic. Summer breeding migrant to se. Aust., (Aug.–April); winters inland and n. Aust. Casual s. and w. Vic., King I. Sedentary in coastal n.; migratory/nomadic elsewhere. Also Torres Strait, Fiji to PNG, Indonesia, Philippines.

WHITE-BROWED WOODSWALLOW *Artamus superciliosus* 18–21 cm

Other names: Blue Martin, Summerbird.

Male: *strong white eyebrow over small black mask; upperparts/upperbreast deep blue–grey, cut off sharply by chestnut to pale rufous underparts; rump/tail paler grey above, tail broadly tipped white.* **Female:** *paler, duller.* **Immature:** like female; streaked, scalloped paler. Pairs, parties, flocks of thousands: on warm days drifts high overhead, rich underparts contrast with whitish underwings. Noisy at water or in woodlands abundant with insects, e.g. grasshoppers, hatching termites; nectar. Forages with bee-eaters, trillers, honeyeaters. In e. Aust., flocks include small numbers of Masked Woodswallows; ratio reversed in WA. **Similar species:** Masked Woodswallow. **Voice:** musical 'chap chap' (or 'chyep'); sweet, miner-like notes; rattling scolds; quiet song includes mimicry. **Habitat:** margins of rainforests; woodlands, inland/coastal scrubs; vineyards, orchards, golf-courses, parks, suburban streets. **Breeds:** Aug.–Dec., or after rains. **Nest:** flimsy, of twigs, grass, rootlets; in fork, bark against tree-trunk, spout, stump, cavity in fence-post, 1–6 m high. **Eggs:** 2–3; buff–white/grey–green; spotted, blotched brown–grey. **Range and Status:** Aust., mostly w. of Gt Divide; *absent* n. C. York Pen. (Q); scarce Top End (NT). Mostly *absent* from WA, except for regular small numbers with flocks of Masked Woodswallows, ratio reversed in e. Aust. Loose colonies breed mostly from s. Q to c. Vic.–se. SA, arriving irregularly mid–late spring, departing Feb.–March, movement modified by temperature/rainfall. In drought, large flocks irrupt into coastal e. and se. Aust., including suburbs of Brisbane, Sydney, Melbourne; may breed where previously unrecorded. Vagrant Kangaroo I. (SA), Bass Strait islands, n. Tas. Common to uncommon. Highly nomadic.

MASKED WOODSWALLOW *Artamus personatus* 17.5–19 cm

Other names: Bluebird, Blue or Bush Martin, Skimmer.

Male: *silvery-grey above, white below; large, black mask over forehead/face/throat bordered by slim white crescent; outer tail-feathers broadly tipped white.* **Female:** duller; lightly washed brown; mask shadowy, *without white border.* **Immature:** like female; streaked, mottled paler. *Overhead, mask contrasts with whitish underparts/underwings, especially in males.* Pairs, parties, flocks of thousands. In e. Aust., small numbers accompany White-browed Woodswallows; occasionally interbreed. In WA, ratio is reversed: Masked often occurs alone. Also associates with Black-faced, Dusky Woodswallows. **Similar species:** White-browed, Black-faced Woodswallows, Black-faced Cuckoo-shrike. **Voice:** musical 'chap, chap'; sweet, miner-like notes. **Habitat:** open forests/woodlands; lightly timbered ranges; sparse inland scrubs; timber on inland watercourses; coastal heaths, pastoral country, farmlands, orchards, vineyards, golf-courses. **Breeds:** Aug.–Dec. **Nest:** scanty, of twigs, grass, rootlets; in fork, branch of living/dead shrub/tree, protruding bark, spout, stump, cavity in fence-post; 1–6 m high. **Eggs:** 2–3; variable, grey–white/green–grey/pale brown; speckled, blotched brown, grey. **Range and Status:** mainland Aust., mostly inland of Gt Divide, breeding in desert regions when conditions suitable; sparse Kimberley (WA), n. C. York Pen. (Q). Highly nomadic, influenced by temperature/rainfall; regular seasonal migration s. in spring, often to breed in inland se. and sw. Aust., where conditions suitable; frequently reaches s. coast in SA–WA; irregular to e. and se. coasts, mostly during drought. Has reached Kangaroo I. (SA), King I. (Bass Strait).

WHITE-BREASTED
WOODSWALLOW

WHITE-BROWED
WOODSWALLOW

MASKED
WOODSWALLOW

BLACK-FACED WOODSWALLOW *Artamus cinereus* 17.5–20 cm

Bill bluish with black tip; *plumage ashy grey–brown with black 'face' around base of bill/eye; black tail broadly tipped white.* Widespread nominate race has black under tail-coverts, often tipped white; in race *albiventris* of ne. Q, *under tail-coverts are wholly white.* **Immature:** paler; streaked pale brown. Singles, pairs, open companies: a bird of open country, perches shrubs, fence-posts, telephone wires; works into wind, darts down after insects; *often hovers, showing silvery white underwing;* takes nectar. Associates with other woodswallows; White-winged Triller. **Similar species:** Dusky, Masked Woodswallows. **Voice:** soft, sweet notes: scratchy 'chiff, chiff' or 'chap, chap'; animated song includes mimicry. **Habitat:** open country — gibber, spinifex; sandhills; saltbush, grasslands: nearly treeless plains often far from water; open woodlands/scrublands; lake-margins, wetlands, irrigation areas. **Breeds:** communally, Aug.–Jan., or after rain in arid regions. **Nest:** sparse cup of grass, twigs, rootlets; lined with grass, horsehair; low in small tree, stump, grasstree, artificial structure. **Eggs:** 3–4; glossy white/blue–grey; spotted, blotched red–brown; purplish grey spots/dashes. **Range and Status:** Aust.; mostly inland of Gt Divide in Q–NSW–Vic., coastal islands. Absent from forested sw. corner WA; sparse n. C. York Pen. (Q). During drought may reach coastal districts where previously little known, e.g. Kangaroo I. (SA); Illawarra (NSW). Race *albiventris* occurs in ne. Q, s. to *c.* Rockhampton. Common. Sedentary and nomadic.

DUSKY WOODSWALLOW *Artamus cyanopterus* 17–18 cm

Other names: Skimmer, Summer-bird, Woodmartin.
Bluish bill tipped black; plumage smoky brown; *wings gunmetal-grey, with white streak on leading edge. the only woodswallow with this marking.* Tail black, tipped white. **Immature:** mouse-brown; streaked paler. Pairs, colonies, travelling flocks. Sits watchfully on exposed branches, wags tail; makes soaring flights after flying termites, etc.; *dark body contrasts with white underwings; note white streak on leading edge.* Birds often huddle closely along branches; may form dense roosting clusters of dozens/hundreds, like bees, in cavity on trunk. **Similar species:** Little, Black-faced Woodswallows. **Voice:** brassy chirps, chirrups; soft, low 'vut, vut'; brisk 'peet peet'; quiet, animated sub-song includes mimicry. **Habitat:** open forests/woodlands; timbered paddocks; coastal/sub-inland scrubs; golfcourses, orchards, roadside timber, street trees. **Breeds:** Aug.–Jan. **Nest:** scanty, of twigs, rootlets; lined with finer rootlets; 1–20 m high on horizontal branch, against trunk on lifting bark, stump, end of broken branch, fallen limb, cavity in fence-post. **Eggs:** 3–4; oval, glossy; white/buff–white; spotted, blotched purplish brown, grey; in zone. **Range and Status:** e. Aust. and Tas.: from Atherton Tableland (ne. Q) to Kangaroo I. and Bight coast (SA); in WA, from Bight coast inland to *c.* Menzies–Paynes Find, w. to Moora. Summer breeding migrant (Oct.–March) in se. Aust./Tas. Some overwinter, but most appear to winter in inland NSW–Q w. to upper Flinders R.–Windorah (Q); Paroo R.–Broken Hill (NSW); Flinders Ras.– Kingoonya–Cook (SA). Movements in s. WA less extensive. Common. Sedentary; in parts, migratory.

LITTLE WOODSWALLOW *Artamus minor* 12–14 cm

Bill bluish with black tip; *plumage smoky chocolate-brown; wings/rump/tail deep gunmetal-grey;* tail tipped white. **Immature:** paler, streaked, scalloped. Small flocks, colonies. Often in rocky gorges, tiny against grandeur as it sails along rockfaces. In woodlands, groups huddle closely along dead limbs. Clusters in roosts of hundreds at night. Flight floating, graceful with curves, dips: looks almost black; *brown-washed underwing contrasts less with dark body than in Dusky Woodswallow; no white wingstreak.* Companies hawking insects over wetlands can be confused with martins; also takes nectar. **Voice:** brisk 'peet, peet', somewhat like Azure Kingfisher in 3–4 evenly spaced notes, or single note followed by two quick notes; pleasing song. **Habitat:** rocky gorges with permanent water; open scrubs; grassy woodlands with living/dead tall timber; belar; acacia scrubs with spinifex. **Breeds:** Aug.–Jan., or after rain. **Nest:** flimsy, of twigs, rootlets; in rock cavity, hole in tree. **Eggs:** 3; white buff–white, spotted, blotched brown, dark grey, in zone. **Range and Status:** widespread, patchy in n. and w. inland Aust. and islands off w. and n. coasts: most NT/Q, *except* Simpson Desert. In NSW, e. to *c.* Grafton, s. to Warrumbungle NP–Lachlan R.; casual sw. to Wentworth (NSW), w. Vic. In SA, mostly in inland rocky ranges (Everard, Flinders Ras.); occasional s. to Murray R.–Gawler Ras.–Eyre Pen. In WA, Kimberley–Pilbara s. to Lower Greenough R.–*c.* Southern Cross. Sedentary; part-nomadic.

BLACK-FACED WOODSWALLOW

race
albiventris

race
albiventris

DUSKY WOODSWALLOW

LITTLE WOODSWALLOW

459

BLACK BUTCHERBIRD *Cracticus quoyi* 40–44 cm

Powerful black butcherbird with massive, finely hooked silver–blue bill, tipped black; tail large. Rufous morph of race *rufescens*: deep rufous with paler rufous streaks and fine black bars below (both plumages may occur in same brood). Singles, pairs, family parties: hunts on edges of rainforest, mangroves. **Voice:** rich, deep, organ-like: 'choi', chopped short; rollicking, deep, butcherbird yodel. **Habitat:** rainforests, monsoon forests, coastal scrubs, paperbarks, mangroves; well-treed parks, gardens. **Breeds:** Oct.–Jan. **Nest:** untidy, of sticks, twigs; in upright fork to *c.* 6 m high. **Eggs:** 3–4 (5); cream–brown/grey–green, spotted brown, dark grey. **Range and Status:** coastal n. and ne. Aust. and islands: from Port Keats (NT)–Top End–Arnhem Land, inland *c.* 50 km on rivers. C. York Pen. (Q) s. to Archer R. in w., coastally s. to *c.* Rockhampton in e. Race *rufescens* from *c.* Cooktown s. to *c.* Ingham–Hinchinbrook I., inland to Atherton Tableland. Fairly common in dense, coastal habitats. Sedentary. Also PNG.

GREY BUTCHERBIRD *Cracticus torquatus* 24–30 cm

Other names: Silver-backed Butcherbird, Derwent or Tasmanian Jackass.
Finely hooked blue–grey bill, tipped black; crown/cheeks black; partial white collar. **Female:** crown/upperparts browner. **Immature:** dark brown, white areas dirty fawn — resembles a 'little kookaburra'; bill dark grey. Birds in c. and nw. Aust. silver–grey above; underparts/collar pure white. Race *latens* (Kimberley (WA)): black 'necklace' forms partial breastband; birds in s. WA also have partial black 'necklace'. Singles, pairs, family parties: sits watchfully, darts to ground or through trees. Flight direct, with rapid shallow wingbeats; note whitish rump. Calls loudly in flight; wings quivering. Aggressive near nest. **Similar species:** Pied Butcherbird, imm.: shadowy buff–grey head/throat. **Voice:** territorial song — loud, mellow piping, phrasing varies. In aggression, staccato, rollicking shriek; 'karr karr'. **Habitat:** margins of rainforests, monsoon forest; vine-scrub, paperbarks, eucalypt forests, woodlands, coastal/inland scrubs; timber on roadsides and watercourses; shelterbelts, golf-courses, parks, gardens. **Breeds:** July–Jan. **Nest:** untidy, of twigs; lined with grass, rootlets; 2–10 m in sapling, scrubby tree. **Eggs:** 3–5; dull green/light brown; speckled, blotched dull red, chestnut–brown. **Range and Status:** widespread but patchy s. of Tropic, n. to s. C. York Pen.(Q); race *argentius* Top End (NT); race *latens* n. Kimberley (WA). Mostly uncommon except Tas., where common in lowlands (Green, 1993). Sedentary; locally nomadic.

BLACK-BACKED BUTCHERBIRD *Cracticus mentalis* 26–28 cm

Like Grey Butcherbird but boldly black and white; broader white partial collar joins white throat and underparts. **Immature:** black areas brownish, white areas washed buff–grey. Habits like Grey; tame around camps, habitation. **Similar species:** Pied Butcherbird: black hood/upperbreast. **Voice:** like Grey Butcherbird, not Pied; soft mellow carolling; mimics. **Habitat:** open forests/woodlands; watercourses, agricultural areas, settlements. **Breeds:** June–Nov. **Nest:** like Grey; in tree-fork, to 25 m. **Eggs:** 2–3; green–grey/pale grey–brown; spotted, blotched dark brown. **Range and Status:** n. C. York Pen. (Q), s. to Mitchell R. on w. coast and to near Cooktown in e. Common. Sedentary. Also PNG.

PIED BUTCHERBIRD *Cracticus nigrogularis* 32–36 cm

Bill blue–grey, finely hooked, tipped black; white body with black hood extending well down upperbreast, broad white rear collar; rump white; tail black with white corners. **Immature:** hood brownish grey; white areas greyish cream. Singles, pairs, family parties, loose companies. Perches, sings from overhead wires, dead trees; flies to ground to seize food. Hunts in pairs; co-operates with Australian Hobby pursuing small birds. Flight strongly undulating. **Similar species:** Black-backed Butcherbird. **Voice:** superb slow, flute-like, mellow notes, by two/three birds alternately; day or night. Quieter sub-song; mimics. **Habitat:** drier woodlands, sub-inland/drier coastal scrubs; watercourses, pastoral lands, treed plains, farmlands, croplands, roadsides, picnic areas, gardens. **Breeds:** Aug.–Nov. in s. Aust.; May–June in tropics. **Nest:** untidy, of twigs, sticks; lined with rootlets, dry grass; in fork to 15 m. **Eggs:** 3–4 (2); olive–green to brownish; spotted darker brown, red–brown. **Range and Status:** mainland Aust., coastal islands. *Mostly absent from:* driest deserts, Nullarbor region; Sydney and s. coast NSW; e. and s. Vic.; much of s. SA; forested sw. WA. Common. Sedentary.

BLACK BUTCHERBIRD

race *rufescens*
rufous morph
imm.

GREY BUTCHERBIRD

imm.

BLACK-BACKED BUTCHERBIRD

imm.

PIED BUTCHERBIRD

imm.

461

MAGPIE-LARK *Grallina cyanoleuca* 26–30 cm

Other names: Little or Murray Magpie, Mudlark, Peewee, Peewit.

Now regarded as a giant monarch flycatcher (pp. 440/541), but because often seen skirmishing with Australian Magpie, and linked by association of names, they are grouped together here. **Male:** bill white; eye yellowish white; legs black; head/breastpatch black; *prominent white eyebrow and broad white panel down side of neck below eye.* **Female:** *forehead/throat white; broad black band from crown down through eye to black breastband.* **Immature:** bill and eye dark; pattern differs — brownish black of forehead/crown/nape extends in band down through eye to black breastband, leaving white throat. Pairs, family parties, loose autumn–winter flocks. Noisy, demonstrative, particularly before roosting. Males may hold territories throughout year, frequently skirmishing with neighbouring pairs, magpies, raptors. Forages on ground, walks with back-and-forward head-movement; wades. In flight, *rounded wings make lapping strokes;* flutters, lifts, dodges lightly. Calls on wing while flying with exaggerated, catchy wingbeats. Note *white tail with broad subterminal black band pointing up centre.* Birds in n. Aust. smaller. **Similar species:** White-winged Triller: smaller; bill/head black; underparts white. Pied Butcherbird: robust, hooked bill; hood black; longish tail black with large white corners. **Voice:** mated pairs duet; one bird utters loud, metallic 'knee-deep', immediately answered antiphonally by the other, 'tee-o-wee', 'pee-o-wit'; with rhythmically opening wings, spread tails. Liquid, mellow 'cloop, cloop, cloop' or 'clue-weet, clue-weet'. Alarm-call: brassy, strident, emphatic 'tee! tee! tee!'. **Habitat:** virtually anywhere there are trees and mud for nest-building; trees by rivers/wetlands; widespread in urban areas; *absent* from dense forests, waterless deserts. **Breeds:** Aug.–Nov.; almost any month after rain in arid and n. Aust. **Nest:** frequently near that of Willie Wagtail and/or White-winged Triller; bowl-shaped, of mud, bound with grass; lined with hair, grass, feathers; on horizontal branch 6–15 m high, often over water or on artificial structure. **Eggs:** 3–5; white/pale pink; spotted, blotched reddish, purplish brown, violet. **Range and Status:** Aust. and coastal islands, e.g. Kangaroo I. (SA), Lord Howe I.; casual Bass Strait islands; vagrant n. and e. Tas. Common, often abundant. Sedentary, nomadic; winter migration to Top End (NT), C. York Pen. (Q). Also s. PNG; Timor.

AUSTRALIAN MAGPIE *Gymnorhina tibicen* 38–44 cm

Other names: Black-backed, Western or White-backed Magpie.

Conspicuous large black-and-white bird with pointed whitish, black-tipped bill. **Nominate race *tibicen*, 'Black-backed Magpie':** male: mostly glossy black with prominent white nape, white shoulder and wingband, white rump, under tail-coverts and tail, latter broadly tipped black; eye red–brown. Female: nape greyer; duller black. Immature: duller, mottled; bill shorter, grey, eye black. **Race *hypoleuca*, 'White-backed Magpie':** male: *back pure white from nape to tail.* Female: *white upperparts mottled grey.* Immature: like dull, mottled female; bill shorter, grey; eye black. **Race *dorsalis*, 'Western Magpie':** male: like White-backed. Female: *back black, feathers edged white, in contrasting scalloped pattern.* Immature: like White-backed. Familiar: feeds mostly on ground; resident territorial groups and other aggregations noisily play and skirmish; flight swift, direct, with characteristic noisy lashing of wings, showing angled white bar on black underwing. Aggressive to humans near nest; kills smaller birds, house mice. Tame in parks, gardens. **Voice:** rich, mellow, organ-like carolling, often by several, at night. Quiet sub-song includes mimicry. In aggression, brisk high-pitched yodel. Alarm-call: short harsh shout, repeated; also drawn-out, descending 'pew, pew'. **Habitat:** almost wherever there are trees and open areas of bare soft ground or grass; orchards, golf-courses, playing fields, suburban areas, gardens, crops. **Breeds:** June–Dec. **Nest:** compact shallow bowl of sticks, twigs; lined with grass, rootlets, wool, hair; occasionally of wire; in fork or branch in outer part of tree 5–16 m high; sometimes in shrub near ground; rarely on ground. **Eggs:** 2–3 (5); variable — grey, brown, pale blue; typically blue–green spotted brown. **Range and Status:** entire continent except driest deserts, far Top End (NT) and far n. C. York Pen.(Q), but white-backed race *eylandtensis* occupies e. coastal Top End–Groote Eylandt (NT). Race *hypoleuca* extends throughout Vic. and s. SA, nw. to central ranges, s. NT, being nearly surrounded by nominate race *tibicen*. Race *dorsalis* occupies coastal sw. WA from head of the Bight to *c.* Shark Bay, with a wide zone of contact with *tibicen*. White-backed race *leuconota* inhabits Tas. and islands of Bass Strait. The principal mainland races, particularly *tibicen* and *hypoleuca*, readily hybridise, producing intermediates with varying amounts of black and/or white on their backs (observable along the Melbourne–Sydney highway). Has benefited greatly from land-clearing and establishing of crops, pastures, waterholes. Common and now very abundant in developed farming/cropping country of e. Aust.; rare, sparse (and more shy) in inland and n. Aust. Sedentary; locally nomadic. Also PNG; introduced NZ.

MAGPIE-LARK

imm.

♀

♂

nominate race

imm.
nominate
race

♀

♂

imm.
race
hypoleuca

♂

♀

race
hypoleuca

AUSTRALIAN MAGPIE

♀ race
dorsalis

BLACK CURRAWONG *Strepera fuliginosa* 47–49 cm. Male larger.

Bill black, massive; eye bright yellow; plumage black with small white tips to flight-feathers/tail. **Immature:** duller; gape yellow, eye dark. Pairs, family parties; winter flocks to 100+. Noisy; forages on ground in paddocks, swampy areas; in branches, bark, foliage. Flight loose, easy. **Similar species:** Grey Currawong, race *arguta*. Forest Raven. **Voice:** noisy; musical 'kar-week, week-kar'. **Habitat:** mountain/lowland forests/woodlands; high moors, coastal heaths, grazing country, orchards, suburban areas. On Bass Strait islands, more open habitats; forages on beaches. **Breeds:** Aug.–Dec. **Nest:** large, deep, of sticks, twigs; lined with roots, grass; in fork 3–20 m high. **Eggs:** 2–4; pale grey–brown, purplish buff; spotted, blotched red–brown, purplish brown. **Range and Status:** throughout Tas; sole currawong on King, Flinders, other islands. Common. Sedentary, altitudinal migrant.

PIED CURRAWONG *Strepera graculina* 42–50 cm. Male larger.

Black bird with robust black bill, yellow eyes, *white window in the wing, white base to tail-feathers, white under tail-coverts/tail-tips.* Note that in sw. Vic., white markings in wings and at base of tail are smaller than on e. coast. **Female:** greyer. **Immature:** grey–brown; breast mottled; feathers have paler edges; has less white; eye dark. Singles, pairs, autumn/winter flocks. Noisy, especially in rough weather; forages on ground, trunks, limbs, in foliage. Flies with deep, lapping wingbeats/swoops; silhouette flat, showing small-to-large white *base* to tail-feathers — *the only currawong so marked.* Tame around settlement, picnic areas, ski villages. In winter, noisy communal roosts. **Similar species:** White-winged Chough. Grey Currawong: no white *base to tail-feathers,* but see race *melanoptera* ('Black-winged Currawong'), below. **Voice:** loud, falsetto, wailed, descending; 'crik, crik, bewaiir'; 'currar-awok-awok-currar', or 'jabawok! jabawok!'; in e. Aust., long wolf-whistle 'weeeooo'. **Habitat:** alpine forests/woodlands to *c.* 1500 m; rainforests, forests, woodlands, inland/coastal scrubs; farmlands, garbage tips, picnic grounds, parks, gardens. **Breeds:** Aug.–Dec. **Nest:** flattish, of sticks; lined with roots, grass, bark; in leafy fork, 5–25 m high. **Eggs:** 3; light-brown, freckled, blotched darker. **Range and Status:** e. Aust. and islands from C. York (Q) to sw. Vic.–far se. SA. Inland in Q to *c.* upper Mitchell R.–Longreach–Idalia NP–Morven; in NSW to Collarenebri–Hillston–Barham. In Vic., inland on Murray R. to *c.* Kerang, sw. to Grampians NP. Breeds in forested ranges, coasts, foothills; flocks disperse to coastal lowlands, inland plains, April–Sept. Year-round resident in highlands of ne. Q. Common. Sedentary; dispersive.

GREY CURRAWONG *Strepera versicolor* 45–50 cm. Male larger.

Other names: Black-winged, Brown or Clinking Currawong, Squeaker.
Furtive large grey bird with robust bill, shaded black around the bright yellow eye; white patch at base of primaries, visible in flight; white tips to primaries; prominent white under tail-coverts and white tips to tail, but no white at base of tail. Flies with flat silhouette, pulsing wingbeats. **Immature:** duller, browner; gape yellow; eye dark. Mostly, the white markings remain constant, but in w. Vic.–se. SA–sw. NSW, race *melanoptera* ('Black-winged Currawong') can be black, with white in wings reduced or *absent.* Birds on Yorke Pen.–Eyre Pen.–nw. SA–sw. NT–s. WA browner. Largest, darkest race is *arguta* ('Clinking Currawong') of Tas. Singles, pairs, family parties: loose autumn/winter flocks in parts. Forages noisily in loose bark; raids nests/eggs; steals food; small birds; eats phasmids, etc., in foliage. **Similar Species:** Pied Currawong: in e. Aust., has conspicuous white base to tail-feathers, visible in flight. In w. Vic., this marking, *and white in wings,* is often much-reduced, causing confusion with dark race *melanoptera* of Grey Currawong, especially those with short, new, white tipped feathers in tail. Take care, listen to *calls.* **Voice:** ringing 'chling chling' or 'chding, chding'; ringing 'cree'. Conversational notes like mewing cats, toy trumpets. In Tas., race *arguta* calls 'keer-keer-kink', or 'klink, klank', like striking anvil. **Habitat:** forests/woodlands; mallee, coastal scrubs, heaths, roadside timber; orchards, suburban areas. **Breeds:** Aug.–Dec. **Nest:** large, shallow, of sticks; lined with rootlets, grass; 3–20 m on horizontal fork. **Eggs:** 2–3 (4); light-brown to reddish buff; spotted, blotched red–brown, lilac–grey. **Range and Status:** s. Aust., n. and e. Tas.: all Vic; in NSW, ranges n. to Blue Mts, exceptionally to Hunter Valley, inland to *c.* Willandra NP; in SA, widespread n. to s. Flinders Ras.–Gawler Ras.–Nullarbor Plain, w. to s. WA, n. to Laverton–Wiluna–Shark Bay. Common to uncommon. Sedentary, seasonally nomadic. (Little-known, far-inland population from Everard–Musgrave Ras. (nw. SA), n. to Victory Downs–Mt Olga–Petermann Ras. (NT), w. to Warburton Ras. (WA).)

BLACK CURRAWONG

imm.

e. form

PIED CURRAWONG

w. form

imm.

'Black-winged
Currawong'.
race
melanoptera

browner
SA, NT, WA
form

race
melanoptera

imm.

GREY CURRAWONG

MAGNIFICENT RIFLEBIRD *Ptiloris magnificus* 28–33 cm. Male larger.

Note range. **Male:** splendid; bill longish, curved; tail short; plumage black with iridescent blue–green crown, nape, central tail-feathers; throat/upperbreast have scale-like iridescent blue–green feathers, forming broad, erectile shield in display; *narrow band of bronze–green/deep-red separates this from blackish underparts. Long, black hairlike tufts on flanks.* **Female:** bill long, curved: long whitish eyebrow; dark eyemark; *off-white whisker-mark with dark line below.* Crown/mantle grey–brown; wings/rump/ tail rufous brown. *Entire underparts off-white, with very fine dark brown, wavy bars.* Forages on trunks, branches, hammering into decayed wood for large beetles, etc.; hangs upside down, works through sprays of foliage, vines; feeds on fruits, holding them under foot. Male makes heavy rustling sound in flight. Males display spectacularly on high branches, shaking plumage like heavy silk, suddenly spreading, flicking wings; crouching, posturing; head thrown back, bill open, tail cocked, head swinging side to side. 'Brown birds' also display. **Similar species:** Victoria's, Paradise Riflebirds: note range. **Voice:** very loud, mellow whistle with dip in the middle, rising to a high 'whiip', as though whistling to attract attention. During breeding season, 3 loud, clear whistles and a long-drawn diminishing note; each of the first 3 notes sounding like 'wheeoo', ending abruptly in a note like 'who-o-o'. **Habitat:** rainforest, monsoon forest, scrubs. **Breeds:** Sept.–Feb. **Nest:** deep, loose cup of plant-stems, large dry leaves, twigs, vines; lined with ribs of leaves, plant-fibre; in fork of tree, butt of leaves of pandanus, or on tall stump among secondary growth, 1–10 m high. **Eggs:** 2; cream, streaked brown/greyish. **Range and Status:** coastal n. C. York Pen. (Q) s. to Weipa on w. coast and to McIlwraith Ra., n. of Coen, on e. coast. Fairly common. Sedentary. Also PNG.

PARADISE RIFLEBIRD *Ptiloris paradiseus* 28–30 cm

Note range. **Male:** spectacular; longish curved black bill and velvet-black plumage, offset by iridescent green crown/throat/upperbreast and middle tail-feathers; shafts of primary feathers glossy; *black feathers of underparts broadly margined glossy olive–green.* **Female:** bill dark horn, long, curved; crown/cheeks grey–brown, lightly streaked paler, separated by pale cream rear eyebrow. Mantle grey–brown; wings/tail bright rufous-brown; underparts off-white; *flanks/belly/under tail-coverts broadly scalloped dark brown.* **Immature:** like female. Singles, pairs: often discovered by call or sound like rustling silk as male flies. Forages vigorously; climbs trunks, branches, flicks tail; hammers bill into cavities, rotting logs, stumps, to remove large beetles, etc.; feeds on fruits; hangs acrobatically. Courting males fly between treetops, calling. Displays spectacularly on horizontal limbs in canopy, tops of large stumps; fanning, opening, shutting, flicking wings, cocking tail, turning side to side, opening lime-green mouth. **Similar species:** Victoria's Riflebird: note range. **Voice:** distinctive rasping 'y-a-a-a-ss' or 'yaass yaass', about once every four minutes; also deep, mellow whistle. **Habitat:** rainforests, mostly in mountains/foothills; nearby wetter eucalypt forests; paperbark woodlands; occasionally open woodlands. **Breeds:** Sept.–Jan. **Nest:** shallow cup of green stems, vine-tendrils, dead leaves; lined with fine stems, twigs; usually in vines or canopy, top of treefern, 5–30 m high; rim may be decorated with snakeskin. **Eggs:** 2; pink–buff, spotted/slashed/streaked chestnut, purplish red, grey. **Range and Status:** mostly in highland rainforests of Gt Divide to *c.* 1200 m: Calliope Ra. s. of Gladstone (Q) (isolated population); and from Cooroy–Nanango–Bunya Mts NP (Q), s. to upper Williams R.–Barrington Tops NP–Gloucester Tops (NSW); casual s. to Dungog–Mt Royal near Singleton (NSW); inland on Dividing Ra. exceptionally to Gibraltar Ra. NP–Murrurundi. Fairly common; uncommon in s. of range. Sedentary.

VICTORIA'S RIFLEBIRD *Ptilotis victoriae* 23–25 cm

Note range. **Male:** like small male Paradise Riflebird, *with broader black breastband between blue–green throat-shield and olive–green glossed underparts.* **Female:** like small female Paradise Riflebird but underparts deeper, buffer; irregular lines of sparse, dark, V-shaped spots to slight barrings on flanks; shows rufous patch in wing-feathers in flight. Habits and display generally like Paradise Riflebird. **Voice, Habitat and Breeding:** like Paradise Riflebird. **Range and Status:** mostly mountain rainforests of ne. Q from near Cooktown s. to Mt Spec NP, near Townsville; also lowland rainforests, some coastal islands. Fairly common. Sedentary.

MAGNIFICENT RIFLEBIRD

♀

♂

PARADISE RIFLEBIRD

♀

♂

VICTORIA'S RIFLEBIRD

♀

♂

467

TRUMPET MANUCODE *Manucodia keraudrenii* 28–32 cm

Other name: Trumpetbird.

Male: glossy, red-eyed, black bird, somewhat larger than Metallic Starling; bill/legs blackish. *Strong violet–blue tone to feathers of head/mantle/foreneck; incl. cluster of long, slender plumes that fall from sides of head down nape. Tail longish, blunt, rounded and 'gabled'; often flicked.* **Female:** duller; eye orange. **Immature:** eye brown. Singles, pairs, loose feeding companies: forages in foliage high and low, mostly on berries, fruits; often hard to locate. Flight described as rather loose, disorganised. Call of male distinctive, uttered from high branch. Display spectacular: facing female, male raises and spreads wings, erects body-feathers, calls loudly. **Similar species:** Koel, male: bill horn-coloured, no crest; calls, habits differ. Spangled Drongo: in display, raises feathers at side of crown; this coupled with reduced 'fish-tail' during moult could cause confusion with Manucode (Frith, 1994). Metallic Starling: smaller; tail pointed. **Voice:** single, level, slightly elongated 'yaaah'; or 'skowlp' (Frith, 1994): resonant quality imparted by lengthened windpipe under skin of breast. **Habitat:** rainforest, vine-scrubs, eucalypt forest/woodland. **Breeds:** mostly Oct.–Jan. **Nest:** shallow basket of vine-tendrils, open in construction; usually slung in foliage in top of tree in tropical scrub or eucalypt forest, 6–22 m high; often near nest of Black Butcherbird. **Eggs:** 2; pale pink, spotted red–brown, grey. **Range and Status:** n. C. York Pen. (Q): from C. York and coastal islands s. to Weipa on w. coast and McIlwraith Ra. on e. coast. Fairly common. Sedentary. Also PNG, Indonesia.

SPANGLED DRONGO *Dicrurus bracteatus* 29–32 cm

Bill black, robust, with prominent hairlike feathers at base; eye bright red. An often frantically active black bird with large head and longish 'fishtail' (temporarily reduced when moulting); head/back dull black, wings/tail more glossy; subtle glossy green spots on crown/neck/upperbreast. **Immature:** dull smoky black, with brown eye, scattered white spots on underwing, under tail-coverts. Singles, pairs, migratory parties or open companies to 100+. Noisy, pugnacious; sits motionless, shrugs shoulders, flicks tail, dashes into air in pursuit of insects (or small birds); forages on trunks/limbs and in foliage; feeds on blossom nectar. Birds display facing one another, sides of crown raised in curious crest shape, wings spread. Flight swift, swooping, erratic. Courting males fly up c. 30 m; dive with wings arched back, tail cocked, calling. **Similar species:** Koel, male: pale bill; rounded tail. Manucode. Metallic Starling: smaller, glossier with pointed tail. Black Butcherbird: larger, with hooked blue–grey bill, tipped black; dark eye; straight tail. **Voice:** harsh chatterings — tearing 'shashashash' while perched and in flight; strange metallic notes, some like a tight fence-wire being twanged. Mimics. **Habitat:** rainforest, mostly at edges; isolated leafy trees in farmland; eucalypt forests/woodlands, paperbarks, coastal scrubs, mangroves; leafy trees on watercourses; roadsides, parks, gardens. **Breeds:** Sept.–March; may return annually to same site. **Nest:** delicate, deep basket of twigs, vine-tendrils, spiders' web; slung in horizontal fork in outer foliage, 10–20 m high. **Eggs:** 3–5; pinkish or purplish white, blotched and with wavy streaks of pinkish red, brown, purple. **Range and Status:** coastal n. and e. Aust. and coastal islands: from Kimberley (WA) through Top End (NT), s. to c. Katherine; e. to c. Oenpelli and NT Gulf Coast; e. Aust. from C. York Pen. (Q) coastally s. to Moruya–Batemans Bay (NSW); inland on Gt Divide to Carnarvon Ra. NP (Q)–Blue Mts (NSW). In NSW, s. to c. Macksville, it is a summer breeding migrant, arriving Sept.–Oct. to breed, many migrating n. through coastal Q in March–April, some crossing to PNG. S. of Macksville, it is a *winter migrant,* arriving c. March–April, departing c. Sept.–Oct. Casual e. Vic., w. to near Melbourne; vagrant n. Tas., SA, including Kangaroo I. Present all year in Kimberley (WA) and Top End (NT) (Blakers et al, 1984). Also Solomon Is., PNG, Indonesia to Malaysia and s. Asia.

TRUMPET MANUCODE

SPANGLED DRONGO

Metallic
Starling
(not to scale)

imm.

AUSTRALIAN RAVEN *Corvus coronoides* 48–52 cm. Male larger.

Other name: Crow.

Long throat-hackle feathers form shaggy bunch as throat balloons out when calling. Bill robust, longish; eye white. In all three ravens, in wind, note grey down at base of feathers of head/neck. Birds in s. WA smaller, with less-developed hackles; voice more guttural. (Debus, 1995). **Immature:** duller; eye brown, then hazel; white in third year. Pairs hold territories throughout year; imms/unmated adults form small nomadic flocks. Wary at nest, slips off, flies away low. In display, flies on shallow-beating, quivering wings. **Voice:** loud, wailing 'aah-aah-aah-aaaaaahh', drawn out, descending. Also high-pitched, descending, baby-like wavering wail; throaty rattles, 'chucks'. **Habitat:** pastoral regions, farmlands; alpine regions up to 1500 m; dunes, beaches, islands, mangroves, rubbish dumps, urban areas. **Breeds:** July–Oct. in permanent territory of *c.* 100 ha. **Nest:** substantial, of sticks; lined with bark, hair, wool; 10 m+ high in fork of living, or dead tree; on pylon, cross-arm of telephone-pole; occasionally on ground. **Eggs:** 3–5; blue–green, blotched, freckled olive–brown, dark brown. **Range and Status:** e. Aust. and sw. WA. Mostly *absent* from C. York Pen.; sparse coastal e. Q–ne. NSW. Ranges w. to e. NT, n. to Nicholson R.–Brunette Downs, s. to w. Macdonnell Ras. In SA, w. to Oodnadatta–Tarcoola, along Bight coast to sw. WA, inland to *c.* Menzies, n. coastally to Shark Bay. The common corvid of Perth, Sydney. Common.

FOREST RAVEN *Corvus tasmanicus* 52–54 cm

Other name: Tasmanian Raven.

Two races: s. (nominate) race: *big, heavy bird with the most massive bill of any Aust. corvid and shortest tail. When calling, throat fills out, but hackles do not form large, shaggy 'bag' as in Aust. Raven*; points tail downwards as it calls (Debus, 1980). Flight ponderous. N. race, *boreus*: bill less massive; tail longer. In both races, mated pairs hold permanent territories of *c.* 40 ha; nonbreeding birds form locally nomadic flocks of *c.* 30–40 (up to 100 in winter in Tas.) (Blakers et al, 1984). **Voice:** powerful, deep, slow, baritone 'kaarr, kaarr, kaarr (kaarr)'; lacks wail of Aust. Raven. **Habitat:** in Tas., ranges from alpine forests/high moors to wet eucalypt forests, woodlands, coastal scrubs/beaches; orchards, pine plantations; adjacent open country autumn/winter. **Breeds:** Aug.–Nov. **Nest:** large stick nest lined with bark, wool; 10 m+ high in fork in forest tree. **Eggs:** like Aust. Raven; slightly larger. **Range and Status:** nominate race is *the only corvid in Tas. proper*; common, widespread, incl. urban areas. Also Flinders I., King I. (but see Little Raven, below), other Bass Strait islands; s. Vic., coastally from West Gippsland/Wilsons Prom. NP to se. SA, inland to Grampians NP (Vic.)–Naracoorte–Fairview Conservation Park (SA). Race *boreus*: isolated populations in ne. NSW, from Glen Innes s. to *c.* Barrington Tops NP, coastally s. from *c.* Coffs Harbour to Port Stephens. Uncommon.

LITTLE RAVEN *Corvus mellori* 48–50 cm

Slightly smaller than Aust. Raven; bill less massive, more curved. Throat-hackles shorter, divided at tip; *throat bulges less when calling.* (But when gathering food for young, note small gular pouch under base of bill, giving head distinctive outline.) **Immature:** duller black; eye brown, then hazel; white in third year. Calls and actions are diagnostic; *gives a quick upward flip with both wings with each note.* When breeding, parties forage near territories in open country; after breeding, travel far in high-flying flocks to forage in woodlands/open farming, cereal growing country of coastal se. Aust. More insectivorous than Aust. and Forest Ravens, scavenges less. On winter/early spring evenings, flocks perform massed, noisy, aerial displays/chases. Roosts communally. **Voice:** harsh, short, level, rapid 'car, car, car, car, car'. Notes hard, clipped. **Habitat:** alpine woodlands to over 1600 m; forests, woodlands to almost treeless plains, sub-inland woodlands and scrubs; pastoral country, farmlands, coasts, suburbs, cities. **Breeds:** Aug.–Dec.; sometimes autumn–winter. Semi-colonial, some nests only a few metres apart. **Nest:** shallow cup of sticks, twigs; lined with bark, grass, wool, felted into thick mat. Rarely over 10 m high, often in light fork in outer canopy. **Eggs:** 4; pale blue–green, blotched, freckled brown, olive. **Range and Status:** se. mainland Aust. from n. tablelands of NSW to Eyre Pen., Kangaroo I. (SA), w. to Cook on Nullarbor Plain; also King I. (Bass Strait). Ranges inland to beyond Lachlan R. (NSW); s. Flinders Ras.–Gawler Ras. (SA). Absent from forested parts of West Gippsland–Wilsons Prom. NP–Otway Ras.(Vic.), where replaced by Forest Raven. The common urban corvid of Adelaide, Melbourne. Nomadic.

AUSTRALIAN RAVEN

FOREST RAVEN

LITTLE RAVEN

TORRESIAN CROW *Corvus orru* 48–53 cm

Resembles Aust. Raven, *but call differs, and on alighting, bird characteristically lifts and shuffles wings.* In wind, adults *show snow-white down at base of feathers on head/neck.* **Immature:** duller black; eye brown in first year, then hazel; white in third year. In c. Aust./WA, where it overlaps Little Crow, occurs mostly in pairs or small parties (though the two form mixed foraging flocks). In coastal n. and e. Aust., *in nonbreeding season,* forms flocks in cultivated lands, towns, abattoirs, rubbish dumps; pest in crops of grain, peanuts, fruit. In flight, wings rounder, tail shorter, looks smaller, more agile than Aust. Raven (Debus, 1980). Like Little Crow, flight display includes undulating 'shooting', in which bird misses wingbeat, keeps wings to sides, uttering a single 'uk' (Debus, 1980). **Voice:** nasal, clipped, staccato 'uk-uk-uk-uk', sometimes drawn out at end. In aggression, harsher, nasal 'arr-arr-arr', warbles or rattles; in WA, reported to utter high-pitched yodelling or falsetto, stuttering call. (Debus, 1995). **Habitat:** rainforest margins; open forest, woodlands, taller inland/coastal scrubs; beaches, tidal areas; in arid regions, ranges, gorges, timber on larger watercourses. Also farms, settlements. **Breeds:** Aug.–Oct in s.; Nov.–Feb. in n. **Nest:** of sticks; high in eucalypt or tall mulga. **Eggs:** 3–5; pale blue, sparsely, lightly spotted, blotched olive–brown, dark brown. **Range and Status:** from c. Raymond Terrace (e. NSW), throughout n. and inland Aust. (*except* far sw. Q and driest deserts); s. through s. NT to Mann, Musgrave and Everard Ras.–Eringa (nw. SA); in WA, s. coastally to c. Geraldton, s. to c. Corrigin–Norseman. Common but patchy. Adults sedentary, with local seasonal movements; imms nomadic. The common corvid of coastal towns n. from c. Forster (NSW) to Brisbane and e. Q; also Darwin (NT). Also Bismarck Arch., PNG, e. Indonesia.

LITTLE CROW *Corvus bennetti* 45–48 cm

Smallest, shortest-legged Aust. corvid, with slender bill; snow-white down at base of feathers of head/neck. **Immature:** duller black; eye brown in first year, then hazel, white in third year. Tame, in inland/w. coastal towns, where it scavenges in streets, shopping arcades. Sociable when nesting; in nonbreeding season forms mixed flocks of 100s of adults/imms (often with Torresian Crows) where food abundant, e.g. grasshopper swarms. Flocks often travel high (70–100 m) in steady direction, calling; soar high, swoop, dive, turn. Wings blunt, tail slender; wingbeats quick, shallow; when soaring, wings markedly backswept from 'wrist'. Like Torresian Crow, has undulating display flight, missing a wingbeat and uttering short call. (Curry, 1978; Debus, 1980). **Voice:** quick, hoarse, nasal 'nark-nark-nark-nark'; high-pitched 'kup-kup-kup'; bubbling calls and a long, creaky call (Debus, 1980). **Habitat:** mallee, mulga, other acacia scrubs; timber on watercourses; grasslands; deserts, near-treeless plains; coastal woodlands, farmlands, abattoirs, towns. **Breeds:** July–Oct. **Nest:** small, of sticks, mud, clay; cup lined with feathers, fur, wool, bark-strips; in scrubby tree; often in loose colony; also on mill-platform; cross-arm of telephone-pole; on ground. **Eggs:** 4–6; small, round, greenish blue, heavily freckled, spotted, blotched olive–brown. **Range and Status:** Inland and w. Aust., coastal islands. In Q, n. to Burketown, e. to c. Roma; mostly *absent* from e. coastal areas–C. York Pen. In NSW, e. to Warrumbungle NP– Condobolin–Berrigan. In Vic., small numbers resident Mildura and nw. mallee areas. In SA, s. to Murray mallee–Port Germein–n. Eyre Pen.–w. on Bight coast to Nullarbor Plain. In WA, widespread s. from Pilbara region, avoiding heavy forests/driest deserts. Widespread in s. NT; sparse coastal n. NT–Kimberley (WA). Common. Nomadic, breeding in response to rainfall; moves coastwards in inland drought. In s. WA, moves s. in spring–summer into Darling Ras./wheatbelt; may remain until June–July.

HOUSE CROW *Corvus splendens* 43 cm

Other names: Colombo or Indian Crow.
Smallish crow with *pale grey to mouse-brown nape/back/breast, emphasising blackness of crown/face/throat.* Bill fairly short, legs fairly long; *eye black.* In India and Sri Lanka, familiar scavenger in towns/villages; destructive of eggs/nestlings. Forms communal roosts. **Voice:** short, flat, clipped 'caw', repeated. **Habitat:** urban areas, dockyards, farmlands, shores, zoological gardens. **Nest:** (Indian data) platform of twigs, often incl. wire, with cup-like depression lined with tow, coir fibre; 3 m or higher in tree. **Eggs:** 4–5; pale blue–green speckled, streaked brown. **Range and Status:** native of India, Sri Lanka, s. Asia. Occasionally self-introduced to Aust. ports on ships, principally Fremantle (WA), also Geelong, possibly Melbourne (Vic.). Should immediately be reported and destroyed wherever identified.

TORRESIAN CROW

LITTLE CROW

HOUSE CROW

APOSTLEBIRD *Struthidea cinerea* 29–33 cm

Other names: Grey Jumper, Happy Family, Lousy Jack, Twelve Apostles.
Sociable dark, ashy grey bird with short, robust black bill, brown flight-feathers and full black tail. Usually in groups of 6–10, sometimes 20+. Garrulous, restless, aggressive; forages on ground, walking slowly, running, occasionally hopping; tail flicked upwards, slowly subsiding. When disturbed, flies direct and low to cover, *wingbeats broken by glides, wingtips upswept, showing coppery tone on flight-feathers*; leaps from branch to branch with wings/tail spread, calling. Dust-bathes on roadsides; rests, preens in groups; associates with White-winged Chough. Tame around campgrounds, farmsteads; often feeds with poultry. **Voice:** scratchy, like tearing sandpaper; loud, discordant 'ch-kew, ch-kew'; on being disturbed, rough nasal 'git-out!', repeated. **Habitat:** near water in drier open forests, woodlands, scrubs; timber on watercourses; black box/river red gum forests; woodlands of cypress pine; roadside timber, timbered paddocks, golfcourses, orchards. **Breeds:** Aug.–March. **Nest:** large mud bowl, reinforced with grass; lined with fine grass; plastered to horizontal branch 3–20 m high. Members of group co-operate in nest-construction, incubation, feeding young. **Eggs:** 2–5 (more when more than one female lays); white, blue–white; spotted, blotched, occasionally streaked blackish brown, dark grey; some lack markings. **Range and Status:** sub-inland and inland e. Aust.; (? isolate) population in NT, in area of Elliott–Katherine, w. toward Top Springs, e. to upper Roper R.–Borroloola. In Q, widespread s. from lower C. York Pen. (Staaten R.–Laura), e. and s. to Atherton Tableland–Townsville–Rockhampton–Toowoomba, occasional to near Brisbane. In NSW, e. to Glen Innes–Tamworth–Sydney region–Cowra–Albury; casual ACT. Extends far w. in inland Q–NSW. In Vic., now confined to near Murray R. in two regions, Wodonga–Nathalia, and from Swan Hill to Hattah–Kulkyne NP–SA border. In SA, s. to c. Naracoorte, w. through Murray mallee to Mt Lofty Ras.–Adelaide region, n. to c. Barrier Highway. Fairly common, but patchy and local. Sedentary; locally nomadic.

WHITE-WINGED CHOUGH *Corcorax melanorhamphos* 43–47 cm

Other names: Black Jay or Magpie.
Note: the name is pronounced 'chuff'. Gregarious black bird, smaller than a raven, with a *full, mobile, black tail and large round white patch on flight-feathers, conspicuous in flight.* Bill black, slender, arched; eye orange–red; legs longish, black. **Immature:** smaller; tail shorter; eye brown. Highly sociable: parties of 5–10; in autumn–winter, where food plentiful, up to 100+. Feeds mostly on ground, *moving ahead in spread-out formation, running to share a food-discovery; swaggers with back-and-forward head-motion, tail raised/lowered.* Dust-bathes; indulges in anting. When disturbed, flies noisily to cover *with quick flaps/glides on flat wings, large white wingpatches prominent;* climbs branches in flying bounds. **Similar species:** Pied Currawong: bill more robust; eye yellow; *prominent white on base of tail, under tail-coverts, tail tips.* Ravens/crows: all black; bills more robust; tails shorter; eye white in adults. **Voice:** mournful, mellow, descending whistles; when alarmed, grating 'hass'; small throaty clicks. **Habitat:** drier forests, woodlands of eucalypts, incl. mallee; belar, cypress pine, mulga; timber on watercourses; introduced pines; crops, pastures, homestead gardens, lawns, poultry-runs, outer suburbs. **Breeds:** Aug.–Dec. **Nest:** large bowl of mud, other material, incl. manure; bound/lined with shredded bark, grass, fur; on horizontal branch, to 6 m+; sometimes on old nest of babbler, corvid. Members of territorial group build nest, co-operate in incubation, feeding young. **Eggs:** 3–5; up to 9 when more than one female lays; creamy white; blotched brown, lilac. **Range and Status:** e. and se. mainland Aust.: from Charters Towers (ne. Q) inland to Longreach–Idalia NP–Hungerford; most NSW *except* far nw.; most Vic. *except* denser forests and cleared, closely settled coastal areas; widespread in s. SA s. of Flinders Ras., w. to near Tarcoola and along coast of Gt Aust. Bight, w. to c. Eucla. (In WA, unconfirmed sight records near Eyre Highway c. Madura–Cocklebiddy.) Common; patchy; reduced by loss of habitat. Sedentary; locally nomadic.

APOSTLEBIRD

WHITE-WINGED CHOUGH

imm.

SPOTTED CATBIRD *Ailuroedus melanotis* 26–30 cm

Bill bone–white; eye dark red; *plumage green, with heavier markings.* Race *maculosus: crown/nape/ear-coverts brownish black with plentiful fine buff spots; throat/breast buff–white, with chainmail pattern of bold, pointed olive–black feather-margins.* Race *joanae:* similar, but *crown/nape/ear-coverts blacker.* **Habits, Voice, Habitat and Breeding:** like Green Catbird. **Range and Status:** race *maculosus:* coastal ne. Q, from Paluma Ra., near Townsville, n. to near Cooktown, inland on Atherton Tableland and other mountain rainforests. Race *joanae:* ne. C. York Pen., from Rocky R. n. to Claudie R., incl. rainforests of McIlwraith Ra. and Iron Ra. NP. Sedentary; with probable movement to habitats below 500 m in winter (Blakers et al, 1984). Also PNG and islands.

GREEN CATBIRD *Ailuroedus crassirostris* 24–32 cm

Robust, handsome, rich-green bird with a sturdy bone–white bill, brownish head, dark red eye with partial white eye-ring, white spots on tips of wing-coverts, secondaries and outer tail-feathers; legs grey–brown. **Immature:** duller, bill greyer; eye brown. Pairs, autumn–winter flocks of 20+: usually first noticed by calls. Not shy, but often difficult to see in foliage; feeds on fruit in rainforest canopy, vine-tangles, occasionally on ground; raids orchards, fruit trees in gardens. Reported to construct a display-ground, but unlike bowerbirds, mates share nest-duties. **Similar species:** Satin Bowerbird, imm.: eye blue; upperparts grey–green, with unspotted yellow–brown flight-feathers; underparts fawnish, with scaly pattern. **Voice:** like yowling cat: loud, nasal, drawling, human-like 'here-I-are'. Contact and alarm-call: slight, sharp 'pik!', or 'tik', seemingly feeble for such robust bird, but a sure guide to its presence. **Habitat:** mountain and lowland rainforests and margins; densely foliaged gullies; paperbarks and other watercourse timber; nearby cultivated areas; gardens. **Breeds:** Sept.–Feb. **Nest:** substantial open cup of vines, twigs, leaves, moss; lined with vines, rootlets, bark-fibre; in tangle of vines, sapling, fork of tree, treefern, 3–6 m high; occasionally to 30 m. **Eggs:** 2; plain creamy white. **Range and Status:** on and coastward of Gt Divide, and some coastal islands (incl. Fraser I.) from s. of Gladstone (Q) to *c.* Mt Dromedary, s. of Narooma (NSW). Occasional visitor to well-treed Sydney suburbs; regular Royal NP.

TOOTH-BILLED BOWERBIRD *Scenopoeetes dentirostris* 26–27 cm

Other names: Stagemaker, Tooth-billed Catbird.
Bill robust, dark brown, with serrations on cutting edge of both mandibles; eye dark red–brown; bare tan eye-ring. Plumage olive–brown above, fawn below, heavily streaked and mottled brown. Seldom seen or heard Feb.–July, but from *c.* Sept.–Jan., when males attend 'display-courts', easily located by calls. Male occupies concealed song-perch 1–6 m above display-court — a roughly oval cleared space 1–3 m in diameter, surrounding at least one tree-trunk, and decorated with large leaves, picked green by bird chewing through leaf-stem and usually laid pale underside uppermost. Perched bird produces stream of very loud song/mimicry (to this observer, seemingly louder/harsher than the originals). Also a softer sub-song of perfect mimicry: species mimicked include King Parrot, Crimson Rosella, Bower's Shrike-thrush, Mountain Thornbill, Bridled Honeyeater (Frith & Frith, 1993). When a female visits court, male drops to ground and displays, lunging forward or sideways with spread wings and twisting or flicking tail, wide open bill showing gleaming, white interior of tip to lower mandible, contrasting with black mouth-interior and spread fawn–white throat-feathers (Frith & Frith, ibid). Outside breeding season, forages in rainforest canopy, singly or in small, loose companies, on fruit, insects, leaves, moving with planing glides between trees. **Voice:** strange, powerful and varied: low chuckling notes develop into medley of calls and mimicry against background of noise like cloth being ripped; softer sub-song includes mimicry; also loud cheerful chirp; soft low rasping notes. **Habitat:** highland rainforests and vine-scrubs; occasionally to nearby thickets, plantations. **Breeds:** Oct.–Jan. **Nest:** flimsy saucer of twigs; in vine-tangle or fork in rainforest canopy, 5–30 m high. **Eggs:** 2; oval; cream to creamy brown. **Range and Status:** highlands of ne. Q, between 500 and 1400 m, occasionally lower; from Mt Amos, near Cooktown, s. to Mt Elliot near Townsville (Q). Common. Sedentary.

SPOTTED CATBIRD

GREEN CATBIRD

TOOTH-BILLED BOWERBIRD

GOLDEN BOWERBIRD *Prionodura newtoniana* 23–25 cm

Smallest bowerbird. **Male:** *glossy golden olive above, with yellow erectile patches on crown, nape. Throat/underparts golden yellow.* **Female:** *olive–brown above, ashy grey below; tail shorter; bill brown; eye yellow; legs black.* **Immature:** like female; eye brown; imm. males tinged golden. Singles, pairs: takes fruit, insects, among foliage, on ground. **Bower:** maypole-type; largest of any Aust. bowerbird: two columns of sticks up to 3 m tall, joined at base, built around vertical saplings. Between columns is a display-perch, where bird places clusters of lichen, pale cream flowers. Male frequents bower Sept.–Jan.; preening, calling, arranging decorations, displaying in spectacular hovering, posturing on vines, trunks: crest, wings raised, tail fanned; head jerking, or thrust forward to meet tail. **Voice:** near bower, frog-like croaks; sound like briskly-wound fishing reel; mimicry. **Habitat:** highland rainforests. **Breeds:** Oct.–Jan. **Nest:** cup of dead leaves, ferns, dry moss; lined with twigs; in low cavity in tree-trunk. **Eggs:** 2; oval, glossy, creamy white. **Range and Status:** highlands of ne. Q; from Mt Cook, near Endeavour R., s. to Mt Elliot NP, near Townsville, above 900 m; lower in winter. Locally common. Sedentary.

REGENT BOWERBIRD *Sericulus chrysocephalus* 25–30 cm. Female larger.

Male: *glossy jet-black; crown/nape/inner wing-feathers bright golden orange; bill/eye yellow.* **Female:** longer-tailed; bill blackish; gape yellow in breeding season; *eye yellow with brown flecks;* upperparts olive–brown with *black patch on nape, grey mottling on mantle;* fawn–white below, black mark down throat; underparts with brown netted pattern. **Immature:** like female; eye dark brown; imm. males may have yellow bill/eye; imms of either sex may have yellow feathers on crown/nape. Dark-eyed females known to breed. Males aquire adult plumage at *c.* 5 years. Singles; flocks of 40+ in nonbreeding season, mostly 'brown birds' on rainforest-margins, clearings, dense gullies. Males mostly seen as a flash of gold/black in quick flight between cover. **Bower:** smallest Aust. avenue-type; shallow layer of twigs forms base for two parallel walls of twigs 15–20 cm long, 24–30 cm high, *c.* 9 cm wide. Display-objects: shells, seeds, leaves, berries. **Voice:** low chattering, tearing rattles, scratchy, wheezy ventriloquial calls; mimics. **Habitat:** rainforest; margins; coastal scrubs; thickets of raspberries, wild tobacco, inkweed; secondary growth, orchards, gardens. **Breeds:** Oct.–Jan. **Nest:** loose saucer of twigs; 4–10 m+ high in creepers in rainforest. **Eggs:** 2; pale brownish buff; irregular lines of dark brown, purple. **Range and Status:** on and coastward of Gt Divide: from Eungella NP near Mackay (Q), s. to *c.* Gosford–Cattai–Baulkham Hills, on nw. fringes of Sydney; casual Royal NP–Illawarra region (NSW). Fairly common. Sedentary; moves to lowlands in winter.

SATIN BOWERBIRD *Ptilonorhynchus violaceus* 28–32 cm

Male: *glossy blue–black; bill bluish white; eye blue; legs greenish white; tail short.* **Female:** bill dark brown; eye blue; legs grey-brown; upperparts olive grey–green; wings/tail rufous-brown; *underparts washed yellow buff, with fine brown scaly pattern on throat becoming bolder on breast/flanks.* **Immature:** like female; third- and fourth-year males acquire *green throat, with fine white spots, streaks; green zone across upperbreast.* Bill progressively paler; adult plumage in sixth/seventh year. Singles, winter flocks of 20–50+, mainly 'green birds': robustly active; feeds on lilly pilly, crab apples, grapes, seedlings, blossom nectar. Hops vigorously; leaps between branches; flies strongly, wingtips upswept on each downstroke. **Bower:** avenue type; layer of twigs on ground 5–7.5 cm deep. Two parallel arched walls of twigs form avenue *c.* 35 cm high, 45 cm long. Display-objects mostly blue or yellow: flowers, feathers, berries, glass, plastic, etc. Male seizes objects in bill, adopts trance-like poses, head low, eyes suffused lilac–pink, leaps sideways, flares wings/tail, utters wheezing, whirring notes; mates with females attracted. **Similar species:** Koel, Spangled Drongo, Green Catbird. **Voice:** in ne. NSW–se. Q, dingo-like 'wee-ooo'; harsh scolds, wheezes, rattles. **Habitat:** rainforests, eucalypt forests/woodlands; in autumn–winter, open woodlands, scrubs, paddocks, orchards, parks, gardens. **Breeds:** Sept.–Jan. **Nest:** saucer of sticks; lined with leaves; in fork, mistletoe, 2–16 m high; near active bower. **Eggs:** 2 (1–3); cream; blotched, streaked brown, slate-grey. **Range and Status:** (1) race *minor*: highlands of ne. Q, above *c.* 900 m, from Big Tableland (s. of Cooktown) to Seaview Ra., near Townsville, inland to Herberton Ra.; (2) Nominate race: coastal se. Aust., from Kroombit Tops NP (se. Q) to *c.* Benalla–Gembrook–Strzelecki Ras. (Vic.); casual Mt Macedon (Emison et al, 1987); (3) Otway Ras. (Vic.), sw. from *c.* Aireys Inlet. Common. Autumn dispersal to lowlands. Sedentary; seasonally nomadic.

GOLDEN BOWERBIRD

♀

♂

REGENT BOWERBIRD

♂ imm.

♀

♂

SATIN BOWERBIRD

♂ imm.

♂

♀

FAWN-BREASTED BOWERBIRD *Chlamydera cerviniventris* 26–30 cm

Grey–brown *above, feathers tipped buffy white; face/throat/breast streaked buff–white; underparts yellow–buff.* Singles, small parties: wary; more often heard than seen; feeds in fruiting trees. **Bower:** avenue-type; under leafy branch; on deep pile of sticks; walls 22–30 cm high, 37 cm long, *c.* 7.5 cm apart. Decorated with green fruit, berries, greyish leaves, shells, bones. In display, male arches neck, twists tail, runs/bounds around bower, wings trailing. **Similar species:** Great Bowerbird. **Voice:** explosive 'kaa-kaa-ka'; churrings; hissing, grasshopper-like notes; mimicry. **Habitat:** dense coastal vegetation: cypress pine scrubs, mangrove fringes; eucalypts, paperbarks, with tall grass, scattered bushes; thickets on watercourses. **Breeds:** mostly Sept.–Dec. **Nest:** bulky saucer of sticks, twigs, bark; to *c.* 10 m in tree, pandanus. **Egg:** 1; creamy white, scribbled with browns, greyish purple. **Range and Status:** from C. York (Q) s. to *c.* Silver Plains, e. of Coen (Blakers et al, 1984). Locally fairly common. Sedentary. Also PNG.

WESTERN BOWERBIRD *Chlamydera guttata* 25–28 cm

Darker, richer than Spotted Bowerbird: *upperparts, neck, upperbreast and rump blackish brown patterned with red–buff spots.* On nape, erectile pink crest; *lower nape blackish brown.* Singles; loose parties in nonbreeding season. In rocky inland hills, frequently visits rock figs, *Ficus platypoda.* **Habits, Bower, Voice and Breeding:** like Spotted. **Range and Status:** interior and WA: from Everard–Musgrave Ras. (nw. SA), through ranges of s. NT, e. to Jervois Ra., n. to MacDonald Downs–Mt Allan, w. to Rawlinson/Warburton Ras. (WA), Pilbara to coast *c.* Eighty Mile Beach, s. to Gascoyne R.–Cue–Kathleen Valley–Leonora. Uncommon. Sedentary; nomadic in nonbreeding season.

SPOTTED BOWERBIRD *Chlamydera maculata* 25–30 cm

Bold rich-buff spots on pale brown mantle/wings/rump; on nape, erectile pink crest; ash-grey patch on lower nape. **Female:** crest smaller. **Immature:** heavily marked throat/breast; lacks crest. Singles, parties: active around human habitation, camps. Feeds in foliage, branches. Flight swooping, wingtips upswept. **Bower:** avenue type; under leafy branch or lignum; thick layer of twigs, at one end a double, arched wall of twigs, *c.* 35–75 cm long, 25–50 cm high, 15–22 cm wide. Red, white, shiny display-objects: bones, snail/mussel shells, green native figs, berries, glass, cartridges, nails, spoons, coins, plastic, etc. **Similar species:** Great Bowerbird. **Voice:** loud churring grating, hissing; 'throat-clearing' noises; mimicry. **Habitat:** inland scrubs, brigalow; open woodlands of cypress pine, belar; river red gums/black box; lignum; homestead gardens, peppercorn/fruit trees, vineyards. **Breeds:** Sept.–Dec. **Nest:** flimsy saucer of twigs, leaves; in fork to 16 m, near active bower. **Eggs:** 2 (3); grey to greenish, blotched grey–mauve, with dark brown, thread-like markings. **Range and Status:** inland e. Aust. to *c.* coast (Q); now rare sw. NSW; nearly extinct nw. Vic., far-e. SA. Uncommon. Sedentary; locally nomadic.

GREAT BOWERBIRD *Chlamydera nuchalis* 34–38 cm

Large, fawn–grey bowerbird with *erectile pink crest on nape; upperparts* grey–brown, *heavily scalloped grey–white;* tail tipped whitish. **Female:** smaller, paler; often lacks crest. **Immature:** like female. Singles, small flocks: active, inquisitive; bounds on ground and between branches. Flight strongly undulating, wings abruptly out-thrust, tips upswept. Male displays away from bower; half-spreads wings, with 'knee-bends'. At bower, stretches; holds object in bill; ticks; hisses; head lowered, jerked, crest expanded. Runs/bounds, ruffles feathers, cocks tail. **Bower:** largest avenue-type; under shrub, leafy branch; platform of twigs, with two arched walls 60–120 cm long, *c.* 45 cm high, form avenue *c.* 15 cm wide; with bones, shells, stones, pale leaves, flowers, green fruits, red objects, glass, nails, cartridge-cases. **Similar species:** Spotted Bowerbird. **Voice:** whistles, chatterings, explosive hisses; mimicry; harsh alarm-churr. **Habitat:** drier woodlands, scrubs/thickets; near water; outer urban areas, parks, gardens. **Breeds:** Aug.–Feb. **Nest:** saucer of twigs; lined with leaves, finer twigs; to *c.* 5 m in open tree. **Eggs:** 1–2; oval; grey–green with blackish brown, purplish squiggles. **Range and Status:** from *c.* Broome (WA) through Kimberley, Top End (NT) s. to *c.* Elliott; Gulf coast s. to Nicholson, O'Shannassy, upper Flinders Rs.; occasional s. to Mt Isa (Q); C. York Pen., coastally s. to near Mackay. Vagrant s. NT; ne. NSW. Common. Sedentary.

FAWN-BREASTED BOWERBIRD

WESTERN BOWERBIRD

SPOTTED BOWERBIRD

GREAT BOWERBIRD

RED-THROATED PIPIT *Anthus cervinus* 14.5–16 cm

Smaller, tail shorter than Richard's Pipit, also edged white. **Breeding plumage:** *pale rust-red face/throat/upperbreast.* **Nonbreeding and immature:** *facial area/throat/breast washed reddish buff, with black whisker-streak; buff-edged black streaks on back, prominent buff edges to blackish wing-coverts; heavy black streaks on breast and flanks, underparts white.* **Similar species:** Singing Bushlark. **Voice:** described as high-pitched, musical or piercing 'psee', 'psee-eep' or 'psee-oo.' **Range and Status:** breeds n. Scandinavia–e. Siberia: migrates to Africa, India, se. Asia, Philippines, Borneo, Indonesia. First Aust. sight-record: Broome (WA), Jan. 1992, on sports oval with Yellow Wagtails (Carter, 1992). WA Museum has specimen found dead on wharf in Albany, May 1983, near ship from Singapore.

RICHARD'S PIPIT *Anthus novaeseelandiae* 16–19 cm

Other name: Groundlark.

Slender, pale brown 'groundlark': *wags longish white-edged tail up/down.* Note *slender pale–brown bill; fawn–white eyebrow; fine black streak down side of throat* joins fine dark breast-streaks; *long, pinkish brown legs.* **Immature:** buffer, more finely marked. Singles, pairs: walks/runs easily, perches on fences, rocks, stumps. Flight fluttering, head raised, *tail folded, or depressed and spread; white edges prominent.* Courting male, in flight, repeatedly swings up with wings quivering, tail elevated; at each swing, utters high, quavering 'tzweeer'. **Similar species:** Common Skylark, Singing Bushlark, Rufous Songlark. **Voice:** brisk, splintered 'pith!'; trilled, drawn-out 'tzweeer'. **Habitat:** grasslands, crops, pastures; roadsides, alpine meadows, open woodlands, coastal dunes, paddocks, golfcourses. **Breeds:** Aug.–Dec. **Nest:** deep cup of grasses; in shelter of tussock, stone. **Eggs:** 3–4; grey, buff–white, finely freckled grey, slate-brown. **Range and Status:** Aust. and Tas. Common; widespread. Sedentary. Also e. Europe, Africa to Asia, Indonesia, PNG, NZ, sub-Antarctic islands.

SINGING BUSHLARK *Mirafra javanica* 12.5–15 cm

Other names: Australian Skylark, Croplark.

Smaller, stockier than Common Skylark; *tail shorter.* Colour variable: *sandy, reddish grey or blackish above; bold rufous margins to wing-feathers form strong pattern; often has heavy blackish mottling on breast.* **Immature:** finer scalloped pattern on upperparts. Singles, open flocks: runs nimbly, legs bent, or flutters, *wings half-closed in shivery, jerky tail-down manner; rufous in wings, white edges to tail prominent.* Perches on fences, telephone-lines over crops, grasslands. **Similar species:** Common Skylark, Richard's Pipit. **Voice:** when disturbed, chirrups. Song: tinny, spasmodic; thinner, less melodious and throbbing than Common Skylark, but carries far. Sings while hovering high, in low undulating flight, or perched on stump, fence, or ground; mimics. **Habitat:** tropical, temperate grasslands, with rank cover; open woodlands/scrublands; cereal crops, lucerne, sparse sugar cane. **Breeds:** Sept.–Jan. **Nest:** flimsily domed cup; in depression. **Eggs:** 2–4; glossy; greyish stone to whitish; speckled, blotched pale grey, dark brown. **Range and Status:** n. and e. Aust., w. to Eyre Pen. (SA), s. on w. coast to *c.* Shark Bay (WA). Summer breeding migrant in se. Aust., although many may overwinter, unnoticed because silent. Vagrant Tas. Uncommon; locally irruptive/abundant. Also PNG to Asia, Africa.

COMMON SKYLARK *Alaúda arvensis* 17–19 cm.

Other name: English Skylark.

Bill sparrowlike; pale eyebrow encircles darker ear-coverts; crown feathers form low, cap-like crest; upperbreast boldly streaked; tail edged white. **Immature:** less 'crest'; more scalloped. Singles, pairs, companies: crouches, turns back, flattens itself on ground. Flushes with chirrup, flies in strong undulations on *broad triangular wings with pale trailing edge, slightly forked tail edged white.* Song-flight: hovers up, or mounts in spirals to great heights, *singing.* **Similar species:** Singing Bushlark, Richard's Pipit. **Voice:** mellow chirrup, heard overhead, spring/autumn. Song: sustained, clear, beautiful runs, trills, throbbing phrases. **Habitat:** cultivated grasslands/crops; wastelands, coastal dunes. **Breeds:** Sept.–Jan. **Nest:** grass-lined cup by tussock. **Eggs:** 3–5; grey white, freckled/blotched brown. **Range and Status:** se. Aust.: introduced from Britain in 1850s; ranges from Yorke Pen. (SA) to Hunter Valley (NSW), inland to *c.* Macquarie Marshes. Common Tas., Vic., s. SA, NSW Riverina. Nomadic; part-migratory.

Richard's
Pipit

RICHARD'S PIPIT

RED-THROATED PIPIT

SINGING BUSHLARK

dark
individual

imm.

COMMON SKYLARK

imm.

*YELLOW WAGTAIL *Motacilla flava* 16.5–18 cm

Other names: Blue-headed or Siberian Wagtail.

Dark-legged wagtail of many races; tail shorter than other species. *Most races have uniform grey–green or olive–green backs/rumps. In breeding plumage, underparts bright yellow from breast to vent.* Breeding males of races known to visit Aust. differ. **Race simillima:** crown blue–grey; eyebrow whitish; ear-coverts dark blue–grey; back/rump olive–green. **Race taivana:** crown to rump olive–green, with yellow eyebrow and throat, and dark olive–green ear-coverts. **Race tschutschensis:** crown blue–grey; eyebrow whitish; back/rump greyish olive; ear-coverts dark grey–brown; throat white; some have speckled brownish 'necklace'. **Other races** (e.g. Asian *lutea*) have yellow heads and could be confused with Citrine Wagtails, *but most have a darkish mark from bill through eye to ear-coverts.* **Nonbreeding adults** have greyish brown upperparts and simple white or yellowish eyebrows *over well-defined dark ear-coverts and buff–white underparts;* some have traces of a spotted brownish necklace and breastband, or yellow patches. *Their dark grey wing-coverts and secondaries have white or yellowish margins in a netted pattern.* **Immature:** browner than nonbreeding, with bolder spotted necklace and breastband; *whitish under tail-coverts.* Before departure from Aust. in March–April, traces of yellow breeding plumage appear on head and underparts, with green wash on upperparts. In Aust., singles, to mixed-race flocks of 50+. Shy, active; walks with back-and-forward head-movement, bobs tail, leaps for insects; perches on shrubs and trees. Flight strongly undulating, *with no obvious wingbar or pale rump.* **Similar species:** Grey Wagtail (all plumages): yellowish rump and under tail-coverts contrast with grey upperparts; legs pink–brown; *tail very long.* Citrine Wagtail, nonbreeding adult: upperparts blue–grey, with two broad white wingbars; *yellow sides of face and neck surround 'hollow' brownish ear-coverts.* Imm. Citrine: like imm. Yellow; dull white to buff sides of face, brownish ear-coverts; bolder white wingbars; speckled brown breastband. **Voice:** high-pitched 'sweet' or 'tzeep', on each undulation in flight. **Habitat:** short grass and bare ground; swamp-margins, sewage ponds, saltmarshes, playing fields, airfields, ploughed land, town lawns. **Range and Status:** breeds from Europe to Siberia and w. Alaska, migrating to Africa, s. and se. Asia, Indonesia and PNG. Regular summer migrant to mostly coastal Aust. especially Darwin (NT) to Broome (WA), but also ne. Q, usually in Nov.–April. Most abundant visitor is probably race *simillima* of e. Siberia and Kamchatka, but *taivana* of e. Asia to n. Japan and *tschutschensis* of far e. Siberia and far w. Alaska (and probably other races) occur.

GREY WAGTAIL *Motacilla cinerea* 18–19 cm

Very long tailed wagtail; grey above with a contrasting greenish yellow rump and rich yellow under tail-coverts; legs always flesh pink to pale brown. **Male, breeding:** grey crown separated from dark grey face by white eyebrow; bold white 'whisker' separates face from large black throat-patch; underparts yellow; flight-feathers black with long white streaks forming conspicuous narrow white wingbar in flight.* **Male, nonbreeding (and female all year):** duller; throat white; breast washed yellow. **Immature:** similar: eyebrow indistinct; upperparts grey–brown; breast whitish or buffish; rump and under tail-coverts buff–yellow. Singles or pairs locally: usually in or near shallow water, walking busily with see-saw tail movements; *long tail makes flight even more dipping and undulating than other wagtails.* **Similar species:** Yellow and Citrine Wagtails. **Voice:** clear, metallic 'chitik'; 'tzit-zee' or 'tchit', repeated. **Habitat:** in Aust. near running water in disused quarries; sandy, rocky streams in escarpments and rainforests; sewage ponds, ploughed fields, airfields. **Range and Status:** breeds from w. Europe to Asia: migrates to Africa, Malaysia, Indonesia and PNG, (where it is 'the usual wagtail'). Nonbreeding summer visitor mostly to n. Aust., Nov.–April.

*Note: Despite their name, the Wagtails, family Motacillidae, are related to Pipits, and are wholly unrelated to the Willie Wagtail, a fantail flycatcher. Eurasian and African in distribution, with many differing races, they mostly reach n. Aust. during our summer as nonbreeding migrants from Asia.

YELLOW WAGTAIL

♀ and
nonbreeding ♂

race *simillina*
♂ breeding

imm.

♂ race *taivana*

♂ race
tschutschensis

♂ race *lutea*

♀ and
nonbreeding ♂

♂ breeding

imm.

GREY WAGTAIL

CITRINE WAGTAIL *Motacilla citreola* 16–18 cm

Other names: Yellow-headed or Yellow-hooded Wagtail.

Male, breeding: distinctive, *yellow head and breast, black rear collar and blue–grey or blackish back and rump; black wings, with two broad white wingbars.* Legs black. **Male, nonbreeding (and female all year):** *crown to rump grey, with broad white wingbars;* face yellowish or buff–white, surrounding *hollow brownish mark on ear-coverts;* throat/breast yellow, sides of breast often suffused grey; *under tail-coverts white.* **Immature:** browner, with buff–white eyebrow and underparts; faint brown 'necklace'; *under tail-coverts white.* Shy; walks like typical wagtail; flirts tail up and down; flight strongly undulating, *showing strong white double wingbar on grey/black wings; white edges to black tail.* **Similar species:** Grey Wagtail. Yellow Wagtail: usually has darkish area from bill to eye; eyebrow simpler and shorter; ear-coverts bolder; upperparts greener; wing-coverts edged white or yellow. Imm. Yellow: nearly indistinguishable, but usually has simpler, shorter eyebrow, bolder ear-coverts, finer whitish edges to wing-coverts and more distinct brownish 'necklace' and breastband; *under tail-coverts often yellowish.* **Voice:** harsh, sharp 'tzreep', or 'dzeep', like Richard's Pipit. Also a high 'tseew' or a soft 'chit chit'. **Habitat:** saltmarshes; shallow muddy wetlands. **Range and Status:** breeds from w. Russia and Turkey to Siberia: migrates to India, China, Burma; vagrant Thailand. Vagrant coastal mainland Aust., summer *and* winter.

WHITE WAGTAIL *Motacilla alba* 18–20 cm

Several races of this widespread Eurasian wagtail reach Aust. as vagrants. Only males in breeding plumage are identifiable as to races. **Race *ocularis*:** *forehead/face/underparts white; crown/nape/line from bill through eye, throat and 'bib', black; back/scapulars grey; rump darker; large white patch on shoulder; flight-feathers/tail black with white edges; legs black.* **Race *leucopsis*:** *no black eyeline; throat white above black bib; back black.* **Race *baicalensis*:** *black eyeline faint or absent; back grey; much less white in wing; wing-coverts/flight feathers black with strong white margins in netted pattern.* **Female and nonbreeding male, all races:** *upperparts greyer; less white in wing; blackish wing-coverts have white edges in netted pattern; thin U-shaped black breastband; flanks grey.* **Immature:** duller; upperparts mottled brownish; face and throat washed yellowish; wing-coverts greyish black, tipped white. Smutty patch on breast or deep U-shaped black band. Walks with head bobbing back and forward, tail jerking. Flight strongly undulating, showing blackish wings with double white wingbar, grey rump, white-edged black tail. **Similar species:** Black-backed Wagtail. White-winged Triller, male. **Voice:** harsh, distinctive 'tzchissick'. **Habitat:** stubblefields, freshwater wetlands, sewage ponds, wharves, lawns, house roofs and gutters. **Range and Status:** breeds from Britain to e. Asia, Japan, Alaska, Greenland. Migrates to Africa, s. and se. Asia, Borneo, Philippines. Scarce autumn–winter visitor to coastal Aust.

BLACK-BACKED WAGTAIL *Motacilla lugens* 16–18 cm

Male breeding: very like black-backed White Wagtail race *leucopsis*, but has *black scapulars, black line from bill through eye to nape and black throat joining large black bib;* underparts and flanks white. **Female, nonbreeding:** back greyer; black on breast reduced to deep U-shaped breastband; white wingpatch smaller than male. **Immature:** resembles imm. White Wagtail. Behaves like White Wagtail. *In flight, wing largely white, with black shoulders and outer wingtips, contrasting black back and white-edged black tail.* **Voice:** like White Wagtail. **Habitat:** as above. **Range and Status:** breeds far e. Siberia: migrates through Aleutians to Alaska and s. to Japan. Vagrant Aust.: Fraser I. (Q), May–Sept. 1987; Derby (WA), Dec. 1995–Jan./Feb. 1996.

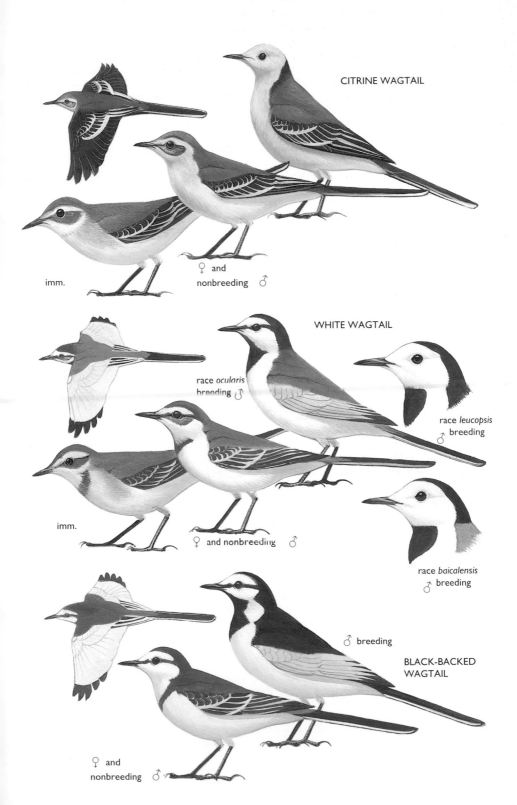

CITRINE WAGTAIL

imm.

♀ and
nonbreeding ♂

WHITE WAGTAIL

race *ocularis*
breeding ♂

race *leucopsis*
♂ breeding

imm.

♀ and nonbreeding ♂

race *baicalensis*
♂ breeding

♂ breeding

BLACK-BACKED
WAGTAIL

♀ and
nonbreeding ♂

DOUBLE-BARRED FINCH *Taeniopygia bichenovii* 10–11 cm

Other names: Banded or Black-ringed Finch.
Face/underparts white, two thin black bars across lower throat and breast; rump white; tail black. Race annulosa: *rump black.* **Immature:** duller; plain fawn below, bars indistinct. Pairs, flocks: forages in seeding grasses. Retreats in bouncing flight to cover. **Similar species:** Banded Whiteface, White-fronted Chat. **Voice:** high-pitched, 'tiaat, tiaat'. **Habitat:** vegetation on watercourses; near water in grassy scrublands/woodlands; farmland, crops, canefields, roadsides, golfcourses, plantations, parks, gardens. **Breeds:** July–Dec. in se. Aust.; Feb.–May in n. **Nest:** scruffy bottle-shaped, of dry grass; lined with plant-down, feathers; 1–5 m in pandanus, tall grass, shrub; stump, fence-post; old nest of finch, babbler; near active wasp nest; under verandahs, in gardens. **Eggs:** 4–5 (6); white, oval. **Range and Status:** n. and e. Aust., coastal islands. Race *annulosa*: from Kimberley (WA) e. through Top End (NT) to Groote Eylandt, s. to Pine Ck. Nominate race: s. and e. from *c.* Katherine (NT), along Gulf to n. and e. Q, s. to Sydney area–Blue Mts (NSW), s. coastally to *c.* Bermagui. Inland to Mt Isa–Longreach–Hebel (Q); Walgett–Cobar–Mt Hope (NSW); s. to s. NSW tablelands–Albury; ACT; casual far e., ne. Vic. Common. Nomadic.

MASKED FINCH *Poephila personata* 12.5–13.5 cm. Male larger.

Bill heavy, yellow–orange; face/chin black; crown red–brown; upperparts cinnamon brown; breast paler; underparts/rump white with heavy black flank-mark, long pointed black tail. **Immature:** duller, no black mask; bill blackish. **Race leucotis,** 'White-eared Finch': *redder brown; face, ear-coverts white.* Parties, flocks of 20–30; breeding colonies; companies gather to drink, bathe, preen at waterholes. Feeds much on ground. **Similar species:** Long-tailed, Black-throated Finches. **Voice:** low 'twaat, twaat'; somewhat like Zebra Finch; groups chatter. **Habitat:** near water in grasslands with shrubs, scattered timber; paperbarks. **Breeds:** Feb.–June. **Nest:** globular; of broad grasses, seed-heads; lined with plant-down, fur, feathers, paper, charcoal; in bushes, low trees, ground near stump, log; old nest-hole of kingfisher in termite mound. **Eggs:** 4–5 (6); white, oval. **Range and Status:** nominate race: from Broome (WA), through Kimberley; Top End (NT) s. to Victoria R. Downs–Newcastle Waters–Brunette Downs; Gulf lowlands s. to *c.* Camooweal (Q). Race *leucotis*: s. C. York Pen. (Q) from *c.* lower Leichhardt R., n. to Watson R., Princess Charlotte Bay; s. to *c.* Georgetown-Chillagoe. Fairly common. Sedentary.

LONG-TAILED FINCH *Poephila acuticauda* 15–16.5 cm

Other name: Blackheart.
Bill yellow in n. WA, orange–red in NT/Q; head grey, earpatch white, large black throat-patch. Rump/underparts white, with black flank-mark and bar across rump; long, black pointed tail. **Immature:** bill blackish; short tail more pointed than Black-throated Finch; legs black. Pairs, to flocks in which pairs persist. Forages on ground and in grasses, takes flying insects. **Similar species:** Black-throated, Masked Finches. **Voice:** mournful, descending 'peew'. Alarm-call: staccato, 'cheek-chee-chee-cheek'. **Habitat:** grassy woodlands near water; coastal plains with pandanus. **Breeds:** Feb.-June. **Nest:** domed, with entrance-spout, of dry grass, creepers; lined with fine grass, plant-down, feathers, charcoal; 15–20 m high in foliage, mistletoe, pandanus; or low in grass, incl. spinifex. **Eggs:** 5–6; white, oval. **Range and Status:** coastal n. Aust.: from Broome (WA), through Kimberley, Top End (NT), s. to *c.* Elliott; e. into nw. Q, to *c.* Burketown-Leichhardt R., s. to Mt Isa region. Common. Sedentary.

BLACK-THROATED FINCH *Poephila cincta* 10 cm

Other names: Black-rumped, Black-tailed or Parson Finch.
Note black bill, short black tail; reddish legs. Nominate race has white rump; race *atropygialis,* 'Black-tailed Finch', has *black rump.* **Immature:** paler; legs black. Habits like Long-tailed Finch. **Voice:** like Long-tailed; deeper. **Habitat:** grassy scrublands/woodlands/dune woodlands/pandanus near water. **Breeds:** Sept.–Jan. in s.; Feb.–June in n. **Nest:** like Long-tailed; or in hollow limb, tree-termite mound. **Eggs:** 4–5 (6); white, oval. **Range and Status:** ne. Aust. Race *nigrotecta*: n. C. York Pen., (Q). Race *atropygialis*: s. C. York Pen. Nominate race: w. to Doomadgee, s. to *c.* Cloncurry–Winton–Clermont, e. to *c.* Townsville–upper Burdekin R. Sparse population in New England region (ne. NSW). Sedentary; locally nomadic. Vulnerable.

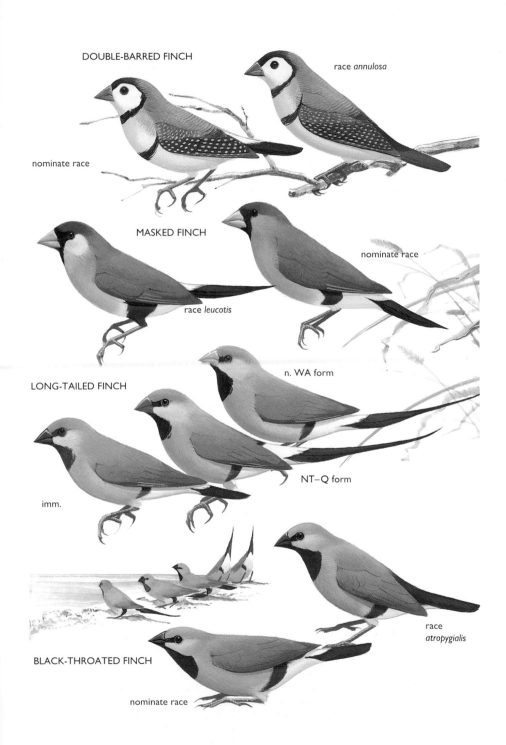

DOUBLE-BARRED FINCH

race *annulosa*

nominate race

MASKED FINCH

nominate race

race *leucotis*

LONG-TAILED FINCH

n. WA form

NT–Q form

imm.

BLACK-THROATED FINCH

race *atropygialis*

nominate race

RED-BROWED FINCH *Neochmia temporalis* 11–11.5 cm

Scarlet bill, eyebrow and rump; upperparts olive–green; tail black. **Immature:** bill black; lacks eyebrow. Pairs, family parties, autumn–winter flocks in grass, lawns; darts to cover in bouncing flight. **Similar species:** imm. Beautiful, Red-eared Firetails. **Voice:** high-pitched squeak; sharp 'dup'; brisk chatter. **Habitat:** grassy clearings in forests, woodlands, coastal scrubs/heaths; mangroves, canefields, crops, roadsides, blackberries, lantana, golfcourses, orchards, parks, gardens. **Breeds:** Sept.–Jan. in se.; Dec.–April in ne. **Nest:** bottle-shaped, untidy; of grass; lined with plant-down, feathers, fur; 1–10 m high in prickly bush, citrus, cypress pine, leafy tree, palm. **Eggs:** 4–6; white. **Range and Status:** widespread coastal e. and se. Aust.: from C. York (Q) to Mt Lofty Ras.–Kangaroo I. (SA); inland to western slopes, Murray R. tributaries; all Vic. except nw.; n. to Barossa Valley, (SA). Common. Sedentary; locally nomadic. In s. WA, established in Darling Ra., from aviary escapes *c.* 1960.

STAR FINCH *Neochmia ruficauda* 10–12 cm

Nominate race, male: *small, white-spotted, pale olive–brown finch with red bill/scarlet forehead/face/throat;* underparts whitish; *dull purplish red tail;* legs yellowish. **Female:** duller; less red on 'face'. **Immature:** bill black; crown/cheeks/breast greyish olive–brown. Race *clarescens:* brighter red face; upperparts pale olive–green; underparts yellow. Pairs to flocks: forages in grasses; takes flying insects; flight undulating; large flocks swift, with rapid turns. **Voice:** loud 'ssit' or 'sseet'. Contact-call, 'tlit'. **Habitat:** near water; grassy flats with bushes, low trees; reeds, rushes; irrigated crops, sugar cane. **Breeds:** Dec.–May. **Nest:** domed, of grass; lined with feathers; 1–6 m in tall grass, shrubby tree. **Eggs:** 3–5 (6); white. **Range and Status:** nominate race: once widespread from s. C. York Pen., (Q) to inland ne. NSW; decimated by earlier trapping, destruction of waterside vegetation etc. Sparse and rare. Endangered (Garnett, 1993). Race *clarescens:* patchily from *c.* Shark Bay–Ashburton R. (WA), to Top End (NT), s. to Katherine; e. on Gulf coast to s. C. York Pen. n. to Staaten R., possibly further.

CRIMSON FINCH *Neochmia phaeton* 12.5–14 cm

Male: bill/*face/breast/flanks crimson; back/wings/tail earth-brown, washed crimson;* white spots on flanks; underparts black. **Female:** breast/underparts grey–brown; white spots on flanks. **Immature:** bill blackish. Race *evangelinae,* 'White-bellied Crimson Finch': male has white abdomen/under tail-coverts. Both sexes: base of bill pale blue. Pairs, parties, flocks: longish tail flicked up/down, sideways. Forages on ground, long grass; *flies up to trees, scarlet rump/tail conspicuous.* Adapts to settlement. **Similar species:** Painted Finch. **Voice:** brisk 'che-che-che'; sharp 'chip'. Flocks make brittle tinkling. **Habitat:** near water: canegrass, pandanus; paperbarks, crops, tall rank growth, roadsides, gardens. **Breeds:** Oct.–April. **Nest:** domed, bulky, of strips, blades of grass, paperbark, leaves; lined with plant-down, feathers; 2–16 m in grass, pandanus, paperbark, hollow limb; pineapples, bananas; house eaves, sheds, verandahs. **Eggs:** 5–6 (8); small, white. **Range and Status:** nominate race: from Broome (WA), through Kimberley, Top End (NT), s. to *c.* Mataranka, e. along Gulf coast to Leichhardt R. (nw. Q); inland to 300 km on streams. Race *evangelinae:* w. coast C. York Pen. (Q). Race *iredalei:* e. coastal Q, s. to *c.* Mackay, inland to *c.* Georgetown. Common. Sedentary. Also s. PNG.

ZEBRA FINCH *Taeniopygia guttata* 10 cm

Male: grey, bill red; *orange–tan cheekpatch/flanks, latter spotted white; rump white; tail black, barred white.* **Female:** bill red; black/white face/tail-markings; otherwise greyish. **Immature:** like female; bill black. Pairs, large flocks at water: forages on ground; takes flying insects. Flight undulating; *rump/tail prominent.* **Similar species:** Southern Whiteface. **Voice:** loud 'tya', like toy trumpet. **Habitat:** near water, in mulga, spinifex, gibber; grasslands, open woodlands/shrublands/scrubs, saltbush, crops, orchards, gardens. **Breeds:** most months. **Nest:** untidy, domed, of grass, twigs, rootlets; lined with feathers, plant-down, fur; 2–4 m high, in shrub, tree, hollow branch, fence-post, termite-mound, tussock; old nest of babbler, Fairy Martin. **Eggs:** 4–5 (6); pale blue. **Range and Status:** mainland Aust., islands. Except in drought, mostly *absent* from wetter/coastal districts of se., sw. Aust.; sparse n. Kimberley (WA); Top End (NT); C. York Pen. (Q). Common. Sedentary; nomadic. Also e. Indonesia.

RED-BROWED FINCH

imm.

race
clarescens

STAR FINCH

imm.

CRIMSON FINCH

♂

♂ race *evangelinae*

♀

ZEBRA FINCH

imm.

♀

BEAUTIFUL FIRETAIL *Stagonopleura bella* 11.5–13 cm

Sturdy dark finch with red bill, black mask, blue eye-ring, glossy scarlet rump; underparts finely barred black/white; under tail-coverts black. **Male:** abdomen black. **Immature:** duller, bill blackish. Pairs, family parties, small autumn–winter flocks: forages near cover. Hops through grass like plump dark mouse; flies to cover with burr of wings, scarlet rump conspicuous. Feeds in seeding saw-sedges; she oaks, hazel pomaderris, etc. **Similar species:** Red-browed Finch. **Voice:** mournful, drawn-out 'pee-ee-ee', dipping in middle; three high notes end in staccato downward run. **Habitat:** dense, damp vegetation: coastal heaths; paperbarks; eucalypt forests/woodlands with dense undergrowth; she oaks, near creeks. **Breeds:** Sept.–Jan. **Nest:** bulky, bottle-shaped; of green grass, stems of creepers; lined with plant-down, feathers; 1–6 m in dense shrub, tree. **Eggs:** 4–5 (6); white, oval. **Range and Status:** from Hunter Valley (NSW) to Mt Lofty Ras.–Adelaide Plains–Kangaroo I. (SA). Inland to Blue Mts–Braidwood–ACT; in Vic., coastal in suitable habitat, inland on lower slopes of Divide, e.g. Yellingbo–L. Eildon–Mt Beauty; Bass Strait islands (not King I.); in Tas., coast to mountains (1000 m) *except* drier e. woodlands (Green, 1993). Rare to locally common. Sedentary; local seasonal nomad.

RED-EARED FIRETAIL *Stagonopleura oculata* 11–13 cm

Note range: Ear-coverts deep scarlet in male, orange–scarlet in female; underparts black, spotted white in dense pattern. **Immature:** bill blackish; lacks red ear-coverts. Singles, pairs, family parties: secretive; forages in grass, sedges, low shrubs; on ground, hops. Flight low, slow, without undulation; showing scarlet rump. **Similar species:** Red-browed Finch. **Voice:** mournful, directionless 'wee-ee' or 'oo-wee'. **Habitat:** forest undergrowth; vegetation on creeks; gullies with she oaks, saw-sedge; coastal scrubs, heaths, paperbarks. **Breeds:** Sept.–Jan. **Nest:** bulky, bottle-shaped, of green grass blades, plant-stems, tips; lined with fine grass, plant-down, feathers; in shrub, sapling, leafy branch up to 16 m. **Eggs:** 4–5 (6); white, oval. **Range and Status:** sw. WA: from Darling Ras., near Perth, s. to Manjimup–Pemberton, e. coastally to Cape Arid NP, inland to Stirling Ras. NP. Uncommon. Sedentary.

PAINTED FINCH *Emblema pictum* 10.5–11.5 cm

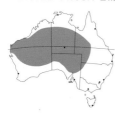

Male: bill *fine-pointed, black and-crimson, blue at base; eye white; face/throat/belly/rump glossy scarlet; underparts black, heavily spotted white.* **Female:** less red; larger white spots. **Immature:** duller; bill blackish; less red, none on rump. Pairs, flocks to 30+ among rocks, spinifex; perches boulders, bare branches. Flushes with chatter; flight fast, rumps glowing. **Similar species:** Crimson Finch, Crimson Chat. **Voice:** scratchy, staccato 'chek chek'; rapid 'chek-did-did-dit', reedy 'ched up, cheddy up'. **Habitat:** spinifex in rocky hills over permanent water, plains; acacia scrubs; citrus orchards. **Breeds:** any month, after rain. **Nest:** globular, poorly constructed with verandah; of spinifex, twigs, bark, rootlets, soft grass; lined with plant-down, feathers; on platform of bark, roots; in spinifex or on ground. **Eggs:** 3–4; white, rounded. **Range and Status:** patchy through arid inland and w. coastal Aust.: e. to Winton–Opalton (Q); n. to Mt Isa–Nicholson R.–Alexandria–Wave Hill (NT); w. to s. Kimberley–Pilbara (WA), to w. coast *c.* Eighty Mile Beach–Carnarvon; s. inland to upper Murchison R.–Menzies; in SA, s. to *c.* Oodnadatta–n. Flinders Ras.–L. Frome. Often casual beyond 'normal' range; nomadic.

DIAMOND FIRETAIL *Stagonopleura guttata* 12–13 cm

Note crimson bill, bold black band across white breast joining boldly white-spotted black flanks; scarlet rump, black tail. **Female:** breastband narrower. **Immature:** bill black; breastband absent/shadowy. Pairs to autumn–winter flocks: feeds among native grasses with bouncing hops; flies to high branches, scarlet rump prominent. **Voice:** penetrating, rising 'p-a-i-r-r'; soft chatters. **Habitat:** open eucalypt forests/woodlands; river red gums; mallee, buloke; cypress pine, acacia scrubs; golfcourses. **Breeds:** Aug.–Jan. **Nest:** bulky, bottle-shaped; of grasses; lined with grass, feathers, plant-down; 2–3 m in eucalypt, citrus, or mistletoe clump; shed roof. **Eggs:** 4–6; white, oval. **Range and Status:** se. mainland Aust., extends patchily to coast from *c.* Rockhampton (Q) to s. Eyre Pen.–Kangaroo I. (SA); inland to *c.* Longreach–Cunnamulla (Q); Bourke–Euston (NSW), casual Mootwingee; river red gums woodlands on R. Murray downstream into se. SA, n. to s. Flinders Ras. Uncommon. Sedentary; local migrant.

BEAUTIFUL FIRETAIL

imm.

RED-EARED FIRETAIL

imm.

PAINTED FINCH

♀

♂

DIAMOND FIRETAIL

imm.

YELLOW-RUMPED MANNIKIN *Lonchura flaviprymna* 11–12 cm

Robust silver bill; fawn–white head; deep chestnut upperparts; yellow–chestnut rump/tail; throat/underparts washed yellow–buff; under tail-coverts black. **Immature:** like imm. Chestnut-breasted. Pairs to flocks of *c.* 5–100 (Garnett, 1993): feeds, roosts and, in parts, interbreeds with Chestnut-breasted, producing intermediates. **Voice:** like Chestnut-breasted; deeper, more bell-like. **Habitat:** tall seeding grasses near water; grassy flats with shrubs/trees; mangroves; rice, sorghum; roosts in reedbeds. In 'wet', drier, more inland grasslands, open woodlands. **Breeds:** Jan.–March. **Nest:** like Chestnut-breasted. **Eggs:** 4–5; white, oval. **Range and Status:** from Ord R. (e. Kimberley, WA) and coastal w. NT, n. to King R. in Arnhem Land, inland to Victoria R. Downs, e. to upper Roper R. Generally scarce; locally abundant, e.g. irrigated areas on Ord R. Locally nomadic: coastwards in dry season, inland in 'wet'.

CHESTNUT-BREASTED MANNIKIN *Lonchura castaneothorax* 11.5–12.5 cm

Robust silver bill/black face; upperbreast chestnut, separated from white underparts by black band; flanks barred black; under tail-coverts black; rump/tail yellow–chestnut. **Female:** paler, duller. **Immature:** bill darker; underparts plain brownish buff; tail ashy-brown. Pairs, flocks, imms predominating. Feeds on tall seeding grass, rice, sorghum, millet; roosts in reeds, ricefields; takes flying insects. Normal flight undulating, but large flocks fly fast with swift turns. Forages, roosts, interbreeds with Yellow-rumped Mannikin. **Voice:** bell-like tinkling. **Habitat:** grasslands near water; swamp-vegetation, coastal heaths, mangroves, wastelands, roadsides, lantana thickets, canefields, ricefields, sorghum, millet. **Breeds:** Nov.–April; any month. **Nest:** small, globular; of green/dry grass; lined with grass, plant-down; low in long grass, reeds, crop, shrub, bamboo. **Eggs:** 5–6; white, oval. **Range and Status:** from Kimberley (WA), Top End (NT), e. on Gulf coast to C. York Pen. (Q), s. on e. coast to Shoalhaven R. (NSW); inland to Richmond–Carnarvon Ras. NP (Q); Glen Innes–Gloucester (NSW). Sedentary, seasonally nomadic. Feral colonies from aviary escapes reported elsewhere. Also PNG. Introduced New Cal., Tahiti.

PICTORELLA MANNIKIN *Heteromunia pectoralis* 11–11.5 cm

Male: *robust, silver–grey bill; face/throat black, separated by broad band of white scallops from pinkish fawn underparts; tail black; legs pink.* **Female:** face brownish; *breast-scallops black/white.* **Immature:** bill black; *face grey; underparts whitish fawn; legs dull pink.* Pairs, parties; flocks in nonbreeding season. Feeds in tall grasses; takes flying insects; mixes with other mannikins. **Similar species:** other imm. mannikins have black legs. **Voice:** single 'pik'; flocks make continual 'chip's. **Habitat:** tall grass in woodlands near water; grassy flats, sparse, trees/shrubs; also spinifex, crops. **Breeds:** Jan.–April. **Nest:** untidy, bottle-shaped; of grass, rootlets; lined with feathers; low in bush, grass, spinifex. **Eggs:** 4–6; white. **Range and Status:** from Fitzroy R. (WA), through Kimberley to NT, s. to *c.* Wave Hill. Gulf lowlands (Q) e. and n. to Edward R., w. C. York Pen., e. to *c.* Georgetown–Charters Towers, s. to *c.* Mt Isa–Richmond. Moves coastwards in dry season, inland in 'wet'. Locally common.

NUTMEG MANNIKIN *Lonchura punctulata* 10.5–11.5 cm

Face/throat dark brown; underparts whitish, with fine scaly cinnamon–brown pattern. **Immature:** pale brown above, plain brownish yellow below; *tail yellow–grey.* Pairs, flocks: forages in grasses, weeds, climbs stems; flicks wings, swings tail; perches fences, overhead wires. Flocks fly fast with simultaneous turns; drop. **Similar species:** imm. Chestnut-breasted paler below. **Voice:** sharp 'kit-tee'. **Habitat:** grasslands, crops, rank roadside growth, urban wastelands, lantana thickets, vineyards. **Breeds:** spring–summer, se. Aust., all months ne. Q. **Nest:** bottle of coarse green grass, leaves, bark; lined with grass, seed-heads; 1–10 m in shrub, tree, often in colony; sheds, buildings. **Eggs:** 4–7; white. **Range and Status:** native from India to s. China, Malaysia, Philippines to e. Indonesia. Introduced from aviary escapes near Brisbane, Townsville, Rockhampton (Q), Sydney (NSW), from *c.* 1930. Widespread from *c.* Cooktown (Q) to Moruya (NSW), mostly coastal, but inland to Miles (Q), Mudgee (NSW). Also Canberra, Melbourne, Adelaide, from local escapes. Common; expanding.

YELLOW-RUMPED
MANNIKIN

imm.

CHESTNUT-
BREASTED
MANNIKIN

imm.

PICTORELLA
MANNIKIN

imm.

imm.

NUTMEG MANNIKIN

GOULDIAN FINCH *Erythrura gouldiae* 13–14 cm

Polymorphic throughout range — most are black-headed, but about a quarter are red-headed; a few have golden heads. **Black-headed**, male: bill whitish, tipped pink; *head black, finely margined pale blue; breast purple; underparts yellow/white; rump sky-blue; tail black, ending in two long fine points.* Female: duller, breast paler. Immature: bill blackish above, pale below; head greyish; shading to greenish olive back/wings/tail; underparts pale grey–brown; legs dull pink. **Red-headed**, male: *head dull crimson; chin/throat black.* Female: duller. **Golden-headed**, male: *head rich ochre–yellow; chin black.* Female: duller. Pairs, parties in breeding season; flocks to 30+ (formerly thousands) in nonbreeding season. Sunbathes, active in heat of day; feeds in seeding grasses, on flying insects; disturbed, flies to nearby trees. Gathers in late afternoons to feed, bathe. **Similar species:** Star Finch, Blue-faced Parrot-Finch. **Voice:** quiet, contact-call, sibilant 'si-i-i-it', sharply in alarm. **Habitat:** breeds in savannah woodland on stony hills with eucalypts over dense, tall (2 m) native grasses (Woinarski & Tidemann, 1992); grassy flats, trees near water; vegetation on watercourses; scrublands with spinifex. **Breeds:** Dec.–May, to Aug. **Nest:** globular, poorly made, some without roof; of dry grass lined with soft grass; 6–14 m in hollow in tree or termite mound; low scrub, tall grass; sometimes simply on debris in hollow. Several pairs may use same hollow. **Eggs:** 4–6 (8); white, oval. **Range and Status:** from near Broome (WA), e. through Kimberley, to s. of L. Argyle; e. to Top End (NT), s. to *c.* Victoria R. Downs; sparse along Gulf coast to s. C. York Pen. (Q), e. and s. to *c.* Georgetown. Some sedentary; most are seasonally nomadic, moving coastwards in dry season, returning inland in wet. Population seriously depleted by infection with fatal air-sac mite, *Sternostoma tracheacolum* (Tidemann, 1991). Seasonal burning defoliates trees needed for cover/nest-hollows. Endangered.

BLUE-FACED PARROT-FINCH *Erythrura trichroa* 12–13 cm

Rich grass-green finch with black bill, cobalt-blue forehead/face; tail olive–brown washed dark red. **Female:** duller; less blue on face. **Immature:** dull green, without blue face. Pairs, family parties to flocks of 20–30; elusive. Forages in seeding grasses, bamboos, rainforest trees; flocks fly swiftly through the forest mid-strata (Schodde & Tidemann, 1986). **Habitat:** coastal mangrove fringes to margins of, and grassy clearings in, mountain rainforests over 1000 m. **Breeds:** Nov.–April. **Nest:** oval, with side-entrance; of green moss, dark fibrous material, vine strands; lined with coarse grass; low to 7 m high in sapling or tree in or at edge of rainforest. **Eggs:** 3–6; oval, white. **Range and Status:** imperfectly known. Usually stated as from near Cooktown (Q), to Mt Lewis, near Julatten, and Atherton Tableland, but breeding reported from Iron Range, e. C. York Pen. and near Ingham. (John Young, quoted by Garnett, 1993). Also Micronesia, Solomons, PNG, to e. Indonesia. Seasonal nomad or migrant, to highlands in summer, coastal lowlands in winter. Rare.

PLUM-HEADED FINCH *Neochmia modesta* 10.5–11.5 cm

Other names: Cherry, Plain coloured or Plum-capped Finch.
Most sombre Aust. grass-finch. **Male:** *forehead/chin plum–purple, cheeks white; underparts barred brown/white; upperparts brown with white spots on wings,* whitish barring on rump; tail blackish, tipped white. **Female:** purple forehead *separated from eye by white eyebrow; throat whitish.* **Immature:** brownish above, with some white spots on wings; no head-markings or barring. Pairs, parties, flocks; occasional influxes of thousands, e.g. near Townsville (Q) (Britton, 1992). Forages on ground; climbs grasses; attracted to cultivated millet, maize, sorghum. Flight strong, slightly undulating. Small parties quiet; flocks noisy. **Similar species:** Nutmeg Mannikin. **Voice:** single 'tlip' or 'tleep'. **Habitat:** tall grasslands; reeds, cumbungi fringing rivers/wetlands; lightly timbered grassy river flats; lowland pastoral country to tablelands. **Breeds:** Sept.–Jan. **Nest:** small, rounded, taller than wide; no entrance-spout; of grass plucked green; lined with feathers; in tall grass, low shrub, tree. Living grasses frequently interwoven. **Eggs:** 4–7; white. **Range and Status:** e. Aust.: coastally s. from *c.* Burdekin R. (Q) to Rockhampton; mostly *absent* coastal se. Q–ne. NSW; ranges inland in Q to Julia Ck–Winton–Windorah; in NSW, to Bourke–Weddin Mts NP, casual s. to Murrumbidgee R., e. to Newcastle–Hawkesbury R.–Richmond/Windsor, near Sydney; casual ACT; vagrant w. Vic. Migrates n. in autumn–winter, reaching Atherton Tableland–Georgetown (inland ne. Q); returning in spring. Migratory, locally nomadic, irruptive. Locally common.

imm.

GOULDIAN FINCH

Red-headed ♂

Golden-headed ♂ ♀

♀

BLUE-FACED
PARROT-FINCH

imm.

PLUM-HEADED
FINCH

EUROPEAN GOLDFINCH *Carduelis carduelis* 12–13.5 cm

Sharp, whitish bill; deep-red face, bordered white; crown/nape black; wings black, with broad golden wingbar. **Immature:** plain grey–buff, streaked darker; wings/tail like adult. Pairs, autumn–winter flocks: feeds in thistles; perches fences, telephone wires; switches about, calling. Flight dancing, accompanied by tinkling; *note golden wingbar, whitish rump,* black fish-tail. **Similar species:** European Greenfinch. **Voice:** pretty, tinkling song, 'twiddle-ee-twiddle-ee-dee'; scratchy, canary-like tweet; rasping scolds. **Habitat:** grasslands, weedy wastelands, farmlands, orchards, roadsides, dune-wastes; nests/roosts mostly in introduced trees. **Breeds:** Sept.–Dec. **Nest:** cup of fine twigs, rootlets, grass; lined with plant-down, fur; 1–10 m in leafy shrub, fruit-tree, cypress, pine. **Eggs:** 4–6; blue–white, finely spotted/blotched pale red–brown. **Range and Status:** native from w. Europe, n. Africa to c. Asia; introduced se. Aust., Tas, from 1860s. Widespread but patchy s. from Brisbane–Darling Downs (Q); e. and s. NSW, inland to Moree–Warrumbungle NP–Roto, w. on Murray R. to c. Dareton, Darling R. n. to Menindee; most Vic., Bass Strait islands, Tas. to c. 1200 m; vagrant Macquarie I.: in SA, n. to c. Barrier Highway, w. to Yorke Pen.–s. Eyre Pen.–Kangaroo I. Common. Locally nomadic.

EUROPEAN GREENFINCH *Carduelis chloris* 14–16 cm

Robust dull yellow–green finch. *Bill pale, robust; yellow panels on wing and blackish forked tail.* **Immature:** dull brown, streaked darker; less yellow. Pairs, autumn–winter flocks: forages on ground, beach-dunes; flight bouncing, *revealing yellow wing/tail-panels.* Male sings from treetops and in slow, wavering flights. **Similar species:** European Goldfinch. **Voice:** deep, grasshopper-like 'birrzz'; canary-like trills, twitterings; harsh, 'tsooeet?'. **Habitat:** farmlands, weedy wastelands, coastal dune, swamp-woodlands, roadsides, orchards, parks, golf-courses, gardens; favours introduced trees. **Breeds:** Sept.–Dec. **Nest:** cup of twigs, bound with hair; lined with rootlets, feathers; in pine, cypress. **Eggs:** 4–6; whitish blue, spotted, streaked red–brown, violet. **Range and Status:** native of Europe, n. Africa, Middle East; introduced to se. Aust. from 1860s; self-introduced to Tas. from 1940s. Patchy from Sydney (NSW) to Adelaide plains (SA); inland to c. Orange; casual Roto (NSW). Commonest coastally. Sedentary.

EURASIAN TREE-SPARROW *Passer montanus* 13–15 cm

Bill black, smaller than House Sparrow; *crown/nape pale chestnut; black earmark on whitish cheek;* smaller blackish throat-patch; yellow–brown rump. Sexes alike. **Immature:** paler, markings less distinct. Pairs to winter flocks; often with House Sparrows. Forages on ground or in foliage; takes flying insects. **Voice:** short metallic 'chik', repeated 'chit-tchup' and rapid twitter; flight-call, 'tek, tek'. **Habitat:** suburbs, rural towns, farm buildings/homesteads. **Breeds:** Sept.–Jan. **Nest:** smaller than House Sparrow; in hole in building, tree. **Eggs:** 4–6; smaller, browner, more glossy than House Sparrow. **Range and Status:** native to Eurasia, s. to Philippines, e. Indonesia. Introduced to se. Aust. from 1860s: established in Melbourne and towns from c. Dimboola (w. Vic.) and Hay (NSW) n. to Narromine–Gilgandra; e. to Cowra–ACT–Albury. Status in Sydney–Newcastle uncertain. Locally common. Sedentary.

HOUSE SPARROW *Passer domesticus* 14–16 cm

Male: bill blackish, robust; *crown grey; nape/sides of neck chestnut; cheeks grey-white, unmarked.* Throat/upperbreast *black;* smaller in winter. **Female:** bill horn-coloured; *buff eyebrow;* upperparts brown with paler/darker streaks; *single pale bar across wing-coverts.* **Immature:** like female; gape yellow. Singles, pairs, flocks: bold, perky, forages in grainfields, poultry-yards, parks; raids food-tables. **Similar species:** Tree Sparrow. **Voice:** insistent 'cheep'; tinny rattle. **Habitat:** cities, towns, parks; homesteads/farm buildings; farmlands; dead trees in pastoral, cereal-growing areas; mallee, mulga. **Breeds:** mostly spring–summer. **Nest:** bulky, domed; of dry grass; lined with feathers; in dense shrub/tree, hollow limb; eaves, ceilings, ventilators, cavities in buildings. **Eggs:** 4–6; grey–white, spotted/freckled grey, brown. **Range and Status:** native to nw. Africa, Eurasia. Introduced s. Aust. from 1860s. Widespread in e. Aust. *except* driest deserts, heaviest forests; extending toward Top End settlements (NT); Oodnadatta–Mt Willoughby and w. to Cook (SA); Kangaroo I., other coastal islands; also Torres Strait. Sparrows *anywhere* in WA should be *immediately* reported to fauna authorities.

EUROPEAN
GOLDFINCH

imm.

EUROPEAN
GREENFINCH

imm.

Tree
Sparrow

EURASIAN
TREE-SPARROW

House Sparrow

♂ winter

HOUSE SPARROW

♂ summer

♀

YELLOW-BELLIED SUNBIRD *Nectarinia jugularis* 11–12 cm

Other name: Olive-backed or Yellow-breasted Sunbird.
Male: note *long curved bill; throat/upperbreast burnished blue–black; slight yellow eyebrow and whisker-streak; upperparts olive–green; underparts yellow;* tail black with whitish corners. **Female:** *eyebrow, whole throat/breast lemon-yellow.* **Immature:** like female; young males develop dark 'bib' from centre. Singles, pairs, temporary groups: assertive; flits about blossoms, hovers to feed; takes spiders, dismembering them while hovering at web. Direct flight swift, darting; mixes with smaller honeyeaters. Groups gather in animated display, uttering brisk calls. Tame; nests about houses/tropical gardens. **Voice:** splintered squeaky notes, staccato in display; loud, rising, canary-like 'tweeet'; brisk twittering song. **Habitat:** margins of rainforest; vegetation on watercourses; coastal scrubs, paperbarks, mangroves, lantana thickets, agricultural areas, streets, orchards, gardens. **Breeds:** Oct.–March; most months. **Nest:** beautiful, pendulous, 30–60 cm long; with hooded side-entrance; of bark, grass, leaves, spiders' web, incl. web-debris; lined with plant-down, feathers; suspended from sapling, vine, low branch, sometimes over water; houses, sheds, verandahs, etc. **Eggs:** 1–2 (3); grey–green, mottled brownish, in zone at large end. Parasitised by Gould's Bronze-Cuckoo. **Range and Status:** coastal n. Q and many coastal islands: from C. York s. to near Normanton on w. coast and to *c.* Bundaberg on e. coast. Vagrant Coffs Harbour, Stroud, Hawks Nest (NSW) (Lane, 1994). Common. Sedentary. Also Solomon Is., PNG, to parts of Indonesia, se. Asia, se. China.

MISTLETOEBIRD *Dicaeum hirundinaceum* 9.5–11 cm

Other name: Mistletoe Flowerpecker.
Male: tiny; bill black, sharp; *upperparts glossy blue–black; throat/upperbreast, under tail-coverts scarlet; underparts grey–white with black mark down centre.* **Female:** bill dark grey; upperparts grey; tail black; underparts whitish; *under tail-coverts pale red.* **Immature:** like female; *bill/gape pale orange.* Pairs when breeding, otherwise solitary; difficult to observe because small, quick, often high in foliage. Flight swift, darting on longish, pointed wings. Seems to develop regular local circuits linking clumps of fruiting mistletoes. Posture upright when perched; restlessly switches this way and that, depositing excreted, sticky mistletoe seeds on branch. Also eats nectar, pollen, insects, berries/fruit of native/introduced plants. **Similar species:** behaviour separates male from other red-breasted Aust. birds. **Voice:** has glancing, splintered quality. Flight-call: sharp 'dzee!'; clear brisk 'pretty-sweet'!; or 'tsew!'; clear penetrating 'kinsey-kinsey-kinsey'; 'wait-a-bit', 'wait-a-bit, zhipp!'; or 'swizit, swizit, weet-weet-swizit'. Quiet, warbling sub-song includes mimicry. **Habitat:** any vegetation that supports mistletoes. **Breeds:** Oct.–March. **Nest:** beautiful pear-shaped purse with slit-like upper side-entrance; of plant-down, spiders' web, egg-sacs, web-debris, lichen or faded wattle-blossom; hung from leafy twig, 1–15 m high. **Eggs:** 3 (4); white. **Range and Status:** mainland Aust., many coastal islands. Absent from driest, treeless deserts, agricultural areas without native trees; rare above 1000 m in Snowy Mts (Blakers et al, 1984). Also islands in Torres Strait, e. Indonesia. Common. Nomadic.

YELLOW-BELLIED
SUNBIRD

♀

♂

MISTLETOEBIRD

♀

♂

WELCOME SWALLOW *Hirundo neoxena* 15 cm

Other names: Australian or House Swallow.

Our familiar house swallow: *forehead/face/throat dull tan; upperparts glossy blue–black; underparts mid-grey; tail deeply forked, with lacelike white spots on inner tail-feathers.* **Immature:** duller, tail shorter. Singles, pairs, large autumn–winter companies: mixes with Tree, Fairy Martins; and with Barn and other swallows in n. Aust. Flight swift, slipping, low and high, wing-linings grey; hawks insects over water; many perch together on overhead wires, esp. in autumn. Courting males descend on stiffly downheld, quivering wings. **Similar species:** Barn Swallow. Tree and Fairy Martins have shorter tails, white rumps. **Voice:** single 'chep', usually in flight; spirited twittering song; rising 'seep, seep, seep'; in alarm, high-pitched, puny 'seeet'. **Habitat:** open woodlands, grasslands, coasts, rivers, wetlands, urban areas. Roosts or nests in cavernous dead trees, overhung banks, cavities in cliffs, rock-shelves. Nowadays often uses built structures: wharfs, bridges; cranes, boats, factories, house eaves, verandahs, garages, deserted buildings. **Breeds:** Aug.–Dec. **Nest:** open cup of mud-pellets bound with grass; deeply lined with feathers, fur, hair, grass. **Eggs:** 2–5; whitish; streaked, spotted red–brown, lavender. **Range and Status:** mainland Aust. and Tas. *Scarce* in arid zone, driest deserts, n. NT, Kimberley region (WA). Many birds from Tas. and se. Aust. migrate n. in autumn–winter to e. and ne. Q, Torres Strait islands. Self-introduced to NZ from 1920s. Common. Sedentary; part-migratory.

PACIFIC SWALLOW *Hirundo tahitica* 13–14 cm; (not illustrated).

In 1995 small numbers of Pacific Swallows were recognised in the Mossman–Daintree region, ne. Q (Lloyd Nielsen, pers. comm.). Very similar to Welcome Swallow: *bill deeper, tail shorter — outer tail-feathers about equal length of wingtips.* Inner tail-feathers *have white spot near tip and white edge to inner web.* When wind ruffles feathers of neck/body, under-down shows white, not dull grey as in Welcome Swallow. **Range:** widespread from s. India and se. Asia to Melanesia; the common resident swallow in Indonesia–PNG. Also reported Weipa (Q).

BARN SWALLOW *Hirundo rustica* 16–17 cm

Other names: Common or European Swallow.

Widespread house swallow of n. hemisphere: resembles Welcome Swallow, but markings more contrasting: *face/throat dark chestnut, separated from pure white underparts by black breastband;* wing-linings white; tail-streamers longer. **Immature:** paler, variable; upperparts dull black with browner feather margins; chestnut areas paler, or dirty, mottled white; underparts whitish, without breastband or patchy band; tail-streamers shorter. Occurs in Aust. mostly in migratory companies, including many imms. In s. Aust., vagrant with Welcome Swallows, whose habits/habitat it shares. **Voice:** high-pitched 'tswit', becoming rapid twitter. Alarm call: high 'tswee'. Song pleasant, weak mixture of rapid twitterings, warblings (European data). **Habitat:** open country; agricultural land, especially near water; railyards, towns, overhead wires. **Range and Status:** widespread in n. hemisphere, 'winters' in s. hemisphere. East Asian race *gutturalis* regular summer migrant to Philippines, Indonesia, PNG and n. Aust., mostly Sept.–March. Now seen nearly annually from Kimberley (WA) to ne. and se. Q; vagrant e. NSW, c. SA, n. Vic.

RED-RUMPED SWALLOW *Hirundo daurica* 16–18.5 cm.

Large Eurasian swallow that migrates to Borneo and parts of Indonesia, occasionally reaching n. Aust. *Note size; rusty rear eyebrow/collar, rusty or chestnut rump; underparts whitish, washed buff, rusty or uniform chestnut, with or without dark streaks. No white spots in tail; wing linings buff; under tail-coverts black.* **Immature:** buffer, plainer below. Flight slower, heavier and more soaring than other swallows; *note broad wings and rather thick tail-streamers.* Mixes with other swallows. **Voice:** harsher than Barn Swallow; flight-call, nasal 'tweit', like Tree Sparrow; warbling twitter (European data). **Habitat:** open country, overhead wires, swamps, grasslands, coasts. **Range:** breeds Eurasia, migrating to Africa, India, se. Asia; uncommon summer migrant to n. Sumatra, Borneo, PNG. First recorded Aust. Feb. 1983, when J. Squire saw *c.* 9 with Tree Martins on overhead wires and hawking over roadside swampy area between Mossman and Daintree R. (ne. Q). Subsequent sight-records: in Gulf of Carpentaria, Dec. 1990; Garradunga (Q), Jan. 1991; Yungaburra (Q), Broome (WA), Jan. 1992; Mossman region, Jan. 1996 etc.

WELCOME SWALLOW

imm.

BARN SWALLOW

imm.

RED-RUMPED WALLOW

imm.

503

WHITE-BACKED SWALLOW *Cheramoeca leucosternus* 14–15 cm

Unmistakable black-and-white swallow of drier habitats across mainland Aust. Usually in small, loose flocks or colonies: forages with Tree Martins, *flight similar: more clipped and fluttering than Welcome Swallow*. Perches on dead trees, overhead wires. In winter cold snaps, uses nest-burrows, for communal roosting: over 20 temporarily torpid birds have been found in one burrow. **Similar species:** both Martins have *dark* backs, white rumps, shorter tails. **Voice:** dry 'jk, jk' in flight; attractive twittering song. **Habitat:** open inland areas; watercourses, dunes; ranges and foothills; inland lakes, river valleys; creek-banks, sandpits; quarries in areas with suitable sandy soil for nesting. **Breeds:** Aug.–Dec. **Nest:** sparse lining of grass, leaves, at end of tunnel 30–100 cm long, 5 cm in diameter, in sandy or gravelly creek-bank, road-cutting, sandpit; usually in a colony with other pairs. **Eggs:** 4–6; pure white. **Range and Status:** widespread in drier regions across mainland Aust., mostly inland of Gt Divide and s. of Tropic (Blakers et al, 1984); to coasts in WA (s. from Eighty Mile Beach); SA; ne. NSW–e. Q. *Avoids driest deserts*, (except in good seasons); rainfall zones over *c.* 600 m (Emison et al, 1987), wetter coastal forests/farmlands of far sw. WA and coastal se. Aust. Resident or regular visitor to drier parts of Adelaide, Sydney, Brisbane; uncommon, casual Perth, Melbourne, Canberra. Sedentary; locally nomadic; possible regular n. movement in dry season to *c.* Broome (WA)–Barkly Tablelands (NT)–Charters Towers (Q). In s. Aust., coastward during droughts.

TREE MARTIN *Hirundo nigricans* 12.5–14 cm

Other name: Tree Swallow.

Small dark swallow, *stubbier than Welcome Swallow, with dull white rump and short tail.* Note deep-buff forehead, black crown, smutty cheeks; underparts whitish, washed buff, finely streaked darker. Flight clipped, erratic; wingbeats shallow, fluttering, with quick turns. Forms loose colonies in large river red gums, sweeping blithely around their heads, plunging into high nest-hollows. Flocks roost communally in their high foliage. In nonbreeding season, migrating or nomadic companies of hundreds to thousands form temporary roosts in reedbeds, pouring into them at dusk. Resident in some urban areas, e.g. Brisbane, Sydney, Canberra. Associates with Welcome Swallows, Fairy Martins; perches overhead wires. **Similar species:** Fairy Martin: crown ginger; cheeks pale; whiter rump; call distinctive. **Voice:** animated sweet twittering, elaborated in song. **Habitat:** open country with large trees; e.g. river red gums, on watercourses, rivers, lakes/wetlands. **Breeds:** July–Jan. **Nest:** loose grass, leaves, in hollow tree-spout, partly walled off by mud. Several pairs may use one entrance. Sometimes in hole in cliffs, hole or ventilator in city building, or abandoned Fairy Martin nest. **Eggs:** 3–5; pinkish white, finely freckled pale rusty brown at large end. **Range and Status:** Aust. and Tas., coastal islands; avoids driest deserts. Breeds mostly s. of Tropic (Blakers et al, 1984); many migrate n. to NT, n. Q, PNG, in Feb.–May, returning s. July–Oct. Common. Also Indonesia, PNG, New Cal.

FAIRY MARTIN *Hirundo ariel* 12–13 cm

Other name: Bottle Swallow.

Small white-rumped swallow, very like Tree Martin, but note *ginger crown, pale cheeks, whiter rump and underparts.* Looks chunky and compact on wing; tail square, slightly forked; flies with quick, clipped wingbeats and glides. Dozens circle vicinity of breeding colonies, filling air with calls. Often in mixed flocks with Tree Martins, other swallows. *Distinctive call immediately indicates its presence in mixed flocks.* **Similar species:** Tree Martin: crown dark; cheeks smutty, rump less persil white; voice differs. **Voice:** short, dry, churring 'drr, drr', wholly unlike twitter of Tree Martin. **Habitat:** open country; rivers, creeks, wetlands; vicinity of cliffs, banks, bridges, caves, culverts, where nests are situated. **Breeds:** Aug.–Jan. in s. Aust.; after rain in inland. **Nest:** the only Aust. bird to build a mud-bottle nest with drooping, narrow entrance-spout. In colony of a few to dozens, nests often fused together: on walls, ceilings of caves, overhung banks, cavernous trees near water, but now often in large, concrete road-culverts; under bridges, eaves of masonry buildings. Old nests used by pardalotes, House Sparrows, Tree Martins, small bats. **Eggs:** 4–5; whitish, finely freckled reddish or yellowish brown. **Range and Status:** mainland Aust. *except* driest deserts; breeding not reported C. York Pen. (Q) or far Top End (NT). Vagrant Tas. and PNG. (Blakers et al, 1984). Regular migration from se. Aust. to n. Aust. in March–April, returning to breed Sept.–Oct. Uncommon.

WHITE-BACKED
SWALLOW

imm.

TREE MARTIN

imm.

FAIRY MARTIN

imm.

CLAMOROUS REED-WARBLER *Arocephalus stentoreus* 16–17 cm

Other names: Australian Reed Warbler, Reedbird, Reedlark, Water Sparrow. Outstanding singer of the summer reedbeds. *Plain pale olive–brown above, with faint fawn eyebrow*; *plain fawn–white below*. Clings to reed-stems, forages on floating vegetation. Singing, mouth yellow. In flight, *note tawny rump*. **Similar species:** Oriental Reed-Warbler, Tawny Grassbird. Song of Brown Honeyeater can be confused. **Voice:** rich, liquid, guttural phrases, 'chutch chutch, dzee-dzee-dzee, quarty-quarty-quarty'. Alarm-call: sharp 'tuk!'. Rattling scolds. **Habitat:** reeds, cumbungi, pencil rush, over water; river red gum regrowth; weeping willows, bamboos, crops near irrigation channels; public gardens. **Breeds:** Sept.–Dec. **Nest:** deep cup, narrowing at rim; of reed-sheaths, woven around reed-stems, willow-strands. **Eggs:** 3–4; blue–white/buff–brown; spotted, blotched blue–grey, brown. **Range and Status:** widespread e. Aust. and coastal WA, mostly s. of Tropic; uncommon Tas. In se. Aust. and sw. WA, summer breeding migrant, arriving Aug.–Oct., most departing March–April. Some overwinter. In tropical n. Aust., mostly winter visitor from s. Common. Also PNG to se., s. Asia, to ne. Africa.

ORIENTAL REED-WARBLER *Acrocephalus orientalis* 19–20 cm

Other names: Eastern or Great Reed-Warbler.

Very like Clamorous Reed-Warbler: *bill slightly shorter, heavier; lores darker, fine grey streaks on sides of throat/upperbreast.* **Voice:** 'loud, harsh 'chack'; song hard, guttural, croaking' (Darnell in King et al, 1980); calls quicker, lower-pitched than Clamorous. **Habitat:** dense reeds, cumbungi, over and near water. **Range and Status:** Breeds e. Asia; migrates to Indonesia. Vagrant PNG. Rare, summer migrant to coastal n. and e. Aust. (Jan.–March); records from Kununurra (WA) to ne. Q, e. NSW.

SPINIFEXBIRD *Eremiornis carteri* 14–16 cm

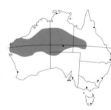

Best identified by its preference for spinifex. Bill longish; eyebrow buff; upperparts *unstreaked tawny brown* (some rufous, others greyer); *underparts plain buff–white; dark brown tail nearly equals length of body, carried part-raised.* **Immature:** browner. Climbs to sing or watch intruder; scrambles to hide; runs between clumps, tail cocked; flies with tail pumping. **Voice:** loud, repeated 'cheery-wheat', like Stubble Quail; also 'cheerit' repeated *c.* every 3 seconds, followed by repeated descending 'cheeroo'. Alarm-call, sharp 'tk!'. **Habitat:** spinifex clumps, dense grasses, near creekbeds, lower slopes,; mostly in hilly country above *c.* 300 m (Ford & Parker, 1974). **Breeds:** Aug.–Nov. **Nest:** cup of grasses lined with rootlets, in spinifex-clump. **Eggs:** 2–3; pink–white, freckled pale lilac, purplish, red–brown. **Range and Status:** patchy in arid inland and WA: from *c.* Winton–Jundah (Q), n. to *c.* Mt Isa (Q)–Barkly Tableland–upper Victoria R. (NT); to w. coast WA from Eighty Mile Beach to *c.* Carnarvon; n. to n. upper Fitzroy R., s. to *c.* Minilya R.; also Dampier, Montebello Is. groups. Locally common. Sedentary.

TAWNY GRASSBIRD *Megalurus timoriensis* 17–19 cm

Larger than Little Grassbird; crown plain rufous–tawny; upperparts similar, with heavy black streaks; tail tawny, longish, pointed; underparts whitish fawn, unstreaked. Singles, pairs in loose colonies: climbs stems, utters alarm-call, drops. Breeding male makes fluttering, tail-down song-flights over cover. **Voice:** sweet, descending song, somewhat like Rufous Songlark, Superb Fairy-Wren. Alarm-call: sharp 'jk-jk'. **Habitat:** coastal heaths, rank grasses, canegrass; cumbungi swamps; grassy dunes, crops. **Breeds:** Aug.–Dec. se. Aust; Feb.–April n. Aust. **Nest:** deep cup of fine grasses; in rank grass. **Eggs:** 2–3; pink–white, freckled purplish brown, grey. **Range and Status:** Kimberley (WA) to Shoalhaven R. (NSW); inland to Atherton Tableland–Charters Towers–Tambo–Carnarvon Ras. NP (Q); Moree–Macquarie Marshes–Gilgandra (NSW); vagrant King I., Bass Strait (Blakers et al, 1984). Uncommon. Possibly spring–summer breeding migrant in se. Aust. Also Torres Strait, PNG to Philippines.

LITTLE GRASSBIRD *Megalurus gramineus* — see p. 508.

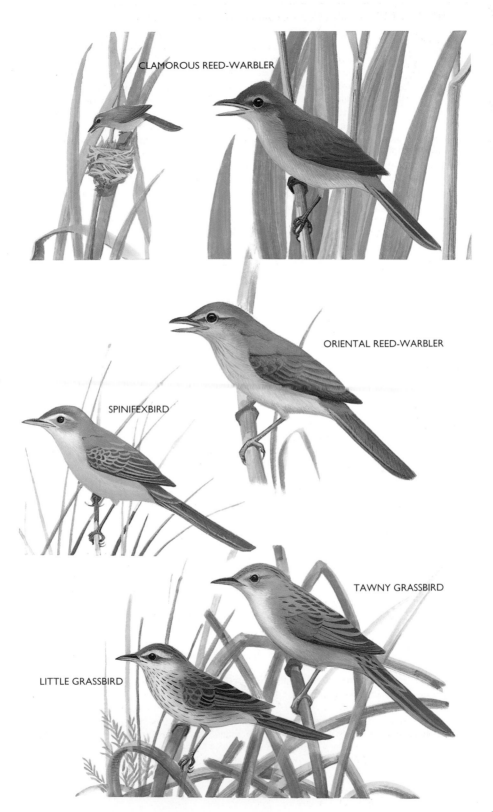

CLAMOROUS REED-WARBLER

ORIENTAL REED-WARBLER

SPINIFEXBIRD

TAWNY GRASSBIRD

LITTLE GRASSBIRD

BROWN SONGLARK *Cinclorhamphus cruralis* male 24–26 cm, female 18–19 cm

Male, breeding: bill black; crown/nape fawn, contrasting with *sooty-brown face/throat/breast; legs long, flesh-brown.* **Male, nonbreeding:** bill light brown; *lores blackish, eyebrow pale; feathers of upperparts patterned by brown centres, paler margins; rump coloured like back; face/underparts pale grey–brown; throat whitish; centre of breast/abdomen blackish brown.* **Female:** similar, much smaller, paler; bill/lores pale brown. **Immature:** like female. Mostly silent, solitary, or in loose companies when not breeding; walks, runs through grass. In spring/summer, *displaying males sit upright on stumps, fences, telephone-poles/wires over grassland, tails cocked.* Take off singing, rising on long, circling, line in fluttering flight broken by glides, *wings upswept, long undercarriage lowered;* descend in shallow glide, drop. Normal flight swift, undulating, with glides. **Similar species:** Common Starling, imm. Rufous Songlark: like female Brown; rump rufous. Richard's Pipit. **Voice:** song of male catchy, metallic, guttural; hence schoolchildren's name 'skit-scot-a-wheeler'. **Habitat:** pastures, cereal crops; in inland, open grassy country, saltbush etc. **Breeds:** Sept.–Feb. in s. Aust., after rain in inland. **Nest:** deep cup of grasses; in shelter of tussock or tuft of grass. **Eggs:** 3–4; salmon-pink, speckled pinkish red, mostly on large end. **Range and Status:** mainland Aust., mostly s. of Tropic and inland of Gt Divide: Reaches coasts in ce. Q, w. Vic., SA, incl. Kangaroo I.; most of WA s. of Broome. Summer breeding migrant in s. Aust., arriving from June onwards, departing by March; winters inland. Highly nomadic; moves to coasts during inland drought, may breed. Locally, irregularly common.

RUFOUS SONGLARK *Cinclorhamphus mathewsi* male 19 cm, female 16–17 cm

Male larger than female: in both sexes note *distinctly rufous rump and upper tail-coverts.* **Male, breeding:** bill black; *slight dark eyeline; pale fawn eyebrow; netted pattern to wing-feathers;* underparts greyish fawn with slight necklet of spots/streaks. Singing, male shows *black mouth-lining* (female pink). **Male, nonbreeding:** like female. **Female:** bill grey–brown, paler on sides; lacks dark eyeline; note pale eyebrow/throat, rufous rump/upper tail-coverts. Tail mid-brown, *without* white edges; *feathers pointed.* Singles or loose flocks. Male territorial behaviour conspicuous, attracting females to mate and build nests in or near his territory. Otherwise quiet, easily missed; moves unobtrusively through grass and foliage of shrubs, trees. **Similar species:** Brown Songlark, female. Richard's Pipit. White-winged Triller, female. **Voice:** male song has sweet, splintered, ventriloquial quality; begins with clear loud trill, develops into full, loud ringing refrain, sweet, high-pitched and strong 'a-witchy-weedle', repeated; uttered from high perches in territory, e.g. large dead or live tree, telephone wires, and in flight between such high points or while descending to ground. Also scolding rattle; alarm-call, sharp 'tik'. **Habitat:** open grassy woodlands/scrublands; with dead and living trees. **Breeds:** Sept.–Dec. **Nest:** deep cup of grasses; in depression or in shelter of tussock. **Eggs:** 3–4; white, speckled reddish, mostly at large end. **Range and Status:** widespread across mainland Aust. *except* n. C. York Pen. (Q); driest, treeless deserts, heavy forests and closely settled coastal regions. Patchy, irregular e. and s. of Gt Divide. Migratory, moving s. in spring to breed, n. in autumn. Winter visitor to n. Aust., but many overwinter inland. Breeds mostly in se. Aust. s. inland of Gt Divide, and in coastal/subcoastal WA s. of Tropic (Blakers et al, 1984). Uncommon to seasonally common.

LITTLE GRASSBIRD *Megalurus gramineus* 13–15 cm. Illustrated on p. 506.

Skulking little bird of wetlands. *Olive–brown crown/upperparts heavily streaked black; eyebrow pale; underparts greyish–fawn, with fine black streaks; tail longish, pointed.* Sneaks to tops of bushes to view intruder, drops out of sight; *runs over mud, floating vegetation.* In flight, *tail without bars or white tips.* **Similar species:** Tawny Grassbird. **Voice:** mournful, trisyllabic 'p-peee-pee'; scolding rattle. **Habitat:** dense wetland vegetation: cumbungi, reeds, rushes, canegrass, lignum; vegetation on bore-drains; tidal marshes, salt lakes; mangroves. **Breeds:** Aug.–Dec., or after rain. **Nest:** deep, cup; of grass, stems; lined with feathers; in grass, reeds, low shrubs. **Eggs:** 3–5; whitish/pink–white, speckled greyish, red–purple, in zone on large end. **Range and Status:** e. and sw. Aust., Bass Strait islands, Tas., w. to Eyre Pen. (SA), Gulf coast (Q). Patchy through inland in pockets of suitable habitat to Kununurra (n. WA) (Blakers et al, 1984). Locally common. Sedentary; dispersive. Also PNG.

BROWN SONGLARK

♂ breeding

♀

♂ breeding

RUFOUS SONGLARK

♀

♂

GOLDEN-HEADED CISTICOLA *Cisticola exilis* 9–11.5 cm

Other names: Barleybird, Cornbird, Golden-headed Fantail Warbler, Tailorbird.

Spirited diminutive dweller of tall ground-cover in moist situations. *Bill grey–brown above, pink on sides; eye yellow–brown; legs long, pinkish.* **Male, breeding:** *head/neck bright, plain golden buff; upperparts golden buff; back and wing-coverts heavily streaked black;* underparts whitish, flanks/underparts washed rich buff; *tail short, blackish, tipped buff.* **Female and nonbreeding male:** less golden; tail longer. **Immature:** underparts washed yellowish.

Breeding males call incessantly from grass-tops, fences, telephone wires; flutter up in bouncing song-flights in wide, high circuits over territory before dropping to cover. Unobtrusive when not breeding. **Similar species:** Zitting Cisticola. **Voice:** perched and in flight, breeding males utter incessant, far-carrying insect-like 'bhzzt' followed by liquid 'lek' or 'pillek', or 'WEEZ, wit-wit-wit', varying locally; also diminutive high-pitched chatterings, scolds. **Habitat:** shrubs, tall grass, rushes, other rank herbage around wetlands; river flats, sewage farms, drainages, wet neglected paddocks; floodplains, samphire on margins of saltmarshes; roadsides; overgrown margins of irrigation channels; irrigated pastures, grain crops, blackberries. **Breeds:** Sept.–March. **Nest:** small, domed, with side-entrance; of fine grass, plant-down, bound with spiders' web, *several broad living green leaves stitched in with spiders' web, plant-fibre* (hence 'Tailorbird'); under 1 m in low shrub, rush, reeds, tussock, grapevine. **Eggs:** 3–4; blue, spotted, dotted, blotched red–brown. **Range and Status:** coastal n., e. and se. Aust. and coastal islands (incl. Gt Barrier Reef): from Pilbara/Kimberley regions (WA), to mouth of Murray R. (SA); also King I., Bass Strait; vagrant Tas. Widespread to *c.* 300 km inland in suitable habitat, e.g. Murray/Murrumbidgee irrigation systems in NSW Riverina. Common. Sedentary; part-migratory. Also Bismarck Arch.–PNG to Indonesia, Philippines, se. Asia, s. China, India.

ZITTING CISTICOLA *Cisticola juncidis* 9.5–10.5 cm

Closely resembles Golden-headed Cisticola but lacks golden tonings. Bill grey–brown above, pinkish below; eye mid-brown; long legs pinkish brown; *lores, eyebrows and underparts fawn–white, washed tawny on flanks.* **Breeding:** crown/upperparts fawn–brown with long black streaks, *shadowy dark streaks on nape; conspicuous fawn–white feather-margins on back emphasise strongly black-streaked effect; rump tawny buff;* tail short, dark grey–brown with buff–brown panels on edges, blackish subterminal band, dull-white tips. **Nonbreeding:** tail longer. **Female:** duller, more streaked. **Immature:** like female; eye brown. Singles, pairs; parties in nonbreeding season. **Voice:** when breeding, males fly up from grass to heights of *c.* 15–30 m, calling. Hover, head-to-breeze, bouncing up and down in time with double 'zit-zit' or 'lik-lik' call, or fly in wide circles with fluttering undulations and calls, before diving to grass. **Habitat:** long grass on temporarily inundated coastal plains; margins of mangroves, saltmarshes. **Breeds:** Dec.–March. **Nest:** very deep cup, with restricted top opening, binding together several converging grass-stems; externally of spiders' web and felted plant-down, lined with plant-down, fine rootlets; in grass less than 1 m tall. **Eggs:** 3–4 (5); oval, smooth, unglossy, pale blue with very fine reddish brown specks evenly over surface (Hitchcock & Givens, 1953). **Range and Status:** three separated races on coastal plains of n. Aust.: from coastal plain n. of Kununurra in far n. WA to Darwin region (NT); Gulf lowlands of n. Q and w. coast C. York Pen.; coastal e. Q from *c.* Townsville s. to Curtis I., near Gladstone (Arnold et al, 1993). Sedentary.

ARCTIC WARBLER *Phylloscopus borealis* 11.5–12.5 cm

Member of a large, confusing Eurasian complex: *dark olive–green above, with yellowish white eyebrow over long, slim blackish eyeline. Pale tips to wing-coverts form two pale lines across wing (upper line often indistinct). Throat white; underparts off-white; flanks washed brownish olive; legs pale brown.* **Similar species:** Greenish Warbler, *P. trochiloides:* smaller; head/bill shorter; underparts, incl. flanks, whitish; legs dark grey. Not recorded in Aust. **Voice:** call described as 'loud, husky *"dzeet"'* (King & Dickinson, 1980); also 'characteristic *zit* occasionally given by wintering birds' (MacKinnon & Phillipps, 1993). **Habitat:** in Indonesia reported to frequent open wooded areas, mangroves, secondary forests and forest edges. **Breeds:** from n. Scandinavia e. to Alaska. Migrates to se. Asia, Philippines, and to Indonesia in small numbers. Placed on Aust. list with discovery of freshly dead bird on treeless Sandy I. on Scott Reef (WA) (14°03'S; 121°46'E) on 7 Nov. 1979 by the late John McKean (McKean, 1980).

GOLDEN-HEADED CISTICOLA

♂ breeding

♀

♂ nonbreeding

ZITTING CISTICOLA

♂ breeding

♀

ARCTIC WARBLER

PALE WHITE-EYE *Zosterops citrinellus* 10–11 cm

Bill robust; *upperparts pale olive–yellow, yellower on head and rump; underparts off-white; flanks washed grey or buff; throat/upperbreast and under tail-coverts pale yellow.* **Immature:** paler. Pairs, parties, small flocks: forages in foliage, behaves like other white-eyes. **Similar species:** Yellow White-eye: underparts bright yellow; note range. **Voice:** described as less plaintive than Silvereye; presumed contact calls louder, resembling White-throated Honeyeater (Holmes, 1986). **Habitat:** wooded and forested islands. **Breeds:** probably Dec.–June. **Nest:** small neat cup of fine grass bound with spiders' web; suspended in slender fork of shrub or foliage of tree. **Eggs:** 2–4; pale blue–green. **Range and Status:** islands in Torres Strait and off ne. C. York Pen. (Q) e.g. Quoin, Eagle, Palfrey Is., and other islands, s. to Rocky Islets, n. of Cooktown (Q). (Holmes, 1986). Also islands off s. PNG, e. Indonesia. Sedentary.

YELLOW WHITE-EYE *Zosterops luteus* 9.5–11 cm

Bill like Silvereye: *upperparts yellow–olive; forehead/underparts bright yellow.* **Immature:** duller. Colours blend well with yellow–green leaves of mangroves. Habits like other white-eyes; but note specialised habitat. **Similar species:** Pale White-eye. **Voice:** like other white-eyes, with distinct dialect; reportedly lower in pitch, more nasal and metallic than Silvereye; song canary-like; perhaps loudest of any Aust. white-eye. **Habitat:** coastal mangroves, acacia thickets; adjacent eucalypt, paperbark woodlands; monsoon thickets; vegetation on coastal rivers; trees, gardens in coastal towns. **Breeds:** Oct.–March. **Nest:** deep cup of soft grasses, spiders' web; suspended from horizontal fork, usually of mangrove. **Eggs:** 3–4; paler blue than Silvereye. **Range and Status:** coasts and some coastal islands of nw. and n. Aust.: from Shark Bay (WA) to Edward R., C. York Pen. (Q). Isolate colony in region of Ayr–mouth of Burdekin R. (e. coastal Q). Extends some distance inland along rivers. Common. Sedentary.

SILVEREYE *Zosterops lateralis* 10–12.5 cm

Other names: Blightbird, Grape-eater; Grey-backed, Grey-breasted or Western Silvereye or White-eye; Ringeye, Silvey, Tauhou, Waxeye.
In most of e., se. Aust. and sw. WA, *the only small grey and olive–green bird with conspicuous white eye-ring.* Colours (especially of underparts) vary:
Race *chlorocephala*: largest race; with robust bill (plumage like *ramsayi*).
Race *ramsayi*: throat/under tail-coverts citrine yellow.
Race *familiaris*: throat yellow; flanks grey or buffish; under tail-coverts lemon.
Nominate race (*lateralis*): throat grey; flanks buff to chestnut; under tail coverts whitish.
Race *gouldi*: upperparts more olive–green; throat olive–yellow; breast grey; flanks washed buff.
Race *halmaturina* (not illustrated): throat/under tail-coverts greyish; breast grey; flanks pale rufous.
Races interbreed: e.g. intergradation between *halmaturina* and *gouldi* is seen in green-backed birds from Eyre Pen.–Kangaroo I. (SA). Pairs when breeding, otherwise parties to flocks, in which pairs persist. Flocks cohesive; banded parties retrapped together several years apart. Moves rapidly through bushland, orchards, gardens, calling constantly. Migrating, flocks gather in trees, dash into air on next stage of journey. Pest in orchards/vineyards; aggressive at bird-tables; has intimidating threat-display of flared eye-rings, yellow gape, quivering wings. **Similar species:** Pale and Yellow White-eye. **Voice:** thin peevish 'psee'. Alarm-call: wavering 'wee-ee-ee-ee-ee'; territorial song rapid succession of high-pitched notes, trills, warbles. Autumn sub-song includes mimicry. Calls of *gouldi* harsher: flight-note staccato 'chip chip'. **Habitat:** most vegetational types in coastal/sub-coastal s. Aust. **Breeds:** Sept.–Jan. **Nest:** suspended cup of grass, thistletown, moss, spiders' web, usually in shrub. **Eggs:** 2–4, usually 3; delicate pale blue. **Range and Status:** e. and se. Aust., sw. WA and coastal islands. Race *chlorocephala*: Bunker/Capricorn Groups, Gt Barrier Reef. Race *ramsayi*: breeds ne. Q, n. of Mackay, n. to Pascoe R. Race *familiaris*: breeds from c. Vic. to c. Rockhampton (Q). Race *lateralis*: breeds Tas., Bass Strait islands, s. Vic. Race *halmaturina*: breeds w. Vic. to Kangaroo I., w. to c. Ceduna (SA). Race *gouldi*: sw. SA, s. of Nullarbor Plain w. along Bight coast, and throughout sw. WA, n. to Wongan Hills–Shark Bay, and coastally n. to c. Pt Cloates. Common, often very abundant; some races nomadic and/or migratory. Part of *lateralis* population leaves Tas. from mid-summer through autumn, dispersing through coastal se. Aust., n. to se. Q; returns to Tas. Aug.–Oct. Birds on Gt Barrier Reef islands n. of Bunker/Capricorn Groups sedentary; some resemble Pale Whiteyes; status confused (Blakers et al, 1984). Also NZ, Pacific islands, to Fiji.

PALE WHITE-EYE

YELLOW
WHITE-EYE

SILVEREYE

race *chlorocephala*

race *ramsayi*

nominate race

race *familiaris*

race *gouldi*

SONG THRUSH *Turdus philomelos* 23 cm

Other name: English Thrush.

Small neat thrush; *underparts whitish, washed buff, with dark arrow-streaks; legs pale flesh-coloured.* **Immature:** mantle speckled buff. Singles, pairs, autumn flocks: forages on lawns in bouncing hops, short runs. Smashes shells of garden snails on rocks. Flight slipping; note buff wing-lining. **Voice:** clear, fragmented song; mimics Australian species; scolding chatter; quiet 'sip'. **Habitat:** parks, gardens, woodlands, forests, thickets. **Breeds:** Sept.–Dec. **Nest:** bowl of grasses, roots; smoothed inside with mud, horse-manure, wood-pulp; in dense bush, creeper against wall, bank. **Eggs:** 3–5; pale blue, black. **Range and Status:** native to Europe, n. Africa, w. Asia: introduced Melbourne 1860s; later (unsuccessfully) elsewhere. Patchy Dandenong Ras.–Mt Macedon, Melbourne and suburbs; Mornington Pen.; Geelong–Lorne. Local. Also introduced Lord Howe, Norfolk Is., NZ.

COMMON BLACKBIRD *Turdus merula* 25–26 cm

Male: *dull black with yellow–orange bill/eye-ring; black legs.* **Female:** bill yellow–brown; plumage dark brown; *throat dull white, finely streaked darker.* **Immature:** like female; bill brown, plumage mottled rufous. Singles, pairs: hops, runs on lawns; droops, flicks wings, jerks longish tail; jabs bill into soil. Short flights low, undulating; sustained flight fast, direct. Aggressive, territorial, vocal; pest in fruit, berries, grapes, seedlings. Part-albinos occur, mostly in urban populations. **Similar species:** Common Starling, Song Thrush. **Voice:** serene, mellow, song; in alarm, ringing 'tchink, tchink'; anxious 'tsooi?'; screeching chatter; thin 'tseeep'. **Habitat:** gardens, lawns, parks, orchards, citrus, vineyards, woodlands/forests, watercourses, coastal scrubs, islands. **Breeds:** Sept.–Dec. **Nest:** robust cup of grass, rootlets, bark, with mud, horse-manure. **Eggs:** 3–5; blue–green, freckled, streaked, blotched red–brown, grey. **Range and Status:** native to Europe, Asia; introduced Melbourne by 1862, later Sydney, Adelaide, Hobart, ACT. Common, widespread Tas., much of Vic., ACT and s. SA, from s. Flinders Ras. to s. Eyre Pen., Kangaroo I.; in NSW, patchy Sydney and s. coast; on Murray R., tributaries, irrigated areas of s. Riverina, casual n. and w. to Cobar, Broken Hill. Sedentary; dispersive.

RUSSET-TAILED THRUSH *Zoothera heinei* 25–27 cm

Slightly smaller than near-identical Bassian Thrush, with somewhat plainer honey-brown upperparts. Outer tail feather on either side has *more white, visible in flight.* **Voice:** distinctive: ethereal, high-pitched 'peer, pooee' or 'peer, purr', tending to fall, then rise; repeated at slow intervals. **Breeds:** Sept.–Dec. **Nest:** like Bassian. **Eggs** differ: 2–3; pale greenish blue, with minute flecks of pale chestnut-red. **Range and Status:** mountain rainforests, wetter woodlands in coastal e. Aust., from Hawkesbury R. (NSW) to highlands of ne. Q, to n. of Cairns. In ne. NSW, occurs on Gt Dividing Range up to *c.* 775 m; Bassian present above *500 m*; the two thus overlap without interbreeding (Holmes, 1984). Sedentary; autumn movement to coastal lowlands in n. NSW–se. Q.

BASSIAN THRUSH *Zoothera lunulata* 26–29 cm

Other names: Ground, Mountain, Scaly or White's Thrush.

Olive–brown to golden brown above, whitish below, with *heavy overall pattern of dark half-moons.* Singles, pairs, family parties: inconspicuous in leaf-litter; stands motionless, ducks head, runs forward, rocks a little, jabs bill into soil; flies away low, *showing black-and-white underwing-bar;* slim white tail corners. **Similar species:** Russet-tailed Thrush. **Voice:** wild, beautiful: two clear loud notes connected by upward slide, 'tlee-oo-whee'; quieter, sustained, song of many small notes, like Common Blackbird. Contact-note: thin, high-pitched 'seeet'. **Habitat:** rainforests, forests, woodlands, coastal scrubs, pine plantations; in winter, sub-inland scrubs, riverine woodlands, secondary growth. **Breeds:** Aug.–Dec. **Nest:** large bowl of rootlets, bark strips, green moss, lichen; in fork, 2–10 m high. **Eggs:** 2–3; stone to pale green, freckled red–brown. **Range and Status:** coastal e. Aust.: from Tas., Bass Strait islands and (isolated population) Kangaroo I.–Mt Lofty Ras. (SA) to ne. Q. From *c.* Hunter R. (NSW) to n. Atherton Tableland (Q) mostly above 500 m in mountain rainforests. Isolated large race *cuneata* on Atherton Tableland (Q). Sedentary; disperses to more open lowlands in winter, inland to Murray Valley. Also PNG to se. Asia, Siberia, e. Europe.

SONG THRUSH

COMMON
BLACKBIRD

♂

♀

RUSSET-TAILED
THRUSH

BASSIAN THRUSH

race *cuneata*

515

METALLIC STARLING *Aplonis metallica* 21–24 cm

Other names: Glossy or Shining Starling, Whirlwindbird.
Highly sociable, migratory black bird with oily green/purple gloss, bulging bright red eye and pointed tail; neck-feathers long, pointed. Bill, legs blackish. **Immature:** dark brown shot green above, *whitish below, streaked darker;* eye brown, then red. Parties to large flocks after breeding. Forages on fruit/seeds of rainforest trees, nectar, insects. When nesting, incessant, noisy coming/going to colonies. Some breed while still in imm. plumage. Tight, chattering flocks hurtle with rush of wings over rainforests, like lorikeets. In sustained flight, e.g. to offshore islands, flocks rise and fall, like Common Starlings. In ne. Q roosts in street trees, overhead wires; raids fruit. **Similar species:** Spangled Drongo; Koel; Trumpet Manucode. **Voice:** reedy wheezings, jeerings, chatterings; song canary-like, but briefer, more fluty. **Habitat:** rainforest, coastal woodlands, scrubs, mangroves, gardens. **Breeds:** Aug.–Jan., in colony of dozens/hundreds, in large trees, native/introduced, in or near rainforest; suburban allotments. **Nest:** bulky, oval, of straws, vine-tendrils, palm-leaves, fibre, occasionally paper; suspended from branch 10–20 m high. **Eggs:** 2–3 (4); pale blue–white; spotted, speckled brown, grey. **Range and Status:** from C. York (Q) s. to c. Mackay; inland to Big Tableland near Cooktown–Atherton Tableland. Migratory; arrives from PNG mostly Aug.–Sept. to breed; departs Feb.–April; some overwinter. Common in coastal lowlands to 750 m; less common on highlands and s. of Innisfail. Also Solomon Is., PNG, e. Indonesia.

COMMON STARLING *Sturnus vulgaris* 21 cm

Note longish *fine, pointed bill and short tail; plumage blackish, glossed bronze–green and purple.* In autumn, feathers tipped buffish, underparts tipped white, *giving finely spotted appearance. By spring,* tips worn, *birds appear glossy black,.* Bill pale yellow in summer (base blue–black in male, pinkish in female); *bill blackish in winter; legs red–brown.* **Immature:** plain dull mouse-brown; whitish on throat; bill/legs blackish. Singles to large flocks. Runs about jerkily with quick jabs of open bill into soil in sewing-machine action. Flight swift; *flocks rise and fall.* Conspicuous at roosts in reedbeds, street trees, city buildings. Sings from roofs, chimneys, TV aerials. Pest in soft fruit, berries, grapes; beneficial in pastures. **Similar species:** Common Blackbird. Metallic Starling. **Voice:** sings with slowly flapping wings: wheezes, clicks, rattles; loud descending whistle; mimics; harsh descending 'tcheer'; sharp 'dick!'. **Habitat:** urban areas, pastoral country, open woodlands, mallee, mulga; river red gums on watercourses; reedbeds, tidal mudflats, beaches, islands, resorts, gardens, orchards. **Breeds:** Aug.–Jan. **Nest:** rough, cup of grass, straw, wool, feathers, leaves; in tree-hollow, stump, fence-post, cliff, wall, ceiling, ventilator; old nest of babbler. Nests harbour vermin hazardous to human health. **Eggs:** 4–5; plain blue–white. **Range and Status:** native to Europe, n. and w. Asia. Introduced to Aust. in 1860s. Now established mostly throughout se. Q, NSW, Vic., Tas., s. SA, w. to Cook–Bight coast. Many destroyed annually at Nullarbor Station (WA) to prevent colonisation of WA. In n. NT, Q, slowly expanding n. and w.: records from Darwin; Iron Range; Cairns, Port Douglas, Port Moresby (PNG). Common; abundant. Dispersive; nomadic; migratory. Vagrant Lord Howe I.

COMMON MYNA *Acridotheres tristis* 23–25 cm

Other names: Indian Myna or Mynah.
Sturdy *cocoa-brown bird: yellow bill; bare yellow skin behind eye; glossy black head/throat; yellow legs.* **Immature:** duller, plain brown. Pairs to loose flocks: garrulous; forages on ground; scavenges, raids soft fruits, berries; walks bandily, hops exaggeratedly. In flight: *large white patch on rounded black wings, broad white tips to black tail.* Roosts communally in street-trees, buildings, bridges. **Voice:** creaky, growls, rattles; in flight, mellow liquid note. Alarm-call: harsh 'scairr!'. **Habitat:** urban areas; pastoral/agricultural districts near towns; disperses along highways. **Breeds:** Oct.–March. **Nest:** of grass, twigs, straw, feathers, paper; in cavity of building, tree-hollow, or bulky open nest in dense foliage. **Eggs:** 4–5; glossy, pale blue. **Range and Status:** native to Asia. Introduced Aust. early 1860s and later. Patchy through coastal e. Aust. from c. Laura –Mossman (casual Cooktown) (ne. Q) to c. Melbourne–Ballarat–Swan Hill (Vic.); n. Tas.; reported Adelaide (SA); extends inland to Darling Downs (Q); Murrurundi–Goulburn (NSW); ACT separately introduced. Spasmodic reports Tas., apparently not established (Green, 1993). Locally common. Sedentary; dispersive.

Spangled
Drongo
(not to
scale)

imm.

METALLIC STARLING

COMMON
STARLING

imm.

winter   summer

COMMON MYNA

imm.

517

CLASSIFYING AND NAMING AUSTRALIAN BIRDS

To put the right name to *anything*, you must first know precisely what the thing *is*. In recent times, the classification of Australian birds has undergone a fundamental reappraisal from application of radical new molecular techniques for comparing the structure of their DNA — the molecules that encode genetic inheritance.

Since Karl von Linne (1707–1778), the Swedish founder of systematic biological classification, the world's 9000+ species of birds have been described and allotted to orders, families, genera and species, mostly on the basis of body-size, structure and function, plumage structure and colours.

Until the revolutionary work of Darwin the following century, it was thought that a species, once described and allotted a place in that Linnaen system, was fixed for all time.

We now know that species are not unchanging. Birds, like other animals (even plants), show astonishing plasticity — an ability *over time* to alter their size, plumage patterns and colours, the shape of bills, wings, legs, feet, even the structure of their skeletons, to pursue particular ways of life.

To give an example: penguins are now known to be descended from petrels, which depend on their graceful wings to carry them over immense ocean distances when foraging and migrating. Secure on some remote southern oceanic islands, surrounded by fish-rich seas, ancestral petrel-penguins nevertheless found it profitable to modify their wings into swim-flippers and to acquire heavy, solid skeletons, plump heat-retaining bodies, dense down and scale-like outer plumage for more efficient undersea foraging. For them, trading flight for flightlessness was advantageous. But who, from visual appearance alone, would pick a graceful, aerial petrel as a penguin's evolutionary grandparent?

A contrasting phenomenon is that of convergent evolution — the tendency for unrelated animals that follow similar ways of life to assume *similar* body-structure, colours, markings, even habits. Convergent evolution is especially evident in Australia where, because many of our birds evolved in isolation and free of outside competition, there was opportunity for a few ancestral forms to radiate into many ways of life, some with many surprising similarities to those of unrelated birds on other continents. Thus the bark-gleaning Australian sittellas bear an astonishing resemblance to the northern hemisphere nuthatches, and thus when the first European settlers reached Sydney Cove in January 1788, they saw and heard birds apparently very like those they knew at 'home'.

Naturally the nostalgic newcomers gave the Australian birds the names of their supposed English counterparts: small brown birds with cocked tails became 'wrens'; red-breasted insect-eaters became 'robins'; crested, yellow-breasted small birds with hooked bills 'shrike-tits'; crow-like, black-and-white birds were 'magpies', while tree-climbing small birds with big feet had to be 'treecreepers'. Dozens of such names were bestowed; almost all were wrong in terms of precise classification.

In giving those names, the marines, convicts and settlers of the day and the naturalists who followed them were guilty not only of false labelling: they unconsciously established the notion that Australian birds were descended from northern hemisphere ancestors.

Undoubtedly some songbird groups have colonised Australia from Eurasia in comparatively recent geological time: Australia's pittas, sunbirds, mistletoebirds, swallows, larks, reed-warblers, cisticolas, white-eyes, thrushes and starlings all belong to largely northern hemisphere, African and/or Eurasian families which moved down the islands of the Indonesian archipelago to reach this continent. But by far the most numerous, most typical assemblages of Australian songbirds, totalling some 300 species, and many of our larger non-passerine birds as well — emus, cassowaries, parrots, cockatoos, some birds of prey and some waterfowl — had other origins.

While bird-classification remained based on the old criteria of form, size, plumage, bones and behaviour, it proved next-to-impossible for taxonomists to penetrate the thickets of suggestive or misleading clues and achieve a clearer understanding of just how those wholly native Australian birds had arisen.

In the 1970s a new branch of science — molecular biology — began to provide an aggressive new breed of biologists with radical diagnostic techniques, able to cut through the old barriers of feathers and bones and the red-herrings of plasticity and convergent evolution to reveal the true genealogy below.

Two American evolutionists in particular, Prof. Charles Sibley and Jon Ahlquist of the Peabody Museum of Natural History at Yale University, set about systematically comparing the DNA of some thousands of bird-species — including many Australian songbirds, whose isolated origins make them of particular interest. In a landmark succession of publications over several decades*, Sibley and Ahlquist have demonstrated that Australia's old endemic songbirds, as well as many non-passerines, were not derived from Eurasian families, as tradition (and a succession of renowned biologists) had claimed, but had arisen from ancestors present on this continent from the start.

In order to appreciate just *how* ancient and how different our birds *are*, it is necessary to recall a little geomorphological history. In the 1950s and 1960s, international geophysical investigations produced the first positive evidence confirming the long-disputed phenomenon of continental drift. Australians began to hear startling affirmation of the previously debunked proposition that this continent had, as long ago as 100 million years, once been part of the supercontinent Gondwana, lying at the bottom of the world and consisting of Antarctica, Africa, India, New Zealand, South America and other pieces, in a monstrous continental jigsaw puzzle.

At that time, unlike Antarctica today, the combined landmass supported humid rainforests which sheltered many flowering trees and shrubs populated by ancestral birds, mammals, reptiles, amphibians, insects and the rest. Where *they* had come from is beyond the scope of this outline.

After other continents had separated and drifted away north, the combined continent of Australia–New Guinea, riding on its own tectonic plate, separated from Gondwana some 50 million years ago and drifted north in lonely isolation, an ark loaded with ancestral wildlife, before ploughing into the Indonesian Sunda plate some 20 million years later — a garagantuan collision which pushed up the mountains of Papua-New Guinea and helped preserve rich examples of rainforest life in the damp coolness of higher altitudes.

According to Sibley and Ahlquist, during that long isolated drift Australia's endemic songbirds had radiated from a small group of corvine ancestors already present on Gondwana before the ark departed and had begun to evolve into the diversity we know today. By this hypothesis, our songbirds are seen to have evolved in tandem with our great marsupial fauna — the bandicoots, quolls, possums, koalas, wombats and kangaroos for which this continent is justly famous.

Perhaps even more significantly, our bush birds also prove to have co-evolved with plants of the more adaptable rainforest plant families, as they learned to live with poor soils, rising temperatures and advancing aridity, eventually producing Australia's characteristic tough, hard-leafed woodland vegetation, with its high incidence of bird-pollinated blossoms. That ancient partnership between our birds and our plants is beautifully confirmed in many recent ecological studies.

With those majestic geomorphological and evolutionary events providing a vast time scale onto which to project their DNA studies, Sibley and Ahlquist were able to postulate a plausible, and much longer than previously accepted, time sequence for the evolution of Australian birds.

Their explanation of the origins of our endemic songbirds carried its own compelling logic: only a sweep of some 20 million years in isolation, from the time of Australia's departure from Gondwana to its arrival within flying distance of Indonesia, could have provided the necessary time and opportunity for a handful of small, ancestral, corvine songbirds to radiate into the present diversity of hundreds of species we now know: lyrebirds, treecreepers, fairy wrens, grasswrens, honeyeaters, monarchs, pardalotes, thornbills, shrike-tits, fantails, woodswallows, birds of paradise, bowerbirds and others.

Those old endemic families provide an essential, characteristic component of Australia's avifauna, along with the even more ancient, Gondwanan-evolved emus and cassowaries, parrots and cockatoos, mound-builders, some endemic raptors, frogmouths, as well as early cosmopolitan families like grebes, petrels, herons, waterfowl, waders, cuckoos, kingfishers and others.

As well, a diverse company of seabirds — penguins, albatrosses, petrels, gulls, terns — made their Australian landfall and, perhaps as 'recently' as the Pleistocene ice-ages, birds from many families, mostly originating from Asia, either colonised the continent, as already mentioned, or began to come to Australia as nonbreeding migrants during the northern winter — our summer. A large and fascinating company of over 50 species of migratory sandpipers and plovers is outstanding among these.

Sibley and Ahlquist's proposals were dropped into the still pond of Australian ornithology in the 1970s. This was an era when many biologists tended to view Australia as a sort of biological dead end which had acquired its 'primitive' birds, mammals, reptiles and so on as refugees fleeing before the rise of 'more successful' species in a series of waves from Asia. The proposals should have been explosive.

But the perceived preposterousness of the notion of Gondwanan origin, as well as distrust of accepting an unknown set of laboratory techniques in place of older methods of classification, gave it all a

For example:
Sibley, C.G. & Ahlquist, J.E. (1985), The phylogeny and classification of the Australian-Papuan passerine birds, *The Emu* 85 (1): 1–14.
Sibley, C.G & Ahlquist, J.E. (1990), *Phylogeny and Classification of Birds, A Study in Molecular Evolution*, Yale University Press, New Haven and London.
Sibley, G.C. & Monroe, B.L. Jr. (1990), *Distribution and Taxonomy of Birds of the World*, Yale University Press.

dreamlike quality. The implications of Sibley and Ahlquist's work were so vast that embracing them demanded a huge mental leap into the unknown. There was also the practical consideration that uncritical adoption of the new proposals, so radically different in their views of origins and family relationships, would play havoc with the existing Australian bird checklist, which had long been a bible to most ornithologists.

Since 1926, the accepted 'family tree' of Australian birds had been *The Official Checklist of the Birds of Australia*, Second Edition, Royal Australasian Ornithologists Union, Melbourne 1926 (with Supplements 1–9, 1941–67). In 1975, the Royal Australasian Ornithologists Union (RAOU) published two works aimed at bringing the 1926 Checklist up to date: H.T. Condon's *Checklist of the Birds of Australia: Part 1: Non-Passerines* and Richard Schodde's *Interim List of Australian Songbirds*.

Schodde undoubtedly appreciated the significance of Sibley and Ahlquist's work, and this was reflected in some of the new family arrangements he made in the Interim List, and in his own researches. Molecular biology was, however, still in its infancy in 1975 and insufficient work had been done for any but the most tentative conclusions about Australian bird families to be drawn from it.

So apart from some amendments in 1976 and 1978, and 'Recommended English Names for Australian Birds' by CSIRO (*Emu* 77, pp. 245–307, 1978), the official naming and classification of our birds remained inert, apparently mesmerised by the implications of DNA, until the early 1990s.

Then, the task of producing a new 'official' Australian list fell to Dr Leslie Christidis, Curator of Birds at the Museum of Victoria, and Walter E. Boles of the Australian Museum, Sydney.

Instigated by the nation's top scientific bird research organisation, the RAOU, 'The Taxonomy and Species of Birds of Australia and its Territories' (RAOU Monograph 2, Melbourne, 1994) gained immediate and wide acceptance.

The work recognises traditional relationships yet incorporates many changes in family order and composition, reflecting the determinations of Sibley and Ahlquist and other workers, including Richard Schodde, Christidis himself and other Australian biologists.

Accordingly, Australia's birds now fall into 20 orders, some 85 families (see below) and some 793 species, including a number of recently reported visiting species accepted by the RAOU's Record Appraisal Committee, and species found on outlying Australian island territories. A Supplementary List includes mostly rare visitors not officially validated at date of publication.

This guide closely follows Christidis and Boles, confining itself to some 778 species of birds recorded (or likely to be reported) in Australia and Tasmania, coastal seas and nearer islands. It deviates in only a few cases where the appearance or size of a bird is sufficiently like another species to justify placing them on the same plate. Examples are Australian Pelican (p. 109); Magpie-lark (p. 463); Spangled Drongo (p. 469); and Arctic Warbler (p. 511).

There follows below a complete summary of Australian bird families, in the sequence of Christidis and Boles. Reading it will help you to more satisfactorily place the species in the main body of the book in their family (or world) context.

Common Names: the key to familiarity

When it instigated the compilation of Christidis and Boles's work, the RAOU took the opportunity to amend a number of common names for Australian birds. This was done by a plebiscite of Australian ornithologists and birdwatchers, conducted in 1993–1994 through the RAOU's quarterly, *Wingspan*. The results were announced in *Wingspan* Vol.5, no.1, March 1995.

Thus Christidis and Boles's *Taxonomy* was able to incorporate a number of popularly agreed changes to common names, including welcome restoration of some traditional names such as Bush Stone-curlew, Nankeen Night Heron and White-necked Heron. These had been rejected in the 1978 'Recommended English Names' in favour of 'Bush Thicknee', 'Rufous Night Heron' and 'Pacific Heron'. Some other well-loved names were similarly restored. As such, today we have a combined up-to-date bird taxonomy and a widely accepted list of common names, democratically chosen.

The long-term stability of common names is a matter of extreme importance, both culturally and in terms of conservation. The interested public needs a feeling of comfortable first-name familiarity with the nation's wildlife. Passed down the generations, that familiarity has become an essential part of Australian cultural heritage for many. Such stability is made doubly important by the need for scientific names to remain flexible, able to change as scientific advancement enables ever-increasing understanding of our birds' relations, one to another.

FAMILY INTRODUCTIONS

OSTRICHES Family Struthionidae
EMUS AND CASSOWARIES Family Casuariidae

PP. 18–19

Largest living birds, sharing a common flying ancestor when southern continents were one land-mass. The Ostrich has a spreading foot of only two toes and huge, bare legs, for walking and running on sandy or stony African desert-steppe, and for heat-dispersal. The Emu, dweller of Australia's arid plains and woodlands, has powerful legs and shaggy, divided plumage for protection from sun, snow and sleet. The Southern Cassowary, of tropical rainforests of ne. Aust. and PNG (where two other cassowary species occur), has a horn-covered bony helmet and coarse, hairlike plumage, for pushing through spiny vines and to shed tropical rains.

Food: nearly omnivorous: insects, fruits, berries, seeds, cultivated grain, grasses, herbage, blossoms, small dead animals and other carrion.

Range: Ostrich: n. and s. Africa. Introduced to Aust. in 1860s and in 1980s–1990s for farming. Feral populations doubtfully present in s. SA. Emu: mainland Aust., except driest deserts and closely settled areas (extinct in Tas., King and Kangaroo Is. — the last two having had separate species). Southern Cassowary: ne. Q, PNG, Aru Is., Seram.

Number of species: Ostrich: 1 (Aust. 1, introduced). Emu: 1, formerly 3, (Aust. 1, formerly 3). Cassowary: 3 (Aust. 1).

MOUND BUILDERS Family Megapodiidae

PP. 20–21

Specialised fowls of the Australian region that lay large progressive clutches in incubating mounds of decomposing vegetation, mixed with earth or sand. They have complex routines for maintaining temperature, humidity and aeration of these mounds for successful incubation.

Food: insects, herbs, buds, seeds, fallen fruits and small vertebrates.

Range: Aust. and PNG, Indonesia, w. to Nicobar Is., n. to n. Borneo and Philippines, e. to c. Polynesia (Marchant and Higgins, 1993).

Number of species: 12 (Aust. 3).

TRUE QUAILS, RED JUNGLEFOWL, COMMON PHEASANT, INDIAN PEAFOWL, WILD TURKEY Family Phasianidae
CALIFORNIA QUAIL Family Odontophoridae

PP. 22–25

Except for the Red Junglefowl, Common Pheasant, Indian Peafowl, Wild Turkey and California Quail (all introduced), members of this family in Aust. are typical quails: small, plump, ground-living birds, with short bills and legs, four toes and short wings. Red Junglefowl are descended from domestic fowls permitted to go feral on some Gt Barrier Reef islands in the 19th century, but only successful on Heron I. where in the absence of new genes, the birds reverted to ancestral type, the Red Junglefowl, *Gallus gallus*, of se. Asia.

Food: insects and other invertebrates; seeds of native plants and introduced cereals; legumes and weeds; other vegetation.

Range: all temperate continents; many islands.

Number of species: Phasianidae: 210 (Aust. 8, 5 introduced). Odontophoridae: *c.*30 (Aust. 1, introduced).

MAGPIE GEESE Family Anseranatidae

PP. 32–33

The Magpie Goose is ancient and possibly related to the South American screamers, Anhimidae. The structure of its bill, neck, legs and part-webbed, clawed feet, and the progressive moult of its flight-feathers ensuring that it is never completely flightless, reflect long adaptive development to seasonally drying Aust. coastal wetlands. The bird has a long, convoluted windpipe, which produces loud, mellow honks.

Food: underground bulbs of spike-rush; sedges, seeds of grasses incl. wild rice.

Range: Aust. and PNG.

Number of species: 1 (Aust. 1).

SWANS, GEESE AND DUCKS Family Anatidae

PP. 26–41

Broad-bodied waterbirds with dense, water-resistant plumage. Necks are slender; bills adapted for filtering small plants and animals from water; also for grazing, browsing, picking up seeds and grain, seizing molluscs, crustaceans, young waterfowl, pulling up waterplants, digging underwater for corms, etc. Adapting to irregular rainfall, some Australian species are highly mobile and nomadic.

Food: omnivorous.

Range: cosmopolitan.

Number of species: 184 (Aust. 24, incl. 2 introduced species, 2 vagrants).

The following are the main groups within the family.

WHISTLING DUCKS (*DENDROCYGNA*)

Small-bodied, longish necked, long-legged ducks, lacking a speculum; some species have decorative flank-plumes. The group is without clear affinities with other waterfowl. Most species occur in warmer regions. Sexes alike: they share incubation of eggs; both accompany ducklings.

AUSTRALIAN WOOD DUCK (*CHENONETTA*)

With a short, grazing bill with serrated cutting edges, long legs and partly webbed feet, the Australian Wood Duck is a dabbling duck that has become a goose-like grazer on wetland margins, pastures, crops and in open woodlands.

FRECKLED DUCK

With a scooped swan-like bill (red at base in breeding males) and lacking the strong plumage patterns and glossy wing-mirror (speculum) of most other dabbling ducks, the Freckled Duck is thought to represent an early stage of waterfowl evolution. Accorded a subfamily of its own, Stictonettinae, it is one of world's rarest, and probably one of world's earliest waterfowl.

STIFFTAILS — BLUE-BILLED AND MUSK DUCKS

Members of a world group of eight diving ducks so-called because of their many stiff, pointed tail-feathers (18 in Blue-bill, 24 in Musk). They possibly diverged early from the mainstream of waterfowl evolution. The two Aust. representatives are alike in their ability to swim and dive, propelled by large, rear set feet; they walk awkwardly on land. The male Musk Duck is distinguished by a large, leathery lobe under the bill, prominent in its bizarre mating display.

SWANS

Very large waterfowl with simple plumage patterns; their long necks are adapted for reaching underwater plants while upending, assisted by large dark webbed feet. They have long bills with a horny, broad, hooked nail at tip for tearing up bottom-growing plants; the interior sides of the bill are equipped with a long set of combs (*lamellae*) to drain water from small plant food, e.g. duckweed. Like most other members of the family, swans moult their flight feathers either annually or at irregular longer intervals, becoming flightless for up to six weeks.

CAPE BARREN GOOSE

The taxonomic position of the endemic Cape Barren Goose is unclear. Adaptation for life on small islands off s. Aust. (its world stronghold), has given it a short, sturdy bill for grazing tough herbage, well-developed salt-excreting glands, a sturdy frame and strong legs with heavily clawed, part-webbed feet. Drinking saltwater if need be, it breeds on these islands in winter. When the herbage dries out in spring-early summer, many geese leave the breeding islands for larger islands or mainland areas, where they seek developed pastures with introduced grasses and legumes. The total world population has been estimated at *c.* 17 000 (Marchant & Higgins, 1990).

SHELDUCKS

Large, boldly marked, showy ducks, with small heads, slightly upturned bills and a large coloured wing-mirror or speculum. They take their food by upending, suzzling, grazing in short green grasslands and developed pastures, or gleaning cereal grain. When breeding, males take up wetland feeding territories which they defend. Many pairs with young gather annually on certain wetlands, where young of varying ages are occasionally grouped in creches of scores of ducklings. After breeding, the birds moult their flight feathers and become temporarily flightless, gathering on traditional, secure large waters.

PYGMY-GEESE

Members of a diverse group of so-called 'perching ducks', subfamily Anatinae. Exquisite, very small, tropical waterfowl, they have short bills for foraging on aquatic vegetation and seeds on the surface, and when upending and diving. Males, in particular, have differing breeding/nonbreeding plumages.

POCHARDS

A world group of ducks that mostly feed by diving. With legs set well back for efficient swimming, they walk awkwardly. Starting with a little leap, they dive deep, propelling themselves underwater with large feet, wings closed. They also feed by dabbling and upending. To take off they must run across surface.

DABBLING DUCKS

'Typical' ducks; most species have a glossy, iridescent blue–green 'window' or speculum in the wing. They feed by 'suzzling' and upending for animal and plant-food, drawing in a stream of water and mud through the open tip of the bill and discharging it through combs (*lamellae*) in sides of upper mandible, retaining small food items. Shovelers have enlarged bills for filter-feeding; the Pink-eared Duck has food-guiding 'flanges'; both have specialised foraging techniques. Most species have a double annual moult, males in particular assuming bright plumage in autumn and maintaining this into the spring breeding season, when they moult temporarily into duller 'eclipse' plumage. Molecular studies reveal little genetic differentiation between the perching, diving and typical dabbling ducks (Christidis & Boles, 1994). Sexes are alike in some species, but not others; males usually larger.

GREBES Family Podicipedidae $\qquad$ PP. 42–43

Very small to medium, sharp-billed, slender-necked, nearly tailless aquatic birds of uncertain, ancient origin. Feet lobed rather than webbed, they dive expertly, locating much of their prey underwater. They usually dive rather than fly to escape danger, but fly long distances to new waters, usually at night.
Food: fish, tadpoles, insect-larvae, crustaceans.
Range: nearly cosmopolitan.
Number of species: 19 (Aust. 3).

PENGUINS Family Spheniscidae $\qquad$ PP. 44–49

Descended from flying, petrel-like ancestors, penguins have flippers rather than wings. On land they mostly walk upright. To render them less conspicuous while swimming, plumage is strongly counter-shaded, i.e. dark above, pale below; recognition markings are mostly on the head. Feathers are small, close and scale-like, over thick waterproof down. For survival in cold seas, the plumage forms a complete, water-resistant sheath. Once a year, after breeding, old plumage must be completely replaced. This moult takes weeks and must be completed ashore while fasting. Species from the sub-Antarctic are frequently found moulting ashore in s. Aust. Because bulky bodies retain warmth more efficiently than slimmer ones, the larger, rounder species have tended to evolve in Antarctic regions, smaller ones in temperate zones. To avoid aerial predators, small species such as the Little Blue Penguin nest in burrows and come and go from breeding colonies under cover of darkness.
Food: fish, crustaceans, molluscs.
Range: Antarctica, sub-Antarctic islands and seas, ranging n. to c. 30°S (one to n. of Equator). NZ region has most species.
Number of species: 18 (Aust. 11).

PETRELS, SHEARWATERS AND PRIONS Family Procellariidae $\qquad$ PP. 50–77

Very small to very large oceanic birds. Most (but not the Diving Petrels) have two nostrils united in a nostril-tube along the top of the bill. They have a keen sense of smell, capable of locating swarming fish or plankton. Coupled with typical musky petrel odour, sense of smell may help locate breeding islands at night. Most species use the energy of the wind to provide motive power in their constant foraging flights far from land, differing migratory patterns taking them to certain zones of surface-water at critical times of the year across apparently trackless oceans. The various groups (outlined below) have evolved differing foraging techniques and physical structures for taking particular prey.
Food: planktonic crustaceans, molluscs, fish, other seabirds, carrion.
Range: oceans, seas, bays, islands and mainland coastal areas worldwide.
Number of species: 70 (Aust. 44).
The following are the main groups in the family.

DIVING PETRELS
Very small stocky petrels. They 'fly' underwater on short, stubby wings in pursuit of prey.

FULMARINE PETRELS
Seven species of huge to large, sturdy petrels with prominent nostril-tubes and stiff-winged flight. Six species, incl. the Giant-Petrels, breed on or near the Antarctic continent, nesting in surface scrapes, not burrows.

GADFLY PETRELS
Graceful, slender-winged petrels, of dramatic high-speed arcing and soaring flight, with occasional quick, shallow wingbeats. *A black, short, narrow bill with a prominent hooked nail and short nostril-tube separates them from shearwaters.* Most species nest in burrows, or in cavities under rocks and/or roots. Most (but not all) come and go from nesting/roosting sites during darkness.

PRIONS OR WHALEBIRDS
Specialised plankton-feeders — *the upper mandibles of their bills, narrow or grotesquely wide, are edged with fine bristle-like combs, which retain small plankton while expelling water.* Form and size of bill differ greatly between species, and between different populations faithful to particular oceanic islands, where they nest in burrows and rock crevices and mostly come and go under cover of darkness. Most can be safely identified at sea only as 'prions'.

Bills noticeably longer, more slender than in gadfly petrels, usually dark; feet usually dark, but in some, pale bill/feet are useful field marks. With long, narrow wings, broader in some, large shearwaters have a banking, gliding flight, hugging the water; medium species slice fast on fixed wings in undulating streams; small ones fly low with bursts of fluttering wingbeats and glides. Gregarious, some feed in dark rafts, churning spray and swimming underwater on half-closed wings. Several are among the world's most numerous birds. Most nest in burrows, coming and going under darkness.

ALBATROSSES Family Diomedeidae   PP. 78–89

Fabled oceanic birds with extremely long, slender wings. Bills are large, shapely, nearly hooked at tip, with short, well-separated nostril-tubes. Most species live in the far s. oceans where effortless sailing flight using wind-energy enables them to cover great distances economically while foraging. Most southern albatrosses are regular winter visitors to s. Aust. seas. Only one species breeds in Aust. Some species have suffered unsustainable levels of mortality caused by long-line fishing operations.
Food: cuttlefish, fish and other marine organisms (some caught at night), carrion and offal at sea.
Range: oceans and bays mostly s. of the equator, and N. Pacific Ocean; some vagrant to N. Atlantic; also many oceanic islands, some parts of mainland coasts.
Number of species: 13 (Aust. 9).

STORM-PETRELS Family Hydrobatidae   PP. 90–93

Tiny, dark petrels with slight, hooked bills surmounted by a nostril-tube, usually slanted upward. Northern storm-petrels, subfamily Hydrobatinae, have long, narrow, angled wings, short legs and rounded or forked tails. They swoop and skim in almost tern-like flight. Southern storm-petrels, subfamily Oceanitinae, have shorter, rounded wings, more or less square tails, very long legs and butterfly-like fluttering as they hop, skip and bounce over waves, running or trailing legs as sea-anchors. Most species are migratory. They breed in burrows and rock cavities on islands, coming and going in darkness.
Food: plankton, crustaceans, molluscs, fish.
Range: world oceans, bays, islands and some mainland coastal areas incl. Antarctica.
Number of species: Hydrobatinae: 14 (Aust.2). Oceanitinae: 7 (Aust. 5).

TROPICBIRDS OR BOSUNBIRDS Family Phaethontidae   PP. 94–95

Related to gannets, tropicbirds resemble large-bodied terns, with strong, slightly down-curved bills and elongated ribbon-like central tail-plumes. They make high, gannet-like plunges for prey, and hover or display spectacularly in vicinity of nest-site.
Food: fish, squid, other molluscs.
Range: tropical and subtropical oceans, bays, islands and some mainland coastal areas.
Number of species: 3 (Aust. 2).

GANNETS AND BOOBIES Family Sulidae   PP. 96–101

Gannets are large, high-diving seabirds: plumage mostly white, with partly or wholly black flight-feathers and tail. They inhabit some temperate coastal waters and form a single world superspecies. Boobies inhabit tropical and subtropical seas: they have coloured facial skin and throat-pouches and some have brightly coloured feet. Both are streamlined in silhouette, with long pointed wings and body, tapering to a pointed, cone-shaped bill with serrated holding edges, and pointed tail.
Food: fish, squid, other molluscs.
Range: Gannets: coasts of w. Europe and ne. N. America; s. Africa; s. Aust. and NZ. Boobies: mostly tropical oceans, bays and islands.
Number of species: 9 (Aust. 5).

DARTERS Family Anhingidae   PP. 102–103

Fishing birds related to cormorants, with smaller head, stiletto-like bill with serrated holding edges at base, and a kinked snake-like neck with a trigger-like hinge in the vertebrae to impart a sudden thrust of the slightly opened bill to impale fish while swimming underwater. Easily saturated plumage necessitates frequent drying of wings. All four toes are webbed and the short legs are rear-placed for efficient swimming; when walking, the wings are spread for balance. Sexes dissimilar.
Food: mostly fish; reptiles, crustaceans, aquatic insects, spiders, plant material incl. seeds.
Range: tropical and subtropical regions, mostly coastal and inland.
Number of species: 2 (Aust. 1).

CORMORANTS Family Phalacrocoracidae PP. 102–105

Black, or black-and-white fishing birds, with bills hooked at tip, long flexible necks, tails rather long, feet totipalmate. Plumage is sparse and cormorants conspicuously dry their open wings on piles, piers, rocks, buoys, branches. (This action may also assist digestion of food.) They seldom venture far to sea from coasts or islands. Some species hunt co-operatively in flocks; all roost and breed communally.
Food: Fish, eels, frogs, crustaceans, insects and larvae; occasionally ducklings and small mammals.
Range: nearly cosmopolitan.
Number of species: 29 (Aust. 5).

FRIGATEBIRDS Family Fregatidae PP. 106–107

Frigatebirds have modified the characteristic features of their order to a remarkable degree. Bills are long, slender and hooked, throat-pouches are modified in males to inflatable red balloons, used in mating displays; webbed feet are miniaturised for weight-loss, but clawed for perching. Black plumage, extremely long crank-shaped wings and long, pointed or scissor-forked tails distinguish them. Spending hours in effortless soaring, they seldom alight on water, but snatch prey (incl. flying fish) from sea or land, in spectacular swoops. They also harry flying seabirds, especially boobies, until they disgorge, seizing food as it falls.
Food: fish, squid, crustaceans, young turtles, young birds, carrion.
Range: tropical and subtropical coasts, islands and oceans.
Number of species: 5 (Aust. 3).

PELICANS Family Pelecanidae PP. 108–109

Like other members of the Order Pelecaniformes (tropicbirds, gannets and boobies, cormorants and frigatebirds) pelicans have totipalmate feet and large, expandable throat-pouches of bare, elastic skin — in their case, developed to a remarkable degree. Filling with water as the bill is plunged forward, the huge bill-pouch is used as an expansible dip-net for capturing small fish, crustaceans, etc. On shadeless islands where pelicans breed, the pouch, fluttered as the bird pants, probably helps disperse body heat. Flushing deep pink in mating displays, it also serves as a secondary sexual character. Flying formations of Australian Pelicans use rising columns of warm air to lift them to great heights. Scanning a wide area, they head to where other pelicans are feeding.
Food: fish, frogs, tadpoles, crustaceans, large insects; occasionally ducklings.
Range: warm temperate and tropical parts of all continents; some oceanic islands.
Number of species: 8 (Aust. 1).

HERONS, EGRETS, NIGHT-HERONS, BITTERNS Family Ardeidae PP. 108–119

Medium to very tall wading birds with long necks and legs, and straight, sharp bills with finely serrated gripping edges for seizing slippery, active prey. They plunge the bill forward while wading, standing still, or stirring ahead with one foot to disturb prey. Most species have a specialised arrangement of the neck-vertebrae for suddenly straightening the curved neck to increase speed of thrust. Most herons and egrets nest in treetop colonies (some on ground), and most develop long, slender plumes on head, back and/or breast when breeding. Egrets are mostly white; the colours of their bills, facial skin, legs (and in some, plumage) alter when breeding. Most herons produce powder down in tracts under the plumage of the rump, breast and elsewhere. Broken up as the bird preens, it is spread through the plumage as a feather-dressing.
Food: fish, amphibians, reptiles, small mammals, small birds, crustaceans, insects and other invertebrates.
Range: all continents except Antarctica; many oceanic islands.
Number of species: 62 (Aust. 14).

IBISES AND SPOONBILLS Family Threskiornithidae PP. 120–123

Readily recognised by their long, sickle-shaped bills, ibises feed by probing, fossicking or seizing prey in water and on land. Spoonbills sweep the opened, sensitive tips of their submerged flattened, wide-tipped bills from side to side, locating prey by touch in water too turbid for location by sight alone. They also occasionally feed in dry grasslands.
Food: fish, eels, reptiles, frogs, tadpoles, small or young mammals; birds and eggs or young; crustaceans, insects, spiders and other invertebrates, molluscs.
Range: temperate and tropical parts of all continents.
Number of species: 31 (Aust. 5).

STORKS Family Ciconiidae PP. 108–109

Very tall, striking birds with bold plumage patterns and heavy, straight pointed bills; storks fly with long necks and legs extended, wingbeats slow and shallow. Some are nearly voiceless, but clatter and snap bills in display. Sexes nearly similar; eye colour may differ.
Food: fish, reptiles, rodents, frogs, crustaceans, insects, molluscs, small birds.
Range: almost cosmopolitan in temperate and tropical regions.
Number of species: 17 (Aust. 1).

OSPREY, HAWKS, EAGLES AND HARRIERS Family Accipitridae PP. 124–137 &
PP. 142–143

Mostly diurnal (day-flying) birds of prey with strongly hooked, sharp bills for cutting and tearing (but not primarily for killing prey). All have taloned feet, from large and powerful (eagles) to small and feeble (Black Kite, Pacific Baza). Most species use their feet to seize, hold, and/or kill prey. Females are larger than males. All build or add to their own nests, though some may pirate nests of other raptors or corvids.
The main groups in the family are as follows.

OSPREY

Cosmopolitan fish-hunting raptor with closeable nostrils; water-resistant plumage, long legs and massive feet, with strongly curved talons, reversible outer toe and sharp spicules on soles of feet and toe-pads for gripping and carrying struggling fish head-first, to reduce drag.
Food: in Aust., mostly fish; also sea-snakes, terns, petrels; on other continents, frogs, small mammals.
Range: Eurasia, n. Africa, N. and C. America, se. Asia to Aust.
Number of species: 1 (Aust. 1).

ELANID (HOVERING) KITES

Beautiful small grey-and-white hawks, mostly rodent-hunters. They hover gracefully, 'parachuting' with upraised wings onto prey. One Aust. species is largely nocturnal.
Food: rodents, small reptiles, birds or their young.
Range: Africa, Eurasia, N., C. and S. America; se. Asia to Aust.
Number of species: 4 (Aust. 2)

BAZAS OR CUCKOO FALCONS

With small, upright crest, long, broad, barred 'paddle-shaped' wings, feeble feet and talons, they often take small prey by flopping into foliage canopy.
Food: large insects, e.g. phasmids; frogs, reptiles, fruit.
Range: Africa, s. Asia to China, se. Asia, Philippines, Indonesia, PNG, Solomon Is., n. and ne. Aust.
Number of species: 4 (Aust. 1).

MILVINE (SOARING) KITES

Broad-winged, soaring raptors with small to medium feet and claws; predators on mostly small prey; consummate scavengers. They soar on long, broad wings with prominent 'fingertips'.
Food: insects, fish, small reptiles, birds, small mammals; a wide range of carrion.
Range: Eurasia, Africa, se. Asia to PNG, Aust.
Number of species: 4 (Aust. 3).

OLD ENDEMIC RAPTORS

Despite their familiar European names — Square-tailed Kite, Black-breasted Buzzard, Red Goshawk — the species are of uncertain relationships. They may represent an early raptor development on this continent, from a common, buzzard-like ancestor (Debus, 1991).
Food: birds, eggs and young; small mammals, reptiles, insects.
Range: mainland Aust.
Number of species: 3 (Aust. 3).

GOSHAWKS AND SPARROWHAWKS

Bird-hunting hawks with long legs and long toes, broad wings and longish tails for rapid acceleration and fast manoeuvering in flight through woodlands. Females are mostly much larger than males: difference in size between sexes and between species helps to lessen potential overlap in choice of prey.
Food: birds, small mammals, reptiles, insects.
Range: all continents except Antarctica.
Number of species: 46 (Aust. 3).

SEA-EAGLES

Sea-eagles in the genus *Haliaeetus* include several of the world's largest raptors. With broad wings, small tails and powerful legs and feet with bare tarsi, they take surface-swimming fish in spectacular dives without submerging.

Food: fish, reptiles, birds, small mammals, carrion.

Range: N. America, Greenland, n. Europe, sub-Saharan Africa, e. coastal Siberia, Asia, se. Asia to PNG, Aust.

Number of species: 8 (Aust. 1).

EAGLES

Powerful, medium to very large birds of prey; they have very robust, hooked bills, long legs feathered to the 'ankle' and strong, piercing talons with which to kill their prey.

Food: mammals, birds, fish, reptiles, carrion.

Range: all continents except Antarctica.

Number of species: 14 (Aust. 3, incl. 1 vagrant).

HARRIERS

Long slim hawks with long wings, legs and tails, small heads and owl-like facial discs of raised, stiff feathers that probably assist hearing when hunting small ground-living or wetland prey. Best-known for their low sailing flight on upswept wings over open country; they sometimes hover heavily. Most species nest on ground, in crops and swamp-vegetation, but one Aust. species builds a stick-nest in trees — the only harrier to do so.

Food: ground and water-living birds, small mammals, reptiles, insects.

Range: all continents except Antarctica.

Number of species: 12 (Aust. 3, incl. 1 vagrant).

FALCONS Family Falconidae   PP. 138–141 & 144–145

Swift, dark-eyed birds of prey with short necks and long, powerful wings which sweep back to a point in high speed chases and dives. Kestrels, a world group of delicately built small falcons, are consummate hoverers. Falcons mostly kill prey by a bite to the neck-vertebrae, employing a sharp projection ('tomial tooth') on the cutting edge of the upper mandible, which meshes with a corresponding notch in the lower mandible. They nest on sheltered cliff-ledges, ledges of tall buildings, in large tree-hollows, or usurp the stick nests of other raptors or corvids. Females are larger than males.

Food: birds, mammals, reptiles, frogs, insects.

Range: all continents except Antarctica.

Number of species: 60 (Aust. 6).

CRANES Family Gruidae   PP. 146–147

Long-legged, long-necked birds of stately carriage; long tertiary feathers droop over rump in graceful 'bustle'. Adults have bare coloured heads. Cranes fly with neck and legs extended, with powerful, slow wingbeats and, often, a distinctive upward wing-flick. In display, pairs or groups leap, bow and 'dance'. They breed mostly in permanent, solitary pairs and form post-breeding mixed companies of hundreds on wetlands, floodplains or grain-stubbles.

Food: seeds, roots, bulbs and other vegetation; reptiles, frogs, fish, small mammals and birds, insects and larvae.

Range: cosmopolitan except S. America, NZ.

Number of species: 14 (Aust. 2).

CRAKES, RAILS AND GALLINULES Family Rallidae   PP. 148–157

Very small to medium, slim and often shy, secretive waterbirds with sharp to long, slender bills, small heads, longish necks, strong legs and slender toes for swimming, running, climbing or walking on floating vegetation. Upright tails are flicked when walking, running or swimming. Gallinules are large rails with coloured bills extending in a shield onto forehead. One group, the Coots, have flattened lobes on all four toes, enhancing diving ability. Most rails have strident, shrieking, clacking or purring voices. Despite apparently feeble flight, most species are capable of substantial movements between areas of suitable habitat. Some island forms have become flightless, e.g. the Tasmanian Native-hen, *Gallinula mortieri*, and the Woodhen, *Gallirallus sylvestris*, of Lord Howe Island.

Food: seeds, insects, frogs, crustaceans, molluscs, water-insects, eggs, young birds, small mammals, carrion, aquatic (and other) green plants.
Range: all continents except Antarctica.
Number of species: 123 (Aust. 16).

BUSTARDS Family Otididae   PP. 158–159

The heaviest of flying birds; foraging, roosting and nesting on the ground, bustards are stately dwellers of plains and grassy woodlands. Male bustards are much larger than females, and have spectacular mating displays.
Food: insects, especially caterpillars, locusts and beetles; scorpions, centipedes, spiders, small birds, small mammals, reptiles, molluscs, succulent plants, seeds, fruit.
Range: Africa, Eurasia, Australia and PNG.
Number of species: 24 (Aust. 1).

BUTTON-QUAILS Family Turnicidae   PP. 160–163

Plump, short-legged, quail-like birds of grasslands, woodlands and open forest. They have intricate protective colouring and short, broad wings to propel them into rapid flight. Unrelated to true quail, they lack a crop and hind-toe. Females are larger, more colourful/strongly marked than males. With accelerating 'ooming' calls, they establish territories and initiate courtship; both sexes may build the cup-shaped, partly hooded nest. The smaller, plainer male does much of the brooding and overseeing of young. When feeding, woodland species scratch backward with both feet while rotating in either direction. Characteristic soup-plate depressions result.
Food: invertebrates, seeds, green shoots.
Range: Africa, sw. Europe, s. Asia, Aust., PNG, Solomons and Pacific islands.
Number of species: 15 (Aust. 7).

PLAINS-WANDERERS Family Pedionomidae   PP. 162–163

A monotypic family, endemic to Australia. The Plains-wanderer somewhat resembles a small, lanky button-quail but is related to the S. American seed-snipes (Thinocoridae) in the wader Order, Charadriiformes. As in button-quails, the male does much of the incubation and overseeing of chicks. Plains-wanderers inhabit sparse, open native grasslands that survive in inland se. Aust.
Food: seeds and green parts of plants, insects and other soil invertebrates.
Range: se. mainland Aust.
Number of species: 1 (Aust. 1).

SNIPE, GODWITS, CURLEWS, SANDPIPERS, STINTS AND PHALAROPES Family Scolopacidae   PP. 164–195

Wading birds with medium-long to very long, slender bills with more sensitive tips for locating animal food by probing. Eyes are smaller, heads narrower than plovers. Legs are medium-long to very long. Plumages are mottled or patterned with streaks, notchings and/or barrings. Colourful breeding plumage contrasts with drab brown to grey or white nonbreeding plumage. Except for some snipe and woodcock, all breed in the n. hemisphere. In the northern autumn–winter they migrate to tidal mudflats, beaches, coral and rock reefs, and freshwater habitats throughout the s. hemisphere. They are active at low tide, day and night. With bills, legs, body-structure and size, and specialised foraging techniques differing subtly or markedly from one group to the next, few families demonstrate the diversity of adaptive radiation better than this.
Food: aquatic and terrestrial invertebrates, small fish, small reptiles, molluscs, crustaceans, marine worms, earthworms, seeds and vegetation.
Range: all continents except Antarctica.
Number of species: 85 (Aust. c. 48).
The following are the main groups in the family.

SNIPE

Short-legged, specialised sandpipers of soft, muddy ground. The sensitive tips of their long, straight bills can locate and seize prey underground. Solitary or loosely gregarious, snipe keep to low cover in marshy habitats, made inconspicuous by cryptic behaviour and disruptive plumage patterns. As their large eyes indicate, they forage and travel much at night. Note that the Painted Snipe (family Rostratulidae, p. 196) is not related.

Godwits

Elegant, medium-to-large waders with long, tapering, straight or slightly upswept bills (longer in females), longish legs and subtle plumage patterns; breeding plumage colourful. They feed by probing the sensitive tips of their bills into the tidal ooze to locate prey. Godwits fly in lines or echelons often low to the water, their long bills, swept wings and slightly tubby outlines distinctive.

Dowitchers

Resemble small, rather heavy godwits with untapering black bills which they carry downpointed.

Curlews

With bills of differing size, curlews that annually migrate to Australia form an adaptive 'set'. The largest sandpiper, the Eastern Curlew, has a very long, sickle-shaped bill which it rams deep into crab-holes. The Whimbrel has a medium-long, less-curved bill. Little Curlews, with the shortest, straightest bills, regularly migrate in flocks of many thousands to the grasslands of inland n. Aust. The mottled plumage-patterns of curlews are subtle, with less seasonal differences than most other waders.

Greenshanks, Redshanks and other medium to small sandpipers; Common Sandpiper, Tattlers

Contrasting the probing techniques of godwits and curlews, the so-called Tringine sandpipers peck rapidly on either side as they wade, picking and probing; they dash after small fish in shallow water, or turn quickly to stab. Some swim and upend. Nervously alert, they bob heads, or wag rear of body up and down. Flight swift, wings often held arched down in glides between clipped wingbeats.

Ruddy Turnstone

With its short, pointed, upswept bill, backed by a squat body and strong orange legs, it flips over shells and pebbles, and bulldozes piles of seaweed, uncovering small crustaceans, invertebrates and molluscs.

Knots, Stints, Caliditrine Sandpipers, Broad-billed and Stilt Sandpipers, and Ruff

Caliditrine Sandpipers and their allies are small to medium-sized, swift flying waders of subtly distinctive structures and habits. Bills are straight or slightly downcurved, short to medium-long. Breeding, nonbreeding and immature plumages are distinctive. Despite confusing similarities, no two species share precisely the same build, behaviour or choice of micro-habitat. The species accounts give brief sketches of the characteristics of each. The curiously named Ruff is best known for the extravagant breeding plumes of males on n. hemisphere display grounds. The Buff-breasted and Upland Sandpipers are unusual sandpipers that breed in N. American grasslands and prairies and migrate to S. America, occasionally straying to Aust.

Phalaropes

Elegant, aberrant sandpipers, with slender bills, small heads, slender necks, broad, buoyantly feathered bodies, and short, laterally-flattened legs and lobed toes for efficient swimming. Females are larger, and initiate courtship, becoming strikingly colourful in breeding plumage. The smaller, less colourful males brood eggs and attend young. In nonbreeding plumage both sexes are grey and white, with a distinctive dark grey or black 'phalarope-mark' on face/ear-coverts. Two species winter mostly at sea off w. S. America, w. Africa, Arabian Sea and n. Indonesia, at times gathering in flocks among surfacing whales to feed on plankton. Straying to Aust., phalaropes occur mostly in singles on shallow, fresh or saline waters, noticeable by their buoyancy, whiteness and habit of spinning like tops while feeding.

PAINTED SNIPE Family Rostratulidae   PP. 196–197

Strikingly patterned, rail-like waders, not closely related to true snipe. Females, larger and more colourful than males, initiate courtship; males incubate eggs, (but not so in the related South American Painted Snipe, *Nycticryphes*, in which sexual roles are conventional). Part-nocturnal, Painted Snipe have a preference for shallow freshwater wetlands with ooze and low cover of green and dead marsh plants. They have become rare and spasmodic in occurrence, though faithful to particular locations.
Food: worms, molluscs, insects, vegetable matter.
Range: Africa, s. and se. Asia, China, Japan, Philippines, Indonesia, Aust., S. America.
Number of species: 2 (Aust. 1).

JACANAS ('LOTUSBIRDS') Family Jacanidae   PP. 196–197

Unusual wetland birds, related to rails, with spurs on wings; long legs with enormously long, slender toes and hind claws support them on lily pads and other floating vegetation as they forage. Their nests are small collections of floating waterplants in which the eggs are constantly wet. Aust. has one widespread species and one vagrant. The name Jacana is Brazilian; in Aust. the alternate name 'lotusbird' is well established.

Food: molluscs, insects; seeds, other vegetable matter.
Range: South and Central America, Africa, tropical Asia to Aust.
Number of species: 8 (Aust. 2).

STONE-CURLEWS Family Burhinidae PP. 158–159

Large plover-like waders with large heads, large yellow eyes, and grey, brown, buff, black or white plumage with strong streaks and/or strong, disruptive patterns. Part-nocturnal, secretive by day; when disturbed they take cover, freeze flat, move slowly with neck held stiffly forward, run, or fly away on bowed, contrastingly marked wings. Active at night, groups display noisily. The two Aust. species differ in build, markings and habits in response to demands of bush and beach habitats. Voices are clear, high-pitched whistlings, wails and pipings, mostly heard at night — the celebrated 'wail of the curlew'.
Food: insects, crustaceans (principally crabs), other arthropods, small rodents, reptiles, frogs, molluscs, other marine invertebrates.
Range: Africa, Eurasia, Malaysia, Philippines, Borneo, Indonesia, PNG, Aust., Solomon Is.
Number of species: 9 (Aust. 2).

OYSTERCATCHERS Family Haematopodidae PP. 198–199

Gregarious, noisy, demonstrative, sturdy black, or black-and-white wading birds with straight, laterally flattened red bills used to pry limpets off rocks, open bivalves in hard, wet beach-sand by hammering, or by stabbing to dismember crustaceans. In Aust. two species occupy sandy and rocky shores, respectively. Oystercatchers are mostly sedentary, with local autumn-winter dispersals.
Food: molluscs, crustaceans, seaworms, earthworms.
Range: coasts of Europe, S. Africa, Red Sea, Arabian Peninsula, Persian Gulf, India, se. Asia, Japan, PNG-Aust., NZ, Alaska, Aleutians, w. and s. N. America, w. and se. S. America. Inland in parts of Eurasia, S. America.
Number of species: 7 (Aust. 2).

STILTS AND AVOCETS Family Recurvirostridae PP. 200–201

Slender waders with long, very fine, straight bills (stilts) or upturned bills (avocets), and extremely long thin legs, feet partly or fully webbed. Foraging in shallow waters, fresh and salt, they wade, probe, sweep bill from side to side, pick from surface while swimming, or upend. In Aust. they are not regular, long distance migrants, although there is a seasonal regularity about their opportunistic movements. Breeding habits and habitat requirements of the Banded Stilt are notable — see species entry.
Food: aquatic and terrestrial insects, spiders, water mites, crustaceans, molluscs, marine worms, earthworms, small fish, seeds, vegetable matter.
Range: all continents except Antarctica; se. Asia to PNG, NZ (possibly colonised from Aust. early in 19th century), (Marchant & Higgins, 1993).
Number of species: 7 (Aust. 3).

PLOVERS, DOTTERELS AND LAPWINGS Family Charadriidae PP. 202–215

Small to medium waders with characteristic short bills, large eyes, rounded heads, short necks, medium-long legs, usually no hind toes, and bolder, simpler patterns than sandpipers. When foraging, plovers typically walk or run a short distance, pause watchfully upright, tilt forward to lunge and jab at prey, before moving on. Seven resident and 12 migratory species (incl. three rare vagrants) occur in Aust. The flight of the long-winged migrants is especially swift and graceful. They breed mostly in n. hemisphere, though one breeds in NZ and migrates across the Tasman Sea to Aust. in autumn–winter, returning to NZ in spring. In Aust. they are mostly seen in nonbreeding plumage, but newly arrived or soon-to-depart individuals often show traces of, or complete, breeding plumage. Note that several species formerly called dotterels are more correctly called 'plovers', though two native species whose relationships remain unclear are still called 'dotterels'. Two large, broad-winged native species, formerly known as 'plovers', are now placed with the worldwide lapwings, subfamily Vanellinae.
Food: insects and larvae, molluscs, crustaceans, spiders, marine worms, earthworms, small reptiles, small fish, birds' eggs, seeds, fruits, vegetable matter.
Range: all continents except Antarctica.
Number of species: 65 (Aust. 19).

Pratincoles (subfamily Glareolinae) are graceful, long-winged aberrant wader-like birds of plains and dry margins of wetlands, now linked with terns, family Laridae. Bills are short and curved, with a wide gape. With short legs and longish, deeply forked tails, they run like waders but fly easily like terns, taking insects on the wing and on the ground. One species migrates to Aust. during the southern summer. The Australian Pratincole, regarded by some as a courser (subfamily Cursoriinae), has long legs, very long wings and a short tail. It stands more upright than pratincoles and wags rear of body up and down. Unlike either pratincoles or coursers, it lacks pectinations (comb-like processes) on the claw of the middle toe. Like coursers but unlike pratincoles, it has no hind toe. Its flight is strong, swift and graceful.

Food: mostly insects.
Range: temperate and tropical Europe, Africa, Asia, Aust., vagrant NZ.
Number of species: 16 (Aust. 2).

SKUAS, JAEGERS, GULLS, TERNS, NODDIES   PP. 218–241
AND TERNLETS Family Laridae

Skuas and Jaegers

Robust predatory seabirds, now united with gulls, family Laridae. With hooked bills, swift, direct flight and distinctive elongated central tail-feathers, most species pursue other seabirds, forcing them to disgorge. They are also powerful predators and scavengers, following ships for scraps. The Great Skua has widely separated discrete breeding populations in N. Atlantic and far s. hemisphere. The widespread sub-Antarctic race *lonnbergi* is the usual form on our coasts. Large and blunt, it harries birds as large as gannets, often forcing them to disgorge prey, which it seizes in flight. The Arctic, Pomarine and Long-tailed Jaegers breed in far n. hemisphere. All are summer migrants to Aust. waters. Smaller and lighter than skuas, jaegers are identified by swift, almost falcon-like flight, the comparative width of their swept pointed wings, length of tail, and size/shape of elongated central tail-feathers. They frequently harry gulls and terns. They have distinctive light and dark plumage morphs, with variable intermediates. Immatures have different, mottled plumages, difficult to identify safely.

Gulls

Sturdier, broader-winged and longer-legged than terns; bills deeper and more robust, tails mostly squared or rounded. Most gulls have white bodies with grey or black wings and backs; their young are usually brown and mottled and can be difficult to identify. Smaller gulls, e.g. Silver Gull, attain adult plumage with adult bill, eye and leg-colours in two years. Larger species, e.g. Pacific Gull, take up to four years. Northern hemisphere gulls that occasionally reach Aust. have distinct breeding and nonbreeding plumages. Profiting greatly from human settlement, gulls are increasingly abundant scavengers in cities around the world.

Terns

In general terns have sharper, finer bills than gulls and are more slender, with longer narrower wings and deep forked or short, nearly square tails; they fly gracefully and take live food by plunging below, or skimming, the surface. A few feed over land. Typical terns have black caps, greyish wings, white underparts; in nonbreeding plumage they typically become whiter on the head. One subgroup is the marsh terns (*Chlidonia*): small, delicate terns, they prefer freshwater wetlands, hovering and dipping, working into the wind, seldom plunging.

Noddies and Ternlets

Five mostly tropical, oceanic terns; three are sooty, with white or pale grey caps. Two others belong to different genera and are frequently called ternlets; one is pale grey, the other spotless white. Most terns (and some gulls) lay their eggs in a scrape in sand; or in cavities in rocks; gulls typically build large cup-nests on the ground or in low bushes, noddies typically nest in bushes or trees. Most species breed in colonies, some immense. Sexes alike, females are smaller.

Food: whole prey disgorged by other seabirds; flotsam, scraps, refuse from whaling and fishing operations and other carrion; fish, crustaceans, molluscs, insects, small mammals, birds, eggs and nestlings, reptiles, carrion, human refuse, berries and other vegetable matter.
Range: worldwide.
Number of species: Skuas: 4 (Aust. 2). Jaegers: 3 (Aust. 3). Gulls: 46 (Aust. 9). Terns: 37 (Aust. 17). Noddies: 5 (Aust. 5).

PIGEONS AND DOVES Family Columbidae

PP. 242–257

Plump, small-headed, densely-plumaged, seed or fruit-eating birds. Generally, larger members of the family are called pigeons and smaller ones doves. Species of rainforests and similar dense, humid habitats of e. and n. Aust. include colourful, boldly marked fruit pigeons and others which feed mostly on whole fruit and berries. Pigeons and doves of drier, more open habitats are mostly modestly-coloured, ground-feeding, seed-eating birds. They include the Bronzewings, which have a brightly coloured bronze patch (speculum) on the wing. Some members of both groups are highly gregarious, travelling, feeding (or watering) in flocks. Most pigeons and doves have strong, direct flight; many take off with a characteristic clatter. When courting, some make clapping sounds with their wings in conspicuous aerial displays. Males tend to be larger and more boldly marked and/or coloured.

Food: seeds, shoots, fruit, berries, insects and other invertebrates.

Range: almost cosmopolitan; absent from high latitudes and some oceanic islands.

Number of species: 297 (Aust. 25, 3 introduced).

COCKATOOS, CORELLAS & COCKATIEL Family Cacatuidae

PP. 258–265 &
PP. 274–275

Cockatoos are large, simply coloured parrots with mobile crests and powerful articulated bills for cutting and tearing wood, opening seed-capsules and digging, according to species. Strong feet, with two toes forward and two back, are adapted to efficient climbing and grasping. The Australian region is their stronghold: beyond PNG, a few species range to the Philippines. Most have loud voices. The small, parrot-like cockatiel is now regarded as a cockatoo.

Food: seeds, nuts, berries, fruits, blossoms, corms and roots, palm shoots, and invertebrates (especially large wood-boring larvae of moths and beetles).

Range: Australian region, incl. PNG; Solomon Is., Indonesia, Philippines.

Number of species: 18 (Aust. 14).

PARROTS, INCL. LORIKEETS, FIG-PARROTS, ROSELLAS, RINGNECKS AND BUDGERIGAR Family Psittacidae

PP. 266–291

Most parrots are very colourful birds with strong curved bills with both mandibles articulated for manipulating seeds, fruit and insects, digging, crushing or tearing hard objects. Their mostly short legs have muscular, zygodactylous feet. Species of arid inland habitats are mostly nomadic, moving and breeding irregularly in response to rainfall. Following good rains and growth of seeding grasses, species like the Budgerigar enjoy spectacular increases. Most Australian parrots nest in tree-hollows but the small group of 'anthill' parrots burrow in termite mounds; one grass-parrot nests in rock-cavities. The Ground and Night Parrots, alone, build nests of plant-material on or near ground in heavy low cover. Most parrots are gregarious, forming small to large flocks, especially after breeding. Some have become more abundant and widespread following pastoral and agricultural development; one species is probably extinct, and at least four are in danger of extinction, or have been seriously reduced by loss or change of habitat, or by illicit trapping.

Food: seeds and grain, green vegetation, fruits (incl. cultivated fruit and berries), nectar and pollen, insects and larvae.

Range: throughout the tropics, extending into temperate, cool temperate and even alpine zones in Asia, N. and S. America, Africa, Aust. and NZ and some oceanic and even sub-Antarctic islands.

Number of species: 328 (Aust. 40).

The main groups in the family are as follows:

LORIKEETS

Small to medium, highly energetic, swift-flying, glossy green parrots of Aust. region. Their brush-tipped tongues and simplified digestive systems are adapted for feeding on nectar and pollen. Lorikeets have a high level of daily and seasonal mobility as they search for nectar-flows in eucalypt, paperbark, banksia and other forests and woodlands, attracting attention with thin, piercing shrieks. Sexes alike.

TYPICAL PARROTS

Medium-sized, short-tailed parrots that feed on fruits in rainforest but also forage in eucalypt woodlands. They are represented in Aust. by the Eclectus and Red-cheeked Parrots, regarded as relics of PNG fauna. Sexes markedly dissimilar, especially in Eclectus Parrot.

FIG-PARROTS

Tiny fruit-eating parrots with broad, robust bills, rather large heads, and very short, rounded tails. Sexes dissimilar. Three races of one species from PNG occur in Aust.

LONGTAILED PARROTS
Medium to large long-tailed parrots of easy graceful flight. They comprise the Australian King, Red-winged, Superb, Regent and Princess Parrots. They occupy habitats from inland semi-deserts to coastal rainforests and are identified by usually strong plumage-patterns and characteristic calls, often uttered in flight. Sexes dissimilar.

BROADTAILED PARROTS: ROSELLAS, AUSTRALIAN RINGNECKS, RED-CAPPED, BLUE BONNET, SWIFT PARROT, THE PSEPHOTUS GROUP, BUDGERIGAR AND GROUND AND NIGHT PARROTS
Perhaps the most characteristically Australian parrots, they inhabit temperate, subtropical and tropical forests, woodlands and grasslands. Most are generalised feeders in grasses or low herbage or in foliage and blossoms. One has a brush-tongue and feeds on nectar, much like a lorikeet. Most nest in tree-hollows. The flight of most broadtails is strong and undulating; that of the Swift Parrot is impetuous and lorikeet-like.

ROSELLAS
The Rosellas are divided into two groups; both groups consist of closely related species or races which replace one another geographically, and may interbreed.
(1) White-cheeked Rosella complex: proceeding anti-clockwise around the continent, the group comprises the Eastern, Pale-headed, Northern and Western Rosellas.
(2) Blue-cheeked Rosella complex: consisting of two species — Crimson Rosella, *Platycercus elegans*, of e. Aust. (with one crimson, one yellow and one intermediate race) and the isolated Green Rosella, *P. caledonicus*, of Tas. and Bass Strait islands.

AUSTRALIAN RINGNECK COMPLEX
Medium-large green parrots related to rosellas, with distinctive yellow rear-collar. Several geographic forms replace one another across inland and w. Aust. There is considerable interbreeding where they overlap. For purposes of simplicity and clarity they are treated in this guide as two species, Eastern Ringneck, *B. barnardi* and Western (or Port Lincoln) Ringneck, *B. zonarius*, each with one or more distinctive geographical races.

PSEPHOTUS COMPLEX
The genus *Psephotus* contains five species of extremely beautiful small to medium grass-seed and blossom-eating parrots widespread across parts of Aust. One, the well-known Red-rumped Parrot, appears to be able to adapt well to clearing and farming development. It is present, and perhaps expanding, on the outskirts of eastern mainland cities. Other members, especially the three species that make nest-burrows in termite-mounts, have become much scarcer from habitat alteration. One, the Paradise Parrot, is probably now extinct. A former member of the genus, the Blue Bonnet, *Northiella haematogaster*, is widespread in three races across inland s. Aust.

BUDGERIGAR
Widespread across inland Aust. In the wild it is always green and yellow: all other colours result from selective aviary breeding.

GRASS PARROTS (GENUS NEOPHEMA)
Small, charming parrots, identified by size, colour, head-markings, calls and darting flight: wings briefly left open between beats, giving a hesitant, wader-like, flight-pattern. They include one of Aust. rarest and threatened birds, the Orange-bellied Parrot, which breeds in Tas. and migrates in autumn to coastal se. Aust. where its saltmarsh habitat has drastically declined.

GROUND AND NIGHT PARROTS
Green, barred parrots with legs adapted for walking. The Ground Parrot inhabits coastal heaths in se. sw. Aust. and 'buttongrass' moors in Tas. The secretive, 'lost' Night Parrot inhabits inland spinifex, *Triodia*, and low, succulent, shrubby vegetation around inland salt lakes. Both make nests of plant-material in grass-tussocks and low shrubs.

CUCKOOS Family Cuculidae PP. 292–299
Cuckoos look much like graceful, long-tailed songbirds; the main external difference is that their feet are zygodactylous: two toes point forward, two back. All species in Australia are brood-parasites, depositing their eggs in nests of other birds, often removing an egg of the host at the same time. Over 100 species of Australian birds have their nests parasitized by cuckoos. Their eggs are either adapted to resemble those of the host, or the cuckoos select nests with eggs similar to their own. Young cuckoos, whether in the nest or following foster-parents when fledged, can be recognised by their insistent sibilant begging calls, often causing birds other than their foster-parents to feed them. Most cuckoos in Aust. are migrants, many birds moving s. to breed in spring, returning n. in nonbreeding season to inland or n. Aust., PNG or beyond. Two come here as nonbreeding migrants. In spring cuckoos call insistently from the tops of

dead trees or overhead wires and in noisy courtship flight. They feed in foliage or in the open, perching on fences or stumps, flying down to take food on or near the ground. Often the prey is a hairy caterpillar. In Aust. they can be divided into three broad groups. (The Pheasant Coucal, long regarded as an aberrant cuckoo, is now placed in its own family, Centropodidae.)

Typical cuckoos
Graceful, mostly greyish, slender birds somewhat like large honeyeaters, whose wingtips often droop; longish tails hang vertically or are raised and lowered. Flight swift, graceful, undulating and rather hawk-like on swept wings.

Bronze-cuckoos
Widespread from NZ to Asia and in Africa. The Aust. species are rather like small honeyeaters, but their wingtips often droop and plumage patterns differ.

Koel and Channel-billed Cuckoo
The only Australian cuckoos to lay more than one egg in the same nest; broods of up to five young of the latter have been reported. Hosts include friarbirds, blue-faced honeyeaters, magpie-larks, currawongs and corvids. Soon after hatching, the nestlings of most other parasitic cuckoos instinctively expel the eggs and/or young of the host from the nest. Young Koels and Channel-bills grow quickly and outcompete the young of the host, which starve and die.

Food: insects and larvae (especially hairy caterpillars); larger species take fruits, berries and vertebrates incl. small lizards, mice and the young (and eggs) of other birds.
Range: almost cosmopolitan in tropical to temperate regions.
Number of species: 126 (Aust. 13).

PHEASANT COUCALS Family Centropodidae   PP. 298–299
Long-tailed, ground-foraging birds, long regarded as aberrant cuckoos, which differed from others in building their own nests and rearing their own young. DNA and other investigations now determine that there is some evolutionary distance between parasitic cuckoos and coucals. Thus the latter have been placed in their own family.
Food: insects, frogs, crustaceans, small mammals, birds eggs and young, carrion.
Range: from w. and e. Africa and Madagascar to s. Arabia, India, Sri Lanka, s. China, se. Asia, Philippines, Borneo, Indonesia, PNG, Solomon Is., New Britain, New Ireland.
Number of species: c. 24 (Aust. 1).

HAWK-OWLS Family Strigidae   PP. 300–303
MASKED (OR BARN) OWLS Family Tytonidae   PP. 304–307
To house their large eyes, and to direct these and other receptive senses, owls have broad heads on long, flexible necks, concealed by plumage. An asymmetric arrangement of the ear openings provides precise, directional hearing. Silence of flight is achieved by soft plumage and a comb-like ridge on outer flight-feathers that softens the flow of air. Legs are usually feathered; feet powerful, outer toe reversible, usually directed sideways, permitting wide spread of talons.
Hawk Owls have large, tubular, forward-directed yellow eyes capable of acute binocular night-vision. Our familiar Boobook and eagle-sized Powerful Owl are well-known representatives.
Masked or Barn Owls have dark eyes surrounded by a heart-shaped facial disc of part-erectile stiff feathers which serves as a sound-dish, augmenting hearing. Guided by ears alone, under experimental conditions a Barn Owl has been shown capable of capturing a house mouse on dry leaves in a wholly darkened room.
Food: mammals (possums, flying foxes, rabbits, rodents), reptiles, amphibians, insects, other invertebrates.
Range: worldwide except Antarctica; many islands.
Number of species: Hawk-Owls: 135 (Aust. 4). Barn Owns: 12 (Aust. 5).

FROGMOUTHS Family Podargidae   PP. 308–309
Often mistaken for owls, with silent flight assisted by soft, moth-like plumage, frogmouths are more lightly-built, with smaller, weaker feet. Related to nightjars, they are named for their very broad, slightly hooked bills, which they use to seize live prey on the ground and branches at night. Relaxed, they look large, with big, round red or yellow eyes. Disturbed by day, eyes close to slits, the bill lifts, the intricately patterned grey, tawny, marble and streaked plumage slims, and the bird imperceptibly becomes a jagged dead branch.

Food: large insects, spiders and other arthropods, small reptiles, rodents and occasionally small birds.
Range: se. Asia to Melanesia, Aust., Tas.
Number of species: 13 (Aust. 3).

NIGHTJARS Family Caprimulgidae

PP. 310–311

Nocturnal, aerial insectivorous birds with large eyes, short bills, huge gapes, long wings and ample tails. Their legs are very short and feet tiny; the claw on the middle toe has a comb-like process for grooming. The plumage is beautifully patterned like dead leaves, in black, grey, chestnut, buff, cream and white. Nightjars usually roost by day (and nest) on the ground, lying among leaf debris with large dark eyes closed to slits. Difficult to see, they often wait until they are almost underfoot before taking flight with startling suddenness, looking dark and long-winged. They often settle lengthwise on open branches. Mostly they are seen hawking for insects at dusk over treetops, clearings, roads or waterways, with stiff-stroking flicks, glides and turns on raised wings. Silence of flight is enhanced by flight feathers with slightly abraded edges, softening the flow of air. Their calls are unusual and diagnostic.

Food: mostly flying insects.
Range: almost worldwide except for far n. Eurasia and n. N. America, s. S. America, NZ and oceanic islands.
Number of species: 75 (Aust. 3).

OWLET-NIGHTJARS Family Aegothelidae

PP. 310–311

Small night-birds with the features of both nightjars and frogmouths. The tiny broad bill is surrounded by prominent cat-like bristles; the large, non-reflective eyes are forwardly directed and the head has an almost owl-like mobility; the feet are rather feeble. The single Aust. species nests and roosts by day in tree-hollows. At night it captures large insects in the air and on the ground.

Food: mostly insects
Range: Australasian region, PNG, Moluccas, New Cal.
Number of species: 8 (Aust. 1).

SWIFTS AND SWIFTLETS Family Apodidae

PP. 312–315

Fastest and most aerial of birds; flight much swifter, direct and more impetuous than that of swallows. Plumage blackish to glossy blue-black, typically with white on rump, throat or under tail-coverts. Wings swept, bladelike, long and tapering; tails deeply forked or short and square, with feather-shafts extending as short spines in some. The feet have strong, sharply curved claws; in some species, all four toes are directed forward for clinging to vertical surfaces, with the short, spine-tipped tail acting as a prop. True swifts cannot perch: they roost and nest clinging to walls of cliffs, caves, tree-trunks and foliage, in hollow trees or on buildings. They build tiny bracket-like nests of hardened saliva reinforced with fine twigs or similar material, attached to the wall of a cave, hollow tree, or chimney. Once thought even to sleep in flight, White-throated Needletails in Aust. have been seen to alight in high foliage after dark and remain until dawn. Swifts form small to large open companies, feeding high on flying insects ahead of thundery weather fronts or along mountain ridges, rising under some conditions to several thousand metres.

Food: flying insects.
Range: nearly worldwide, except polar regions and some oceanic islands; vagrant NZ.
Number of species: 82 (Aust. 6; 1 breeding resident, 2 regular summer migrants, 3 vagrants).

KINGFISHERS Families Alcedinidae and Halcyonidae

PP. 316–321

Plump, mostly short-tailed, colourful birds with large heads and oversized bills, short legs and syndactylous toes. Despite their name, only two Aust. species are river kingfishers, family Alcedinidae. They typically sight prey from a perch or while hovering and dive into the water to seize it. Other Aust. species are tree kingfishers, family Halcyonidae. They forage mostly over land and are often seen perched on telephone wires, fence posts, branches. Sighting live prey, they make a long descending glide or dart to ground, foliage, surface of water or mud to seize it. But all our kingfishers sometimes plunge into shallow water after prey or when bathing. Their calls are usually harsh, those of kookaburras being among our loudest and most famous bush sounds.

Food: small mammals; small birds, nestlings and eggs; insects, reptiles, fish, amphibians, crustaceans.
Range: cosmopolitan; absent from high latitudes and some remote islands.
Number of species: 90 (Aust. 10).

BEE-EATERS Family Meropidae

Distinctive colourful birds with slender curved bills and small, syndactylous feet. Fine shafts of two central tail-feathers extend 25 mm or more, slightly enlarged at tip when new. Flight swift, graceful and soaring, like swallows or woodswallows. The single Aust. species is migratory and nomadic, gregarious on migration, nesting in communal groups. Like other bee-eaters, it removes or renders harmless the stings of bees or wasps before swallowing or feeding to mate or young.

Food: flying insects, incl. bees and wasps; also dragonflies.

Range: Europe and Africa through Asia to Australasian region; not NZ.

Number of species: 24 (Aust. 1).

ROLLERS ('DOLLARBIRDS') Family Coraciidae

PP. 321–321

Robust, colourful birds with large heads, short, wide, somewhat hooked bills and small syndactylous feet. Wings are long and broad, and flight strong. During courtship, they typically perform spectacular swooping, looping and rolling displays. Sexes similar.

Food: mostly insects caught in flight and in outer foliage of trees.

Range: Europe and Africa, through s. Asia to Aust.

Number of species: 11 (Aust. 1).

All families from the Pittas onwards belong to the single great songbird order, Passeriformes, named after the Old World Sparrows, family Passeridae. See 'passerine' in the glossary, p. 548.

PITTAS Family Pittidae

PP. 322–323

Brightly coloured, stumpy, thrush-like, long-legged, ground-feeding songbirds of rainforests, mangroves and tropical scrubs. With strong, whistling voices, they are heard more than seen. They stand upright, hop briskly over leaf-litter, give tail a few brisk wags, throw leaves aside with bills. Noisily striking shells of large land-snails on rock 'anvils', they remove the flesh, leaving tell-tale discarded shells. Flight strong, usually low, displaying flashing electric-blue shoulders and white wingpatches. They roost high and often call from perches high in canopy. Some species are migratory, moving seasonally from highlands to lowlands, or across open sea, apparently travelling at night.

Food: molluscs, earthworms, small crustaceans, insects, other invertebrates, fruit, berries.

Range: tropical Africa to India, se. Asia, China, Borneo, Philippines, Indonesia, PNG, Solomon Is., coastal tropical and subtropical Aust.

Number of species: 26 (Aust. 4).

LYREBIRDS Family Menuridae

PP. 324–325

Very large 'Old Endemic' songbirds which feed on mostly soil-invertebrates, digging deep in humus with powerful claws, leaving tell-tale workings. Males have spectacular tails of 14–16 feathers: two main 'lyrate' plumes, two ribbon-like guard plumes and 10 or 12 filamentary plumes, black above, silver below; normally carried horizontally. In Superb Lyrebird, lyrates, when raised and spread, resemble shape of a Greek lyre; in Albert's Lyrebird they are less developed. Females have simpler, long, broad, drooping tail-feathers, with short lyrates. Lyrebirds have highly developed, powerful, directional voices. In autumn-winter, males claim territories highly variable in size (c. 2.5–35 ha.), where they sing and display. With their own song-patterns, they interweave skilled mimicry of other bird calls, from thornbills to black-cockatoos and eagles. Male Superb Lyrebirds display on low, circular mounds scratched clear of vegetation. Male Albert's Lyrebirds display from tangles of vines, logs, etc. In both, as the performance develops, spread tail is suddenly inverted over the bird's head/body in a silvery umbrella. Males mate indiscriminately with any submissive female attracted to the display. Establishing their own territories nearby, each female builds a large, domed nest, incubates the single egg and rears the offspring unaided.

Food: earthworms, molluscs, soil-crustaceans, insects, spiders and other invertebrates.

Range: forests of temperate and subtropical se. Aust.; introduced to se. Tas.

Number of species: 2 (Aust. 2).

SCRUB-BIRDS Family Atrichornithidae

PP. 326–327

'Old Endemic' Australian family, possibly related to the much larger lyrebirds. Strongly territorial and extremely elusive, they dwell in undergrowth and fly feebly. They are almost invariably heard before (and usually without) being seen. Voices of males have astonishingly sharp, penetrating quality; they may mimic other species. Their present distribution reflects a wide former range, divided by climatic change.

Food: invertebrates in leaf-litter.
Range: two restricted, widely separated ranges in Gt Divide in n. NSW-se. Q, and coastal s. WA.
Number of species: 2 (Aust. 2).

AUSTRALIAN TREECREEPERS Family Climacteridae

PP. 328–331

Robust, upright smallish birds with strong legs and very large feet and claws for gripping bark of trees and strong, slightly curved bills for probing bark and rotting wood. Of Australian origin, their precise relationships are unclear. They make downward, planing glides from high in one tree to base of another, climbing in shuffling runs, one foot leading the other. Having one foot always attached enables them to 'hop' along the underside of limbs, a foraging niche denied most others. Several species often feed on ground. They build untidy nests concealed in hollow trunks or limbs. Most Australian treecreepers (but not White-throated) breed co-operatively, two or three males feeding the young of one female (Noske, 1980).

Food: insects (especially ants), other small invertebrates, seeds.
Range: Aust. and PNG.
Number of species: 7 (Aust. 6).

FAIRY-WRENS, EMU-WRENS AND GRASSWRENS Family Maluridae

PP. 332–345

DNA hybridisation studies by Sibley and Ahlquist (1990), and allozyme studies by Christidis (1991) and Christidis and Schodde (1991a), indicate that the modified family Maluridae, embracing the Fairy-wrens, Emu-wrens and Grasswrens (but not the Bristlebirds), is part of a larger assemblage that includes the (newly enlarged) family Pardalotidae and the honeyeaters, Meliphagidae.

Fairy-wrens

A genus of three distinct groups. Males are colourful, females and young are usually brownish above (blue–grey in two) and paler below. They differ in subtle ways, e.g. in colour of bills and lores, and tail length. For details see species entries.

(1) The so-called 'blue wrens' — the Superb and Splendid Fairy-wrens, the first in coastal e. Aust. and Tas., the second in three distinctive races ranging from coastal sw. WA to inland Vic., NSW and Q.
(2) The four chestnut-shouldered wrens: Variegated Fairy-wren (and races) and the Lovely, Blue-breasted and Red-winged Fairy-wrens, identified by the colour of crown, back and breast of males and the subtle colour-tones and tail-lengths of the brown females and young.
(3) Three unmistakable species: Purple-crowned, White-winged and Red-backed Fairy-wrens, all with brown females identified by colour-tones, colour of bills and/or lores, and length of tails.

Emu-wrens

Like small rich-buff, dark-streaked fairy-wrens with very long thin tufty tails of only six feathers, curiously like emu-feathers in their coarse open structure and colour. No other Aust. bird has such a tail and no known bird has fewer tail-feathers. Males have beautiful lavender-blue throats and/or ear-coverts — the latter a diagnostic feature. One emu-wren lives in mostly humid coastal and sub-coastal heathlands; the other two are spinifex-dwellers in arid lands. Their ranges are largely well separated, but care is needed where ranges approach one another in coastal se. SA and Shark Bay area, WA.

Grasswrens

Marked by fine white double streaks, reflecting their preferred habitat: mostly spinifex, *Triodia* and *Plectrachne*; canegrass, lignum thickets, low shrubs. The ground-colour of their plumage — black, red-brown, cinnamon to grey — repeats the colours of sand, soil or rocks in their arid homes. Members of one group have white throats and black whisker-marks. Most females have chestnut flanks.

Food: insects and other small invertebrates, earthworms, seeds.
Range: Aust. and PNG.
Number of species: 25 (Aust. 20).

PARDALOTES, BRISTLEBIRDS, SANDSTONE WARBLERS, SCRUBWRENS, HEATHWRENS, FIELDWRENS ETC., GERYGONES, THORNBILLS & WHITEFACES Family Pardalotidae

PP. 346–369

Pardalotes

Very small, colourfully marked Australian warblers with broad heads and stubby, notched bills adapted to removing lerps and other small invertebrates from leaves, mostly of eucalypts. Competing with honeyeaters for insect food and manna, they are frequently pursued by the larger birds. Their habit of nesting in tree-hollows and/or earth-tunnels may be for protection from this threat. In autumn-winter pardalotes make extensive migrations and/or dispersals, companies flying at treetop height, exploiting lerp outbreaks. They have adaptive strategies for sharing the canopy between species.

Bristlebirds

Characterised by four or more stiff bristles curving forward from near the base of bill, bristlebirds are the giants of the Pardalotidae. Their behaviour is furtive and they are easily confused with scrub-birds. They have subtle dark or rufous markings on brownish plumage and large, frequently cocked or fanned tails. Their calls are silvery, clear and far-carrying. Widely divided east-west ranges indicate that they were formerly widespread but are now in decline. The western race of the Rufous Bristlebird may be extinct.

Sandstone Warblers

The Rock Warbler, the only bird found solely in NSW, and the Pilotbird, have simple patterns and unusual deep-rufous or orange–buff underparts. Differing habits and habitats ensure that they present no serious problems of identification. They remain in a separate, monotypic genera.

Scrubwrens (incl. Scrubtit and Fernwren)

Forest and undergrowth-dwelling small Australian warblers of strong distinctive voices and sombre plumage, with characteristic patterns on face, throat, breast and bend of wing. DNA hybridisation studies do not support the case for inclusion of two monotypic genera, the Scrubtit (*Acanthornis*) of Tas. and the Fernwren (*Oreoscopus*) of ne. Q in the Scrubwren genus *Sericornis*. They are placed near the scrubwrens, but for the present remain in separate genera.

Heathwrens and Fieldwrens

Closely related to scrubwrens, each with a coastal and an inland member, they are distinctive in their ways, as are two other 'independants', the Redthroat and the Speckled Warbler. All have clear, sweet, distinctive voices; each is capable of skilled mimicry. The Chestnut-rumped Heathwren is the outstanding singer of heathlands in Sydney's sandstone/shale convergence; the Redthroat claims that distinction inland. For the present, all retain their existing generic identities.

Weebill

With voice, foraging and nesting habits reflecting both thornbills and gerygones, the Weebill may represent an ancestral form of both. Reflecting this, and with the distinction of being the smallest Australian bird, the single species is placed in a genus of its own, (*Smicrornis*).

Gerygones

Small, fine-billed Australian warblers formerly known as fairy-warblers. Their Greek generic name, approximately pronounced 'jerriganee' (with emphasis on the second syllable), means 'born of sound'. Their shape is characteristic, their patterns simple. They typically hover outside foliage of trees and saplings, taking leaf insects or flying insects with an audible snap. Their songs are sweet, plaintive, silvery 'falling-leaf' melodies in minor key.

Thornbills

Endlessly active, tiny, fine-billed warblers — Australia's quintessential 'small brown birds'. There is a thornbill for every major woodland niche in s. Aust.: leaf-canopy; branches and understorey; rough-barked trunks and fallen limbs; feathery acacias; open, short, grassland. Thornbills have a reputation for being hard to identify. But if one concentrates on head-patterns and colours, calls, habits, and choice of habitat, they *can* be separated.

Whitefaces

Small warblers with short, stout bills for seed and insect-eating, distinctive facial patterns and tinkling, twittering voices. One species is rare and confined to n. SA.

Food: insects, other small invertebrates, lerp-insects, manna, earthworms, small molluscs and soil crustaceans.
Range: Aust., PNG, NZ.
Number of species: 67 (Aust. 47).

HONEYEATERS Family Meliphagidae PP. 370–407

Owing their diversity to the dominance of nectar-producing, bird-pollinated trees and shrubs in the Aust. flora, honeyeaters are our strongest endemic family, occupying every major vegetational zone. Bills are short to long and curved, with extensile, partly tubular tongues finely split and brushlike toward the tip for nectar-gathering. Several groups have bare colourful skin on heads, others have knobs on bills or coloured wattles. In others, gape skin (at corners of mouth) and eye-ring are yellow in winter, but black in breeding condition (young birds typically have yellow gapes). With their high-energy diet, honeyeaters are active, vigorous and aggressive, defending food resources, flying to snap airborne insects — an essential source of protein, mostly gathered toward the end of the day when blossom-nectar is depleted. Competition has resulted in the development of a diversity of physical sizes, shapes and feeding strategies. In a given area of scrubland, woodland or forest there is usually a 'guild' of six to a dozen or more honey-eaters, of complementary shapes, sizes and foraging habits. Dependence on blossoming plants causes much transience. Some species have become 'blossom nomads'. Others eat mostly insects, berries and fruit, incl. mistletoe-fruits, as well as sugary sap, manna and the sweet exudates of sap-sucking insects. Some are regular migrants: the northward, autumn migration of Yellow-faced, White-naped Honeyeaters and Noisy Friarbirds in coastal e. Aust. is notable, with thousands of birds passing daily in some locations.

Australian Chats

Endemic, mostly colourful, small birds now included in the family Meliphagidae. Four species have brush-tipped, honeyeater-like tongues. One certainly eats nectar, but all may use their tongues to take up moisture from dew. Several are inland dwellers and extreme nomads, irrupting in large numbers as a result of drought, or conversely, good seasons. One coastal wetland specialist is expanding its range inland by exploiting artesian bore-drains. The fifth species, whose habits are somewhat pipit-like, is a desert-dweller.

Food: insects, blossom nectar, sugary excretions of sap-sucking insects, sap, manna, fruits, berries incl. mistletoe-berries.
Range: predominantly Aust. and PNG; also NZ. One or more species extend to Indonesia, Bonin Is., Pacific islands.
Number of species: 178 (Aust. 72).

AUSTRALIAN 'ROBINS' Family Petroicidae PP. 408–419

Three *Microeca* 'flycatchers' head the family as it is now assembled. Small graceful flycatcher-like birds with flat triangular bills and soft tones of plumage, they perch high or low and sally into the air for insects, hover low over grassland or make high, wavering songflights. They build tiny shallow nests — the smallest of any Australian bird. (Their generic name *Microeca*, is derived from the Greek *micros*, small, and *oikos*, house.) Australian robins look plump and round-headed. Most perch upright, lowering or flicking their wingtips. Male 'red robins' are fairly easily identified; colours and markings of brown females and immatures are subtle, if reliably different between species. Identification is based on general shade; presence or absence of red on breast or cap, shade/extent of 'broken arrow' wingbar, presence or absence of white panel in wing and/or tail. 'Yellow' robins present few identification problems, though several have more or less completely lost the yellow pigmentation. The two thrush-like scrub-robins, of widely separated geographic ranges, are more completely adapted to ground-dwelling. With cryptic colours and patterns, long legs and longish balancing tails, they walk and run easily and nest on the ground, behind a protective barricade of sticks and leaves.
Food: chiefly insects and invertebrates; small reptiles.
Range: Australasia, Oceania.
Number of species: 46 (Aust. 20).

LOGRUNNERS Family Orthonychidae PP. 420–421

Terrestrial songbirds with robust legs and feet, and tails with exposed feather-shafts extending in resilient spines. They locate food by rapid scratching, throwing debris out sideways and behind, sometimes briefly propping on the spread, spine-tipped tail and using both feet alternately to excavate. Logrunners are very noisy, especially at dawn and dusk: the Chowchilla takes its name from its unmistakably distinctive loud calls; it is an accomplished mimic. The two species are widely separate in range. Curiously, only the more southern species occurs in PNG.
Food: insects, larvae, small crustaceans and other soil invertebrates.
Range: Aust. region.
Number of species: 2 (Aust. 2).

AUSTRALIAN BABBLERS Family Pomatostomidae

PP. 422–423

Gregarious, noisy, energetic, babblers live in groups of three to about a dozen, foraging, preening, dust-bathing, roosting together. They co-operate in building numerous domed stick-nests, one for nesting, others for roosting. Members of the group help rear the young. Babblers feed on the ground, hammering into the soil to expose insect-larvae, and on trunks and larger branches, moving in bouncing hops and searching crevices in the bark, anchored by strong feet. They fly low, follow-my-leader, from cover to cover, with rapid wingbeats and short glides. Groups take up residence in the vicinity of homesteads, though one species at least is declining, as a result of expanding settlement.

Food: Insects, larvae, spiders and other invertebrates, small amphibia, crustaceans, reptiles, fruits, seeds.
Range: Aust., PNG.
Number of species: 5 (Aust. 4).

WHIPBIRDS, WEDGEBILLS AND QUAIL-THRUSHES Family Cinclosomatidae

PP. 424–427

Whipbirds

With unmistakable voices, which include duets between mated pairs, whipbirds have crests and bold patterns in sombre colours: they feed mostly on or near the ground, but Eastern Whipbirds will ascend rainforest trees. The Western Whipbird has adapted to drier habitats. It is rare, and declining.

Wedgebills

Plainer than whipbirds, they live in more open habitats. Vocal contact and territorial advertisement is important: the two present species, which are physically nearly identical, were identified on the basis of differing song-patterns.

Quail-thrushes

Unrelated to either namesake, quail-thrushes are birds of bold but cryptic patterns. They live on the ground in open forests of se. Aust. and in scrubs or open stony ground in the inland. Shy and secretive, they move in pairs or small groups, freeze when disturbed, run, dodge, or burst up with a quail-like whirr, flying low, fast and straight in spurts, displaying white-tipped dark tails. Colours of upperparts match the soil of their habitats, but their markings below, important for recognition and display, remain more alike. The females of inland forms are difficult to separate.

Food: insects, their larvae and other invertebrates.
Range: Australia and PNG.
Number of species: 9 (Aust. 8).

SITTELLAS Family Neosittidae

PP. 428–429

Small branch and trunk-foraging birds now thought to be related to Whistlers, Pachycephalidae. With longish, slightly upturned bills, large wings, white rumps, short tails and robust yellow legs and feet, the family in Aust. consists of a single species, with five main races, most of which converge in Q, w. of the Divide. Mostly resident in woodlands, flocks of up to nine (average five) travel between trees in bouncing flight. Settling on high branches, they mostly work downward, or toward the trunk, with jerky, rocking-horse actions, making short flights between branches, opening and quivering their contrastingly banded wings, possibly to disturb prey. They prefer to forage in rough-barked eucalypts and other trees such as cypress-pines. Foraging habits differ between sexes: males tend to use their longer bills to lever off bark-flakes to uncover prey; shorter-billed females tend to probe cracks in dead wood. They nest co-operatively, with up to seven birds building the beautiful nest and feeding the young; the female alone broods.

Food: insects and larvae, spiders, other small invertebrates (but few ants).
Range: mainland Aust., PNG.
Number of species: 3 (Aust. 1).

SHRIKE-TITS, CRESTED BELLBIRD, WHISTLERS AND SHRIKE-THRUSHES Family Pachycephalidae

PP. 430–439

Shrike-tits

Songbirds with large rounded heads and robust bills, short in some but longish and hooked in others. Now regarded as races of a single species, the Crested Shrike-tit. In structure and colouring they have superficial similarity to true tits, Paridae, of n. hemisphere, hence their early-bestowed name. (The word 'shrike' refers to their hooked bills, supposedly similar to those of Old World shrikes, used by shrike-tits to tear away bark and dismember large beetles and spiders.)

Bellbirds
The monotypic Crested Bellbird (*Oreoica*) is a ground-foraging dweller of arid habitats and mallee. Not to be confused with the 'bellbird' (Bell Miner — Meliphagidae) of e. Aust., its name derives from the male's beautiful deep, tolling call.

Whistlers
Smaller than shrike-thrushes; their sexes are usually dissimilar. They take large insects and their larvae while methodically scrutinizing surrounding leaves and branches, then flying to seize their prey. Courtship displays include see-saw posturings with heads and tails cocked. Their voices are higher-pitched than those of shrike-thrushes and sequences of notes are longer. Memorable explosions of song by several species place them among our most outstanding vocalists. Their small notes, especially in species like Red-lored and Olive Whistlers, are distinctive, pensive small voices of indrawn quality.

Shrike-thrushes
Unrelated to true thrushes (pp. 514–515), shrike-thrushes are active, medium-sized birds of soft, simple browns, greys or rufous; sexes nearly alike. They take prey as large as a feathertail glider and a green tree-frog. Their voices are strong, mellow and beautiful; song-patterns shorter than those of whistlers.

Food: insects and other invertebrates; small mammals; birds, eggs and nestlings; small reptiles, amphibians.
Range: Aust. region, Pacific islands, PNG, Indonesia, Malaysia, se. Asia.
Number of species: 47 (Aust. 14).

BOATBILLS, MONARCHS, FLYCATCHERS, MAGPIE-LARKS, FANTAILS AND DRONGOES Family Dicruridae

PP. 440–449, 462–463, 468–469

Members of this newly constituted family of small to large, robust insect-eaters mostly have broad, ridged bills and extensive bristles around the bill to assist insect-catching.

Boatbills and Frill-necked Flycatchers
The tropical boatbills are represented in n. Q rainforests by a small, colourful, boldly marked foliage gleaner, with the grotesquely broad, insect-catching bill of its genus. Two other tropical species are small, distinctive, black-and-white trunk-gleaning birds with decorative neck frills.

Monarchs
The four monarchs are larger, with bold simple patterns and loud, distinctive voices. They mostly take their insect prey in foliage and by sallying into surrounding air-space. Three are seasonal migrants, wintering in ne. Q or PNG. The fourth species, the White-eared Monarch, is a local migrant and vivacious insect-gleaner in outer foliage. Its resemblance to the related, larger Magpie-lark is noted below.

Flycatchers
The Broad-billed, Leaden, Satin, Shining and Restless Flycatchers of the genus *Myiagra* are generalised flycatchers of tropical rainforests, temperate woodlands, paperbark groves and open woodlands; the Shining Flycatcher lives mostly in mangroves. Several show strong sexual dimorphism. The Leaden and Satin Flycatchers are annual spring-summer migrants to se. Aust. and/or Tas., wintering in n. Aust. or PNG. They are distinguished by the rapid *vertical* quivering of their tails. In coastal n. Aust., from C. York (Q) to Kimberley (WA) their females can be confused with the Broad-billed Flycatcher.

Fantails
The well-known Fantails, agile catchers of small flying insects, have been augmented by a new species, the Mangrove Grey Fantail, confined to mangrove habitats in nw. and n. Aust. The Willie Wagtail, largest of the group, takes large insects on or near the ground, and eats many butterflies.

Magpie-Lark
Long classified as a mud-nest builder, the Magpie-Lark appears to be a giant monarch. It has a strong resemblance to the imm. White-eared Monarch. Its diet reflects its foraging habitat — damp ground and shallow fresh waters, where it seeks water-insects, their larvae, earthworms and molluscs.

Drongoes
The other giants of the family, the mostly tropical drongoes, are represented by the Spangled Drongo (sub-family Dicrurinae), an energetic insect-eater and predator with spectacular aerial agility, swooping, twisting and curving after large flying insects and memorable aerial displays when courting. It is a summer breeding migrant, mostly from PNG; there is a curious winter migration to s. coastal NSW.

Food: insects, invertebrates incl. molluscs and small crustaceans; possibly small reptiles and small birds.
Range: mostly tropical, from Africa to Asia and Aust. region, NZ and parts of Oceania.
Number of species: 139 (Aust. 19).

CUCKOO-SHRIKES, CICADABIRD AND TRILLERS Family Campephagidae

PP. 450–453

Neither cuckoos nor shrikes, but related to orioles, the seven Australian species of this widespread Afro-Asian family take their name from their somewhat shrike-like bills, cuckoo-like form and undulating flight. Mostly grey, with black and/or white markings and barrings, several of the Aust. species shuffle and refold the wings on alighting. Most have thick-matted, slightly spiny feathers on the lower back and rump, erected during display or on the approach of a predator while brooding; when the head and tail are depressed, the raised mound of rump-feathers become the highest part of the bird, causing it to blend with the branch on which the tiny grey, cobweb-bound nest is situated. Cuckoo-shrikes forage singly, in pairs or small parties, in foliage of trees and on ground. Some hover over foliage, and low over grassland. One forages actively on the ground, running on longish legs. Another, the White-winged Triller, is unusual in moulting twice a year, the male having a separate post-breeding 'eclipse' plumage. Cuckoo-shrikes are co-operative breeders; more than a pair feed the young. Most species in s. Aust. are nomadic and/or migratory, moving in winter to n. Aust., PNG and Indonesia. But some remain through winter in s. woodlands, roosting close together in groups, high in the foliage canopy, using the same site for weeks.
Food: insects, other invertebrates, berries, fruit.
Range: Africa and s. Asia to Aust. region and Samoa.
Number of species: 70 (Aust. 7).

ORIOLES AND FIGBIRDS Family Oriolidae

PP. 454–455

Graceful, slender, thrush-like fruit and insect-eating birds of the forest canopy. Males often have slightly arched, pink bills and bold, simple colours and patterns in which gold, black and greens predominate. Aust. species are more subtly coloured. Females and immatures similar, or brown and streaked. While the Yellow and part-migratory Olive-backed Orioles tend to be solitary, or associate only in pairs or trios, the related Figbird is gregarious, travelling and feeding in small flocks, which often attract a few orioles. All species in Aust. have distinctive, memorable voices.
Food: fruit, insects.
Range: Afro-Asia to Aust.
Number of species: 25 (Aust. 3).

WOODSWALLOWS, BUTCHERBIRDS, AUSTRALIAN MAGPIES AND CURRAWONGS Family Artamidae

PP. 456–465

Woodswallows

Unrelated to true swallows, woodswallows are graceful songbirds with broad, pointed wings; they are among the few songbirds that soar. Their grey, brown, black-and-white plumage has a bloom from powder down (friable, waxy down that grows in patches in the under-plumage and is spread as feather-dressing when preening). Few other songbirds have it. Woodswallows also have brushlike tongues for gleaning nectar from blossoms — although mostly they eat flying insects. Annual routines differ: one is sedentary; others highly nomadic and/or migratory. Drifting south in high, widespread companies on the first warm northerlies of spring, several species breed in s. Aust. when conditions for insect-eaters are optimal, returning north and/or inland in autumn-winter. During drought, or following widespread breeding, numbers may irrupt (and breed) into districts where unseen for years. Woodswallows are contact-species, roosting and preening in packed rows. For shelter or group-safety, all species except White-breasted occasionally form roosting clusters of hundreds on sheltered vertical trunks, like honeybees (Stokes & Hermes 1979).

Butcherbirds

Smaller than magpies and currawongs, butcherbirds have robust, straight, finely hooked bills used to capture live prey, incl. surprisingly large birds (e.g. blackbirds, spotted turtle-doves). Larger victims are wedged into a fork (or an angle in wires of a fence or clothes-hoist) for purchase to tear against. But prey is seldom if ever impaled on thorns. Butcherbirds have memorable voices. Duets or trios of Pied Butcherbirds are some of the purest Australian bush sounds.

Australian Magpies

The familiar Australian Magpie is now regarded as a single species of several races, which differ mostly in back-markings. Interbreeding where ranges overlap, they produce offspring with intermediate patterns. Magpies are unusual in holding permanent territories occupied by groups consisting of a dominant male and female with several subordinate females and one or more supernumerary males, usually their offspring. Birds, mostly males, unable to join territories, form loose nonbreeding companies in open country, with roosting trees.

Currawongs

Currawongs take their name from the rollicking common call of the Pied Currawong. With robust, pick-like bills and yellow eyes, they fly with deep, lapping wingbeats, in rather flat silhouette. Omnivorous, they forage on the ground, tree-trunks, limbs and in foliage, prising off bark to expose hidden prey. They rob birds' eggs and nestlings, exploit rubbish dumps and picnic grounds and can be a pest in orchards and vineyards. They breed in single pairs but form autumn/winter flocks which roost communally, with noisy calling. Breeding in summer in mountain forests of e. Aust., they move to lowlands mostly in autumn/winter, some well inland.

Food: small mammals and reptiles; birds, nestlings and eggs; insects and other invertebrates; carrion, fruit, grain, nectar.
Range: Aust. region to Pacific islands and Indonesia to se. and s. Asia.
Number of species: 20 (Aust. 14).

BIRDS OF PARADISE Family Paradisaeidae   PP. 466–469

Birds of paradise in PNG, their stronghold, are spectacular and varied, typically with brilliant, glossy or shot-colours and exaggerated plumes. The family is represented in Aust. by three riflebirds and the Trumpet Manucode. Male riflebirds have spectacularly rich glossy black, green and blue plumage, moss-like on the head; one has long flank-plumes; females are brownish. Active birds, feeding on trunks, rotting stumps and logs somewhat like giant treecreepers, they also take fruit and berries. Their outstanding behavioural feature is the extraordinary arboreal display of males (see species accounts). The Trumpet Manucode has less spectacular displays, though in courtship it dramatically shows off its long, decorative head-plumes. The male's deep mellow calls are produced by a long, highly-modified trachea under the skin of the breast.
Food: fruits, berries, leaves, insects and their larvae.
Range: PNG and adjacent islands to e. Indonesia, coastal e. and ne. Aust.
Number of species: 43 (Aust. 4).

RAVENS AND CROWS Family Corvidae   PP. 470–473

Although the names 'raven' and 'crow' are used specifically for one or other Aust. species, their superficial differences are slight. All five native corvids are glossy black, with brown to hazel eyes when juvenile and immature, and white eyes when adult. Our three ravens differ from our two crows mostly in size and in the colour of the down at the base of the body-feathers. All species are commonly called 'crows' and are safely identified in the field only with care, practice, and regard to the part of the country where seen. Note:
1. Colour of down at the base of feathers on neck and body: *ashy brown in ravens, snow-white in crows*, visible when wind ruffles feathers of head/neck.
2. Presence or absence of a bunch of long, pointed feathers on neck and throat (throat hackles), forming a shaggy bag when calling.
3. Posture and actions when calling and position from which call is made.
4. The nature of the main aggressive or territorial call: whether a very deep, level 'carrr!'; a hard, descending, sad 'carrr, carrr, caarrrr'; a much quicker 'cah cah cah' or a high-pitched, nasal 'nark, nark' nark'.
5. Relative length and massiveness of bill.
6. Aspects of behaviour: does the bird shuffle wings on alighting, or flip them when calling? Does it live in single pairs, or in flocks? Details of nest-site, nest-construction, and behaviour near the nest can all help build points for satisfactory identification.
7. Location.
Food: omnivorous.
Range: cosmopolitan, except for NZ and many islands.
Number of species: 103 (Aust. 6, incl. 1 introduced).

AUSTRALIAN MUD-NEST BUILDERS Family Corcoracidae   PP. 474–475

A curious family, now of two species only; indicated by DNA hybridisation studies to be close to the Crows, Corvidae. Note that the Magpie-lark, *Grallina cyanoleuca*, a former member, is now regarded as a Monarch Flycatcher, family Dicruridae (p. 541). The remaining two members, the Apostlebird and White-winged Chough, forage, nest and breed in close, constant groups, the nucleus being a dominant male with one or more females and offspring of previous seasons as 'helpers'. Groups cooperate in building the large bowl-shaped mud-nest. One or more females may lay in it, the clutch being larger than when only one bird lays. Members of the group co-operate in feeding the young. Mud-nest builders have harsh to mellow contact-calls. Sexes similar.

Food: small vertebrates and invertebrates generally; also molluscs; seeds, etc.
Range: e. and se. Aust. mainland.
Number of species: 2 (Aust. 2).

BOWERBIRDS Family Ptilonorhynchidae

PP. 476–481

Above all, bowerbirds are distinguished by the construction of bowers where courtship displays and mating take place. Bowers form the actual and psychological centre of male territory. The instincts that in male bowerbirds govern bower-construction and 'painting' were formerly directed to nest-building and feeding of young, duties now performed by females alone. In Aust., bowers are of two main types.
(1) Avenue-bowers: a double avenue of twigs/grass, secured on a platform of sticks on ground.
(2) Maypole-bowers: tall single or double columns of sticks built around adjacent saplings, and partly filling the gap between them.
Owners of bowers deposit in them natural or artificial objects usually of similar colour, or reflectivity, to the bill, eyes or plumage of their own species. During display, the bower 'owner' reacts to these objects as they would to an intruding male, seizing and pecking them. The display might thus be seen as a form of ritualised aggression. Bower-display by males helps stimulate and synchronise the development of male/female sexual organs for successful reproduction, while offering females a shop-window where they can observe and select superior males to father their young. In avenue-builders, bower-display takes the form of a strange, stiff-legged dance, accompanied by flaring wing-movements, whirrs, wheezes and hisses, and brandishing of display-objects. Maypole-builders, represented in Aust. by the Golden Bowerbird, perform spectacular hovering displays over the bower. Nests are shallow cups of twigs, in foliage or branches, usually in vicinity of bower. They are built by single females, which brood the eggs and raise the young unaided by the male.
Food: fruit, berries, leaves, insects and invertebrates.
Range: Aust., PNG and adjacent islands.
Number of species: 19 (Aust. 10).

LARKS Family Alaudidae

PP. 482–483

Smallish birds of grasslands with brown plumage streaked and scalloped buff, blackish or red–brown. They have short, sparrow-like bills, crown feathers erectile in low crest, longish legs, very long hind claws and white outer tail-feathers. They run rather than hop and, when disturbed, crouch. During breeding season, males make conspicuous song-flights, rising vertically or flying over grasslands, grain crops, etc., on quivering wings, pouring out a stream of song, often with mimicry. After breeding, they may form loose flocks. Despite their names, neither Songlarks nor Magpie-larks are true larks.
Food: insects, other invertebrates, seeds, vegetable matter.
Range: cosmopolitan; introduced NZ.
Number of species: 76 (Aust. 2, 1 introduced).

PIPITS AND WAGTAILS Family Motacillidae

PP. 482–487

Note: the familiar Willie Wagtail is a fantail, family Dicruridae, unrelated to Motacillid wagtails.

Pipits ('groundlarks')

Streaked, brownish, ground-dwelling birds somewhat like larks, with longer, more slender bills and legs. They walk with a slight swagger, teetering the longish tail up and down. One resident species is widespread; one Asian species is a rare vagrant.

Wagtails

More boldly marked and colourful than Pipits. They come to n. Aust. mostly in summer and autumn, as nonbreeding migrants and vagrants from Asia. A few reach s. Aust. They prefer open habitats, often near water, on playing fields, lawns. They wag long tails up and down, run after insects with heads nodding backwards and forwards, leap to pursue them in flight. Sustained flight has pronounced dips, accentuated by longish tails. All species have distinct male breeding plumage (male nonbreeding plumage mostly resembles adult female plumage). Nonbreeding adults and immature birds of several species (and races) can look nearly identical. Most species have several geographic races, which can be distinctive, or confusingly similar. Much care is needed to safely identify them.
Food: insects, invertebrates, seeds, vegetable matter.
Range: pipits: all continents except Antarctica. Wagtails: widespread across n. Eurasia, N. America and parts of Africa, migrating to s. N. America, s. and se. Asia, Philippines, Borneo, Indonesia, PNG and Aust.
Number of species: Pipits: 43 (Aust. 2). Wagtails: 12 (Aust. 2 regular summer migrants, 3 vagrants).

OLD WORLD SPARROWS; WEAVERS, WAXBILLS, GRASSFINCHES, MANNIKINS Family Passeridae

PP. 488–489

This radical new assemblage links three subfamilies: Old World Sparrows, Passerinae; African Weavers, Ploecinae and Australian Grassfinches and allies, Estrildinae.

Old World Sparrows
In common with other countries, Australia 'benefited' from the deliberate introduction of English House Sparrows and Eurasian Tree Sparrows in the 1850s and 1860s, to help control insects in the bird-scarce vegetable gardens of new Australian cities. But some of the immigrants became widespread pests.

Grassfinches (subfamily Estrildinae)
Highly social small birds, many species familiar in aviculture. Gathering in small to large flocks, especially in the nonbreeding season, they eat seeds and insects, and gather frequently to drink — some hourly. The pair-bond is strong: some mate for life. Mating displays include posturing with a long piece of grass gripped in the bill of males and tail-quivering by soliciting females. Most species nest in loose colonies. The Gouldian Finch, one of Australia's most gorgeous birds, has declined disastrously in recent decades from widespread infection by an air-sac mite, possibly spread from captive birds. Left untreated, the infection is fatal. The Chestnut-breasted Mannikin is frequently reported feral far from its natural range, from aviary escapes. One exotic species, the Nutmeg Mannikin, has become established in e. Aust. from aviary escapes.

Food: mostly seeds and insects (especially flying termites).
Range: Eurasia, Africa, Asia to PNG, Aust., Fiji and Samoa.
Number of species: 157 (Aust. 19, incl. 1 introduced).

FINCHES AND ALLIES Family Fringillidae

PP. 498–499

Larger than grassfinches, Fringillids have robust, sharp bills for seed-cracking — or in the case of the European Goldfinch, removing seeds from thistles. Their calls are musical chirrupings, expanded into longer song-patterns in spring. They build cup-nests, usually in introduced trees. Two species, introduced in the 1860s and 1870s, have been successful.

Food: mainly seeds; also insects.
Range: worldwide, except for Australasian and Malagasy regions.
Number of species: 122 (Aust. 2, introduced).

SUNBIRDS Family Nectariniidae

PP. 500–501

Sunbirds are small, brightly coloured and/or highly-burnished, nectar-eating birds of Old World tropics and subtropics. Resembling long-billed small honeyeaters, they are related to the flowerpeckers, Dicaeidae (see next family). Most species are found in sub-Saharan Africa. Their bills are mostly long, slender and down-curved, edges of mandibles often serrated. Their slender tongues roll into a partial tube for nectar-sucking. The birds probe and pierce blossoms for nectar and take insects and other invertebrates from flowers, leaves and in flight. Many spiders are eaten, the birds hovering at their webs to dismember them. Sunbirds are volatile and aggressive; group displays are frequent. They build pendulous domed nests, slung from low branches, under verandahs, sheds, etc.

Food: nectar, insects and larvae, spiders, other invertebrates.
Range: sub-Saharan Africa, s. parts of Middle East to s. and se. Asia, Philippines, Borneo, Indonesia, PNG, Solomon Is. and Aust.
Number of species: 118 (Aust. 1).

FLOWERPECKERS Family Dicaeidae

PP. 500–501

Colourful, small, stubby-tailed birds with numerous species in se. Asia. The single Australian species, Mistletoebird, has a fine bill and split tongue adapted to nectar-eating, but its staple is insects and the fruit of mistletoes. Eaten in quantity, the flesh-covered stones of mistletoes pass quickly through the bird and are tacky when excreted. Several seeds are often linked like beads in a glutinous thread hanging from the bird's vent. Assisted by the Mistletoebird's restless switching about, the thread adheres to the branch where the mistletoe seeds may germinate. There is thus a mutual dependence between bird and plant. Australia's 60+ species of mistletoe rely heavily on Mistletoebirds (and some honeyeaters and parrots) for dispersal. Many Asian flowerpeckers behave similarly.

Food: fruits (especially of mistletoes), berries, nectar, pollen, small insects.
Range: Oriental and Aust. regions, excl. Tas. and NZ.
Number of species: 58 (Aust 1).

SWALLOWS AND MARTINS Family Hirundinidae PP. 502–505

Well-loved small, graceful birds mostly seen on the wing in slipping pursuit of flying insects. They superficially resemble swifts, but their flight is less impetuous and dashing. They usually feed at lower levels, and perch in rows on overhead wires, TV aerials, dead branches, twigs over water or settle on ground, which swifts seldom do. Our four native swallows can be recognised by their nests: one builds a cup-nest of mud (often under eaves, in garages, sheds); one tunnels in earth banks; one nests in hollow limbs; and one makes long-necked bottle-nests of mud-pellets, under bridges and in culverts. Three nonbreeding migratory swallows from Asia and/or the Pacific visit Aust. mostly in summer. In Aust. the name 'martin' has been given to smaller members of the family. Note that woodswallows (Artamidae, p. 542) are not true swallows.

Food: flying insects.
Range: all continents except Antarctica.
Number of species: 80 (Aust. 7, incl. 3 summer migrants, mostly to n. Aust).

BULBULS Family Pycnonotidae PP. 430–431

Active, gregarious, fruit, bud and insect-eating birds with bright touches to inconspicuous plumage; noisy, with musical chatterings, pleasant songs. Some species are crested. Sexes mostly similar.

Food: insects, fruit, buds, nectar, etc.
Range: Africa to Asia and Indonesia, where they are well-represented.
Number of species: *c.* 123 (Aust. 1, introduced).

OLD WORLD WARBLERS Family Sylviidae PP. 506–511

Widespread family of songbirds that includes the Nightingale and other forest warblers. The few Australian forms are medium to small birds with streaked/unstreaked brownish plumage and somewhat pointed tails. They mostly favour grassy or swampy habitats. Several have rich voices characteristic of the family. The Clamorous Reed-Warbler, *Acrocephalus stentoreus*, also of PNG to se. Asia and Eurasia, is identified by its outstanding song, plain appearance and choice of habitat. The Oriental Reed-Warbler, *A. orientalis*, is possibly a regular, nonbreeding summer migrant to coastal n. Aust. from Asia. The two grassbirds, *Megalurus* have a mostly coastal distribution, in heavy grass or swamp and saltmarsh vegetation (though one occurs patchily across the continent in vegetation on bore drains, inland lakes, etc.). The Spinifexbird, sole member of its genus, *Eremiornis*, occupies an unusually arid habitat. The two songlarks, *Cinclorhamphus*, are not larks at all, but were so-called because of their conspicuous, though not especially lark-like, song-flights when breeding. The two Cisticolas belong to a complex assemblage that ranges over much of Africa, s. Europe and Asia. The Arctic Warbler, *Phylloscopus*, member of a confusing complex of species widespread across the n. hemisphere, is a rare summer vagrant to n. Aust.

Food: mostly insects and other small invertebrates; seeds and other vegetable matter.
Range: Europe, Africa and Asia, to Aust. and Tas.
Number of species: 400 (Aust. 10, incl. 1 rare summer vagrant).

WHITE-EYES Family Zosteropidae PP. 512–513

A widespread family whose members show remarkable uniformity, suggesting comparatively recent evolution and colonisation. Most have fine, slightly decurved bills, brush-tipped tongues (for nectar-eating), grey to olive–green plumage and a conspicuous eye-ring of fine white feathers, erected to enhance their threatening appearance in confrontations over food and territory, a threat supported by the open yellow mouth and spread, quivering wings. The most widespread Australian member is called 'Silvereye' to distinguish it from the two more restricted native species, which remain as 'white-eyes'. The Silvereye population is divided into five major races, ranging from Tas. and se. mainland Aust. to WA, n. Q and islands of the Gt Barrier Reef. When not breeding, Silvereyes associate in parties or flocks and some populations make long migrations, e.g. from Tas. to near Brisbane. They are an economic pest in orchards and vineyards, but destroy quantities of insects like aphids. Sexes alike.

Food: insects, berries, fruit, nectar.
Range: Africa, Asia, Australasian region, parts of Oceania and some sub-Antarctic islands.
Number of species: 84 (Aust. and Tas. 3).

THRUSHES Family Muscicapidae

PP. 514–515

Rounded, straight-billed, medium-sized songbirds. Feeding mostly on moist ground, they characteristically make a little run, stop, head on side, watch or listen, then plunge the bill vigorously into the soil, often withdrawing a worm or grub. Most have serene, melodious voices; plumage brown to reddish brown, or black, with scallops, spots, speckles and other markings. Most familiar around settlement in se. Aust. are two introduced species — the Blackbird and (in s. Vic.) the Song Thrush. Less familiar is the handsome large native Bassian Thrush of Tas. and e. Aust., whose huge natural range extends from islands in the sw. Pacific to w. Siberia. This species and its sibling, the closely related Russet-tailed Thrush share the humid rainforests of ne. NSW and Q between them. The Bassian Thrush occupies the colder, higher forests; the Russet-tailed living mostly lower. — the fact that their ranges marginally overlap, yet the birds maintain different song-patterns and lay differently coloured eggs, helps confirm that they have reached separate species status (Holmes 1984). Note that the Shrike-thrushes (family Pachycephalidae, p. 540) are unrelated to true Thrushes.

Food: insects, earthworms, molluscs, other invertebrates, seeds, fruits, berries.

Range: worldwide, except Antarctica and NZ (but two thrushes have been introduced to NZ).

Number of species: *c.* 300 (Aust. 4, 2 introduced).

STARLINGS AND MYNAS Family Sturnidae

PP. 516–517

Medium-sized, sharp-billed, gregarious, often glossy songbirds, widespread from Polynesia to Africa. Some have brilliant eyes and gorgeous plumage, fleshy wattles or bare coloured skin on heads. Voices creaking, wheezy or rattling, but some utter pleasant whistling notes; many mimic. They forage in flocks and often breed in colonies. Nesting habits vary; most use tree-hollows, some tunnel in banks. The one native species, Metallic Starling, builds bulky hanging nests in large treetop colonies. The Common Starling and Common Myna often nest in buildings, with attendant mess and risk of infection. Since their introduction to e. Aust. in the 1860s and 1930s respectively they have continued to expand their ranges. The Common Starling in particular displaces many native species from bushland nest-hollows.

Food: omnivorous.

Range: Africa and Eurasia, Aust. region, Polynesia.

Number of species: 106 (Aust. 3, incl. 2 introduced).

GLOSSARY

aberrant: abnormal or unusual.

accidental: species whose normal range is in another area, which has appeared astray, well out of that range. *See also* Vagrant.

adult: bird mature enough to breed.

altitudinal migration: movement of populations of birds that breed at high altitudes down to lower levels in autumn-winter and back to higher levels for the breeding season, usually spring-summer.

aseasonal: without season.

axillaries: feathers covering the 'armpit' area, where the underside of the wing joins the body, sometimes distinctly shaded, e.g. Grey Plover; Hutton's Shearwater.

bar: contrasting dark, light or coloured band across wing, tail or breast.

belly: lowest part of undersurface, before the under tail-coverts.

bib: colloquial term to describe light or dark combined area of throat and upperbreast, e.g. in Peregrine Falcon.

breeding plumage: plumage worn during breeding season; often more brightly coloured than nonbreeding plumage.

cap: patch of colour covering the crown, or part of crown.

carpal joint: the 'wrist', forming the bend of the wing, between the 'arm' and the 'hand'.

casque: an enlargement of the upper part of the bill or crown.

casual: species outside its normal range, though not necessarily outside its normal habitat. Reported more frequently than accidentals or vagrants.

cere: bare, wax-like or fleshy structure at the base of the upper beak containing the nostrils.

chenopods: plants in the family Chenopodiaceae, literally 'goose-foot', referring to the shape of the leaves. Examples are saltbush, bluebush.

chevrons: pointed or V-shaped contrasting marks on bend of wing or in bands across breast.

circumpolar: of or inhabiting the region around the Arctic or the Antarctic.

collar: a band of contrasting colour passing around the neck.

colonial: roosting or nesting in groups or colonies.

colour morph: some members of a species, have darker or lighter (and sometimes differently marked) plumages than typical members of their species, independent of age, sex or time of year. They are not reproductively isolated: light and dark morph birds breed successfully together, producing both light and dark morphs in the same brood. The condition was formerly described as a 'phase', but that implies a passing condition. A morph is genetically determined and the condition is permanent, e.g. Little Eagle and Reef Heron

commensal: literally, a table-sharer, a species which has come to depend, partly or wholly, on the actions or economy of another. The House Sparrow is a commensal of humans. The Pilotbird has a commensal relationship with the Superb Lyrebird. *See* Symbiotic.

communal breeding: when a breeding group contains more than one male and one female.

congenor: a member of the same genus; loosely, a close relative.

conspecific: member of the same species.

cosmopolitan: worldwide in distribution, or at least occurring on all continents except the polar regions.

coverts: small feathers that cover the bases of the large flight-feathers of the wings and tail, or that cover part of body structure, e.g. ear-coverts.

crepuscular: active at dusk (and/or at dawn).

crown: top of the head.

cryptic: hidden — having protective colouring and/or associated behaviour.

diagnostic: a decisively different, distinctive feature or features — build, colours, markings, calls or behaviour that helps to clearly identify a bird beyond reasonable doubt.

dimorphism: the existence of two distinctive forms in one species, not racially distinct, or confined to a geographic area. Usually relates to colour of plumage, e.g. Striated Heron. Sexual dimorphism: where males and females of a species differ in size, structure or in having different plumage, e.g. Brown Goshawk, Varied Sitella, Golden Whistler.

distal: terminal; the outer end.

diurnal: active by day.

dorsal: the upper surface, as opposed to ventral.

duetting: male and female singing together, in response to each other usually uttering differing song-patterns, e.g. Magpie-lark, Pied Butcherbird.

ear-coverts: feathers covering the ear opening and the area immediately around it; often distinctly coloured.

ear-tuft: a tuft of plumes, usually contrastingly coloured, forming, or as a part of, the ear-coverts.

echo-location: emission of high-frequency sounds to locate objects.

eclipse plumage: dull-coloured plumage acquired usually after the breeding season by most male ducks, fairy-wrens, etc., worn for a few weeks or months, followed by a more brightly coloured plumage.

ecosystem: ecological unit embracing interrelationship between animals, plants and their environments.

endemic: confined to a region or country: the Albert Lyrebird is endemic to the border region of se. Q-ne. NSW. *See* 'Old Endemic'.

extinct: no longer in existence.

eyeline: narrow stripe that runs horizontally from the base of the bill through the eye.

face: the lores, orbital area and cheeks, combined.

facial disc: heart-shaped arrangement of feathers on the face of harriers and some owls (especially); probably enhances hearing.

family: the level of organisation between order and genus; it defines a group of related birds sharing fundamental features and ancestry. The scientific name of a bird family always ends in 'idae', e.g. Anatidae — ducks.

feral: domesticated species escaped or released and living wild.

field mark: characteristic colour, pattern, or structure useful in distinguishing a species in the field. Markings that birds themselves use in recognising others.

flank: the side of a bird's breast and/or belly, immediately adjacent to (and under) the closed wing.

fledgling: a young bird partly or wholly feathered, before flight.

flight-feathers: long, well-developed feathers of wings and tail, used in flight. On the wings they are divided into primaries, secondaries and tertiaries. *See* also rectrice.

foreneck: the lower throat.

frons: forehead.

gape: the mouth, from corner to corner of the bill.

genus (pl genera): the level of organisation between family and species; a group of animals or plants having common structural characteristics distinct from those of all other groups, containing one or many species.

glean: to search leaves, branches and bark for food or prey; to seek out fallen grain.

gliding: straight flight on outstretched wings, without flapping.

gorget: patch or shield of brilliantly coloured, iridescent feathers on the chin or throat of certain birds.

gregarious: living in groups.

gular pouch: an expandable pouch of bare skin on the throat of pelicans, cormorants, etc.

hackles: long, slender neck-feathers.

hepatic: brown colour morph found in some cuckoos.

hood: dark-coloured head and throat.

hybridisation: cross-breeding, usually between different species· by definition a rare event.

immature: stage of a bird's life from the time it fledges (flies) until adulthood; all plumages that follow the first moult.

intergradation: merging of one part of a population with another as a result of interbreeding, usually between races of one species, producing birds with intermediate plumage characteristics. *See* hybrid.

iridescence: play of light on feather structure; colours produced by refraction of light, rather than pigment.

irruption: irregular movement in which large numbers of birds, usually of one or a few related species, move into areas where they are not usually found in such numbers. Typically a single event, without a regular, reciprocal movement, and thus not a migration. In Aust., usually caused by: (1) inland drought; (2) conversely, better than normal inland rainfall causing improved breeding success, often followed by an exodus.

jizz: the overall impression or character a bird gives: a combination of colour, size, shape and movement.

juvenile: fledgling to free-flying birds with feathers that first replaced the natal down.

lamellae: small stiff comblike membrane on inner edge of bill, used to sieve food particles.

lanceolate: lance-shaped; slender and pointed.

leading edge: forward edge of wing.

lignum: a tangled shrub, *Muehlenbeckia cunninghamii*, with long, cane-like stems growing in low, dense thickets in wetlands and on inland floodplains.

lobe: fleshy protuberance on the face or throat, or in harder form, on the feet, as an aid to swimming.

local: found only in certain confined areas.

lore (pl. lores): the space between the base of the bill and the eye, sometimes distinctively coloured.

mallee: low, usually arid, scrubland formed by species of small Eucalypts with multiple trunks growing from a central underground lignotuber.

mandibles: the two parts of a bird's bill; respectively the upper mandible and the lower mandible.

mangrove(s): highly productive woodland or forest of small trees, often of various species, growing in (and protecting) the tidal mud of shallow coastlines, river mouths and estuaries. The species of trees are not necessarily related — their essential common feature is adaptation to live and grow in salt water (though there are 'freshwater mangroves').

manna: white, energy-rich, crystalline sugary sap, produced on the small branches of trees following injury, usually by insects.

mantle: unit of plumage, formed by the feathers of back, upper wing-coverts and scapulars.

mask: black or dark area that encloses the eyes and part of the face.

melanistic: blackish morph.

mid-strata: mid-level vegetation of a rainforest, forest or woodland.

migration: regular, usually seasonal, geographical movement, and return.

mirror: white areas in black or dark grey primary wing-feathers of certain gulls.

morph: distinctive plumage, usually dark, light or red–brown, worn by members of certain species irrespective of age, sex, or season. Also called 'phase' (incorrectly). (*See* Striated Heron, Eastern Reef Egret, Grey Goshawk, Little Eagle, Oriental Cuckoo, Black Butcherbird.)

mulga: usually open, mostly arid scrubland formed by certain acacias, especially Grey Mulga, *Acacia aneura*. A widespread important formation in inland Aust.

nail: hook on tip of upper mandible in albatrosses, petrels, some waterfowl.

nocturnal: active at night.

nomadic: of variable, erratic movement — in Aust., often related to the effects of irregular rainfall.

nominate race: when a species has several races, the race that takes the scientific specific name of that species is known as the nominate race. It is always given precedence when several races are listed. The Grey-crowned Babbler has two widespread races. The race in s. Aust., where the species was first described, is known scientifically as *Pomatostomus temporalis temporalis*. It is the nominate race. The other race is *Pomatostomus temporalis rubecula*, in practice often foreshortened to *P. t. rubecula*.

nostrils: the external nostril; in birds located near the base of the upper mandible. In some (raptors), surrounded by a raised, coloured 'cere', in others (petrels), in a tube.

notch: an indentation in outline of feather, wing, tail, etc.

nuchal: pertaining to a bird's nape. Some bowerbirds have a small, erectile fan-shaped crest on the hind-neck or nape — a nuchal crest.

nuptial plumage: breeding plumage.

Old World: region from Africa and Eurasia to Indonesia.

orbital ring: ring of flexible bare or feathered skin surrounding the eye; the eye-ring.

Order: unit of systematic classification below Class and above Family. The name of the Order, always ending in '-formes'. For instance, the Australian Budgerigar, *Melopsittacus undulatus*, is described as follows: Class: Aves, Order: Psittaciformes, Family: Psittacidae, Genus: *Melopsittacus*, Species: *Melopsittacus undulatus*.

Oriental: from Himalayas, India, se. Asia e. to Indonesia.

parasite: organism that draws its sustenance from, or somehow takes advantage of, another, without conferring benefit in return.

passerine: literally, 'sparrow-like' — a member of the Order Passeriformes; a higher songbird, defined by the complexity of muscles of the syrinx (voice-producing organ) and by the arrangement of the toes, always three forward and one back, with ligaments arranged in such a way that the foot locks onto the branch when the bird perches and sleeps. Passerine birds exhibit other highly evolved features, apart from complex songs — in particular, the construction of skilfully woven nests.

pelagic: ocean-living, especially on the surface levels.

pellet: plug of indigestible material — feathers, bones, wing-cases of beetles, hard parts of ants, regurgitated by raptors, owls, corvids, magpies and others.

pied: patterned black and white.

plumage: the total covering of feathers over a bird's body. Its condition and colouration vary with age, sex, time of year.

plume: elongated ornamental feather, usually used in display.

polymorphic: taking several forms.

powder-down: specialised friable, waxy down that grows in tracts on the breast, flanks and/or rump of certain birds and breaks up when preened to form a powdery feather-dressing.

primaries: outermost and longest flight-feathers on a bird's wing. They vary in number from 9 to 11 per wing, always in a fixed number in any particular species.

race: colloquial term for subspecies.

range: geographical area or areas inhabited by a species.

resident: remaining in one place all year; non-migratory.

roost: the act of retiring to sleep; also, a place where a bird or birds sleep, or congregate at certain times, e.g. a high-tide roost used by waders.

rump: area of body plumage below the back and above the tail; includes upper tail-coverts.

saltmarsh: areas, tidal or inland, dominated by salt-tolerant plants, e.g. Samphire, Arthrocnemum and *Sarcocornia*; the ground is often damp and may be irregularly flooded or temporarily covered by exceptionally high tides. Often contains pools.

samphire: low shrubfield species of *Sarcocornia*, *Arthrocnemum*, etc. (Chenopodiaceae), growing on tidal flats and saline lakes that are flooded irregularly.

scapulars: shoulder-feathers, growing along the side of the back, covering the gap between the folded wing and body.

scrape: a shallow depression made by a bird on the ground to serve as a nest.

secondaries: flight-feathers located in a series along the rear edge of the wing, immediately inward from the primaries. They may number from 9 to 20.

sedentary: staying in the same locality throughout the year.

shaft: the central stem of a feather, its lower end (quill) being buried in the skin. Some birds, e.g. Pheasant Coucal, have glossy feather-shafts.

shank: bare part of leg. *See* tarsus.

shoulder: where the wing meets the body. The term is also loosely applied to the bend of the wing when this area is distinctively coloured, as in the Black-shouldered Kite.

skulking: creeping or flitting about in an unobtrusive and furtive manner close to the ground, usually within dense cover.

soaring: rising flight on still, extended wings, using thermals or updraughts to gain height without flapping.

spangles: conspicuous white or shimmering spots in plumage.

spatulate: spoon-shaped or shovel-shaped; describing the bills of certain birds, such as spoonbills.

species: a population whose members breed among themselves but not normally with members of similarly defined populations. Each species has been given a scientific name of two parts. The first name, always beginning with a capital, denotes the genus. The second name, always starting without a capital, denotes the species. *See* subspecies.

speculum: iridescent green patch or mirror on a duck's wing.

spur: sharp, bony projection on bend of wing, or on leg.

storey: a level of the forest.

striations: streaks — fine longitudinal marks.

sub-adult: immature moulting into adult plumage.

sub-Antarctic: southern oceans and islands between 45°S and the Antarctic Circle.

subspecies: population morphologically distinguishable from other populations of the same species; usually a regional or geographic entity within a widespread species. In scientific terminology, the subspecies is indicated by the third scientific name, which always starts without a capital. For example, the full scientific name of the nominate race of the Australian Magpie is *Gymnorhina tibicen tibicen*. A widespread subspecies is s. and inland Aust. is the 'White-backed Magpie', *Gymnorhina tibicen leuconota*.

subterminal: last before the end.

sulcus: groove (sometimes coloured) along bill of albatrosses and some petrels.

superfamily: a group of related families, usually widespread.

symbiotic: a close association or interdependence between two different species.

syndactyl: having the inner and middle toes fused for part of their length.

tail-streamers: elongated, ribbon-like tail feathers or long outer tail-feathers.

talon: robust, strongly curved sharp claw used by raptors and owls to seize and/or kill prey.

tarsus: the lower part of a bird's leg.

taxonomy: science or practice of classification.

terminal: the end.

terrestrial: ground-living.

tertiaries: the innermost flight feathers on a bird's wing, between the secondaries and the body. They grow from the upper 'arm'.

tomial tooth: projection on the edge of a falcon's upper mandible fitting a matching notch on lower mandible; used to kill prey by biting neck-vertebrae.

totipalmate: all four toes connected in a single web, as in cormorants and pelicans.

trailing edge: hind edge of spread wing.

undergrowth: saplings, bushes, ground-cover in a forest.

underparts: undersurface of body from throat to under tail-coverts.

underwing: undersurface of the wing, including wing-linings and flight-feathers.

upperparts: upper surface of body; the dorsal surface.

vagrant: bird found in area not its usual range or habitat, having strayed there by accident or mistake, e.g. blown by gales. Rare and irregular in occurrence; a species that has occurred in the country less than 20 times in total.

vent: area surrounding cloaca.

ventral: the undersurface of body — opposite to 'dorsal'.

washed: suffused with a particular colour or shade.

wattle: usually paired, often brightly coloured, fleshy lobes hanging from the face or neck of certain birds. Often a secondary sexual character, becoming larger and/or brighter in breeding condition: e.g. Southern Cassowary; Red Wattlebird; Brush Turkey.

web: skin stretched between toes; or part of the structure of a feather.

whisker-mark: a streak, coloured or black or white, from the base of the bill along the side of the throat, well below the eye.

window: translucent area in the wing formed by pale bases of primaries in certain birds (e.g. Black-breasted Buzzard) visible from below in flight. *See* roundal.

wingband: band across spread wings formed by white or coloured tips to wing-coverts, or by contiguous coloured parts of primaries and/or secondaries.

wingbar: single or double, white or coloured bar across wing, usually formed by white or coloured tips to wing-coverts (or by pale bases of primaries and/or secondaries part-covered by wing-coverts in flight). Visible either when wing is closed, or when bird is in flight, e.g. in waders. *See* also wingband.

wing-coverts: all or part of the covert-feathers on the upperwing or underwing.

wing-lining: the underwing coverts.

wingspan: measurement between wingtips at maximum natural spread.

winter plumage: plumage worn by many birds during the nonbreeding season. Usually less brightly coloured than breeding plumage. In Aust., it is mostly encountered in migrant waders, and in terns.

zygodactyl: having two toes facing forwards and two backwards.

BIBLIOGRAPHY

Journals

Agar, G., Jaensch, R. & Vervest, R.(1988), 'A Northern Pintail *Anas acuta* in Australia', *Australian Bird Watcher*, 12 (6), p. 204.

Ambrose, S. & Debus, S. (1987), 'Review: the Slater Field Guide to Australian Birds', *Australian Bird Watcher* 12 (4), p. 139.

Arnold, D., Bell, I. & Porter, G. (1993), 'The incidence of the Yellow Chat *Epthianura crocea* (Castelman & Ramsay) on Curtis Island', Curtis Coast Study, Dept. of Environment & Heritage, Queensland.

Barton, D.(1982), 'Notes on skuas and jaegers in the Western Tasman Sea', *Emu* 82 (1), pp. 56–59.

Bartram, Kevin (1988), 'A Glossy Swiftlet *C. esculenta* at Iron Range, Queensland', *Australian Bird Watcher* 12 (5), pp. 165–166.

Beruldsen, G. (1979), 'Ten days at Weipa, Cape York Peninsula', *Australian Bird Watcher* 8 (4), pp. 128–132.

Beruldsen, G. (1990), 'Cape York in the Wet', *Australian Bird Watcher* 13 (7), pp. 209–217.

Beruldsen, G. R. (1992), 'Another Queensland locality for the Carpentarian Grasswren', *Sunbird* 22 (3), pp. 49–50.

Black, A. B. et al (1983), The Yellow Chat *Epthianura crocea* at Pandiluna Bore, north-eastern South Australia', *South Australian Ornithologist*, 29 (2), pp. 42–45.

Boekel, C. (1979), 'Notes on the status & behaviour of the Purple-crowned Fairy-wren *Malurus coronatus* in the Victoria River Downs area, Northern Territory', *Australian Bird Watcher* 8 (3), pp. 91–97.

Bramwell, M., Pyke, G., Adams, C. & Coonts, P. (1992), 'Habitat use by Eastern Bristlebirds in Barren Grounds Nature Reserve', *Emu*, 92 (2), pp. 117–121.

Bravery, J. A. (1971), 'Sight-record of Uniform Swiftlet at Atherton, Queensland', *Emu* 71 (4), p.182.

Britton, P. L. (1990), 'The Queensland Ornitholgical Society Bird Report, 1988', *Sunbird* 20 (1), pp. 18–32.

Britton, P. L. (1992), 'The Queensland Ornitholgical Society Bird Report, 1991', *Sunbird* 22 (3), p. 82.

Brooker, M. G. (1988), 'Some aspects of the biology and conservation of the Thick-billed Grasswren *Amytornis textilis* in the Shark Bay area, Western Australia', *Corella* 12 (4), p. 101.

Brown, P. B. (1975), 'Status of Parrot Species in Western Tasmania', *Tasmania Bird Report* No. 9, Bird Observers Association of Tasmania 1979, Hobart.

Bunkport, K. (1995), 'Little Aussie Tattlers', *Australian Birding*, 2 (1), no page numbers.

Campbell, J. & Minton, C. (1995), 'Long-billed Dowitcher — a new wader species for Australia?', *The Stilt* 27, p. 16.

Carpenter G. & Matthew, J. (1992), 'Western records of the Mallee Emu-wren *Stipiturus mallee*', *South Australian Ornithologist* 31 (5), p. 125.

Carter, M. (1983), 'Streaked Shearwaters in Northern Australia', *Australian Bird Watcher* 10 (4), pp. 113–121.

Carter, M. (1992), 'A new bird for Australia, Red-throated Pipit, *Anthus cervinus*', *Bird Observer* 717, p. 2.

Carter, M. & Sudbury, A. (1993), 'Spotted Redshank, *Tringa erythropus*, in Australia', *Australian Bird Watcher* 15 (4), pp. 149–159.

Carter, M. et al (1994), 'The Comic Terns', *Wingspan* 16, pp. 17 -19.

Clarke, J. H. (1975), 'Observations on the Bush-Hen at Camp Mountain, South-East Queensland', *Sunbird* 6 (1), pp. 15–21.

Cooper, R. M. (1990), '1986 New South Wales Bird Report', *Australian Birds* 23 (4), pp. 68–97.

Corben, Chris & Roberts, Greg (1993), 'Some recent records of the Plumed Frogmouth *Podargus ocellatus plumiferus*', *Sunbird*, 23 (3), pp. 61–72.

Courtney, J. (1986), 'Plumage development & breeding biology of the Glossy Black-Cockatoo, *C. lathami*', *Australian Bird Watcher* 11 (8), pp. 261–273.

Coventry, P. (1989), 'Comments on airborne sightings of White-throated Needletails', *Australian Bird Watcher* 13 (1), pp. 36–37.

Curry, P. J. (1978), 'On the field characters of Little and Torresian Crows in Central Western Australia', *Wingspan* 5 (4), pp. 38–42.

Curry, P. J. (1979), 'Baird's Sandpiper, *Calidris bairdii* at Eyre: a new species for Western Australia', *Western Australian Naturalist* 14 (6) pp. 137–140.

Curry, P. J. (1979), 'Breeding records of the Grey Honeyeater in the Upper Lyons River district', *Western Australian Naturalist* 14 (6), pp. 162.

Debus, S. (1980), 'Notes on the Australian Corvids', *Australian Bird Watcher* 8 (6), pp. 194–198.

Debus, S. (1991), 'Relationships of the Red Goshawk', *Australasian Raptor Association News*, 12 (3), pp. 46–52.

Debus, S. (1995), 'Crows and Ravens', *Wingspan* 5 (4), pp. 38–42.

Estbergs, J. A. et al (1978), 'Observations of the Eastern Grass Owl near Darwin', *Emu* 78 (2), pp. 93–94.

Ford, J. & Parker, S. A. (1974), 'Distribution and taxonomy of some birds from south-western Queensland', *Emu* 74 (3), pp. 177–194.

Franklin, D. C., Menkhorst, P. W. & Robinson, J. L. (1989), 'The ecology of the Regent Honeyeater', *Emu* 89 (3), pp. 140–154.

Frith, C. B. (1994), 'The status and distribution of the Trumpet Manucode *Manucodia keraudrenii* (Paradisaeidae) in Australia', *Australian Bird Watcher* 15 (5), pp. 218–224.

Frith, C. B. & D. W. (1993), 'Courtship display of the Tooth-billed Bowerbird *Scenopeetes dentirostris* and its behavioural systematic significance', *Emu* 93 (3), pp. 129–136.

Frith, C. B. & D. W. (1993), 'Notes on birds found nesting at Iron Range, Cape York Peninsula, November–December 1990', *Sunbird* 23 (2), pp. 44–58.

Garnett, S. (1987), 'An Australian record of Gurney's Eagle', *Australian Bird Watcher*, 12 (4), pp. 134–135.

Givens, T. V. & Hitchcock, W. B. (1953), '*Cisticola juncidis* (Raf.) in the Northern Territory', *Emu* 53 (3), pp. 193–200.

Holmes, G. (1984), 'Ecological evidence for distinguishing two species of Ground-Thrushes in Central Eastern Australia', *Australian Bird Watcher* 10 (5), pp. 164–166.

Holmes, G. (1986), 'Notes on the Pale White-eye, *Zosterops citrinella*', *Australian Bird Watcher* 11 (6), pp. 208–9.

Ibbotson, M. & J. (1996), in 'Bird Reports Series 117 (Part 1)', *Bird Observer* 766, p. 14.

Johnstone, R. E. (1991), 'A Black-faced Monarch *Monarcha melanopsis* (Viellot) in Western Australia', *Western Australian Naturalist* 18 (6), p. 166.

Johnstone, R. E. & Hamilton, N. (1995), 'A Blue-winged Pitta *Pitta moluccensis* in Western Australia', *Western Australian Naturalist* 20 (2), p. 120.

Joseph, L. (1982), 'A further population of the Grey Grasswren', *Sunbird* 12 (4), p. 51.

Joseph, L. (1986), 'The decline and present status of the Black-eared Miner in South Australia', *South Australian Ornithologist*, 30 (1), pp. 5–13.

Lane, S. G. (1994), 'Sunbirds at Coffs Harbour', *Australian Birds* 27 (3), p. 85.

McAllan, I. A. W. (1990), 'Observations on the Green-backed Honeyeater *Glycichaera fallax*', *Australian Bird Watcher* 13 (6), pp. 201–202.

McKean, J. L. (1980), 'The first record of the Arctic Warbler *Phylloscopus borealis* for Australia', *Western Australian Naturalist* 14 (7), p. 200.

McLaughlin, J. (1993), 'The identification of the endangered 'Black-eared Miner *Manorina melanotus*', *Australian Bird Watcher*, 15 (3), pp. 116–123.

Matthew, J. (1994), 'The status, distribution and habitat of the Slender-billed Thornbill *Acanthiza iredalei* in South Australia', *South Australian Ornithologist* 32 (1), pp. 1–19.

Matthew, J., Croft, T. & Carpenter, G. (1995), 'A record of the Red-lored Whistler on Eyre Peninsula, *South Australian Ornithologist* 32 (2), pp. 39–40.

Morris, A. K. (1980), 'The status and distribution of the Turquoise Parrot in New South Wales, *Australian Birds*, 14 (4), pp. 57–67.

Morris, A. K. (1994), 'Third report of the NSW Ornithological Records Appraisal Committee', *Australian Birds* 27 (4), pp. 140–150.

Nagle, P. (1987), 'Yellow-legged Flycatcher reported from the Atherton region of North Queensland', *Sunbird* 17 (2), p. 31.

Niland, D. C. (1986), The Queensland Ornithological Society Bird Report 1985, *Sunbird* 16 (3), pp. 49–67.

Nix, H. (1984), 'The Buff-breasted Paradise Kingfisher in Central Queensland', *Sunbird* 14 (4), pp. 77–79.

Noske, R. (1978), 'Range extensions of the Grey-headed Honeyeater and Fan-tailed Cuckoo', *Sunbird* 9 (1), p. 12.

Noske, R. A. (1980), 'Cooperative breeding by treecreepers', *The Emu* 80 (1), pp. 35–36.

Noske, R. A. (1992), 'The status and ecology of the White-throated Grasswren *Amytornis woodwardi*', *Emu* 92 (1), pp. 39–51.

Noske, R. A. & Sticklen, R. (1979), 'Nest and eggs of the Yellow-legged Flycatcher', *Emu* 79 (3), p. 148.

NSW Bird Report 1986, *Australian Birds*, 23 (4), 1990, p. 91.

Paton, D. C., (1980) 'The importance of manna, honeydew and lerp in the diets of honeyeaters', *Emu* 80 (4), pp. 213–226.

Paton, J. B. (1981), 'The Grey Honeyeater: a review of distribution and variation', *South Australian Ornithologist* 28 (7), pp. 185–190.

Pavey, C. R. (1991), 'Comments on range, seasonality and behaviour of some North Queensland birds', *Sunbird* 21 (1), pp. 13–18.

Pavey, C. R. (1994), 'Observations on the ecology of the Green-backed Honeyeater *Glycichaera fallax* at Iron Range, Cape York Peninsula', *Sunbird* 24 (3), pp. 66–69.

Pavey, C. R. (1994), 'Records of the food of the Powerful Owl *Ninox strenua* from Queensland', *Sunbird* 24 (2), pp. 30–39.

Pettigrew, J. D. et al (1986), 'Incubation period of the Australian Grass Owl *Tyto capensis longimembris*', *Emu* 86 (2), pp. 117–118.

Ragless, G. B. (1977), 'The Chestnut Rail at Darwin', *South Australian Ornithologist* 27 (7), pp. 254–255.

Rix, C. E. (1970), 'Birds of the Northern Territory', *South Australian Ornithologist* 25 (6), pp. 147–191.

Roberts, G. J. (1980), 'Records of interest from the Alice Springs region', *South Australian Ornithologist* 28 (4), pp. 99–102.

Roberts, G. J. (1981), 'Field observations of the Grey Honeyeater in Central Australia', *South Australian Ornithologist* 28 (7), pp. 190.

Robertson, D. (1980), 'First record of the House Swift *A. affinis* in Australia', *Australian Bird Watcher* 8 (8), pp. 239–242.

Robertson, J. S. (1961), 'Mackay report', *Emu* 61 (4), pp. 270–274.

Rowland, P. (1994), 'A northern sighting of the Cinnamon Quail-thrush *Cinclosoma cinnamomeum* in Queensland', *Sunbird* 24 (4), pp. 94–95.

Rowley, I. (1965), 'The Life History of the Superb Blue Wren *Malurus cyaneus*', *Emu* 64 (4), pp. 251–297.

Rowley, I. (1993), 'The Purple-crowned Fairy-wren *Malurus coronatus*, I. History, distribution and present status', *Emu* 93 (4), pp. 220–234.

Rowley, I. & Russell, E. (1993), 'The Purple-crowned Fairy-wren *Malurus coronatus*, II. Breeding, biology, social organisation', *Emu* 93 (4), pp. 235–250.

Serventy, D. L. (1958), 'A New Bird for the Australian List — The Malay Banded Crake', *Emu* 58 (5), pp. 415–418.

Shields, J. M. & Boles, W. E. (1980), 'Evidence of breeding by the Pink Robin in New South Wales', *Australian Birds*, 15 (2), pp. 30–31.

Smith, F. T. H. (1982), 'Dunlins undone', *The Stilt*, No. 2, pp. 10–11.

Smith, F. T. H. (1992), 'A second Australian sighting of the Stilt Sandpiper, *M. himantopus*', *Australian Bird Watcher* 14 (8), pp. 313–317.

Smith, G. C. et al (1994), 'Home range of Plumed Frogmouth *Podargus ocellatus plumiferus* during the nonbreeding seasons shown by radio tracking', *Emu* 94 (2), pp. 134–137.

Smith, G. T. (1987), 'Observations on the biology of the Western Bristlebird *Dasyornis longirostris*', *Emu* 87 (2), pp. 111–118.

Smith, G. T. & Moore, L. A. (1992), 'Patterns of movement in the Western Long-billed Corella *Cacatua pastinator* in the south-west of Western Australia.' *Emu* 92 (1), pp. 19–27.

Smith, L. A. and Johnstone, R. E. (1985), 'The birds of Lake MacLeod, upper west coast, Western Australia', *Western Australian Naturalist*, 16 (4), pp. 83–86.

Start, A. N. & Fuller, P. J. (1995), 'Grey Honeyeater breeding records and habitat in the Pilbara, Western Australia, *Western Australian Naturalist* 20 (3), pp. 121–123.

Stewart, D. A. (ed.) (1984), 'Queensland Bird Report, 1983.' *Sunbird* 14 (3), pp. 45–65.

Stewart, D. & Nielsen, L. (1996), in 'Bird Reports Series 118 (Part 1)', *Bird Observer* 768, p. 16.

Stokes, T. & Hermes, N. (1979), 'Cluster roosting in the Black-faced Woodswallow', *Emu* 79 (2), pp. 84–86.

Strong, B. W. & Fleming, M. R. (1987), 'Recent observations of the distribution and habitat of the Yellow Chat *E. crocea* in the Northern Territory', *South Australian Ornithologist*, 30 (4), pp. 98–102.

Tidemann, S. (1991), 'Has the finch had its chips?', *Wingspan* 3, p. 1.

Webb, Horace P. (1992), 'Field observations of the birds of Santa Isabel, Solomon Islands', *Emu* 92 (1), pp. 52–57.

White, H. L. (1922), 'A Collecting Trip to Cape York Peninsula', *Emu* 22 (2), pp. 99–116.

Woinarski, J. & Tidemann, S. (1992), 'Survivorship and some population parameters for the endangered Gouldian Finch *Emblema gouldiae* and two other finch species at two sites in tropical northern Australia', *Emu* 92 (1), pp. 33–38.

Wood, G. A. (1984), 'Tool use by the Palm Cockatoo *Probisciger aterrimus* during display', *Corella* 8 (4), pp. 94–95.

Books

Alstrom P. & Colston P. (1991), *A Field Guide to the the Rare Birds of Britain & Europe*, HarperCollins, London.

Baxter, C. (1995), *An Annotated List of the Birds of Kangaroo Island*, (rev. ed.), National Parks and Wildlife Service, South Australia.

Beehler B. M. et al (1986), *Birds of New Guinea*, Princeton.

Beruldsen, Gordon (1980), *A Field Guide to Nests and Eggs of Australian Birds*, Rigby, Adelaide.

Blakers M. et al (1984), *The Atlas of Australian Birds*, RAOU & MUP.

Cooper, R. M. & McAllan, I. A. W. (1995), The Birds of Western New South Wales: A Preliminary Atlas, New South Wales Bird Atlassers Inc., Albury.

Cramp, S. (chief ed.) (1980–), *Handbook of the Birds of Europe and the Middle East and North Africa*, OUP.
  Vol. I Ostrich to Ducks 1977, rep. 1980.
  Vol. II Hawks to Bustards 1980.
  Vol. III Waders to Gulls 1983.
  Vol. IV Terns to Woodpeckers 1985.
de S. Disney, H. J. et al (1974), *Bird in the Hand*, Bird Banders' Association of Australia, Sydney.
Emison, W. B. et al (1987), *Atlas of Victorian Birds*, Dept. of Conservation, Forests & Lands & RAOU, Melbourne.
Falla, R. A. et al (1979), *The New Guide to the Birds of New Zealand* (rev. ed.) Collins, Auckland.
Forshaw, J. M. & Cooper, W. T., *The Birds of Paradise and Bower Birds*, William Collins, Sydney.
Forshaw, J. (1981), *Australian Parrots*, (2nd rev. ed.), Lansdowne Editions Melbourne.
Frith, H. J. (1982), *Pigeons & Doves of Australia*, Rigby, Adelaide.
Green, R. H. (1993), *Birds of Tasmania*, (4th rev. ed.), Potoroo Publishing, Launceston.
Grigson, Geoffrey, (1962). *The Shell Book*, Phoenix, London, p. 190.
Hall, B. P. (ed.) (1974), *Birds of the Harold Hall Australian Expedition 1962–1970*, British Museum, London.
Harrison, P. (1983), *Seabirds: An identification guide*, A. H. & A. W. Reed, Sydney.
Hayman, P. et al (1986), *Shorebirds: An identification guide to the waders of the world*, Croom Helm, London.
Hollands, D. (1991), *Birds of the Night: Owls, Frogmouths and Nightjars of Australia*, Reed, Sydney.
Hollands, D. (1984), *Eagles Hawks & Falcons of Australia*, Nelson, Melbourne.
Hoskin, E. S. (1991), *The Birds of Sydney*, (2nd ed.), Surrey Beatty, Sydney.
Jonsson, Lars (1992), *Field Guide to the Birds of Europe*, Christopher Helm Ltd, London.
King, B. et al (1980), *A Field Guide to the Birds of South-East Asia*, Collins, London.
Lekagul, B. & Round, P. D. (1991), *A Guide to the Birds of Thailand*, Saha Karn Bhaet Co. Ltd., Bangkok.
MacKinnon J. & Phillipps K. (1993), *A Field Guide to the Birds of Borneo, Sumatra, Java and Bali*, OUP, Oxford.
Marchant, S. & Higgins, P. J. (eds), (1990–), *Handbook of Australian, New Zealand & Antarctic Birds*, OUP, Melbourne.
  Vol. 1A Ratites to Petrels 1990.
  Vol. 1B Pelican-Ducks 1990.
  Vol. 2 Raptors to Lapwings 1993.
Mayr, Ernst (1978), *Birds of the South-west Pacific*, Chas. E. Tuttle Co. Inc., Vermont USA.
Morris, Alan K. et al (1981), *Handlist of Birds in New South Wales*, NSW Field Ornithologists Club, Sydney.
National Geographic Society (1983), *Field Guide to the Birds of North America*, Washington D.C.
National Photographic Index of Australian Wildlife Series (1982–1994), Angus & Robertson, Sydney.
Olsen, P. et al (1993), *Birds of Prey and Ground Birds of Australia*, Angus & Robertson, Sydney.
Parker, S. A. et al (1979), *An Annotated Checklist of The Birds of South Australia, Part One: Emus to Spoonbills*, South Australian Ornithological Association.
Parry, Veronica (1970), *Kookaburras*, Lansdowne Press, Melbourne.
Pizzey, G. M. (1991), *A Field Guide to the Birds of Australia*, (rev. ed.), Angus & Robertson, Sydney.
Rand, A. L. & Gilliard, E. T. (1967), *Handbook of New Guinea Birds*, Weidenfeld and Nicolson, London.
Rogers, K. et al (1986), *Bander's Aid: A Guide to Ageing and Sexing Bush Birds*, A. Rogers, St. Andrews.
Schodde, R. (1982), *The Fairy-Wrens: A Monograph of the Maluridae*, Lansdowne, Melbourne.
Schodde, R. et al (eds) (1983), *A Review of Norfolk Island Birds: Past and Present*, ANPWS , Canberra.
Schodde, R. & Mason, I. J. (1980), *Nocturnal Birds of Australia*, Lansdowne Editions, Melbourne.
Schodde, R. & Tideman, S. (eds) (1986), *Readers Digest Complete Book of Australian Birds*, (2nd ed.) Sydney.
Serventy, D. L. (1976), *Birds of Western Australia*, University of Western Australia, Perth, (5th ed.).
Sibley, C. G & Ahlquist, J. E. (1990), *Phylogeny and Classification of Birds, A Study in Molecular Evolution*, Yale University Press, New Haven and London.
Sibley, G. C. & Monroe, B. L. Jr (1990), *Distribution and Taxonomy of Birds of the World*, Yale University Press.
Slater, P. (1986), *The Slater Field Guide to Australian Birds*, Rigby, Sydney.
Smythies, B. (1984), *The Birds of Borneo*, (2nd ed.), Oliver & Boyd, Edinburgh (1968).
Soper, M. F. (1984), *Birds of New Zealand and Outlying Islands*, Whitcoulls, Christchurch.
South Australian Ornithological Association (1977), *A Bird Atlas of the Adelaide Region*, SAOA, Adelaide.
South Australian Ornithological Association (1980), *A Field List of the Birds of South Australia*, (2nd ed.), SAOA, Adelaide.
Storr, G. M. & Johnstone, R. E. (1979), *Field Guide to the Birds of Western Australia*, Western Australia Museum, Perth.
Tuck, G. (1980), *A Field Guide to the Seabirds of Australia and the World*, Collins, Sydney.
Whitehead, J. in B. Smythies (1984), *The Birds of Borneo*.
Wild Bird Society of Japan (1982), *A Field Guide to the Birds of Japan*, Wild Bird Society of Japan, Tokyo.

Papers and Reports

Christidis, L. & Boles, W. E. (1994), *The Taxonomy and Species of Birds of Australia and Its Territories*, Royal Australasian Ornithologists Union Monograph 2, RAOU, Hawthorn East, Victoria.

Garnett, S. (ed.), (1993), *Threatened and Extinct Birds of Australia*, RAOU/Australian National Parks and Wildlife Service, RAOU Report No. 82, (2nd ed).

Garnett, S. (1984) in G. L. Warren & A. P. Kershaw (eds), Australian Rainforest Study Report No. 1. pp. 358–360, Griffith University.

Garnett, S. & Crowley G. (1995), *Recovery Plan for the Golden-shouldered Parrot Psephotus chrysopterygius*, Australian Nature Conservation Agency, Canberra.

Storr, G. M. (1977), *Birds of the Northern Territory*, Western Australian Museum Special Publication No. 7.

Storr, G. M. (1980), *Birds of the Kimberley Division, Western Australia*, Western Australian Museum Special Publication No. 11.

Storr, G. M. (1984), *Birds of the Pilbara Region*, Records of the Western Australian Museum, Supplement No. 16.

BIRDWATCHING ORGANISATIONS WITHIN AUSTRALIA

Australian Bird Study Association
PO Box A313
SYDNEY SOUTH, NSW 2000
Publication: *Corella*

Bird Observers' Association of Tasmania
GPO Box 68A
HOBART TAS 7000
Publication. *Tasmanian Bird Report*

Bird Observers Club of Australia
PO Box 185
NUNAWADING VIC 3131
Publications: *The Bird Observer;*
The Australian Bird Watcher

Canberra Ornithologists Group Inc.
PO Box 301
CIVIC SQUARE ACT 2608
Publication: *Canberra Bird Notes*

NSW Field Ornithologists Club Inc.
PO Box Q277
Victoria Building
SYDNEY NSW 2000
Publication: *Australian Birds*

Queensland Ornithological Society
PO Box 97
ST LUCIA Q 4067
Publication: *The Sunbird*

Royal Australasian Ornithologists Union
415 Riversdale Road
HAWTHORN EAST VIC 3123
Publications: *Wingspan; The Emu*

South Australian Ornithological Association
C/- South Australian Museum
North Terrace
ADELAIDE SA 5000
Publication: *South Australian Ornithologist*

Western Australian Naturalists' Club
PO Box 156
NEDLANDS WA 6009
Publication: *The Western Australian Naturalist*

Personal observations can inform only so much of a book like this. In its preparation I have consulted a good deal of the Australian ornithological literature, from Gould's *Handbook* (London, 1865) on. My debt to those books, journals, special publications and field notes, and to their authors, is considerable and is freely and gratefully acknowledged.

Although only major sources can be named in a field guide, I would like to draw attention to Australia's mostly unsung State and regional bird journals, listed in the above bibliography. Written, edited, designed and published mostly by busy volunteers, they record and make available an expanding store of invaluable data, the collective work of people from many walks, bound by a splendid common interest — the understanding and conservation of birds.

GAZETTEER

Lake Alexandrina, SA	35/139	Maitland, NSW	32/151
Lake Argyle, WA	16/128	Malanda, Q	17/145
Lake Barlee, WA	29/119	Mallacoota Inlet, Vic.	37/149
Lake Boga, Vic.	35/143	Mallapunyah, NT	16/135
Lake Cargellico, NSW	33/146	Mandora, WA	19/120
Lake Cuddapan, Q	25/141	Manjimup, WA	34/116
Lake Eildon, Vic.	37/145	Mann Ras., SA	26/129
Lake Eyre (N.), SA	27/137; 28/137	Manning R., NSW	31/152
Lake Eyre (S.), SA	29/137	Mannum, SA	34/139
Lake Eyre Basin, SA	see map	Manowar I., Q	16/139
Lake Finniss, NT	12/131	Many Peaks Ra., Q	24/151
Lake Frome, SA	30/139	Marble Bar, WA	21/119
Lake George, NSW	35/149	Margaret R., WA (Kimberley)	18/126; 18/125
Lake Grace, WA	33/118	Maria I., Tas.	42/148
Lake Hume, NSW	35/147	Marlo, Vic.	37/148
Lake Hume, Vic.	36/147	Marree, SA	29/138
Lake King, WA	33/119	Mary R., NT	13/132; 12/131
Lake Leake, Tas.	42/147	Maryborough, Q	25/152
Lake Macleod, WA	23/113	Mataranka, NT	14/133
Lake Macquarie, NSW	33/151	McArthur R., NT	15/136; 16/135
Lake Moore, WA	29/117	McGregor Ra., Q	26/142
Lake Torrens, SA	30/137	McIlwraith Ra., Q	13/143
Lake Tuggerah, NSW	33/151	McIntyre R., NSW	28/149; 28/150
Lake Way, WA	26/120	McPherson Ra., NSW	28/152
Lake Woods, NT	17/133	Meekatharra, WA	26/118
Lakefield NP, Q	14/144	Melbourne, Vic.	37/144
Lancelin, WA	31/115	Melrose, SA	32/138
Langhorne Ck, SA	35/139	Melville I., NT	11/131
Larrimah, NT	15/133	Menindee, NSW	32/142
Launceston, Tas.	41/147	Menzies, WA	29/121
Laura, Q	15/144	Merimbula, NSW	36/149
Laverton, WA	28/122	Merredin, WA	31/118
Lawn Hill NP, Q	18/138	Merriwa, NSW	32/150
Lawrence Rocks, Vic.	38/141	Mewstone, Tas.	43/146
Leeton, NSW	34/146	Mildura, Vic.	34/142
Legume, NSW	28/152	Miles, Q	26/150
Leichhardt R., Q	17/139; 20/139	Milton, NSW	35/150
Leigh Ck, SA	30/138	Mingenew, WA	29/115
Leonora, WA	28/121	Mistake Mts, Q	27/152
Lerderderg Gorge FP, Vic.	37/144	Mitchell, Q	26/147
Lightning Ridge, NSW	29/147	Mitchell R., Q	16/144; 15/141; 16/143
Limmen Bight R., NT	15/135; 16/135	Mitchell R. NP, Vic.	37/147
Lismore, NSW	28/153	Moama, NSW	36/144
Little Desert, The, Vic.	36/141	Montague I., NSW	36/150
Liverpool Ra., NSW	31/150	Montebello Is., WA	20/115
Lockhart R., Q	12/143; 13/143	Moon I., NSW	33/151
Longreach, Q	23/144	Moora, WA	30/116
Lord Howe I.	31/159	Moore R., WA	31/115
Lorne, Vic.	38/143	Mootwingee, NSW	31/142
Lower Plenty, Vic.	37/145	Moree, NSW	29/149
Lune R., Tas.	43/146	Moreton Bay, Q	27/153
Maatsuyker I., Tas.	43/146	Morgan, SA	34/139
MacDonald Downs, NT	22/135	Mornington Pen., Vic.	38/144
MacDonnell Ras., NT	23/132	Morphett Ck, NT	18/134
Mackay, Q	21/149	Moruya, NSW	35/150
Macksville, NSW	30/152	Morven, Q	26/147
Macleay R., NSW	30/152	Mossgiel, NSW	33/144
Macquarie I., sub-Antarctic	54/158	Mossman, Q	16/145
Macquarie Marshes, NSW	30/147	Moulamein, NSW	35/144
Macquarie R., NSW	31/147; 32/148	Mount Alexandra, Vic.	37/144
Madura, WA	31/127	Mount Allan, NT	22/132
Magnetic I., Q	19/146	Mount Amos, Q	15/145

INDEX OF COMMON NAMES

Note: *See also* Family Introductions, pp 521–547

INDEX OF SCIENTIFIC NAMES

Note: *See also* Family Introductions pp 521–547